The Christian as Imitator of Christ

"This thought-provoking work invites Christians to reflect deeply on how their lives can authentically mirror the compassion of Jesus toward the poor. I wholeheartedly endorse this clarion call to Christlikeness—the only form of Christianity that has the power to transform individuals and nations. It is time for genuine Christians to rise up! The church desperately needs this message. Thank you, Dr. Achampong, for your important contribution!"

—**Darlingston G. Johnson**, presiding prelate, Harvest Intercontinental Ministries Unlimited

"Professor Achampong brilliantly and admirably argues that Jesus Christ is not only our Lord and Savior, but also our social ethics. This means that the deepest and broadest virtue of the Christian is to embody and express the Christic ideals (devotional and ethical principles) within society. Achampong views the Christian as a living imitation of the moral excellences of Jesus Christ within his or her community. The book calls for a spirituality driven by a desire to transform our character and to care for the 'least of these' in our world."

—**Nimi Wariboko**, Walter G. Muelder Professor of Social Ethics, Boston University

"God created a single human race in Genesis. Science has substantiated a single human origin from Africa. The Catholic priest and theologian, Father Gustavo Gutiérrez, reminds us that at the heart of Christ's gospel is the primacy of the poor in God's kingdom. So, how can Euro-American Christians harbor prejudice towards non-white Christians and the poor? *The Christian as Imitator of Christ* seeks to re-orient Christians by reminding us of the history and the distinguishing marks of our faith. It provides a guide to Christian conduct in our contemporary times, and how living in imitation of Christ would make our world a genuinely better place. This is a book every Christian must read."

—**Emmanuel K. Akyeampong**, Ellen Gurney Professor of History and of African and African American Studies, Harvard University

"Some might argue that Dr. Achampong has redefined what it means to be a Christian in post modernity. I would contend that rather than redefine he has rediscovered the original, biblical definition of what being a Christian means. A brief overview of the chapters makes it clear that all that is fundamental to living our faith out in this world is examined in these pages. My hope is that every Christian leader in America and around the globe will read this great work and decide to imitate our Savior in all we say, do, and promote."

—**COURTNEY MCBATH**, president, Virginia Christian College

The Christian as Imitator of Christ

How That Should Influence Treatment of the Poor and Others Based on Race

Francis Kofi Achampong

Foreword by Antipas L. Harris

WIPF & STOCK · Eugene, Oregon

THE CHRISTIAN AS IMITATOR OF CHRIST
How That Should Influence Treatment of the Poor and Others Based on Race

Copyright © 2025 Francis Kofi Achampong. All rights reserved. Except for brief quotations in critical publications or reviews, no part of this book may be reproduced in any manner without prior written permission from the publisher. Write: Permissions, Wipf and Stock Publishers, 199 W. 8th Ave., Suite 3, Eugene, OR 97401.

Wipf & Stock
An Imprint of Wipf and Stock Publishers
199 W. 8th Ave., Suite 3
Eugene, OR 97401

www.wipfandstock.com

PAPERBACK ISBN: 979-8-3852-3873-6
HARDCOVER ISBN: 979-8-3852-3874-3
EBOOK ISBN: 979-8-3852-3875-0

VERSION NUMBER 04/22/25

Scripture quotations are from New Revised Standard Version Bible (NRSV), copyright © 1989 National Council of the Churches of Christ in the United States of America. Used by permission. All rights reserved worldwide.

Scripture quotations marked (HCSB) are taken from the Holman Christian Standard Bible®, Copyright © 1999, 2000, 2002, 2003, 2009 by Holman Bible Publishers. Used by permission.

Scripture quotations marked (NIV) are taken from the Holy Bible, New International Version®, NIV®. Copyright © 1973, 1978, 1984, 2011 by Biblica, Inc.™ Used by permission of Zondervan. All rights reserved worldwide. www.zondervan.com.

Scripture quotations marked (NKJV) are taken from the New King James Version®. Copyright © 1982 by Thomas Nelson. Used by permission. All rights reserved.

Scripture quotations marked (KJV) are in the public domain.

To the next generation—
Alexandra, Joshua, and Gabriella, and those yet to come

Contents

Foreword by Antipas L. Harris | ix
Acknowledgments | xi
Introduction | xiii

1. Jesus Christ, the Model for Christians to Imitate | 1
2. Who Is a Christian? | 25
3. Practicing the Spiritual Disciplines | 94
4. Understanding and Triumphing over the Devil | 136
5. Trusting in the Lord | 165
6. Being a Good Steward | 192
7. Carrying Out the Great Commission | 222
8. Committing to a Local Church | 250
9. Treatment of the Poor | 272
10. Treatment of Others Based on Race | 314

Conclusion | 403
Bibliography | 407
Index | 425

Foreword

THROUGHOUT HISTORY, FOLLOWERS OF Jesus Christ have wrestled with the timeless question: What does it mean to be a Christian? This book serves as a profound and practical guide for Christians who desire to live as Christ did—fully devoted to God, empowered by the Holy Spirit, and committed to loving all of God's children while advocating for their equal rights and fair treatment. It emphasizes that discipleship is not passive but an active, disciplined lifestyle shaped by spiritual practices. True discipleship begins with hearts surrendered to God's will, attentive to the word of God, and, most importantly, filled with the Holy Spirit.

This book is foundationally an exposition of the life of Jesus, who consistently demonstrated devotion through prayer, fasting, and reflection on what God says. These spiritual disciplines not only connected him with the Father but also equipped him to confront spiritual battles that often accompany faithful obedience. Dr. Francis Achampong aptly explains how these practices are not merely ancient rituals; they are essential tools for resisting temptation, discerning truth, and growing in intimacy with God.

Dr. Achampong inspires us by illuminating the stark reality of the devil's schemes. Through an exploration of diabolical tactics and Jesus's triumph over temptation, it reveals biblical strategies that guide us to stand firm in faith. With the Holy Spirit as empowerment, we discover that victory over the adversary is not only attainable but also a promise for those who trust in God's word and embrace his authority.

At the heart of this work is an inspiring call to trust in the Lord with the unwavering faith that Jesus demonstrated, even amid suffering and death. Through powerful examples from Scripture—spanning both the Old and New Testaments—the author encourages readers to place their confidence in God's faithfulness and to resist the worldly influences that seek to undermine that trust. Trusting in the Lord is not merely a personal virtue; it is a communal act that empowers Christians to share with others compassion, justice, and mercy.

Moreover, this book inspires readers to embrace their lives as sacred stewardship. Just as Jesus dedicated all his resources to advancing God's kingdom, believers are called to be wise and faithful stewards of their time, talents, and treasures. True stewardship is all about serving others, regardless of their backgrounds, and glorifying God in every action.

Finally, this book emphasizes the Great Commission—the ongoing call for all disciples to share the gospel, make disciples, and inspire faithfulness to Christ's teachings. It underscores that true discipleship goes beyond mere conversion; it involves transformation and a lifelong commitment to living out Jesus's message. In a world often divided by various ideologies, Dr. Achampong challenges Christians to rise above these divisions and wholeheartedly embrace Christ's global mission: the salvation and reconciliation of all humanity to one another and to God.

Within these pages lies a compelling blueprint for following Jesus Christ. Though the journey may be challenging, it is imbued with divine purpose, eternal hope, and the empowering promise of the Holy Spirit to support us through our human frailty. As you read, may you find inspiration to draw nearer to God, deepen your trust in Christ, and radiate God's love to a world that desperately needs it.

Antipas L. Harris, PhD, DMin
Harris Institute, Chairman & CEO
Urban Renewal Center, President & CEO

Acknowledgments

I AM ETERNALLY GRATEFUL for the prayers and support of my family and confidants who knew I had embarked on this massive undertaking. Burdened by the need for such a book but grappling with whether to write it, I was already two years in before I shared this project with anyone. I drew strength from their encouragement to persevere.

Amid my feelings of inadequacy, I was reminded by the Scriptures that God chooses the foolish things of the world to shame the wise, the weak things of the world to shame the strong, the lowly things of the world, the despised things, and the things that are not to nullify the things that are, so that no one may boast before him (1 Cor 1:26–29). I remembered that Moses, Gideon, and Jeremiah all felt inadequate. But God used them once they answered the call. I was also reminded of how the high priest, rulers, elders, and teachers of the law were amazed by the boldness of Peter and John as ministers of the gospel because they were uneducated or untrained, ordinary men. So, to God be all the glory for inspiring and enabling this work.

Thanks to Dr. Stephen Mark Heim of Yale Divinity School for helping me narrow the original focus of the book to address the intersecting issues of the class and racial divide in the church. A very big thanks to Dr. Antipas Harris, Chairman and CEO of Harris Institute, for encouraging me to send the manuscript for this book to Wipf and Stock, for providing valuable feedback on the manuscript, and for writing a foreword. Thanks also to the associate editors at Wipf and Stock who provided valuable feedback.

Thanks to the entire editorial and marketing team at Wipf and Stock for shepherding me through this process and for their assistance in proofreading and editing the manuscript throughout the production process.

I also appreciate all the help I received with formatting and compilation of a bibliography.

Finally, my sincerest thanks to everyone who has encouraged me and kept me in their thoughts and prayers. Altogether, this has been a labor of love every step of the way. My only desire is that it enriches the lives of all who read it and helps bridge the class and racial divide in the church and society.

Introduction

TWO-AND-A-HALF BILLION PEOPLE WORLDWIDE profess to be Christians. These include people who espouse ideas about White Christianity, Christian nationalism, Christian libertarianism, racial segregation, and racial purity. It also includes people who see assistance to the poor as handouts that perpetuate poverty. The latter group includes people who espouse ideas about accountable individualism where people are expected to pull themselves up by their own bootstraps and become self-sufficient as a sign of faith in God's grace, and a perversion of crucicentrism which takes the position that it is compassionate to allow poor people to suffer because it can drive them to the cross and salvation in Christ.

This book deals with the subject of what the Bible says about who a Christian is, how a Christian's life ought to imitate that of Jesus Christ, and how that should impact the way professing Christians treat the poor and others based on race, two of the most divisive issues in contemporary society. And race and poverty intersect because of the overrepresentation of Blacks among the poor and the erroneous perception that most of the people on welfare are Black, when they are in fact White.

In this introduction, I will talk about my motivation for authoring this book and provide an outline for the book.

Motivation for Writing This Book

As a legal scholar, I am familiar with, and have taught and written on, various aspects of civil rights laws that protect historically marginalized populations from various kinds of discrimination, especially racial and sex discrimination. I am also familiar with laws and regulations that govern entitlements like social security and public assistance to

INTRODUCTION

the poor. These intersecting issues of race and poverty currently feature prominently in America's culture wars in which professing Christians are deeply embroiled.

The positions that policymakers, lawyers, and judges take on issues of race and poverty are often colored by their ideological influences. As a result, lawyers make opposing arguments and judges make divergent rulings on the same facts.

As an engaged citizen and a Spirit-baptized disciple who is also critically engaged with the church (both predominantly majority and minority churches) and the Scriptures, I have felt a burden to help bridge the divide in the church with respect to treatment of the poor and others based on race. But instead of producing a legal treatise to attempt to bridge this divide, given the limitations of such an approach because of how ideology influences interpretation of the law, I felt that an approach that engages Scripture and biblical scholarship from an evidentiary legal lens that uses many compelling sources to support my arguments would be more effective in the church. I, therefore, bring a different type of hermeneutics to the engagement of Scripture as a legal scholar to produce a professional book for theological consumption that will impact church pews. I merge my critical engagement with Scripture with my skills in legal advocacy to appeal to professing Christians to imitate Christ in the way they relate to the poor and others based on race.

The chapters on treatment of the poor and treatment of others based on race do indeed contain many references to statutes, case law, and legal scholarship. But the book primarily appeals to professing Christians to look to Christ as their model to help bridge the class and racial divide in the church with the Holy Spirit's help and serve as an example to the broader society. Being mindful of the fact that the law that God gave to the Israelites was unable to get them to do the right thing, necessitating Christ's coming, I do not presume to be efficacious in arguing respect for human antipoverty and antidiscrimination laws in bridging the class and racial divide in the church. Instead, this book merges my interpretation of Scripture from a legal perspective with biblical scholarship and commentary to empower church leaders, lay leaders, and church members of all ethnicities in the pews to imitate Christ in their treatment of the poor and others based on race as an example to the broader society.

In approaching a book about imitating Christ, I must observe that, in many respects, the word *Christian* seems to have acquired extra-biblical meanings. I cannot help but ask, with the world in the state that it is

INTRODUCTION

in, could there really be almost two-and-a-half billion Christians living in it, when just a few Christians were said to have turned the world upside down in the days of the early church? In this regard, it seems to me that the term *Christian* is one of the most misunderstood and misused terms in contemporary society. And only an examination of what the Bible says, going back to the first use of that term to describe not just believers but disciples or imitators of Christ, can help illuminate what it means to be a Christian and how that should influence attitudes on race and poverty. That is what this book sets out to do. It deals with how a Christian's life ought to imitate that of Jesus Christ and how that should impact the way professing Christians treat the poor and others based on race, two of the most divisive, intersecting issues of our day.

As would be expected of a legal scholar trained in adducing evidence to provide support for the arguments and interpretative points made in this book, and for readers who want to dig deeper into the topics and issues this book discusses, the book provides extensive citations that make up a rich bibliography. This bibliography includes many Bible commentaries, books, and other scholarship produced by a diverse and highly regarded group of theologians and Bible scholars across several continents, as well as general scholarship by subject-matter experts on the relevant subjects the book tackles.

Chapter Outline

The first chapter is a discussion of attributes of Jesus Christ, the model for Christians to imitate. Because the Bible uses *Christian* to denote a disciple or imitator of Jesus Christ, this chapter is an important foundational chapter. It shows that Jesus Christ is the second person of the Triune God or Trinity and creator of humanity. He as God the Son, along with God the Father and God the Holy Spirit, was involved in creation when they made man or humans in their image. The Bible shows that God only created Adam and Eve as the forebears of all humanity. God, therefore, never created many races, just one race—the human race. Imitators of Christ should, therefore, with the help of the Holy Spirit who is the Spirit of truth, reject the narrative about many races, the superiority of some races over others, racial segregation, racial purity, and the notion of White Christianity. Jesus is the Son of God who loves all humanity. He established his earthly ministry's headquarters in Galilee of the gentiles.

INTRODUCTION

He did not segregate himself from gentiles like Jews normally did. He loved and ministered to all people regardless of their nationality, ethnicity, skin color, or socioeconomic status. This included many Jews, a Roman centurion, a Samaritan leper, a Samaritan woman in Sychar, a Canaanite woman in Tyre and Sidon, and a man from Gadara in Perea. The chapter points out that Jesus himself was of mixed heritage or ancestry, having a Canaanite called Rahab and a Moabite called Ruth in his ancestry. Jesus taught that one should love one's neighbor as oneself, treat others as one would want to be treated, and love other believers as he has loved them.

The chapter also shows that Jesus was the model of compassion to people he encountered. He compassionately preached the good news, healed the sick, fed thousands of poor people, and set people free from demon possession. He healed people suffering from severe pain, seizures, paralysis, leprosy, blindness, deafness, muteness, hemorrhaging, and fever, and raised a dead son of a widow back to life. These were all life-changing events in the lives of the people he ministered to, many of whom would have been impoverished by their condition, and many of whom would have been rendered social outcasts because of their condition. His compassion in restoring them to health gave them hope and a new lease on life. Christians, as imitators of Jesus must—with the help of the Holy Spirit, the Spirit of love—show the same compassion to others regardless of their nationality, ethnicity, skin color, or socioeconomic status.

Jesus was totally devoted to God in prayer, fasting, and expending his time and energy doing the work God sent him to do. He spent many times alone with God in prayer. He also taught his disciples about how to pray as well as how not to pray. He also taught them about how to fast and how not to fast. As imitators of Christ, Christians must also model this devotion to God by being about God's business and by using their time, energy, and gifts to do God's work in ministering to and serving others regardless of their nationality, ethnicity, skin color, or socioeconomic status.

As the head of the church, Jesus instituted a new diverse, blended family comprised of all who do his will regardless of skin color or socioeconomic status. The chapter ends by discussing the fact that he is the ruler of a future diverse kingdom filled with people from every nation, tribe, people, and language, as the apostle John saw in the Revelation of Jesus Christ to him regarding the tribulation saints in heaven. Jesus will

INTRODUCTION

return at the end of the age to rule for one thousand years with his saints in what has been called the millennial kingdom. This is a kingdom rid of the devil and evil where there will be righteousness, peace, and no racism or mistreatment of the poor. The millennial kingdom will be followed by the new heaven and the new earth that God will create. It will be a new universe rid of Satan, sin, and the effects of the fall, where God will live with his people in eternity. It is this future righteous, diverse, eternal kingdom over which Christ will rule that all Christians hope for. This is the place Jesus promised to prepare for his disciples of all time. It is a kingdom made up of Christians from all over the world who will live eternally with God. Christians who aspire to this kingdom should live here on earth in a manner worthy of people headed to a future diverse kingdom where Christ rules in all righteousness and where there are no divisions based on nationality, ethnicity, skin color, or socioeconomic status. The millennial kingdom and the new heaven and new earth will be the ultimate fulfillment of what God has always intended—that his creation live in loving community with him and each other regardless of differences.

Chapter 2 discusses who a Christian is and the history behind the name *Christian*, which was only used to refer to disciples or imitators of Christ, not just believers. In discussing names that the disciples used to describe themselves, as well as those that others used to describe them, the chapter notes that these names did not include *evangelical*. The chapter identifies the Bible's account of the distinguishing marks of a Christian, including the fact that a Christian is not merely a believer or convert, but a born-again disciple, follower, or imitator of Jesus Christ. It discusses the fact that a Christian is one who is regenerated (born again through the work of the Holy Spirit) in Christ, redeemed, justified, sanctified, and indwelt by the Holy Spirit. It also includes the insightful notion that a Christian is a citizen of heaven, a kingdom of people from every nation, tongue, and tribe, as well as the fact that a Christian is one who lives life on what Jesus described as the narrow, difficult road that leads to eternal life. Jesus said that few find this narrow road, even more reason to wonder if almost two-and-a-half billion people have found it. The chapter discusses Bible passages, many spoken by Jesus himself, of the need to stay on this narrow road till the very end of one's life to enter eternal life.

The chapter discusses what life on the narrow road entails for imitators of Christ, including picking up one's cross daily; examining oneself to make sure one is in the faith; living a holy life; and being loving and kind to all, especially members of the household of faith (other Christians), regardless of ethnicity or socioeconomic status. It discusses how Christians, like Jesus, can be sociable people who enjoy, within appropriate boundaries, the company of all kinds of people regardless of their ethnicity or socioeconomic status. It emphasizes that a Christian is not defined by race, ethnicity, or socioeconomic status. Becoming a Christian is a lifelong commitment to aligning one's life with the teachings of Jesus Christ and imitating the life that he lived and how he treated the poor and people of all ethnicities.

The chapter contrasts life on the narrow road with life on what Jesus called the broad road that leads to destruction. Jesus said many find this broad road, where life involves loving the world and the things of the world and practicing a false form of religion based on a mixture of elements of biblical truth and tradition, culture, or ideology. The chapter debunks the notion that Christianity is synonymous with Whiteness and that one can punch an irrevocable ticket to heaven by praying the sinner's prayer, even if one's life after that does not align with God's ways and righteous standards, and one does not imitate Christ and how he related to the poor and people of all ethnicities. It ends by emphasizing that a Christian is not defined by race, ethnicity, or socioeconomic status; that a Christian is a disciple, follower, or imitator of Jesus Christ who endeavors to live like Jesus did with the Holy Spirit's help; and that as imitators of Jesus Christ, Christians must live lives that are obedient to God's word and glorify God. They must love their neighbor as themselves regardless of their ethnicity, nationality, skin color, or socioeconomic status, treat all people, especially members of the diverse family of God, as they would expect to be treated, and show kindness and compassion to the poor and needy as Jesus did.

Jesus Christ, the one Christians imitate, was totally devoted to God his Father. He often spent time alone with God praying and taught his disciples how to pray. He spent time fasting before launching his public ministry. He also taught on fasting. Chapter 3 discusses four core spiritual disciplines: prayer, fasting, studying God's word, and meditating on God's word. It discusses praise and worship as integral parts of prayer. Jesus said that he and the Father are one, and that he only spoke what his Father commanded him. Like Jesus, Christians must be totally devoted to their Father in heaven by disciplining themselves to spend time with him in prayer and fasting, and by studying his word so that they can know and do what he commands, including loving their neighbor as themselves regardless of what they look like, where they are from, or their station in life; treating others as they would want to be treated; and being kind and compassionate to the poor and needy. And the Holy Spirit helps believers in their prayer life and with understanding God's word.

Jesus talked about the devil quite a bit. He said that the mission of false prophets who are of the devil, and by implication the devil's mission, is to steal, kill, and destroy. The devil tempted Jesus at a time when he was hungry after fasting for forty days and forty nights. The devil twisted the Scriptures to try to get Jesus to sin. But Jesus rebuffed all his temptations using the Scriptures and triumphed over him. Chapter 4 discusses how Christians, with the Holy Spirit's help as teacher, must know what the Bible says about the devil so that they can rebuff his temptations and triumph over him like Jesus did. The chapter discusses the devil's origins and his attributes, including being an adversary, slanderer, deceiver, liar, accuser, and enemy of Christians, as well as his power of suggestion. He is also described as the prince or ruler of this world, hence the admonition to not love the world or the things of this world. The chapter discusses the devil's designs, schemes, and devices, including not wanting people to be saved, attempting to turn the hearts of disciples from God, using persecution to discourage and undermine faith, offering worldly rewards to get people to do things his way, breaking bonds between disciples, spreading misinformation and twisting the truth, getting people to worship money, getting disciples to fight spiritual battles with worldly weapons, causing division, and inciting fear of others who are different.

The chapter ends by discussing the devil's fate and how to triumph over him through knowledge of God's word, resisting him, putting on the whole armor of God, prayer, fasting, believing in Christ's saving power through his shed blood, confessing Jesus as Lord, sharing the good news about him, and totally surrendering one's life to him. This will empower Christians, with the Holy Spirit's help, to triumph over Satan and live by Christ's commands to love their neighbor as themselves, regardless of what they look like and their station in life, and to treat others as they would want to be treated.

Chapter 5 discusses trusting in the Lord and what that means. Jesus trusted God to the point of surrendering to death knowing that God would raise him up. Christians must trust in the Lord the same way Jesus trusted his Father knowing that he is faithful and that he will do everything he has promised in his word for those who love him and do his will. The chapter examines examples of Old and New Testament saints who trusted in the Lord, including Abraham, Rahab, Ruth, Daniel and his three friends (who were taken to Babylon as captives), the Roman centurion, and the Canaanite woman Jesus encountered in the region of Tyre and Sidon. The chapter examines things that Satan uses to undermine trust in the Lord—money, weapons, and powerful people. It also examines things that hinder trusting in the Lord, such as fear, doubt, worry, suffering, and persecution. Trusting in the Lord means Christians must, with the Holy Spirit's help, be willing to obey his word, which exhorts Christians to love their neighbor as themselves, treat others as they would want to be treated, and extend love and compassion to the poor and needy, believing that the Lord will bless them and meet their needs. The chapter also looks at the benefits of trusting in the Lord and how to grow in one's trust in the Lord.

Jesus was the perfect steward of everything he had, totally devoting his time, energy, divine power, anointing, and gift as a master teacher, to the work of God's kingdom. Chapter 6 examines the topic of being a good steward and how Christians should view themselves as stewards of God and use their time, talents (gifts and abilities), and treasure (money and possessions) in the service of God for God's glory. Serving God invariably involves serving others regardless of who they are or their station in life. It discusses the qualities of a good steward—including being faithful, wise, industrious, and productive, all of which were qualities Jesus exemplified—and the consequences of failing to be a good steward. It stresses that the Holy Spirit, the Spirit of power and wisdom, is able to give believers strength and wisdom to be faithful stewards.

Jesus was constantly on the move on foot, preaching the good news in the towns and cities in Israel. When the people of Capernaum tried to keep him from leaving their town because of all the miracles he performed there, he told them that he must preach the good news of the kingdom of God to the other towns also, because that is why he was sent. So, he kept on preaching and teaching in the temple in Jerusalem, in the synagogues of Judea, and throughout all of Galilee. Chapter 7 discusses the Great Commission. This is the only commission Jesus gave to his disciples of all time, to share the gospel (or good news), get new converts to make their newfound faith public through baptism, and teach them to observe all of Jesus Christ's commandments. And they were not to embark on this task until they had received the baptism of the Holy Spirit. Jesus did not commission his disciples to take over government, society, or the world,

INTRODUCTION

the latter representing the notion of Christian nationalism. The imperative to teach new disciples to keep Jesus's commandments makes it clear that becoming a believer or convert is only the beginning of the Christian journey. One cannot follow or imitate Jesus Christ, the essence of being a Christian, without knowing and obeying what he taught. Jesus made it clear that one must continue in his word to be his disciple. It is his word and obedience to it that transforms one into a Christlike disciple with the help of the Holy Spirit, and sets one free from the power and bondage of sin. Only disciples were called Christians in the Bible. Without becoming a disciple or imitator of Christ, one cannot love one's neighbor, including the poor and people of different ethnicities, as oneself. The chapter also discusses refuting, or simply not teaching, what Jesus did not command, such as Christian libertarianism and Christian nationalism. Instead, it is the Jesus of the Bible—the one who came to save all humanity regardless of ethnicity, nationality, skin color, or socioeconomic status—and his word that must be preached diligently, both locally and globally.

Jesus was often found teaching in the synagogue and engaging with all kinds of people, from Pharisees, Sadducees, scribes, and teachers of the law to ordinary Jews. As imitators of Jesus Christ, Christians must also commit to a local assembly or church where they can fellowship and engage with others and grow spiritually from biblical teaching that equips them to treat others like Jesus did. Chapter 8 examines the Christian's relationship with the church, referred to in the Bible as the body of Christ, and the expectation that Christians will make a commitment to a local church where they can use their God-given spiritual gifts for the edification of other believers and support the work of the kingdom of God both locally and globally. The chapter examines practical demonstrations of the Christian's commitment to the local church, including giving one's time, energy, gifts, and talents, as well as finances, to the work of the church, just as Jesus gave all his time, energy, and life to the work of God's kingdom. It examines practical aspects of committing to a local church, including the way church members relate to, love, serve, encourage, and forgive one another as Christ has forgiven them. This commitment also includes refraining from negative, un-Christlike behaviors like envying and speaking evil of each other.

The chapter ends by noting that as Christians emulate Christ's example and commit to engaging and fellowshipping with other believers in a local assembly, they will realize certain benefits. In addition to these benefits, to commit to a local church is to be obedient to the exhortation to not forsake assembling together. When this commitment causes believers to walk together in love as God's family, receive biblical teaching, use their gifts to strengthen each other, and give of their time, energy, and resources to advance the work of the kingdom of God on earth, it all brings glory to the name of the Lord and equips them through the Holy Spirit to live like Jesus did, including how he treated the poor and people of all ethnicities.

Having discussed the life of Jesus, his model of devotion to God, love for God and all people, and how Christians, with the help of the Holy Spirit, should imitate Christ by being devoted to God, rejecting the devil's ways of division and lies, trusting in God and surrendering to his way, seeing themselves as God's stewards, sharing the good news with all people, and committing to fellowship and service in a local church, the last two chapters discuss how a Christian, having become an imitator of Christ in all these areas, should now be prepared and empowered by the Holy Spirit to treat others like Christ did, regardless of their socioeconomic status, the color of their skin, or their ethnicity.

Jesus Christ loved, healed, delivered, preached to, and fed thousands of people, many of whom would have been poor. Chapter 9 deals with how Christians, as followers and imitators of Jesus Christ, must treat the poor. God was so concerned about the poor that he instituted the practice of gleaning in ancient Israel for the benefit of the poor. He also instituted the law of the tithe whereby every third year, a tenth of produce and animal herds were brought to storehouses and the temple to feed widows, orphans, immigrants (foreigners), and priests who did not get an allotment of land in ancient Israel, and to sustain the sacrificial system. God also protected the poor by instituting the Year of Jubilee, a year when slaves were freed, debts forgiven, and foreclosed lands restored to the original owners. The chapter discusses poverty in America, factors contributing to poverty, and attitudes toward the poor that may not reflect God's heart and concern for the poor. Jesus said the poor will always be with us. With the Holy Spirit's help, how a Christian relates to the poor must reflect the heart of God and the biblical record we have of his care of the poor and needy. It must also reflect how Jesus, who was himself poor, treated the poor, and how the early church treated the poor, remembering that Jesus takes all acts of kindness extended to the poor personally. He promises a place in his kingdom for the righteous who show love and compassion to the poor and needy while warning of eternal punishment for those who withhold love and compassion from them.

INTRODUCTION

The chapter points out that race and poverty intersect because of the overrepresentation of Blacks among the poor and the misconception that most welfare recipients are Black, although the data show that most welfare recipients are White. Studies show that there are Whites who support cutting or restricting aid to the poor because they mistakenly assume Black people are benefiting and White people are being disadvantaged. The chapter notes that this is un-Christlike because Jesus Christ showed compassion to all poor people regardless of their ethnicity. The chapter ends by noting that, as the apostle Paul taught and modeled, modern-day Christians must have a heart to help the poor without encouraging idleness, while also being cognizant of contemporary societal issues that complicate gainful employment. These include employment discrimination, mental health challenges, barriers to reentering society after incarceration, and low wages that disincentivize hard work. It argues that professing Christians must commit to advocating and working for change in these areas.

Chapter 10, the closing chapter in this book, examines how a Christian, as an imitator of Christ, should treat people based on race, using a biblical lens. It looks at biblical teaching on whether there is more than one race or whether God only created one race—the human race. Considering its finding that the Bible references only one human race, the chapter examines where the notion that there are multiple races comes from. It posits that racism is a deceptive satanic device and discusses how Satan manages to pull off his lies about race. It also examines how God feels about racism, given that the Bible says he is no respecter of persons, and that he accepts as his children all who love and serve him. It finds that slavery was the most sinister form of racism and examines how the Bible views slavery, the principle of reparations for freed slaves, and racism. It probes whether, and how extensively, Satan has sewn racism into society's fabric, investigating whether there is evidence of systemic or institutional racism in areas of American society like education, employment, the criminal justice system, healthcare, and the church and, if so, what a Christian's stance should be on these matters.

The chapter discusses ideas about how to combat racism. It looks at how Jesus Christ related to people of all ethnicities and puts this model forward as what a Christian, with the Holy Spirit's help, ought to emulate or imitate. It examines the lunacy of racism by pointing to scientific research tracing the origins of modern humans to common ancestors who

INTRODUCTION

lived in Africa and by referencing the Human Genome Project that has established that humans share 99.9 percent of genes in common.

It argues that one who professes to be a Christian can neither condone nor practice racism in any of its manifestations. It argues that from a spiritual perspective, a racist is one who opposes God's will for others because of the color of their skin. And one cannot oppose God's will and consider oneself a Christian. In light of Christ's love for all humanity and his example in ministering to people regardless of who they were or their life circumstances, professing Christians, as people who purport to imitate Christ, must soberly ponder whether they can practice or condone racism; believe that there are many races with some superior to others when that contradicts the biblical narrative that there is only one race created in the image of God; believe they will live together with disciples of Christ from every nation, tongue, and tribe in the new heaven and the new earth, even though they segregated themselves, wanted nothing to do with people of certain ethnicities, or may even have harmed them, on earth. The chapter ends with a look at what the future holds for a world rid of racism at the end of the age and what disciples, followers, or imitators of Jesus Christ must do in the meantime to make the world a kinder, gentler place. It suggests that Christians—disciples, followers, and imitators of Christ, people who have accepted him as their Lord and Savior and desire to do his will—must, with the Holy Spirit's help, love him with all their heart, soul, strength, and mind, and their neighbor, regardless of nationality or ethnicity, as themselves.[1] They must do unto others as they would have others do unto them.[2] They must do what is just, love mercy, and walk humbly with God.[3] And they must treat others like Jesus did, regardless of their nationality, ethnicity, or skin color. It argues that this is a huge part of the antidote to racism as we work toward a more just and equitable society and wait for the appearing of the Lord Jesus Christ to make things right.

The conclusion wraps things up by reiterating that a Christian is a citizen of heaven who traverses this world on the narrow road that leads to eternal life. A Christian is a believer who, led by the Holy Spirit, has

---

1. Matt 22:37–40; Mark 12:30–31; Luke 10:27. Jesus said in Matthew's account that these are the two greatest commandments, and that the law and the prophets hang on them.

2. Matt 7:12; Luke 6:31. Jesus said in Matthew's account that this sums up the law and the prophets.

3. Mic 6:8.

transitioned to becoming a disciple by continuing in Jesus's word, knowing his truth, and being set free from the power of sin, including the lie and sin of racism and related notions of White Christianity, racial segregation, and racial purity. The notion of racial purity leads to the absurd conclusion that even Jesus was racially impure, being of mixed Jewish, Canaanite, and Moabite heritage. Because Jesus said few find the narrow road that leads to life, the conclusion wonders whether 2.4 billion people have found it, given the state the world is in, and the fact that two disciples who did find it, Paul and Silas, were said to have turned the whole world upside down. It challenges every professing Christian to examine themselves to see if they are in the faith as Paul admonished. It asks what they will do if an honest self-examination reveals that they are not the imitators of Christ that they claim to be. To do nothing will make one's claim of being a Christian an act of hypocrisy. The conclusion notes how Jesus hated hypocrisy. He said that even though the hypocritical Pharisees were not on their way to heaven, they were hindering others from going to heaven. It ends by asking every professing Christian to soberly reflect on whether they are indeed Christians imitating Jesus Christ, or whether they are putting on an act that may be hindering others from accepting Christ and going to heaven. This sober reflection must be done remembering the warning that everyone will face death and judgment.

1

Jesus Christ, the Model for Christians to Imitate

THE BIBLE ONLY USES the term *Christian* to describe disciples of Jesus Christ, not just believers.[1] Jesus told the Jews who had believed in him that if they continued to hold on to his word, they would be his disciples indeed, that they would know the truth, and the truth would set them free from the power of sin.[2] Jesus said that he is the truth.[3] He also said God's word is truth.[4] Thus, holding on to Jesus's word and living by it will bring one into intimacy with Jesus, make one his disciple, and empower one to live victoriously over sin.

The Greek word for disciple is *mathētēs* and denotes a learner, student,[5] or pupil who not only learns from, but actually follows, the teaching of another.[6] It was used to describe the followers of Jesus, espe-

---

1. Acts 11:26. See Johnson, *Acts of the Apostles*, 204–5, where he interprets *christianoi* to mean a follower of someone.

2. John 8:31–36. See Moloney, *Gospel of John*, 275–77, where he explains that some of the Jews had partially believed in Jesus, and that Jesus is now attempting to draw them into authentic, full faith by exhorting them to abide in his word and become disciples who are no longer slaves to sin.

3. John 14:6.

4. John 17:17.

5. Matt 10:24–25; Luke 6:40, NIV.

6. See Vine et al., *Vine's Complete Expository Dictionary*, 171 (New Testament Section).

cially the twelve apostles,[7] but also others who came to believe in him.[8] It includes all who hold to Jesus's teaching and live by his word.[9] A Christian is, therefore, a follower or imitator of Jesus Christ.

In this chapter, we will examine attributes of Jesus Christ that Christians should imitate in the way they live and treat others, regardless of nationality, ethnicity, skin color, or socioeconomic status.[10]

Jesus Christ, the Second Person of the Triune God and Creator of Humanity

The Bible teaches that during creation, the Triune God, consisting of God the Father, God the Son, and God the Holy Spirit, created man, Adam, in the image of God.[11] God formed him out of the dust of the earth and breathed life into him. God placed him in the garden of Eden to tend it and take care of it.[12] God said it was not good for Adam to be alone, so he created Eve to be Adam's companion and helper. The Bible says that Adam and Eve wore no clothes. They were naked and unashamed of it.[13]

The Bible says that God made all the nations from one man, Adam, or from one ancestor; and that God allotted the times of their existence and the boundaries of the places where they would live.[14] Adam and Eve were, therefore, the forbears or common ancestors of all humanity—the human race. In other words, God only created one race, not many races.

---

7. Matt 10:1.

8. Acts 9:10 referring to Ananias as a disciple and Acts 16:1 referring to Timothy as a disciple.

9. John 8:31.

10. For further insights into Jesus's life, see Johnson, *Living Jesus*; *Real Jesus*; Keener, *Historical Jesus of the Gospels*, arguing that the Gospels present a coherent and plausible picture of the historical Jesus; and Allen Dwight Callahan, "God's Only Begotten Thug," in Smith et al., *Bitter the Chastening Rod*, 39–52, noting that Jesus was penniless, landless, and homeless—a thug in the sense of one who has nothing.

11. Gen 1:26–28.

12. Gen 2:7–8.

13. Gen 2:18–25.

14. Acts 17:26.

In all his interactions with people, whether they were Jews, Samaritans,[15] Romans,[16] from other nationalities or ethnicities like the woman from Tyre and Sidon[17] or the demoniac in Gadara,[18] Jesus showed the same love, concern, and compassion for them all.

One who has believed in Jesus, continued in his word, and become a disciple—that is, a Christian—will know the biblical truth that there is only one race, not many races, and will be set free from the power of the sin of racism to imitate Jesus Christ's example in how he treated everyone he encountered. The Christian must imitate Jesus's love, concern, and compassion for all people, regardless of their nationality, ethnicity, or skin color. They must reject false notions like White Christianity and racial purity, as well as un-Christlike behaviors like racial segregation.

Jesus Christ, the Son of God Who Loves All Humanity

The Bible says that God so loved the world that he gave his only son, that whoever believes in him will not perish, but have everlasting life.[19] The world God loved is filled with people of different nationalities and ethnicities. God loves them all just as much. Jesus also loved them all and came to lay down his life as a ransom for them all.[20]

When Jesus launched his public ministry, he left Nazareth and retuned to Galilee where he established his headquarters in Capernaum. The upper part of Galilee bordered Phoenicia.[21] That region was called "Galilee of the gentiles." Isaiah had prophesied that the people of that region would see a great light.[22] Matthew notes that Jesus centered his

---

15. Luke 17:11–19; John 4:4–42. See Johnson, *Gospel of Luke*, 260, where he notes the shock of a Samaritan leper, an outcast who was only marginally part of Israel, giving a positive example of faith.

16. Matt 8:5–13; Luke 7:1–10; John 4:46–54.

17. Matt 15:21–28; Mark 7:24–30.

18. Matt 8:28–34; Mark 5:1–17; Luke 8:26–37.

19. John 3:16.

20. Matt 20:28; Mark 10:45. See Harrington, *Gospel of Matthew*, 287–89, where he comments that the word *ransom* describes the deliverance of a captive by means of a purchase and the giving of Jesus's life meant martyrdom. See also Boring, *Mark: A Commentary*, 302–3, interpreting Jesus's coming to lay down his life as a ransom for many as referring to the servant ministry of the Christ event as a whole and to his death as salvific for everyone.

21. See Smith, *Smith's Bible Dictionary*, 203.

22. Isa 9:1–2.

ministry here to fulfill the prophecy in Isaiah.[23] It was, therefore, in a region of great diversity that Jesus lived the greater part of his life and carried out most of his ministry. He did not segregate himself from gentiles. This was consistent with God's love for all humanity and contrary to the tendency of Jews to look down on, and disassociate from, gentiles, and to the racial strife that we are experiencing in our society today.

Jesus demonstrated this love in his interactions with all kinds of people. A centurion once came to Jesus and asked him to come and heal his servant who was paralyzed and suffering greatly. A Jew would normally not enter the home of a gentile. But Jesus was willing to go to the centurion's house. It was the centurion who said he was not worthy to have Jesus come under his roof. He asked Jesus to just say the word, believing that Jesus's word would go and heal his servant. Jesus commended the centurion's great faith.[24] Another encounter involved a Canaanite woman who came to Jesus to ask him to heal her demon-possessed daughter while he was in the region of Tyre and Sidon. Jesus commended her great faith for her persistence in seeking healing for her daughter.[25] Jesus did not withhold his favor from anyone because of the person's ethnicity, nationality, or skin color.

Jews despised Samaritans. When Jesus upset some Jews by telling them that the devil was their father, not Abraham, because their hearts were not right, they accused him of being a demon-possessed Samaritan.[26] Samaritans were part Jewish but were the offspring of intermarriages between Jews and people from other nations that the Assyrians transplanted in Israel when they conquered the northern kingdom in 726 BC. Samaria was the region between Judea in the south, where Jerusalem was, and Galilee in the north, where Capernaum was.

Jews traveling from Judea to Galilee would add days to their travel by going around Samaria instead of through it. But not Jesus. On his way back to Galilee from Judea on one occasion, he went through Samaria. There was a woman there whose life and community he wanted to touch with the good news of the kingdom of God. He met the woman at the well in the heat of the noon hour. When he asked her for a drink of water, she was puzzled and reminded Jesus that Jews did not associate with Samaritans. Jesus came to Samaria to break down this barrier and to teach

---

23. Matt 4:15–16.
24. Matt 8:5–10; Luke 7:1–10.
25. Matt 15:21–28; Mark 7:24–30.
26. John 8:42–48.

JESUS CHRIST, THE MODEL FOR CHRISTIANS TO IMITATE

her about salvation and true worship. Many in the town of Sychar where she lived became believers. Jesus spent two days with them at their urging. Jesus modeled to his disciples, the Samaritans, and to everyone who professes to be a disciple, follower, or imitator of Christ how to relate to and treat others, regardless of who they are.[27]

At another time, an expert in the law tested Jesus by asking him what he needed to do to inherit eternal life. Jesus asked him what the law said, and the lawyer correctly answered that it was by loving the Lord with all one's heart, soul, strength, and mind, and one's neighbor as oneself. Jesus commended him for his right answer and told him to put it into practice in order to have eternal life. The lawyer than asked Jesus who his neighbor was. Jesus used what has come to be known as the parable of the good Samaritan to illustrate his answer. In this parable, neither a priest nor a Levite stopped to help a wounded Jew, but a Samaritan did. The man's own countrymen did not prove themselves to be a neighbor to him. But a Samaritan did. Jesus told the lawyer to go and do likewise.[28] In other words, in order to please God, one's life must model love for God and others regardless of who they are or what they look like. One can imagine the surprise of his Jewish audience when Jesus portrayed a Samaritan, someone Jews would normally despise, as the model of neighborliness in his parable.

It is noteworthy that Jesus was of mixed heritage. He was of Jewish, Canaanite, and Moabite ancestry. Regarding the history of his Canaanite ancestry, when the people of Israel were finally ready to enter Canaan after wandering in the wilderness for forty years, Joshua, who now led the Israelites after Moses's death, sent a couple of spies to spy out the land. They went to the house of a prostitute named Rahab. The king of Jericho heard that spies had entered his country and were in Rahab's house, so he sent a message to Rahab to give up the men. But Rahab hid them and helped them escape.

Rahab had heard how God had parted the Red Sea and how he had given the Israelites, a ragtag group of former slaves, victory in battle over the kings of the Amorites. She was convinced that God had given Jericho to the Israelites. She figured that Jehovah, the God of the Israelites, was real and that he was the God in whom she was going to put her trust. She was willing to put her life in the hands of this God. So, she made a deal

---

27. John 4:3–42.
28. Luke 10:25–37.

with the spies to protect her and her family in return for her protection of the spies.[29] The Israelites did conquer Jericho. They saved Rahab and her family. Rahab became a part of the nation of Israel[30] and appears later in the genealogy of Jesus.

The history of Jesus's Moabite ancestry is intertwined with the history of his Canaanite ancestry. When Rahab came to Israel, she married a man by the name of Salmon and had a son named Boaz.[31] Boaz later married a woman by the name of Ruth, a young widow who had returned with her widowed mother-in-law, Naomi, from the land of Moab. Naomi and her husband, Elimelech, had settled in Moab during a time of famine in Israel.[32] Ruth and Boaz had a son by the name of Obed, who was the grandfather of king David.[33] Jesus is the root of David,[34] a descendant of Rahab and Ruth, two foreigners who put their faith in God and settled in Israel. Jesus, the Son of God, was therefore of mixed heritage, having Jewish, Canaanite, and Moabite ancestors in his lineage.

When Rahab and Ruth gave up their gods for Jehovah, the God of Israel, and put their faith in him, the prohibition that they were off limits to the Israelites as spouses no longer applied. God had no reason to be concerned that they would lead an Israelite astray. He allowed them to be part of the lineage of Jesus to emphatically show that he accepts all who put their faith in him regardless of ethnicity or nationality. Jesus Christ came to reconcile humanity to God and to one another. He came to tear down the wall of hostility between Jew and gentile.[35] In Christ there is neither Jew nor Greek, slave nor free, male nor female.[36]

Jesus redefined family for Christians. He instituted a new family—those who do the will of God regardless of who they are or what they look like. He drove this new reality home when his mother and brothers came looking for him as he spoke to the crowd. When he was told that his mother and brothers wanted to speak to him, he pointed to his disciples and said they were his mother and brothers. He reiterated that whoever

---

29. Josh 2.
30. Josh 6:25.
31. Matt 1:5; Luke 3:31.
32. Ruth 1:1–7.
33. Ruth 4:13–17.
34. Rev 5:5; 22:16.
35. Eph 2:11–14.
36. Gal 3:28.

JESUS CHRIST, THE MODEL FOR CHRISTIANS TO IMITATE

does the will of his Father in heaven is his brother, sister, and mother.[37] Jesus loves them all regardless of their nationality, ethnicity, or socioeconomic status. As imitators of Christ, every Christian must do the same.

On one occasion, Jesus and his disciples crossed over Lake Gennesaret[38] from Capernaum, the headquarters of his ministry, and headed southeastward to Gadara or the land of the Gadarenes, sometimes referred to as the land of the Gergesenes. The Gadarenes were non-Jews. According to Mark's and Luke's accounts, when they arrived they encountered a demon-possessed man who was mentally disturbed.[39] The man lived in a cemetery, or among the tombs. Attempts to confine him with chains and shackles were futile as he would break them and go out to the tombs. He was tormented, crying out day and night, and cutting himself with stones.[40]

When the man saw Jesus from afar, he ran to Jesus and bowed down to him in worship. The demons recognized Jesus and spoke through the man's voice. When Jesus commanded the demons to come out of the man, they acknowledged Jesus's sovereignty and lordship by addressing him as "Jesus, Son of the Most High God."[41] The demons implored Jesus not to torment them and begged him earnestly not to send them into the abyss, a place where evil spirits are bound and where Satan will be bound during the millennial reign of Jesus Christ on earth after the world as we know it comes to an end.[42]

There were so many demons in this man that when Jesus asked the demon about his identity, he said his name was Legion because they were so many. A Roman legion was a military unit consisting of anywhere between 3,000 men in early times to over 5,200 men in imperial times. When Jesus commanded the demons to come out of the man, they begged him to allow them to go into a herd of pigs that was feeding on the hillside, and Jesus gave them permission. When they entered the swine, the herd ran violently down the hill into the lake. The shepherds ran into

---

37. Matt 12:46–50; Mark 3:31–35; Luke 8:19–21.

38. Also known as the Sea of Galilee or Lake Tiberias, a freshwater lake that supported a fishing industry.

39. Matthew's account says there were two demon-possessed men.

40. Matt 8:28; Mark 5:1–6; Luke 8:26–28.

41. One of the many Hebrew names of God is *El Elyon*, meaning "God Most High" or the "Most High God." In Luke 1:32 the angel Gabriel told Mary that the son she was about to have would be called "the Son of the Most High." See Johnson, *Gospel of Luke*, 37, where he notes that this is a favorite Lukan designation for God.

42. See Rev 9:1–11; 20:1–3.

town and told the townsfolk what had happened. When the townsfolk came to see for themselves what had happened, they found the mentally deranged, demon-possessed man healed and in his right mind, clothed, and sitting at Jesus's feet.[43]

Seized with great fear, the Gadarenes asked Jesus to leave. Before Jesus left, the man who had been healed asked to come with him. But Jesus asked him to stay behind and tell his people the great things God had done for him. The man became an evangelist in a ten-city area known as the Decapolis, in the region of Perea, telling people what this man named Jesus had done for him.[44] Out of his great love for all humanity, Jesus went out of his way to Perea to minister to a non-Jew and set him free so that he could fulfill his divine purpose.

In addition to demonstrating love and compassion for all humanity, Jesus also taught love and compassion for all humanity. Jesus taught that there are two great commandments that sum up everything in the Law and the Prophets. The first is to love God with all one's heart, soul, and mind. The second is to love one's neighbor as oneself.[45] This love of neighbor is regardless of that neighbor's nationality, ethnicity, skin color, or socioeconomic status.

Jesus also taught that, in everything, people should treat others as they would want to be treated. Again, he said that this rule, referred to as the Golden Rule, sums up the Law and the Prophets.[46] Everyone wants to be shown kindness and compassion. No one wants to be mistreated, oppressed, or harmed by others. Neither should anyone treat another person in any of those ways. And that is regardless of their nationality, ethnicity, skin color, or socioeconomic status. Many of the evils that have been done in this world, including slavery and colonialism, are inconsistent with the Golden Rule.

Jesus also taught that Christians should love one another as he has loved them. He said that this was a new command. He said that in doing so, all people would know that Christians are indeed his disciples or imitators. That is because people tend to love those who look like them, mingle in their social circles, or of whom they approve. But Jesus was now issuing a new command to Christians not to love that way, but to love all other Christians, regardless of who they are, just as he

---

43. Mark 5:8–16; Luke 8:29–36.
44. Mark 5:17–20; Luke 8:37–40.
45. Matt 22:25–40.
46. Matt 7:12; Luke 6:31.

has loved them.⁴⁷ Jesus loved all people unconditionally. As imitators of Jesus, Christians ought to do the same, particularly with respect to other Christians, regardless of their nationality, ethnicity, skin color, or socioeconomic status.

Jesus Christ, Model of Compassion

Jesus's ministry was driven by compassion for humanity. It consisted of teaching and preaching the good news of the kingdom of God, healing the sick, and setting free those who were possessed by demonic spirits.

Matthew said Jesus preached the good news of the kingdom in Galilee and healed every disease and sickness. News about him spread and people brought all manner of sick people to him—people possessed by demons, those suffering from severe pain, epilepsy, and paralysis. Out of compassion, he cured them.⁴⁸

Once, Jesus left the synagogue and went to the house of Simon Peter, one of his disciples. Jesus was informed that Simon's mother-in-law was in bed with a fever, so he went to see her. Jesus took her by the hand and rebuked the fever. The fever left her and she waited on them.⁴⁹ When word got out that Jesus was in Simon's house, people brought all kinds of sick people to the house after sunset, and he healed many people of all kinds of diseases by laying hands on them. He also drove evil spirits out of many people who were demon possessed.⁵⁰

Jesus once preached an extensive sermon that has been called the Sermon on the Mount. When Jesus came down from the mountain where he preached this sermon, a leper came and bowed down to him, assuming the posture of worship. The man, acknowledging Jesus's lordship, made a declaration of faith and a request, telling Jesus that he believed Jesus could heal him and make him clean if he was willing to do so. Jesus answered him by telling him that he was indeed willing to heal him. Jesus reached out his hand and touched the leper as he said to him, "I am willing; be made clean."⁵¹ The man was immediately healed from his leprosy.⁵²

---

47. John 13:34–35.
48. Matt 4:23–24.
49. Matt 8:14–15; Mark 1:29–31; Luke 4:38–39.
50. Matt 8:16; Mark 1:32–34; Luke 4:40.
51. Matt 8:3.
52. Matt 8:1–3; Mark 1:40–42; Luke 5:12–13.

Leprosy was a chronic and infectious skin condition. Lepers had to live outside the community. Touching a leper made one ritually unclean.[53] Nonetheless, because of his compassion, Jesus broke with tradition by touching this leper and healing him. Jesus ordered him not to tell anyone, but instructed him to go and show himself to the priest as the Old Testament law required. The priest would examine him and declare him clean so that he could return into society.[54] He would now be able to live a normal life and no longer be an outcast. The man was so overwhelmed with joy that he could not help spreading the word about what Jesus had done for him. This made it difficult for Jesus to openly enter the city. It drew "many crowds"[55] to him to hear his teaching and be healed of their sicknesses.[56]

Jesus also healed a paralyzed man who was brought to him lying on a bed. Jesus was preaching in a house that was besieged by people. Four men were carrying the paralytic's bed. Not being able to get into the house, they climbed onto the roof, made an opening in it, and let the paralyzed man down through the roof. Jesus was impressed with their faith and told the paralyzed man to get up, pick up his bed, and go home. The man did just that in full view of all. The whole crowd was in awe and gave God the glory.[57]

Then there was the woman who had suffered from a chronic menstrual disorder for twelve years. Jesus healed her on his way to attend to a sick girl.[58] The woman's condition would have made her ritually unclean and, therefore, a social outcast. Even beds she lay on or chairs she sat on became unclean and anyone who came into contact with these objects had to wash his or her clothes and bathe in water. After a discharge

---

53. See Lev 13:1–46. The modern form of leprosy is Hansen's disease. In ancient times, *leprosy* was used generically to describe various infectious skin conditions and was not the same as what is now known as Hansen's disease. See Harrington, *Gospel of Matthew*, 112, making this distinction.

54. Matt 8:4, 43–44; Luke 5:14; Lev 14:1–22.

55. Luke 5:15.

56. Mark 1:43; Luke 5:15.

57. Matt 9:2–8; Mark 2:1–12; Luke 5:18–26. See Harrington, *Gospel of Matthew*, 122, commenting that the complete cure of the man establishes the extraordinary authority of Jesus and renders at least plausible his power over sins. See also Boring, *Mark: A Commentary*, 78, commenting that the paralyzed man is given back not just the use of his legs, he is given his life back, which points to God's redemptive act for humanity in raising up Jesus.

58. Matthew actually states that the girl had already died. Matt 9:18–19; Mark 5:22–24; Luke 8:41–42.

beyond the normal menstrual cycle ended, a woman was considered clean seven days later and was required on the eighth day to bring prescribed offerings to the priest to sacrifice on her behalf.[59] This woman became so desperate that she spent all her money on physicians. As long as she kept hemorrhaging, she was in a perpetual state of uncleanness. To add to her desperation, she actually got worse in spite of spending all her money on physicians. Having heard of Jesus and believing in his power to heal, she surmised that she only needed to touch the hem or tassel[60] of his garment in order to be healed.

When she reached out in faith and touched the hem of Jesus's garment, her bleeding stopped immediately. Mark and Luke record that Jesus felt healing power go out of him when he was touched. He asked who touched him and the woman came forward and told him everything. Showing compassion to this woman, Jesus told her to go in peace because her faith had made her whole or well.[61] She could now offer the required offering and live a normal life as a full-fledged member of society.

As a compassionate healer, Jesus once went into the synagogue on the Sabbath and noticed a man with a withered or shriveled hand there. Luke notes that it was his right hand.[62] Unless this man had inherited wealth, it is unlikely that he could live a productive life with a withered hand. Unless he owned land and could hire workers, he would hardly be able to work as a farm hand and handle implements such as a plough. He certainly could not make a living as a fisherman like some of Jesus's disciples did prior to their call. And he could not be a tradesman like Joseph, Jesus's earthly father, who as a carpenter would have needed both hands to handle tools. This man's healing would, therefore, be a life-changing event.

Despite this reality, the Pharisees, who interpreted the law strictly without any compassion, were against doing anything on the Sabbath that could remotely be construed as work. It would be against their tradition for Jesus to heal this man on the Sabbath. Jesus asked the Pharisees whether it was lawful to do good and to save life on the Sabbath. They did not respond. Jesus was grieved by the hardness of the hearts of the Pharisees who put ideology above human need. Jesus asked the man to step forward and stretch out his hand. As he did so, it was restored to the

---

59. Lev 15:25–33.

60. Jews were to wear tassels on their garments to remind them to keep all God's commandments.

61. Matt 9:20–22; Mark 5:29–34; Luke 8:43–48.

62. Luke 6:6.

same health as his other hand.⁶³ Despite the fact that this man could now live a productive life, the Pharisees were filled with rage that Jesus had done something inconsistent with their ideology and they plotted as to how to destroy him.⁶⁴

Then there was the episode that happened as Jesus and his disciples were heading out of Jericho. Matthew recounts that two blind men heard that Jesus was passing by and shouted out a plea for mercy. Mark's and Luke's accounts only mention one man, whom Mark identified as a beggar called Bartimaeus. Determined not to miss this once-in-a-lifetime opportunity to regain his sight, he continued to cry out to Jesus despite attempts by many in the crowd to silence him.⁶⁵ He refused to allow them to talk him out of his miracle.

Having attracted Jesus's attention, Jesus asked Bartimaeus what he wanted done for him. Bartimaeus replied that he wanted his sight. Showing Bartimaeus great compassion, Jesus gave him his sight, telling him to go on his way, that his faith had made him well. Bartimaeus praised God for his miracle and became a follower of Jesus.⁶⁶ In Matthew's account involving two blind men—Bartimaeus and a second blind man, who might have been begging along with him—Jesus touched their eyes out of compassion, and they immediately received their sight.⁶⁷

We have already seen how Jesus showed compassion to a centurion's servant and the daughter of a Canaanite woman. He healed both of them by sending his word, without ever seeing them.⁶⁸ Jesus did not withhold his compassion from the centurion and the Canaanite woman despite their ethnicity or nationality.

A dramatic example of Jesus's compassion is seen in his raising of a widow's dead son. Jesus was entering a city called Nain when he saw a funeral procession heading out of the city to the cemetery. The mourners were carrying the coffin of a young man. His mother was a widow and

---

63. Matt 12:9–13; Mark 3:1–5; Luke 6:6–10. See Boring, *Mark: A Commentary*, 93, commenting that the man's present condition connoted death because in a dry land where moisture means life, having a withered hand implies death. Therefore, his healing is narrated in resurrection language.

64. Matt 12:14; Mark 3:6; Luke 6:11.

65. Matt 20:29–31, noting that the two blind men persisted in their attempts to get Jesus's attention. Mark 10:46–48; Luke 18:35–39.

66. Matthew's account says both blind men received their sight and immediately followed Jesus. Matt 20:32–34; Mark 10:49–52; Luke 18:40–43.

67. Matt 20:34.

68. Matt 8:5–10//Luke 7:1–10; Matt 15:21–28//Mark 7:24–30.

he was her only son. This means that she had no husband to provide for her. And now she had lost the only son who could support her. Jesus had compassion on her when he saw her weeping. He told her not to weep and came and touched the coffin. He spoke to the dead young man and raised him from the dead. Jesus presented him to his mother who would now have her means of support back.[69]

Then there was the memorable example of Jesus's compassion when he fed five thousand men and their families with five loaves and two fish.[70] When Jesus heard that John the Baptist had been beheaded by Herod, he and his disciples got into a boat and headed to a deserted place in Bethsaida. However, many saw them leave and ran on foot ahead of them. When Jesus got out of the boat upon arriving in Bethsaida, there was already a crowd waiting. Looking on them with compassion, Jesus gave up the solitude he had sought there and taught them. As evening came, his disciples came to him and expressed concern that the crowd had not eaten, that it was getting late, and that it was a good idea to dismiss them so that they could go into the neighboring villages to get something to eat.

Instead of doing that, Jesus told his disciples to give the crowd something to eat. The disciples estimated that it would cost two hundred denarii to feed the crowd. A denarius was the equivalent of a penny in the Roman realm and was a day's wages. Philip estimated that it would cost two hundred denarii to feed all these people.[71] Jesus asked how much food they had. Andrew, Peter's brother, told him that there was a boy with five small barley loaves and two fish.[72] This lad's mother had packed him lunch, but one can only surmise that he was so engrossed in listening to Jesus's teaching that he had not even taken time to eat his lunch. Not only had the boy not eaten his lunch, but he was also willing to part with it and let Jesus have it. He had no idea what was about to happen. Little becomes much when put in Jesus's hands.

---

69. Luke 7:11–15. See Johnson, *Gospel of Luke*, 118, where he notes that this widow would have had no means of economic support in losing her only son. Jesus's compassion for her describes an inner emotion that accompanies mercy, the same compassion Jesus enjoined on his disciples.

70. Matt 14:15–21; Mark 6:35–44; Luke 9:12–17; John 6:5–13.

71. John 6:7. This was more than eight months' wages.

72. John 6:8–9.

THE CHRISTIAN AS IMITATOR OF CHRIST

In order to ensure orderly distribution of the food and avoid a stampede, Jesus asked his disciples to have the crowd sit in groups of fifty.[73] He then took the loaves and the fish, looked up to heaven, blessed them, broke them, and gave the pieces to his disciples to distribute. They kept breaking and distributing the pieces until the crowd all ate their fill. They collected twelve basketfuls of leftovers afterward. Matthew records that there were five thousand men besides women and children.[74]

At another time, after his brief sojourn in Tyre and Sidon, he came back to Galilee and sat on a mountainside. Great crowds came to him with lame, blind, crippled, mute, and many other sick people, and Jesus healed them all. After ministering to them for three straight days, Jesus said he felt compassion for them because they had nothing to eat. He said he did not want to send them away because they might collapse of hunger on the way. With just seven loaves and a few small fish, Jesus fed four thousand men in addition to the women and children who were there. But they all had enough to eat and were satisfied, with seven basketfuls of small pieces left over. He then sent the crowd away.[75]

Many of the people in this crowd would have been poor people. Jesus did not expect them to prove themselves to be self-sufficient in feeding themselves. Neither did he think that he was enabling dependency.[76] It is this same compassion that Christians, as imitators of Jesus, must demonstrate in their dealings with all people, regardless of their nationality, ethnicity, or socioeconomic status. Christians cannot withhold compassion from the poor to drive them to the cross and salvation in Christ[77] or withhold assistance to the poor because they expect them to pull themselves up by their own bootstraps as a show of faith in God's grace. That is not the example that Jesus Christ, the model for Christians, set during his ministry.

In fact, Jesus considered it so important to show compassion to the poor that he said he takes it personally when compassion is extended to or withheld from the poor. Jesus said this in the parable of the sheep

---

73. Luke 9:14. Mark's account says there were one hundred people in some groups and fifty in others (Mark 6:40).

74. Matt 14:21.

75. Matt 15:29–39; Mark 8:1–10.

76. Some evangelicals espouse the notion of accountable individualism, whereby the poor should fend for themselves and not be encouraged to become dependent. See Hendricks, *Christians Against Christianity*, 142.

77. A notion which is a perversion of the theory known as crucicentrism. Hendricks, *Christians Against Christianity*, 142.

and the goats, where he talked about his return to earth as king to judge the nations. At some point after his return, Jesus said he will separate the righteous (sheep) from the wicked (goats). He said the righteous will inherit the kingdom and the wicked will suffer eternal punishment. He said he (the king) will commend the righteous because they fed him when he was hungry, gave him drink when he was thirsty, took him in as a stranger, clothed him when he was naked, and visited him in prison. Jesus said the righteous will ask when they did all this for him and he will tell them that they did these things for him when they did it for the least of his brethren, believers who were suffering. Jesus said that he will tell the wicked how they failed to feed him when he was hungry, give him drink when he was thirsty, take him in as a stranger, clothe him when he was naked, or visit him in prison. They too will ask when they failed to do all these things for him. He will respond that when they failed to do it for the least of his brethren, they failed to do it for him.[78]

Jesus Christ, Total Devotee of God

Jesus was totally devoted to God, his Father in heaven. This devotion included spending time in prayer and fasting. The Bible records many instances of Jesus praying. One evening, while Jesus was in the home of Simon and his brother Andrew, many sick and demon-possessed people were brought to him. He healed many of the sick and cast many demons out of those who were possessed. Very early the next morning, while it was still dark, Jesus left the house and went to a solitary place to pray.[79] Jesus often withdrew from the crowds that followed him to quiet or solitary places where he could spend time alone with God in prayer.[80] After the miraculous feeding of five thousand men and their families with two fish and five loaves, Jesus dismissed the crowd, sent his disciples in the boat to the other side of the lake ahead of him, and went on a mountainside to pray.[81] He sometimes prayed alone, privately, or by himself even when his disciples were near him.[82] And he sometimes prayed in their presence.[83]

78. Matt 25:31–46.
79. Mark 1:32–35.
80. Luke 5:15–16.
81. Matt 14:22–23.
82. Luke 9:18.
83. Luke 11:1.

THE CHRISTIAN AS IMITATOR OF CHRIST

Jesus prayed when John the Baptist baptized him. The Holy Spirit visibly descended upon him and God audibly spoke to affirm that Jesus was his son with whom he was very pleased.[84] Jesus prayed for himself on the eve of his crucifixion after he and his disciples had eaten the Passover supper. He affirmed that he had completed the work or mission God sent him to earth to carry out, and prayed that God would glorify him with the glory he shared with the Father before the world began.[85]

Jesus prayed fervently in the garden of Gethsemane after the Passover supper. He prayed three times that God would spare him this cup—the separation from God that would take place because he would be carrying the sins of the world. But he surrendered to God's will by praying that God's will and not his own be done.[86]

Not only did Jesus live a life of prayer, but he also taught about prayer because he wants Christians, his disciples, to be devoted to God in prayer. During his Sermon on the Mount, Jesus taught about how not to pray. He said that prayer should not be motivated by a desire to be seen and admired, calling that hypocritical. He warned that the only reward one who prays like that gets is the admiration of the people who are impressed by it because God does not reward that kind of prayer. Instead, prayer should be private. And even though private, the answer and reward from God will be given openly and, therefore, seen by others.[87]

Jesus also taught that prayer should not be a rambling rant. Jesus explained that pagans pray that way because they think that the more words they say, the more likely their gods will hear. God, being omniscient, already knows the needs of believers. Believers should get to the point and not beat about the bush.[88] Jesus taught that prayer should not be conceited and self-righteous. He told a parable of a Pharisee who went up to the temple to pray along with a tax collector. Instead of honoring God in his prayer, the Pharisee prayed about himself by elevating himself above others, including the tax collector, and touting how he fasted and gave tithes of all he owned. Jesus said that, unlike the tax collector who

---

84. Luke 3:21–22.
85. John 17:1–5.
86. Matt 26:36-44; Luke 22:39-45. See Johnson, *Gospel of Luke*, 351, noting that the cup represents Jesus's suffering, as his words at the last supper made plain.
87. Matt 6:5–6.
88. Matt 6:7–8.

prayed a humble and penitent prayer, the Pharisee went home without having received justification from God.[89]

Jesus did not just teach his disciples how not to pray, but he did teach them how to pray by giving them a model for prayer.[90] This model prayer was part of the Sermon on the Mount, given after one of Jesus's disciples asked him to teach them to pray as John the Baptist taught his disciples. The prayer Jesus taught them is always referred to as the Lord's Prayer. Jesus was offering a pattern on which his disciples were to model their prayers. Jesus, therefore, prefaced it by telling them that this was how they should pray.[91]

Jesus's devotion to God included fasting. Before his temptation by Satan in the wilderness, Jesus fasted for forty days and nights. After his fast, the devil tempted him to sin, but he overcame all the devil's temptations.[92] And not only did Jesus fast, but he also provided guidance for when a believer fasts, suggesting that it is something that a Christian ought to practice regularly. He told believers to avoid making a show of fasting to impress people, describing that as a hypocritical fast that God will not honor. The admiration that fasting to show off attracts will be its only reward. Instead, fasting ought to be a private matter between the believer and God. It is that kind of fast that God will reward because it is not done with wrong motives.[93]

As imitators of Jesus Christ, Christians also ought to be totally devoted to God in prayer and fasting because doing so builds intimacy with God, matures Christians to become more like God, makes them more eager to please him as Jesus did, and empowers them to do his will.

In addition to being devoted to God in prayer and fasting, Jesus was also devoted to God by spending all his time and energy doing God's work. Jesus began to preach about the kingdom of God after John the Baptist was imprisoned.[94] While in prison, John was kept informed about the things Jesus was doing. He sent messengers to Jesus to ask him if he

---

89. Luke 18:9–14.

90. Matt 6:9–13; Luke 11:1–4. See Johnson, *Gospel of Luke*, 179, noting that this prayer Jesus taught his disciples authenticates his prophetic mission by showing that what he proclaims and performs in his ministry expresses the deepest reality of his own relationship with God. See also González, *Teach Us To Pray*; Packer, *Praying the Lord's Prayer*; Towns, *Praying the Lord's Prayer*; and Wright, *Lord And His Prayer*.

91. Matt 6:9.

92. Matt 4:1–11; Luke 4:1–13.

93. Matt 6:16–18.

94. Matt 4:12–17.

was the expected Messiah, or whether they should be expecting someone else. Jesus told the messengers to go back and tell John what they had heard and seen. Blind eyes were seeing, and the lame were walking. Lepers were being healed, deaf ears were being opened, dead people were being raised, and the good news was being preached to the poor.[95] This included those who were poor in spirit and had humbled themselves to acknowledge their need for God, as well as those who were oppressed, disadvantaged, and looked down on in society, especially by the wealthy and privileged.

Jesus ministered in Capernaum on the Sabbath in the early days of his ministry. He taught the people, cast out demons, and healed many people. The people of Capernaum wanted to keep him there, but Jesus told them that he could not just stay there; he had to preach the good news of the kingdom of God to the other towns also, because that is why he was sent. So, he preached in the synagogues of Judea.[96] Jesus traveled about on foot from one town and village to another, proclaiming the good news of the kingdom of God.[97] Jesus had a sense of urgency about the work God sent him to do. He said that he must do God's work while it was day because the night comes when no one can work.[98]

As imitators of Christ, Christians must also model this devotion to God by being about God's business, and by using their time, energy, and gifts to do God's work in ministering to and serving others, regardless of their nationality, ethnicity, skin color, or socioeconomic status.

Jesus Christ, the One with Power over the Devil

Jesus talked often about the devil. Jesus talked about the mission of false leaders or shepherds—hirelings who did not operate under God's authority, which meant they were of the devil—as coming to steal, kill, and destroy. That must be understood to be the devil's mission too. In contrast, Jesus is the good shepherd who came to give all who believe in him abundant life.[99] As the Son of God and second person of the Triune

---

95. Matt 11:4–5.

96. Luke 4:31–44; Mark 1:38, where Mark records that Jesus told his disciples that they must go to the nearby villages and preach there also. He traveled throughout Galilee, preaching in the synagogues.

97. Luke 8:1.

98. John 9:4.

99. John 10:10. See Moloney, *Gospel of John*, 303–4, where he explains Jesus's words

JESUS CHRIST, THE MODEL FOR CHRISTIANS TO IMITATE

God or Trinity, all power and all authority in heaven and on earth has been given to Jesus.[100] He, therefore, has power over the devil who, as the adversary of Christians,[101] works overtime to undermine the ability of Christians to obey God's commandments, love one another as Jesus has loved them, love their neighbor as themselves, treat others as they would want to be treated, and live by the truth of Jesus's word.

Before Jesus began his public ministry, and right after his baptism by John, he had his first confrontation with the devil. After Jesus was baptized, the Spirit of God descended on him, and God audibly affirmed him as his son with whom he was well pleased.[102] Jesus was tempted by the devil after a forty-day fast. Jesus used the Scriptures to repel Satan's attempts to compromise his loyalty to God by trying to get him to put comfort before obedience by turning stones into bread; test God by leaping from the pinnacle of the temple; or worship Satan in return for worldly possessions and power.[103] After Satan departed, Jesus returned to Galilee. He settled in Capernaum and launched his public ministry after John the Baptist was imprisoned.

Like Jesus, a Christian must become intimately familiar with God's word by studying the Scriptures.[104] The Scriptures reveal the devil's devices so that Christians may not be ignorant of them.[105] They also equip the Christian to overcome temptation and see through the devil's lies. Jesus said that the devil is a liar and the father of lies.[106]

We saw that God only created one race. Yet there is the narrative about many races, and false notions that some races are superior to others. Knowing the truth of God's word as revealed in the Bible enables one to reject the lie of multiple races. It enables the Christian to reject the lie of racial purity and the un-Christlike practice of racial segregation. It

---

to refer to the fact that there was nothing life giving about those who came before Jesus claiming to be shepherds. They were thieves and robbers. But Jesus offers salvation and pasture and gives the sheep abundant life.

100. Matt 28:18.
101. 1 Pet 5:8.
102. Matt 3:16–17.
103. Matt 4:1–11; Mark 1:12–13.
104. John 8:31.
105. 2 Cor 2:11.
106. John 8:44–45. See Moloney, *Gospel of John*, 280, where he explains that through lies and deceit, the devil robbed Adam of God's original promise of immortality, making him a liar and a murderer. Because of the devil's role of deceit and lies in human history, this makes him "the father of lies."

enables Christians to love other people, especially other Christians, as Christ loves them, regardless of their nationality, ethnicity, skin color, or socioeconomic status. It also enables Christians to reject the lie that it is acceptable, even compassionate, to withhold assistance to the poor so that hardship may drive them to faith in Jesus Christ and salvation. Jesus did not just preach the good news to the poor, but he also healed them, set them free from demonic spirits, and fed them. And he said that he takes it personally when others do the same or refuse to do the same to the least of Christ's brothers and sisters.

One of the devil's devices is to break the bonds between people. He desires to break the bonds of love among disciples by driving wedges between them. Christians must use their knowledge of God's word to reject the devil's attempts to use ethnic and socioeconomic differences, as well as differences in nationality, to divide them contrary to Christ's teaching and example.

Another of the devil's devices is division. Satan knows that a house divided against itself cannot stand.[107] Because of this, Paul exhorted the church in Ephesus to make every effort to keep the unity of the Spirit through the bond of peace. The way to do that is to walk worthy of the calling of God to be his disciple by being humble, gentle, patient, and by bearing with each other in love.[108] Disciples of Christ must resist the temptation to be used by Satan to divide the church based on nationality, ethnicity, skin color, or socioeconomic status.

Jesus Christ, Ruler of a Future Diverse Kingdom

The kingdom of God is a diverse kingdom. It is a blended family made up of people from all over the world, people from all nationalities and ethnicities.

At one point during Jesus's ministry, his mother and brothers came looking for him as he talked to a crowd. When he was told that his mother and brothers were outside wanting to speak to him, Jesus rhetorically asked, "Who is my mother, and who are my brothers?"[109] He then pointed to his disciples as his family and said whoever does the will of his Father in heaven is his family. Jesus's statement makes it clear that the

---

107. Matt 12:25; Mark 3:25; Luke 11:17.
108. Eph 4:1–3.
109. Matt 12:46–50.

JESUS CHRIST, THE MODEL FOR CHRISTIANS TO IMITATE

kingdom of God is a diverse, blended family of all who do the will of his Father, Jehovah.

The apostle Paul emphasized that all who have put their faith in Christ are children of God. He said that there is neither Jew nor Greek, slave nor free, male nor female, because all Christians are one in Christ.[110] There are no national, ethnic, gender, or socioeconomic divisions or barriers in the kingdom of God.

In the Revelation of Jesus to the apostle John, John saw a scene in heaven where a great multitude from every nation, tribe, people, and language stood before the throne of God and Jesus Christ, the Lamb. They were wearing white robes and waving palm branches. These were saints who had died during the great tribulation, a period of great suffering under the rule of the antichrist that will take place in the last three-and-a-half years of history.[111] Their diversity reflects Christ's statement about the family of God. The only identifying characteristic of God's diverse, blended family is their obedience to God, not their nationality, ethnicity, skin color, or socioeconomic status.[112]

The great tribulation will be followed by Christ's second coming and the establishment of Christ's millennial kingdom on earth. John saw a vision of Jesus's second coming at the end of the tribulation period with the title "King of Kings and Lord of Lords" inscribed on his robe and on his thigh.[113] Upon Jesus's return, there will be a final world war, called the Battle of Armageddon, which will be centered in the Middle East. Armageddon means the mountain of Megiddo and is located in northcentral Palestine. Under the instigation of evil spirits, the antichrist

---

110. Gal 3:26–28.

111. Rev 7:9–14; 13:1; 1 John 2:18. See Blount, *Revelation*, 150–51, noting the vast crowd's universal nature, meaning that Jews and gentiles—metaphorically grafted onto Israel's family tree through Christ—stand together in their worship, praise, and identification as the people of God. Also see Yong, *Revelation*, 110–15, where he comments that this huge group of persons invites consideration of how they might speak theologically to the church today—namely, whether we will be welcoming of others different from us and stand out now from the world's crowds in order to be counted among the eschatological multitude tomorrow.

112. For how God uses the diverse people he calls to enrich the body of Christ with their unique interpretative insights of the Bible, see McCaulley et al., *New Testament in Color*, and Adeyemo, *Africa Bible Commentary*, interpreting and applying the Bible in the light of African culture but also providing insights that benefit readers from around the world.

113. Rev 19:11–16.

will lead armies from many nations to destroy Israel and Christians.[114] But Jesus will return and fight against and defeat these enemies.[115] The antichrist and the false prophet, a powerful false prophet who will support the antichrist, will be captured and thrown into the lake of fire than burns with sulfur.[116] The rest of the ungodly living on earth, all who rejected Christ, will be gathered for judgment and destroyed.[117] The nations will only be populated by believers in Christ after the destruction of the wicked. Christ will rule over the earth as king and believers from the nations will go on pilgrimages to Jerusalem to seek him[118] and celebrate the Feast of Tabernacles.[119]

Satan, described as the dragon, the serpent of old, the devil, will be bound and thrown into a bottomless pit called the Abyss for one thousand years. Jesus Christ will reign here on earth with his saints, those who believed in him, for those thousand years in what is known as the millennial kingdom. These saints will include those who will be raptured, transfigured, and taken to heaven during the first stage of Christ's second coming; believers who are alive when he returns; and believers who died during the great tribulation who will come to life upon his return at the end of the tribulation period.[120]

Jesus's millennial kingdom will be headquartered in the new Jerusalem and people who live there shall experience the blessing of longevity and safety. The prophet Zechariah prophesied the return of Christ to Zion and the blessings that will follow. He prophesied that peace will come to Jerusalem with Christ's return and millennial rule.[121]

After the thousand years, Satan will be released from the Abyss and will attempt one final time to deceive those who live in the nations that exist outside of the beloved city and center of Christ's millennial rule. He

---

114. Rev 16:13–14, 16. In Zech 12, the prophet prophesied the Lord's return and intervention in the battle of Armageddon, and the defeat of Israel's enemies.

115. Zech 14:1–5.

116. Rev 19:19–20. Another name for this lake is the lake of fire and sulfur (Rev 20:10). When the Kilauea Volcano in Hawaii erupted in May of 2018, its molten lava was said to be emitting sulfur dioxide, among other gases.

117. Rev 14:19–20; 19:15, 21.

118. Isa 2:2–3.

119. Zech 8:20–23; 14:9, 16.

120. Rev 20:4.

121. Zech 8; 9. In Isa 2:2–5; 4:2–6; 11; 24:23; 25:6–8; 32:1–5; and 62, the prophet Isaiah prophesied about Christ's rule in Jerusalem. In Jer 3:17, the prophet Jeremiah also prophesied of Christ's millennial rule from Jerusalem.

will attempt to form an alliance with them to attack the beloved city and wage one final attempt to change the course of history and his prophesied doom. Some of those who join him will be people born during Christ's millennial rule who reject Christ's rule, choosing instead to believe Satan's lies. They are born to believers who live in the nations who do not have glorified bodies like the raptured saints or those who were raised on Christ's second return who reign with him in his kingdom.[122]

However, the devil and his cohorts will fail in this final attempt. The Bible says fire will come down from heaven and devour them as they surround the city. The devil will be thrown into the lake of fire and sulfur, which was created for him and his fallen angels.[123]

God will create a new heaven and a new earth, a new universe[124] rid of Satan, sin, and the effects of the fall, and he will live with his people in eternity. There will be holiness and righteousness.[125] Creation will be liberated from the bondage to decay in the new heaven and new earth.[126] A city called the new Jerusalem, which is a heavenly city, will be relocated to the new earth. God himself will live with his saints in the new earth. They will have glorified, imperishable, immortal bodies like Christ's

---

122. Since these believers do not have glorified bodies and are still giving birth, they will also die and go to heaven to be with God till the end of the millennial rule when God himself comes and lives with his redeemed in a new earth. They will return with God and be unified with resurrected glorious bodies. It is important to note that the Bible acknowledges more than one resurrection. There's also the rapture of living believers and dead believers (1 Cor 15:51–52; 1 Thess 4:16–17). The first resurrection of saints who died during the tribulation will happen on the second return of Christ at the end of the great tribulation (Rev 20:4), and the second resurrection of all else who have died after the end of the thousand-year reign of Christ on earth (Rev 20:5). This second resurrection will include the Old Testament saints, deceased believers who lived in the nations during the millennial reign of Christ, as well as the wicked who will be raised for judgment (Rev 20:11–12, 15). See Blount, *Revelation*, 367–68, explaining that the first resurrection restores the martyrs to life for their millennial reign, and the second brings all the dead before the great white throne. Also see Yong, *Revelation*, 233–36, explaining that the millennial kingdom is bookended by two resurrections, and that it is an interim period to reward the martyrs and to grant reprieve from the dragon's (Satan's) claws.

123. Rev 20:7–10.

124. The stars and galaxies as we know them will no longer exist. Isaiah prophesied that the stars of the heavens will be dissolved, the sky rolled up like a scroll, and all the starry host will fall (Isa 34:4 NIV). He also prophesied about the new heavens and the new earth that will follow Christ's millennial reign (Isa 65:17–25).

125. Second Peter 3:13 says it will be the home of righteousness.

126. Rom 8:21.

resurrected body.[127] There will be no more death, sorrow, crying, or pain, for the old order of things has passed away, and God himself will wipe every tear from the eyes of his people.[128]

It is this future righteous, diverse, eternal kingdom over which Christ will rule that all Christians hope for. This is the place Jesus promised to prepare for his disciples of all time.[129] It is a kingdom made up of Christians from all over the world who will live eternally with God and Christ in glorified bodies. It will reflect the scene in heaven that John saw with people from every nation, tribe, people, and language. There will be no racial segregation there. There will be no racial discrimination there. There will be no talk of racial purity or White Christianity there. And there will be no distinction on the basis of socioeconomic status there. If life on earth is a dress rehearsal for Christians headed to heaven, then there should be nothing un-Christlike or unbiblical in the lives of Christians and their interactions with others here on earth.

Everyone who claims to be a Christian should imitate the model Jesus provided in his interactions with all the people he encountered. They should live here on earth in a manner worthy of people headed to a future diverse kingdom where Christ rules in all righteousness and where there are no divisions based on nationality, ethnicity, skin color, or socioeconomic status.

The millennial kingdom and the new heaven and new earth will be the ultimate fulfillment of what God has always intended—that his creation live in loving community with each other, regardless of differences, and with him. That was his intent in the garden of Eden before Satan cunningly engineered the fall of humankind, and that was his intent in sending his son Jesus Christ to redeem and reconcile the world to himself. For all who receive him and become his disciples, living with him in the millennial kingdom and later with him and his Father in the new heaven and new earth is the culmination of, and reward for, their faith and obedience.

---

127. 1 Cor 15:52–55.

128. Rev 21:1–4. See Blount, *Revelation*, 379–80, explaining the staggering results of God's direct relationship with the peoples participating in this covenant relationship. God will remove the cause of tears, including pain and even death itself. Also see Yong, *Revelation*, 243, noting that the covenantal language of the Old Testament is enlarged to include all the peoples of the earth.

129. John 14:2–3.

2

Who Is a Christian?

ONE MIGHT HEAR IT said that someone is a good Christian man or woman, or that a family is a Christian family. Some schools, colleges, or universities are referred to as Christian schools, colleges, or universities. One may even hear a country referred to as a Christian country. And people may point to someone as having or believing in Christian principles or as having Judeo-Christian ethics or values. What does this all mean? Who is a Christian? And what does that mean?

Definitions of Christian

There are many secular ideas and definitions of Christian that may be insightful but not necessarily biblical. For example, Merriam-Webster defines a Christian as a person who believes in Jesus Christ and follows his teachings, one who professes belief in the teachings of Jesus Christ, or a member of a Christian church. It defines Christianity as the religion that is based on the teachings of Jesus Christ.[1] The Cambridge English Dictionary defines a Christian as a person who follows or belongs to a religion based on the worship of one God and the teachings of Jesus Christ as described in the Bible, or one who follows or belongs to the Christian religion. It defines Christianity as a religion based on the worship of one God and the teachings of Jesus Christ as described in the Bible.[2] The

1. Merriam-Webster, "Christian (n.)" and "Christianity (n.)."
2. Cambridge, "Christian (n.)" and "Christianity (n.)."

Oxford Learner's Dictionaries defines a Christian as one who relates to or professes Christianity or its teachings, a person who has received Christian baptism, or who is a believer in Christianity, and Christianity as the religion based on the person and teachings of Jesus Christ, or its beliefs and practices.[3] One concordance[4] defines a Christian as a follower of Jesus Christ and an expository dictionary of Bible words defines a Christian as an adherent of Jesus.[5]

Notions of who a Christian is are also influenced by popular culture or history. Historically, some laws in colonial America, such as penal laws or laws governing who could run for elected office, defined who a Christian is in terms of being White. In 1680, slaves were punished in Virginia after a quelled rebellion for laying their hands on "any Christian," meaning White people.[6] And in 1705, Virginia lawmakers made it a requirement for one to be a "Christian White servant" in order to hold public office.[7] Sometimes even political ideology influences what people believe about who a Christian is. However, extrabiblical definitions cannot truly and fully capture who a Christian is. The full import of who a Christian is can only be fully gleaned and understood by examining the Bible.

Biblical References to *Christian*

The first use of the word *Christian* was in the first century in a place called Antioch in the Roman province of Syria. Writing in the Acts of the Apostles, Luke, a physician and companion of the apostle Paul, who also wrote the Gospel of Luke, records that the disciples were first called Christians in Antioch.[8] It is important to stress that those who were called Christians were disciples of Jesus Christ, not just born again, converts, or believers. The Greek word for disciple, *mathétés*, denotes a learner or someone who follows the teaching of another. Thus, it has been pointed out that a disciple is not just a pupil but an adherent who

---

3. Oxford Learner's, "Christian (n.)" and "Christianity (n.)."

4. See Strong, *New Strong's Concordance*, 111.

5. See Vine et al., *Vine's Complete Expository Dictionary*, 101 (New Testament Section).

6. See Kendi, *Stamped from the Beginning*, 54.

7. Kendi, *Stamped from the Beginning*, 68.

8. Acts 11:26. Luke authored this book in AD 62. It is believed that the term *Christian* was first used in Antioch ca. AD 43. See Smith, *Smith's Bible Dictionary*, 116.

imitates his or her teacher.[9] Jesus told believers that they must live by his word or teaching to become his disciples.[10] And it is only after becoming a disciple, an imitator of Jesus, that one can accurately and biblically be called a Christian.

When the disciples were first called Christians in Antioch, it carried with it the connotation that they were followers of Christ. It meant "little Christs." The name derived from *Christ* and was rendered *christianos* in Greek. It is quite possible that the pronunciation of the word in its inception in Antioch, especially given the scorn that was attached to it,[11] was probably more like "Christ-ian," with a full enunciation of the "Christ" in Christian. The modern pronunciation of the word hardly enunciates the "Christ" in Christian and the term has acquired a cultural or even secular meaning vastly different from its New Testament origins, hence modern definitions that define a Christian as one who is a member of a Christian church, or one who professes belief in the teachings of Jesus Christ. Professing to believe in something is one thing. Living out that profession as a lifestyle is another.

It was not the disciples who called themselves Christians. It was the gentiles among whom they lived who called them by this name, which carried a scornful connotation. This is seen when the apostle Paul appeared before King Agrippa on charges by his Jewish antagonists, who had plotted to kill him.[12] For his own safety, Roman soldiers took Paul to Caesarea where he was tried by Governor Felix and his successor Governor Festus.[13] Pending his appeal to Emperor Caesar, King Agrippa visited Governor Festus while Paul was still being held in Caesarea, and asked to hear from Paul.[14] Paul shared his personal testimony about his former life as a persecutor of disciples of Christ until his dramatic conversion. He then asked King Agrippa if he believed in the prophets of the Old Testament. King Agrippa responded by asking Paul if he thought he could "so quickly," or in such a short time, persuade him to become a Christian.[15]

---

9. Vine et al., *Vine's Complete Expository Dictionary*, 171 (New Testament Section).

10. John 8:31–32.

11. See Johnson, *Acts of the Apostles*, 204–5, where he notes that *Christian* appears to have originated as a somewhat slighting designation, given not by the believers themselves but by hostile observers.

12. Acts 23.

13. Acts 23; 24; 25.

14. Acts 25:22.

15. Acts 26:28.

The Christian as Imitator of Christ

Writing to encourage disciples who were being persecuted for their faith, the apostle Peter exhorted them to glorify God that they bear the name Christian and not to consider it a disgrace to suffer for being identified as one.[16] In all three cases of the use of the word in the Bible, therefore, there was a tone of scorn.[17] It wasn't until the second century that believers themselves accepted this name as a name of honor.[18]

Names Followers of Christ Used to Describe Themselves

Followers of Christ referred to themselves variously as believers,[19] brothers or brethren,[20] disciples,[21] saints,[22] or holy ones.[23] *Saints* or *holy ones* denoted that followers or disciples of Christ were separated or set apart from the world unto Christ to live holy lives. They were, therefore, imitators of Christ who, being tempted in every way as we are, was yet without sin.[24]

In his trial before Governor Felix, the apostle Paul referred to himself as a follower of the Way.[25] This was probably a reference to Jesus himself. Before his crucifixion, Jesus told his disciples he was going away and that they knew where he was going and the way there. When Thomas said they did not know where he was going or the way there, Jesus told his disciples that he is the way, the truth, and the life, and that no one comes to the Father except through him.[26]

It is noteworthy that nowhere in the Bible did Christians or believers refer to themselves as evangelicals.

---

16. 1 Pet 4:16.
17. Acts 11:26; 26:28; 1 Pet 4:16.
18. Vine et al., *Vine's Complete Expository Dictionary*, 101 (New Testament Section).
19. Acts 5:14.
20. Acts 15:1, 23; 1 Cor 7:12.
21. Acts 9:26.
22. Rom 8:27; 15:25.
23. Jude 1:14.
24. Heb 4:15.
25. Acts 24:14. See Johnson, *Acts of the Apostles*, 412–13, 416, where he interprets *the Way* (*hodos*) as a reference to the Messianists' claim to represent a legitimate, authentic form of Judaism, not heresy.
26. John 14:6.

Other Names Used to Describe Believers

We have already seen that it was not the disciples who called themselves Christians. It was the gentiles among whom they lived who called them by this name. And as already pointed out, it was meant to carry a scornful connotation.

Believers were also referred to as members of the sect of the Nazarenes. During Paul's trial before Governor Felix, the lawyer for the high priest and the elders who came to testify against Paul called him a ringleader of the sect of the Nazarenes,[27] although Paul did not seem to accept that description, choosing instead to describe himself as a follower of the Way.[28]

Again, it is noteworthy that not only did believers not refer to themselves as evangelicals in the Bible, but neither did others refer to them that way.

Identifying Characteristics of a Christian

A Christian Is a Follower of the Way

Before his crucifixion, Jesus comforted his disciples by telling them about his Father's house in heaven. He told them that there were many mansions or rooms in his Father's house and that he was going away to prepare a place for them. He assured them that he would come again for them. He told them that they knew where he was going and the way there.[29] To this, Thomas, one of his disciples, said that they did not know where he was going and asked how they could know the way. In one of his "I AM" statements recorded in the Gospel of John, Jesus answered Thomas by telling his disciples, "I am the way and the truth and the life. No one comes to the Father except through me."[30]

During Paul's trial before Governor Felix, although the lawyer for the high priest and the elders who came to testify against Paul called him a ringleader of the sect of the Nazarenes,[31] Paul told Governor Felix

---

27. Acts 24:5.
28. Acts 24:14.
29. John 14:1–4.
30. John 14:6.
31. Acts 24:5.

The Christian as Imitator of Christ

that he was a follower of the Way,[32] the term Jesus had used to describe himself in his discourse with Thomas. It is noteworthy that before he became a disciple of Christ, Paul had asked for letters from the high priest to go to Damascus to arrest followers of the Way and bring them back to Jerusalem. Another reference to the Way is found in the book of Acts during Paul's initial ministry in Ephesus while he was on his third missionary journey. He taught about the kingdom of God in the synagogue for three months. However, some of the Jews refused to believe and publicly maligned or spoke evil of the Way. Paul left the synagogue as a result. He took his disciples with him and taught at a location that was referred to as a lecture hall or school.[33]

The word *way* is derived from the Greek word *hodos* and denotes more than receiving or professing belief in Jesus. It denotes a road or path that the believer in Christ walks in faith and fellowship with Christ to the very end.[34] In referring to himself as the way, Jesus was saying that he is the only path to God.

A Christian Is One Who Has Been Regenerated

To become a disciple or follower of Jesus, one must be regenerated. This is also variously referred to as being saved or born again. While Jesus was in Jerusalem to celebrate the Passover, a man called Nicodemus, a Pharisee, came to Jesus at night wanting to know more about him.

Pharisees were Jewish leaders who insisted on keeping the law of Moses and Jewish traditions strictly. This made them very ritualistic and legalistic, even in their tithing. They were also often self-righteous and proud. But a few, like Nicodemus, Gamaliel, and Joseph of Arimathea, showed a good and open heart. In a parable that Jesus told about pride, he used the character of a Pharisee who boasted about how he fasted twice a week and gave a tenth of all he got as an illustration of pride.[35] Jesus also called the Pharisees hypocrites for tithing even their spices but ignoring justice, mercy, and faithfulness, which he called the more

---

32. Acts 24:14.
33. Acts 19:8–9.
34. See note to Acts 24:14 in Stamps and Adams, *Life in the Spirit Study Bible*, 1720, commenting that salvation in Christ is not only an experience to receive but also a road to walk in faith and fellowship with Jesus to the end in order to enter final salvation in the world to come.
35. Luke 18:12

important matters of the law.[36] Pharisees had great political influence and formed much of the Jewish ruling council, known as the Sanhedrin. It was made up of the chief priests, scribes, and lawyers who were learned in the Jewish law. The high priest headed it. One could liken it to a Jewish Supreme Court with power over religious matters. It had the power of capital punishment, except this was taken away by the Romans in Jesus's day. They needed Pilate's permission to have Jesus crucified and have his legs broken to hasten his death. However, since Jesus had already died when they got to him, they did not break his legs.[37]

Nicodemus was a member of this Jewish ruling council. With all the miracles Jesus was performing, Nicodemus was curious about whether Jesus could be the promised Messiah prophesied about in the Old Testament.[38]

Jesus engaged Nicodemus in a discourse about salvation and told him that no one can see the kingdom of God, that is, God's rule and presence in their lives, unless they are born again.[39] Because of the disobedience and fall of Adam and Eve, sin entered the human race. Since then, every human being is born a sinner.[40] And with sin comes spiritual death and separation from God.[41] It is this spiritual chasm that Jesus came to bridge[42] by shedding his own blood for the remission of sin.[43] Jesus made it clear to Nicodemus that everyone who believes in him has eternal life.[44] This new birth, called *palingenesia* in Greek, is a spiritual regeneration,[45] a new life that results from the work of the Holy Spirit when one hears and

---

36. Matt 23:23.

37. John 19:16, 31, 33. For more on the Sanhedrin, see Smith, *Smith's Bible Dictionary*, 588–89.

38. John 3:1–2.

39. John 3:3, 5. See Moloney, *Gospel of John*, 91–93, where he explains that Jesus was challenging Nicodemus to expand his notion of what the kingdom of God might be by saying one must be born again from above, meaning one must both be born of water in time (a ritual of rebirth solemnized by water baptism) and of the Spirit by experiencing the inbreaking of God.

40. Ps 51:1.

41. Gen 2:17.

42. John 14:6.

43. Rom 5:8; Heb 9:22, 27, 28; 10:4–10.

44. John 3:14–18. In Acts 4:12, Peter told his hearers that salvation is found in no one else but Jesus Christ.

45. See "Regeneration" in Vine et al., *Vine's Complete Expository Dictionary*, 517 (New Testament Section).

THE CHRISTIAN AS IMITATOR OF CHRIST

receives the message of salvation in the gospel.[46] It results in the gift of salvation, called *soteria* in Greek, signifying deliverance, preservation, or salvation.[47] Paul emphasized this aspect of salvation by reminding Titus, his son in the faith whom he had placed over the ministry in Crete, that God saved us not because of any righteous works we have done, but only because of his mercy. Paul then explained the role of the Holy Spirit in this process. God saves us through the water of rebirth and renewal by the Holy Spirit.[48] In other words, the Holy Spirit serves as God's agent in washing away our sins and causing us to be spiritually reborn and renewed.

To be saved, one must repent of sin and turn to God.[49] When Jesus began his public ministry and started preaching after the imprisonment of John the Baptist, his forerunner who had prepared the way for him,[50] his very first call was for people to repent. He told them that the kingdom of heaven was at hand and urged them to believe the good news.[51] The Greek word for repentance is *metanoia*, which means a change of mind that involves a turning from sin to God.[52]

Jesus warned that all who do not repent will perish.[53] And God graciously works in the sinner through the Holy Spirit to stir repentance.[54] It is God himself who lovingly draws the sinner to faith in Christ upon hearing the good news of salvation.[55] The Holy Spirit is the one that convicts the sinner of sin and the need to repent and receive the salvation that God offers in Christ. Before his crucifixion, Jesus told his disciples that he was going away but promised to send a Counselor, the Holy Spirit, who would convict the world of guilt with respect to sin.[56] The convicting

---

46. Titus 3:5; Jas 1:18; 1 Pet 1:23.

47. See "Salvation" in Vine et al., *Vine's Complete Expository Dictionary*, 545 (New Testament Section).

48. Titus 3:5.

49. Acts 3:19; 16:31. See Johnson, *Acts of the Apostles*, 57, 68, where he interprets repenting and turning to God as involving a change of mind and conversion.

50. John the Baptist prepared the way for Jesus in fulfillment of Isaiah's prophecy in Isa 40:3. He called on his hearers to repent, telling them that the kingdom of heaven is near (Matt 3:1–3; Mark 1:1–4; Luke 3:3–4).

51. Matt 4:17; Mark 1:14–15.

52. See "Repentance" in Vine et al., *Vine's Complete Expository Dictionary*, 525 (New Testament Section).

53. Luke 13:3, 5.

54. Acts 11:18.

55. John 6:44, 65.

56. John 16:7–8.

work of the Holy Spirit was evident when the apostle Peter preached in Jerusalem on the day of Pentecost and his hearers, cut to the heart, asked what they should do. Peter told them to repent and be baptized in the name of Jesus Christ for the forgiveness of their sins and the gift of the Holy Spirit.[57]

Turning to God in repentance requires forsaking sin. During the apostle Paul's third missionary journey, many of those in Ephesus who believed in Jesus Christ came and openly confessed the evil things in which they had been involved. Some of them had practiced sorcery or magic but now repudiated it and publicly burned their books or scrolls.[58]

In addition to repenting of sin, one must also confess with one's mouth that Jesus is Lord and believe in one's heart that God raised him from the dead. Paul explained that it is with the heart that one believes and is justified, and it is with the mouth that one confesses and is saved.[59] Everyone who meets these conditions and calls on the name of the Lord will be saved.[60] To be saved is to be recreated or born again. Jesus told the Jews that whoever hears his word and believes in the one who sent him has eternal life and has crossed over from death to life.[61] It is God who grants this gift of salvation and offers spiritual and eternal deliverance from sin and death to all who accept his son as Lord and Savior.[62]

In Isaiah's day, God showed how he detested outward forms of godliness and empty religion. He sent Isaiah to extend an invitation to the nation to come and allow him to reason with them to repent. If they did, though their sins were like scarlet, he would make them as white as snow. And though their sins were as red as crimson, he would make them as wool. In other words, he would replace their sinfulness with purity. In calling the nation of Israel to repent of its sin, it is significant to note

---

57. Acts 2:37–38.

58. Acts 19:18–19.

59. Rom 10:9–10. See Jarvis J. Williams, "Letter to the Romans," in McCaulley et al., *New Testament in Color*, 278, 301, commenting that the Jews who reject Christ stumble over Christ in their efforts to keep the Torah. However, the gentiles receive the promise of Christ's righteousness because they confess with their mouth that Jesus is Lord and believe in their hearts that God raised him from the dead so that they could be saved. See also Adeyemo, *Africa Bible Commentary*, 1366, noting that the only thing that is required now for salvation is to respond to the gospel by confessing Jesus is Lord and believing God has raised him from the dead.

60. Rom 10:13.

61. John 5:24.

62. John 3:16.

that God uses the color red or scarlet to describe sin. This is probably because it takes blood to remit and wash away sin.[63] Nonetheless, some inaccurately ascribe the color black to sin or to a sinful heart, although it is unscriptural.

Salvation is God's will for all humankind. Paul told Timothy that God wants everyone to be saved and come to a knowledge of his truth.[64] The apostle Peter made it clear that God does not want anyone to perish. He wants everyone to repent and be saved.[65] But God gives everyone the freewill, autonomy, and choice to accept his son Jesus. He does not compel anyone to believe in him. And neither can anyone compel another to believe in the name of Jesus or accept him as Lord. A professing Christian cannot take the life of another for not believing in Christ. To purport to do that, as happened in the Crusades of the Middle Ages, is contrary to the will of God as revealed in the Scriptures and is un-Christian. During the Crusades, there were unspeakable acts of cruelty against unbelievers (Muslims and pagans) that did not reflect Christ and could not have been inspired by his Holy Spirit, the Spirit of truth and love.

Salvation is a gift from God. It cannot be earned by good works or by being a good person. It is conferred by the grace of God upon repenting, confessing Jesus as Lord, and believing that he has been raised from the dead. Thus no one can boast about their salvation.[66]

Being born again or regenerated results in eternal life.[67] It also results in a transformation from being a sinner to becoming a child of God.[68] One who is born again is a new person or creation. The old way of thinking and living is replaced by a new way of thinking and living with the help of the Holy Spirit.[69] One who is born again has been rescued by God from the dominion or power of darkness or Satan's rule and brought into the kingdom of Jesus Christ in whom there is forgiveness and redemption.[70] That person no longer lives according to the ways of an evil

---

63. Heb 9:22.
64. 1 Tim 2:4.
65. 2 Pet 3:9.
66. John 3:16; Rom 6:23; Eph 2:8–9.
67. John 3:16; 1 John 5:11.
68. John 1:12–13; Gal 3:26.
69. Rom 12:2; 2 Cor 5:17; Col 3:5–10.
70. Col 1:13–14.

world that is under Satan's control and where people live to gratify the sinful nature and follow its desires and thoughts.[71]

Becoming regenerated or born again makes one a citizen of heaven and puts one by deliberate choice on the narrow and difficult road that leads to eternal life. Just as one who is born in a certain country has a birth certificate that proves his or her citizenship in that country, one's spiritual birth certificate, acquired by being born again through faith in Jesus Christ, is proof of one's citizenship in heaven. One cannot claim to be a citizen of heaven without this proof of citizenship. And just as a citizen of a country is loyal to that country, a citizen of heaven's first loyalty is to the kingdom of God and to doing God's will on earth as an ambassador of Christ representing his kingdom on earth. Paul described himself as an ambassador in chains because of the gospel that he preached.[72]

Although the process of being born again is a spiritual process that is not observable, its effects are. Jesus spoke to this by comparing the work of the Holy Spirit—in the process of conviction, confession of sin, repentance, and salvation—to the wind. He talked about how we hear the wind blowing but cannot tell the direction in which it is blowing just by its sound.[73] But we can see its activity and effects. We likewise may not observe the spiritual process of regeneration, but we can see and tell its impact on the lives of those who have been born again.

Jesus commissioned his disciples after his resurrection to take the gospel message to the whole world.[74] The disciples began to fulfill this commission on the day of Pentecost, a harvest celebration that brought Jews living in diaspora all over the world to Jerusalem. Peter preached a sermon on that day that saw the regeneration of three thousand souls who were added to the church.[75] The subsequent ministry of the apostles resulted in many more being saved in Judea,[76] Samaria,[77] and Antioch.[78]

---

71. Eph 2:1–5.

72. Eph 6:20. See Esau D. McCaulley, "Letter to the Ephesians," in McCaulley et al., *New Testament in Color*, 414, 436, commenting that Paul requested the Ephesians to partner with him in prayer so that he might engage in his ministry with boldness as an ambassador in chains.

73. John 3:8.

74. Matt 28:18–20.

75. Acts 2:41.

76. Acts 4:4; 5:14.

77. Acts 8:12; 9:31.

78. Acts 11:21.

A centurion and his entire household were regenerated when Peter preached the gospel to them[79] and an Ethiopian eunuch who was a high-ranking official in Ethiopia was born again when Philip, a deacon in the church, explained the gospel to him as he was returning to Ethiopia from worshipping in the temple in Jerusalem.[80] Many people all over Europe were regenerated during Paul's three missionary journeys as they received the gospel and put their faith in Jesus Christ. Others were saved during the two years he spent under house arrest in Rome while awaiting trial.[81]

A Christian Is One Who Has Been Redeemed

Jesus laid down his life to rescue sinners who receive him by faith from darkness and the dominion of Satan. He gave himself to redeem humankind from all wickedness so he could purify them for himself, make them his own, and empower them to eagerly do what is good.[82] He paid the price or ransom required to deliver or rescue sinners from Satan's rule and control so that he could bring them into his own kingdom. Sinners, therefore, find redemption and forgiveness of sins in him.[83] He secured the sinner's release from Satan's rule through the payment of ransom in the form of his own life.

The Greek word for this act of spiritually redeeming the sinner is *lutroo*, denoting the securing of one's release on receipt of ransom. This results in the redemption of the sinner. One who has been saved or regenerated is, therefore, one who has been redeemed or ransomed by Christ with his own blood. It is by this redemption that the sinner's salvation is accomplished. The Greek word for redemption is *apolutrosis*, which denotes forgiveness and justification, the result of being delivered from the guilt of sin.[84]

---

79. Acts 10:48.
80. Acts 8:38.
81. Acts 13:48; 14:1; 16:5, 15, 34; 17:4, 12, 34; 18:8; 19:10, 20; 28:24.
82. Titus 2:14.
83. Col 1:13–14.
84. Rom 3:24. See "Redeem" and "Redemption" in Vine et al., *Vine's Complete Expository Dictionary*, 515–16 (New Testament Section).

A Christian Is One Who Has Been Justified

When one believes in the Lord Jesus Christ and is saved, the believer is now declared by God, as judge, to be just and righteous. The believer is, therefore, acquitted from guilt and punishment solely by grace based on the believer's redemption through faith, not because of the believer's own righteousness or works.[85] It is a gift that cannot be earned because all have sinned and fall short of God's glory.[86] The Greek word for justify is *dikaioo*, which means to deem to be right.[87] And it is God who justifies those who have faith in Christ Jesus.[88]

Paul used the patriarch Abraham as a good example of justification by faith. Because Abraham believed God, God declared him righteous by crediting righteousness to him.[89] It was not because Abraham was righteous in his own right. Righteousness was imputed to him as an act of grace on God's part because Abraham demonstrated faith in God. And just as God did for Abraham, God will also credit righteousness to all who believe in Jesus Christ. Jesus Christ died and rose from the dead for the justification of believers; in other words, that he might declare those who believe in him to be righteous.[90] The fact that justification is an act of grace on God's part is also clearly articulated by Paul in his Letter to Titus where he points out that we become heirs who have the hope of eternal life as a result of having been justified by grace.[91]

One of the results of being justified by faith in Christ is that those who are justified have peace with God. They are no longer at enmity with God and subject to his wrath and judgment. Instead, they now have God's unmerited favor[92] and no longer stand condemned.[93] It is by Jesus's

---

85. Rom 3:24. On being justified by grace as a gift, See Jarvis J. Williams, "Letter to the Romans," in McCaulley et al., *New Testament in Color*, 278, at 295, commenting that Paul's remarks about justification remind us that God justifies a diverse people and makes them right before him and with him by faith in Christ so that every ethnic group is placed on an equal footing before God in the judgment and can participate in the soteriological blessings now and at the end of the age.

86. Rom 3:23.

87. See "Justify" in Vine et al., *Vine's Complete Expository Dictionary*, 339 (New Testament Section).

88. Rom 3:26.

89. Rom 4:3.

90. Rom 4:23–25.

91. Titus 3:7.

92. Rom 5:1–2.

93. Rom 8:1.

shed blood that believers are justified and saved from God's wrath in response to sin.[94] I have heard being justified by faith explained in these simple terms: when I become *justified*, it is *just as if I'd* never sinned.[95]

Even though being regenerated, redeemed, or born again results in one's justification as if one had never sinned and removes all condemnation,[96] it does not stop Satan, who is called the accuser of the brethren, from throwing one's past life of sin in one's face. Satan is said to accuse Christians constantly before God.[97] He also wrestles with believers about their own worth, particularly if they make themselves available to do the work of God's kingdom on earth. He throws their past sins, though forgiven, in their faces, with the aim of discouraging or shaming them from making themselves available for God's service. Recall how the apostle Paul was reminded of his past life as a persecutor of Christians. He told the believers in Corinth that he was the least of the apostles and did not even deserve to be called an apostle because he persecuted the church of God. But he was thankful for God's grace in transforming and using him.[98]

Not only does Satan accuse believers to their faces and to God, but he also instigates others to accuse them. These might be former partners in sin or people against whom a believer may have sinned before being born again. Or it might be people who are offended by the truth of the gospel that a believer shares or teaches because it challenges and contradicts their beliefs and lifestyles. The apostles and followers of Christ were accused by people whose lifestyles and beliefs were challenged by their teaching. Stephen, a deacon in the early church, was accused of blaspheming against Moses and God at the instigation of antagonists.[99] Paul was accused of propagating teaching that was anti-Jewish and against the Mosaic law.[100]

Satan knows that God can use redeemed sinners who are willing to be salt and light to an unsavory and dark world to redeem and change

---

94. Rom 5:9.

95. A clear play on words from the word *justified*.

96. Rom 8:1.

97. Rev 12:10. He accused Job before God of serving God just because of God's blessings and protection, not out of genuine love for God. Job 1:9–11.

98. 1 Cor 15:9–10.

99. Acts 6:11–14.

100. Acts 21:28.

lives for his glory.[101] His goal is to keep people in darkness and separated from God. Satan had no issues with Saul when he was zealously persecuting Christians in spiritual ignorance. But the moment he saw the light after his encounter with the living Christ and turned his zeal to work for Christ, Satan instigated persecution and trouble seemingly at every turn during his three missionary journeys and afterward. Paul and his companions often had to flee for their lives from the very people to whom they lovingly brought the message of eternal life in Christ and were frequently mistreated and sometimes physically harmed.[102] Paul told the Corinthians about his sufferings for Christ, which included floggings, lashes, beatings, and danger from fellow Jews as well as gentiles.[103]

A Christian Is One Who Has Been Forgiven

When Adam and Eve disobeyed God in the garden of Eden, sin entered the human race.[104] Sin denotes a missing of the mark in relation to God's righteous requirements or an act of disobeying divine law.[105] All of humankind became sinners because they inherited moral corruption

---

101. Matt 5:13–16. See Harrington, *Gospel of Matthew*, 80, 83, commenting that Jesus's disciples are challenged to active engagement in their "good works," so that other people might come to praise God. Salt and light serve to define the identity of those who follow Jesus faithfully. See also Culpepper, *Matthew*, 101–2, commenting that Jesus is warning the disciples that if they cease to be "poor in spirit," they will become like salt that has lost its savor, lose the power that is theirs in the kingdom of heaven, cease to bring change to the world, and therefore become as worthless as salt that has lost its saltiness. The disciples are not to hide the light that is already at work in them. They should fulfill their mission by bringing change in the world, salting and enlightening.

102. Acts 14:6 where Paul and his companions fled from Iconium because of a plot to harm them; Acts 14:19 where Paul was stoned in Lystra; Acts 16:19–23 where Paul and Silas were thrown into prison for casting a demon out of a slave girl; Acts 17:5–10 where Paul and Silas were dispatched from Thessalonica to Berea because of trouble they were facing; Acts 21:27–32 where Paul was beaten by a mob for preaching a gospel that challenged their beliefs and was subsequently arrested and tried; and Acts 22–28 documenting Paul's trials before Roman governors, his journey to Rome to have Emperor Caesar hear his appeal, and his house arrest in Rome.

103. Acts 11:23–27.

104. Gen 3:1–6.

105. In Greek, the noun *hamartia*, defined as sin, means a missing of the mark. In another form, *hamartēma*, it refers to the act of disobeying God's law. See Vine et al., *Vine's Complete Expository Dictionary*, 576–77 (New Testament Section). See also Strong's Reference Number 266, defining *hamartia* as sin or failure. Also, Strong's Reference Number 265, defining *hamartēma* as sin.

through Adam.[106] All have sinned and fall short of the glory of God.[107] But God made provision for the forgiveness of sin by giving his son Jesus to pay the penalty for sin through his death on the cross. Jesus Christ offered himself as a sacrifice for sin.[108] He is the perfect sacrifice for sin.[109] God forgives sin when one confesses it and repents.[110] As the apostle Paul pointed out, the wages of sin is death, but the gift of God is eternal life in Christ Jesus our Lord.[111] Forgiveness is a gift of God. It is available to all as an extension of God's grace.[112] But as with any gift, one may choose to accept or reject it. Those who accept it are forgiven and Christ's righteousness is imputed to them.[113] Christ died for sin once. His sacrifice has paid for all sin. But even after becoming a Christian, one must continue to appropriate the gift of forgiveness when one falls short. Of course, believers are not to commit deliberate sin for grace to abound.[114] The fact, however, is that until believers are glorified at the end of the age, they will fall short from time to time. But if the believer who sins confesses it, God forgives and cleanses that believer of all unrighteousness.[115] Believers must, therefore, continually appropriate the gift of forgiveness. A believer cannot cherish sin in his or her heart. God is holy and cannot condone sin.[116] Unconfessed sin will block the flow of God's grace and forgiveness.[117] And having been forgiven, God expects believers to extend the same gift of forgiveness to others.[118] In other words, believers are to forgive because they have been forgiven.

106. Rom 5:12, 19.
107. Rom 3:23.
108. Heb 9:25–26.
109. Heb 10:14.
110. The Greek word for repentance is *metanoia*, which denotes a change of mind or a transformative change of heart. First John 1:9 states that if we confess our sins, God, who is faithful and just, will forgive us our sins and cleanse us from all unrighteousness.
111. Rom 6:23.
112. Rom 5:8.
113. 2 Cor 5:21.
114. Rom 6:1–2.
115. 1 John 1:9.
116. 1 Pet 1:15–16.
117. Ps 66:18.
118. Eph 4:32; Col 3:13.

A Christian Is One Who Has Been Sanctified

In the evening before his crucifixion, as Jesus and his disciples shared the Passover meal, he prayed for them and for all who would later believe. During this prayer, which has been called the farewell prayer or high priestly prayer, Jesus prayed that God would sanctify his disciples by the truth of his word. He stated that, for the sake of his disciples, he sanctified himself or set himself apart to do the will of God by being willing to die for them in order that they, too, may be truly sanctified.[119]

Sanctification, as defined from the Greek word *hagiasmos*, denotes separation unto God in a relationship that is made possible by the death of Christ and through faith in him.[120] It is a separation from sin and the world and a consecration to the will and service of God in holiness. Thus, *hagiasmos* is also defined as holiness in some contexts.[121] Although still subject to the temptations of this world, sanctification empowers believers to live victoriously over temptation and sin.[122]

Sanctification is produced in several ways by different agents including God the Father, Jesus Christ, and the Holy Spirit. In his first Epistle to the Thessalonians, Paul prayed that God himself would sanctify them completely (spirit, soul, and body) and keep them blameless at Christ's second coming.[123] God uses the truth of his word to sanctify believers as they study and obey his word.[124] The writer of Hebrews also makes clear that it is Jesus who sanctifies or makes believers holy so that they can belong to the family of God as Christ's brothers and sisters.[125] Jesus, by shedding his blood for humankind, provides the means for their sanctification or holiness.[126] His blood purifies our consciences from dead works or sinful acts so that we may worship or serve the living God.[127] The Holy

---

119. John 17:17, 19. See Moloney, *Gospel of John*, 465–69, explaining that Jesus was praying that the disciples be made holy in the truth, and that God extend his holiness to the disciples that they may repeat the holiness of Jesus as they were being sent into the world. Their mission to make God known demanded holiness.

120. See "Sanctification" in Vine et al., *Vine's Complete Expository Dictionary*, 545 (New Testament Section).

121. It is used in this sense in 1 Thess 4:7 and Heb 12:14.

122. 1 John 2:1; 3:6.

123. 1 Thess 5:23.

124. John 17:19.

125. Heb 2:11.

126. Heb 13:12.

127. Heb 9:14.

THE CHRISTIAN AS IMITATOR OF CHRIST

Spirit is also involved in the sanctification of the believer as God's agent in bringing the believer to faith and a life of obedience in Christ.[128] Writing to the church in Thessalonica, the apostle Paul told them that their sanctification was God's will for their lives. In that regard, they were to abstain from sexual immorality and learn to control their bodies in a holy and honorable way, not in passionate lust like those who do not know God. Paul made it clear that living a holy life was God's intent or purpose in calling them into relationship. God did not call them to be impure or unholy.[129] The need to learn to live a holy life stems from the fact that humans are born in sin. Living a holy life must, therefore, be learned from God through the study of his word, which is truth.[130] David wrote that he had hidden God's word in his heart so that he would not sin against God.[131]

The believer plays a role in his or her sanctification by desiring and pursuing it. The writer of Hebrews exhorts believers to make every effort to be holy because without it no one will see the Lord.[132] Believers must, therefore, separate themselves from the ungodliness of the evil world system. Once a believer is saved or redeemed, that person is no longer of this world, just as Jesus was not of this world.[133] Followers or disciples of Christ must not allow themselves to be polluted by the ways of this evil world.[134] One who chooses to be a friend of the world becomes an enemy of God, as the Bible makes clear that friendship with the world is enmity with God.[135]

One who becomes a born-again believer or convert but does not grow into a disciple who lives by Jesus's word[136] and surrenders to the sanctifying power of the Holy Spirit to deny self and crucify the sinful nature risks being carnal though regenerated. The person does not go on to become a Christian, as only disciples can accurately and biblically be called Christians.[137] Paul warned some in the Corinthian church of

128. 1 Pet 1:2.
129. 1 Thess 4:3–7.
130. John 17:19.
131. Ps 119:11.
132. Heb 12:14, NIV.
133. John 17:16.
134. Jas 1:27.
135. Jas 4:4.
136. John 8:31–32.
137. Acts 11:26.

this. He said they were carnal or worldly.[138] They were spiritual babies or infants who were not maturing in Christ. They had been fed milk by being taught the elementary truths of the faith. But they were not ready for the deeper truths, or solid food. They were still acting like worldly, unsaved people, caught up in envy and divisions.[139] As such, Paul said he could not speak to them as spiritual people.[140] These Corinthians may not have been living in persistent disobedience to God's word, but they were compromising with the world and their own sinful nature in some areas of their lives.

The danger with a believer who is not growing in Christ but who is compromising with the world and living according to the flesh is that they might drift into habitual unrighteous behavior and immorality, fall away, and become disqualified from the kingdom of God.[141] Paul warned the Corinthians that one cannot practice certain behaviors or engage in certain lifestyles characterized by pre-marital sex, same sex, and extra-marital sex, and inherit the kingdom of God.[142]

Paul appealed to the believers in Corinth to separate themselves from unbelievers, reminding them that they were God's temple now and that God promises to dwell in his people, walk among them, and be their God and Father.[143] Given these promises from God, Paul exhorted the

138. In 1 Cor 3:3, NKJV, carnal is derived from the Greek word *sarkinos*, denoting consisting of flesh but not antispiritual. However, in 1 Cor 3:4, NKJV, carnal is derived from the Greek word *sarkikos* denoting being governed by human nature instead of the Spirit of God, given the behaviors in which they were engaging. See Vine et al., *Vine's Complete Expository Dictionary*, 89–90 (New Testament Section). See also Strong's Reference Number 4559, defining *sarkikos* as pertaining to the flesh or carnal. Also Strong's Reference Number 4560, defining *sarkinos* as of the flesh.

139. 1 Cor 3:1–3.

140. The Greek word for spiritual as used here is *pneumatikos*. One who is led by the Spirit is spiritual. One who is immature is unspiritual. See Vine et al., *Vine's Complete Expository Dictionary*, 594–95 (New Testament Section), stating that a spiritual state is reached through diligent prayer and Bible study and maintained by obedience and self-judgment in a continuing process of growth in the grace and knowledge of Jesus Christ. See also Strong's Reference Number 4152, defining *pneumatikos* as spiritual.

141. 2 Cor 6:14–18; 11:3.

142. 1 Cor 5:1, 9–11; 6:9–10. If not interested in marriage as instituted by God between Adam and Eve, a follower of Christ must remain celibate. 1 Cor 7:7–9. See Yusufu Turaki, "Homosexuality," in Adeyemo, *Africa Bible Commentary*, 1355, noting that the Bible clearly defines homosexuality as a sin as seen in the punishment of Sodom and Gomorrah and in Paul's words in 1 Cor 6:9–10 and Rom 1:24–27. He urges gay people, like all believers, to be willing to surrender their sexuality to Christ and to accept the help of fellow believers.

143. 2 Cor 6:14–18.

THE CHRISTIAN AS IMITATOR OF CHRIST

Corinthians to purify themselves from everything that defiles body and spirit, perfecting holiness out of reverence for or in the fear of God.[144]

Believers in Christ who are sanctified are called saints or holy ones, denoting their separation unto the Lord. The word *saints* comes from the Greek word *hagioi*, plural of *hagios*, and denotes "saints," "sanctified," or "holy ones."[145]

Writing to the church in Rome, the apostle Paul addressed the Letter to them as people loved by God or beloved of God and called to be saints.[146] In his first Letter to the Church in Corinth, Paul addressed them as those who had been sanctified in Christ Jesus and called to be saints or called to be holy.[147] He addressed his Letter to the Ephesians as being written to the saints in Ephesus who are faithful in Christ Jesus[148] and his Letter to the Colossians as being written to the saints and faithful brothers in Christ who are in Colossae, or to the holy and faithful brothers in Christ at Colossae.[149]

When Paul encountered the risen Christ on the road to Damascus to arrest Christians and was blinded in the encounter, God instructed a disciple called Ananias to go and lay hands on him so Paul would receive his sight back.[150] Ananias protested by telling God that he had heard of the harm Paul had done to God's saints in Jerusalem. And after Paul became a Christian, he himself recounted to King Agrippa how he had persecuted Christians before his conversion and put many of the saints in prison.[151]

In the Revelation of end times to the apostle John, John saw an angel who announced the fall of the evil world system called Babylon the Great. He then heard a voice from heaven exhorting heaven, the saints, apostles, and prophets to rejoice over the destruction of the evil world

---

144. 2 Cor 7:1.

145. See "Holy" and "Saint" in Vine et al., *Vine's Complete Expository Dictionary*, 308 and 544, respectively (New Testament Section). This use of the term in the Bible is different from the sense in which it is used in some denominations to describe believers who have died and have been canonized. For an insightful account of the holiness experience in Black religion and culture, see Sanders, *Saints in Exile*.

146. Rom 1:7.

147. 1 Cor 1:2. The NRSV uses the word *saints*.

148. Eph 1:1.

149. Col 1:2.

150. Acts 9:13.

151. Acts 26:10.

system because God had judged Babylon for the way it treated them.[152] John had earlier heard an angel declare that God's judgment on the evil world system was just because they had shed the blood of his saints and prophets.[153]

In several of the psalms he wrote, David referred to those who served the Lord as his saints. He exhorted God's saints to sing to the Lord and praise his holy name,[154] and to fear the Lord because those who fear him lack nothing.[155] And one of the most comforting verses from the Scriptures is found in a psalm of David where he assures believers that precious in the eyes of the Lord is the death of his saints[156] because they are finally delivered from the evil of this world to live in the presence of God and their Savior Jesus Christ.

A Christian Is One Who Is Indwelled by the Holy Spirit

God the Father and God the Son are the first two persons of the Holy Trinity. God the Holy Spirit is the third. He is not just a force or influence, but a person. All three persons of the Holy Trinity are introduced at the very beginning of the Bible in the account of creation. From that account, God had already created an uninhabitable earth that was formless, empty, and dark.[157] But it did have water, which is needed to sustain life. It is to this earth that God consigned Satan and the angels who rebelled against him in Satan's bid to usurp God's power and seize his throne.[158] The Spirit of God hovered over the waters of the earth during the process of creation as God began to speak the world into existence.[159] He then spoke to the other two persons in the Trinity saying, "Let us make man in our image, in our likeness."[160] During Old Testament times, God would fill people with the Holy Spirit or cause the Holy Spirit to come upon them to empower them for a task to which he had called them. While in the

---

152. Rev 18:20.
153. Rev 16:6.
154. Ps 30:4.
155. Ps 34:9.
156. Ps 116:15.
157. Gen 1:1–2.
158. Jude 1:6 says that some of these fallen angels, called demons, are chained in dungeons until judgment day.
159. Gen 1:3–25.
160. Gen 1:26.

THE CHRISTIAN AS IMITATOR OF CHRIST

wilderness after the exodus from Egypt, God filled a man called Bezalel with the Holy Spirit and equipped him with the skills and knowledge of a craftsman to lead other craftsmen in building the tent or tabernacle in which the Israelites met, as well as the ark of the covenant.[161] And after the prophet Samuel anointed Saul to become king of Israel, he told him that the Spirit of God would come upon him with power at a subsequent point and that he would prophesy and be changed into a different person.[162] However, the Spirit of the Lord departed from Saul when his disobedience led to his rejection by God.[163] David was anointed by the prophet Samuel to become Israel's king after Saul's rejection. Unlike Saul, the Spirit of the Lord came upon David with power from the day Samuel anointed him as king.[164]

Early in the New Testament, an angel of the Lord appeared to a priest called Zechariah, father of John the Baptist, and told him of John's impending birth. He also told Zechariah that John, who would prepare the way for Jesus's public ministry by preaching a message of repentance, would be filled with the Holy Spirit from birth.[165] And when John's mother Elizabeth was pregnant with John, her cousin Mary, Jesus's mother, came to pay her a visit in her home in Judea. When Mary greeted Elizabeth as she entered her home, the baby leaped in Elizabeth's womb and she was filled with the Holy Spirit.[166] And when Jesus was baptized by John, the Holy Spirit descended like a dove and came and rested on him.[167] Jesus was, therefore, empowered by the fullness of the Holy Spirit before his public ministry.[168] After his baptism, Jesus, full of the Holy Spirit, was led by the Spirit into the desert or wilderness where the devil tempted him for forty days.[169] Jesus prevailed over Satan because he operated in the fullness of the Holy Spirit's power.[170] After his triumph over the devil

---

161. Exod 31:2–5.
162. 1 Sam 10:6, 10.
163. 1 Sam 16:14.
164. 1 Sam 16:13.
165. Luke 1:8–17.
166. Luke 1:39–41.
167. Matt 3:16; Mark 1:9–10; Luke 3:21–22; John 1:32–33.
168. Luke 4:1; John 3:34.
169. Luke 4:1.
170. Matt 4:1–11; Mark 1:12–13; Luke 4:3–13.

in the wilderness, Jesus returned to Galilee in the power of the Spirit to begin his public ministry.[171]

Why did Jesus, the Son of God, need the anointing of the Holy Spirit for his ministry on earth? The prophet Isaiah had prophesied that the Messiah would be empowered by the fullness of the Holy Spirit. Isaiah prophesied of the Spirit, wisdom, understanding, counsel, power, knowledge, and the fear of the Lord that the Messiah, Jesus Christ, would possess. These seven characteristics of Jesus's anointing in the Holy Spirit signify the fullness of his anointing.[172] Jesus was conceived by the Holy Spirit in Mary's womb and was born into this world as a human being to redeem humanity from sin.[173] As one who was holy, fully divine, and fully human, Jesus was sinless and, therefore, qualified to redeem humanity from sin. However, because of his humanity, he needed the fullness of the power of the Holy Spirit operating in his life to equip him to successfully carry out his ministry.[174] And it was through the power of the Holy Spirit that he was able to face the cross.[175] It was also through the power of the Holy Spirit that he was raised from the dead.[176]

On his last night on earth, after he and his disciples had eaten the Passover supper and Judas had left to consummate his betrayal, Jesus made an invaluable promise to his disciples. He said that he would ask his Father to send another Counselor or Helper to his disciples who love him and keep his commandments. Jesus called this Counselor or Helper the Spirit of Truth. Jesus told them that this Spirit of Truth was already living with them. However, the time would come when he would live in them.[177] The Greek word for Counselor is *parakletos* or one who is called alongside to help; a comforter, intercessor, or advocate, in the sense of one who pleads the cause of another, much like a defense attorney does.[178] Jesus had filled this role till now, but now that he was going back to the Father, he

---

171. Luke 4:14.

172. Isa 11:2–4; 61:1–3. The number seven represents completeness or perfection in the Scriptures. See Gen 2:1–3, where God rested on the seventh day after creation because his work was complete. See Got Questions, "Biblical Significance of Seven/7."

173. Matt 1:18, 23; Luke 1:26–35.

174. Acts 10:38.

175. Heb 9:14.

176. Rom 8:11.

177. John 14:15–17.

178. See "*Parakletos*" in Vine et al., *Vine's Complete Expository Dictionary*, 111 (New Testament Section).

would be taking on a new role as the Advocate or *parakletos* in heaven,[179] and would send a replacement Advocate or Counselor much like himself to assume his role on earth in the lives of his obedient followers.

Jesus then told his disciples more about the role that this Counselor, whom he later identified as the Holy Spirit, would play in the lives of his disciples. He would teach them all things and remind them of Jesus's teachings.[180] He would also convict the world of guilt regarding sin, righteousness, and judgment. He would convict sinners of unbelief so that they might repent and be saved, convince sinners that Jesus Christ is the righteous Savior and Son of God, and convince sinners that Satan, the prince of this world whom sinners follow, stands condemned.[181] He would testify of Christ.[182] He would guide his disciples into all truth. The Holy Spirit would not speak on his own but would only convey what he hears (from the Father). He would tell Jesus's disciples things that were yet to come, and he would glorify Christ by taking from what is Christ's and revealing it to his disciples.[183] So, in addition to the convicting work the Holy Spirit does to bring sinners to salvation in Christ, he also works in the lives of disciples to guide them into God's truth, to make Christ real to them, and to help them become imitators of Christ.

After Christ's death and resurrection, he gave his disciples the Holy Spirit to indwell them. This happened when he appeared to the disciples as they were huddled in fear behind locked doors. He gave them the traditional peace greeting and showed them his hands and side. He told them that as the Father had sent him, he was now sending them. He then breathed on them and told them to receive the Holy Spirit.[184] This was the point in time when Jesus's disciples were born again or regenerated. Jesus Christ, described by the apostle Paul as a life-giving spirit[185] following his death and resurrection, gave new life to his disciples by breathing on

---

179. 1 John 2:1.

180. John 14:26. In the KJV, the Holy Spirit is called the Comforter in this verse. It corresponds to the Hebrew *Menahem* or Messiah. See also Moloney, *Gospel of John*, 408–10, explaining the role of the Holy Spirit as replacing Jesus's physical presence upon his departure, teaching the disciples all things, and recalling for them everything Jesus has said and revealed to them about God.

181. John 16:8–11.

182. John 15:26.

183. John 16:13–14.

184. John 20:19–22.

185. 1 Cor 15:45.

them in much the same way as God breathed new life into Adam.[186] The result was a new creation in both instances. The disciples had now experienced the promise Christ made to them on his last night with them and had entered a new relationship with him based on the new covenant, not the old covenant under which they had previously come to faith in God as Jews. They, therefore, became the first members of the body of Christ, the church, of which Christ is the head.[187] And when people come to faith in Christ, it is the Holy Spirit who incorporates them into the body of Christ and makes them one.[188] One who is unsaved may join a local church and become a member of that local congregation. But unless saved, that person is not a member of the body of Christ, the true church.

Jesus sent the Holy Spirit to serve as an agent of salvation and sanctification in those who would believe in him and receive him by faith. He made clear that without the cleansing of the Holy Spirit, one cannot enter the kingdom of God.[189] Upon hearing the message of salvation, the Holy Spirit works to bring conviction that results in repentance and salvation.[190] God saves the sinner through the water of rebirth and renewal by the Holy Spirit[191] and the sanctifying work of the Holy Spirit.[192] The Holy Spirit, therefore, serves as God's agent in washing away sin and causing the sinner to be spiritually reborn and renewed. The Holy Spirit is also involved in the sanctification of the believer as God's agent in bringing the believer to faith and a life of obedience to Christ.[193] The Holy Spirit enables the believer to live according to the Spirit instead of the sinful nature.[194] It is, therefore, not what one professes but how one lives that serves as an indication of whether one is born again and has received the Holy Spirit.[195]

After the disciples had received the indwelling of the Holy Spirit, Jesus met with them again before his ascension into heaven and exhorted them not to leave Jerusalem until they had received a gift that God had

186. Gen 2:7.
187. Eph 1:22; Col 1:8.
188. 1 Cor 12:13.
189. John 3:5.
190. John 16:8–9; Titus 3:5; Jas 1:18; 1 Pet 1:23.
191. Titus 3:5.
192. 2 Thess 2:13.
193. 1 Pet 1:2.
194. Rom 8:3–4; Gal 5:16–17.
195. Gal 5:19–25.

THE CHRISTIAN AS IMITATOR OF CHRIST

promised to those who would believe in Christ.[196] Jesus said they had heard him speak about this gift before. He told them that John the Baptist baptized with water, but they would be baptized with the Holy Spirit in a few days.[197] John the Baptist had prophesied that one more powerful than he was coming after him who would baptize with the Holy Spirit.[198] John also testified that when he baptized Jesus, he saw the Spirit descend like a dove from heaven and come to rest on Jesus. John testified that God told him that the one he saw the Spirit descend on would be the one who would baptize with the Holy Spirit.[199] Jesus told his disciples that this baptism in the Holy Spirit, the gift that they were to wait for, would give them the power[200] to be his witnesses beginning in Jerusalem and Judea, and from there to Samaria and the whole world.[201]

This promised gift came as the disciples were all huddled together in a house on the day of Pentecost. Pentecost was a harvest celebration or festival, also known as the Festival of Weeks, during which the first fruits of the grain or wheat harvest were presented to God.[202] A sound like that of a violent wind came from heaven and filled the whole house. What seemed like tongues of fire came and rested on each of them and they were all filled with the Holy Spirit. They began to speak in other tongues as the Spirit enabled them.[203]

Jews from all over the world had come to Jerusalem to celebrate the Festival of Weeks. They heard the violent wind and came outside to find the disciples, who had spilled out of the house, speaking in the languages of the nations where their hearers lived. The crowd was amazed by the fact that they could hear the disciples, who were all Galileans, speaking in

196. Joel 2:28–29.
197. Acts 1:4–5.
198. Matt 3:11.
199. John 1:32–33.
200. The Greek word for power as used here is *dunamis*, denoting might or ability. Dynamite and dynamic come from this Greek word. See Strong's Reference Number 1411, defining *dunamis* as miraculous power, might, or strength.
201. Acts 1:8.
202. About this festival, see Exod 23:16; 34:22; Lev 23:15–21; Num 28:26–31; and Deut 16:9–12.
203. Acts 2:1–4. See Johnson, *Acts of the Apostles*, 42, where he interprets speaking in tongues as speaking in other languages because Luke is stressing the communicative rather than the ecstatic dimensions of their speech. However, he points out that *glossolalia* originally referred to a form of ecstatic (speech-like) babbling. It was a form of prophecy that was highly esteemed because it was thought to derive from direct possession by the deity.

their native languages, fifteen of which are mentioned. They were declaring the wonders of God in these languages. Some of their hearers made fun of them thinking they had had too much to drink.[204] The tongue or utterance inspired by the Holy Spirit may be a known but unlearned language, as happened at Pentecost,[205] or an unknown tongue. Paul described these two as the tongues of men and of angels, respectively.[206]

The apostle Peter spoke up and assured the people that they had not been drinking at this early hour. It was only nine o'clock in the morning. He explained to them that what they had witnessed was the fulfillment of the promise God made through the prophet Joel to pour out his Spirit on all people in the last days—the days that began with the ascension of Jesus Christ. Peter then preached the gospel to them, telling them about Jesus of Nazareth whom God had sent to save the world from sin, but who had been unjustly crucified despite the miracles and wonders he had performed. Death, however, could not hold him down, and God had raised him from death in fulfillment of prophecy.[207] Peter explained that it was Jesus, who was now exalted at the right hand of God, who had poured out the Holy Spirit which they had just witnessed.[208]

Peter's message brought conviction to his hearers. They asked him what to do.[209] Peter urged his hearers to repent and be baptized in the name of Jesus Christ so that they would be forgiven of their sins and receive the gift of the Holy Spirit. About three thousand people received Peter's message, were baptized, and became born again that day.[210]

The disciples received the indwelling of the Holy Spirit when they were regenerated after Jesus breathed on them following his resurrection. But they were still timid until they received the baptism of the Holy Spirit and, with it, the power to be bold witnesses.

The apostles were not the only ones who received the baptism of the Holy Spirit. Others did too as the church began to grow. After a deacon in

---

204. Acts 2:3–13.

205. The Greek word for this phenomenon of speaking in an unlearned tongue is *glossa*. See "*Glossa*" in Vine et al., *Vine's Complete Expository Dictionary*, 636 (New Testament Section).

206. 1 Cor 13:1.

207. King David, from whom Christ descended, prophesied that the Christ would neither be abandoned to the grave nor see decay. Ps 16:8–11.

208. Acts 2:14–36.

209. Jesus told the disciples that when the Holy Spirit came, he would convict the world of sin, righteousness, and judgment. John 16:8–9.

210. Acts 2:37–41.

the early church by the name of Stephen was stoned to death for asserting to the Sanhedrin that Jesus was the promised Messiah,[211] persecution arose against the church. Except for the apostles who stayed in Jerusalem, all the other followers of Christ were scattered throughout Judea and Samaria,[212] preaching the gospel as they fled. Philip, who had been appointed a deacon along with Stephen and five others, went and preached the gospel in Samaria. Many believed and were baptized.[213] News of this reached Jerusalem, and the apostles sent Peter and John to minister to them. When they arrived, they prayed for the new believers to receive the Holy Spirit. They would have received the indwelling of the Holy Spirit when they were regenerated, but they had not received the baptism of the Holy Spirit. Peter and John placed their hands on them, and they received the baptism of the Holy Spirit.[214]

There must have been a visible manifestation of the baptism of the Holy Spirit in the Samaritan believers because a former sorcerer called Simon, who had also received Jesus Christ on Philip's preaching, saw that the Holy Spirit came on the Samaritans when hands were laid on them. He offered Peter and John money to confer on him this gift of imparting the Holy Spirit by the laying on of his hands. Peter rebuked him for thinking the Holy Spirit could be bought and chastised him for having a heart that was not right before God. Peter told him to repent.[215] This visible manifestation Simon saw was, most probably, the Samaritans speaking in tongues, as had happened with the disciples at Pentecost in Jerusalem.

During the apostle Paul's third missionary journey, he came to Ephesus and encountered several disciples. He asked them if they had received the Holy Spirit when they were born again. It turns out that they had not even heard of the Holy Spirit. They had been baptized according to the baptism of John the Baptist. When Paul explained that John himself was only preparing the way for Jesus, they were baptized into the name of the Lord Jesus. Paul then placed his hands on them, and they received the baptism of the Holy Spirit and spoke in tongues and prophesied.[216]

211. Acts 7:51–52.
212. Acts 8:1, 4.
213. Acts 8:5, 12.
214. Acts 8:14–17.
215. Acts 8:18–22.
216. Acts 19:1–7.

It is not necessary for one to receive the baptism of the Holy Spirit in order to be born again. However, after being born again, one needs it in order to boldly share the gospel with others. There seems to usually be a time lag between being regenerated (and indwelled by the Holy Spirit) and receiving the baptism of the Holy Spirit, as was the case with the apostles and the Samaritans. However, on at least one occasion in the Scriptures, the baptism of the Holy Spirit was imparted simultaneously with regeneration and the indwelling of the Holy Spirit.

This happened as Peter preached the gospel to a Roman centurion by the name of Cornelius and his family. Cornelius and his family were God-fearing and devout people and Cornelius was a man of prayer who gave generously to the poor. As he prayed one afternoon, an angel appeared to him in a vision and directed him to send for Peter. When Peter arrived, he preached the gospel of Jesus Christ to them. As he was preaching, Cornelius and all in his house who heard the message received the baptism of the Holy Spirit and they spoke in tongues and praised God. They were then baptized in water as a public declaration of their newfound faith in Jesus Christ.[217]

While Jesus was in Jerusalem to observe the Feast of Tabernacles, a commemoration of the years the Jews spent in the wilderness after their exodus from Egypt, he spoke about the subsequent outpouring of the Holy Spirit. He invited anyone who was thirsty, which symbolized anyone who desired the Holy Spirit, to come to him and drink. This was an invitation to establish an intimate relationship with him. If a person did this, Jesus said that streams of living water, a reference to the Holy Spirit, would flow within that person as the Scriptures had promised.[218] One must, therefore, be born again and desire an intimate relationship with Jesus in order to receive the baptism of the Holy Spirit.

Jesus also made it clear to his disciples that they had to be his obedient followers for him to ask the Father to give them the Holy Spirit. He told them that the world, or unbelievers, cannot accept the Holy Spirit because they do not know him. However, the Holy Spirit would come and live in his disciples.[219] Jesus promised his disciples that their Father in heaven will give the Holy Spirit to those who ask him. He pointed out that even evil, worldly fathers give their children good gifts. How much more, then, will God give anything other than the Holy Spirit to

217. Acts 10:1–8, 34–48.
218. John 7:37–39.
219. John 14:15–17.

those who ask?.[220] Since believers are immediately indwelled by the Holy Spirit upon regeneration, Jesus was referring to asking for the baptism of the Holy Spirit. One who desires to be an effective and bold witness for Christ needs and must ask for the baptism of the Holy Spirit. It is, of course, also possible to receive the baptism of the Holy Spirit as Cornelius and his household, as well as the twelve Ephesian disciples, did without first asking. In both cases, however, although the recipients did not specifically ask for the baptism of the Holy Spirit, there was a desire on the part of the recipients, who served God, for more of God and his presence in their lives.

The apostles also emphasized the importance of being an obedient follower of Jesus to receive the baptism of the Holy Spirit. When he and his fellow disciples were dragged before the Sanhedrin for continuing to preach in the name of Jesus despite having been warned not to do so, Peter told the Sanhedrin that they would rather obey God instead of men. He told them that Jesus, whom they had crucified but whom God had raised from the dead, was now at God's right hand and that they and the Holy Spirit, whom God had given to those who obey him, were witnesses to these things.[221]

Jesus said the Holy Spirit will remind his disciples of his teachings.[222] For that to happen, a disciple of Christ must become a serious student of the Scriptures. The Holy Spirit cannot remind one of what one does not know, much like one cannot retrieve data that has not been stored or saved on a device. The apostle Paul urged Timothy to study the Scriptures so that he could appropriately handle and impart the word of truth.[223]

Jesus also said the Holy Spirit would guide his disciples into all truth. This again reinforces the need to seriously study God's word because God's word is truth and has sanctifying power.[224] And Jesus himself is the truth.[225] Receiving the Holy Spirit is essential to understanding God's word and his truth to empower the believer to become an imitator of Christ. It is through God's word that the believer receives teaching, correction, training in living a righteous life, and the equipping that is needed

220. Luke 11:9–13.
221. Acts 5:27–32.
222. John 14:26.
223. 2 Tim 2:15.
224. John 17:17.
225. John 14:6.

to do what is right.[226] Having the Holy Spirit is evidence of being a believer in Christ.[227] The apostle Paul wrote to the Colossians about this phenomenon of Christ coming to live in a believer through the Holy Spirit as the believer hopes for the future glory of eternal life. He described it as a mystery that was hidden for ages but has now been revealed.[228]

Becoming an imitator of Christ also means the believer must be willing to surrender his or her will to God[229] and live a holy life as Christ did.[230] God requires everyone who confesses the name of Christ to forsake sin.[231] One cannot, therefore, claim to have the Holy Spirit and live a sinful lifestyle that manifests what Paul described as the acts of the sinful nature,[232] or a lifestyle that is disobedient to God's commands.[233] On the other hand, the Holy Spirit helps believers develop and manifest love, joy, peace, patience, kindness, goodness, faithfulness, gentleness, and self-control in their lives.[234] These qualities attest to the fact that a believer has received a genuine experience of the indwelling of the Holy Spirit. The Holy Spirit also helps the believer to develop a deeper love for God and all humanity, particularly the diverse family of God.[235] The apostle John flat-out calls anyone who claims to love God but hates a brother a liar.[236] He warned believers to test what spirit a person has since not every spirit is of God.[237]

It is important for one who becomes a believer to surrender to the Holy Spirit and not to grieve the Spirit[238] by failing to yield to his teaching, guidance, or prompting. Believers are to be continually filled with the Holy Spirit as they live the Christian life.[239] The early church

226. 2 Tim 3:16.
227. 1 John 4:13.
228. Col 1:27.
229. Matt 16:24; Mark 8:34; Luke 9:23.
230. John 17:19.
231. 2 Tim 2:19.
232. Gal 5:19–20. These include sexual immorality, hatred, discord, envy, and idolatry, which is putting anything ahead of God.
233. 1 John 5:3.
234. Gal 5:22–23.
235. 1 John 4:8, 20–21.
236. 1 John 4:20.
237. 1 John 4:1.
238. Eph 4:30.
239. Eph 5:18.

picked seven deacons who were known to be full of the Holy Spirit[240] and sent Barnabas, a leader in the Jerusalem church who was full of the Holy Spirit, to minister to new believers in Antioch.[241] As with the early believers, as one surrenders to the Holy Spirit, grows in Christ, and commits to serving the Lord, God may also impart a specific gift or gifts of the Holy Spirit to the believer that God can use to edify or strengthen other believers in the church or the body of Christ. These gifts are beyond the indwelling of the Holy Spirit or the baptism in the Holy Spirit. God imparts these gifts as he sees fit. The apostle Paul discussed these gifts in detail in his first Letter to the Church in Corinth.[242]

A Christian Is a Disciple of Christ

A Christian is a disciple of Christ. Secular definitions of disciple abound. For example, Merriam-Webster defines a disciple as one who accepts and assists in spreading the doctrines of another. Merriam-Webster also uses it to refer to one of the twelve in the inner circle of Christ's followers according to the Gospel accounts.[243] A disciple has also been defined as a person who believes in the ideas of a leader, especially a religious or political one, and tries to live according to those ideas.[244] The Oxford Learner's Dictionaries defines a disciple as one who believes in and follows the teachings of a religious or political figure. It also defines it in the context of the Bible as one of the people who followed Jesus Christ and his teachings when he was living on earth, especially one of the twelve apostles.[245]

The Greek word for disciple[246] in the biblical context is *mathétés* and denotes a learner, student, or pupil who not only learns from, but actually

---

240. Acts 6:3, 5.
241. Acts 11:22–24.
242. 1 Cor 12.
243. Merriam-Webster, "Disciple (n.)."
244. Cambridge, "Disciple (n.)."
245. Oxford, "Disciple (n.)."

246. Matt 10:24–25; Luke 6:40. See Johnson, *Gospel of Luke*, 114, noting that a disciple could become fully trained to teach as the teacher does. See also Adeyemo, "Discipleship," in Adeyemo, *Africa Bible Commentary*, 1223, noting that a disciple is a learner who follows another's teaching, and that discipleship implies a personal attachment to a particular person who shapes the disciple's whole life. Disciples are adherents and imitators who put Christ above all else. He notes that discipleship in the New Testament sense is rare today because of the preaching of cheap grace.

WHO IS A CHRISTIAN?

follows, the teaching of another.[247] It was used to describe the followers of Jesus, especially the twelve apostles,[248] but also others who came to believe in him,[249] including some like Joseph of Arimathea who followed him secretly out of fear.[250] Jesus told Jews who were already believers that they would become his disciples if they continued in his word.[251] Only disciples were first called Christians in Antioch.[252] So, one can be a believer or born again and yet not a disciple—a Christian. When Saul of Tarsus, who later became known as Paul, was converted and became a follower of Christ, the apostles were at first afraid of him because they were skeptical that he had really become a disciple.[253]

A disciple has certain important characteristics worth noting. A disciple does not merely profess belief in or love for Christ. A disciple is one who obeys Christ's commands.[254] A disciple is also one who remains in Christ and bears fruit as a result.[255] This fruit is the fruit of Christ-likeness evidenced in one's lifestyle and manifests itself in the fruit of the Spirit, which includes love, joy, peace, patience, kindness, goodness, faithfulness, gentleness, and self-control.[256] This is in stark contrast to a carnal or sinful lifestyle characterized by things like sexual immorality, idolatry, witchcraft, hatred, discord, jealousy, selfish ambition, dissensions, factions, envy, and drunkenness. Paul warned that those who live like this will not inherit the kingdom of God.[257]

A disciple also perseveres in the faith and holds on to Christ's teaching to the end. A disciple does not give up in the face of difficulties. Jesus warned that the love of most will grow cold toward the end of the age. But he assured his followers that the one who stands firm to the end will be

---

247. See Vine et al., *Vine's Complete Expository Dictionary*, 171 (New Testament Section).

248. Matt 10:1.

249. Acts 9:10 referring to Ananias as a disciple and Acts 16:1 referring to Timothy as a disciple.

250. John 19:38.

251. John 8:31.

252. Acts 11:26.

253. Acts 9:26.

254. John 14:15.

255. John 15:8.

256. Gal 5:22–23.

257. Gal 5:19–21.

saved.²⁵⁸ In addition to the quality of perseverance, a disciple's life is also characterized by love²⁵⁹ and humility²⁶⁰ as Christ's own life was.

Salvation is free because Christ paid the price by laying down his own life. One is saved by grace through faith.²⁶¹ However, discipleship is not free. It is costly. Indeed, being a disciple demands that one surrender all by putting Christ above all things in one's life. It demands that one pick up one's cross and follow Jesus.²⁶² In other words, everything in one's life, including plans, ambitions, interests, possessions, families, and work must be surrendered to and aligned with Christ's will. Therefore, one cannot wear the Christian label without wanting to bear the cost of being a disciple.

But cost aside, there are also great temporal and eternal rewards for being a disciple. Peter asked Jesus what their reward will be for leaving everything to follow him. Jesus promised the twelve disciples that they would sit on thrones in heaven and promised everyone who has forsaken all for his sake a hundredfold return in the present age and eternal life in the age to come.²⁶³ Jesus also said that the one who serves him will be where he is, and God will honor that person.²⁶⁴

A Christian Is a Follower of Christ

A Christian is a follower of Christ or one who follows Christ. Secular definitions of follower include Merriam-Webster's definition of a follower as one who follows the opinions or teachings of another or one who imitates another.²⁶⁵ The Cambridge Dictionary defines a follower as one who obeys or supports another person or that person's ideas,²⁶⁶ while the Oxford Learner's Dictionaries defines a follower as a person who supports and admires a particular person or set of ideas.²⁶⁷

---

258. Matt 24:13; John 8:31.
259. John 13:35.
260. Isa 53:7.
261. Eph 2:8–9.
262. Luke 14:26–27.
263. Matt 19:27–29; Mark 10:29–30; Luke 18:28–30.
264. John 12:26.
265. Merriam-Webster, "Follower (n.)."
266. Cambridge, "Follower (n.)."
267. Oxford, "Follower (n.)."

The Greek word for follower in the biblical context is *akolouthos*, denoting one going the same way in a literal sense.[268] Metaphorically, it is used to denote discipleship.[269] When Jesus called Simon Peter and his brother Andrew to be his disciples, he invited them to follow him and promised to make them fishers of men. They left their nets and followed him. He did the same with James and his brother John.[270] Jesus said anyone who wants to be his disciple must deny self, pick up his or her cross, and follow him.[271] Jesus invited the rich young ruler to liquidate his assets, give to the poor, and come and follow him, but he declined because his wealth was his god.[272] Jesus called himself the good shepherd. He said his sheep, his disciples, know his voice and follow him or do his will.[273] He also said the one who serves him must follow him or do his will.[274] The apostle John made clear that whoever claims to be a Christian must follow Jesus's example and live as Jesus did.[275] The apostle Paul exhorted the believers in Corinth to follow his example even as he followed the example of Christ.[276] Therefore, a Christian is one who is Christlike, demonstrating love for God and fellow human beings, regardless of the color of their skin or socioeconomic status, and committed to God's word, will, and glory.

A Christian Is an Imitator of Christ

A Christian is an imitator of Jesus Christ. Secular definitions of an imitator include the Cambridge English Dictionary's definition of an imitator as one who copies someone or something that they think is good.[277]

---

268. Large crowds followed Jesus. Matt 4:25. See Harrington, *Gospel of Matthew*, 75, noting that this crowd provided an audience for the Sermon on the Mount.

269. See Vine et al., *Vine's Complete Expository Dictionary*, 244 (New Testament Section), noting that *follower* is used seventy-seven times in the Gospel accounts of people following Christ.

270. Matt 4:18–20; Mark 1:16–20; Luke 5:11.

271. Matt 16:24; Mark 8:34; Luke 9:23.

272. Matt 19:21–22; Mark 10:21–22; Luke 18:22–23.

273. John 10:4, 11, 27.

274. John 12:26.

275. 1 John 2:6. Jesus said the one who follows him will not walk in darkness. John 8:12.

276. 1 Cor 11:1.

277. Cambridge, "Imitator (n.)."

The Christian as Imitator of Christ

Merriam-Webster defines an imitator as a person who adopts the appearance or behavior of another, especially in an obvious way.[278] And the Oxford Learner's Dictionaries defines it as a person or thing that copies somebody or something else.[279] The Greek word for the verb "to imitate" is *mimeomai* and the Greek word for the noun "imitator" is *mimetes*. It has been noted that the exhortation to imitate Christ is always used in a good sense and in a way that suggests making it a habit or practice.[280]

Paul commended the Thessalonians for becoming imitators of him and his fellow workers as well as of the Lord, and for becoming a model for other believers in the region.[281] He also told them that he and his fellow workers set an example for them by not being a burden to them. Instead, they worked to pay for their own needs. Paul exhorted them to imitate this example of working for one's living.[282] He urged the believers in Corinth to imitate him as their spiritual father.[283] He also urged the believers in Ephesus to imitate God as his children and live a life of love as Christ did and sacrificed his life for them.[284] The writer of Hebrews told his audience to imitate the faith of their leaders who spoke the word of God to them.[285] The apostle John urged the believers to whom he wrote to imitate what is good, not what is evil, since the one who does what is evil does not know God.[286]

---

278. Merriam-Webster, "Imitator (n.)."

279. Oxford, "Imitator (n.)."

280. See Vine et al., *Vine's Complete Expository Dictionary*, 245, 319–20 (New Testament Section). They note that the Revised Version translates *mimeomai* as "to imitate" whereas the KJV translates it as "to follow," and that it is always used in a good sense and in exhortations that suggest making it a habit or practice.

281. 1 Thess 1:6–7.

282. 2 Thess 3:7–9.

283. 1 Cor 4:15–16. See Gene L. Green, "First Letter to the Corinthians," in McCaulley et al., *New Testament in Color*, 312, 325, commenting that the Corinthians had a triumphalist theology not joined with a theology of suffering. As one who suffered for Christ, Paul appeals to them as their spiritual father to be imitators of his way of life which was so despised among them.

284. Eph 5:1–2. See Kempis, *Imitation of Christ*, 1, where he cites John 8:12 and advises Christians to imitate Jesus's life and habits so as not to walk in darkness. He urges patterning one's whole life on that of Christ to fully understand Christ's words.

285. Heb 13:7.

286. 3 John 11.

As an imitator of Christ, a Christian must exemplify or imitate his compassion,[287] gentleness, humility,[288] self-denial,[289] love,[290] obedience,[291] forgiveness,[292] wrongful suffering at the hands of ungodly people,[293] and his purity. The apostle John said that all who hope for Christ's return purify themselves even as Christ himself is pure.[294]

The apostle Paul lamented the behavior of some in the Corinthian church who were worldly or carnal and not spiritual. They had failed to grow spiritually by moving from feeding on the milk of God's word to solid spiritual food or the deeper truths of God's word. Their lives were still characterized by jealousy, quarreling, division, pride, and immorality.[295] Their lives did not imitate Christ or demonstrate that they had the mind of Christ. They had not grown to become disciples of Jesus.

If a Christian is a disciple, follower, or imitator of Christ, then a "carnal Christian" or "worldly Christian" is a misnomer or an oxymoron because Christ was neither carnal nor worldly. It is tantamount to saying that one can be a "carnal little Christ" or a "worldly little Christ." But one can be a carnal or worldly believer or convert if one has not transitioned to becoming a disciple. Being carnal means that one's life is lacking in evidence of transformation, a renewed mind,[296] and a regenerated life that has been substituted for the old sinful self.[297]

The idea that one can pray the sinner's prayer and thereby punch an irrevocable ticket to heaven, regardless of whether one lives a godly life that imitates Christ's love and demonstrates obedience to God's will, puts one at risk of finding oneself on the wrong side of eternity and hearing Jesus Christ utter the words "I never knew you; go away from me, you

---

287. Matt 9:36.
288. Matt 11:29; Phil 2:5–8.
289. Matt 16:24.
290. John 13:34.
291. John 15:10.
292. Col 3:13.
293. 1 Pet 2:21–23.
294. 1 John 3:3.
295. 1 Cor 3:1–3; 3:21; 4:7; 5:21.
296. Rom 12:1–2.
297. 2 Cor 5:17.

who behave lawlessly."[298] In this regard, one cannot overemphasize Jesus's words that many are called but few are chosen.[299]

A Christian Is a Citizen of Heaven

No one is born a Christian. One becomes a Christian by accepting Jesus Christ as one's Savior, leading to the new birth. Once one becomes born again, one becomes a citizen of heaven and becomes registered or enrolled[300] in heaven. Becoming a citizen of heaven also makes one an ambassador of Jesus Christ on earth. As Christ's ambassadors on earth share the gospel with the lost, they, too, can be saved and become citizens of the kingdom of heaven.

In the natural realm, one can become a citizen of a country in which one was not born by going through the process of naturalization. It is by a similar process, albeit a spiritual one, that everyone who becomes a Christian after hearing the good news becomes a citizen of heaven. Through this process of spiritual adoption, believers are brought into the family of God and become his children.[301] As members of God's household of faith, believers acquire citizenship in God's kingdom. As citizens of heaven, they now have a spiritual passport to heaven. Their calling now is to live according to the values and principles of the kingdom of God—to live for God, exemplify Christ, and bring others along with them to heaven. Anything in the societies and cultures in which disciples or followers of Christ live that is contrary to or inconsistent with biblical teaching and the principles of God's kingdom must give way to obedience to God's word and his truth, as the apostles exemplified. When the Sanhedrin reminded them that they were flouting the strict orders they had been given not to preach in the name of Jesus, Peter and the other apostles replied that they must obey God rather than men.[302]

Jesus taught extensively about the kingdom of heaven, sometimes also referred to as the kingdom of God. The kingdom of heaven or the kingdom of God is a reference to the spiritual rule or reign of God, how God reigns, and those over whom he reigns. God rules in the lives of

---

298. Matt 7:23.
299. Matt 22:14.
300. Heb 12:23. The NIV says one's name is written in heaven.
301. Gal 4:5.
302. Acts 5:27–29.

believers who have made him King or Lord over their lives through faith in Jesus Christ his Son, whom he sent to reconcile the world to himself and to redeem a fallen world from sin and death.[303] The kingdom of God is also God's power revealed against the works of the devil[304] and the ways of this corrupt world.[305] Those who are part of this kingdom show the characteristics of righteousness, peace, and joy in the Holy Spirit.[306] The kingdom of God will eventually be fully consummated in both time and eternity when Jesus returns to reign with his saints[307] and establishes a new heaven and a new earth.[308]

Jesus told Nicodemus that no one can enter the kingdom of God unless they are born again.[309] He said that unless one is converted or unless one changes through repentance, one cannot enter the kingdom of heaven. He also taught about the values of the kingdom of heaven.[310] Unlike the kingdoms of the world where greatness is measured by wealth, power, and fame, humility is the mark of greatness in the kingdom of heaven.[311]

The kingdom of God on earth started small. It began with Jesus's disciples but grew beyond Jerusalem, Judea, and Samaria to the ends of the earth. Jesus told his disciples that this was going to happen in two parables he told from a boat on the Sea of Galilee, using the mustard seed and yeast as illustrations. Jesus compared the kingdom of God to a mustard seed, which a man took and planted in his garden. It grew and became a tree, and birds nested in its branches.[312] Like the mustard seed, which was the smallest seed sown by farmers in Israel in Jesus's day, the kingdom of God started small but has grown and given life to many. Jesus also compared the kingdom of God to yeast that a woman mixed into a large amount of flour until it spread all through the dough, signifying how the kingdom of God started with his disciples but spread throughout the world.[313]

303. John 14:23.
304. John 12:31; 16:11.
305. John 16:8–11.
306. Rom 14:17.
307. Rev 19:11–15; 20:1–6; 21.
308. Rev 21:1–3.
309. John 3:3.
310. Matt 18:3.
311. Matt 18:4.
312. Matt 13:31–32; Mark 4:30–31; Luke 13:18–19.
313. Matt 13:33; Luke 13:20–21.

Jesus told a parable about the kingdom of heaven that illustrated that entering into God's kingdom is a privilege. It is a gift of God's grace. It is not earned or based on merit. In this parable, Jesus compared the kingdom of heaven to a landowner who went into the marketplace, the equivalent of an employment agency or office, to hire laborers at various times of the day to work in his vineyard. He hired four groups of laborers at various times of the day, including one at the eleventh hour. That group only worked one hour compared with the first group that worked twelve hours.[314] However, the landowner paid them all the same wage, much to the chagrin of those who labored all day.[315] Although rewards may be different based on what one did for the kingdom of God on earth, everyone who is saved receives the same gift of eternal life regardless of when they were born again.

In this regard, it is worth noting that when Jesus was crucified, two criminals were crucified along with him, one on each side. One of them asked Jesus to remember him when he comes into his kingdom. Jesus answered with an assurance that he would be with him in paradise that day.[316] This criminal was saved at the eleventh hour. But he found eternal life by believing in Jesus Christ at the last minute.

Jesus also told a parable about the fakes who will populate the church before his return. The parable had two parts. In the first part, which he told from a boat from which he taught on the Sea of Galilee, he compared the kingdom of heaven to a man who sowed good seed in his field. However, at night, when everyone was asleep, his enemy came and sowed weeds among the wheat and went away. The wheat sprouted and produced a crop, but the weeds also grew. The owner's servants wondered where the weeds came from since the owner had sowed good seed only. The owner told them that an enemy was responsible. The servants asked the owner if he wanted them to go and pull the weeds. The owner said no because they would also uproot the wheat in the process. He instructed his servants to allow both to grow together until the harvest, at which time he would instruct the harvesters to first collect the weeds and tie them into bundles to be burned. They would then gather the wheat to bring into his barn.[317]

---

314. Matt 20:1–7.
315. Matt 20:8–15.
316. Luke 23:32, 39–43.
317. Matt 13:24–30.

Jesus told the second part of this parable, where he explained its meaning, when his disciples asked him to explain the parable to them after they came into the house. He explained that he is the one who sowed the good seed, that the field is the world, and that the good seed are the sons of the kingdom—those who have received him as Savior and do his will. He explained that the weeds are the sons of the evil one, Satan, and that the enemy who sows them is the devil. The harvest is the end of the age, and the harvesters are angels. He explained that he will send his angels at the end of the age to weed all who do evil out of his kingdom. They will then be thrown into the fiery furnace where there will be weeping and gnashing of teeth. Then the righteous will shine like the sun in his Father's kingdom. Jesus ended by exhorting his disciples to pay attention and take to heart what he had just shared.[318]

Just as some hear the gospel, repent of their sins, receive Jesus Christ as Savior, and make him Lord by obeying his commandments, there will be others who have not had a genuine conversion experience or submitted to the lordship of Jesus Christ that Satan will plant in the church alongside genuine believers. These are not citizens of the kingdom of God. They will undermine the truth of God's word and promote unrighteousness and false doctrine. They will coexist with God's elect in the church until the end of the age, when angels will separate them from true believers. Jesus said that not everyone who calls him Lord will enter the kingdom of heaven, except those who do the will of his Father in heaven.[319]

Jesus told them another parable comparing the kingdom of God to a net that was let down into a lake for a catch. The fishermen pulled it up to shore when it was full of fish. They then sorted out the fish, putting the good fish in baskets and throwing the bad fish away. Jesus then explained that this is what will happen at the end of the age. Angels will come and separate the wicked from the righteous. The wicked will be thrown into the fiery furnace, where there will be weeping and gnashing of teeth.[320]

It cannot be overemphasized that the kingdom of heaven is not of this world. When Jesus came to save humanity, he did not come to establish a worldly, political kingdom, although many in his day wanted him to be a political messiah who would liberate them from Roman colonial rule and establish his own political kingdom. And it is not only the people

318. Matt 13:36–43.
319. Matt 7:21–23.
320. Matt 13:47–50.

THE CHRISTIAN AS IMITATOR OF CHRIST

in Jesus's day who wanted his kingdom to be a political kingdom. Many today also want the kingdom of God to be a political kingdom. They have woven political ideology and beliefs into the faith and are heavily engaged and deeply embedded in the political sphere. They seem to believe that it is through that sphere that the kingdom of God will be advanced. But when Jesus was brought to stand trial before Pontus Pilate, the Roman governor, and Pilate asked Jesus if he was the king of the Jews, Jesus told him that his kingdom was not of this world. Jesus said that if his kingdom were of this world, his servants would be fighting to prevent his arrest. He said his kingdom was from another place, not from here.[321]

Becoming a citizen of heaven by accepting Jesus Christ as Savior and Lord is not the end of being a Christian. It is only the beginning. A Christian must maintain his or her heavenly citizenship. As the apostle Peter pointed out, living in anticipation of the Lord's return ought to motivate believers to live holy and godly lives. He warned his audience to be on their guard against people who distort the Scriptures lest they fall from their secure position.[322] Believers must persevere to the end as Jesus exhorted.[323] This means that believers must be diligent to maintain their heavenly citizenship.

In the natural realm, someone who has become a naturalized citizen of a country can renounce their citizenship, surrender their passport, and return to their original country. Indeed, it was reported that 5,411 people renounced their American citizenship in 2016. One of them was Boris Johnson, then foreign secretary and later prime minister of England.[324] In the same way, a Christian can also renounce their faith or heavenly citizenship and return to the world. Paul was deserted by his fellow believers during his first trial, presumably out of fear for their safety, as the Roman authorities were persecuting Christians.[325] But Paul specifically said that a believer called Demas deserted him because he loved this world more.[326] When one is saved, one is called out of the world to become part of the *ekklesia*, the called-out ones who have become

---

321. John 18:36.

322. 2 Pet 3:11–17.

323. Matt 24:13.

324. See Wintour, "Boris Johnson."

325. 2 Tim 4:16.

326. 2 Tim 4:10. Paul also said Hymenaeus and Alexander had shipwrecked their faith in 1 Tim 2:13.

separated unto God.[327] To return to the world out of a greater love for the world is to renounce one's heavenly citizenship. The apostle James made it clear that friendship with the world is enmity with God.[328]

After one becomes a citizen of heaven, one must maintain one's heavenly citizenship by persevering in the faith till the end.[329] Jesus promises that no one can snatch a believer who has accepted him as Savior, hears his voice, and follows him, from his or God's hand.[330] But the believer may choose to walk away in exercise of their free will as Demas did. Peter warned that a person who comes to know Christ and goes back to the world is worse off than the one who never knew the way of righteousness. That person is like a dog that returns to its vomit or a washed sow that returns to wallowing in mud.[331] This means that the believer must continue to follow Jesus, abide in him as the vine,[332] remain faithful to the Lord with steadfast devotion,[333] or remain true to him till the end.[334]

As citizens of heaven and ambassadors of Jesus Christ on earth, Christians must exemplify Christ. They must follow in his footsteps because he is the one they imitate.[335] Being citizens of heaven does not mean that followers of Jesus are not good, engaged citizens in the nations and societies in which they live. They are not so heavenly minded that they are no earthly good. Writing to followers of Christ in the Roman province of Asia Minor, Peter reminded them that they are aliens and exiles[336] in this world and that they should, therefore, live good lives among those who do not believe so that their good deeds may be seen to the

---

327. 2 Cor 6:17.
328. Jas 4:4.
329. Matt 24:13.
330. John 10:28–29.
331. 2 Pet 2:20.
332. John 15:5.
333. Acts 11:22–23.
334. Acts 11:23, NIV. Paul warned in 1 Tim 4:1 that the Spirit has revealed that some will abandon the faith in later times to follow deceiving spirits. He said in 1 Tim 5:15 that some had turned to follow Satan.
335. John 13:15; 1 Cor 11:1; 1 Pet 2:21.
336. 1 Pet 2:11. The NKJV speaks of sojourners and pilgrims and the NIV speaks of aliens and strangers.

glory of God.[337] Peter also exhorted followers of Christ to be law-abiding citizens who respect and honor political authority.[338]

Paul urged Timothy to pray and intercede for monarchs and all those who have political authority, regardless of political ideology. Paul stressed that this pleases God because he wants everyone to be saved and come to know his truth. Furthermore, these prayers and intercessions are to be offered in the hope that those in authority will become followers of Jesus Christ and foster societies in which followers of Christ can live peaceful, quiet, godly, and holy lives.[339] He also urged the believers in the church in Rome to submit to the authority of the government because government as an institution and, therefore, governmental authority is ordained by God for a fallen world where sin can lead to chaos, lawlessness, and anarchy. Paul described government as God intended it to be, one that is just and only punishes wrongdoers, not one that punishes the innocent or oppresses the helpless. However, where authority is used as an instrument of injustice or takes positions contrary to God's will or truth as revealed in his word, disciples or followers of Christ are to obey God instead of unjust laws.[340]

Paul exhorted the believers in Rome to do what is right, not because of fear of punishment, but out of good conscience. He reminded them that this is why believers pay taxes to the government.[341] Disciples and followers of Christ can be comforted in the knowledge that when Jesus Christ returns to earth after the great tribulation and establishes his millennial kingdom on earth, his reign will be characterized by peace, justice, and righteousness, just as God had in mind for the institution of government.[342]

Being engaged citizens requires discernment in order not to become so entangled with the world and the things of the world that the loyalties and priorities of the follower of Christ begin to shift to the point that unbelievers do not see the difference between themselves and professing Christians. Paul warned Timothy about this by likening a follower or disciple of Christ to a soldier and exhorted Timothy to be a good soldier of

---

337. 1 Pet 2:12.
338. 1 Pet 2:13–16.
339. 1 Tim 2:1–4.
340. Acts 5:29.
341. Rom 13:1–7.
342. Isa 9:7; Rev 20:1–4.

Jesus Christ who, being engaged in spiritual warfare,[343] does not become entangled in civilian affairs or the affairs of this life because his aim is to please his commanding officer or the one who enlisted him as a soldier.[344]

Jesus reminded his disciples that if salt loses its flavor, it is worthless and gets thrown out and trampled by people. This was a warning to his disciples about allowing themselves to become ineffective witnesses who end up being overrun by the ungodly values of secular society.[345] Instead, believers are to let the light of Christ that is in them shine so that people may see their good deeds and glorify or praise God.[346] Being engaged citizens, therefore, requires wisdom, understanding, and knowledge of God's word.[347] It requires a delicate balance of civic engagement without entanglement in the things of this world. As tempting as it might be for followers of Christ to become embroiled in culture wars because they feel strongly about some of the issues involved, it must remain uppermost in believers' minds and hearts that imitating Jesus Christ and carrying out the Great Commission in love ought to be their foremost priority.

A Christian Is One Who Takes the Narrow Road That Leads to Eternal Life

Toward the end of the Sermon on the Mount in which Jesus taught his disciples on a wide range of topics from a mountainside, he talked about two different gates and paths or roads that lead to different destinations. Jesus exhorted his disciples to enter through the narrow gate, warning that there is a wide gate and an easy road that leads to destruction. Unfortunately, Jesus said that the wide gate and the easy, broad road or way are what many find. He said many live their lives in this world on the broad road. On the other hand, there is a narrow gate and a hard or difficult road that leads to life. However, Jesus indicated that only a few find it.[348] Jesus was, of course, speaking of spiritual choices that lead either to eternal life or to eternal destruction.

---

343. In Eph 6:10–19, Paul told the believers in Ephesus that they do not wrestle with people. On the contrary, believers are engaged in spiritual warfare with Satan and demonic forces and should, therefore, put on the whole armor of God to stand firm in their faith and prevail.

344. 2 Tim 4:4.

345. Matt 5:13–14.

346. Matt 5:16.

347. Prov 24:3–6.

348. Matt 7:13–14. The NRSV speaks of a narrow gate and easy road. The NIV

The truth is that everyone is born guilty as a sinner at conception[349] being descendants of Adam in a fallen world.[350] As such, everyone starts life on the broad road. But God provides a way of escape. Through faith in Jesus Christ, one can get off the broad road and onto the narrow road that leads to eternal life.[351] So, what does life look like on the narrow and difficult road or path that leads through the narrow gate to eternal life? While with his disciples in the region of Caesarea Philippi, Jesus told them what becoming his follower or disciple requires. It requires denying oneself, picking up one's cross, and following him. Jesus explained that in losing one's life by surrendering control of it to him, one will find it. On the other hand, in trying to save one's life by living independently of him and assuming lordship over one's own destiny instead of surrendering control of it to Christ, one will actually end up losing one's life.[352] The one who surrenders control of his or her life to Jesus Christ will find it by having a fulfilled life lived under God's rule, direction, care, and blessing here on earth, and eternal life with him in the new heaven and new earth that God will establish at the end of the age. On the other hand, the one who does not surrender control of his or her life to Jesus will lose the very life that he or she tried to keep or save by living under Satan's deception and rule on earth. Moreover, that person will live in eternal damnation and separation from God.

A cross was used to crucify someone. Jesus carried his own cross toward the place where he was crucified. Carrying one's cross means being willing to be crucified to self in order to do God's will. In his Letter to the Galatians, Paul told them that he had been crucified with Christ and that he lived his life by faith for Christ who was really the one living in

uses the terms *narrow* and *road* to describe this path that leads to eternal life and the NKJV uses the terms *difficult* and *way* to describe it. See Harrington, *Gospel of Matthew*, 107–8, commenting that the image of a gate is probably that of a city gate through which people would enter a city. Since the topic of the sermon is entering the kingdom of God, the point behind the images of the narrow gate and the hard way is the difficulty involved in bringing the task to its eschatological conclusion. The image of a hard road is one that is hard pressed, a warning to the audience that to enter the kingdom is hard and only a few do so.

349. Ps 51:5. The NKJV says we are conceived in sin and born in iniquity.

350. Rom 3:23; 5:12.

351. John 3:16.

352. Matt 16:24–25; Mark 8:34–35; Luke 9:23–24. According to Matthew and Luke, Jesus was addressing his disciples. However, according to Mark he was addressing a crowd of people along with his own disciples. Mark 8:35 also adds that Jesus said that the one who loses his or her life for his sake and for the gospel's will save it.

him.³⁵³ Since as a sinner Paul deserved death, but Christ took his place, he owed his life to Christ and now lived for him.

Right after making the statement about discipleship, Jesus revealed the motivation behind the choice to live one's life independently of God. It is because those who make that choice value the things of the world more than the kingdom of God. So, Jesus asked the rhetorical question as to what good it will do if a man should gain the whole world but lose or forfeit his own soul. He then followed up with another rhetorical question, asking what a man could give in exchange for his soul.³⁵⁴

Jesus's question about what could make losing one's soul worthwhile reveals an important truth—namely, that the soul is one's most precious or prized possession. As such, it is the prize most sought after by Satan. Humans are spiritual beings who happen to live in a physical body while here on earth.³⁵⁵ Each one is created by God and sent to this world with a finite amount of time, gifts, talents, a purpose, and a specific calling that is unique to him or her. And when that finite time ends, each one is accountable to God for how they stewarded what was entrusted to them.³⁵⁶

The outcome of that account, whether at the judgment seat of Christ or the white throne of judgment, determines the fate of one's soul. The ungodly and unjust who appear before the white throne of judgment will suffer eternal damnation in the lake of fire and brimstone and thus lose their souls. In asking his rhetorical question about what one can give in exchange for one's soul, Jesus was asking whether anything in this world is worth going to hell for. The fact, however, is that beginning with Eve in the garden of Eden, Satan always tempts humans to reject God's way in favor of his way in return for independence from God and the promise of worldly rewards. Since his fate is sealed and he is destined for the lake of fire and brimstone, Satan's goal is to take as many of the people God so loves to hell with him. He hates that disciples are headed to heaven from which he was evicted while he is headed to hell.

---

353. Gal 2:20.

354. Matt 17:26; Mark 8:36–37; Luke 9:25.

355. In 2 Cor 4:7, Paul pointed out that we are earthen vessels or jars of clay in which the power of God dwells. In Gen 3:19, after the fall of Adam and Eve, God told Adam that he is dust, having been made from dust, and that he would return to it.

356. Heb 9:27 makes clear that judgment will come after death. Believers will be judged at the judgment seat of Christ per Rom 14:10–12 and unbelievers at the white throne of judgment per Rev 20:11–15.

Jesus said that many find the broad road that leads to destruction. Its attraction lies in living on one's own terms independently of God. It is this same attraction that caused Eve to be deceived by Satan in the garden of Eden. Satan deceived Eve into believing that she would become like God if she ate the fruit of the forbidden tree because she would know good and evil.[357]

Denying oneself and picking up one's cross involves a daily decision to resist temptation and sin. The apostle Paul exhorted Timothy to shun youthful passions and pursue righteousness, faith, love, and peace along with those who call on the Lord out of pure hearts and are, therefore, on the path that leads to life.[358] Although the path that leads to life is not devoid of temptation to sin, God is faithful in not allowing disciples of Christ to be tested beyond their strength and in providing a way out so that the disciple can endure the test.[359] Paul compared life on this path that leads to life with a race, the prize being eternal life. He urged the Corinthians to run purposefully, not aimlessly. As a fellow runner on this path, Paul told them how he disciplines his body and makes it his slave (instead of the other way around) so that he himself would not end up being disqualified after having preached to others.[360] Paul thus recognized that one must stay on this path and persevere to the end to enter eternal life.

In the parable of the sower, which is about the kingdom of God, Jesus used the image of a farmer who was sowing seed. Some of the seeds fell along the path as the farmer scattered them by hand and the seeds were eaten by birds. Some fell on rocky places where the shallow soil caused the seed to spring up quickly only to die in the withering heat of the sun because they had no root. Other seed fell among thorns which choked the plants, but others fell on good soil and produced a crop—some one hundred, some sixty, and some thirty times what was sown.[361]

Jesus explained that the farmer is one who shares the gospel, and the seed is God's word. The seed that fell along the path represents those who hear the gospel about Jesus but do not understand it. The devil then

---

357. Gen 3:1–5.

358. 2 Tim 2:22.

359. 1 Cor 10:13.

360. 1 Cor 9:24–27. The Greek word for being disqualified is *adokimos* and denotes being rejected or failing the test. See Strong's Reference Number 96b, defining *adokimos* as not standing the test or being rejected.

361. Matt 13:3–9; Mark 4:3–8; Luke 8:5–15.

snatches the word that they heard but did not understand so that they are unable to receive it, act on it, and be born again into the kingdom of God. The seed that fell on rocky places represents those who hear and receive the gospel with joy. However, they have no root and so they abandon the faith when trouble and persecution come because of their newfound faith.

The absence of root speaks to the absence of discipleship where believers are taught and given a grounding in the word of God in line with Jesus's command that all who receive him be made into disciples by being taught to obey all his teachings. Jesus was making it clear here that one can fall away from the faith after coming to believe. There is nothing like an irrevocable one-way ticket to heaven after one professes faith in Christ by praying the sinner's prayer and confessing one's sin. One must live a life of obedience to God's word and persevere to the end. No wonder Paul the apostle urged the believers in Corinth to run this race called the Christian life in such a way as to get the crown of eternal life. And no wonder that Paul disciplined himself so that he would not become disqualified after having preached to others. This discourse, which took place on the Mount of Olives, is referred to as the Olivet discourse.[362] Before his crucifixion, Jesus had a discourse with his disciples about signs of the end of the age. He warned them repeatedly of false prophets who would come and deceive many people. Jesus said that the love of many will grow cold but the one who stands firm to the end will be saved.[363]

While in Jerusalem for the Feast of Dedication, also known as Hanukkah, the Jews came to Jesus in the temple area and asked him to tell them plainly if he was the Messiah. Jesus answered that he had told them, but they didn't believe. He asserted that the miracles he had been doing in his Father's name spoke for him. He said they did not believe him because they were not his sheep; that his sheep listen to his voice, and that he knows his sheep and they follow him. He then made it clear that he gives his sheep eternal life; that they shall never perish; and no one can snatch or pluck[364] them out of his hand or his Father's hand.[365] Jesus was

362. 1 Cor 9:24–27.

363. Matt 24:11–13. The NKJV says the love of many will grow cold. The NIV says the love of most will grow cold.

364. John 10:28–29. The NRSV and NIV use the word *snatch* and the KJV uses the word *pluck*. See Moloney, *Gospel of John*, 315, where he explains that Jesus is saying belief in him as the Messiah on his terms will bring life. The believer cannot be snatched away from Jesus because the life received from being attached to Jesus is a gift of the Father. Since no power is greater than God, the believer's union with Jesus is assured.

365. John 10:22–29.

referring to his disciples as his sheep and pointing out that his disciples follow his teachings or obey his commandments. He gives eternal life to his disciples or followers, not to those who are not following him. And he makes a priceless promise to his followers—that as long as they are following and being obedient, they will not lose their salvation. One who is not in God's or Christ's hand or who was at one point, but has since walked way, does not need to be snatched or plucked. Being snatched or plucked is an involuntary act of separation from God and Christ. It is a forcible taking against one's will that Jesus promises will not happen, but walking or falling away is not.

When the believers in Jerusalem were scattered by the persecution that started after the martyrdom of Stephen the deacon, some of them ended up in Antioch where they preached the gospel, first to Jews, and subsequently to gentiles also. This resulted in a harvest of souls with a considerable number of people becoming believers. When the church leaders in Jerusalem heard about this, they sent Barnabas to Antioch. He encouraged the new believers to remain faithful to the Lord with steadfast devotion with all their hearts, or to cleave to the Lord with purpose of heart.[366] The Greek word for cleave is *prosmeno*, which means to abide with or stay with. And if one abides with the Lord, one can count on the Lord's promise that no one can snatch the believer from his or God's hand.

Along these same lines, the apostle Paul reminded the believers in Colossae how they had once been alienated from God but had now been reconciled to him in Christ, and how Christ would present them to God holy and free from blame if they continued in their faith, established and firm, and did not allow themselves to be moved from the hope of the gospel that they had heard and received.[367]

Paul warned the believers in Rome that they would die if they lived according to the sinful nature or flesh. On the other hand, if they put to death the misdeeds of the body with the help of the Holy Spirit, they would live.[368] Paul was warning the believers that if they surrendered to the desires of the sinful nature and did not live holy lives, they could revert from having been made spiritually alive in Christ to being spiritually

---

366. Acts 11:19–23. The KJV says to cleave to the Lord and the NIV says to remain true to the Lord.

367. Col 1:21–23.

368. Rom 8:13.

dead like they once were before they became saved. He went on to point out that it is those who live by the Spirit who are God's children.[369]

Paul also told the church in Galatia that those who belong to Jesus Christ have crucified the sinful nature with its passions and desires. But those who have not live by the dictates of the sinful nature. Paul recited a litany of the kinds of sins that are evident in the lives of those who have not crucified the sinful nature and warned that those who live like that will not inherit the kingdom of God.[370] To this end, Paul exhorted believers in his Letter to the Corinthians to examine and test themselves to make sure they are in the faith, reminding them that Christ Jesus lives in them, unless they fail the test, in which case he does not.[371] Jesus himself addressed this when he told his disciples that he is the vine and they are the branches, and that they must remain or abide in him to bear Christlike fruit. If they do not remain in him, they will be like a branch that is thrown away and withers. He reminded his disciples that withered branches are burned in fire.[372] The Greek word for abide is *meno*, meaning to continue. Continuing in Christ is made possible with the help of his Holy Spirit as the believer communes with God in prayer, discovers God's will through the study of his word, and lives in obedience to God's revealed will.[373] Jesus was making it clear that being saved is not a one-and-done transaction or experience. On the contrary, one must make a conscious decision every day to remain on the narrow road that one embarks on when one becomes a follower of Jesus. It is entirely possible for one to turn back and lose one's salvation and end up in the lake of fire and brimstone.

Regarding Paul's exhortation to the Corinthians to examine and test themselves to make sure that they are in the faith, the apostle John gives believers a lot of guidance on doing just that. In his first Epistle, which he is believed to have written from Ephesus to churches in the province of Asia, he debunks the false teaching that holiness and separation from

---

369. Rom 8:14.

370. Gal 5:19–24. The sins Paul listed included sexual immorality, idolatry (putting anything above God), hatred, discord, jealousy, fits of rage, selfish ambition, dissensions, factions, envy, and drunkenness.

371. 2 Cor 13:5. On being a Christian, see McKinley, *Am I Really a Christian?* See also Rainer, *I Am a Christian*.

372. John 15:5–6.

373. See Vine et al., *Vine's Complete Expository Dictionary*, 1 (New Testament Section).

the world are not necessary to be saved and states the express purpose of the Letter as being to provide them with biblical criteria or standards for being assured of their salvation. These standards include believing in the name of the Son of God,[374] obeying the commands of the Lord,[375] loving the Father instead of the things of the world,[376] remaining in Christ and the Father by letting his word remain in the believer,[377] doing what is right instead of what is sinful,[378] and being conscious of the indwelling Holy Spirit.[379]

The writer of Hebrews warned against drifting away by not paying careful attention to the truth of God's word that the Jewish believers to whom he was writing had heard.[380] He warned them against turning from the living God[381] and falling away after having tasted the gift of salvation, sharing in the Holy Spirit, and tasting the goodness of God's word.[382] Instead, they were to keep in mind that they were God's house if they held on to their courage and hope[383] and that they had to hold firmly till the end the confidence they had in the beginning in order to share in Christ.[384] He also reminded them that they could not deliberately keep on sinning after coming to a knowledge of the truth without expecting judgment,[385] and exhorted them to see to it that they did not miss the

---

374. 1 John 5:13.

375. 1 John 2:3–5.

376. 1 John 2:15–16.

377. 1 John 2:24.

378. 1 John 3:7–10.

379. 1 John 4:13.

380. Heb 2:1–3.

381. Heb 3:12.

382. Heb 6:4–6. See Madison N. Pierce, "Letter to the Hebrews," in McCaulley et al., *New Testament in Color*, 581, 593, commenting that this is part of one of the "warning passages," warning that if after believers have been enlightened, tasted the heavenly gift, shared in the Holy Spirit, tasted the good word of God, and the powers of the age to come, they fail to complete their journey and enter the promised rest, then it is impossible for them to be restored since Christ's work cannot be repeated. See also Adeyemo, *Africa Bible Commentary*, 1497, noting that if we do not grow toward maturity, we can easily lapse into immaturity and willful apostasy. Those who reject Christ after being enlightened and receiving the gift of God's Spirit and word will find it difficult, even impossible, to come back to him through repentance.

383. Heb 3:6.

384. Heb 3:14.

385. Heb 10:26–27.

grace of God.[386] They had to persevere to the end in order to receive the promise of eternal life.[387] They had to keep in mind that God will not be pleased with those who draw back. The latter will end up destroyed, not saved.[388] Writing to believers who were being besieged by false teaching in Asia Minor, Jude, the brother of James and half-brother of Jesus, exhorted them to contend for the faith and not to buy into the false notion that being saved by grace permitted sin without condemnation. He warned against turning the grace of God into a license for immorality and reminded his readers that not all the Hebrews who were delivered from slavery in Egypt made it into the promised land. Many were consigned to die in the wilderness because of their unbelief even though they had begun the journey to the promised land.[389] It is not enough to begin the journey of faith to heaven. One must continue in that faith till the very end in order to inherit eternal life. Jude reminded his audience of the apostles' warning that there would be scoffers or mockers in the last days who would live by their sensual desires.[390] Jude described these mockers or scoffers as self-gratifying and boastful faultfinders.[391] Instead of following this un-Christlike example, Jude urged his audience to live holy lives by faith through the power of the Holy Spirit as they awaited eternal life through the mercy of Jesus Christ.[392]

In Jesus's Revelation of end-time events to the apostle John in which Jesus gave John messages for seven local churches in Asia Minor, there are many references to remaining faithful and persevering to the end in order to inherit eternal life. In his message to the church in Thyatira, Jesus warned against the consequences of sexual immorality in that church and made it clear that he searches hearts and minds and will repay according to one's deeds. He urged the faithful in the church to hold on to

---

386. Heb 12:12–15. These warnings are warnings against personal apostasy, which involves falling away from faith in Christ or abandoning one's relationship with Christ. *Aphistēmi* in Greek means to turn away, abandon, or defect. See Strong's Reference Number 647, defining *aphistēmi* as *apostasion* or a forsaking.

387. Heb 10:36.

388. Heb 10:38–39.

389. Jude 1:3–5.

390. Jude 1:17–18. Jude was referring to Peter's warning in 2 Pet 3:3 about scoffers who would follow their own desires in the last days.

391. Jude 1:16.

392. Jude 1:20.

THE CHRISTIAN AS IMITATOR OF CHRIST

what they had till his return and promised that the one who overcomes and does his will to the end will receive authority over the nations.[393]

Jesus also gave a message to John for the church in Sardis, which had a reputation for being alive. However, Jesus told them that they were a dead church. He pointed out that there were nonetheless a few believers in that church who were living right because they had not soiled their clothes. They were unspotted or unpolluted by the world.[394] Jesus promised that they will walk with him in heaven dressed in white because they were worthy. He promised that those who overcome will also be dressed in white like these faithful ones, that he will not erase their names from the Book of Life, and that he will confess their names before his Father and the angels.[395] The Greek word for blot out is *exaleiphó*, meaning to wipe out or obliterate.[396] Thus, Jesus Christ himself warned in no uncertain terms that one must persevere, overcome the lure of this corrupt world, and remain faithful to him to the end in order to inherit eternal life. Identifying himself to the apostle John in Revelation as the Alpha and the Omega, the Beginning and the End, Jesus told John that the one who overcomes will inherit the new heavens and the new earth where there is no more death, mourning, or crying. Jesus Christ promised to be that person's God. But he also told John in stern terms that the place of the cowardly, the unbelieving, the vile, the murderers, the sexually immoral, those who practice magic arts, the idolaters, and all liars will be in the fiery lake of burning sulfur, which is the second death.[397] Despite all these warnings by Jesus and the New Testament writers, many throughout history have believed that they can live contrary to God's word on the broad road and still make it to heaven. They believe that once they pray the sinner's prayer, they have punched an irrevocable one-way ticket

---

393. Rev 2:18–26.

394. Jas 1:27.

395. Rev 3:1–5. The NIV and NKJV use blot instead of erase. See Blount, *Revelation*, 71–72, explaining that the Book of Life registers those who have an eternal relationship with God. Entries are made from the creation of the world. Those whose names are not written in it have lost their connection with God and are due eschatological punishment. See also Yong, *Revelation*, 70, where he argues that this Scripture ought to prompt not anxiety about the state of our souls but self-reflection about the condition of our hearts and lives in the present world.

396. See Vine et al., *Vine's Complete Expository Dictionary*, 71 (New Testament Section). Also, Strong's Reference Number 1813, defining *exaleiphó* as to wipe out, erase, or obliterate. In Ps 69:22–28, David prayed that judgment would come on the wicked and that they would be blotted out of the book of the living or the Book of Life.

397. Rev 21:6–8.

to heaven regardless of whether they live contrary to Jesus's teachings, and in spite of his warning that not all who call him Lord will enter the kingdom of heaven, except those who do God's will.[398]

The apostle Paul warned the Corinthians not to be ignorant of the fact that not all the Jews who were freed from slavery in Egypt, crossed the Red Sea, ate manna, and drank water from the rock made it into the promised land. They lusted after evil things and committed idolatry and sexual immorality. As a result, they missed the promise of God, and their bodies were scattered in the desert because God was displeased with them. Paul said that what happened to them serves as an example and a warning to us to keep us from setting our hearts on evil like they did. Paul warned the Corinthians to be careful if they thought they were standing firm, lest they fall.[399] God did not tolerate Israel's sins of idolatry and immorality in the wilderness. Neither will he tolerate the sin of professing believers under the new covenant. Knowing that few find the road that leads to life, Jesus warned the crowds that followed him around of the real cost of being his disciple. The Gospel writer Luke records that Jesus turned to large crowds of people who were traveling with him at one point and told them that a person cannot be his disciple unless they hate their father, mother, wife, children, brothers, sisters, and even their own life. And neither can they be his disciple unless they carry their cross and follow him.[400]

After finding the narrow road that leads to eternal life through faith in Jesus Christ and adoption into the family of God,[401] Christians must stay on that road and resist the lure to get back on the broad road that leads to destruction. Christians are citizens of heaven who have a spiritual passport to heaven. But just as someone who becomes a naturalized citizen of a country can renounce their citizenship and return to their original country, a Christian can also renounce their faith and return to the world as Demas chose to do. Regarding the lure of the broad road, in the Sermon on the Mount Jesus exhorted his disciples to store up treasures in heaven where their treasures are safe. He explained that one's heart follows one's treasure. If one is earthly minded, one's heart will be on earthly things, and one is likely to travel the broad road or path that leads to destruction. On the other hand, if one is heavenly minded or has

---

398. Matt 7:21–23.
399. 1 Cor 10:1–12.
400. Luke 14:25–27.
401. Rom 8:15; Gal 4:4–5; Eph 1:5.

THE CHRISTIAN AS IMITATOR OF CHRIST

an eternal perspective, one will value the things of God more, choose the narrow road or path that leads to eternal life, and stay on it.[402] Paul told Timothy that, because they were eager for money, some people had wandered away from the faith.[403] To wander from the faith, they must have once been in the faith. This means that they were once true believers who walked on the narrow road.

Like Abraham, those who travel on the narrow road that leads to eternal life are looking forward to the new Jerusalem, the city whose architect and builder is God. They, like Abraham and the Old Testament saints who are commended in the book of Hebrews for their faith, consider themselves citizens of heaven who are looking forward to their heavenly home. They consider themselves to be aliens and strangers or pilgrims on earth. And God, who is not ashamed to be called their God, has prepared a city for them.[404] Paul warned the Philippians of the destruction that awaits those whose minds are focused on earthly things. He reminded them that followers of Christ are citizens of heaven who eagerly await the return of the Lord Jesus Christ.[405]

Living on the narrow path that leads to eternal life does not mean followers or disciples of Christ are unsociable people who live drab, boring, and dull lives. Jesus himself was very sociable and enjoyed the company of people. Jesus's very first recorded miracle in the Gospel of John took place while Jesus was at a wedding as one of the invited guests. Not only did Jesus and his mother and disciples attend a wedding and enjoy themselves, but Jesus also saved the day by sparing the bridegroom the embarrassment and disgrace of running out of wine on his and his bride's big day.

Jesus also loved to spend time with people over a meal. He spent time with Mary and Martha, the sisters of Lazarus. Martha busied herself with preparing the meal while Mary sat at Jesus's feet listening to him, much to Martha's chagrin.[406] While passing through Jericho once, Jesus saw a man by the name of Zacchaeus who, being short, had climbed up a sycamore-fig tree to get a look at Jesus. When Jesus reached the spot where Zacchaeus was, he looked up, called him by name, and told him

---

402. Matt 6:19–21. *Thesaurizo*, the Greek word for lay, denotes laying up or storing up. See Vine et al., *Vine's Complete Expository Dictionary*, 358 (New Testament Section).

403. 1 Tim 6:10. The NKJV says they have strayed from the faith.

404. Heb 11:10–16.

405. Phil 3:20.

406. Luke 10:38–41.

he was going to be staying at Zacchaeus's house that night.[407] As was the custom in those days, Zacchaeus would have hosted Jesus to dinner. Jesus also once went and enjoyed a meal at the home of a prominent Pharisee on the Sabbath.[408] And Peter's mother-in-law waited on Jesus once after he had healed her of a fever.[409] Moreover, Jesus himself threw two big miraculous dinner parties. At the first, he fed five thousand men and their families with fish sandwiches out of two fish and five loaves a lad was willing to hand over to him. There were twelve basketfuls of leftovers.[410] At another time he miraculously fed fish sandwiches again to four thousand men and their families out of seven loaves and a few pieces of fish. This time there were seven basketfuls of leftovers.[411]

Jesus also participated in the Jewish feasts. He went to the Feast of Tabernacles.[412] He observed the Feast of Passover, eating the Passover meal with his disciples the very night he was betrayed.[413] Even after his resurrection, Jesus continued to be sociable. Two disciples Jesus had walked with to Emmaus hurried back to tell the disciples they had seen the risen Christ. As they spoke, Jesus appeared in the room in his glorified body and asked for something to eat. They gave him a piece of broiled fish and he ate it.[414] His last meal on earth after his resurrection was a meal of broiled fish and bread that Jesus himself served to his disciples early one morning by the lake. They had toiled all night without catching any fish. As they came toward shore, Jesus called out to them and directed them to throw the net on the right side of the boat. They got such a haul of fish that John realized it was Jesus. When they got to

---

407. Luke 19:1–7.
408. Luke 14:1.
409. Matt 8:14–15; Luke 4:38–40.
410. Matt 14:15–21; Mark 6:35–43; Luke 9:10–17; John 6:5–13.
411. Mark 8:2–9.
412. Also called the Feast of Tents or Festival of Booths. See John 7. This feast was a commemoration of the time the Israelites spent in the wilderness when they lived in tents or tabernacles. See Lev 23:34–43.
413. Matt 26:14–29; Mark 14:12–25; Luke 22:3–20. John 13:1–2. The Passover Feast or the Feast of Unleavened Bread was a commemoration of the sparing of the Israelites and the destruction of the firstborn of the Egyptians. The death angel passed over the homes of the Jews whose door posts had been marked with the blood of a lamb. The Jews ate unleavened bread, or bread without yeast, in haste in preparation for their exodus. See Exod 12:1–20 and Lev 23:5–8.
414. Luke 24:36–43.

THE CHRISTIAN AS IMITATOR OF CHRIST

shore, Jesus asked them to bring some of the fish they had just caught and invited them to breakfast.[415]

As imitators of Christ, Christians can also have fun and enjoy themselves in ways that are consistent with living holy lives. The only caveat is to avoid things that are harmful to both body and soul, and potentially harmful to one's walk with the Lord, such as unholy relationships, drugs, alcohol, and tobacco.

All believers do not live on this narrow road the exact same way. There are believers who choose to live their lives on the narrow road in solitude, celibacy, and sacrifice, devoting themselves to prayer and service to God in a convent or monastery. Some take a vow of poverty and devote themselves to ministering to others, while many choose a different way to honor God.

Living life on the narrow road does not mean that followers of Christ are perfect by any means. Since all are born into sin because of the fall of Adam, no one is automatically born onto this narrow path. It is a path that one must find through a conscious decision to become a follower of Christ after hearing and receiving the gospel. Paul reminded the Corinthians that some of them used to live in sexual immorality, greed, and drunkenness before being justified in the name of Jesus and sanctified or set apart to live for him.[416]

Those who have chosen to live on the narrow road have answered the call to put off the old self that is corrupted by evil desires and to put on the new self that imitates the righteousness and holiness of God. Paul pointed out that this is made possible by a new attitude of mind—a different way of thinking.[417] With renewed minds, instead of lying, they are to tell the truth; instead of stealing, they are to work and be a blessing to others; instead of unwholesome speech, they are to speak in a way that builds others up.[418] In his Letter to the Church in Rome, Paul urged them not to be conformed any longer to the pattern of the world but to become transformed by the renewing of their minds so that they could discern God's will.[419] Living on the narrow road means relating to the things of

---

415. John 21:1–14.
416. 1 Cor 6:9–11.
417. Eph 4:22–24.
418. Eph 4:25–29.

419. Rom 12:2. See Jarvis J. Williams, "Letter to the Romans," in McCaulley et al., *New Testament in Color*, 279, 307, where unlike the tribal and divisive pattern of this world, he emphasizes the importance of love without which Christians will live

this world differently—from a godly perspective, having the mind and attitude of Christ.[420] So Paul urged the Galatians to view the freedom that Christ had given them from sin differently. They were not to use their freedom as an opportunity for self-indulgence[421] or do whatever they wanted, as some view freedom. Instead, Paul urged them to act for the good of others instead of acting selfishly. This means not insisting on their right to do something that happens to be permissible or lawful if it will not be edifying to other believers.[422]

The pilgrims on the narrow road that leads to life are the family of God. Regarding this family, Jesus gave great insight as he was teaching in a place that had attracted a crowd. His mother and brothers came to talk to him, and someone informed him that his mother and brothers were outside looking for an opportunity to talk to him. Jesus asked a puzzling rhetorical question: "Who is my mother, and who are my brothers?"[423] He then answered his own question by pointing to his disciples and saying that his family members are those who do the will of his Father in heaven.[424] Jesus was making it clear that faith in him and living by his teaching makes one a member of the family of God.

Jesus's statement was a radical shift from the normal paradigm of blood relationship as a determinant of membership in a natural family. Jesus was elevating spiritual relationship with him above blood relationship and identifying the true people of God as the ones who do God's will. This was a redefinition of God's covenant community from the nation of Israel descended from Abraham to all who put their faith in Christ, a new creation called the Israel of God, comprised of all of God's people under the new covenant.[425]

---

isolated, selfish, and fragmented lives, like the pattern of this world, in opposition to the multiethnic redemptive vision for which Jesus died and to which the gospel calls us. See also Adeyemo, *Africa Bible Commentary*, 1368–69, noting that this renewing of the mind is a reorientation of our worldview as we seek to live the way Christ lived and think as he thought so that we can please God.

420. 1 Cor 2:16; Phil 2:5.

421. Gal 5:13. The NIV says not to use their freedom to indulge the cravings of the sinful nature. The NKJV says not to use liberty as an opportunity for the flesh.

422. 1 Cor 10:23–24.

423. Matt 12:48.

424. Matt 12:46–50; Mark 3:31–35; Luke 8:19–21. Luke 8:21 says Jesus said that his mother and brothers are those who hear God's word and do it (NRSV and NKJV) or put it into practice (NIV).

425. Gal 6:15–16.

THE CHRISTIAN AS IMITATOR OF CHRIST

Christians must understand that other Christians, regardless of their nationality, ethnicity, skin color, or socioeconomic status, are their family. Notions of White Christianity, racial purity, racial segregation, and socioeconomic class are inconsistent with Christ's definition of the Christian family.

The apostle Paul picked up on this new paradigm of family in his Letter to the Romans and explained to both Jews and gentiles that salvation is now based on a relationship with God in Christ.[426] He also told the Ephesians that although as gentiles they were once excluded from citizenship in Israel and were foreigners to the covenants of the promise, through faith in Christ, they were no longer foreigners and aliens, but fellow citizens with God's people and members of God's household. In Christ, both Jew and gentile can now live together in peace, the wall of hostility between them having now been destroyed.[427]

This new capacity to live together in peace is not only true for Jews and gentiles, but for all the people of this world who are willing to entrust their lives to Jesus Christ as Lord and Savior and become his disciples or imitators. As he talked to his disciples about his impending death, Jesus told them that he was giving them his peace and leaving them peace. He stated further that he was not giving them his peace as the world gives.[428] Indeed, the world's way of peace is oftentimes tenuous and illusory. Peace treaties, ceasefires, and truces are conditional, and are sometimes broken before the proverbial ink in which they are written is dry. But as simplistic as it may seem, Jesus's breaking down of walls of hostility that once existed between former enemies by becoming disciples and imitators of Christ who walk in love contains the secret to world peace. The secret is love, not fear. Fear is not of God[429] because he has not given Christians a spirit of cowardice, but of power, love, and self-discipline.[430]

Jesus taught his disciples to reject the practice of retaliation captured in the expression "an eye for an eye and a tooth for a tooth." Instead, he taught them to turn the other cheek. He also turned the idea that one should love one's neighbor and hate one's enemies on its head, pointing out that there is no reward in only loving those who also offer love in

---

426. Rom 9:6–8.

427. Eph 2:11–19.

428. John 14:27.

429. 1 John 4:18.

430. 2 Tim 1:7. The NKJV says God has not given us a spirit of fear. It says God has given us a spirit of power, love, and a sound mind.

return. He taught his disciples that they should love their enemies and pray for those who persecute them. In this way, disciples imitate their Father in heaven and seek to become perfect like their heavenly Father.[431] Jesus also taught his disciples to treat others as they would expect to be treated. He revealed to them that this principle sums up everything in the Mosaic law and the prophetic books.[432]

Christ's capacity to bridge divides and bring peace is alluded to when Isaiah prophesied of the birth of the Messiah. One of the titles he used to describe him was that he would be the Prince of Peace. His eventual rule on earth when he returns to establish his millennial kingdom will also be characterized by peace.[433]

When one becomes a disciple of Christ, one becomes a member of the family of God and embarks on a lifelong journey on the narrow road that leads to life with all the other members of the family of God. Members of this family recognize that they are citizens of heaven. They understand that they and all the other members of the family of God are pilgrims headed to the heavenly Jerusalem, the city of God not made with human hands, the same city Abraham was looking for. They recognize that this is a difficult road as Jesus said. Followers of Christ, therefore, recognize that they need each other on this road as they journey toward heaven. Pilgrims will get sick on this road and need access to medical care. Many will experience poverty and need compassion and assistance. Many will suffer persecution and need refuge. Many who are vulnerable for whatever reason will need to feel safe without fear of being exploited or subjected to physical or emotional harm. They will need none of these things when they make it to their heavenly home. It is, therefore, here on earth that those who profess to be Christians ought to show them love, compassion, and empathy, and offer help and protection.

In the Revelation of Jesus Christ to the apostle John, he gave John a glimpse of the family of God in heaven. He saw a great multitude that no one could count, from every nation, tribe, people, and language, standing before the throne of God and in front of the Lamb of God,[434] Jesus Christ. They were wearing white robes and holding palm branches in their hands. One of the elders standing around the throne explained to John

---

431. Matt 5:38–48.
432. Matt 7:12; Luke 6:31. This principle is referred to as the Golden Rule.
433. Isa 9:7.
434. Jesus is the Lamb of God because he was sacrificed for the sins of humankind.

that these people had come out of the great tribulation.[435] The family of God on earth and in heaven is a diverse, blended family that transcends nationality, ethnicity, skin color, or socioeconomic status. Paul exhorted the believers in Galatia to do good to all people as the opportunity arises, but they were to do good especially to the family of God. Paul described this family as consisting of those belonging to the household of faith or the family of faith.[436] Therefore, one cannot be a member of the family of God yet refuse to love or have anything to do with other members of the family of God because they have a different ethnicity, nationality, or skin color, or because they have a different socioeconomic status.

Also, for believers sojourning together on the narrow road that leads to eternal life, there is no such thing as a Black, White, Latino, Asian, or any kind of church that is based on skin color or ethnicity. The church is the body of Christ, and it is color neutral.

Jesus Christ told his disciples that he was giving them a new commandment to love one another as he had loved them. He made it clear that it was by their love for one another that all will recognize them as his disciples.[437] This means that the only criterion by which people will recognize the disciples or followers of Jesus Christ is the love that they have for the diverse, blended family of God, unlike the people of the world who have a problem with diversity. And only the Holy Spirit makes this possible. Thus, it will not be by their miracles, anointing, resources, or preaching that people will recognize disciples of Christ. Neither will it be by their ideological stances, political alliances, influence, earthly resources, or power, but by their love for all members of the diverse family of God.

Many people on the broad road are religious, although they have not surrendered to God. The Pharisees, Sadducees, elders, and teachers of the law in Jesus's day were the religious leaders of Israel. Jesus told the elders and teachers of the law that they did not believe John the Baptist and repent even though they saw evidence of the impact of John's ministry because tax collectors and prostitutes repented. He told them that these tax collectors and prostitutes were entering the kingdom of God ahead of them.[438] They had failed to recognize that it is better to

---

435. Rev 7:9.

436. Gal 6:10. The NIV calls them the family of believers. The NKJV calls them those who are of the household of faith.

437. John 13:34–35.

438. Matt 21:28–32.

acknowledge sin and repent than to be self-righteous and perish. Jesus also called the Pharisees blind guides, hypocrites, and snakes[439] although they appeared to be righteous and outwardly worshipped God.

Through the prophet Isaiah, God revealed how he saw the people of Israel. They honored him with their lips while their hearts were far from him. God said their worship was made up of rules taught by men.[440] Although they appeared to love and serve God, they really did not. They only had a form of godliness devoid of doing God's will. They followed religious rituals while living for themselves. They worshipped God on their own terms, not according to God's will. Their traditions were more important to them than God's word and they followed their traditions instead of God's word. Jesus explained during one of his many confrontations with the Pharisees and teachers of the law that Isaiah's prophecy was about them, and that Isaiah was right. He said they had nullified the word of God for the sake of their tradition and called them hypocrites to their faces.[441]

The Pharisees were the spiritual leaders of Israel who were supposed to lead others to God. But Jesus said that not only were they not entering the kingdom of heaven, but they were also shutting the kingdom in the faces of others and hindering them from entering.[442] Jesus condemned their hypocritical and legalistic giving of tithes while ignoring justice, mercy, and faithfulness, things that Jesus characterized as weightier matters of the law.[443] He pointed to their seeming outward righteousness when in truth they were full of greed and indulgence on the inside. He challenged them to be cleansed from within first so that their outward appearance of righteousness would be genuine.[444] Because they were full of hypocrisy and wickedness but appeared righteous to people, Jesus compared the Pharisees to whitewashed tombs that look beautiful on the outside but are full of uncleanness inside.[445] Jesus accused them of

---

439. Matt 23.

440. Isa 29:13.

441. Matt 15:6; Mark 7:13.

442. Matt 23:13. On hindering others from entering the kingdom of heaven, see Harrington, *Gospel of Matthew*, 325, where he explains that this charge assumes the scribes and pharisees have an authoritative position. By hindering the spread of the gospel of Jesus, they close themselves and others out of the kingdom.

443. Matt 23:23.

444. Matt 23:25–26.

445. Matt 23:27–28.

killing the prophets and being the descendants of their forefathers who had killed the prophets God had sent.[446]

Eventually, it was these same Pharisees and the high priests who railroaded Jesus and subjected him to the injustice of an undeserved death penalty by bringing unjust accusations against him before the Roman governor Pontius Pilate. Ironically, it was the raising of Lazarus from the dead by Jesus, one of the greatest miracles ever recorded in human history, which unnerved the Pharisees and the chief priests and caused them to resolve to kill Jesus. Their response to this miracle was the opposite of many Jews who had seen the miracle and put their faith in Jesus. They were more concerned about losing their place if there was a repressive response from the Roman government against the nation because they mistakenly thought Jesus was projecting himself as a political savior or messiah and, therefore, pitting himself against Rome's authority.[447] What they did not know was that Jesus came to give his life as a ransom, not just for the nation of Israel, but for all of humankind. No one could take his life from him. He was laying it down himself and would reclaim it three days after his crucifixion.[448] He did not come as a power broker or political savior as many wanted him to be.

As with the Pharisees, there are many people today who want Jesus to be something other than who he is. To want to serve God on one's own terms is to create one's own religion. In the Revelation of Jesus Christ to the apostle John, an angel described all false religion, including a secular, false form of Christianity, as the great whore.[449] This false or apostate church is part of the evil world system controlled by Satan, referred to as Babylon.[450]

Consider this disconnect between what professing Christians say and what they believe: according to the Pew Research Center's "Religious Landscape Study," conducted in 2007 and 2014, a little over 70 percent of thirty-five thousand Americans surveyed identified themselves as Christian.[451] Ironically, however, the survey also revealed that not all

---

446. Matt 23:33–35. Jesus specifically mentioned the prophet Zechariah, who was murdered between the temple and the altar.

447. John 11:45–52.

448. Matt 20:28; Mark 10:45; John 2:19; 15:13.

449. Rev 17:1. The NIV calls this religious system the great prostitute while the NKJV calls it the great harlot.

450. Rev 17:5; 18.

451. Pew Research Center, "Religious Landscape Study."

professing Christians are certain of their belief in God. Not only were some uncertain of their belief in God, but others also did not believe in God. Since the term *Christian* is used in the Bible only to describe disciples—those who live by Jesus's word—it would seem that Satan has succeeded in deceiving many people into thinking they are Christians when they are not.

It is estimated that 2.4 billion people in the world identify themselves as Christians.[452] These numbers are in tension with Jesus's statement that few find the narrow and difficult road that leads to eternal life, and that many find the broad road that leads to destruction. During Paul's second missionary journey into Europe, he and his companion Silas were thrown into prison for casting an evil spirit out of a slave girl who made her owners a fortune through fortune telling. After they were released from prison, Paul and Silas went on to Thessalonica.[453] On reaching Thessalonica, Paul and Silas were accused by Jews who opposed their message of having turned the whole world upside down with the gospel message.[454]

After a brief respite from his second missionary journey, Paul embarked on a third journey that eventually brought him to Ephesus. He taught there for two years. Luke notes that as a result of Paul's ministry in Ephesus, all the Jews who lived in the province of Asia heard the word of the Lord.[455]

If two followers of Christ could be said to have turned the world upside down by faithfully preaching the gospel message in fulfillment of the Great Commission, and an entire province heard the word of God because of the faithful ministry of one man, what would be said of almost two-and-a-half billion disciples, followers, or imitators of Christ, "little Christs," keeping Jesus's commandments, sharing the gospel, loving their neighbor as themselves regardless of their nationality, ethnicity, skin color, or station in life, and treating others as they would want to be treated?

The truth is that throughout history, God's will and work has been done by his remnant—the relative few who believe and obey his word—not those who profess to believe but do not live in obedience to his

---

452. The world's population in 2022 was estimated at 8.05 billion, with 31.1 percent of them identifying as Christians. See Central Intelligence Agency, "People and Society."

453. Acts 16:16–40.

454. Acts 17:1–7.

455. Acts 19:10.

word.[456] There have always been many of the latter and few of the former. But it is those few who are on the narrow road that leads to eternal life.

Jesus's statement that few find the narrow road was true in the time of the prophet Elijah. Ahab was king of Israel and he and his wife Jezebel, a Sidonian princess, practiced and promoted Baal worship.[457] After exposing the prophets of Baal to be false prophets in a showdown on Mount Carmel to prove that Jehovah was the only true, living God, Elijah fled for dear life after Jezebel threatened his life. He became depressed and felt alone. He thought he was the only one in Israel who served God. But God revealed to him that there were seven thousand true believers in Israel who served him and were faithful to him.[458] There had to be several million Israelites in Elijah's day, many of whom professed to serve Jehovah. But only seven thousand really did. Consider that one hundred years earlier during David's reign there were 1.3 million fighting men in Israel and Judah. If one counted all the women, children, elderly, and disabled people who could not fight, there had to be several million Israelites at that time and probably more during Elijah's time. Because Jesus is the truth, his word is truth, and his words shall never pass away, his statement that few find the road that leads to life is still true today.

The Essence of Who a Christian Is

A Christian is not just someone who is born again—a convert, or a believer. A Christian is a born-again follower, disciple, or imitator of Jesus Christ who endeavors to live a Christlike, Bible-based life with the help of the indwelling Holy Spirit. Only disciples, not just believers, were first given the name Christian in the Bible.[459] And Christ told believers that they only become disciples if they live by or continue in his word.[460] A Christian is not merely someone who attends a church service, someone who has been baptized, someone who professes belief in the teachings of Jesus Christ, or someone who has been converted. Mere profession of belief in Jesus, conversion, baptism, or attendance at church services

---

456. Isaiah prophesied in Isa 10:20 about the remnant of Israel whom God would preserve and restore despite impending punishment and exile at the hands of the Babylonians.

457. 1 Kgs 16:29–33.

458. 1 Kgs 19:2–3, 10, 14, 18.

459. Acts 11:26.

460. John 8:31–32.

does not equate with being a disciple, follower, or imitator of Jesus Christ who endeavors to live like he did. In the Great Commission, Jesus did not charge his disciples to just make believers or converts of the nations. He charged them to go and make disciples who would obey his commands.[461] In the Revelation of Jesus to the apostle John, believers raptured at the beginning of the great tribulation who return with the Lord on his second coming are described as his "faithful followers."[462] It is clear from all this that *Christian* is one of the most misunderstood and misused terms in history.

Followers, disciples, or imitators of Christ, regardless of their nationality, ethnicity, skin color, or socioeconomic status, are members of the family of God. They are citizens of heaven. They are supposed to have more in common with each other than with the people in the secular societies in which they were born or live who are not Christians. They are a nation unto themselves, a people transcending race, nationality, ethnicity, skin color, or socioeconomic status. Their "brothers" and "sisters" are not the unbelievers with whom they share the same nationality, ethnicity, or skin color, but those with whom they have been redeemed into the family of God. This counter-cultural perspective needs to be embedded in the understanding of everyone who professes to be a Christian.

When the disciples first started to carry out the Great Commission, they first concentrated their preaching in Jerusalem to other Jews. But a centurion—a gentile—and his entire household got regenerated when Peter preached the gospel to them.[463] And after Stephen, a deacon in the church in Jerusalem, was martyred for his faith in Jesus Christ and the church came under great persecution,[464] many of the disciples were scattered. As they fled, they preached wherever they went. The ministry of the disciples in flight resulted in many more being saved in Judea[465] and Samaria.[466] As they preached in flight, they continued to preach the gospel only to Jews. They reached as far as Phoenicia,[467] Cyprus, and Antioch.[468] However, other believers from Cyprus and Cyrene (in North

461. Matt 28:18–20.
462. Rev 17:14. They are also described as called and chosen.
463. Acts 10:48.
464. Acts 7:54–59.
465. Acts 4:4; 5:14.
466. Acts 8:12; 9:31.
467. An area that included Lebanon and Syria.
468. Acts 11:21.

THE CHRISTIAN AS IMITATOR OF CHRIST

Africa) went to Antioch and preached to gentiles also and a considerable number of them believed and became followers of Christ.[469]

An Ethiopian eunuch, the treasurer of Queen Candace of Ethiopia, was born again when Philip, a deacon in the Jerusalem church, explained the gospel to him as he was returning to Ethiopia from worshipping in the temple in Jerusalem.[470]

Many people all over Europe were born again or regenerated as a result of the ministry of Paul and his fellow workers in the ministry, including Silas, Barnabas, Luke, Timothy, Titus, Phoebe, Priscilla and her husband Aquila, Tychicus, Epaphroditus, and others.[471] Many people got saved during Paul's three missionary journeys. He preached in many European towns and cities including Athens, and planted churches in Corinth, Galatia, Ephesus, Philippi, Colossae, and Thessalonica,[472] places that are now found in Greece and Turkey. During his imprisonment in Rome, he ministered to many people, including a runaway slave called Onesimus.[473] He wrote letters to the churches in Ephesus, Philippi, and Colossae, and to Philemon, Onesimus's master, who lived in Colossae, and to whom he appealed to treat Onesimus as a brother and not as a slave.[474] He wrote to Titus, a spiritual son, who ministered in Crete and Dalmatia,[475] which is now in Croatia, and to Timothy, also a spiritual son, who ministered in Ephesus.[476]

After receiving the gospel from faithful Jews and believing gentiles who suffered much to bring the gospel to Europe,[477] Europeans were positioned to take the gospel to the whole world in fulfillment of the Great Commission. Many missionaries from Europe and the Western Hemisphere did carry, and continue to carry, the gospel message to

---

469. Acts 11:19–21.

470. Acts 8:26–40.

471. Acts 13:48; 14:1; 16:5, 15, 34; 17:4, 12, 34; 18:8; 19:10, 20; 28:24.

472. See Acts 13 and 14 (Paul's first missionary journey); 15:36—18:22 (Paul's second missionary journey); and 18:23—21:16 (Paul's third missionary journey).

473. Phlm 1:10.

474. Phlm 1:15–16.

475. 2 Tim 4:10.

476. 2 Tim 1:18; 4:19.

477. In 2 Cor 11:23–28, Paul pointed out to the Corinthians his legitimacy as a servant of Christ by telling them about the things he had suffered for Christ—imprisonments, floggings, lashes, beatings, stoning, shipwrecks, continual exposure to death and danger from gentiles, fellow Jews, bandits, and false prophets, hunger and thirst, exposure to the elements, and the burden of his concern for all the churches.

other nations. Unfortunately, however, missionary work, beginning in the fifteenth century until the abolition of slavery around the world, was conflated with support for and the defense of two other exports from Europe that have had profound and long-lasting negative impacts on the cause of Christ—slavery and colonialism.

Unfortunately, many people reject the gospel and Jesus because of misconceptions of who a Christian is and what that means. Evils that many who profess the name of Jesus Christ have engaged in throughout the centuries—including the bloodshed during the so-called crusades, and particularly the harms and lingering effects of slavery and colonialism—have turned many people around the world off Christianity. There are White supremacists who talk about "White Christianity" and people of color who have bought into the false notion that Christianity is a "White man's religion."[478]

A Christian is not defined by race, ethnicity, skin color, or socioeconomic status. A Christian is a disciple, follower, or imitator of Jesus Christ. A Christian endeavors to live like Jesus did with the Holy Spirit's help. As imitators of Jesus Christ, Christians must live lives that are obedient to God's word—lives that glorify God. They must love their neighbor as themselves, regardless of their ethnicity, nationality, skin color, or socioeconomic status, treat all people, especially members of the diverse family of God, as they would expect to be treated, and show kindness and compassion to the poor and needy as Jesus did.

---

478. See Harris, *Is Christianity*, debunking the notion that Christianity is the White man's religion and noting that it is good news to people of color.

3

Practicing the Spiritual Disciplines

JESUS CHRIST, THE ONE Christians imitate, was totally devoted to God the Father. He often spent time alone with God praying. He taught his disciples how to pray and how not to pray. He spent time fasting before launching his public ministry. He also taught about fasting. On the night he was betrayed, Jesus and his disciples sang a hymn after supper before heading out to the Mount of Olives where Jesus prayed intensely in the garden of Gethsemane.

Prayer and fasting are part of what are called spiritual disciplines. Studying the Scriptures, praise, and worship are also part of spiritual disciplines. Some include other things like fellowship, giving, serving, and being thankful.[1] These are called spiritual disciplines because they require a commitment to discipline oneself to practice them on a regular basis. Jesus said that he and the Father are one,[2] and that he only spoke what his Father commanded him.[3] Like Jesus, Christians must be totally devoted to their Father in heaven by disciplining themselves to spend time with him in prayer and fasting, and by studying his word so that they can know and do what he commands, including loving their neighbor as themselves, regardless of what they look like or their station in life, and treating others as they would want to be treated.

---

1. See, for example, Altrogge, "5 Spiritual Disciplines."
2. John 10:30.
3. John 12:49–50.

This chapter focuses on four core spiritual disciplines—prayer, fasting, studying God's word, and meditating on God's word. Although this chapter does not discuss praise and worship in their own right, it must be emphasized that they are often part of prayer. When Christians come to God in prayer, they praise and thank him for who he is and for what he has done in their lives. They humble themselves and bow in worship to him as they communicate with him in prayer.

Prayer[4]

There are many secular definitions of prayer. It has been defined as an address (such as a petition) to God in word or thought, or the act or practice of praying to God.[5] It has also been defined as words that you say to God to give thanks or ask for help.[6] Prayer can be defined as talking to God or making a request to God. For a believer or disciple of Christ, since prayer is accompanied by a desire for an answer from God, it may more accurately be defined as communicating with God. When one communicates with another, one does more than just talk; one also listens to what the other has to say. Likewise in prayer, not only does one communicate what is on one's heart and mind to God, but one must also listen for God's voice or what God has to say—his answer, assurance, guidance, or direction. Christians must persevere in prayer even when God seems silent.[7] And during those trying times when believers are hard-pressed to pray, or do not know what to pray for, God's Holy Spirit graciously helps them in their weakness by praying fervently for them according to God's will.[8]

Communication is essential to building a relationship and developing intimacy with another person. It is a way of getting to know someone in a very personal way. Communication cultivates transparency. Since

---

4. Numerous books have been written on prayer and fasting. A few that I found useful include Bright, *Transforming Power of Fasting and Prayer*; Fletcher, *Prayer and Fasting*; and Hickey, *Power of Prayer and Fasting*.

5. Merriam-Webster, "Prayer (n.)."

6. Oxford, "Prayer (n.)."

7. For an excellent resource for believers struggling to listen for God, to whom God seems silent amidst the din and press of worldly demands and distractions, see Weems, *Listening for God*.

8. Rom 8:26–27. See Adeyemo, *Africa Bible Commentary*, 1363–64, commenting that while we wait patiently for what God has promised, the Spirit continually helps us to pray and intercedes for us with wordless groans. After all, in our suffering, we often do not know even how to pray or for what to pray.

THE CHRISTIAN AS IMITATOR OF CHRIST

God has revealed himself to humankind through his word and his Son, Jesus Christ, the human manifestation of the word, it is the believer or disciple who must become transparent before God when communicating with God in prayer. God, being omniscient, already knows the heart of the believer, but requires and expects the believer to be honest and transparent with him. David laid himself bare before God by asking God to search him to know his heart and to try him to know his thoughts. He asked that God might free him from any wickedness or offensiveness within him, to the end that God might lead him in the way that leads to eternal life.[9]

Several synonyms are used in the Bible for *pray*, such as ask,[10] petition,[11] or request.[12] Synonyms for *prayer* include petition, request, intercession,[13] and supplication.[14]

When it comes to prayer, Jesus is the model for every follower, disciple, or Christian. Jesus, the second person of the Triune God, was sent by God to redeem fallen humanity from sin by laying down his own life. He was the full representation of the deity in bodily form[15] and laid down his will to do the will of God.[16] Jesus and the Father are one.[17] Those who saw Jesus saw the Father through him[18] and those who knew him knew his Father.[19] Yet Jesus sought God the Father in prayer constantly. How much more should Christians who profess to follow and imitate Jesus fervently seek God in prayer?

The Bible records many instances of Jesus praying. One evening, while Jesus was in the home of Simon and his brother Andrew, many sick and demon-possessed people were brought to him. He healed many of the sick and cast many demons out of those who were possessed. Early the next morning, while it was still dark, Jesus left the house and went

---

9. Ps 139:23–24.

10. Matt 7:7; Eph 3:20; Phil 1:9; Jas 1:5–6; 4:2–3; 1 John 3:22; 5:14–15.

11. 1 John 5:15.

12. Rom 1:10; Phil 1:4.

13. Rom 8:26; 1 Tim 2:1. In intercession, one approaches God in prayer on behalf of another. The church interceded for Peter while he was in prison. Acts 12:5, 12.

14. 1 Tim 2:1; Heb 5:7.

15. Col 2:9.

16. John 6:32.

17. John 10:30.

18. John 14:9.

19. John 14:7.

to a solitary place to pray.[20] Jesus was often followed by crowds or multitudes of people who came to hear him teach and to receive healing from sicknesses. But he often withdrew from the crowds to quiet or solitary places where he could spend time alone with God in prayer.[21]

Luke records that one evening, many sick and demon-possessed people were brought to him to heal and set free. He laid hands on every single one of the sick and healed them. When daybreak came, he left for a deserted place.[22] He likely spent this time with his heavenly Father in prayer. And after the miraculous feeding of five thousand men and their families with two fish and five loaves, Jesus dismissed the crowd, sent his disciples in the boat to the other side of the lake ahead of him, and went on a mountainside to pray.[23] He sometimes prayed alone, privately, or by himself even when his disciples were near him.[24] And he sometimes prayed in their presence.[25]

In a world filled with hustle, bustle, and competing demands on one's time, how does a disciple of Christ find time to pray? The answer is in Christ's example—giving God the very first and best moments of one's day before the hustle and bustle begins. It is not unlike the Old Testament principle of giving God the first fruits of one's harvest.[26]

As it was with Christ, spending time with God when we are at our freshest needs to become a lifestyle. God deserves our best. But it will require the same discipline Jesus showed in getting up early to pray.

Jesus prayed when John the Baptist baptized him. The Holy Spirit visibly descended upon him, and God audibly spoke to affirm that Jesus was his Son with whom he was very pleased.[27] Jesus spent an entire night praying by a mountainside before choosing his twelve disciples.[28] On a mountainside where he had taken Peter, James, and John to pray, he was transfigured and the appearance of his face changed while in

---

20. Mark 1:32–35.
21. Luke 5:15–16.
22. Luke 4:40–42.
23. Matt 14:22–23.
24. Luke 9:18. The NKJV says his disciples joined him as he prayed alone.
25. Luke 11:1.
26. Exod 23:16, 19; Prov 3:9.
27. Luke 3:21–22.
28. Luke 6:12–13.

prayer, as Moses and Elijah appeared and talked to him about his impending crucifixion.[29]

When Jesus and the disciples came down from the mountain, they encountered a scene of commotion. A father had brought his demon-possessed son to the disciples Jesus left behind, but they could not cast it out. Jesus rebuked the spirit and cast it out of the boy.[30] The disciples asked Jesus privately why they were unable to cast the demon out. Jesus told them in Mark's Gospel account that this kind of demon can only be cast out by prayer. In Matthew's account, Jesus said that it takes a lifestyle of prayer and fasting that builds up faith to take authority over that kind of evil spirit.[31]

Jesus prayed for himself on the eve of his crucifixion after he and his disciples had eaten the Passover supper. He affirmed that he had completed the work or mission God sent him to earth to carry out and prayed that God would glorify him with the glory he shared with the Father before the world began.[32] God answered Jesus's prayer in raising him from the dead, seating him at his right hand, and giving him a name that is above all names.[33]

But Jesus did not only pray for himself after the Passover meal. He also prayed for his disciples. He prayed that, as he was about to leave them, God would protect them from the devil; that they would be one as he and the Father are one;[34] and that God would sanctify them by his word of truth.[35] And then he prayed for all believers who would accept him as Savior and Lord through the preaching of the gospel. He prayed that believers of every age would be one in him and in God; that believers would live in complete unity as a testimony to an unbelieving world that their Savior, Jesus, was indeed sent by God; and that believers would be with him and behold his glory in heaven.[36] In a divisive and conflict-rid-

---

29. Luke 9:28–31.

30. Matt 17:14–18; Mark 9:14–26.

31. Mark 9:28–29. Matthew 17:21 says this kind does not go out except through prayer and fasting in the NKJV.

32. John 17:1–5.

33. Eph 1:20–23; Phil 2:8–11.

34. This speaks to a continual, abiding unity of heart, mind, and purpose. It is therefore a spiritual unity grounded in believers' faith in and obedience to God and his son Jesus.

35. John 17:6–19.

36. John 17:20–26.

PRACTICING THE SPIRITUAL DISCIPLINES

den world, when Christians are able to live in unity with other Christians regardless of their nationality, ethnicity, skin color, or socioeconomic status, it serves as a testimony to unbelievers of Jesus's power to change lives, legitimating his claim of being sent by God.

Jesus prayed fervently in the garden of Gethsemane after the Passover supper. He prayed three times that God would spare him this cup—the separation from God that would take place because he would be carrying the sins of the world. But he surrendered to God's will by praying that God's will and not his own be done. He chided his disciples, whose eyes were heavy and couldn't seem to watch and pray with him for even one hour in his time of need. He exhorted them to watch and pray so that they would not fall into temptation given that even though the spirit may be willing, the body is weak.[37] Disciples of Christ must likewise watch and pray in order not to fall into the many temptations of our modern world.

Jesus even prayed on the cross as he was being executed. He interceded for those who were carrying out his execution since they had no idea what they were doing.[38] He prayed for God to receive his spirit before breathing his last on the cross.[39] He prayed over the meal with the believers in Emmaus after his resurrection.[40] And he continues to pray for believers to this day, as he is seated at the right hand of God where he intercedes for believers and those who come to God through him for salvation.[41] The Holy Spirit, whom Christ sent to be a helper to believers, also intercedes on behalf of believers in whom he dwells in accordance with God's will.[42]

Not only did Jesus live a life of prayer, but he also taught about prayer. During his Sermon on the Mount, Jesus taught about how not to pray. He said that prayer should not be motivated by a desire to be seen and admired, calling that hypocritical. He warned that the only reward one who prays like that gets is the admiration of the people who are impressed by it because God does not reward that kind of prayer. Instead, prayer should be private, between the one who prays and God, flowing out of an intimate, personal relationship. And even though prayer is

37. Matt 26:36–44; Luke 22:39–45.
38. Luke 23:34.
39. Luke 23:46.
40. Luke 24:30.
41. Rom 8:34; Heb 7:25.
42. Rom 8:26–27.

offered in private, the answer and reward from God will be given openly and, therefore, seen by others.[43]

Jesus also taught that prayer should not be a rambling rant characteristic of heathen or pagan prayers. Jesus explained that pagans pray that way because they think that the more words they say, the more likely their gods will hear. God, being omniscient, already knows the needs of believers. Believers should get to the point and not beat about the bush.[44] However, a time of prayer may be long because it is filled with praise, thanksgiving, intercession, and petitions, or because of the momentousness of the circumstances occasioning the prayer, not because of vain repetition. Jesus himself prayed all night before choosing his disciples.[45] Although God already knows what believers need, he still desires for believers to come to him in prayer as a way to nurture their relationship with him by keeping the lines of communication open. He wants believers to renounce self-sufficiency by acknowledging their dependence on him. And God makes good on his desire for us to come to him in prayer by waiting for us to ask before he gives.[46]

Jesus taught that prayer should not be conceited and self-righteous. He told a parable of a Pharisee who went up to the temple to pray along with a tax collector. Instead of honoring God in his prayer, the Pharisee prayed about himself by elevating himself above others, including the tax collector, and touting how he fasted and gave tithes of all he owned. Jesus said that unlike the tax collector who prayed a humble and penitent prayer, the Pharisee went home without having received justification from God.[47]

Jesus didn't just teach his disciples how not to pray. He did teach them how to pray by giving them a model for prayer.[48] Matthew records

---

43. Matt 6:5–6. See Harrington, *Gospel of Matthew*, 96, where he comments that those who make acts of personal piety, including prayer, into public displays will have to be satisfied with public recognition as their reward. They will get no reward from God. But God will reward those who keep secret their private acts of piety. See also Adeyemo, *Africa Bible Commentary*, 1121–22, commenting that the person who gives prayers in order to gain a reputation for piety falls into the trap of being a hypocrite.

44. Matt 6:7–8.

45. Luke 6:12.

46. Jas 4:2.

47. Luke 18:9–14.

48. Matt 6:9–13; Luke 11:2–4. Many books have been written on this model prayer. See, for example, González, *Teach Us to Pray*; Packer, *Praying the Lord's Prayer*; Towns, *Praying the Lord's Prayer*; and Wright, *Lord and His Prayer*. See Johnson, *Gospel of Luke*,

this model prayer as part of the Sermon on the Mount. Luke records it in the context of a scene where Jesus had just finished praying in the presence of his disciples, which prompted one of his disciples to ask him to teach them to pray as John the Baptist taught his disciples. The prayer Jesus taught them is always referred to as the Lord's Prayer. It has also been called the Disciple's Prayer because the Lord taught it to his disciples and it can only be offered by a disciple. The prayer was not really a prayer that Jesus was praying. He was offering a pattern or outline on which his disciples were to model their prayers. Jesus, therefore, prefaced it by telling them that this was how they should pray.[49] Of course, it is recited in corporate prayer in church services and people may pray it literally in their private prayer time. But one must understand the spirit behind the prayer so that it is not rote.

Jesus's model prayer begins with an acknowledgment of the disciple's relationship with God. He is our Father in heaven, and we are his children.[50] We must also approach God in an attitude of worship and reverence by exalting his name and acknowledging that his name must be hallowed or honored as being holy or sacred. This means we should not start asking God for things without first approaching him in the right spirit and with the right attitude.

This model would appear to be meant for quiet times alone with the Lord. It probably would not be the pattern for a desperate and immediate need in an emergency situation such as where a pilot has just announced that a plane is in distress and flight attendants are preparing passengers for a crash or water landing. A desperate and quick prayer in that context might be a whole lot shorter and focused. Nor would this model likely be used by a sinner desperately pleading to God for mercy. In a parable about prayer, Jesus spoke of a tax collector who went to the temple to pray but while still a distance away and without even looking toward heaven, beat his breast in acknowledgment of his sin and asked God for mercy. Jesus said that the tax collector's humility caused him

---

179, commenting that Luke's version of the Lord's Prayer is a series of five imperatives. The first two concern the holiness of God and the establishment of his kingdom. The final three ask for necessary provisions, forgiveness of sins, and freedom from testing. See also Adeyemo, *Africa Bible Commentary*, 1122, commenting that the first three petitions are all concerned with God: his name, his kingdom, and his will. These form the background for the second set of three petitions about human needs: food, forgiveness, and guidance.

49. Matt 6:9. The NKJV says they should pray in this manner.

50. Matt 9:9; Luke 11:2. The beginning of the model prayer is the invocation.

THE CHRISTIAN AS IMITATOR OF CHRIST

to go home having received justification because he repented, and God forgave him.[51] Jesus answered the prayer of the thief on the cross who acknowledged his lordship and asked that Jesus remember him when he came into his kingdom. Jesus promised him that he would be with him in paradise that day.[52]

In his model prayer, Jesus next expressed the desire that God's name be honored as holy.[53] And this happens to be the very first petition in Jesus's model prayer. One of the Ten Commandments prohibits misusing God's name.[54] The prohibition was accompanied by a warning that God would hold accountable anyone who misuses his name. Falsely swearing in God's name is an example of misusing God's name.[55]

Jesus then made his second petition by praying that God's kingdom would be established on earth.[56] This includes God's rule in and through the lives of believers to accomplish his will on earth, Jesus's eventual establishment of his millennial kingdom on earth, and the establishment of the new heaven and the new earth. In the Revelation to the apostle John, Jesus promised that he would come soon. In response, John prayed for Jesus to come.[57] Likewise, every believer must pray for the return of the Lord to establish his kingdom on earth.

Jesus's third petition was for God's will to be done on earth just as his will is done in heaven.[58] Believers are to pray that God's will, as revealed in his word, will be done in this world. This includes praying for God's will to be done in the lives of believers themselves by submitting to discipleship in the teachings of Jesus Christ and the will of God and turning from disobedience to living in obedience to God's will. It also includes praying for God's will to be done in the lives of unbelievers through their acceptance of the gospel and the salvation God offers in Christ. Wanting God's will to be done on earth also requires praying that Satan, sin, and evil will be defeated through the power of Jesus's name.

---

51. This was in contrast to a Pharisee who prayed a self-righteous and conceited prayer and was not justified. Luke 18:10–14.

52. Luke 23:39–43.

53. Matt 9:9; Luke 11:2.

54. Exod 20:7; Deut 5:11.

55. Lev 19:12.

56. Luke 6:10; 11:2.

57. Rev 22:20.

58. Luke 6:10; 11:2.

The first three petitions in Christ's model prayer all have to do with God's position, sacredness, reverence, rule, and will. The believers's own needs have not yet been addressed. God is, therefore, foremost in the model prayer.

It is not until the fourth petition that the prayer begins to ask for the needs of the believer by asking for our daily bread from God.[59] This petition is not for what we will need in the future but for what we need today. Our daily bread would encompass all our daily needs—physical, material, emotional, directional, and spiritual. This is consistent with Jesus's teaching not to worry about material needs like food, drink, and clothing as if God is oblivious to our needs, or about tomorrow. Jesus said to let tomorrow worry about itself because today has enough trouble of its own. Believers are instead to seek God's rule and righteousness and have faith that God will supply their needs.[60]

The fifth petition asks for forgiveness of sins but is conditioned on forgiving others whatever wrongs they have committed against the petitioner.[61] This means that the petitioner must deal with any unrepented sin. The reason is because sin separates or disconnects us from God. The psalmist understood that if he cherished sin in his heart, the Lord would not hear him. He therefore dealt with sin in his life and was assured that God had heard and answered his prayer.[62] Christians do not live a lifestyle of sin. But if they fall short because of their humanity, the apostle John assured them that God is faithful and just to forgive them when they confess their sins and cleanse them from all unrighteousness.[63]

In order to be forgiven for sin, the disciple must also forgive others. The requirement to forgive others means that being unforgiving is a sin that separates us from God. After completing the model prayer, Jesus returned to the issue of being unforgiving before moving on to address other issues by emphasizing that God will forgive us if we forgive others. On the other hand, God will not forgive us if we refuse to forgive others.[64]

The apostle Peter once asked Jesus how many times he was supposed to forgive someone. Seven times? Peter evidently thought seven times would be plenty. After all, the number seven was also the number

---

59. Matt 6:11; Luke 11:3.
60. Matt 6:25–34; Phil 4:19.
61. Matt 6:12; Luke 11:4.
62. Ps 66:18–19.
63. 1 John 1:9.
64. Matt 6:14–15; Mark 11:25.

of completeness or perfection in Jewish numerology. Jesus's answer was that Peter would have to forgive his brother, not seven times, but up to seventy times seven.[65] Jesus then proceeded to tell his disciples a parable in which he likened the kingdom of heaven to a king who settled his accounts with his servants. One servant, who owed 10,000 talents, did not have the money. The king ordered that the servant be sold along with his family to repay the debt. However, the king had mercy when the servant begged for forgiveness. The king canceled the debt. That same servant was owed one hundred denarii by a fellow servant who also begged for time to repay it. However, the servant who had been forgiven of his debt refused to have mercy on his fellow servant and had him thrown into prison. When the king heard about what the unforgiving servant had done, he reversed his earlier debt-cancellation decision and had the servant thrown into jail until his entire debt was repaid.[66]

A talent in Roman currency was about 6,000 denarii or drachmas, the currency used in Israel. A denarius or drachma was a daily wage in Jesus's time. That means one hundred denarii were a little over three months' wages. On the other hand, 10,000 talents represented a colossal sum to owe; one that couldn't possibly be paid by the servant in a lifetime. It amounted to 60 million denarii or drachmas. It would literally take 164,384 years for a servant earning a daily wage to pay it back. Jesus's use of this sum was hence a depiction of the debt of sin humankind couldn't possibly repay—a debt that was canceled only because Christ paid the debt with his own life. Jesus said at the end of the parable that this is how his heavenly Father will treat each of us unless we forgive our brother from the heart.[67] Forgiving from the heart means forgiveness must be genuine, not phony.

As difficult as it might be, a disciple of Christ must forgive even the most egregious wrongs in order to remain in vital relationship with God. As desirable as an apology might be, the disciple cannot condition forgiveness on an apology and must be willing to forgive unconditionally. Of course, forgiveness does not mean a prior relationship can be maintained. Relationships are based on trust and where trust is completely destroyed, a relationship may no longer be possible. But there must still be forgiveness even if a relationship has to be permanently severed.

---

65. Matt 18:21–22.
66. Matt 18:23–34.
67. Matt 18:35.

The sixth and final petition in the model prayer instructs disciples to pray that God will not lead them into temptation, but that he will deliver them from evil or the evil one.[68] James, the half-brother of Jesus and leader of the church in Jerusalem, wrote that God does not tempt anyone. Instead, people are tempted and enticed by Satan who exploits the evil desires in their own hearts. If those desires are not dealt with through the power of the Holy Spirit, prayer, fasting, and the word of God, the evil desires culminate in sin, resulting in spiritual death or separation from God.[69]

Even though God does not tempt anyone, he may allow us to go through temptation to strengthen, purify, and mature us. He never allows temptation that exceeds a believer's capacity to successfully endure and always provides a way of escape from it.[70] It is up to the believer to draw on the power of the Holy Spirit, prayer, and God's word to triumph over the temptation and use the escape hatch God provides. And God even graciously works through his Holy Spirit in us to will and act according to his good purpose or pleasure.[71] God allowed Job to go through great suffering knowing that Job would come through victorious.

Jesus ended the model prayer in the same spirit in which he began it, by acknowledging and recognizing God's sovereignty, power, glory, authority, kingdom, or rule, for eternity.[72]

How often should a disciple or follower of Christ pray? And in addition to the things Jesus taught his disciples to pray about in the model prayer, what other things should a believer pray about or pray for? Jesus prefaced his teachings on prayer with the phrase "whenever you pray" indicating that prayer should be a regular feature of a believer's life.[73] Jesus once told his disciples a parable to illustrate how believers should always pray and not give up or lose heart. He assured them that God will administer justice in answer to the prayers of believers. But he asked whether believers will faithfully persist in prayer till his return.[74] Jesus also taught about persistence in prayer during his Sermon on the Mount. He

---

68. Matt 6:13; Luke 11:4. The NKJV asks to be delivered from the evil one—Satan.
69. Jas 1:13–14.
70. 1 Cor 10:13.
71. Phil 2:13.
72. Matt 6:13. The ending of the model prayer is the doxology.
73. Matt 6:5, 6; Luke 11:2. The NIV and NKJV say "when you pray."
74. Luke 18:1–8.

exhorted believers to persevere in prayer by persistently asking, seeking, and knocking, with the assurance that God will answer their prayers.[75]

Jesus conditioned answers to prayer on a life of obedience made possible by remaining or abiding in him and his words abiding in the believer.[76] A life of obedience pleases God and results in answered prayer. Prayer must be offered in faith in order to be answered.[77] And Jesus also made it clear that it is in his name that believers come before God and ask.[78] James said that God does not answer prayers that have wrong motives.[79] John pointed out that believers can be confident that God hears prayers that are in line with his will.[80] Prayers that have wrong motives or are not in line with God's will cannot be said to be offered in the name of Jesus, who did God's perfect will. John also assured his readers that God answers the prayers of those who obey his commands and do what pleases him. He then articulated what God's command is—namely, to believe in the name of his son Jesus Christ and to love one another.[81] How much prayer goes unanswered because professing Christians refuse to love other Christians because of their nationality, ethnicity, skin color, or socioeconomic status?

In the final instructions he gave in his first Epistle to the church in Thessalonica, the apostle Paul exhorted them to pray continually or without ceasing.[82] They were to maintain an attitude or spirit of prayer so as to be ready, willing, and able to pray wherever and whenever. Paul urged the church in Rome to be faithful or to remain steadfast in prayer[83] and exhorted the Ephesians to pray in the Spirit on all occasions with all kinds of prayers and requests. He asked that they pray for all the other believers and for him to be able to boldly proclaim the gospel while imprisoned in Rome.[84] He also urged the Colossians to devote themselves

---

75. Matt 7:7–11; Luke 11:9–13.
76. John 15:7.
77. Matt 11:24; Heb 11:6.
78. John 14:13–14; 15:16; 16:23–24.
79. Jas 4:3.
80. 1 John 5:14.
81. 1 John 3:22–23.
82. 1 Thess 5:17. See Adeyemo, *Africa Bible Commentary*, 1464, commenting that Paul's vision for the church is that it will always be a joyful community, with a life of prayer nourished by thanksgiving and by meditation on the word under the direction of the Holy Spirit.
83. Rom 12:12.
84. Eph 6:18–20.

to, or to continue earnestly in prayer,[85] and urged Timothy to pray for kings and all those in authority (local, state, national, and world leaders) to be saved so that we may live peaceful and quiet lives.[86] Believers are not just to pray for leaders they like or for those in the political party they support.[87] There would indeed be peace on earth if leaders everywhere lived godly lives in Christ Jesus and governed according to God's righteous standards.[88]

Jesus told his disciples at one point that there was a plentiful harvest of souls to be reaped and brought into the kingdom of God but few laborers. He therefore urged them to pray for God to send more laborers or workers into his harvest field—laborers who would share the gospel and disciple souls.[89]

After the disciples received the baptism of the Holy Spirit following Jesus's death and resurrection, they devoted themselves to the teaching of the apostles, to fellowship, and to prayer.[90] Later, Peter and John were arrested and threatened by the Sanhedrin, the Jewish ruling council, for healing a crippled beggar in the name of Jesus. When they were released, they and the rest of the congregation prayed about the threats they were facing and for boldness to preach the gospel. They also prayed that God would confirm their preaching through healing and miracles. After their prayer, their meeting place was shaken and they all received a fresh infilling of the Holy Spirit, which emboldened them to preach the word of God.[91] The apostles later suggested the appointment of deacons to oversee the care of widows while they devoted themselves to prayer and ministering the word.[92] The apostle James encourages those who lack wisdom to pray for it in faith with the assurance that God will answer their prayer offered through Christ.[93]

---

85. Col 4:2.

86. 1 Tim 2:1–3. Paul told Timothy that such prayers please God because he wants all to be saved.

87. Unfortunately, I have seen prayer lists circulated in churches for some political administrations but not others.

88. The angels who announced Jesus's birth to the shepherds wished for peace on earth and goodwill toward men with Jesus's coming. Luke 2:14.

89. Matt 9:37–38.

90. Acts 2:42.

91. Acts 4:23, 24, 29–31.

92. Acts 6:1–4.

93. 1 Cor 1:30. It is the Lord who gives wisdom to believers. Prov 2:6.

THE CHRISTIAN AS IMITATOR OF CHRIST

This all means that disciples or followers of Christ may pray wherever or whenever, silently or audibly, as circumstances allow. Prayers may be offered while standing,[94] kneeling,[95] sitting,[96] bowing,[97] lying down on one's bed,[98] prostrated with one's face to the floor or ground,[99] and with hands uplifted.[100] Prayers may be private,[101] public,[102] individual,[103] or corporate (group) prayers.[104]

Believers may pray about any issue or topic on which they feel moved to pray.[105] Furthermore, believers must have the same eagerness to pray that motivated Jesus to get up early to meet with God. It is this same eagerness the psalmist expressed when he said his soul panted and thirsted for God in the same way that a deer pants for water, and that he was eager to go and meet with God or appear before him.[106] And believers must pray by the enabling power of the Holy Spirit,[107] whether with the mind or spirit.[108]

The apostle James encouraged believers to pray for one another's healing and assured them that the prayer of a righteous person is powerful and effective.[109] The power and effectiveness of prayer are not measured by the prayer's decibel level, frequency, length, or the admiration people have or express for someone's prayerfulness. It is measured purely by results—whether God hears and answers the prayer. In this regard, I have read about and heard people express great admiration for the prayerfulness of Confederate Generals like General Thomas Jonathan

---

94. Neh 9:5.
95. 1 Kgs 8:54; Luke 22:41.
96. 1 Chr 17:16.
97. Exod 34:8.
98. Ps 63:6.
99. Matt 26:39; Mark 14:35.
100. 1 Kgs 8:54; 1 Tim 2:8.
101. Matt 6:6.
102. Acts 21:5.
103. Matt 6:6.
104. Matt 18:20.
105. One pastor has written prayers that may be prayed centering on the different names of God. See Evans, *Praying Through the Names of God.*
106. Ps 42:1–2.
107. Jude 1:20.
108. 1 Cor 14:15.
109. Jas 5:16.

"Stonewall" Jackson while failing to reconcile that admiration with the fact that the loss of the war by the Confederacy means that God did not answer whatever prayers they may have been praying for the Confederacy to win the war. Slavery was a great sin, and the Confederacy fought for the right to choose to be slave holding states. The psalmist acknowledged that God does not hear those who cherish sin in their hearts.[110] Through the prophet Isaiah, God said that when the Israelites who lived contrary to his will spread out their hands in prayer, he would hide his eyes from them; even if they offered many prayers, he would not listen because their hands were full of blood.[111]

Other than Jesus's prayers and those of the apostles, there are many prayers in both the Old and New Testaments that were offered in varying circumstances by people of faith across the ages who trusted in God. Here I will discuss one from each Testament.

One of the simplest but most powerful prayers from the Old Testament is the prayer of Jabez. Ezra, a priest who had led a group of exiles back to Israel from Babylon in 457 BC,[112] is the Chronicler of the genealogies in which Jabez appears. As Ezra chronicled the genealogy of the tribe of Judah, one of the twelve tribes of Israel, he mentioned all the sons of Helah, a descendant of Judah, but paused to say more about Jabez. Ezra stated that Jabez was more honorable than his brothers and sheds light on why. Jabez's mother had given birth to him in pain and named him Jabez to reflect that painful experience. Jabez obviously did not want his life to be defined by the circumstances of his birth and he prayed to God for a future and destiny that would break free of the constraints of his name and launch him into a realm of God's supernatural blessing and protection. This suggests that Jabez must have been a man of prayer who believed in the power of prayer.

Jabez prayed that God would indeed bless him, that God would enlarge his territory, that God's hand would be with him, and that God would keep him from hurt and harm or evil.[113] And Ezra notes that God granted his prayer.[114] This means that Jabez experienced the blessing,

---

110. Ps 66:18.

111. Isa 1:14–15.

112. Ezra 7:1–9.

113. The NKJV uses *evil*. Jesus also taught in his model prayer to pray for deliverance from evil or the evil one. Matt 6:13. Perhaps Jabez recognized that the evil one could trip him up even in the midst of a blessed life.

114. 1 Chr 4:9–10. The NKJV says he asked that he be kept from evil so as not to

expansion, and protection he prayed for. It also means that he became a blessing to others rather than a cause of pain. This blessed state distinguished Jabez from his brothers and made him more honorable. One author has written about Jabez's prayer as a model for Christians today to pray for God's blessing in a bold way so that they can impact the world for him.[115]

One example of the power of prayer in the New Testament comes from Peter's ministry. Peter was traveling about the country and went to Lydda to visit the believers there. While there, two men from Joppa came to inform him of the death of a beloved disciple called Tabitha (Dorcas) and urged him to come with them. When they arrived, Peter was taken to the upstairs room where Dorcas's body was lying. He put out the crying widows, got on his knees, and prayed. He then spoke to the dead woman and commanded her to get up. Dorcas opened her eyes and Peter helped her up by the hand and presented her alive to the believers. Many people believed in Jesus Christ as a result of this miracle.[116] And that is ultimately the purpose of prayer—that God's presence and power will be made manifest through his answers to prayer so that others will put their trust in him.

Sometimes we have no idea of the impact of our prayers. When I became chancellor of a Penn State campus in southwestern Pennsylvania, I committed the campus to God in prayer. I prayed for wisdom to lead the campus and asked for God's protection over the campus. One morning I read a story in the local newspaper about two people who had been arrested after they set out on a cross-country killing spree. One of them confessed that he came to my campus earlier that day with the intent to randomly kill someone. He parked in a secluded location on campus and waited for someone to come that way, but nobody did. People do normally walk for exercise around the campus. In any event, he left and went to a bar in Morgantown, West Virginia, about thirty minutes away. There he met another man and the two of them decided to go on a killing spree. They had obviously had one too many drinks and crashed their car. When the police arrived and questioned them, they confessed to their nefarious plot. Imagine my shock reading this in the paper the day after it happened. God had answered my prayer to protect my campus without my even knowing it.

---

cause pain. His mother named him Jabez for causing her pain in childbirth.

115. Wilkinson, *Prayer of Jabez*.

116. Acts 9:32–43.

It is my prayer that followers or disciples of Christ all over the world will commit to a ministry of prayer and intercession that fervently seeks and desires for God's will to be done on earth and for Christians to love and treat others as Christ did, regardless of their skin color, where they come from, or their station in life.

Fasting

Fasting is when one abstains from food[117] or does not eat food, especially for religious or health reasons,[118] for a period of time.[119] The Greek word for fasting is *nesteia*, denoting abstinence from food. Fasting is not a hunger strike to twist God's arm to do something. Neither is fasting aimed at weight loss, although one may lose weight while fasting. When one fasts, one denies the flesh and brings it into subjection to one's spirit in order to draw nearer to God in spirit. Jesus told his disciples to watch and pray in order not to fall into temptation. He said the flesh or body is weak even when the spirit is willing.[120] Fasting is a way to discipline the weak flesh and strengthen one's spirit. Seeking the Lord in fasting signals that one is seeking him with seriousness and fervency.

Fasting was a customary practice among Jews that Christians continued.[121] Jesus provided guidance for when a believer fasts, suggesting that it is something that a Christian ought to practice regularly. He told believers to avoid making a show of fasting to impress people, describing that as a hypocritical fast that God will not honor. The admiration that fasting to show off attracts will be its only reward. Instead, fasting ought to be a private matter between the believer and God. It is that kind of fast that God will reward because it is not done with wrong motives.[122]

---

117. Merriam-Webster, "Fasting (n.)."
118. Oxford, "Fasting (n.)."
119. Cambridge, "Fasting (n.)."
120. Matt 26:41; Mark 14:38.
121. See Vine et al., *Vine's Complete Expository Dictionary*, 227 (New Testament Section).
122. Matt 6:16–18. See Harrington, *Gospel of Matthew*, 96, where he comments on Jesus's teaching on three acts of piety—almsgiving, prayer, and fasting—and notes that it is ostentatiousness in personal piety that is criticized here. See also Adeyemo, *Africa Bible Commentary*, 1121–22, commenting that the feeble accolades and admiration someone who fasts to gain a reputation for piety receives from people is their payment in full.

The disciples of John the Baptist asked Jesus once why they and the Pharisees fasted, but Jesus's disciples did not. Jesus answered them by saying that his disciples, whom he compared to guests of a bridegroom, did not fast because he (the bridegroom) was still with them. But they would fast after his departure.[123] Jesus therefore expected believers to fast after his death, resurrection, and ascension as an act of spiritual discipline and devotion while they await his return.

There are different forms of fasting in the Bible. There is the normal fast when one abstains from food but not water. Before his temptation by Satan in the wilderness, Jesus did a normal fast by abstaining from food for forty days and nights. The Bible says he was hungry at the end of his fast but did not say he was thirsty.[124] He must, therefore, have been drinking water. The second type of fast is an absolute fast where one abstains from both food and water. Abstaining from water for more than three days will result in dehydration except in supernatural circumstances such as when Moses was sustained in the presence of God on Mount Sinai for forty days without food or water.[125] Elijah was supernaturally sustained for forty days and forty nights after eating food and drinking water that an angel provided to him.[126] Esther, her maids, and the Jews in Susa did an absolute fast for three days while they prayed and sought God's favor.[127] Finally, the third type of fast is the partial fast where one abstains from certain foods but not from food completely. Daniel received a revelation from God after abstaining from choice or pleasant food (delicacies), meat, and wine during a twenty-one day fast.[128]

Fasting was done on many different occasions and for many different purposes in biblical times. Looking at a number of them will help us understand this spiritual discipline, the various contexts in which it may be done, its proper practice, God's perspective on it, and its results.

Each year, the Jews observed the Day of Atonement when the high priest offered a sacrifice for his own sins and for the sins of the people. The Israelites were to humble themselves and do no work on this day.[129]

---

123. Matt 9:14–15; Mark 2:18–20; Luke 5:33–35.
124. Matt 4:2.
125. Exod 34:28; Deut 9:9.
126. 1 Kgs 19:6–8.
127. Esth 4:16.
128. Dan 10:2–3.
129. Lev 16:29–31; 23:27, 32. The NKJV says they were to afflict their souls (through fasting). This was in a spirit of repentance for their sins. The NIV says they were to deny

This was the only day of the year that God required the entire nation of Israel to fast as part of the law of Moses. They were commanded to fast from the evening of the ninth day of the seventh month until the following evening, an approximate twenty-four-hour fast.[130]

Fasting is usually accompanied by prayer,[131] confession, and humbling oneself. In biblical times, it was also sometimes accompanied by mourning as an act of repentance. The practice and power of prayer and fasting are seen in many accounts in the Bible.

At one point in the history of the Israelites, when the prophet Samuel led them, they were again facing the prospect of war with the Philistines. They had suffered defeat at the hand of the Philistines two decades earlier and lost the ark of the covenant because of their idolatry. The ark was later returned but now hostilities had emerged again. Samuel exhorted them to put away their idols and return to the Lord with all their hearts. Samuel assembled the Israelites before the Lord, and they fasted and confessed their sins. The Lord supernaturally intervened in the ensuing battle with the Philistines and the Israelites experienced victory.[132]

Later, after Israel became a monarchy, King Jehoshaphat and the entire nation of Judah sought God in prayer and fasting because a coalition of armies from Ammon, Moab, and Mount Seir was coming to wage war against him. He prayed before the gathered people in the temple, acknowledged that they were no match against the great armies that were coming against them, but also acknowledged the power and sovereignty of God and the fact that they were looking to him for deliverance. They sang praises to God as they marched to battle. God answered their prayers by creating confusion among the invading armies. They turned against each other and destroyed each other. The people of Judah didn't even have to fight. When they came to the place where the invaders had encamped, they found only dead bodies. It took them three days to gather the jewelry and valuables of the dead soldiers. They blessed the

---

themselves. This happened on the tenth day of the seventh month of the ecclesiastical year in the Jewish calendar, the month of *Tishri* (September–October on the Gregorian calendar). The Day of Atonement is also known as Yom Kippur, the holiest day of the year in Judaism.

130. Lev 23:32. See Adeyemo, *Africa Bible Commentary*, 163, noting that the Day of Atonement was observed with rest and fasting.

131. There are many books that discuss fasting and prayer together. See, for example, Bright, *Transforming Power of Fasting and Prayer*; Fletcher, *Prayer and Fasting*; and Hickey, *Power of Prayer and Fasting*.

132. 1 Sam 4:1–10; 6:1–15; 7:1–11.

Lord on the fourth day and returned to Jerusalem with joy, with King Jehoshaphat at the head of the procession. The nations around Israel were in fear of God when they heard that it was the Lord himself who had fought against Israel's enemies.[133]

While a captive in Babylon where the Babylonians had deported him in 605 BC, Daniel fasted and interceded on behalf of himself and the nation of Israel by confessing his and their sins and praying for their restoration according to Jeremiah's prophecy that the captivity would last seventy years.[134] He acknowledged that the captivity was God's just punishment for their rebellion and disobedience. Before they entered the promised land, Moses had prophesied to the Israelites that if they disobeyed God after being blessed to live in the promised land, they would end up in captivity in a foreign nation.[135] God heard Daniel's prayer and sent the angel Gabriel to give him insight and understanding about end-time events.[136] On another occasion, Daniel mourned and fasted for twenty-one days while abstaining from delicacies, meat, and wine. Three days later, an angel appeared to him in a vision to explain to him what would happen on the global political scene at a future time, including end-time events.[137]

Again, while the Jews were in captivity in Babylon, a Jewish virgin by the name of Hadassah or Esther was selected as King Xerxes's queen in place of the deposed Queen Vashti.[138] She became queen in 478 BC after the first group of exiles in Babylon returned to Jerusalem but before the second group of exiles returned. When Haman, the highest-ranking official next to the king, conceived a plot to annihilate the Jews in the Babylonian kingdom and got the king to enact a law to carry it out, Mordecai, Esther's cousin and guardian, implored her to help by speaking to the king on behalf of the Jews. Since it was against the law to approach the king without

---

133. 2 Chr 18:1–30.

134. Jer 25:11–12; 29:10–14.

135. Deut 28:15, 36–37.

136. Dan 9. The angel Gabriel told Daniel that there would be a gap of 483 years (sixty-nine periods of seven years each) between the restoration of Israel from the Babylonian captivity and the coming of Jesus. And there will be a further gap between the sixty-ninth period of seven years when Jesus, the Anointed One, would be crucified, and the seventieth seven-year period that will usher in the great tribulation and the rule of the antichrist. The antichrist will desecrate the temple in the middle of the tribulation period, three-and a half years before Jesus's return.

137. Dan 10–13.

138. Esth 2:1–18.

invitation, Esther asked all the Jews in Susa to do an absolute fast for three days without eating or drinking anything. She and her maids would do the same. She would then approach the king.[139] Esther found favor with the king when she approached him uninvited.[140] Haman ended up being executed when his plot was exposed[141] and an edict was issued giving Jews the right to defend themselves if attacked on the day they were to be killed. Thus, the Jews prevailed against their enemies.[142]

After the Babylonian captivity, Ezra, who was a priest, led a group of Jews back from exile in Babylon in 457 BC. Before they left, he and the Jews fasted and humbled themselves before the Lord and prayed that he would keep them safe on their journey back to Jerusalem. They had professed their faith in God's ability to keep those who look to him, so they prayed that God would honor their faith, and he did.[143] God protected them from bandits and enemies on their journey till they arrived safely in Jerusalem.[144]

Nehemiah, a Jew who was born in captivity in Babylon and served as the king's cupbearer, was burdened by news that Jerusalem's walls were still in shambles and that the Jews who had survived the exile were living in disgrace.[145] He fasted and prayed for months about the plight of his people, confessing his and their sins, reminding God of his promise of restoration for repentance and obedience,[146] and asking for God's favor with the king.[147] He asked the king for permission to go back to Judah to help rebuild. Not only did the king grant Nehemiah's request, but he also gave him letters to the governors of the territories he would be traveling through to provide him with safe passage. The king also provided him with a letter to the keeper of the king's forests to provide him with the lumber he needed to rebuild Jerusalem's walls and gates, as well as his residence. The king also sent army officers and mounted soldiers with

---

139. Esth 3–4.
140. Esth 5.
141. Esth 7.
142. Esth 8–9.
143. Ezra 8:21–23.
144. Ezra 8:31–32.
145. Two waves of exiles had returned to Israel—the first in 538 BC (under the leadership of Zerubbabel, who became governor) and the second under Ezra, the priest, in 457 BC.
146. Deut 30:2–4.
147. Neh 1.

THE CHRISTIAN AS IMITATOR OF CHRIST

Nehemiah.[148] Nehemiah led a third and final wave of exiles back from Babylon to Jerusalem in 444 BC and served as governor.

Ezra and Nehemiah teamed up to lead spiritual revival among the returned exiles. They assembled together and read the book of the law of Moses. They fasted as a nation, confessing their sins and the wickedness of their fathers that had led to their punishment in exile. They worshipped God and made a collective commitment to live in obedience to God's will.[149]

Fasting was practiced not only in the Old Testament. The New Testament also records many instances where people fasted. When Jesus was presented to the Lord in the temple by his parents as a baby, a prophetess by the name of Anna came up to them and gave thanks to God for Jesus. She was devoted to God and was a fixture at the temple, fasting and praying day and night.[150]

In the church in Antioch, two apostles, Paul and Barnabas, were chosen at the Holy Spirit's direction to carry the gospel into Europe after the church had been worshiping and fasting. Before the church sent them off, they fasted and prayed.[151] Before the end of their missionary journey, Paul and Barnabas went back to a number of cities where they had preached and planted churches. They appointed elders in each of these churches and committed them to the Lord with prayer and fasting.[152]

In what spirit must fasting be done to be acceptable to God? A time in the history of the Jews who returned from exile in Babylon sheds light on this.

The law of Moses required the Israelites to fast on the Day of Atonement. However, when the Babylonians burned down Jerusalem, the temple, and the palace in 586 BC, the Jews added a day of fasting to commemorate that fateful day. The temple was rebuilt by the exiles who returned under the leadership of Zerubbabel.[153] With the rebuilding of the temple, the people asked the priests and prophets of the time whether to continue to observe this fast as they had done for the past seventy years. The Lord spoke through the prophet Zechariah and asked the people whether they really fasted and mourned for him. In other words,

---

148. Neh 2:1–9.
149. Neh 8:1–3; 9:1–3; 10:29.
150. Luke 2:36–37.
151. Acts 13:2–3.
152. These churches were in Lystra, Iconium, and Pisidian Antioch. Acts 14:21–23.
153. Ezra 3:8; 4:24; 6:15.

God was questioning whether their fasting was an acknowledgment of the sins that had led to the exile and the manifestation of a desire to live in obedience to his commandments, or whether it was a mere formalistic act devoid of any real desire to do God's will.[154]

The Lord then spoke through Zechariah to tell the people what he expects from their fasting. God challenged them to administer justice, show mercy and compassion to one another, and to not oppress the downtrodden and disadvantaged—widows, orphans, the poor, and immigrants.[155] In other words, fasting was supposed to make them more like God—just, loving, merciful, and compassionate. And God made it clear through the prophet Zechariah that it was for refusing to do these things due to the hardness of their hearts and their disobedience that he had sent them into captivity in Babylon.[156]

God's message through the prophet Zechariah is one to which every believer and the church needs to pay close attention. It is a message that God also communicated through the prophet Isaiah. The people of Judah in Isaiah's day had an outward and hypocritical righteousness without a true love for God and others. Nor did they have a sincere desire to know and do God's will. They seemed to seek God constantly and appeared eager to know his will and yet they did not do what was right or obey God's commands in his word. It is in this spirit that they fasted. And God ignored them.[157]

The people wondered why God was not noticing their fasting, so God answered them through the prophet Isaiah and addressed the condition of their hearts. God pointed out that, even as they fasted, they did whatever they wanted and exploited or took advantage of their laborers or workers. They resorted to quarreling and fighting when their fasts ended. They exhibited meaningless outward forms of humility like lying

---

154. Zech 7:2–6.

155. Zech 7:9–10.

156. Zech 7:11–14. See Adeyemo, *Africa Bible Commentary*, 1083, noting that the Day of Atonement was the only fast God had commanded the Israelites. However, after the destruction of Jerusalem and the temple, the people instituted fasts to commemorate these events. They now asked the priests and prophets if they should continue to fast since the temple was almost finished, suggesting that the fast had become wearisome to them. Zechariah rebuked the people for fasts that had nothing to do with any desire to obey God and his word or to change.

157. Isa 58:1–2.

on sackcloth[158] and putting ashes on themselves. These empty outward gestures were meaningless to God and could not attract his favor.[159]

But God did not just tell the people of Judah what kind of fast was unacceptable to him. He told them the kind of fast that would be acceptable to him. He wanted their fasting to cause them to become more like him in the way they related to and treated others. Specifically, he wanted their fasting to cause them to do away with injustice and oppression. He wanted them to help feed the hungry, shelter the homeless, clothe the naked, and help their fellow humans. He also wanted them to stop pointing fingers at each other while engaging in malicious talk.

God promised that if fasting were genuinely from the heart and resulted in right relationship with him and others, he would respond in a positive way. He would extend his light and healing and have their backs. He would answer their prayers and extend help in times of trouble. He would deliver them from darkness. He would always guide them and take care of them even in tough times. He would strengthen and prosper them and bring restoration.[160]

So that is really what God is after when we fast. He wants fasting to result in pure hearts and love for him and our fellow human beings. He does not want it to be a mere religious ritual that results in no real change in our hearts and our attitudes toward others. Fasting that does not result in Christlikeness is meaningless to God and therefore pointless. God expects fasting to result in more Christlikeness where, like Jesus, professing Christians love others, regardless of their nationality, ethnicity, or skin color, and show kindness and compassion toward the poor. And God has given his Holy Spirit to indwell, help, and empower believers do that.

Studying the Scriptures (God's Word)

The apostle John began his Gospel account of the life, teachings, and miracles of Jesus by noting from the outset that Jesus is the personification or

---

158. Sackcloth was a coarse fabric made out of goat's hair. It was used to make sacks. Mourners in ancient Israel wore sackcloth. See Smith, *Smith's Bible Dictionary*, 577.

159. Isa 58:3–5.

160. Isa 58:6–12. See Adeyemo, *Africa Bible Commentary*, 847, commenting that Isaiah is addressing those who offer false worship to the Lord, thinking that they can win favor by fasting. The people were hypocritically fasting once a year on the Day of Atonement as God commanded to obtain pardon for their sins while continuing to behave badly on that very day. Isaiah informs them that fasting is useless if it is not accompanied by abstaining from evil.

embodiment of the word of God. The Word was there in the beginning with God and, as the second person of the Triune God, the Word was God himself.[161] The Greek word used in this context for Word is *logos*, denoting the expression of thought or reasoned speech.[162]

John later stated that God so loved the world that he gave his only Son so that everyone who believes in him may not perish but may have eternal life.[163] God did this by sending Jesus into the world. Thus Jesus, the Word, took on human flesh and came and lived with humanity in order to redeem them.[164]

Reference to the word of God sometimes denotes the totality of what God has spoken as revealed in the Scriptures.[165] This includes God's own words spoken directly, as when God spoke to Adam and Eve,[166] Abraham,[167] or Moses;[168] God's word spoken through the prophets as recorded in the prophetic books of the Old Testament; God's word spoken through the apostles;[169] and God's word spoken through Christ who, as the second person of the Triune God and embodiment of the Word, had inherent divine authority to speak God's word.[170]

God inspired the authors of the books in the Bible at various times to proclaim his word as he revealed himself and his will to humankind. In giving Moses the Ten Commandments, God instructed him to write

---

161. John 1:1–2.

162. See Vine et al., *Vine's Complete Expository Dictionary*, 683 (New Testament Section).

163. John 3:16. The KJV and NKJV describe Jesus as God's only begotten son. The NIV says one and only son.

164. John 1:14. See Moloney, *Gospel of John*, 38–39, where he comments that the preexistent Word, so intimately associated with God, now enfleshed, can be the communication and revelation of God in the human situation, where he now dwells. To gaze on the incarnation of the Word was to see the revelation of the divine in the human story. See also Miguel G. Echevarria, "Gospel of John," in McCaulley et al., *New Testament in Color*, 176, where he comments that John declares that the Word is one and the same with Jesus who "took on flesh and dwelt among us."

165. Mark 7:13; Rev 1:2.

166. See Gen 2:16–17, where God spoke to Adam, and Gen 3:9–19, where he spoke to both Adam and Eve.

167. See Gen 12:1–3, where God made a covenant with Abraham.

168. See Exod 3–4, where God called and sent Moses to deliver the people of Israel from slavery in Egypt.

169. In 1 Thess 2:13, Paul said that the word that he and his fellow workers preached to the Thessalonians was not the word of men but, in truth, the word of God.

170. John 1:1, 14; Rev 19:13.

THE CHRISTIAN AS IMITATOR OF CHRIST

down the words he was giving him to serve as a covenant between God, Moses, and Israel.[171] The Spirit of the Lord spoke through David, who was called Israel's singer of songs, the author of a significant number of psalms in the book of Psalms.[172] God also inspired many prophets to declare his word at different points in time. He sent his word to Jeremiah, put his words in Jeremiah's mouth, and appointed him as a prophet to the nations.[173] God put his word in Ezekiel and sent him to speak to the exiles who had been taken captive to Babylon.[174] The apostle Peter exhorted the believers to whom he wrote to pay attention to the words of the prophets because prophecy does not originate in humans' will. Rather, men who were inspired by the Holy Spirit spoke from God.[175] The Scriptures are, therefore, God's word. They are given by inspiration of the Holy Spirit.[176]

With the coming of Jesus Christ and the ushering in of the church age, God spoke directly through his own Son. He sent Jesus to redeem humanity from sin[177] and show them what God is like.[178] Jesus and the Father are one. Therefore, the words Jesus spoke are the very words of God.[179] Because the Scriptures represent who Jesus is and the sum total of God's utterances and revealed will, the study of the Scriptures or God's word is central, not only to knowing God, his Son Jesus Christ, and the Holy Spirit, but to doing their will and living a victorious Christian life. This makes the hearing and study of God's word imperative in the life of a faithful follower, disciple, or imitator of Jesus Christ. Luke observed that those who heard Jesus teach were listening to the word of God,[180] and that the apostles spoke the word of God boldly after being baptized with the Holy Spirit.[181]

---

171. Exod 34:27–28. Moses wrote the first five books of the Bible and compiled them into the Book of the Law. Deut 31:24–26.

172. 2 Sam 23:1–2. Seventy-three of the 150 psalms are attributed to David.

173. Jer 1:1–3, 9.

174. Ezek 2:1–3, 7, 9; 3:1–4.

175. 2 Pet 1:19–21.

176. 2 Tim 3:16.

177. Heb 1:1–2.

178. John 14:9–10. See Moloney, *Gospel of John*, 396, commenting that the words Jesus speaks are the words of his Father.

179. John 14:10–11; Col 2:9.

180. Luke 5:1. See Johnson, *Gospel of Luke*, 23, where he states that the theme of God's word is intimately connected to that of the Prophet (Jesus) and the people. It is through the prophetic word that God addresses the people.

181. Acts 4:31.

In his Letter to the Galatians, the apostle Paul told them that after his encounter with the risen Christ on the road to Damascus, he spent three years in Arabia before going to Jerusalem to meet with Peter and James. Paul told them that he received the gospel that he was preaching by revelation from Jesus Christ. He was not taught by anyone.[182] It is believed that Paul spent these three years studying the Scriptures in order to understand how Christ fulfilled all the prophecies in Scripture about the Messiah, the one that the Old Testament foreshadowed and to whom Judaism pointed. It is this gospel that Paul preached untiringly to his fellow Jews and to gentiles on his three missionary journeys.

Just as Paul had once zealously but blindly held on to Judaism and rejected the gospel, many Jews to whom he preached the gospel did the same. On his second missionary journey, Paul encountered opposition from jealous Jews in Thessalonica. Fearing for his life, the believers there sent him and his fellow worker Silas to Berea.[183]

The Scriptures reveal something admirable about the Bereans that all professing Christians would do well to emulate. The Scriptures state that the Bereans were of more noble character than the Thessalonians. Not only did they receive the message of the gospel with great eagerness, but they also examined or studied the Scriptures every day in order to determine if what Paul preached was indeed true.[184] Studying the Scriptures is the surest way to spot false doctrine and false teaching. Jesus prayed that God would sanctify or set apart his disciples with his truth, which is his word.[185] He also said that if one continues in his word, then one is truly his disciple. And one will know the truth, and the truth will make one free from sin.[186] Knowing God's truth as revealed in his word is the only way to discern error. The Scriptures give Christians a measuring rod or yardstick for evaluating what they hear or read, and for vetting the things that demand their loyalty, including their "tribe," political party, leaders, traditions, and culture. Paul admitted that his life prior to his conversion was characterized by blind zeal for the tradition of his

---

182. Gal 1:11–19.

183. Acts 17:5–10.

184. Acts 17:11.

185. John 17:17.

186. John 8:31. See Moloney, *Gospel of John*, 275, where he comments that Jesus is attempting to draw Jews who had partially believed in him into authentic belief by abiding in the word of Jesus that they are struggling to grasp so that they can be regarded as disciples. A disciple is always at the school of Jesus.

THE CHRISTIAN AS IMITATOR OF CHRIST

fathers.[187] Jesus accused the Pharisees of putting their tradition ahead of the commands of God and of nullifying the word of God with their handed-down tradition.[188]

In his very last Letter written from the Roman prison where he was held before his execution by Emperor Nero, the apostle Paul exhorted his spiritual son Timothy to study or be diligent to show himself approved by God so that he would not be ashamed to stand before God as one who had correctly handled or taught God's word of truth.[189] Paul noted that Timothy had known the Scriptures from his infancy and urged him to continue in what he had learned and become convinced of because of those from whom he had learned it. Paul reminded Timothy that the Scriptures have the capacity to make one wise to gain salvation through faith in Christ, and that all Scripture is God breathed or given by inspiration of God. As such, the Scriptures are useful for teaching, rebuking, correcting, and training in righteousness, so that the people or servants of God may be thoroughly equipped for every good work.[190]

Unlike disciples of Christ who read or study the Bible for spiritual insight and divine guidance with the help of the Holy Spirit, many read or study the Bible for other reasons. Some read or study it as literature, poetry, ancient Jewish history, culture, theology, philosophy, or mythology. And some non-Christians who read the Bible find it to be archaic, inconsistent, or even nonsensical. But as Paul pointed out to the believers in Corinth, the unsaved person without the Holy Spirit does not receive the things of the Spirit of God because they see it as foolishness. Nor can they understand the things of God because those things are spiritually discerned.[191] Paul went on to say that the message of the cross is foolishness to those who are perishing because it is inconsistent with worldly wisdom or philosophy. But it is the power and wisdom of God to those who are called and are being saved.[192] Bible study must, therefore, be undertaken prayerfully, seeking the guidance of the Holy Spirit, whom

187. Gal 1:14.
188. Matt 15:3–6; Mark 7:1–13.
189. 2 Tim 2:15. See Osvaldo Padilla, "Pastoral Letters," in McCaulley et al., *New Testament in Color*, 556, where he comments that Paul is highlighting the word of God, both its right use and misuse by false prophets. Paul is encouraging Timothy to be a servant who rightly explains the word of truth and uses God's word well, with precision, in order to lead the believers in right living and rebuking false teachers.
190. 2 Tim 3:14–17.
191. 2 Cor 2:14.
192. 1 Cor 1:18–24.

Jesus sent to guide disciples into all truth.[193] David recognized this need and prayed that God would open his spiritual eyes so that he might see wonderful things in God's law.[194]

The apostle Peter urged the believers to whom he wrote his first Epistle to crave or desire the pure spiritual milk of God's word, just as newborns crave natural milk, so that they would grow up or mature in their salvation.[195] The Greek word for desire or crave in this context is *epipotheó*, which means to long for or desire greatly.[196] Thus, believers are to long for the word of God greatly by studying it diligently in order to grow and mature in Christ. By implication, just as a newborn's growth and health would be greatly impaired without the nourishment newborns get from milk, a believer's growth and spiritual health will be impaired or compromised without a diligent study of God's word. One cannot know what God has spoken unless one studies and is familiar with his word. In studying God's word, one progresses from knowing and understanding basic truths to gaining deeper insights as one matures in Christ and digs deeper into his word.

The apostle Paul likened these deeper insights and a greater understanding of God's word to meat or solid food and the basics to milk. During his second missionary journey, Paul spent eighteen months in Corinth where he founded the Corinthian church along with his fellow laborers in Christ and a ministering couple called Priscilla and Aquila.[197] While in Ephesus during his third missionary journey, Paul got word of troubles in the Corinthian church.[198] The church later sent a delegation to Paul in Ephesus with a letter from the church's elders asking for instruction and direction on a number of issues.[199] Paul wrote his first of two Letters to the Corinthians in answer to this request.

In his first Letter to the Church in Corinth, Paul lamented to them that they had not grown in Christ and were acting in worldly ways as the unsaved do. As such, he couldn't address his Letter to them as he would

---

193. John 16:13.

194. Ps 119:18.

195. 1 Pet 2:2

196. See Vine et al., *Vine's Complete Expository Dictionary*, 161, 376 (New Testament Section). See also Strong's Reference Number 1971, defining *epipotheó* as to long for or desire greatly.

197. Acts 18:1–11.

198. 1 Cor 1:11.

199. 1 Cor 16:17.

THE CHRISTIAN AS IMITATOR OF CHRIST

to people who were spiritual. He had to address it to them as infants in Christ who were still worldly. He pointed out that when he was with them during his eighteen-month ministry in Corinth, he fed them milk, not solid food, because they were not ready to receive solid food. Regrettably, they were still not ready.[200] There was quarreling and jealousy among them just as among the worldly. In other words, after receiving Christ and coming into the church, the believers in Corinth had not become transformed. They did not have renewed minds that caused them to think and act differently as disciples of Christ.[201] They had factions and divisions,[202] abused the gifts of the Spirit,[203] showed no compassion for the poor among them during fellowship meals,[204] resisted apostolic teaching,[205] tolerated immorality,[206] and attended idolatrous festivals.[207] The problems in the Corinthian church demonstrate the importance of studying God's word and maturing by feeding on it.

The writer of the book of Hebrews picks up this very point. Writing to Jewish Christians living outside Israel, he explains the status of Christ as a great high priest in the order of Melchizedek, the king of Salem and priest of God during Abraham's time. Melchizedek's genealogy was unknown as if he had neither beginning nor end. It is in this sense that Christ's priesthood is like Melchizedek's, since Christ, being the second person of the Triune God, has no beginning and no end. He is a priest whose priesthood is everlasting, and he is King of kings.[208]

The writer of Hebrews indicated that he had much more to say about this topic of Christ as the great high priest, but it was hard to explain it to his audience because they were slow to learn. He lamented that they should, at this stage of their Christian journey, have grown up enough in Christ to be in a position to teach others, yet they themselves still needed to be taught the elementary truths of God's word. These elementary teachings about Christ include what the Bible teaches about

---

200. 1 Cor 3:1–3.
201. Rom 12:2.
202. 1 Cor 3:4–9.
203. 1 Cor 12; 14.
204. 1 Cor 11:17–22.
205. 1 Cor 14:36–38.
206. 1 Cor 5:1–2.
207. 1 Cor 8; 10.
208. Heb 5:6–10; 7:1–17. Rev 19:16 reveals Jesus's name as King of kings and Lord of lords. Melchizedek appears for the first time in the Bible in Gen 14:18–20.

repentance from sin, faith in God, baptisms, the laying on of hands, the resurrection of the dead, and eternal judgment.[209] They needed to move on from an understanding of these elementary teachings to a place of maturity. Unfortunately, they still needed milk and not solid spiritual food. He pointed out that those who still feed on milk as spiritual infants are unacquainted with or unskilled in the word of righteousness or the teaching about righteousness. They, therefore, lacked the spiritual sensitivity and ability to discern between what is good and evil in this world. On the other hand, solid food, which consists of the deeper insights of God's righteous word, is for the spiritually mature who, by constant use through study and obedience to the word, have trained themselves or have become spiritually sensitive enough to distinguish between good and evil.[210]

As the Israelites were getting ready to enter Canaan, Moses reminded them to obey the Lord. He told them that humankind does not live by bread alone but on every word that comes from the mouth of God.[211] In other words, they were not to become preoccupied with their physical needs, but with their relationship with God. It was their relationship with God and their obedience to his word that would serve as the basis of their security, provision, and prosperity.

The role of the Scriptures in overcoming the devil's temptations is seen in the temptation of Jesus. Before Jesus began his public ministry, he spent forty days fasting in the wilderness. He was naturally hungry when the Holy Spirit led him to the wilderness where Satan came and tempted him to prove that he was the Son of God by speaking to stones and commanding them to become bread. Satan was essentially tempting Jesus to put his physical needs ahead of obedience to God. Satan was also tempting him to be prideful and vain by proving who he was by misusing his

---

209. Heb 6:1–2.

210. Heb 5:11–14. See Adeyemo, *Africa Bible Commentary*, 1497, commenting on the writer's rebuke of his audience for failing to grow spiritually. They had an apathy toward the word of God, were unable to teach and pass on the word of God, preferred an infant diet whereby they were not acquainted with the teaching about righteousness or ready for solid teaching about our Lord's ministry in heaven as the preeminent high priest, and lacked spiritual sensitivity and discernment. They had failed to study the word of God regularly to learn how it applies to daily life and to develop the ability to distinguish between what is good and what is evil. See also Madison N. Pierce, "Letter to the Hebrews," in McCaulley et al., *New Testament in Color*, 592, commenting that the writer expresses the desire that the audience be able to hear more of what he has to say, but then they are effectively infants not mature enough to partake of solid food.

211. Deut 8:3.

power. Jesus responded to Satan's temptation by quoting Moses's words in Deuteronomy.[212]

Satan also tempted Jesus to prove that he was the Son of God by committing a reckless act of self-endangerment—leaping off the pinnacle of the temple with the expectation that God would fulfill his promise of protection by commanding his angels to keep Jesus safe. Jesus refused to oblige by quoting the scriptural admonition Moses gave to the Israelites not to put God to the test.[213] Satan also tried to get Jesus to worship him in return for worldly power and splendor. Again, Jesus quoted the Scripture in Deuteronomy where Moses exhorted the Israelites to worship and serve God only.[214] In all these instances of temptation, Jesus used the Scriptures to rebuff Satan. Jesus was the embodiment of the word of God, yet Satan twisted the word of God to tempt Jesus to sin.

In his Letter to the Ephesians, Paul reminded them that believers are not to be distracted into thinking that their battle is with people because Satan also uses people in much the same way as God uses ordinary people to accomplish his will on earth. Instead, believers must understand that they are in a spiritual battle with Satan and evil forces. Borrowing from the image of a Roman soldier, with which the Ephesians and all who lived in a Roman-dominated world in which the Roman soldier was a ubiquitous presence would have been familiar, Paul exhorted them to fight this spiritual battle by putting on the whole armor of God. The pieces of the armor include the belt of truth, God's word, which holds the armor together and allows free movement; the breastplate of righteousness, which protects the heart, the source of all the issues of life; the shoes of the gospel of peace to keep one firmly planted while taking the gospel to others; the shield of faith to intercept and extinguish Satan's flaming arrows; the helmet of salvation to guard one's mind; and the sword of the Spirit, which is God's word.[215]

Jesus's encounter with the devil in the wilderness could be seen as a spiritual battle in which Jesus skillfully used the sword of the Spirit, the word of God, to defeat Satan. In overcoming Satan's temptations with Scripture, Jesus teaches all believers the importance of knowing God's word. And that requires careful study and memorization of the Scriptures, not merely casually reading the Bible like a novel or newspaper.

212. Matt 4:1–4; Luke 4:1–4.
213. Matt 4:4–7; Luke 4:9–12. Jesus quoted Deut 6:16.
214. Matt 4:8–10; Luke 4:5–8. Jesus quoted Deut 6:13.
215. Eph 6:11–17.

PRACTICING THE SPIRITUAL DISCIPLINES

There will be times like those Jesus faced in the wilderness when Christians will not have access to a Bible or an electronic device and will have to rely on the Holy Spirit to bring to their remembrance what they have studied and memorized.

Moses shared ways to remember God's word with the Israelites. He told them to put the commandments of God that he was conveying to them in their hearts. They were to teach them diligently to their children in every setting, in and out of the home, upon waking up, and upon retiring to bed. They were to become so intimately familiar with God's commandments that they would be unlikely to forget him in their times of blessing after entering the promised land.[216]

Jesus also talked about an aid to remembering God's word. He promised his disciples that the Holy Spirit would teach the believer and help the believer recall his teaching.[217] This teaching happens as the believer studies the Scriptures and listens to the preaching of the word. The Holy Spirit cannot remind people of what they have not studied or committed to memory, in the same way that one cannot retrieve data from a blank hard drive or device on which nothing is stored.

Christians must have faith in and love the totality of God's word as the psalmist does in Ps 119. He mentions the various aspects of God's law or word, including his "statutes" or requirements; his "ways" or the manner in which he operates; his "precepts" or instruction; his "decrees" or regulations; and his "commands" or his authoritative rules.[218] The psalmist wrote that the only way for a young person to keep their way pure or live a holy life is to live according to God's word.[219] He intimated that he had hidden God's word in his heart as a safeguard against sinning against God.[220] Living according to God's law and hiding it in the psalmist's heart would require study and memorization of God's word. The psalmist's life was guided by God's word which he metaphorically described as a lamp

---

216. Deut 6:6–12.
217. John 14:26.
218. Ps 119:1–9.
219. Ps 119:9.
220. Ps 119:11. See Adeyemo, *Africa Bible Commentary*, 722, commenting that the authors of the Bible thought of the heart as the central place that directed one's emotions, thoughts, and actions. That was why it was so important that God's word should have a central place in one's heart. Jesus provided a clear example in Matt 4:11 of how knowing God's word and having it in our hearts can help us to avoid sinning when we face temptation.

unto his feet and a light unto his path.[221] It was this light that illuminated his life and decisions—his moral compass.

Professing Christians must likewise have a deep love for, and a fervent desire to know and live by, God's word. Jesus told his disciples that if they love him, they will obey what he commands.[222] As the second person in the Holy Trinity, Jesus demands obedience of his followers or disciples. To them, he issues commands that impart life to those who obey. And since one cannot obey what one does not know, studying and understanding God's word, memorizing as much of it as possible, internalizing it, hiding it in one's heart, and meditating on it, is imperative. Merely reading the Bible like one reads a newspaper, magazine, or novel, or out of a sense of duty, is unlikely to be profitable.[223]

There are many approaches to studying God's word and many resources to guide Bible study. New converts are usually counseled to start Bible study with the Gospel accounts of the life of Jesus, particularly the Gospel of John, because it was written to convince the reader that Jesus is the Christ, the Son of God, so that the reader might have eternal life.[224] One author recommends that new believers begin studying the Bible with the New Testament, beginning with the Epistle of 1 John because it assures believers of their salvation, followed by the Gospel of John to increase their faith.[225]

I have heard people say that they have read the Bible from cover to cover (from Genesis to Revelation) many times. But reading the Bible is different from studying it for understanding, insight, and application to one's personal life. Reading the Bible may give one a "telescopic" view of the books of the Bible. But it is a "microscopic" approach, one that requires drilling down deeper to extract its truths verse by verse, that will help one understand and live out the Bible.[226] There are study Bibles and other resources that offer schedules for reading the Old Testament, the New

---

221. Ps 119:105.

222. John 14:15.

223. Dwight L. Moody confessed to a point in his life when he read several chapters of the Bible a day to meet his own set quota, but not to grow. He said he hardly remembered what he read even a few hours later. See Moody, *How to Study the Bible*, 54.

224. John 20:30–31.

225. LaHaye, *How to Study the Bible*, 46–47.

226. Moody, *How to Study the Bible*, 124, discusses the telescopic and microscopic approaches to Bible study. He also shows how one can study the Bible by studying types, characters, names, words, and topics, and by marking up one's Bible as a study or memory aid.

Testament, or the entire Bible, in one year. Although one can read the Bible in a year, it is highly unlikely that one can study it in one year. Bible study must transform and empower one to imitate Christ for it to be profitable. One author offered a schedule to read the Bible in three years.[227]

The Bible may be studied in some orderly or systematic way. For example, one may study the books in a particular section of the Bible, such as the prophetic books (from Isaiah to Malachi), the major prophets (Isaiah, Jeremiah, Ezekiel, and Daniel), or the minor prophets (Hosea to Malachi). One may study what are called the wisdom and poetic books (Job, Psalms, Proverbs, Ecclesiastes, and Song of Solomon). One may study the Gospel accounts of the life and works of Jesus Christ, or the Epistles, or the Epistles of a particular apostle like Paul or John. All of this will require reading, studying, and thinking about the books, chapters, verses, words, topics, subjects, and characters in the passages being studied.[228]

One may also study the Bible topically or thematically with the assistance of study aids such as a topical Bible or a theme finder or subject index in a study Bible.[229] Topics, subjects, or themes may cover things like repentance, forgiveness of sin, salvation, sanctification, baptism, the Holy Spirit, the gifts of the Spirit, the fruit of the Spirit, living an obedient life, overcoming temptation, sharing the gospel, the resurrection of the dead, the great tribulation, the second coming of Christ, or God's judgment.

Another way of studying the Bible is by using what is called the inductive method. This involves discovering for oneself through personal study, book by book, what the Bible says (observation), what it means (interpretation), and how it works (application).[230] In studying the Bible, one may find guidance from one or more of numerous books written about how to study the Bible.[231]

---

227. LaHaye, *How to Study the Bible*, 56, offers a three-year Bible reading schedule.

228. LaHaye, *How to Study the Bible*, 11, 75–93, 109–18, talks about reading, studying, learning, and thinking about the Bible's books, chapters, verses, topics, and subjects. At 113, he says he found subject analysis combined with memorization of key verses to be the best way to study God's word.

229. Examples of topical bibles include MacArthur, *MacArthur Topical Bible*; and Nave, *Nave's Topical Bible*.

230. Arthur et al., *How to Study Your Bible*. See also Navigators, "How to Study the Bible."

231. See, for example, Warren, *Bible Study Methods*, where he discusses twelve methods of Bible study—the devotional, chapter summary, character quality, thematic,

THE CHRISTIAN AS IMITATOR OF CHRIST

There are numerous resources that provide Bible study tips, many of which can be found online.[232] Study aids are extremely important in helping one navigate and study the Bible in a meaningful way that fosters spiritual growth. A concordance is a particularly useful tool in Bible study. It may include an alphabetical index of the principal words in a book or an alphabetical list of the words (especially the important ones) present in a text or texts, usually with citations of the passages concerned with information about where the words can be found and in which sentences. Perhaps the best-known Bible concordance is the one by James Strong.[233]

Bible dictionaries are also especially useful tools in Bible study.[234] They provide great insights into the people, places, currencies, organizations, and nations of biblical times. They also help gain a proper understanding of Bible words, putting them into proper context by exploring and explaining their Greek roots.

One may study the Bible with the assistance of a daily devotional that provides subjects, Scriptures, and commentary to help the believer understand and apply the principles being studied. Devotionals are available online or in print and may be geared toward new converts or more mature believers. Some may also be tailored to younger believers and are, therefore, age appropriate.[235] In choosing a devotional, it is important to find one whose only aim is to help the believer know and grow in

---

biographical, topical, word study, book background, book survey, chapter analysis, book synthesis, and verse-by-verse methods.

232. See, for example, Velarde, "Devotional Bible Study Is Not an Option." He emphasizes consistency, prayer for understanding, and memorization as important aspects of devotional Bible study. See also Navigators, "How to Study the Bible." They recommend and provide guidance on the inductive method of Bible study, where one makes observations about Scripture passages, interprets them, and applies them.

233. There are several concordances by James Strong: *New Strong's Concordance of the Bible: Concise Edition*; *New Strong's Exhaustive Concordance of the Bible*; and *Strong's Exhaustive Concordance of the Bible*.

234. Perhaps the best-known Bible dictionary for lay people is Vine et al., *Vine's Complete Expository Dictionary*. Other dictionaries I have found useful include Brand et al., *Holman Illustrated Bible Dictionary*; and Smith, *Smith's Bible Dictionary*.

235. Perhaps the most spiritually helpful devotional I have used as an adult is Chambers, *My Utmost for His Highest* (utmost.org). Another very well-known devotional that has been around a long time is *Our Daily Bread* (odbm.org). Scripture Union also produces devotional aids such as "Discovery" and "Encounter with God."

Christ.[236] One author believes devotional reading is basic spiritual food, but not enough to equip someone to share God's word.[237]

In the parable of the sower, Jesus spoke about a farmer who was sowing seed by scattering the seed manually. Some of the seed fell along the path and was eaten by birds. Some fell on rocky places where the shallow soil caused the seed to spring up quickly only to die in the withering heat of the sun because it had no root. Other seed fell among thorns which choked the plants, but other seed fell on good soil and produced a crop—some one hundred, some sixty, and some thirty times what was sown.

As Jesus explained the parable privately to his disciples, he revealed that the farmer is one who shares the gospel, and the seed is God's word. The seed that fell along the path represents those who hear the gospel about Jesus but do not understand it. The devil then snatches the word that they heard but did not understand so that they are unable to receive it, act on it, and become born again into the kingdom of God.[238] Although this parable shows that it is imperative that the gospel be preached in a way that makes it simple and understandable, we can also extrapolate from it that it is unfruitful to read the word of God without understanding it and growing from it. And if one does not understand the Bible, one cannot apply its truths and live them out.

The importance of understanding the word of God is seen in the story of the Ethiopian eunuch. After Jesus's death, resurrection, and ascension into heaven, persecution arose against his disciples as they preached the word of God and performed miracles, and the church grew in number. This persecution intensified after the death of Stephen, a deacon in the early church. Other than the apostles, the church in Jerusalem was scattered throughout Judea and Samaria.[239] Philip, a deacon in the church in Jerusalem, fled to Samaria, from where an angel directed him to go down to a desert road that led from Jerusalem to Gaza. There, he

---

236. One must exercise discernment in determining whether a devotional provides the sincere, unadulterated milk of the word and the meat or solid food that the believer needs to grow in Christ. There are devotionals that may promote a certain historical or ideological viewpoint. One devotional I looked through wove selected Bible passages with what seemed like a pro-Confederate view of the Civil War.

237. LaHaye, *How to Study the Bible*, 71.

238. Matt 13:3–9; Mark 4:3–8; Luke 8:5–15. See Johnson, *Gospel of Luke*, 134, commenting that the parable's lesson is that it is possible to lose what one has initially been given or what one thinks one has. Protection of the word and perseverance in it mean everything.

239. Acts 5:17–18; 7:57–60.

THE CHRISTIAN AS IMITATOR OF CHRIST

met an Ethiopian eunuch, Queen Candace's treasurer. A convert to Judaism, he was returning from Jerusalem, where he had gone to worship. Philip drew near to the chariot on the direction of the Holy Spirit and heard the Ethiopian reading a passage in the book of Isaiah about Jesus's crucifixion. He admitted to Philip that he did not understand what he was reading and needed someone to explain it to him. Philip explained the passage and shared the gospel of Christ with the eunuch. As a result, the eunuch received Jesus Christ as his Savior and was baptized.[240] It is clear from the Ethiopian eunuch's story that God wants us to study, understand, and act on his word.

Given how important understanding God's word is, it makes sense to use a version or translation of the Bible that one can understand and study aids that help one understand. As one grows in understanding, one may consult other versions to gain insights from different translations. There are study Bibles that have study aids such as notes, articles, charts, and maps, to help explain passages and put them in proper context. Study Bibles may give insights into the historical context for each book of the Bible, information about the author, the time when it was written, the purpose for which it was written, its distinctive features, and how it connects with other books of the Bible. Study Bibles may also contain a reading schedule which, if followed, will help the reader complete reading a book within a certain time.

Before he ascended into heaven, Jesus directed that the gospel be preached to all people. But he didn't stop there. He also directed that all who receive him be made into disciples by being taught to obey all his teachings. And only disciples, not just believers, were called Christians in the Bible. Jesus said one becomes a disciple by continuing in his word, knowing the truth, and being set free from the power of sin.[241]

When all is said and done, it is pointless to read or study God's word without being willing to obey it and be changed by it. The apostle James pointed out that faith without works is dead and as useless as a corpse.[242] James compared the one who hears but does not live by the word of God to one who looks into a mirror and walks away without remembering what the mirror revealed, without fixing what it showed as needing to be fixed.[243] Some talk about people, especially certain venerated historical

---

240. Acts 8:1–5; 26–38.
241. John 8:31–32.
242. Jas 2:26.
243. Jas 1:23–24.

figures, as having Christian virtues, as being students of the Bible, or as being men of prayer, without addressing the all-important question of whether their lives, particularly what they believed and espoused, and how they treated other human beings, imitated Jesus Christ. It is in living out what Christ modeled and taught, including loving all people regardless of what they look like and being kind to the poor, that one demonstrates that one is a Christian.

Meditating on the Scriptures (God's Word)

Moses died before the Israelites entered the promised land. Joshua, Moses's assistant, became the new leader of Israel. God spoke to him and told him to be strong and courageous and not to allow the book of the law, the five books of Moses,[244] to depart from his mouth. He was to meditate on it day and night and carefully observe everything written in it so as to be prosperous and successful.[245] As one commentary has noted, Moses had written down the five books of the Pentateuch, known together as the Law, and given it to the priests, sons of Levi, and the elders of Israel. Joshua was to study this law carefully, meditating on its teachings and applying them to all his activities. God had hitherto revealed his will through dreams, visions, angels, and prophets, and even directly in person. But now God was telling Joshua that whatever he may need to know has already been revealed and recorded by Moses in the book of the law. Joshua was, therefore, not to wait for dreams, visions, angels, prophets, or God's personal appearance. Instead, he was to study and meditate on the book of the law and faithfully put it into practice. That would bring blessing and success.[246]

The Greek word for meditate as used in this Scripture is *hagah*, which means to utter or speak, and may depict the subdued sounds one makes as one muses on God's word.[247] Meditating in this sense can, therefore, be described as muttering or musing on the word of God in order to internalize it and let it sink into one's spirit. In giving Joshua

---

244. These five books of Moses are referred to as the Torah, which means law in Hebrew. It could also refer to the scroll on which the law is written. The Torah is referred to as the Pentateuch in Greek.

245. Josh 1:8.

246. Adeyemo, *Africa Bible Commentary*, 259.

247. See Vine et al., *Vine's Complete Expository Dictionary*, 150 (Old Testament Section).

this command, God was instructing him to be faithful to God's law by muttering, uttering, musing on, or speaking it in order to facilitate his obedience to it. Joshua would have to study and know the law in order to be able to reflect on it, mutter, or speak it.

One author has compared meditating in this sense to the act of a cow chewing the cud over and over, extracting all the nutrients out of it.[248] The prosperity and success that result from meditating on and obeying God's word come from acquiring understanding and wisdom to live a righteous life that fulfills God's purpose for one's life,[249] although this may not necessarily be material prosperity and success in a worldly sense. Another author has described meditating on God's word as thought digestion and has offered helpful tips on meditating on Scripture passages. He suggests visualizing the scene in one's mind, emphasizing different words in the passage, paraphrasing it, and personalizing it.[250]

The kind of meditation God commanded Joshua to practice is different from meditation in a general sense or a religious sense outside of the Judeo-Christian context, such as Transcendental Meditation.[251] Definitions of meditation include the act of focusing one's mind in silence or with the aid of chanting for a religious or spiritual purpose or as a method of relaxation; or to think deeply or carefully about something or to plan mentally.[252] Other definitions include to engage in contemplation or reflection or mental exercise for the purpose of reaching a heightened sense of spiritual awareness.[253] These types of meditation do not capture the essential element of muttering or musing on God's word or Scripture passages in order to internalize them so that one can align one's lifestyle accordingly in fulfillment of God's purpose and will.

Regarding the blessings that come from meditating on God's word, the psalmist wrote that the one who shuns a lifestyle of sin, delights in God's law, and meditates on it day and night is blessed. He compares this

---

248. Burke, *How to Meditate God's Word*.

249. In Ps 19:99, the psalmist recognized that meditating on God's statutes gave him more insight than his teachers.

250. Warren, *Bible Study Methods*, 38–40.

251. This type of meditation, developed by the Maharishi Mahesh Yogi, involves using a mantra to meditate in silence while sitting and with one's eyes closed.

252. Oxford, "Meditation (n.)." The Cambridge Dictionary defines it as to think seriously about something, especially over a period of time. The Cambridge Dictionary states that this can be done as a religious activity or as a way of calming or relaxing one's mind. Cambridge, "Meditation (n.)."

253. Merriam-Webster, "Meditation (n.)."

person to a tree planted by streams of water that brings forth its fruit in season and whose leaves do not wither. The psalmist says that whatever this person does prospers.[254] In other words, the one who desires to do God's will loves God's word and seeks direction from it by searching it, studying it, reflecting on it, and applying it. Doing this will result in the blessing of becoming close to God as Jesus Christ was and being empowered to do his will like Jesus did.

Jesus was totally devoted to God in prayer, fasting, and revealing him to humanity. His devotion was seen in his obedience to God and in sacrificing his life to redeem humanity from their sins. He also showed the love and compassion of God to everyone he came into contact with, regardless of their nationality, ethnicity, skin color, or socioeconomic status. Christians, like Jesus whom they profess to imitate, must likewise be totally devoted to God in prayer, fasting, studying, and meditating on God's word, so that they too can draw close to God as Jesus was, know his will, and model Jesus's example of loving all humanity, especially other Christians, regardless of what they look like or where they are from, treating others as they would want to be treated, and being kind and compassionate to the poor and needy.

---

254. Ps 1:1–3. See Adeyemo, *Africa Bible Commentary*, 609, commenting that the Scriptures give us guidelines for life, that we should delight to study God's word, meditate on it, and live by it. This will result in a fruitful life of service, renewal by the word and the Holy Spirit, and a prosperous life in the sense of being worthwhile and satisfying.

4

Understanding and Triumphing over the Devil

JESUS TALKED ABOUT THE devil, also called Satan, quite a bit. Jesus also dealt with Satan a lot. Whenever he cast demons out of people who were demon possessed, he was tearing down Satan's kingdom.

The devil tempted Jesus when he was hungry, after fasting for forty days and forty nights. The devil twisted the Scriptures to try to get Jesus to sin. But Jesus rebuffed all his temptations using the Scriptures and triumphed over him.[1]

The devil is called the adversary of Christians.[2] His goal is to undermine the faith of Christians and their relationship with God by inducing them to disobey God. This includes inciting racial and class conflicts among Christians contrary to Christ's example and command to love one's neighbor as oneself[3] and to show compassion to the poor.[4] As imitators of Christ, Christians must commit to prayer and fasting and study the Scriptures to understand the devil and his schemes so that they too can rebuff his temptations and triumph over him. Jesus affirmed this

---

1. Matt 4:1–11; Luke 4:1–13.
2. 1 Pet 5:8. See Janette H. Ok, "First Letter of Peter," in McCaulley et al., *New Testament in Color*, 681, commenting that Peter's warning about the devil is a warning about the desires of the flesh, the battle against which he gives a named, personified foe. Peter urges believers to resist the devil's attacks by standing firm in the faith and in solidarity with other believers experiencing the same suffering.
3. Matt 22:36–40; Mark 12:30–31.
4. Matt 6:2; 25:31–40.

when he told his disciples privately that it is only by prayer and fasting that certain kinds of evil spirits can be cast out.[5]

Many, if not all, of the world's religions feature the devil in some form or another. Whether in cultural narratives, folklore, or religious beliefs, the devil is always cast as a sinister, evil character. There are many secular ideas and definitions of the devil. One definition of the devil is that he is an evil being, often represented in human form but with a tail and horns.[6] Another says he is the personal supreme spirit of evil often represented in Christian belief as the tempter of humankind, the leader of all apostate angels, and the ruler of hell.[7] And yet another defines him as the most powerful evil being in Christian, Jewish, and Muslim religions, also referring to him as an evil spirit.[8]

Many books have been written about the devil, some as cultural or historical narratives, and others as books of poems, works of literary criticism, or religious books based on the Bible.[9] The Bible is God's revelation to Christians. So, what does the Bible say about the devil, his origins, how he operates, and how to overcome him? It is these questions that this chapter will address.

Origins of Satan

According to the prophet Isaiah, Satan was an archangel in heaven. His name was Lucifer, meaning "light bearer."[10] The prophet Ezekiel's prophecy against the king of Tyre contains veiled references to Satan as the real ruler of Tyre. The prophecy describes him as the model of perfection, full of wisdom, perfect beauty, and as having been present in the garden of Eden. He was adorned with every precious stone and anointed as a guardian cherub. His heart became proud because of his beauty and his wisdom became corrupted because of his splendor. He was on the holy mount of God, created blameless, till wickedness was found in him. He

---

5. Matt 17:21; Mark 9:29.
6. Cambridge, "Devil (n.)."
7. Merriam-Webster, "Devil (n.)."
8. Oxford, "Devil (n.)."
9. See, for example, Carus, *History of the Devil*; Defoe, *Political History of the Devil*; Dendle, *Satan Unbound*; Milton, *Paradise Lost*; Ramirez, *Unmasking the Devil*; and Stanford, *Devil: A Biography*.
10. Isa 14:12.

THE CHRISTIAN AS IMITATOR OF CHRIST

was cast out of the mountain of God to the ground.[11] Ezekiel's prophecy referred to how the workmanship of Satan's timbrels and pipes was prepared for him on the day he was created.[12] This appears to refer to Satan being imbued with innate musical qualities. This has led to speculation that he may have led the worship that is constantly offered to God in heaven.[13]

Satan's heart was filled with pride. He desired to be like God Most High. He desired to occupy God's throne.[14]

Both Isaiah's and Ezekiel's prophecies about Satan reference a prideful heart and attitude. Satan managed to deceive a third of the angels to join his rebellion and coup attempt against God, but they were defeated and cast out of heaven to earth. This event is captured in the description of the devil as an enormous red dragon whose tail swept a third of the stars out of the sky and threw them to the earth.[15] Jesus told his disciples that he saw Satan fall like lightning from heaven and that he had given them authority over satanic forces of spiritual evil.[16] Evidently, not all the fallen angels were cast down to earth. Some are chained in what the Bible refers to as gloomy dungeons in the spirit world to be held there until judgment.[17]

---

11. Ezek 28:12–18. See Adeyemo, *Africa Bible Commentary*, 964–65, interpreting the "guardian cherub" in Ezek 28:16, Isa 14:13–14, and Rev 12:9 to refer to Satan, who became inflamed with pride and was expelled from heaven, even as the passages also speak against the king of Tyre and the king of Babylon.

12. Ezek 28:13.

13. Rev 4:8–11. See Blount, *Revelation*, 94–95, explaining that the four creatures in Revelation play the role of heavenly liturgists praising God's holy and glorious lordship, to which the twenty-four elders respond in worship. Blount argues it calls for Christians to emulate them and give exclusive allegiance to God. Also see Yong, *Revelation*, 84–85, explaining that God receives relentless worship from the four creatures who represent the full expanse of the creaturely cosmos and the twenty-four elders who represent all the people of God from the old and new covenants. He argues it is an explicit invitation to worship God and offer our allegiance to him alone.

14. Isa 14:12–15.

15. Rev 12:4–9. The NIV says they were flung to the earth. See Blount, *Revelation*, 234, noting that John makes clear that this dragon who was cast out of heaven is the ancient serpent who deceives the whole world, beginning with Adam and Eve. Also see Yong, *Revelation*, 156, noting that Satan and his angels being thrown down to earth is consistent with Jesus's words in Luke 10:18 that he watched Satan fall from heaven like a flash of lightning.

16. Luke 10:18–19.

17. 2 Pet 2:4; Jude 1:6.

As punishment for their rebellion, God also created the lake of fire as a place of eternal punishment for Satan and his demonic hordes.[18] In the meantime, before the time for their consignment to the lake of fire comes, Satan and his demonic hordes do everything they can to pervert and disrupt God's will, purposes, and plan for humankind whom he made in his image and loves. Satan's ultimate goal is to subvert God's will for people to glorify him as his image bearers. Instead, Satan seeks to influence people to live in rebellion against God so that he can take as many of them as possible with him to the lake of fire. It is God's will that no one should perish or end up in hell, but that everyone should repent, be saved, and spend eternity with him, his angels, and those whom he has redeemed.[19] As Satan did with Adam and Eve, he manipulates people to doubt God.[20] He also incites evil by influencing peoples' thoughts and emotions. The Bible says he decided that Judas Iscariot would be the one to betray Jesus.[21] He prompted Judas to betray Jesus.

The Devil's Attributes as Revealed in the Bible

The Bible reveals a lot about the devil's nature and attributes. His many names provide deep insight into his character, his schemes, how he spends his time on earth, and what he works tirelessly to accomplish. The following are insights into some of his attributes.

Slanderer

Devil, *diabolos* in Greek, means "slanderer."[22] To slander someone is to make a false spoken statement about them that is intended to damage the good opinion people have of them,[23] or that damages their reputation.[24]

---

18. Matt 25:41.
19. 2 Pet 3:9.
20. Gen 3:1.
21. John 13:2. The NKJV says he put it into the heart of Judas to betray Jesus. See Moloney, *Gospel of John*, 374, where he notes that the design of God, manifested in and through Jesus's love for his own, clashes with the design of Satan that one of these would betray Jesus.
22. This name occurs over thirty times in the New Testament.
23. Oxford, "Slander (v.)."
24. Cambridge, "Slander (v.)." Also, Merriam-Webster, "Slander (v.)."

The devil slanders God to humans by casting doubt on God's character. Appearing as the serpent in the garden of Eden, the devil did just that with Eve. God had told Adam that he would surely die the day that he ate of the tree of the knowledge of good and evil.[25] Adam must have shared this with Eve, because Eve repeated what God said in her dialogue with the devil. The devil assured Eve that she would not surely die if she ate of the fruit of the forbidden tree.[26] The devil was saying that God was lying to them. The devil also suggested to Eve that God had an ulterior motive in commanding them not to eat of the tree of the knowledge of good and evil. They would become just as knowledgeable as God if they did, and God did not want that.[27] The devil was saying that God was not being honest with them.

These statements the devil made about God were as slanderous as can be. That is because God is true.[28] He is not a man that he should lie.[29] Jesus said that he is the truth.[30] The Holy Spirit, the third person of the Godhead or Holy Trinity is the Spirit of truth.[31] God's word is truth.[32] God does what he says he will do.[33] Adam and Eve found this out the hard way. In slandering God, the devil lied to them and succeeded in orchestrating the fall of humankind. Adam and Eve did indeed die spiritually that day. They became spiritually separated from God by their sin of disobedience. And they did eventually die physically.

The devil also slanders humans to God by questioning their motives for serving God. He questioned Job's motives for serving God, telling God that Job was only serving God for God's blessings.[34] Of course, Job did really love God. The devil was slandering Job by saying he did not.

The devil also instigates humans to slander other humans by believing and saying things about people that are not true. Before Roman governor Pontius Pilate, Jesus was accused of subverting the Jewish

---

25. Gen 2:17.
26. Gen 3:3–4.
27. Gen 3:5.
28. 1 John 5:20.
29. Num 23:19.
30. John 14:6.
31. John 14:17; 15:26; 16:13.
32. John 17:17.
33. Num 23:19.
34. Job 1:9–11. See Yong, *Revelation*, 156, commenting on the devil's history of bringing charges against the righteous, the story of Job being the most prominent.

nation and opposing paying taxes to Caesar,[35] when in fact he did say to give to Caesar what belongs to Caesar.[36] Many slanderous things are said about certain nationalities, ethnic groups, or the poor. These slanders incite mistrust among people. To what extent does Satan instigate some of this so that people, including professing Christians, will be unwilling or unable to love each other as Christ has loved them or treat each other as they would want to be treated?[37] The inability of professing Christians to love others who do not look like them or those who are not in their socioeconomic class compromises their witness to the world because it makes them appear no different from the unredeemed.[38]

Adversary

The name *devil* is translated *Satan* in Hebrew, meaning "adversary." Satan is the most frequently used name for the devil in the New Testament, occurring fifty times.[39] He first appears as adversary with his accusations against Job of serving God only for the blessings God bestows.[40] In doing so, he was also insinuating that God was naïve in thinking that Job served him out of a pure and loving heart.

Ancient Serpent

The devil is referred to as the ancient serpent or serpent of old. It is to this serpent that the temptation of Adam and Eve in the garden of Eden is attributed. The serpent in the garden of Eden is later identified as the ancient serpent or serpent of old, the devil, or Satan.[41]

---

35. Luke 23:1–2.
36. Mark 12:17.
37. John 13:34–35.
38. John 13:35.
39. 1 Pet 5:8. See Yong, *Revelation*, 157 noting that Satan is the ancient adversary not just of the Most High God but also of the people of God.
40. Job 1:9–11; 2:4–5.
41. Rev 12:9; 20:2. See Yong, *Revelation*, 156, where he comments that besides duplicity and trickery, the deceiver of the world also engages in accusations against believers, and that this is consistent with the ancient Hebraic understanding of Satan as a heavenly being with access to the divine council and a history of bringing charges against the righteous.

Deceiver/Liar

From his early deception of Adam and Eve and his ongoing deception of the world, the devil has also earned the name of deceiver.[42] Jesus revealed that the devil is a liar and the father of lies. He invented lying. Jesus said that there is no truth in the devil; that when the devil lies, he is speaking his native language.[43] He is a pathological liar. He lies naturally. This means that the devil is the source of all falsehood. Lying is a character trait of the devil. That is why Christians can neither condone nor practice lying. Lies about others based on their nationality, ethnicity, skin color, or socioeconomic status cause mistrust and make it difficult, even for Christians, to love and do good to other members of the family of God.

What are some of the lies Satan perpetrates on humanity? One is that God does not exist. Many at one point or another have asked, "How can there be a God, one who is good, loving, and omnipotent, when there is so much suffering, tragedy, disaster, and death in the world?" The truth is that there is a God who created a perfect world. Everything he created was very good.[44] He gave humanity free will; Adam and Eve allowed Satan to deceive them into using it to disobey God. Because of this sin, the human race and all of creation came under a curse—the curse of sin and death. It is this curse that has brought suffering, tragedy, disaster, and death into the world. And all of creation—believers, nature, animals—groans for the end of the age to come, for Christ to return, and for all suffering to end.[45] It is the devil who controls the ungodly world system, not God. He influences sinful people to act in evil, cruel, and unjust ways.[46] Satan's influence under God's permissive will is temporary, however, until the appointed time when God will destroy Satan and evil and establish his kingdom on earth.[47]

Paul reasoned that humanity has no excuse for not believing in God because the marvels of nature and creation are a clear demonstration, not

---

42. Rev 20:10.

43. John 8:44. See Moloney, *Gospel of John*, 280, where he explains that through lies and deceit, the devil robbed Adam of God's original promise of immortality, making him a liar and a murderer. His deceits also led to the first murder, Cain's killing of Abel. Because of the devil's role of deceit and lies in human history, this makes him "the father of lies."

44. Gen 1:31.

45. Rom 8:22–23.

46. 2 Cor 4:4; 1 John 5:19.

47. Rev 11:5.

just of God's existence, but of God's eternal power and divine nature.[48] The psalmist calls one who believes there is no God foolish.[49] One reason for choosing to believe that there is no God might be that it would mean no accountability for how one lives or the decisions one makes, other than the normal consequences that flow from those decisions. This, then, might justify ungodly living and not loving one's neighbor as oneself as Christ commanded. Loving one's neighbor as oneself is only possible if one first loves God with all one's heart, soul, strength, and mind.[50]

The devil also deceives people to believe that he does not exist—that he is a figment of the human imagination, a mythical figure in cultural and religious narratives. During his ministry, Jesus cast demons out of many people who had been possessed by evil spirits and were being hindered from fulfilling their God-given purpose, including a man in Gadara who was possessed by a legion of demons that hindered him from becoming the evangelist God had created him to be.[51]

Contrary to the belief that Satan does not exist, Jesus talked about the devil quite a bit. In his model prayer, he taught his disciples to pray that God would deliver them from the evil one.[52] Jesus told Jews who were not obedient to God, as Abraham was obedient to God, that their real father was the devil, whom Jesus described as a murderer and a pathological liar, one whose native language is lying.[53]

The fact that Satan is a deceiver does not absolve those who buy into his deceptions from responsibility. That is because God has revealed his truth to humanity. Humans are to live on every word that proceeds out of the mouth of God.[54] Jesus said that those who continue in his word are his disciples; that they will know the truth, and the truth shall set them free.[55] That is the antidote to satanic deception. God cursed the serpent for deceiving humanity but that did not absolve Adam and Eve from responsibility for buying into Satan's deception and disobeying God. They, and all of humanity after them, became subject to the curse of the fall.

48. Rom 1:20.
49. Pss 14:1; 53:1.
50. Matt 22:37; Luke 10:27.
51. Mark 5:1–20; Luke 8:26–38.
52. Matt 6:13.
53. John 8:44.
54. Matt 4:4, quoting Deut 8:3.
55. John 8:31–32.

Death came to all after sin got transmitted through the lifeblood of the human race.[56]

One of the most sinister deceptions of Satan is his deception of humanity about race. In chapter 10, we will discuss whether God created more than one race or just one race—the human race—and how Christians, as imitators of Christ, should treat others based on race.

Satan deceives humans to believe his lies instead of God's truth. The apostle Paul warned the Colossians not to allow themselves to be deceived by hollow and deceptive philosophy of humanistic and worldly origin.[57] Notions of White Christianity, racial segregation, racial purity, Christian libertarianism, accountable individualism, and a perverted crucicentrism are all humanistic and worldly in origin because they are inconsistent with how Jesus Christ lived and what he taught.[58] And it is his example that Christians must imitate. It is his word that Christians must continue to live by. Paul warned Timothy that some will abandon their faith in later times to follow teachings that originate with demons and are propagated by hypocritical liars who have a dulled conscience.[59] Every professing Christian must guard against that.

Accuser of the Brethren

Another name of the devil is the accuser of the brethren. Day and night, he accuses believers before God.[60] He accuses all believers of whatever sin or unrighteousness is in their lives, thus pointing to their unworthiness to receive God's grace, blessing, or answers to their prayers. He also accuses them of having ulterior motives in serving God. Satan's goal in doing all of this is to get God to remove his favor from his people so that he can come against them, harm them, oppose them, undermine their faith in God, compromise their relationship with God, and pervert their divine purpose. That was Satan's goal with Job. He accused Job of serving God out of ulterior motives.[61] By God's grace, Job persevered because his

---

56. Rom 5:12.
57. Col 2:8.
58. See Hendricks, *Christians Against Christianity*, 139–45, where he discusses these beliefs. The perverse interpretation of crucicentrism is the belief that withholding aid to the suffering poor will lead them to the cross and faith in Christ.
59. 1 Tim 4:1.
60. Rev 12:10.
61. Job 1:9–11; 2:4–5.

faith was genuine. Job was baffled by his plight. Yet, in spite of losing his health, children, and wealth, he remained faithful to God. In the end, God richly rewarded him for his faith.[62]

Regarding Satan's accusations of believers, God revealed a scene in a vision to the prophet Zechariah where Satan was accusing Joshua the high priest before the angel of the Lord, the pre-incarnate Jesus Christ.[63] Joshua was one of the exiles who returned to Jerusalem from captivity in Babylon. He came in the first of three waves of exiles under the leadership of Zerubbabel, who served as governor while Joshua served as high priest. It was this group that rebuilt the temple amid great opposition.[64]

The scene showed that the angel of the Lord rebuked Satan for accusing Joshua because Joshua had been chosen to lead the spiritual restoration of a nation that had been through the fire of suffering in exile. This restoration included the rebuilding of the temple, which Satan used enemies to oppose.[65] The scene showed that Joshua was wearing filthy clothes. There was unrighteousness in his life. The angel of the Lord ordered his filthy clothes to be taken off and rich garments put on him. Joshua also had a dirty turban on his head, symbolizing that his mind and thoughts were not right. The angel of the Lord ordered a clean turban to be put on Joshua's head.[66] He then charged Joshua to walk in the ways of the Almighty God and keep his requirements in order to secure his place as high priest and have access to God's throne room and courts in heaven through prayer.[67] The angel of the Lord also told Joshua of the coming Messiah who would take away sin in one day, the day of his crucifixion.[68]

As imitators of Christ, Christians can overcome Satan's accusations and fulfill their divine purpose by the covering of Jesus's blood, testimony that lines up with God's word, total surrender to God,[69] walking in the

---

62. Job 1:13–22; 2:7; 42:10–16.

63. Zech 3:1. See Yong, *Revelation*, 156, where he cited Zech 3:1 as illustrative of the devil's history of bringing charges against the righteous.

64. Ezra 2; 3; 4.

65. Zech 3:1–2.

66. Zech 3:5.

67. Zech 3:6–7.

68. Zech 3:8–9.

69. Rev 12:11.

light,[70] and the advocacy, defense, and intercession of Jesus Christ.[71] As the angel of the Lord promised Joshua, disciples of Christ can also have access through prayer to God's throne room and courts by walking in God's ways and keeping his requirements.[72]

Enemy

Jesus called the devil "the enemy." He used the parable of the wheat and the weeds, a parable about the kingdom of God, to illustrate what he meant.[73] In this parable, he described the kingdom of God as being like a man who planted good seed in his field. However, an enemy came at night and sowed weeds among the wheat, and both grew together. The man's servants were bewildered and asked how weeds had grown among the wheat knowing that the master only sowed good seed. The master responded that an enemy had done this.[74] He told the servants not to pull up the weeds just yet like they asked to do. Instead, he instructed them to wait until harvest time. He instructed them to pull and burn the weeds first at harvest time, and then gather the wheat for the barn.

Jesus later explained the parable to his disciples. The sower of the seed is Jesus himself. The field is the world, and the good seed represents the children of the kingdom—his disciples, followers, or imitators. The weeds are the children of the devil, or unbelievers, and the devil is the enemy who sows them or plants them among God's people in churches to sow discord, promote unrighteousness, and propagate false doctrine. The harvest is the end of the age when Jesus returns to judge the world. The harvesters are angels who will be sent at the end of the age to weed out sinners and evildoers out of God's kingdom. The evildoers will be cast in the lake of fire where there will be weeping and gnashing of teeth. But the righteous will dwell in the kingdom of God the Father where they will shine like the sun in eternal blessing.

---

70. 1 John 1:7.
71. Rom 8:33–34; 1 John 2:1.
72. Heb 4:14–16.
73. Matt 13:24–30, 39–43.

74. Matt 13:28. See Harrington, *Gospel of Matthew*, 204, 208, explaining that the enemy is Satan, and the weeds are the children of the evil one, opponents of followers of Jesus. The parable counsels patience and tolerance in the present because at the final judgment there will be a separation between the just and the unjust along with appropriate rewards and punishments.

Disciples, followers, or imitators of Christ must understand that not everyone who attends a church service is a disciple or Christian. And not all teaching is consistent with God's truth as revealed in his written word, the Bible. This means that disciples of Christ will need to know God's word through diligent study of the Bible in order to discern false teaching. Teaching about White Christianity, racial purity, racial segregation, Christian nationalism, and Christian libertarianism are not biblical. Neither is withholding aid from the poor and disadvantaged nor withholding compassion from the poor. Such teaching should, therefore, be rejected by any professing Christian.

Thief

Jesus talked about the mission of false leaders or shepherds, hirelings who did not come from God, which meant that they were of the devil, as coming to steal, kill, and destroy.[75] That must be understood to be the devil's mission too. The devil is a thief. Satan aims to steal health, wealth, joy, and peace from the people of God, as he did with Job, with the aim of destroying humanity's relationship with God. He works to destroy hope and faith in order to separate people from God and lead them astray. His goal is to steal souls and take them with him to the lake of fire. He wants to keep people from heaven and eternal blessing in God's presence. He lost heaven because of his rebellion, and he wants no human to be able to enjoy it if he can help it.

Satan stole Job's wealth by destroying his ranching business. He instigated marauders to steal Job's animals and kill his employees. He stole Job's health by afflicting him with sickness. Job overcame Satan's attacks, murderous schemes, and thievery by trusting in God, and believers must do the same. The Scriptures say to submit to God and to resist the devil, promising that he will flee.[76]

---

75. John 10:10. See Moloney, *Gospel of John*, 303–4, where he explains Jesus's words to refer to the fact that there was nothing life-giving about those who came before Jesus claiming to be shepherds. They were thieves and robbers. But Jesus offers salvation and pasture and gives the sheep abundant life.

76. Jas 4:7.

THE CHRISTIAN AS IMITATOR OF CHRIST

Prince or Ruler of this World

Satan is the prince or ruler of this world. The reference to "this world" is a reference to the evil and corrupt world system that Satan runs and controls. Satan stole the dominion God had given to Adam and Eve over the earth by deceiving them into sin. The world he rules or exercises dominion over is a system whose modus operandi is contrary to the will of God.

As Jesus continued to prepare his disciples for his impending death, he told them that he would not speak with them much longer because the prince of this world was coming. In other words, Satan would succeed in instigating the religious leaders of Israel to seek his death. They would succeed in convincing the Roman authorities to crucify him. But Jesus also told them that the prince of this world did not have a hold on him. In other words, Satan, the one who ran the evil and corrupt judicial system that railroaded Jesus and sentenced him to death, could not prevent him from rising from death.[77]

Jesus promised his disciples that he would send the Holy Spirit after his departure. He told his disciples what the Holy Spirit would do. Among other things, the Holy Spirit would convict the world of guilt in regard to sin, righteousness, and judgment. Jesus explained that the Holy Spirit would convict the world of the sin of not believing that he is the Savior of the world. The Holy Spirit would also convict the world of the fact that Jesus is the righteous one because of his resurrection and ascension to heaven to be with the Father. Finally, the Holy Spirit would convict the world of judgment because the prince of this world, Satan, now stands condemned.[78] Satan's present activities as the prince of this world will eventually end when he is cast into the lake of fire.[79]

The apostle John warned the believers to whom he wrote not to love the world or anything in the world because if anyone loves the world, the love of God the Father is not in that person. He said that sinful cravings, the lust of the eyes, and pride about possessions do not come from God the Father. They come from the world.[80] Because the devil is the ruler

---

77. John 14:30. See Moloney, *Gospel of John*, 411, where he comments that "the ruler of this world" refers to the power of evil that opposes Jesus at a metahistorical level, the darkness, in the midst of which the light shines. Jesus's departure is the result of his loving response to his Father, not because the prince of this world has any power over him.

78. John 16:8–11.

79. Rev 20:10.

80. 1 John 2:15–16.

of this world, disciples, followers, or imitators of Christ cannot love the world or the things of this world, such as power and money. It was the love of power and money that fueled slavery and colonialism, two of the greatest evils in human history.

One with Power of Suggestion

After God gave Satan permission to test Job, the Sabeans and Chaldeans attacked and killed Job's servants and carried off his livestock.[81] How did Satan manage to instigate the Sabeans and Chaldeans to do what they did? It would appear that he has the power of suggestion and the ability to plant thoughts in peoples' minds. How did he put it in the heart of Judas to betray Jesus? How did he decide that Judas would be the one to betray Jesus?[82]

David found this out the hard way when Satan incited him to order his army commanders to count the fighting men in Israel. It was God who had given David victory after victory in battle. Counting his fighting men amounted to thinking that his security and strength were in his army. Joab, his top commander, warned him against doing it, but David prevailed upon him to carry out his orders. God was displeased with David's actions and punished Israel for it. When it was all said and done, a plague had killed seventy thousand Israelites. The plague ended when a repentant David offered sacrifices to God.[83]

Where do thoughts to practice racial hatred and racial segregation and to refuse assistance to the poor come from, if they are not biblical? Where do ideas about a segregated White, Black, Latino, or Asian church come from if they do not align with keeping the unity of the Spirit in the bond of peace among all believers?[84] Martin Luther King Jr. sadly observed that the eleven o'clock hour on Sunday is the most segregated hour in Christian America.

---

81. Job 1:14–15, 17. See Adeyemo, *Africa Bible Commentary*, 573, commenting that most commentators try to categorize the four disasters that destroyed Job's family and property as human and natural disasters, but if the conversation between God and Satan is taken seriously, there is no question that all these disasters are from a supernatural source.

82. John 13:2.

83. 1 Chr 21.

84. Eph 4:3–6.

Disciples, followers, and imitators of Christ can overcome Satan's attempts to influence their thoughts and behavior by judging the appropriateness of the thoughts that enter their minds with the word of God, and by rejecting thoughts that are inconsistent with his word. Paul gave the Philippians excellent guidance on what kinds of thoughts to entertain, meditate on, or think about. He told them to think about things that are noble, right, pure, lovely, admirable, excellent, or praiseworthy.[85] To do this is to submit to God and to resist the devil. The apostle James said that Satan will flee from the disciple who does this.[86] Unfortunately, because the unsaved are subject to Satan's power, he can influence them to do his bidding as he did with the Sabeans and Chaldeans. Being outside the kingdom of God, they have no defense against what Satan speaks over their lives. How often have we heard people who have committed heinous acts say they do not know what came over them or that they heard voices instructing them to do what they did? This is not to discount mental illness or suggest that there are always demonic influences involved in the commission of heinous crimes.

Satan's Designs, Schemes, and Devices

Jesus said that false prophets and, by implication, the devil who sends them, come to steal, kill, and destroy.[87] That is Satan's mission. But there are specific designs he seeks to accomplish as he carries out this mission and certain schemes and devices he employs, including the following.

Not Wanting People to Be Saved

Satan does not want people to be saved by hearing, understanding, and believing the gospel. In the parable of the sower, Jesus talked about seed that fell along the path or wayside. The birds came and ate it up. Jesus explained that the seed along the path represents people who hear the gospel, but Satan then comes and snatches the word they heard so that it does not lead to salvation. Matthew explains that these are people who do not understand what they heard. Jesus explained to his disciples later that it is the devil who snatches the word they heard before they can

---

85. Phil 4:8.
86. Jas 4:7.
87. John 10:10.

believe it.[88] Many people who profess to be Christians have little to no understanding of what Jesus taught. They refuse to love others who are different from them or to be compassionate to those in need. They express beliefs like racial purity, racial segregation, and White Christianity that are contrary to Christ's teaching. This raises the question whether they have understood the gospel, received it, and become saved.

Turning the Hearts of Disciples from God

Another design of Satan is to turn the hearts of disciples, followers, or imitators of Christ away from God. In Job's case, he tried to do it through suffering and great loss—of family, business, and health, in the hope that Job would curse God and repudiate his faith in God.[89] Disciples, followers, or imitators of Christ are not immune from misfortune and ill health. Satan can use the failure of a business, unemployment, or sickness (physical and mental health challenges), or life's difficulties, to discourage disciples, followers, or imitators of Christ and undermine their faith. He can use it to raise doubts in their minds about God. Job went through that. As unthinkable as Job's situation was, it was trusting God, no matter what, that brought him through his ordeal even though his wife had doubts about God.[90] And trusting God is essential for disciples, followers, or imitators of Christ to overcome Satan.[91]

Using Persecution to Discourage and Undermine Faith

As was the case with the early church in Jerusalem,[92] using persecution Satan tried to discourage and undermine the faith of the Thessalonians

---

88. Matt 13:4, 19; Mark 4:4, 15; Luke 8:5, 12. See Johnson, *Gospel of Luke*, 134, where he explains that Luke is stressing the need to act in faith after hearing the word. It is possible to lose what one has initially been given, making protection of the word and perseverance in it all important. But Jesus made clear that it is Satan who hinders belief by taking the word from the hearts of hearers.

89. Job 1:11; 2:4–5.

90. Job 1:20–22; 2:9–10; 13:5.

91. See Isa 46:3–4, where God reminded the people of Israel that he was the one who had upheld and carried them as a nation. And he was the one who would sustain and continue to carry them.

92. Acts 6:12–15; 7:54–60; 8:1–4; 12:1–5.

THE CHRISTIAN AS IMITATOR OF CHRIST

who had believed Paul's message,[93] the gentile disciples in Asia Minor to whom the apostle Peter wrote,[94] and the disciples to whom the author of Hebrews wrote.[95] Satan also flat-out opposes the work of those who preach the gospel of Jesus Christ and disciple new believers who come to the faith to help them grow in Christ. Paul left Thessalonica hastily because of intense opposition instigated by Satan. Paul did not have a chance to disciple the young believers there as he wished. He left for Berea where the agitators and antagonists followed him and drove him out.[96] Now in Athens, he desired to return to Thessalonica but said in his first Letter to the Church that Satan stopped him.[97] It was just too dangerous for him to go back. Paul knew he was not just battling "flesh and blood" or the Jews who opposed him. He knew Satan was using them. It was the same way in Philippi,[98] Ephesus,[99] Greece,[100] and back in Jerusalem after Paul completed his third missionary journey.[101] But Paul persevered and finished the work God entrusted to him. So can every believer who perseveres.

Offering Worldly Rewards in Exchange for Doing Things His Way

A big design of Satan is to offer worldly rewards to those who will bow to him and do things his way. He offered wealth, power, and privilege to Jesus in return for worship.[102] Many have taken that deal and secured wealth, power, and privilege in ungodly ways. But as Jesus asked, what shall it profit a man to gain the whole world and lose his own soul? Or what shall a man give in exchange for his soul?[103] Satan is an expert horse

---

93. 1 Thess 2:4–15; 3:4–5.
94. 1 Pet 4:12–16.
95. Heb 10:26–39.
96. Acts 17:1–15.
97. 1 Thess 2:18.
98. Acts 16:22–23.
99. Acts 19:23–41.
100. Acts 20:1–3.
101. Acts 21:27–36; 22:22–24; 23:12–16; 24–26.
102. Matt 4:8–9; Luke 4:5–7. See Johnson, *Gospel of Luke*, 134, where he explains that the devil, as ruler in a counter-kingdom to the kingdom of God, has power to bestow.
103. Matt 16:26; Mark 8:36–37; Luke 9:25. See Boring, *Mark: A Commentary*, 245, stating that there is no one who would choose to keep all the wealth in the world at the expense of his or her own life, and that there is nothing, no matter how valuable, that

trader. When he offers earthly rewards for doing things his way, he is really offering to trade heavenly rewards for earthly rewards. Jesus refused to bow to the devil in exchange for worldly rewards. He was obedient to God, even to the point of death, and has been rewarded by God with power, riches, wisdom, strength, honor, and glory. The apostle John heard every creature glorifying God, who sits on the throne, and the Lamb, Jesus Christ, ascribing to them blessing, honor, glory, and power.[104] Jesus has been given a name that is above every name—a name to which every knee will bow, and to which every tongue will confess lordship, to the glory of God the Father.[105] This is what Satan tried to get Jesus to trade for earthly rewards. How many people throughout history have traded with Satan for the earthly rewards of wealth, power, privilege, and advantage in place of heavenly rewards? Take, for example, the case of slavery where professing Christians enslaved other Christians because of the color of their skin and reaped significant earthly rewards of money, power, and privilege. But at what heavenly cost did they reap these earthly rewards? For now, only they and God know. But we will all know at the end of the age.

Breaking Bonds Between Disciples

A grand design of Satan is to break the bonds of communion between God and his people. He managed to rupture the communion Adam and Eve enjoyed with God before he engineered their fall.[106] He sought to break the bond of communion between Job and the God he worshipped and trusted.[107] He did the same with Joshua the high priest, whom he accused before God.[108] Not only does he desire to break the bonds of communion between God and his people, but he also desires to break the bonds of love among disciples and among people by driving wedges between people. Ethnic and socioeconomic differences, as well as differences in nationality and skin color, divide many professing Christians contrary to Christ's teaching and example.

---

one can offer in exchange for one's own life.
   104. Rev 5:12–13.
   105. Phil 2:8–11.
   106. Gen 3:4–5.
   107. Job 1:9–11; 2:4–5.
   108. Zech 3:1.

The Christian as Imitator of Christ

Spreading Misinformation and Twisting the Truth

Satan also loves to twist the truth and misinform. He does this well as the father of lies.[109] There is so much misinformation in the media, online, chat rooms, and the sphere of public discourse. This includes twisting what the Bible says. The most flagrant example of twisting God's word is the Slave Bible. While purporting to introduce slaves to the Christian faith, the Slave Bible selectively excluded most of the Bible, removing the portions that could inspire hope for freedom while emphasizing portions that were used to justify slavery. Bibles have between sixty-six to seventy-eight books, depending on whether they are Protestant, Catholic, or Eastern Orthodox Bibles. The Slave Bible had fourteen.[110] It was a gross misrepresentation of who God is—his nature, character, and desire for every human being created in his image. Ironically, the fact that the authors of the Slave Bible lied about God to justify slavery is proof that they knew slavery was wrong. What role may the devil, the father of lies and expert twister of the truth, have played in devising this scheme to misrepresent God in order to justify oppression and profit, divide humanity, destroy lives, and lead many astray? And many slave owners were professing Christians who held people who belonged to the family of God in bondage for profit solely because of the color of their skin. Humanity continues to grapple with the legacy of slavery to this day. This demands that Christians, as imitators of Jesus Christ, know the truth of God's word and reject teaching that twists it. Obedience to Christ's commands to love one's neighbor as oneself, treat others as one would want to be treated, and love other believers as Jesus loved them, should have put a quick end to slavery.

Getting People to Worship Money

Perhaps the oldest idol in Satan's toolbox of idols with which he deceives people is wealth and the things wealth brings—power, privilege, and advantage. Satan offered these things to Jesus if Jesus would fall down and worship him.[111] He continues to offer it to many today, including believers. In his Sermon on the Mount, Jesus warned that no one can

---

109. John 8:44–45.

110. The Slave Bible is on exhibit in the Museum of the Bible in Washington, DC. The exhibition is titled *The Slave Bible: Let the Story Be Told*.

111. Matt 4:8–9; Luke 4:5–7.

serve two masters because one can only love and be loyal to one master; one cannot serve God and money.[112] Serving money means putting one's trust in it and looking to it for security, meaning, and fulfillment in life. It means replacing God with money and living independently of God. Paul warned in his first Letter to Timothy that the pursuit of riches carries with it the risk of falling into temptation and a trap, and into many foolish and harmful desires that bring ruin and destruction because the love of money is a root of all kinds of evil.[113] Slavery and colonialism, two of history's greatest evils, were principally about money. They brought wealth and power to the enslaver and the colonizer.

Jesus also warned of the danger of covetousness or greed, pointing out that one's life does not consist in the abundance of one's possessions. He told a parable in which a rich farmer's farm produced a bumper crop. The farmer planned to build bigger barns to store his crops and goods and use his wealth, which he felt would give him security for many years, to take life easy, eat, drink, and be merry. However, God called him a fool and demanded his life the very night he thought these things to himself. Jesus warned that anyone who selfishly hoards wealth or possessions instead of being rich toward God is like that rich farmer in the parable.[114] That is the case where people refuse to show compassion to the poor despite having the means to help them.

Money in itself is not evil. One cannot live without it. One needs it to pay for the necessities of life—food, shelter, clothing, as well as other modern necessities such as transportation, education, and healthcare. One cannot give to others who are less fortunate and financially support the work of the kingdom of God if one has no money. But as descendants of Abraham through faith in Christ,[115] believers must remember that it is God who gives them the power to get wealth so that he may establish his covenant.[116] The security of believers is in God, not in the wealth God

---

112. Matt 6:24. The NKJV and the KJV use mammon instead of money. See Harrington, *Gospel of Matthew*, 104, explaining the saying about not serving two masters as moving the theme of total commitment forward by imagining an attempt at divided commitment and judging it impossible. See also Adeyemo, *Africa Bible Commentary*, 1123, explaining that Mammon was the Carthaginian god of wealth and that a focus on material things can wrest our devotion from God to the god of wealth. Money should be our servant in the service of God, not a god to which we owe allegiance as slaves.

113. 1 Tim 6:9–10.

114. Luke 12:15–21.

115. Gal 3:29.

116. Deut 8:18.

provides, as Satan tempts many to believe. When money and the things of this world that come with money become one's god, one can never have enough. Paul explained to the Galatians that covetousness or greed, the desire and quest for more possessions, is idolatry.[117]

Sadly, no amount of money can make one secure enough. Seeking security in money leads to the vicious cycle of wanting more. And it can all be lost in an instant, as Job discovered. The Great Depression wiped out the wealth of many. So did Black Monday in the late 1980s when the stock market crashed, and the bursting of the tech bubble in the early 2000s when the Nasdaq Composite index tumbled 80 percent. And then there was the Great Recession that wiped out trillions in savings, led to millions of foreclosures of homes, and drove the unemployment rate to double digits. The COVID-19 pandemic wiped out trillions in retirement savings and led to the loss of millions of jobs and the highest unemployment rate since the Great Depression. And natural disasters have wiped out the possessions of many.

Recognizing both his need for sustenance and the danger of riches, Agur, son of Jakeh, prayed that God would give him neither poverty nor riches, but only his daily bread. Otherwise, he feared that he might have too much and forget the Lord, or he might become poor, steal, and dishonor the name of his God.[118] No wonder that in his model prayer, Jesus taught us to ask God for our daily bread, just as Agur prayed.[119]

Getting Disciples to Fight Spiritual Battles with Worldly Weapons

Another device of Satan's is getting believers to use worldly weapons to fight spiritual battles, instead of spiritual weapons like prayer, fasting, sharing the gospel, discipling new converts to obey Jesus's teaching, and modeling Christ by walking in love. Paul told the Ephesians that our struggle is not against blood and flesh but against the rulers, against the authorities, against the cosmic powers of this present darkness, and against the spiritual forces of evil in the heavenly places.[120] To fight a

---

117. Gal 3:5.
118. Prov 30:9.
119. Matt 6:11; Luke 11:3.
120. Eph 6:12. See Adeyemo, *Africa Bible Commentary*, 1437, noting that Paul is reminding Christians that they are in a war that requires both God's power and armor to fight against and defeat the spiritual forces behind the world systems that oppose God. These demonic forces exercise limited authority in opposition to God.

"culture war," as many are doing today, is to become distracted from spiritually battling Satan and his schemes to separate humanity from God and each other and, instead, to become focused on fighting others based on their ethnicity, nationality, skin color, socioeconomic class, ideology, or some other basis that does not imitate Christ's example.

Causing Division

Division is another device Satan uses. Satan knows that a house divided against itself cannot stand.[121] Because of this, Paul exhorted the church in Ephesus to make every effort to keep the unity of the Spirit through the bond of peace. The way to do that is to walk worthy of the calling of God to be his disciple by being humble, gentle, patient, and by bearing with each other in love.[122] Instead of doing this, the church in Corinth was operating in envy, jealousy, strife, quarreling, and divisions.[123] Factions and cliques had arisen among them with some saying they were followers of Apollos, some of Paul, some of Cephas (Peter), and others of Christ.[124]

Disciples of Christ must resist the temptation to be used by Satan to divide the universal church based on ethnicity, skin color, nationality, or socioeconomic status, or to bring division and strife into the local church. As natural as it may be to gravitate toward cliques, disciples of Christ must resist the temptation to form or encourage cliques that exclude fellow believers, because Satan will use it to cause disaffection, disappointment, and discouragement among believers. In some extreme cases, he has used it to divide or even close down a local church. I have seen firsthand what division can do to a church where factions arise, with some for and others against the pastor. In both of the cases I witnessed, the pastor ended up leaving. In one case, many left the church and those who remained were unable to financially sustain the church even though they brought in the pastor they wanted. Sadly, the church closed. But God raised up another church there.

---

121. Matt 12:25; Mark 3:25; Luke 11:17.
122. Eph 4:1–3.
123. 1 Cor 3:3–4.
124. 1 Cor 1:12–13.

Inciting Fear and Anxiety

Fear and anxiety are emotions than can have crippling or debilitating effects. There are anxiety disorders that affect mental health. Traumatic events may leave one suffering from post-traumatic stress disorder. Or a phobia may prove to be oppressive or disruptive in its effect. Such fears and anxieties may require medical treatment in addition to being dealt with on a spiritual plane with prayer, fasting, and meditating on God's word. The fear of death, for example, is common. From a natural standpoint, death is such a drastic thing. But the author of Hebrews explains that Jesus Christ took on human form and experienced death so that by his death he might destroy the one who has the power of death, that is, the devil. And Jesus did this in order to free those who all their lives were held in slavery by the fear of death.[125] Before Jesus raised Lazarus from the dead, he told Martha, Lazarus's sister, that he is the resurrection and the life, whoever believes in him will live even though the person dies, and whoever lives and believes in him will never die.[126] Jesus also said it is God's will that everyone who looks to the Son and believes in him will have eternal life. And Jesus said he will raise them up at the last day.[127] Disciples, followers, or imitators of Christ can live in the assurance that they will one day live eternally with God.[128] Moreover, as Paul told Timothy, God has not given us a spirit of fear, timidity, or cowardice. Instead, he has given us a spirit of power, love, and self-discipline.[129]

Then there are the ordinary, normal anxieties about life and its difficulties and uncertainties. The apostle Paul told the church in Philippi not to be anxious about anything. He said that in everything, disciples should present their requests to God in prayer and supplication with thanksgiving. And having done that, he said that the peace of God which surpasses all understanding will guard their hearts and minds in Christ Jesus.[130]

---

125. Heb 2:14–15.

126. John 11:25–26.

127. John 6:40.

128. 1 Thess 4:13–18; Rev 20:4–6.

129. 2 Tim 1:6–7.

130. Phil 4:6–7. See M. Sydney Park, "Letter to the Philippians," in McCaulley et al., *New Testament in Color*, 476, commenting that just as God granted Paul peace in his imprisonment, Paul told the Philippians how to find that peace that goes beyond human understanding. Whatever stressful and alarming situations may arise, the response should be prayer, supplication, and thanksgiving to God who will hear our concerns and provide his own peace. See also Adeyemo, *Africa Bible Commentary*, 1447,

The Greek word for the verb "guard" as used here is *phroureo*,[131] denoting the protection of a garrison. This means God's peace will literally act as a garrison to protect the hearts and minds of disciples who entrust their cares to him from anxiety.

Unfortunately, Satan has managed to use fear of those who look different to divide Christians to the point that people are talking about how they are afraid of a race war and are arming themselves. It has been reported that Americans are buying guns in record numbers.[132] The apostle John pointed out that there is no fear in perfect love.[133] Fear of others who are different shows an absence of love. And if God has not given us a spirit of fear, then the spirit of fear originates from the devil. Christians must see through this satanic deception, reject fear, and walk in love with all people regardless of ethnicity, skin color, or nationality, as Christ did.

Fear is inconsistent with faith. As long as Satan can intimidate disciples, followers, or imitators of Christ to be afraid, he can compromise the work of the kingdom of God. That is why Paul urged Timothy not to allow fear to hinder his bold proclamation of the gospel. The effect of fear is seen when Jesus was crossing lake Gennesaret with his disciples to the land of the Gadarenes. A squall generated huge waves that swamped the boat. Frightened that they were about to die, the disciples went down to the stern of the boat in panic where Jesus was sound asleep and woke him up. He asked his disciples why they were afraid. He said they had little faith. He then rebuked the winds and the waves, and they calmed down.[134] What if the disciples had not awakened Jesus but had decided to turn the boat around and ride the wind back to shore? There was a demon-possessed man waiting on the other side who needed deliverance and healing. He was the one Jesus was crossing over to set free. As it turns out, he would become an evangelist to ten cities. He was being kept from his divine assignment by a legion of demons who had possessed him.

---

commenting that Paul's exhortation to rejoice in the Lord always and to be gentle or gracious is difficult to do during times of anxiety, hence Paul's counsel to be free from anxiety by coming to God in prayer, letting him share our burdens, and letting his peace protect us and relieve our hearts and minds of all anxiety.

131. See Vine et al., *Vine's Complete Expository Dictionary*, 284 (New Testament Section).

132. See Wernau and Elinson, "Record Numbers of Americans."

133. 1 John 4:18.

134. Matt 8:23–26; Mark 4:35–40; Luke 8:22–25.

Once Jesus set him free and commissioned him, he was able to fulfill his divine purpose and calling and Jesus left.[135]

During Paul's second missionary journey, he spent a year and a half in Corinth teaching them the word of God. Before this, the Lord had spoken to Paul in a vision in which he told Paul not to be afraid because he was with him. The Lord assured Paul in the vision that no harm would come to him because the Lord had many disciples in Corinth.[136] The sons of Korah expressed faith in God as their refuge, strength, and ever-present helper in times of trouble. They, therefore, made up their minds not to be afraid even in the most catastrophic circumstances.[137] David also expressed confidence in the Lord as his light, his salvation, and the strength of his life. He therefore resolved not to fear or be afraid of anyone.[138]

In spite of these biblical examples and assurances, Satan does everything he can to get disciples, followers, or imitators of Christ to live in fear of the unknown and others who are different, even when they are also professing Christians. That is because he knows that this undermines the unity of the Spirit and the bond of peace, weakens faith, and compromises the Christian's witness to unbelievers.

The Devil's Fate

Before Jesus gave his life on the cross to redeem humankind, he said that the prince of this world would be driven or cast out, but that he (Jesus) would draw all men to himself when he was nailed to the cross and hoisted or lifted up.[139] Satan was defeated by Jesus at the cross.[140] With Jesus's crucifixion, the sins of humankind were nailed to the cross. Jesus rose again in victory to give eternal life to all who believe in him and confess him as Lord.[141]

As the prince or ruler of this world, Satan is still actively influencing the world and doing everything he can to undermine God's will for

---

135. Mark 5:1–20; Luke 8:26–39.
136. Acts 18:9–10.
137. Ps 46:1–2.
138. Ps 27:1.
139. John 12:31.
140. Col 2:15.
141. Rom 10:9–10.

humankind. However, his doom is certain. The God of peace will soon crush Satan under the feet of his obedient followers.[142] In Revelation, John saw an angel coming down from heaven, seizing the ancient serpent, also known as the dragon, the devil, or Satan, chaining him, and throwing him into the Abyss, a prison where Satan will be held for one thousand years during Christ's millennial rule on earth. He will eventually be cast into the lake of fire and brimstone or burning sulfur where he will be tormented day and night for eternity.[143] Jesus said that this eternal fire was prepared, not for humans, but for the devil and his fallen angels, the demonic spirits over whom he rules, and who do his bidding in the kingdom of darkness.[144] Unfortunately, through deception, Satan is taking many with him to the lake of fire.

Triumphing over Satan

To triumph over Satan like Jesus did, Christians, as disciples, followers, and imitators of Christ, must live lives of prayer and fasting as Jesus did. They must also know and understand, with the help of the Holy Spirit as teacher, what God's word says about Satan and his schemes and devices. Believers must hold on to Jesus's teaching. Jesus said that holding on to his teaching is the mark of a true disciple. He also said that it will cause one to know the truth, and that the truth will set one free.[145] Jesus was not talking here about political freedom. He was talking about freedom from bondage to sin, satanic deception, and error that can lead to sin. It is not surprising, then, that Jesus commissioned his disciples, not just to get people converted, but to teach new converts to obey all that he has commanded.[146] Jesus resisted the devil's temptations with the word of God. Believers must do the same by living on God's every word.[147] Believers cannot live in sin and expect to triumph over Satan. He accused Job, a righteous man, before God.[148] He also accused the high priest Joshua

---

142. Rom 16:20.
143. Rev 20:10.
144. Matt 25:41.
145. John 8:32.
146. Matt 28:20.
147. Matt 4:1–11; Mark 1:12–13; Luke 4:1–13.
148. Job 1:9–11.

before God.[149] How much more will he accuse a believer who practices sin or falls short?

The apostle James urged believers to submit to God and to resist the devil, assuring them that he will flee from them.[150] But as we saw when Jesus resisted the devil's temptations, the devil left him until an opportune time.[151] Believers must expect him to do the same with them. This means that submission to God must be lifelong through continuing devotion to prayer, fasting, and the study of his word.

To triumph over Satan, believers must recognize that he is the one who battles them in their daily lives. The apostle Paul said that our struggle or battle as Christians is not against flesh and blood or other people, but against Satan and demonic forces who are behind all the evil in this world. He urged believers to put on the full armor of God in order to be able to withstand the devil's schemes or wiles.[152]

The armor, which uses parallels from the armor of a Roman soldier in Paul's day, consists of the belt of truth that is buckled around the waist. A belt held up clothing to allow free movement in battle. In the Christian's case, the belt of truth represents Christ himself, who is the truth, as well as his word, which is truth. He and his word must hold us together. Paul also mentioned wearing the breastplate of righteousness to protect our hearts from being corrupted by Satan and the world. The Bible tells us to guard the heart more than anything else because it is the wellspring of life.[153] Our integrity and character must be free from being impugned by Satan. Believers are also to lace up their sandals in preparation for the gospel of peace, ready to share the gospel that can bring ultimate peace to the world wherever they go, while remaining firmly planted themselves in God's peace in a topsy-turvy world. They are to hold up the shield of faith with which they can extinguish all the flaming arrows of the devil. This speaks to relying on their faith to resist Satan's temptations and attacks. They are to put on the helmet of salvation. Our salvation gives us the hope of deliverance from a wicked world. And since a helmet protects

---

149. Zech 3:1.

150. Jas 4:7.

151. Luke 4:13.

152. See James Nkansah-Obrempong, "Angels, Demons and Powers," in Adeyemo, *Africa Bible Commentary*, 1454–55, commenting on demonic and satanic beings, the need for spiritual weapons to overcome them, and the availability of angels to fight for us and protect us from the wiles and schemes of the evil one.

153. Prov 4:23.

the head, it can also protect the regenerated and renewed minds of Christians from Satan's power of suggestion. And they are to take the sword of the Spirit, which is God's word, which includes the truth about Jesus as the Messiah and Savior of the world. Jesus used God's word to resist and fight against the devil's temptations. Believers must do the same.

Beyond having this full armor on, Paul urged believers to pray constantly under the influence of the Holy Spirit, staying alert, and praying for all believers as they are in this spiritual battle together.[154] Prayer enlists God's help in our conflict with Satan.

Because Satan influences minds, disciples of Christ must seek God's guidance in their decision making. David prospered when he inquired of the Lord.[155] But Satan was able to deceive David when he did not seek God.[156] Seeking God's direction will help believers triumph over Satan by making good, godly decisions.[157]

In Revelation, the apostle John heard a loud voice in heaven saying that believers, whom Satan accuses before God incessantly, overcame him by the blood of the Lamb and by the word of their testimony.[158] Jesus shed his blood to deliver humanity from the power of Satan and sin. Believers triumph over Satan by believing in Christ's saving power through his shed blood, confessing Jesus as Lord,[159] becoming his disciples, sharing the good news about him, living lives of prayer and fasting, studying his word, and totally surrendering their lives to him.[160]

Though once dead through trespasses or sin, those who have put their faith in Christ have been made alive with him, raised up with him, and seated with him in the heavenly realms[161] where he sits above all

---

154. Eph 6:11–18. See Adeyemo, *Africa Bible Commentary*, 1437–38, commenting that the whole armor of God must be put on before the battle starts and that prayer is the climax of preparation for spiritual warfare.

155. 1 Sam 23:2; 30:8; 2 Sam 5:19, 23; 1 Chr 14:10, 14.

156. 2 Sam 24.

157. Prov 3:5.

158. Rev 12:11.

159. Rom 10:9.

160. Rev 12:11. See Yong, *Revelation*, 157–59, commenting that witness of the word and of life via keeping the divine commandments even to the point of death are the saints' tools of defiance of the devil. This means embracing the posture of the slain lamb and bearing witness to his shed blood even to the point of death.

161. Eph 2:4–6. See Adeyemo, *Africa Bible Commentary*, 1429, commenting that believers share not only in Christ's resurrection but also in his authority, power, and rule over principalities and powers in the entire universe as coheirs with Christ. Like Christ, believers are victors over sin, Satan, the world systems, and death. This should

rule, authority, power, dominion, and above every name that is named in this age and the age to come.[162] And that includes Satan. Christians, therefore, have access to the power of Christ through prayer to overcome Satan and his wiles and attacks.

If Christians will commit to prayer and fasting and continually search the Scriptures to understand Satan's schemes and deceptions, they will be able to resist his schemes and deceptions with which he divides humanity and induces them to live in disobedience to God. This will empower Christians, with the Holy Spirit's help, to imitate Christ's example of loving, engaging with, and ministering to all people, regardless of their ethnicity, skin color, nationality, or socioeconomic status. They will be able to live by Christ's commands to love their neighbor as themselves, regardless of what they look like and their station in life, and treat them as they would want to be treated.

---

give Christians a profound assurance of security and protection from menacing evil forces.

162. Eph 1:20–21.

5

Trusting in the Lord

JESUS CHRIST TRUSTED GOD completely. He totally surrendered to God's will to the point of submitting to a gruesome death reserved for criminals so that he might save the world that God so loves.[1] He did that trusting that God would raise him from the dead and exalt his name above all other names.[2] Like Jesus, Christians must also trust in the Lord, knowing that he is faithful and that he will do everything he has promised in his word for those who love him and do his will.

What Is Trust?

To trust someone is to believe that the person one trusts has one's best interest at heart; that one can count on the person not to cause harm or act against one's interests. One dictionary says it is to have confidence in somebody.[3] Another says it is to believe that someone is good and honest and will not harm you,[4] and yet another says it is to place confidence in or rely on someone or something.[5] Trust is indispensable in any relationship.

---

1. John 3:16.
2. Eph 1:20–22.
3. Oxford, "Trust (v.)."
4. Cambridge, "Trust (v.)."
5. Merriam-Webster, "Trust (v.)."

King Solomon exhorted the youth to trust in the Lord with all their hearts, and not to trust in their own understanding.[6] Jesus exhorted his disciples to trust in God and to trust also in him.[7]

In order to trust in the Lord, one must know who he is and have a relationship with him. That means that one must first come to know him and put one's faith in him as Lord.

Who Is the Lord?

In the Bible, *Lord* refers to either Jesus or to God, depending on the context. The Greek word for lord is *kurios*. It may mean lord or master depending on the context.[8]

When the Bible tells us about the story of creation, it says it was the Lord God who made the earth and the heavens.[9] When God called Abraham to leave Ur of the Chaldeans to go to a land that he was going to show him, the Bible says it was the Lord who spoke to Abraham.[10] Centuries later, when the Israelites came out of slavery in Egypt and God gave them the Ten Commandments at Mount Sinai in the wilderness, he prefaced the commandments by reminding them that he was the Lord their God who had brought them out of Egyptian slavery.[11] When God delivered David from Saul's attempts to kill him, David sang a song of praise to God in which he rhetorically asked, Who is God besides the Lord?[12] During Jesus's ministry, he said that the greatest commandment is to love the Lord God with all one's heart, soul, mind, and strength.[13]

Jesus also referred to himself as Lord and was called Lord by many, including his disciples and apostles. Jesus said that not everyone who says to him, "Lord, Lord," will enter the kingdom of heaven but only those who do the will of his Father who is in heaven.[14] Jesus told his disciples after he washed their feet that they call him teacher and Lord, and rightly

---

6. Prov 3:5.
7. John 14:1.
8. See Vine et al., *Vine's Complete Expository* Dictionary, 379–80 (New Testament Section). See also Strong's Reference Number 2962, defining *kurios* as lord or master.
9. Gen 2:4.
10. Gen 12:1.
11. Exod 20:2.
12. Ps 18:31.
13. Mark 12:30. Matt 22:37 does not include strength.
14. Matt 7:21.

so, for that is what he is, yet he had washed their feet and was now calling on them to wash each other's feet or serve each other.[15]

Paul told the Romans that if they confessed with their mouth that Jesus is Lord and believed in their hearts that God has raised him from the dead, they would be saved.[16] Paul further explained to the church in Philippi that because of Jesus's obedience to God, even to the point of surrendering to death, God had exalted him and given him a name above every name; at Jesus's name, every knee will bow and every tongue will confess that Jesus Christ is Lord.[17] Paul exhorted the church in Thessalonica to be alert and self-controlled because the day of the Lord, a reference to Jesus's return, will come as a thief in the night.[18]

The apostle Paul exhorted Timothy to fight the good fight of faith until the return of our Lord Jesus Christ.[19] The apostle John references the battle of Armageddon where Jesus Christ will battle the antichrist and his allies and attributes Christ's victory to the fact that he is Lord of lords and King of kings.[20] And at the very end of the Bible, as the apostle John hears Jesus's promise that he is coming soon, John answers with "Amen. Come, Lord Jesus!"[21]

The context will usually determine whether a reference to the Lord is a reference to God the Father or to Jesus Christ. References to the Lord God[22] or the Lord your God[23] are references to God the Father. Other references to the Lord Jesus,[24] the Lord Jesus Christ,[25] and the day of the Lord[26] are references to Jesus Christ. And sometimes the Lord can be a reference to either God or Jesus Christ as in some of the apostle Paul's

---

15. John 13:13–14.
16. Rom 10:9.
17. Rom 14:11 and Phil 2:8–11, quoting Isa 45:23.
18. 1 Thess 5:2–6.
19. 1 Tim 6:12–16.
20. Rev 17:14.
21. Rev 22:20.
22. Gen 2 has many references to the Lord God.
23. "I am the Lord your God" occurs many times throughout the book of Leviticus. Jesus answered Satan's temptation to jump from the pinnacle of the temple by quoting the Scripture that says, "Do not put the Lord your God to the test." Matt 4:7, NIV, quoting Deut 8:3.
24. Rom 10:9; Rev 22:20.
25. 2 Thess 2:1.
26. 2 Pet 3:10.

writings,[27] or as when, in ordinary, everyday life, a disciple calls on the Lord in prayer.

What It Means to Trust in the Lord

The word "trust" comes from the Greek word *pepoithésis*, meaning trust or confidence.[28] To trust in the Lord is to put one's confidence in God the Father and Jesus Christ the Son, through whom God offers salvation to a fallen world. It is to confidently depend on God and Jesus Christ after coming to believe in their saving power and putting one's faith in them.

Why Trust in the Lord?

It is natural for humans to protect their own interests. It is also natural to want to be in control of one's own destiny and to identify with like-minded people or people in one's own tribe, group, or socioeconomic class. But God challenges Christians to do things that are counterintuitive and countercultural. He commands Christians to deny themselves and pick up their cross to follow him. This means making God the priority in one's life and sharing in the suffering that discipleship can bring.[29] He commands them to love God with all their heart, mind, soul, and strength, and their neighbor as themselves.[30] He also commands Christians to do unto others as they would have others do unto them.[31] And he promises an eternal reward for those who show kindness and

---

27. 1 Cor 7:25; 2 Cor 3:16; 8:21; 1 Thess 4:6.

28. See Vine et al., *Vine's Complete Expository Dictionary*, 120, 646 (New Testament Section), defining *pepoithésis* as confidence and trust, respectively. See also *pepoithésis* in Strong's Reference Number 4006, defined as confidence or trust.

29. Matt 16:24; Mark 8:34; Luke 9:23. See Johnson, *Gospel of Luke*, 155, where he comments that the path that the disciple is to follow must be that already traveled by the Messiah. He notes that what is striking here is that the demand for self-denial applies not simply to the extraordinary person, the sage, but to all, and that here is the essential pattern for Christian identity. He notes that Luke clearly understands imitating Christ to mean something more than a momentary decision or surviving occasional external testing. See also Boring, *Mark: A Commentary*, 244, where he explains that to deny oneself means to no longer make oneself the top priority and the center of one's own universe—to not want to be like God, as with Adam and Eve, but to let God be God. And he explains the voluntary taking up one's cross to mean sharing the suffering involved in discipleship and Christian mission.

30. Matt 22:37–39; Mark 12:30–31.

31. Matt 7:12; Luke 6:31.

compassion to the poor and needy.[32] These commands apply to everyone a Christian encounters, regardless of their nationality, ethnicity, skin color, or socioeconomic status.

Why should Christians trust in the Lord and do as he commands instead of looking out for themselves and those who look like them? Because Jesus Christ, the one Christians follow and imitate, trusted in the Lord and lived out what he commands in his interactions with all people, regardless of who they were. Jesus is the author and finisher of our faith.[33] To trust in the Lord is to follow his example. But beyond following Jesus's example, Christians must trust in the Lord because his promises are pure,[34] and his word promises that those who trust in him will never be disappointed or put to shame.[35] Not only will he take care of those who trust in him here on earth,[36] but he will also live with them in eternity.[37]

How Does One Come to Trust in the Lord?

One cannot trust in the Lord without being in an intimate relationship with him. And for that to happen, one must put one's faith in him. After putting one's faith in the Lord by accepting God's invitation to eternal life through faith in the Son, Jesus Christ, one then begins a relationship with the Triune God.

The Greek word for faith is *pistis*, denoting firm persuasion or faith in God or Christ.[38] It is by God's grace that one who hears the gospel is able to believe it and put their faith in God through the convicting work of the Holy Spirit, leading to salvation.[39] As the hearer believes in their heart, and confesses Christ as Lord, God extends the gift of salvation and the believer begins a new life with the Lord.[40] To become a Christian—a

---

32. Matt 25:34–40.
33. Heb 12:2.
34. Ps 12:6.
35. Isa 28:16; Rom 10:11.
36. Phil 4:19.
37. John 14:2–3.
38. See Vine et al., *Vine's Complete Expository Dictionary*, 222 (New Testament Section), defining *pistis* as firm persuasion or faith in God or Christ. See also *pistis* in Strong's Reference Number 4102, defined as faith, and used to denote trust and confidence.
39. Eph 2:8.
40. Rom 10:9–10; 2 Cor 5:17. See Jarvis J. Williams, "Letter to the Romans," in

disciple, follower, or imitator of Jesus Christ—is to not only believe in him, but to continue in his word and live in obedience to him as Lord.

What Trusting in the Lord Looks Like

Many people in the Bible, including both Old and New Testament saints, trusted in the Lord. Based on conventional wisdom, some of them might be considered unlikely candidates because of their nationality or life circumstances. We can learn from their example that God loves and rewards all who trust and obey him, regardless of their nationality, ethnicity, or socioeconomic status.

Abraham

Abraham trusted God. God called him to leave his country in Ur of the Chaldeans for a place that God would show him—a place that he did not know.[41] Abraham believed God when he promised to give him a son and countless offspring although he was old, and his wife was barren. God credited his faith to him as righteousness.[42] His focus was not the world, but the city whose architect and builder is God.[43] Abraham was a rich and powerful man. But he did not trust in his strength or his riches.[44] He trusted in God.

As a result of Abraham's trust in the Lord and the obedience that flowed from that trust, God made a covenant with him to give him the land of Canaan as an inheritance and to bless the nations of the world through him.[45] God blessed the nations of the world through Abraham because Jesus Christ, the Savior of the world, came from Abraham's lineage.

McCaulley et al., *New Testament in Color*, 278, 301, commenting that the Jews who reject Christ stumble over Christ in their efforts to keep the Torah. However, the gentiles receive the promise of Christ's righteousness because they confess with their mouth that Jesus is Lord and believe in their hearts that God raised him from the dead so that they could be saved. See also Adeyemo, *Africa Bible Commentary*, 1366, noting that the only thing that is required for salvation is to respond to the gospel message by confessing Jesus as Lord and believing God has raised him from the dead.

41. Gen 12:1.
42. Gen 15:6; Rom 4:3.
43. Heb 11:10.
44. Gen 14:14–23.
45. Gen 12:1–3; 15:1, 5, 18. See Adeyemo, *Africa Bible Commentary*, 29, commenting that God's prediction that Abraham would be a blessing and that all peoples on

TRUSTING IN THE LORD

Daniel and His Three Friends

Because of the unfaithfulness of the nation of Judah to the Lord, he allowed the Babylonians to defeat Judah and carry many Jews into exile. Among them were Daniel and his three friends, Hananiah, Mishael, and Azariah, whom the Babylonians named Shadrach, Meshach, and Abednego. Daniel and his three friends trusted in God to take care of them as exiles—foreigners in Babylon.

Nebuchadnezzar, the king of Babylon, had a dream that troubled him and kept him up at night. He asked the wise men in Babylon to do something that seemed impossible. Without telling them the dream, he demanded that they tell him the dream and then interpret it. When the astrologers he first asked said the task was impossible, he ordered all the wise men to be put to death, including Daniel and his three friends. When Daniel heard of this order, he asked the king for time to interpret the dream. He told his three friends about what was going on and asked them to join him to plead with the Lord to reveal the meaning of the dream to Daniel. God did so and Daniel went and told the king what he had dreamed and what it meant. King Nebuchadnezzar was floored. He acknowledged the preeminence of Daniel's God and made Daniel ruler over the entire province of Babylon. He also appointed Daniel's three friends as administrators in Babylon. Daniel worked in the royal court with the king.[46] God elevated four foreigners, people who were taken captive to Babylon, because they trusted in him. Unfortunately, the Babylonian natives became envious of Daniel and his three friends. They had more prestigious positions than most Babylonians. The Babylonians would later seek to get rid of them.

They saw their chance when king Nebuchadnezzar made a gold image of himself and issued a decree that all his subjects were to fall down and worship the image when prompted with music. Anyone who did not do so would be thrown into a fiery furnace. Everyone worshipped the image except the Hebrew boys. The Babylonians sent word to the king that Shadrach, Meshach, and Abednego, did not worship his image. The three Hebrew boys were brought before Nebuchadnezzar and told that they would be thrown into the furnace if they did not bow to the image. They

---

earth would be blessed through him took place when the Savior was born. The salvation he offers will not belong to any one nation like the early Jewish Christians had to learn but will be passed on by and through one nation.

46. Dan 2.

refused. They told Nebuchadnezzar that they trusted the God they served to rescue them. But they also said that even if their God did not rescue them, they would still not worship the image. If God chose for them to die and come to spend eternity with him, they were okay with that.

Infuriated, Nebuchadnezzar had them thrown into the furnace after making it seven times hotter. Even those who threw them in were killed by the heat from the fire. But the Lord sent his angel into the fire to protect the three Hebrew boys. They were not hurt, and the king ordered them out of the fire. When they came out, people crowded around them and observed that the fire had not touched their clothes, hair, or bodies. Nebuchadnezzar praised the God of Shadrach, Meshach, and Abednego in whom they had put their trust. He decreed that anyone who spoke against this God would be put to death because no other god can save in this way.[47]

Daniel also became the target of envious Babylonian natives. After king Nebuchadnezzar died, his son Belshazzar succeeded him. After he died, Darius the Mede succeeded him. Darius appointed 120 satraps over the kingdom with oversight from three administrators, one of whom was Daniel. Daniel distinguished himself more than the other administrators to the point that the king wanted to appoint him over the whole kingdom just as Nebuchadnezzar had done. The natives in the king's administration became green with envy and sought to get rid of Daniel before he could be promoted above them. They wanted to find a way to implicate Daniel in wrongdoing but could not because he was neither corrupt nor derelict of duty as an administrator. His enemies knew one thing about Daniel that they could count on—Daniel trusted in God, and this showed in his prayer life. He prayed three times a day without fail. They figured that the only way to trap Daniel would have to have something to do with his faith. They convinced the king to issue a written decree prohibiting anyone from praying to any god or man other than the king during the next thirty days. Anyone who disobeyed this decree would be thrown into the den of lions.[48]

Daniel was not going to stop trusting in God and stop praying. He continued to pray three times a day. The men who got the king to issue the edict found Daniel praying and came and reported this to the king, telling him that Daniel had no regard for him because he continued to

---

47. Dan 3.
48. Dan 6:1–9.

pray to his God three times a day. The king was distressed because he knew how impressive Daniel was. But he had issued a written decree, and according to the laws of the Medes and the Persians, it was irrevocable. The king reluctantly gave the order for Daniel to be thrown into the den of lions. Daniel was thrown into the den and a stone cover was placed over it and sealed with the king's signet ring and those of his nobles, signifying that Daniel's fate was sealed and irreversible. The king told Daniel he hoped his God to whom he prayed continually would protect him.[49]

The king had a miserable, sleepless night, neither eating nor entertaining himself. He hurried to the lions' den at first light the next morning and frantically called out to Daniel, asking if his God whom he served continually had been able to rescue him from the lions. Miraculously, Daniel answered, assuring him that he was unharmed because his God sent an angel to shut the mouths of the lions. The king ordered that Daniel be lifted out of the den. When he came out, he did not have a single wound. God rewarded Daniel's faith by saving him. Realizing that Daniel's enemies had tried to get him killed, the king had those who had set Daniel up, as well as their wives and children, thrown into the den of lions. They barely hit the bottom of the den before the lions crushed all their bones.[50]

King Darius himself came to hold God in awe. He issued a decree throughout his kingdom that people must fear and reverence the God of Daniel because he is the living God who endures forever, whose kingdom will not be destroyed, and whose dominion will not end. The king attested to the fact that Daniel's God rescues and saves, performs signs and wonders in the heavens and on the earth, and that he had rescued Daniel from the power of the lions.[51]

Rahab

When the people of Israel were finally ready to enter Canaan after wandering in the wilderness for forty years because of their lack of faith in God to deliver on his promise after they came out of Egypt, Joshua, who now led the Israelites after Moses's death, sent a couple of spies to spy out the land. They went to the house of a prostitute named Rahab. The king

---

49. Dan 6:10–17.
50. Dan 6:18–24.
51. Dan 6:25–27.

of Jericho heard that spies had entered his country and were in Rahab's house, so he sent a message to Rahab to give up the men. But Rahab hid them and helped them escape.

Rahab had heard about how God had parted the Red Sea and how he had given the Israelites, a ragtag group of former slaves, victory in battle over the kings of the Amorites. She was convinced that God had given Jericho to the Israelites. She figured that Jehovah, the God of the Israelites, was real and that he was the God in whom she was going to put her trust. She was willing to put her life in the hands of this God. So, she made a deal with the spies to protect her and her family in return for her protection of the spies.[52]

The Israelites did conquer Jericho and save Rahab and her family. Rahab became a part of the nation of Israel.[53] She married a man named Salmon and they had a son called Boaz.[54]

Ruth

Ruth was a Moabite woman. She married a son of Naomi and Elimelech, who settled in Moab because of a famine in Israel. Elimelech and his sons died in Moab. When the famine in Israel ended, Ruth went back with Naomi, vowing to make Jehovah her God and Naomi's people her people.[55] Ruth met and married a relative called Boaz. Ruth and Boaz had a son by the name of Obed, who was the grandfather of king David.[56] Jesus is the root of David,[57] a descendant of Rahab and Ruth, two foreigners who put their faith in God and settled in Israel.

God blessed Rahab and Ruth, two women from foreign countries, for trusting in him. They both appear in the genealogy of Jesus.[58]

---

52. Josh 2.
53. Josh 6:25.
54. Matt 1:5; Luke 3:31.
55. Ruth 1:1–7, 16–19.
56. Ruth 4:13–17.
57. Rev 5:5; 22:16.
58. Matt 1:5; Luke 3:31.

The Roman Centurion

While ministering in Capernaum, a Roman centurion came and asked Jesus for help with his servant who was paralyzed and suffering. Jesus was willing to go to with him, although Jews would normally not enter a gentile's home.[59] But Jesus loved and helped everyone who asked him for help regardless of their nationality, ethnicity, or socioeconomic status. The centurion asked Jesus to just say the word to heal his servant because he was not worthy for Jesus to enter under his roof. The centurion's servant was healed that same hour. Jesus was astonished by the centurion's faith and said he had not found anyone in Israel with such great faith.[60]

The Canaanite Woman

While Jesus was retreating in Tyre and Sidon, a Canaanite woman came and implored him to heal her demon-possessed daughter. Her faith was so strong that she could not be dissuaded by anything Jesus said. Jesus rewarded her faith by granting her wish. Jesus commended her for her great faith and her daughter was healed the same hour he granted her wish.[61]

Jesus did not withhold his favor from anyone because of the person's nationality or ethnicity. He calls on all believers to trust in God and to trust also in him. Christians can trust in him regardless of their nationality, ethnicity, skin color, or socioeconomic status. They can trust that he has their best interests at heart. They can demonstrate their love for him by obeying what he commands. And his word assures Christians that his commands are not burdensome.[62]

Trusting in the Lord in Our Day

I have come to realize that a Christian's trust in the Lord ebbs and flows. Sometimes our faith is strong. Sometimes it is not as strong, and we need more grace to carry us through. Sometimes God seems distant or silent, and faith may waver. One author has shared her personal experiences in these difficult times to encourage others to persevere and keep trusting

---

59. Matt 8:5–10; Luke 7:1–10.
60. Matt 8:5–13.
61. Matt 15:21–28; Mark 7:24–30.
62. 1 John 5:3.

THE CHRISTIAN AS IMITATOR OF CHRIST

till they break through.[63] And as I reflect on the lessons that I have learned about trusting in the Lord, Nehemiah's story comes to mind.

Nehemiah was a godly man who trusted in the Lord. He was the cupbearer to Artaxerxes, the king of Babylon. As a Jew living in exile, he had to be a person of phenomenal character and integrity to hold this position instead of a native Babylonian. Because of his love for his native Judah, Nehemiah was saddened to hear that the walls of Jerusalem that had been torn down when the Babylonians conquered Judah, burned the city, and destroyed and looted the temple were still in ruins. After a period of prayer and fasting and asking God for favor with the king, Nehemiah asked the king for a leave of absence to go and rebuild Jerusalem's walls. The king agreed. In Jerusalem, Nehemiah did not count on encountering antagonists who would oppose the rebuilding of the wall. Three men rose up against Nehemiah—Sanballat, Tobiah, and Geshem. They did not want Nehemiah to succeed. They were against anything that would promote the welfare of the Jews. In spite of their opposition and plots to harm Nehemiah, God prospered him, and the wall was rebuilt in fifty-two days.[64]

Like Nehemiah, I did not count on opposition when I took a job as chief academic officer at a university campus in a rural, conservative community in southcentral Pennsylvania. A handful of antagonists did everything they could to undermine me and make me feel unwelcome. I had taken this job in faith and turned down two others, believing that it was the Lord who had directed my path. But unlike Nehemiah, I allowed my detractors to affect me. I started wondering if I had made a mistake in going there. We had rented a house the first year, intending to buy a house after we became more familiar with the area. I prayed specifically for an all-brick home with two fireplaces, a two-car garage, and acreage, and we found it! I put in an offer. As negotiations ensued, the antagonists at work stepped things up. I stopped negotiating on the house and applied for a new job. But that was not God's will. He did not open a new door. Meanwhile, the chief antagonist left, and things calmed down a bit. But by this time, a housing bubble had blown up home prices and

---

63. See Weems, *Listening for God*. See also Bridges, *Trusting God*, encouraging trusting God more completely even when life hurts; Palmer, *Trusting God*, assuring that faith is well placed even in the face of honest inquiry and deep self-questioning; and Grounds, *Rock Solid Trust*, exploring what it means to trust God with one's whole being.

64. Neh 2:10, 19; 4:7–9; 6:1–15.

we paid a fortune, 50 percent more, for the same type of house we had passed up. However, God sustained me, and I outlasted the antagonists. I had a career spanning twenty-two years at the university, including eighteen at that campus, and was promoted to serve as chancellor at two different campuses. I learned that the Lord can be trusted no matter how challenging the circumstances are, and that he can elevate his servants over the objections of antagonists and detractors.

As a polio survivor, I was always unsure how long I would be able to work. Would I be able to work to full retirement age? Or would I have to retire early because of the polio? Would I be able to save enough for retirement? Would I be able to help my children pay for college? I became doubly apprehensive when my wife became a stay-at-home mom after our second child was born. My apprehensions heightened when our third child was born. My wife took care of the children until our youngest turned fourteen before going back to work full time. As I look back now, I realize that I had absolutely no reason to be apprehensive. During this entire time, I gave to the church and others in need as much as I could and served the Lord. And the Lord took care of us. All three of our children graduated from college debt free. And I was able to work until my late sixties. God's word is true—that the one who believes in him will not be put to shame.[65]

Things That Substitute for Trust in the Lord

The Bible describes the devil as the adversary of Christians. He is a deceiver who works overtime to undermine the faith of Christians. He tempts them to trust in anything but the Lord. He causes divisions and conflicts between people of different nationalities and ethnicities and incites fear so that they cannot love each other as they love themselves or do unto each other as they would expect to be done to them. He instigates hardheartedness so that people will withhold compassion and love from the poor, knowing that Jesus takes it personally when people assist

---

65. 1 Pet 2:6, quoting Isa 28:16. The NIV uses trusts while the NKJV uses believes. See also Ps 25:1 and Rom 10:11. See Adeyemo, *Africa Bible Commentary*, 1519, commenting that Peter is referring to Christ as the chosen and precious cornerstone, a strong foundation stone on which it is safe to erect a building, hence the fact that the one who trusts in him will never be put to shame. In other words, one can securely build one's life on the foundation of Jesus Christ.

the poor. Indeed, Jesus promises an eternal reward to those who help the poor and warns of eternal judgment for those who do not.[66]

The things the devil uses to undermine a Christian's trust in the Lord include the following.

Money

Many people put their trust in wealth. Because their trust in is their wealth, they love wealth and cannot get enough of it. It is their master. Sadly, that means many will do anything to gain wealth, even if it is ungodly. Take slavery, for example. It generated tremendous wealth for the major players in the slave economy. And those who benefited from it found every reason to justify it. Many justified it in the name of God and with the word of God. The apostle Paul told Timothy that the love of money is a root of all kinds of evil. In pursuit of it, Paul said some had strayed from the teachings of the Christian faith and ended up piercing themselves with many griefs.[67]

King Solomon tried to find happiness and fulfillment in wealth and the pleasures wealth can buy. His wealth was vast.[68] But he discovered that if one loves money, one never has enough, and that whoever loves wealth is never satisfied with his income.[69] Solomon only found frustration and despair until he returned to trusting in the Lord.[70]

In one of his parables, Jesus warned of the folly of trusting in wealth. Jesus told his hearers about a rich man whose fields had produced a harvest so plentiful that he planned to build bigger barns and take life easy with food, drink, and merriment. But God demanded his soul of him the very night he made those plans in his heart and his wealth was unable to save him.[71]

66. Matt 25:3–46.
67. 1 Tim 6:10.
68. 1 Kgs 11:14–29; 2 Chr 1:14–17; 9:13–28; Eccl 2.
69. Eccl 5:10.
70. Eccl 12:13.
71. Luke 12:20. See Stephen Adei, "Wealth and Poverty," in Adeyemo, *Africa Bible Commentary*, 762, commenting that wealth in the hands of the righteous is a powerful tool to serve God and others. Money as a purpose for living is not worth it even if one gains the whole world, for this is done at the cost of one's eternal soul. See also Yusufu Turaki, "Secularism and Materialism," in Adeyemo, *Africa Bible Commentary*, 791, commenting that materialism causes peoples' lives to revolve around money, possessions, and the things of the world rather than spiritual values, an inevitable

Jesus told his disciples that no one can serve two masters. He said that the one who tries to do that will hate one and love the other or be devoted to one and despise the other. Jesus said no one can serve both God and money.[72]

Weapons

Today, many people are trusting in weapons to keep them safe. Purchases of firearms have skyrocketed. Many who have never before owned weapons are arming themselves. Some are building arsenals in their homes, including assault-style rifles. Many say they fear a race war. June 2020 saw the highest number of background checks for licenses to carry firearms since the FBI started conducting background checks twenty years earlier. Many say they are buying guns because they see others buying guns.[73] Instead of loving God with all their heart, mind, soul, and strength and their neighbor as themselves, people are preparing to kill or be killed.

One of Jesus's companions might have felt this way at one point because he got a sword and tried to defend Jesus with it when Jesus was arrested in the garden of Gethsemane. He cut off the right ear of the high priest's servant in the process. Jesus put back the ear and chided his companion to put his sword away. Jesus told the sword wielder that those who live by the sword will die by the sword.[74] Of course, in our day, that person would have been carrying a gun, perhaps a concealed weapon, not wielding a sword. And Jesus would tell him the exact same thing, except this time he would not be referencing a sword.

Sadly, many who buy guns to protect themselves end up taking their own lives with them. And many loved ones have lost their lives to the very guns that were meant to protect their households. There were

---

consequence of the failure to love God above all else.

72. Matt 6:24; Luke 16:13. The NKJV uses the word *mammon*, an Aramaic word for riches. It is believed to derive from a Hebrew word signifying treasure. See Vine et al., *Vine's Complete Expository Dictionary*, 388 (New Testament Section). See also Strong's Reference Number 3126, where the Greek *mamónas* is defined as riches and used to denote riches, money, or possessions.

73. See Wernau and Elinson, "Record Numbers of Americans."

74. Matt 26:50–52; Mark 14:47; Luke 22:49–51; John 18:10. The Gospel of John identifies the sword carrier as Peter. See Moloney, *Gospel of John*, 484, commenting that Peter failed to understand the significance of what lay ahead, beginning with Jesus's arrest, and drew a sword in a violent attempt to change the course of events, but he is rebuked. Peter was thwarting God's design even as Judas was thwarting God's design.

39,707 deaths from firearms in the US in 2019. Of this, 23,941 were suicides. Sixty percent of deaths from firearms in the US are suicides. Many are also injured by guns each year. It is estimated that there are 115,000 nonfatal firearm injuries in the US every year.[75] Therein lies how deceptive the devil is. He deceives people to not walk in love but to walk in fear. He induces people to think they can trust in weapons instead of the Lord, leading to even greater insecurity and harm.

No one can suggest that it is imprudent for people to take reasonable steps to protect themselves and their loved ones. But for anyone who claims to be a Christian, weapons can never become a substitute for God. No arsenal will be large enough to keep one safe in a fallen world. Christians, who are followers and imitators of Christ, must understand this more than anyone else, and live in such a way that their lives demonstrate trust in the Lord.

Powerful People

There are those who trust in powerful people, especially powerful politicians. But the Bible exhorts us not to put our trust in princes, in mortal men who cannot save.[76]

After his resurrection, Jesus commissioned disciples, followers, or imitators of Christ, then and now, to share the gospel of Jesus Christ with the entire world. The Great Commission includes discipling those who receive the gospel to become imitators of Jesus Christ by living in obedience to all of Christ's commands.

Unfortunately, instead of sharing the gospel with the lost and trusting God to change lives, many who profess Christ choose to trust in politicians to force people to change through legislation. But laws can only attempt to regulate human behavior. Laws have never been able to transform human beings. Even the Ten Commandments that God himself gave to the Israelites were unable to transform them to live righteous lives. Neither were they meant to do so. They were only a foreshadow of what was to come—namely, salvation through Jesus Christ, God's Son. The Ten Commandments pointed out sin but could not equip one to live above sin. The Ten Commandments showed that unless God himself came to live in humans through his Holy Spirit, they could not live godly lives.

---

75. UC Davis Health, *Facts and Figures*.
76. Ps 146:3.

Trusting in politicians to accomplish what only God can accomplish in a person through Christ's redemptive power and the transformational power of the Holy Spirit, is to put one's trust in people to bring about results that only God can. What are the odds that unredeemed sinners, male or female, will stop having premarital or extramarital sexual relations because of a restrictive abortion law? But the one who is redeemed, sanctified, and filled with the Holy Spirit, can live a holy life.

As necessary as laws are, disciples, followers, or imitators of Christ cannot allow the devil to deceive them to trust in powerful people and man-made laws instead of the Lord, who alone is able to transform those he has redeemed by making them Christlike.

Things That Hinder Trusting in the Lord

Doubt

The devil uses doubt to hinder Christians from trusting in the Lord. When the Israelites left Egypt and were heading for Canaan, they came to a point where they were preparing to invade the land. They sent twelve spies to spy out the land first. For forty days, they spied on the vast land. When they returned to their camp, ten of the spies convinced the Israelites that they were not strong enough to overpower the inhabitants of the land, some of whom were descendants of Anak, men of great physical stature.[77] The ten spies had serious doubts about whether God could deliver on his promise to give them the promised land. They said they looked like grasshoppers in their own eyes compared to the descendants of Anak they saw there. They also believed they looked like grasshoppers in the eyes of the Anakites. However, two of the spies, Joshua and Caleb, believed that they could fully trust in the Lord to give them victory over the inhabitants of the land.[78] They had no doubt that God could indeed deliver on his promise.

However, the ten spies, looking to their own strength instead of trusting in God, managed to discourage the rest of the Israelites from trusting God to give them the land. As a result of the failure of the Israelites to trust God to deliver on his promise to give them the land he had promised to their ancestor Abraham, God decided that none of the

---

77. Num 13.
78. Num 14:6–9.

Israelites who were fit for war, age twenty and above, would enter the promised land, except for Joshua and Caleb. Instead, he would cause them to wander in the wilderness for forty years, one year for each of the forty days they spent spying out the land, until all the people who did not trust in him had died.[79] Their doubt proved costly.

The devil may cause doubt in the hearts of Christians about whether loving one's neighbor as oneself, or practicing the golden rule, instead of looking out for oneself or seeking advantage over others, especially those who look different and do not belong to one's tribe, makes sense. But the devil's way never brings true peace or prosperity, only fear and insecurity, even in the face of power and advantage.

There are people in Jesus's day who lost out on the opportunity for healing or some other miracle because they doubted that Jesus was who he said he was in spite of all the miracles he performed. And as a result of their unbelief, he did not do many miracles in his hometown. He healed only a few sick people there.[80] Christians also stand to lose out on God's blessings if they doubt that they are better off obeying God's commands to love their neighbor as themselves, treat others as they would want to be treated, and extend love and compassion to the poor.

Fear

Fear, a powerful emotion, can be a hindrance to trusting in the Lord. Fear can set in when one thinks or believes that one is in danger or when one feels helpless in the face of a situation outside of one's control. Some fears may lead to mental health challenges that require professional help. The fear of failure can prevent someone from taking on a new challenge such as a new project or job. The fear of being hurt can prevent someone from having a healthy relationship with a trustworthy person. Some are afraid to fly, and others will not get on a ship because they are afraid of water. Indeed, there are all sorts of phobias, which are irrational fears. Not every fear hinders trusting in the Lord, but some do. Fear of other people, especially people who look different, who have a different nationality or ethnicity, or who are in a different socioeconomic class, can

---

79. Num 14:29–34.

80. Matt 13:58; Mark 6:5. See Harrington, *Gospel of Matthew*, 211–13, commenting that Matthew makes Jesus's inability to heal dependent on the faith of the people, an example of the prejudice of familiarity, whereby the people of Jesus's hometown assumed they already knew all there was to know about Jesus and dismissed him.

cause a Christian to live in disobedience to Christ's commands of love and compassion for others.

David dealt with fear by reminding himself of who God is and what that meant to him. David saw the Lord as his light and salvation. As a result, he saw no reason to fear anyone. The Lord was the strength of his life. He had no reason to be afraid of anyone.[81] David made up his mind that even in the face of death, he would not to be afraid, because he was assured of God's presence and comfort.[82] Obviously, being human, there were times when David was afraid and admitted it. But in those times, he put his trust in God.[83]

The apostle Paul reminded his protégé Timothy that God has not given believers a spirit of cowardice, but of power, love, and self-discipline.[84] Believers need to draw on the power, love, and wisdom of the indwelling Holy Spirit to help them overcome fear. Having said all that, it must also be said that there is only one type of fear that actually builds up one's faith or trust in the Lord, and that is the fear of the Lord. The fear of the Lord is not a negative emotion like other fears. It is a healthy reverence and awe for God in acknowledgment of who he is—the all-powerful, all-knowing, and omnipresent God. He is the God whose word we can obey because he has our best interest at heart, and we cannot secure our lives and future better than he can. That fear is the beginning of wisdom.[85] The one who fears the Lord obeys his word and allows God's Holy Spirit to be his or her guide. God's word becomes a lamp to their feet and a light for their path.[86]

---

81. Ps 27:1.

82. Ps 23:4.

83. Ps 56:3.

84. 2 Tim 1:7. The NKJV says God has not given us a spirit of fear, but of power and of love and of a sound mind. See Osvaldo Padilla, "Pastoral Letters," in McCaulley et al., *New Testament in Color*, 554, commenting that the Holy Spirit gives us the strength to live godly lives of ministry and virtuous existence. See also Adeyemo, *Africa Bible Commentary*, 1477, commenting that Paul is telling Timothy to cultivate a spirit of power to counter any appearance of weakness because he is young, love to counter any undeserved criticism, and self-discipline so that the purity of his life will ultimately silence his critics.

85. Prov 9:10.

86. Ps 119:105.

Worry

In his Sermon on the Mount, Jesus addressed the subject of worry. He told his disciples not to worry about their lives. Specifically, he told them not to worry about what they will eat or drink, and about what they will wear. He told them how caring and faithful God is. Because God is caring and faithful, he feeds the birds even though they do not plant and harvest fields or store away food in barns. Jesus reminded them that they were much more valuable than birds. He showed them how pointless worry is because it changes absolutely nothing. One cannot add anything to one's life or stature by worrying—not a single hour to one's span of life or a cubit to one's stature.[87]

Jesus then pointed to the lilies that grow wild. He said they do not work or spin as one spins yarn to make a beautiful article of clothing, yet they look more beautiful than Solomon ever did in all his splendor—royal robes, jewelry, crown, and all. He asked them why God will not clothe them if he cares that much about grass, vegetation that looks good today but is cut down and burned tomorrow. He said it was a matter of faith; worry is an indicator of having little faith. He reiterated his admonition not to worry and said it was a distinguishing characteristic of people without faith. His disciples, therefore, cannot operate that way.

Many people worry about their safety. They are not sure they can trust others. They worry about their financial security. They are not sure it makes sense to give, even to people who are much less fortunate than they are. They worry about scarce resources and would rather look out for themselves. They are not sure it makes sense to love their neighbor, especially those who look different, as themselves.

But Jesus gives us the key to defeating worry. He said it was to seek first the kingdom of God and his righteousness.[88] In other words, disciples are to seek and submit to the rule of God and seek right standing with him through faith and obedience. And as long as they do that, Jesus

---

87. Matt 6:27. The NRSV says one cannot add an hour to one's span of life and the NKJV says one cannot add a cubit to one's stature. A cubit is about eighteen inches in height.

88. Matt 6:25–34. See Adeyemo, *Africa Bible Commentary*, 1123, noting that worry does not advance one's cause at all and is absolutely useless. It can take up so much of one's energy that one is paralyzed and cannot act. The necessities of life, while important, are not to become an all-consuming passion. Instead of worrying, we must learn to focus on serving the Lord wholeheartedly, doing our best, and leaving the rest to him.

promised that God will take care of them and meet their needs. Christians can love their neighbor as themselves. They can treat others as they would want to be treated. They can show love and compassion to the poor. And they can do all that knowing that God, who promises blessings for obedience, will take care of them.

Suffering

Satan uses suffering to discourage faithful believers from trusting in the Lord. He brought untold suffering into Job's life to try to get him to renounce his faith in God. He told God he was sure Job would curse God to his face if God withheld his protection and blessing from Job. God allowed Satan to test Job to prove Satan wrong because he knew that Job fully trusted in him. In just one day, Satan killed Job's children and most of his servants and ransacked and plundered his cattle. Yet Job did not stop trusting in God.[89]

Satan then suggested that if God permitted him to afflict Job physically, Job would surely curse God to his face. God permitted Satan to attack Job's health short of killing him. Although his wife suggested that he curse God and die, Job did not stop trusting in God.[90] Job told his friends that even if God killed him, he would still trust God.[91] Job understood that whether he lived or died would not change who God is—a faithful God who is trustworthy. He knew death would not separate him from God. It would unite him with God. So, even if God chose not to save his life, he would trust God knowing the end of his earthly life would be the beginning of an eternity with God. With this unwavering faith, God eventually restored Job's health, gave him new sons and daughters, and blessed him with even more wealth.[92] The devil failed to get Job to stop trusting in God in spite of the unspeakable suffering God allowed him to inflict on Job.

89. Job 1.

90. Job 2. See Adeyemo, *Africa Bible Commentary*, 573, commenting on how instead of cursing God for his suffering like the adversary predicted, Job worshipped God and surrendered to him. Job's wife could no longer stand the catastrophes that had befallen her family and her husband and urged Job to curse God and die. It is possible that Satan is launching his final attack through her as she urges her husband to utter the curses Satan had predicted. However, Job rebukes her and suggests that the proper response to this suffering is total surrender to God's will.

91. Job 13:15.

92. Job 42:10–16.

Job prayed for his friends who were criticizing him and insisting that his suffering was a result of hidden sin in his life. And it was when Job prayed for his friends that God restored him.[93] As extreme as Job's case was, it serves as an example to modern-day Christians of seeing one's faith as one of one's most valuable assets and holding on to it no matter what. Job's case also shows that even in the face of suffering, Christians can minister to others, and that God will bless them for doing so.

Persecution

Persecution is a perennial tool in Satan's toolbox of devices he uses to try to discourage faithful believers from continuing to trust in the Lord. Working through religious leaders and ordinary Jews, he persecuted Jesus's disciples for their faith and the work they were doing for the kingdom of God. Stephen, a deacon in the church in Jerusalem, was killed and James the brother of John was also killed. The apostle Peter was imprisoned but freed by an angel. Speaking from experience, Peter encouraged believers to remain faithful to the Lord in the face of persecution.[94]

Paul suffered more persecution than all the other apostles. He told the Corinthians about how he had been imprisoned more often, flogged more severely, received thirty-nine lashes from the Jews on five different occasions, beaten with rods three times, stoned three times, and shipwrecked once. He shared how he had been constantly on the move for the Lord and been in danger from Jews and gentiles alike, often toiling without sleep or food, cold and naked.[95] Despite all this, Paul told the church in Corinth that although he and his fellow workers were hard pressed on every side, they were not crushed; they were perplexed but not in despair; they were persecuted but not abandoned; they were struck down but not destroyed. He considered all their earthly troubles to be light and momentary, and believed that their troubles were achieving for them an eternal glory that was much greater. Paul was faithful to the end despite all the persecution Satan incited against him. In the

---

93. Job 42:10.

94. 1 Pet 4:13. See Janette H. Ok, "First Letter of Peter," in McCaulley et al., *New Testament in Color*, 679, commenting that through suffering, Christians share in Christ's sufferings, which gives them reason to rejoice now and overwhelmingly more when his glory is revealed. At present, joy and suffering intermingle, but when Christ returns, only joy will remain.

95. 2 Cor 11:23–27.

very last Letter that he is believed to have written, Paul told Timothy that he had fought the good fight and finished his race. He was now looking forward to the crown of righteousness that the Lord would give him on the day of judgment.[96]

The writer of Hebrews encouraged those to whom he wrote to persevere in the face of persecution. He reminded them of when they first became believers and stood their ground in the face of great suffering, insult, and persecution. They joyfully accepted the confiscation of their property because they knew they had better and lasting possessions. The writer urged them to persevere so that they would receive what God had promised them after doing his will.[97]

Modern-day Christians, as disciples, followers, and imitators of Christ, must do no less than what the writer of Hebrews urged Christians to do in the days of the early church. There are people today who face persecution for their faith. During the times when Iraq was overrun by the group ISIS (Islamic State of Iraq and Syria), many Christians fled their homes in the face of persecution and took refuge in refugee camps. And many, including priests, were killed for their faith.[98] Satan's goal in persecuting Christians is to get them to repudiate their faith and stop trusting in the Lord. Ultimately, it is their souls he is after. But if believers keep their eyes on the Lord knowing that they have an eternal reward that is more precious than anything this life has to offer, God will strengthen them to persevere to the end. They must remember and be encouraged by the words of Jesus that the one who perseveres to the end will be saved.[99]

Benefits of Trusting in the Lord

There are many benefits to trusting in the Lord. Those who trust in the Lord will never lack any good thing[100] or ever be put to shame.[101] In spite

---

96. 2 Tim 4:7–8.
97. Heb 10:31–36.
98. Associated Press, "Timeline of Disaster."
99. Matt 24:13. See Harrington, *Gospel of Matthew*, 335, where he comments that God is guiding human history toward its goal, despite the problems and sufferings of the present time. That goal is the *parousia* (second coming of Christ) at the end of this age/world.
100. Ps 34:10.
101. Ps 25:3; Rom 10:11.

THE CHRISTIAN AS IMITATOR OF CHRIST

of living in a fallen world where unpleasant things happen, those who trust in the Lord can still live a life of joy. They can rejoice in the Lord and be glad in him.[102] It is the Lord who helps them in times of distress. He is the one who delivers those who seek his face from the troubles that besiege them[103] so that they can overcome life's challenges and triumph over those who antagonize them.[104] God extends his goodness[105] and love[106] to those who trust in him. The Lord provides for those who trust in him.[107] He blesses them[108] and keeps them safe.[109] He guides them in their life's decisions.[110] And the greatest benefit of all? An inheritance reserved in heaven that will never perish.[111]

How to Grow in Faith and Trust in the Lord[112]

When the Lord was here on earth, there were times when he commended people for their great faith. He did so with the centurion who understood that Jesus could send his word to heal his servant without setting foot in his house.[113] He also did so with the persistent Canaanite woman who was not going to take no for an answer when she came and pleaded with Jesus to heal her demon-possessed daughter.[114]

But there were also times when he questioned why people had such little faith. He questioned his disciples' faith when they thought they were going to drown in a storm while he was sleeping in the stern.[115] And he

---

102. Ps 5:11.
103. Ps 22:4–5.
104. Ps 25:2–3.
105. Ps 31:19.
106. Ps 32:10. The NKJV says he extends his mercy.
107. Phil 4:19.
108. Ps 40:4.
109. Pss 4:8; 56:4, 11.
110. Prov 3:5–6.
111. 1 Pet 1:4. See Adeyemo, *Africa Bible Commentary*, 1519, commenting that exiles and strangers have often lost hope and have forfeited their inheritance at home. But with God we can be full of enthusiastic hope that our inheritance will be waiting for us in our heavenly home.
112. For books on trusting in the Lord, see Bridges, *Trusting God*; Meyer, *Unshakeable Trust*; and White, *Trusting God When You're Struggling*.
113. Matt 8:10; Luke 7:9.
114. Matt 15:28.
115. Matt 8:26; Mark 4:30; Luke 8:25.

did the same with Peter when Peter began to sink with fear after walking on water.[116]

But these same disciples later grew in faith and trusted in the Lord wholeheartedly. They preached the gospel fearlessly after being baptized with the power of the Holy Spirit and were ready to lay down their lives for the Lord.[117]

So, how can we grow in our faith and trust in the Lord? A good place to begin is to understand and eschew the things that compete with and hinder trusting in the Lord. Beyond that, there are some specific things one can do. One thing is to settle in one's heart that God's word is true, and that one can count on his promises.

Since faith comes by hearing and hearing by the word of God,[118] Christians must also put themselves in a position to hear God's word. But hearing the word of God is not enough. Christians must do what it says so that it may be a blessing.[119] Actions make faith complete. Without acting on faith, faith is merely lip service. The apostle James says faith without works is dead.[120]

Another way to increase in faith and trust in the Lord is to avoid speaking words of unbelief and defeat and, instead, to speak words of faith based on God's promises in his word. The author of Hebrews urges believers to hold fast or unswervingly to the profession of their faith or confession of their hope without wavering, remembering that God is faithful to perform his promises.[121]

A good example of this is seen in the contrast between the words of faith and trust in the Lord spoken by Joshua and Caleb and the words

---

116. Matt 14:31.
117. Acts 2:1–4; 5:12–42.
118. Rom 10:17.
119. Jas 1:22, 25.

120. Jas 2:17–26. See Adeyemo, *Africa Bible Commentary*, 1512–13, commenting that faith that is not demonstrated by works is dead in that it is simply a nominal belief, like that of the demons, who also believe in God but do not obey him. God's word must be put into practice if we are even to be able to speak about faith.

121. Heb 10:23. The NRSV speaks of the confession of our hope and the NKJV speaks of the profession of our faith. See Daniel K. Eng, "Letter of James," in McCaulley et al., *New Testament in Color*, 646–47, where he comments that James reiterates the point that a profession of faith—speaking about having faith—is useless without accompanying deeds that show that faith. The "faith" of demons in God is not good enough for salvation because it is not accompanied by works of obedience of fulfilling God's will.

THE CHRISTIAN AS IMITATOR OF CHRIST

of unbelief and defeat the ten spies spoke after they spied out Canaan.[122] The ten spies said if only they had died in Egypt or this desert, they would not be in this situation.[123] However, Joshua and Caleb said they believed the Lord would give them victory over the inhabitants of the land.[124] The Israelites' words of unbelief came to pass—they did die in the desert. But because of the good report and the words of faith Joshua and Caleb spoke, they lived to see the promised land.[125]

David also gives us a good example of a good confession or profession of faith and trust in the Lord. In faith, David approached Goliath with a sling, five stones, and bold declarations of faith. He said he was coming against Goliath in the name of the Lord God Almighty. He confidently declared that this day the Lord was going to give Goliath into his hands, and that he was going to strike Goliath down and cut off his head. He said the battle was the Lord's and he would give the Philistines into the hands of the Israelites. David did just as he said he was going to do, and the Lord did exactly what David believed the Lord was going to do. Goliath went down and the Israelites won the battle.[126] Christians must also make declarations of faith as David did believing that God will honor their declarations, when those declarations honor God.[127]

To increase in faith and trust in the Lord, one must do what Paul exhorted Timothy to do—guard one's faith and turn away from godless chatter and the opposing ideas of false knowledge.[128] One must also turn away from teaching that is inconsistent with what Christ taught—false teaching,[129] and worldly, humanistic philosophies.[130]

---

122. Num 13:31–33.
123. Num 14:2.
124. Num 14:6–9.
125. Num 14:29–34.
126. 1 Sam 17:40–54.
127. Mark 11:23.
128. 1 Tim 6:20.
129. 2 Tim 2:16–18.

130. Col 2:8. See Dennis R. Edwards, "Letter to the Colossians," in McCaulley et al., *New Testament in Color*, 488, commenting that Paul warns against the impact of being taken captive by following erroneous beliefs, false teaching that is hollow, deceptive, and relies on human traditions, as well as elemental principles of the world. See also Adeyemo, *Africa Bible Commentary*, 1453, commenting that when Paul warns against deceptive philosophy, he is not talking about philosophy as an academic discipline but as a religious system.

One can also grow in one's faith and trust in the Lord by nurturing one's relationship with the Lord through the diligent practice of the spiritual disciplines of praying, fasting, meditating on, studying the Scriptures, and praising and worshipping the Lord in the power of the Holy Spirit.

Finally, to increase in faith and trust in the Lord, disciples must keep looking to Jesus, the pioneer and perfecter or the author and finisher of their faith,[131] and please him by obeying his word instead of just calling him Lord without obedience.[132]

---

131. Heb 12:2. The NRSV says pioneer and perfecter, while the NKJV says author and finisher.

132. Luke 6:46. See Johnson, *Gospel of Luke*, 114–16, commenting that Jesus's rebuke is aimed at Christians who profess faith but don't live it out, and that acting out Jesus's teaching will dig the deep foundation that enables the disciples to resist the floods of opposition they inevitably will face.

6

Being a Good Steward

Jesus was the perfect steward of everything he had. He fully committed his time, energy, anointing, and gifts, to the work of God's kingdom and in service of humanity. That raises the questions of what a steward is, what makes one a good steward, and how Christians can be good stewards.

What Is a Steward?

There are many different meanings that can be ascribed to a steward. However, not all of them capture stewardship in the Christian or biblical sense. Some common definitions of a steward that come close to capturing what a steward is from a Christian perspective include someone employed in a large household or estate to manage affairs like supervising servants, collecting rents, and keeping accounts,[1] or a person employed to manage another person's property, especially a large house or land.[2] The key idea in stewardship is that the steward is not the owner of what he or she oversees or manages. Instead, the steward oversees or manages what another has entrusted to him or her. From a biblical perspective, the Greek word *oikonomos* gives us a picture of what a steward is by using the word to primarily denote the manager of a household or estate.[3]

1. Merriam-Webster, "Steward (n.)."
2. Oxford, "Steward (n.)."
3. See Vine et al., *Vine's Complete Expository Dictionary*, 599 (New Testament Section); also, Strong's Reference Number 3623, where *oikonomos* is defined as the manager of a household.

The earliest mention of a steward in the Bible is during Abraham's time. Eliezer, a man from Damascus, was the manager of Abraham's household. Apparently, in those days, a steward could inherit the master's estate if the master was childless.[4] Abraham trusted Eliezer to the point of entrusting him with the responsibility of finding his son Isaac a wife from his relatives in Ur of the Chaldeans. He gave Eliezer all the resources he needed for the journey, including gold jewelry for the bride-to-be. Eliezer prayerfully sought God's guidance and faithfully carried out his charge. He returned with Rebekah, a grandniece of Abraham's, as a bride for Isaac.[5]

Another early example of a steward in the Bible is Joseph. Out of jealousy, his brothers sold him to Ishmaelite traders on their way to Egypt and they, in turn, sold him to Potiphar, the captain of Pharaoh's guard.[6] Once Joseph arrived in Potiphar's house, because God was with him, Potiphar put Joseph in charge as overseer of his household. He entrusted everything he owned to Joseph's care and put it all under his authority. God blessed Potiphar's household because of Joseph. Potiphar trusted Joseph so much that he had no concern for anything but the food he ate every day. Joseph was such a faithful steward that even when Potiphar's wife tried to seduce him, Joseph refused to sin against God by sleeping with her.[7]

After Joseph became a prominent official in Egypt next only in position and authority to Pharaoh, Joseph also used the services of a steward. His brothers came to Egypt to buy grain during a time of famine in Canaan and the entire known world.[8] They dealt with Joseph without realizing who he was.[9] On a second trip to Egypt after they had run out of food, they dealt not just with Joseph, but also with his steward. Joseph gave his steward instructions to take them to his home and prepare lunch for them. The steward provided them with water to wash their feet and fed their donkeys while they waited for Joseph to come home and have lunch with them.[10]

4. Gen 15:2–3.
5. Gen 24.
6. Gen 37:23–36.
7. Gen 39:1–12.
8. Gen 41:57.
9. Gen 42.
10. Gen 43:16–17, 19–25.

We can also get a sense of a steward as a manager of another's assets from some of Jesus's parables. Jesus once told a parable about a rich man who had a steward who was not managing the rich man's possessions in his best interest. The rich man decided to fire him, but before doing that, he asked the steward to give an account of his stewardship. Knowing that he was about to lose his livelihood, the steward decided to endear himself to his master's debtors by reducing how much they owed so that they would be kind to him and invite him into their homes when he became unemployed. His master commended the dishonest manager because he had acted shrewdly. Jesus made the point that unregenerate, worldly people are shrewder in dealing with their own kind than people of the light. In other words, while worldly people use worldly wealth to promote their own interests and security in this world, disciples of Christ ought to use their worldly possessions to promote God's interest and their desire to secure an eternal reward. Jesus used this parable of the unfaithful steward to warn against the love of money because one cannot serve both God and money as the Pharisees believed.[11]

In another parable, Jesus used the concept of a steward whose master put him in charge as an illustration of the manner in which those who profess faith in him should live between the time he left the earth and his return. A faithful and wise steward is the one whom the master will return to find doing what the master expects, whereas the unfaithful steward does what he or she pleases and incurs the master's displeasure and punishment upon his return.[12]

The Disciple of Christ as a Steward of God

A disciple, follower, or imitator of Christ—that is, a Christian—recognizes that God is the creator of the universe and all living things, including humankind.[13] The psalmist acknowledged that the heavens and

---

11. Luke 16:1–14. See Johnson, *Gospel of Luke*, 245–48, commenting that the manager is praised for having the qualities of a manager in responding to a crisis appropriately to his circumstances. It is this quality of responsiveness rather than the possible morality of the action that is the object of praise. As the manager used possessions to secure a place for himself, so should the disciples use almsgiving to secure a place with God, as the worship of possessions and a clinging to them means separation from God.

12. Luke 12:42–48.

13. Gen 1; 2:1.

the earth belong to the Lord as well as everything and everyone in it.[14] Every creature on earth belongs to God—including birds, cattle, and all the animals.[15] All the mineral and natural wealth—the silver, gold, oil, gas, diamonds, you name it, they all belong to the God of creation.[16] And beyond all that, Christians recognize that whether they live or die, they themselves belong to the Lord.[17]

Because God owns all things, whatever a human being possesses, whether money, material possessions, ability, talent, gifts, or time, is given to him or her by God the creator in stewardship, whether the person acknowledges God or not. Christians acknowledge that God is their source and that it is God who meets their every need. Christians also acknowledge that God is the source of every good gift they have, including the gift of salvation. Christians will all give an account of themselves to God one day at the judgment seat of Christ.[18]

The Gospel writers Matthew and Luke recount two parables of Jesus to illustrate the fact that Christians are God's stewards and are accountable for their stewardship.

The first is the parable of the talents, a parable about the kingdom of heaven recounted by Matthew. In this parable, a man who was about to go on a journey called three servants and entrusted them with some of his property or goods. He gave five talents of money to the first servant, two talents to the second, and one talent to the third servant. He gave these talents to them based on his knowledge of their ability.[19]

A talent, *talanton* in Greek, was a talent in weight and represented a sum of money in silver or gold in the Old Testament. If it was a silver talent, it was worth 3,000 shekels. If it was gold talent, it was worth 10,000 shekels.[20] In Old Testament times, every man over twenty years old in Israel was to give an offering of half of the sanctuary shekel (the half-shekel) to the Lord to be used in the service of the tabernacle of meeting.[21] In the New Testament, the talent was not a weight of silver,

---

14. Pss 24:1; 89:11.
15. Ps 50:10–12.
16. Hag 2:8.
17. Rom 14:8.
18. Rom 14:10, 12. Because Christians will all be judged by God, they are not to judge one another.
19. Matt 25:14–15. The NRSV uses slave instead of servant.
20. Smith, *Smith's Bible Dictionary*, 739.
21. Exod 30:13.

but a unit of money used by the Romans. It was worth 6,000 denarii or drachmas.[22] One denarius or drachma was a day's wages for a laborer.[23] A talent was, therefore, about sixteen-and-a-half years of wages. This means that the first servant received 30,000 denarii or drachmas (worth eighty-two years of wages), the second received 12,000 (worth thirty-three years of wages), and the third received 6,000 (worth sixteen-and-a-half years of wages). Jesus's point here is that these servants or stewards were entrusted with significant resources to put to work on their master's behalf.

The first servant put the master's money to work and earned a 100 percent return, generating five more talents. He presented his master with ten talents. The second servant also put his master's money to work and earned a 100 percent return, generating two more talents. He presented the master with four talents. However, the third servant did not put his talent to work for the master. He buried it in the ground.

When the master returned from his journey, he asked them to account for the money he had entrusted to them. Calling the first two servants good and faithful servants, he commended them for doubling their talents and invited them to enter into the joy of their lord or share their lord's happiness. Although they had different amounts, they had exhibited the same level of industriousness, productivity, and faithfulness.

When the third servant came to settle his accounts, he charged the master with being a hard man who takes what doesn't belong to him. He said the master reaped or harvested where he had not sown and gathered where he had not scattered seed. He said this made him afraid, so he hid the talent in the ground. He presented the master with his talent. The master condemned the servant, calling him wicked and lazy, and reasoning that the servant's view of him was all the more reason why he should have known that it would be unacceptable to the master to just present him with the talent he had entrusted to the servant. The master said that the servant could at least have deposited the talent in the bank so that it would have earned interest for the master. The master ordered the talent to be taken from the third servant and given to the first servant who had ten talents.

---

22. See Vine et al., *Vine's Complete Expository Dictionary*, 617 (New Testament Section). The authors note that the English word *talent*, which is used to denote a gift or ability, was influenced by this parable. Also, see Strong's Reference Number 5007, defining *talanton* as a talent, a sum of money.

23. Matt 20:2. The KJV translates it as a penny.

BEING A GOOD STEWARD

The master then said that the one who has will be given more and will have an abundance. But the one who does not have, even what they have will be taken from them.[24] Jesus was saying that disciples or servants of the Lord are stewards who will one day account for all that has been entrusted to them, whether time, gifts, abilities (talent), or financial resources (treasure). And their heavenly reward and position will depend on how faithful they have been as God's stewards on earth. They will be given greater responsibilities and enjoy fellowship with Jesus Christ in his kingdom.

But the parable did not stop there. The master directed that the worthless servant be thrown into the outer darkness where there will be weeping and gnashing of teeth.[25] This servant had shown contempt for his master. He did not use what his master entrusted to him in the service of his master or in the best interests of his master. He did with it as he pleased and in a spirit that showed that he despised his master. Because God as creator entrusts every human being with time, talent, and resources while on earth, everyone will be held accountable for what was entrusted to him or her at the judgment.

The apostle Paul reminded the believers in Rome that each believer will give an account of himself or herself at the judgment seat of Christ.[26] The writer of Hebrews also reminded his audience that every human being has an appointment with death, after which comes the day of judgment.[27] The unfaithful servant in the parable was thrown outside into the darkness where there was weeping and gnashing of teeth.[28] Based

---

24. Matt 25:16–29. See Adeyemo, *Africa Bible Commentary*, 1163–64, commenting that this parable focuses on the second coming of Christ and the Lord's calling on every one of his disciples to show how well each one has used his or her gifts. God has richly endowed his people with gifts that are not to be ignored or treated as ornaments for display. Instead, they must be seen as investments to be used to gain glory for the master. God will call us to account at some time. Where gifts have been used profitably, more will be added in abundance. Where there has been fruitlessness, the original investment will be lost or taken away.

25. Matt 25:30. See Harrington, *Gospel of Matthew*, 353–55, noting that the outer darkness alludes to the condemnation at the last judgment, and so is the opposite of "enter into the joy of your master." Weeping and gnashing of teeth describes the frustration of those excluded from the master's joy.

26. Rom 14:10–12.

27. Heb 9:27.

28. Jesus talked quite a bit about that place of eternal separation from God where there will be weeping and gnashing of teeth. See Matt 8:12; 13:42; 22:13; 24:51; 25:30; and Luke 13:28.

on what Jesus said elsewhere about weeping and gnashing of teeth in a place of eternal separation from God, did this servant lose more than just rewards? Did he lose his place in the kingdom of God?[29] Since there is no darkness in heaven or the new Jerusalem where God's glory is its light and the Lamb its lamp,[30] does the outer darkness into which he was thrown represent eternal separation from God?

The second parable Jesus told to illustrate the principle of stewardship and accountability to God is one that Luke recounts in the parable of the minas or pounds.[31] Jesus told this parable while in the house of Zacchaeus, a tax collector who came to have faith in God. He told it because he was near Jerusalem and people thought the kingdom of God was going to suddenly appear. Many had mistaken his kingdom for a political kingdom and were hoping he would overthrow Roman rule and institute his kingdom in an independent Israel.

In this parable, a nobleman went away to a far country to receive royal power or to be made king and then to return. He called ten of his servants, gave them each one pound or one mina, and instructed them to put the money to work until he returned. A mina was worth much less than a talent. A mina was fifty shekels whereas a talent was 3,000 shekels. One talent was worth sixty minas. The parable notes that his subjects hated him and sent a delegation after him to say that they did not want him to be their king. He was nonetheless made king, and he returned home. He asked the servants to whom he had entrusted the minas to give an account of their stewardship.

The first servant to give an account had earned ten more minas and the second had earned five more. The master commended them both as good servants and gave them more responsibility. He rewarded the first with oversight of ten cities and the second with oversight of five. Another servant stepped up and presented the master with the mina he had been

---

29. Matt 8:12; 13:42; 22:13; 24:51; Luke 12:28.

30. Rev 21:23.

31. Luke 19:11–26. The NRSV uses *pounds* instead of *minas*. The NRSV uses *slave* instead of *servant*. See Adeyemo, *Africa Bible Commentary*, 1242, commenting that this parable is saying that God has given justified sinners the possibility of earning interest or bearing fruit. Each believer must recognize that they are expected to serve the cause of God in Jesus Christ. Those who faithfully and diligently serve God's cause will be richly rewarded. Those who have been faithful and diligent to a lesser degree will also be rewarded, but in smaller measure. However, a justified sinner who has neglected to do any good works will be rebuked and disgraced. But see a different interpretation by Luke Timothy Johnson in a subsequent footnote.

given. He said he had kept it in a handkerchief this whole time because he was afraid of the master, whom he called a hard man who takes out what he did not put in and reaps what he did not sow. The master called him a wicked servant and said his own words had condemned him. If he felt his master was a hard man who took out what he didn't put in, or who reaped what he didn't sow, then why didn't he at least put the master's money in the bank so that it could have earned interest for the master? The master ordered the mina to be taken away from that servant and given to the one who had earned ten more. Unlike in the parable of the talents, the master did not call the servant worthless or command that he be thrown into the outer darkness. Perhaps this servant had not repudiated his master to the point of becoming an apostate, but the servant in the parable of the talents had?

As with the parable of the talents, Jesus said that those who have will be given more, and those who do not have, even what they have will be taken away, meaning that disciples of the Lord are stewards who will one day account for all that has been entrusted to them. Their heavenly reward or position will depend on how faithful they have been as God's stewards on earth. Those who have been faithful will be given greater responsibilities. Those who have not been as faithful will receive less in terms of position and responsibility.

This parable ends by recounting what happened to the subjects who did not want the nobleman to be made king. The nobleman called them his enemies and instructed that they be killed.[32] Does this denote punishment upon judgment at the end of the age?[33] Jesus will return as King of kings[34] at the end of the age to hold disciples accountable for everything he entrusted to them and offer rewards at the judgment seat of Christ.

---

32. Luke 19:27.

33. See Johnson, *Gospel of Luke*, 298, noting that the usual interpretation of this parable takes it as an allegory to be understood within the framework of early Christian ideas about the end time. However, he argues that the parable is Luke's commentary on the narrative and that the parable does not refer to the end time, but to the events unfolding in Luke's own story. The nobleman is Jesus. The citizens who didn't want to have him as their ruler are the Jewish leaders who rejected him, persecuted his disciples, and found themselves cut off from the people. The servants whose faithful use of possessions is rewarded are the twelve disciples who will exercise power through the Holy Spirit as seen in Acts.

34. Rev 17:14; 19:16.

And those who reject and oppose him will be condemned on their day of judgment at the white throne of judgment.[35]

Areas of Christian Stewardship

Of what are disciples, followers, or imitators of Christ stewards? What has God entrusted to believers that he expects them to account for when their stewardship is over?[36]

Time

Every human being has an amount of time allotted to them by God according to his sovereign will. That time begins to wind down from the moment one is born. Everyone has an expiration date, if you will. The author of Hebrews said it is appointed unto people once to die.[37] In other words, everyone has an appointment with death. Everyone ends up dying, sooner or later. And that will continue to be the case until the world as we know it comes to an end. The crucial question is: how does one use one's allotted time while here on earth? Does one use it to try to gain the whole world? Does one use it in pursuit of worldly knowledge, possessions, power, or pleasure? Does one use it to ride rough shod over others? Does one use it as if one is not accountable, whether here or in eternity,

---

35. Rev 20:11–15. See Blount, *Revelation*, 373–74, commenting on the second resurrection (the first resurrection is before the millennial rule and is of martyrs killed for their witness for Christ) where everybody, both righteous and unrighteous, is raised for judgment after the millennial rule of Christ at the white throne of judgment, and books are opened. Proper works-behavior is rewarded, while improper works-behavior as recorded in a book is punished. However, there is another book, the Book of Life, in which God has graciously written names from creation. Everyone whose name is written in this book will have an eschatological relationship with God. But the final eschatological decision rests with God. Those whose names are not found in the Book of Life are thrown into the lake of fire with the beast (antichrist), false prophet, dragon (Satan), death, and Hades. See also Yong, *Revelation*, 238–39, where he comments that our final destination depends on how we have behaved and what allegiances we have embraced. We "work" and "act out" our way to wherever we are headed.

36. See Evans, *Stewardship*, discussing many aspects of stewardship such as personal, ecological, and financial stewardship, and offering a biblical and theological foundation for giving. See also Amerson, *Stewardship in African-American Churches*, a practical and theological study of stewardship in the context of the African American tradition.

37. Heb 9:27.

for how one uses one's time? Or does one use it as if one is a steward of one's allotted time?

Moses wrote about the brevity of human life in a psalm in which he compared humans to the grass that springs up anew in the morning but dries up and withers by evening. Moses measured the human lifespan as consisting of seventy years, eighty if one happens to be strong or healthy. Even if one lives to be eighty, Moses said those years pass quickly and one flies away or dies. Because of the brevity of life, Moses prayed that God would teach us to number our days aright, that we may gain a heart of wisdom.[38]

Moses is not the only one in the Bible who recognized the brevity of life. David did too. He acknowledged that his life is but a breath and asked to be shown the number of his days and how fleeting his life was. He compared life to a shadow and lamented the fact that someone else ends up with all the riches one heaps up in one's lifetime.[39] David compared the life of a human to dust, grass, and a field flower that flourishes at one moment but disappears when blown away by the wind.[40]

King Solomon also realized the meaninglessness of spending his time and energy trying to find fulfillment and security in worldly knowledge, pleasure, and riches. He eventually acknowledged that one's time on earth is best used fearing God and keeping his commandments. That requires recognizing that one is a steward of the time one has on earth.[41]

As stewards of their time on earth, Christians must not spend their time doing their own thing or doing as they please, as if their time belongs to them. They must see themselves as ambassadors who represent the kingdom of God and determine that whatever they do with the time God has given them must be done as unto the Lord[42] and for his glory.[43] Jesus said that he and his disciples were obligated to do the works of the one who sent him while it was still day because night comes when no one can work.[44] The apostle Paul said the most important thing to him

---

38. Ps 90:5–6, 10, 12.
39. Ps 39:4–6, 11.
40. Ps 103:15–16.
41. Eccl 1:3, 17–18; 2; 5:10, 15; 12:13.
42. Col 3:23.
43. 1 Cor 10:31.
44. John 9:4. See Moloney, *Gospel of John*, 291–92, interpreting this to mean that Jesus was including his disciples in his work. The darkness of night brings the day to an end when Jesus is absent from the human story. In this situation, no one is able to make

was not his life. It was to complete the task or assignment the Lord had given him to testify to the gospel of God's grace.[45] Disciples, followers, or imitators of Jesus must also prayerfully discover their divine purpose and calling and use the time they have been allotted on earth primarily to fulfill that purpose and calling, knowing that their time on earth will eventually run out and they will have to give an account of their use of that time to God.[46]

Talent (Gifts and Abilities)

Everyone is endowed with talent of some kind—gifts and abilities that make them unique. Whatever one's gifts or talents are, if one is a disciple, follower, or imitator of Christ, one must be a good steward of those gifts and use them for the glory of God by being willing to openly acknowledge that God is the source of one's gifts and abilities and by using them for God's glory.[47]

Good stewardship includes a proper stewarding of the returns and rewards that come with one's gifts and talents, be they possessions or money. But there are also spiritual gifts that God gives to believers for the edification of the church. God imparts these gifts as he sees fit.

Paul said he did not want the Corinthians to be ignorant of spiritual gifts.[48] The church in Corinth had written to Paul seeking direction on a number of issues including spiritual gifts and the proper use of these gifts in corporate worship. He explained that there are different kinds of manifestations of the Spirit that are given to individual believers by the Holy Spirit for the common good as the Holy Spirit determines or wills.[49] And believers must also eagerly desire spiritual gifts that may be used for the benefit of the church in corporate worship.[50]

God known. However, Jesus associates the disciples with his work so that this will not happen. The presence of the light of the world will not be limited to the historical life of Jesus; it will continue in the presence of Jesus in his associates, the disciples.

45. Acts 20:24.

46. In 1 Cor 3:8, the apostle Paul said each one will be rewarded for their labor for the Lord.

47. See Exod 35:30–35 and 36:1–2, where gifted artisans like Bezalel and Oholiab used their acknowledged God-given gifts to build the tabernacle of worship for the Israelites in the wilderness.

48. 1 Cor 12:1.

49. 1 Cor 12:7, 11.

50. 1 Cor 12:31; 14:1.

In addition to the manifestations of the gifts of the Spirit, Paul also taught about grace gifts and ministry gifts in which believers operate or function beyond the episodic manifestations of spiritual gifts in a church service or gathering of the body of Christ.

Regarding grace gifts, Paul told the church in Rome that every believer has been given a measure of faith by God and must use their different gifts, extended to them through God's grace, in exercise of that faith. The Greek word for gift in this context is *charisma*, meaning a gift of grace.[51] Believers with the gift of prophesying must use it in proportion to their faith. Those with a gift to serve, teach, or encourage must be faithful stewards of those gifts by exercising them. Those who have a gift to give toward the needs of others must do so generously. Those with a gift of leadership are to lead diligently and those with a gift of showing mercy to others must do so cheerfully.[52] These gifts represent abilities given to individual believers for the good of the congregation.

Regarding ministry gifts, Paul mentioned five ministry gifts in his Letter to the Ephesians[53] and seven ministry gifts in his first Letter to the Corinthians.[54] Both lists included gifts to serve as an apostle, prophet, or teacher. The list to the Ephesians added gifts to be an evangelist or pastor. The list to the Corinthians added gifts of healing, a special ability to help others, gifts of administration, and the gift to minister publicly in different kinds of tongues. And he made it clear that not all believers are given these ministry gifts to edify the body of Christ publicly.[55] These gifts are given by Christ to spiritual leaders in the church to prepare believers for service so that the church body may be strengthened until believers are united in the faith and in the knowledge of Christ, maturing in the process, becoming more like Christ, and no longer gullible to false teaching. Through the use of these ministry gifts, believers will come to the point where they can speak the truth in love and grow in Christlikeness in every way.[56]

---

51. See *"Charisma"* in Vine et al., *Vine's Complete Expository Dictionary*, 264 (New Testament Section). *Charis* in Greek means grace.

52. Rom 12:3–8.

53. Eph 4:11.

54. 1 Cor 12:28.

55. 1 Cor 12:29–30. Although not all believers have the gift to bring a message in tongues to a congregation, every believer can receive the baptism of the Holy Spirit and the manifestation of speaking in another tongue as the disciples in Jerusalem, Paul, the Samaritans, the Ephesian disciples, and Cornelius's household did.

56. Eph 4:12–15. See Adeyemo, *Africa Bible Commentary*, 1433, commenting that

As stewards of God, whatever talents, gifts, or abilities a disciple, follower, or imitator of Christ has, whether spiritual or nonspiritual, must be used, not just to make a living, attract attention, or gain fame and notoriety, but for the glory of God.

Treasure (Money/Finances)

A disciple, follower, or imitator of Christ must be a good steward of his or her money or finances. One cannot live without money. Money is necessary to acquire basic necessities—food, shelter, and clothing. In our modern world, the list of necessities has grown. One needs reliable transportation to get around. One needs good healthcare to stay healthy. Post-secondary education of some kind has become key to earning a family-sustaining wage. All of these things require money. For most, working for a living is a key preoccupation. Some make enough to be able to save. Others do not. Some are able to invest as they earn income. Others are fortunate to benefit from transfers of wealth from previous generations that they are able to build on. However, regardless of one's financial status, as the apostle Paul warned Timothy, getting rich should not be the goal or life's ambition of a Christian. Paul warned that people who want to get rich fall into temptation and a trap and into many foolish and harmful desires that plunge them into ruin and destruction because the love of money is a root of all kinds of evil.[57] In order to avoid the love of money and making the accumulation of wealth one's life's ambition, one must become a good steward of one's treasure or money.

Jesus warned against greed and made it clear that one's life is not measured by the abundance of one's possessions. He told a parable about a rich man who was a poor steward of his money. He had a successful farming operation that yielded a bountiful crop. He decided to tear down his barns and build bigger ones to store his grain and goods. He thought he would be secure for years. Now he could just take life easy, eat, drink, and be merry. But God called him a fool and told him that he would die the very night he thought these things to himself. Christ said that this

---

spiritual gifts are not given for the benefit of church leaders but are intended to be used to help the church to grow physically and spiritually until it reaches maturity. See also Esau D. McCaulley, "Letter to the Ephesians," in McCaulley et al., *New Testament in Color*, 427, where he comments that as these gifts expand the church over the world, the world will be bursting with the presence of God.

57. 1 Tim 6:8–10.

is the way it will be for those who store up things for themselves but are not rich toward God.[58] To be rich toward God is to be a good steward because one acknowledges that God is one's source, and one stewards one's finances in a way that is pleasing to him. The best way to do that is to allow oneself to be used by God as a channel of blessing to the work of his kingdom and to others through one's giving.

Abraham gives us a good example of giving as unto the Lord. Abraham depended on God and looked to God as his source. This became evident in a dramatic incident involving Abraham's nephew Lot. The two had separated earlier. Lot was living near Sodom while Abraham lived in Canaan.[59]

The kings of Sodom and Gomorrah and three other kings with whom they were allied had been subject to Kedorlaomer, king of Elam, for a dozen years. They rebelled in the thirteenth year, and the following year, Kedorlaomer organized a coalition of four kings and came and fought against the coalition of five kings led by the kings of Sodom and Gomorrah. Kedorlaomer's coalition prevailed and carried off food, possessions, and captives from Sodom and Gomorrah, including Lot, his family, and his possessions. When as escapee came and informed Abraham of this, he marshaled 318 men in his household who had been trained to fight, along with three Amorite brothers who were allied with him and launched a night raid against Kedorlaomer and his allies. Abraham and his men defeated Kedorlaomer and his allies and recovered Lot and his family, as well as all the other captives and their possessions.[60]

Melchizedek, the king of Salem, and a priest of God, came out to meet Abraham and blessed him. Abraham, acknowledging that it was God who had given him this victory, gave one-tenth,[61] or a tithe, of everything he had recovered to Melchizedek. The Greek word for tithe, *dekatos*, means a tenth.[62]

The king of Sodom offered to let Abraham have all the goods of the kings he had defeated, but Abraham refused. He asked that the Amorite

---

58. Luke 12:15–21.

59. Gen 13:11–13.

60. Gen 14:1–16. The three Amorite brothers who teamed up with Abraham were Mamre, Eshcol, and Aner.

61. Gen 14:20. The NIV simply says tenth while the NKJV says tithe.

62. See Vine et al., *Vine's Complete Expository Dictionary*, 623, 634 (New Testament Section). See also Strong's Reference Number 1182, defining *dekatos* as tenth. *Dekatos* is an adjective from *deka*, meaning ten.

brothers who went with him be given their share. Other than that, and the food that his men had eaten, Abraham wanted nothing from the king of Sodom. He said he had made an oath to God that he would take nothing from the king of Sodom, lest the king of Sodom claim credit for Abraham's wealth.[63] Abraham knew God was his source and wanted everyone else to know that too. His giving of a tenth or a tithe of everything he had recovered to Melchizedek, described as priest of God Most High, was an act of worship and an acknowledgment that he was a steward of everything God had put in his hands. Abraham wanted God to receive the glory as his provider.

Abraham's giving of a tenth of the goods he had recovered from Kedorlaomer and his allies is the first mention in the Bible of the concept of the tithe. Other than this incident, we have no more information about whether this was a regular practice in Abraham's life with respect to his regular income.

The second time the tithe is mentioned in the Bible had to do with Abraham's grandson Jacob. Jacob had tricked his father Isaac into giving him the blessing Isaac meant to give to Esau, his firstborn son. Fearful that his brother would kill him once Isaac passed away, Rebekah, his mother, sent Jacob to live with her brother Laban in Haran under the guise of sending him to get himself a wife from among Laban's daughters.

As he traveled to Haran, Jacob stopped at dusk to lie down for the night. He had a dream in which God promised to take care of him and give him the land of Canaan, just as he had promised Abraham and Isaac. Recognizing that God had visited him, Jacob built an altar to God there the next morning. Jacob had not really known the Lord up until this point. He did not have a personal relationship with God. When he referred to the Lord earlier in his dialogue with Isaac as he pretended to be Esau, Jacob referred to the Lord as "the Lord your God."[64] In other words, the Lord was Isaac's God, not his God. But now that Jacob had had a personal encounter with the Lord and God had promised to take care of him and bring him back to Canaan to possess it, Jacob made a vow in which he promised to make the Lord his own God if God would indeed take care of him and bring him safely back to Canaan. Moreover, he promised to acknowledge God as his source by giving God a tenth of

---

63. Gen 14:17–24.
64. Gen 27:20.

everything God would give him. In other words, Jacob was willing to be God's steward—one who recognizes that all he has comes from God.[65]

More than five hundred years later, when the Israelites were about to settle into Canaan after being freed from slavery in Egypt, God gave them the law of the tithe.

God made it clear to the Israelites that a tithe of everything from the land, whether grain from the soil, or fruit from the trees, belonged to him. So was every tenth animal in a herd or flock. The tithe was considered holy. If anyone kept their tithe, they had to add a fifth of its value to the tithe when they returned it.[66]

At the end of every third year after settling in Canaan, which was considered the year of the tithe, the Israelites were to bring all the tithes of that year's produce to the Levites to store in storehouses in their towns and some of it in storerooms in the temple so that the Levites—who, unlike the other tribes, were not given an allotment of land or inheritance—aliens or strangers (immigrants), orphans, and widows living in their towns would be provided for. In Nehemiah's time, he directed that when the Levites collected the tithes in their towns, they were to bring a tenth of what they had received to the house of God and the storerooms of the treasury, and that they were to do so in the company of a priest descended from Aaron.[67] God said that he would bless all the work of their hands if they obeyed the law of the tithe.[68] These places where the tithes of produce were stored are not unlike the food banks of our day.

In the two years preceding the year of the tithe, the Israelites were to set aside a tenth of what their fields had produced—grain, oil, and wine, as well as the firstborn of their herds and flocks—and they were to eat it in the presence of the Lord their God in the place where God would designate as the place of corporate worship.[69] They were to do this so that

---

65. Gen 28:10–22.

66. Lev 27:30–33.

67. Neh 10:35–39; 13:4–13. See Adeyemo, *Africa Bible Commentary*, 555, commenting that the people promised to pay a tithe of their crops to the Levites and the Levites, in turn, were obliged to give a tithe of the tithe as laid down by the law. The people made a firm commitment not to abandon God's house, that is, the temple.

68. Deut 14:28–29; Neh 10:35–39; 13:4–13. See Adeyemo, *Africa Bible Commentary*, 230, commenting that the tithe should be treated as a guiding principle, not treated legalistically and seen as a rule binding every believer and as a requirement for satisfying the law, because the NT principle is to give in proportion to how God has blessed us.

69. During the prophet Samuel's time, Shiloh was the place of worship (1 Sam 1:3). Jerusalem later became the place of worship after Solomon built the temple there (1 Kgs 6).

they would learn to revere the Lord always. This reverence would come from their acknowledgment that it was the Lord who had blessed them. If they lived too far from the place of corporate worship to take their tithes with them to eat in the presence of the Lord, they were to exchange the tithe for silver, take the silver to the place of worship, buy meat, wine, or anything they wanted, and eat it with their household in God's presence with rejoicing.[70]

It was not only the tithe of their produce and the firstborn of their animals that they were to bring to the place of worship to eat before the Lord's presence, but they were also to bring their sacrifices, burnt offerings, heave offerings, vowed offerings, choice offerings, and free will offerings. They and their households were to eat with rejoicing at the place of worship in acknowledgment of God's blessing. Although they could eat regular meat or food in their towns, they were not to eat the tithe of their produce and firstborn animals in their own towns. They were to eat it only in the place designated for corporate worship.[71]

In the two years preceding the year of the tithe, the Israelites were instructed not to neglect the Levites who got no allotment of land or inheritance when the Israelites settled in Canaan. The Israelites were to share their blessings with them regardless of whether it was the year of the tithe or not.[72]

Beyond the giving of tithes, in recognition of the fact that their entire lives were lived as stewards of God, there were also a number of offerings that the Israelites had to bring to the Lord through the priests if they fell short of God's requirements. There were other offerings that, although not required, were brought by the Israelites as an act of their own free will. These included guilt offerings, burnt offerings, and grain offerings.

God told Aaron, the high priest, that he was putting him in charge of the offerings that the Israelites presented to God. God told Aaron that, other than offerings that were meant for the fire, he was giving him and his sons the grain, sin, or guilt offerings as their portion and regular share. He also gave Aaron all the first fruits of their grain and olive harvests and their new wine. He gave Aaron and his household the set-asides from wave offerings brought by the Israelites.[73] He also told Aaron that because the Levites did not receive an allotment or inheritance of land as the other

70. Deut 14:22–26.
71. Deut 12:6–7, 11–14, 17–18.
72. Deut 12:19; 14:27.
73. Num 18:8–13.

tribes did, he (God) himself was their inheritance, and he was also giving them as their inheritance the tithes that the Israelites offered to God.[74] God then told Moses to tell the Levites to give a tenth or a tithe of the tithes that they received as an offering to the Lord. They were to present their tithes to Aaron. Moses was also to tell the Levites that the tithes they enjoyed after giving a tenth of it to Aaron represented their wages for their work in the tent of meeting, the place of corporate worship.[75]

The giving of tithes for the benefit of the poor and Levites every third year was an act of obedience to God's command and an acknowledgment on the part of the Israelites that they were stewards of all that they possessed; that it was the Lord who had blessed them. Indeed, before the Israelites settled in Canaan, Moses exhorted them to remember the Lord once they settled there, because he was the one who gave them the power to get wealth so that they would know that God was confirming the covenant he had made with Abraham to bless him and his descendants.[76]

However, after the Israelites settled in Canaan, there were times in their history when they did not obey the Lord. Among other transgressions, they did not uphold justice and righteousness and the giving of tithes. And many who gave tithes gave them in a manner that was legalistic and not pleasing to God. The prophet Amos warned the Israelites about oppressing the poor even though they were still bringing their tithes every third year, in addition to thank offerings and freewill offerings.[77] During his earthly ministry, the Lord Jesus also chastised the Pharisees and the teachers of the law for their hypocrisy, which included tithing legalistically. They even gave a tithe of the herbs and spices they grew—mint, dill, and cumin—yet they neglected the more important matters of the law, things like justice, mercy, and faithfulness. Jesus said they should have observed these more important things in addition to observing the law of the tithe.[78]

There came a time in their history when the Israelites neglected to bring their tithes and offerings as God commanded them to do. Tithes were to be stored in their towns for the benefit of the poor and the Levites and some of it brought to the temple. Offerings were to be brought to the place of corporate worship to offer to the Lord. And as we already saw,

74. Num 18:20–21, 24.
75. Num 18:25–28, 31.
76. Deut 8:18. The NIV speaks of the ability to produce wealth.
77. Amos 4:4–5.
78. Matt 23:23; Luke 11:42.

THE CHRISTIAN AS IMITATOR OF CHRIST

the priests also received portions of certain offerings as part of their food supply.

God used Malachi, the last prophet of the Old Testament, to rebuke the Israelites and to let them know that their failure to bring their tithes and offerings to honor God amounted to robbing him. That was because the tithe belonged to the Lord and was considered holy.[79] Some may have been bringing less than a tenth of their produce and animals that God commanded them to store in the storehouses in their towns every third year for the benefit of the poor and the Levites.[80] Malachi exhorted them to bring the full tithe to the storehouse so that there would be food in God's house.[81]

The tithe was the nation's social safety net. It was for the benefit of the poor—orphans, widows, and immigrants—and for the upkeep of the Levites who did not own land and who were to spend their time ministering to the Lord and offering sacrifices to the Lord on behalf of the people. Not bringing their tithes to the storehouses in their towns and the storerooms in the temple meant the poor were being deprived of the food that they needed, and the Levites were being deprived of their livelihood and inheritance. Not bringing their offerings to the place of worship meant they were undermining the sacrificial system and not observing their covenant responsibilities or acknowledging God's blessings. As a result, Malachi told them that the whole nation was under a curse.[82]

As an agrarian society that depended on farming crops and raising animals, the Israelites needed rain for their crops to grow and for the animals to have pastures to graze. Droughts spelled disaster, including famine. So did pests like locusts. God, through the prophet Malachi, challenged the Israelites to put him to the test by obeying his command to bring their tithes to the storehouse and their offerings to the place of worship. If they did, he would be faithful to open up the windows of heaven and pour down an overflowing blessing. They would have the

---

79. Lev 27:30.

80. Deut 14:28–29.

81. Mal 3:8–9. See Adeyemo, *Africa Bible Commentary*, 1097, commenting that tithes and offerings provided practical support that enabled the priests and Levites to concentrate on serving God, and supplied food for those in need, such as orphans, widows, and aliens. Spiritually, they represented an acknowledgment that all we possess belongs to God. The reference to God's house was a reference to the place where tithes were stored. But could God's house also mean the house of Israel (all Israel), since not only priests and Levites, but the poor and immigrants also benefitted?

82. Mal 3:9.

rain they needed for their crops and pastures. Their crops would be so abundant that their barns would not have enough room to store them. God also promised to prevent locusts from destroying their crops and to protect their vines from failing to produce fruit.[83]

Malachi prophesied four hundred years before Jesus Christ appeared on the scene. The church had not yet been born. However, in the church age, the most extensive New Testament teaching on giving as stewards of God is found in the apostle Paul's second Epistle to the Corinthians.

Paul used the needs of the poor saints in Judea to urge the Corinthians to excel in the grace of giving willingly to help support them. He told the Corinthians about the generosity of the Macedonians, who, although poor themselves, had given generously to help their fellow Christians in Judea. The Corinthians had also expressed a desire to assist in this endeavor while Titus was visiting them. Paul now urged them to follow through with the commitment they made. He was going to send Titus back to Corinth along with two other fellow workers so that there would be accountability for the gift and no room for criticism with respect to the administration of the Corinthians' gift. Paul urged the Corinthians to follow through with their gift to show their love so that the churches these brothers represented would see it and appreciate why Paul was so proud of them.[84] Paul said he would send these brothers ahead of time to help them finish whatever arrangements they needed to make to finalize their gift.[85]

Paul shared a number of key principles about Christian giving in this Letter. First of all, Christians must give themselves to God as the Macedonians did, for it is that relationship of total surrender to God that grounds the Christian's giving.[86] In other words, giving must flow out of intimate relationship with God. Giving is an acknowledgment that the Christian is God's steward. It must be done out of love for God.

---

83. Mal 3:10–11. The NIV refers to the floodgates of heaven. The NIV refers to pests while the NKJV refers to the devourer. See Adeyemo, *Africa Bible Commentary*, 1097, commenting that God promised to flood them with blessings if they obey him. Their land, which evidently had been suffering from drought, will be revitalized. Pestilences and crop failures will cease. He will make their work fruitful and keep away locusts. Their land will be a delight to all who see it.

84. 2 Cor 8.

85. 2 Cor 9:5.

86. 2 Cor 8:5.

THE CHRISTIAN AS IMITATOR OF CHRIST

Paul also taught that giving must be done willingly from the heart, not reluctantly or under compulsion. In other words, one must not give because one feels compelled or pressured to do so. The Macedonians gave willingly to help their fellow Christians in need in Judea. The Corinthians had indicated a willingness to give to this cause too. Now Paul was urging them to match their willingness with action by completing what they had committed to do.[87]

Giving must also be in proportion to what one has or the measure of one's financial blessing. In other words, Christians must give as they are able. Paul told the Corinthians that as long as giving is proportionate to what one has, not what one does not have, the gift is acceptable to God.[88] The Macedonians gave as they were able and, by Paul's estimation, they even gave beyond their ability. Even though they were poor, they literally pleaded with Paul to let them help the saints in Judea. Their giving was sacrificial given their poverty, to the point that they exceeded Paul's expectations.[89]

Giving must also be cheerful. Paul told the Corinthians that God loves a cheerful giver. The Greek word used here is *hilaros*, signifying a joyousness and readiness of mind that prompts one's giving.[90] In other words one must not be glum or sour when one gives.

Giving must be generous. Christians must, therefore, give generously. Paul asked the Corinthians to remember that the principle of sowing and reaping applies to giving. The one who sows sparingly will also reap sparingly, and the one who sows generously will also reap generously.[91] This generosity is not just a reference to the amount given, but to one's motives and the state of one's heart when one gives. Jesus did teach that the measure one uses when one gives is the same one that will be measured back to the giver.[92]

Giving must be sacrificial. The sacrificial nature of one's giving makes it even more meaningful to God. This is seen in a scene that unfolded as Jesus was teaching in the temple toward the end of his ministry. He observed the rich putting their gifts or offerings into the temple

---

87. 2 Cor 8:11.

88. 2 Cor 8:12.

89. 2 Cor 8:3–5.

90. See Vine et al., *Vine's Complete Expository Dictionary*, 98 (New Testament Section). See also Strong's Reference Number 2431, defining *hilaros* as joyous or cheerful.

91. 2 Cor 9:6–7, 13.

92. Matt 7:2; Luke 6:38.

treasury. He also observed a widow who put two mites, two small copper coins worth only a fraction of a penny, into the treasury. Jesus said that she had given more than the rich people because they gave out of their wealth while she gave out of her poverty. And what she gave was actually all she had to live on.[93] Her giving was sacrificial while theirs was not.

Giving must also be regular. In preparation for the gift that they were going to give to help the poor believers in Jerusalem, Paul instructed the Corinthians to set aside a sum of money based on whatever extra income they earned on the first day of the week. In this way, they could save it up or store it up to give, and no special collections would be needed. The gift would then be sent to Jerusalem by men approved by the church. Paul gave these same instructions to the other churches in Galatia that were also giving to help their fellow Christians in need in Jerusalem.[94]

Giving must be systematic. In telling the Corinthians that each one of them should lay aside and save whatever extra they earned, Paul was saying that their giving should be systematic, not sporadic, or inconsistent.[95]

Giving must also be loving. It must flow out of love for God and the work of his kingdom on earth. But giving must also flow out of love for those who benefit from our giving, whether it is the poor, orphans, widows, the homeless, or the church. Paul told the Corinthians to prove their love to the men he was sending to pick up the collection for the believers in Jerusalem by following through with the commitment they had made to contribute. Paul thought it was also important for the other churches to see the love of the Corinthians in action through their giving. The churches in Macedonia, in spite of being poor, had stepped up and made a generous contribution to benefit their poor brothers and sisters

---

93. Mark 12:41–44; Luke 21:1–4. The NRSV says two copper coins. The NIV says two mites. See Johnson, *Gospel of Luke*, 316–19, commenting that the widow exemplifies the righteous poor who receive the good news, as shown by her response of disposing of her own possessions. The widow also symbolizes the kingdom of God. Though left all alone in human terms, she is not only alive herself, but she is capable of giving life by sharing "all her living" with others.

94. 1 Cor 16:1.

95. 1 Cor 16:2. The NIV says to set aside a sum of money in keeping with one's income. The NKJV says to lay something aside on the first day of each week.

in Jerusalem.[96] The churches in Galatia were doing the same.[97] So were the churches in Achaia, which were pleased to do so.[98]

Beyond tithes, offerings, and gifts to the temple treasury for the upkeep of the temple, taxes were also collected every year to support the upkeep of the temple. Every Israelite male above the age of twenty was to pay a half shekel whenever a census was taken. It was an offering to the Lord given as a ransom for the life of the one paying it. The money went to support the tent of meeting.[99] It later supported the temple. It was equivalent to two drachmas, or two days' wages. The collectors of this two-drachma temple tax asked Peter if Jesus would pay the tax. Jesus instructed Peter to go fishing with a line. He told him that he would find a four-drachma coin in the mouth of the first fish he would catch. Jesus instructed Peter to use that coin to pay for both of their temple taxes.[100]

Christians do not live under the sacrificial laws of the Old Testament and do not bring sacrifices and offerings to atone for their sins in our day. However, beyond giving God a tithe of income, Christians today may also bring offerings as gifts to the Lord. These may be offerings of thanks for answered prayer or for a blessing for which they are grateful, or they may be offerings to support a specific need in the church such as a building renovation, a new building, a benevolence fund for those in need, an outreach program to the community, or to support the work of missionaries.

Although Christians are not subject to the Old Testament law of the tithe, good Christian stewardship involves an acknowledgment that God owns everything and that everything the believer owns comes from God.[101] Long before the law of the tithe was given to Israel, Jacob had a personal encounter with God in which God reaffirmed his covenant promises to Abraham and Isaac and passed them on to Jacob. God promised to take care of Jacob and Jacob promised to give God a tenth of everything God gave him. Like Jacob, every Christian must come to a point where they are willing to make a similar commitment as stewards of God.

96. 2 Cor 8:1–5.
97. 1 Cor 16:1.
98. Rom 15:26–27.
99. Exod 30:11–16.
100. Matt 17:24–27. In Jesus's day, this tax is believed to have been collected a month before Passover.
101. Ps 24:1.

Since God owns everything, giving is not to enrich God but to enrich us by strengthening our relationship with him and allowing us to be a part of the work of his kingdom on earth.

There are blessings that accompany giving. Paul addressed these in his Letters to the Corinthians and the Philippians. In urging the Corinthians to follow through with their commitment to give to help the poor believers in Jerusalem, Paul assured them that they would experience God's abundant grace such that all their needs would be met, and they, in turn, would be able to abound in doing good. Paul described the gift that they were about to give as seed that they were sowing. He prayed that God would supply them with more seed and multiply or enlarge the results or harvest of the seed that they had sown in righteousness. Paul assured them that God would enrich them in every way so that they could continue to be generous.[102] Also, because they had blessed others with their generosity, the beneficiaries of their generosity would give thanks and praise to God and remember them in their prayers for showing them God's grace.

To the Philippians, who were the only church that sent Paul financial help when he left Macedonia, and who sent him gifts several more times when he was in Thessalonica, Paul gave the assurance that God would supply all of their needs according to his glorious riches in Christ Jesus. He described the gifts they sent him as a fragrant offering to God, a sacrifice that was acceptable and pleasing to God.[103]

As part of his Sermon on the Mount, Jesus Christ himself also addressed the issue of the blessings that come with giving. He taught his disciples to give in the assurance that what they give will return to them in the same measure as they gave.[104] In other words, God himself will measure what we give and use the same measure to give back to us. The blessings we receive from God will be proportionate to or commensurate with how much of a blessing we have been to others.

As he promised to do through Malachi for those who give faithfully, God is also able to rebuke the devourer. In the case of the farmer or rancher, this could mean protecting their crops and pastures from pests.

---

102. 2 Cor 9:8, 10–11.

103. Phil 4:15–19.

104. Luke 6:38. See Johnson, *Gospel of Luke*, 113–14, commenting that it is God who does the giving in response to those who give and forgive. He notes that this is a truly radical notion, that God adopts for the judgment of humans the standard they use in their relations with each other.

For others, it could mean protecting their businesses and incomes from the devil, thieves, and swindlers, or from the negative effects of recessions and economic meltdowns. But even greater are the spiritual and eternal blessings that believers will receive for storing up treasures in heaven as faithful stewards and loyal disciples of God and his Son, Jesus Christ.[105]

Possessions

In the quest for security in an uncertain world, it is easy for one to become preoccupied or even obsessed with the pursuit of worldly possessions or treasures.

In his Sermon on the Mount, Jesus warned his hearers not to focus on hoarding or storing up worldly treasures because one cannot really count on them; they really don't guarantee security. Jesus used the imagery of the destruction that is caused by moths and rust to convey this and pointed out that thieves are also always out to steal what another has accumulated.

Instead of storing up treasures on earth, Jesus counseled his hearers to store up treasures for themselves in heaven where moth and rust do not destroy, and where thieves do not break in and steal. He pointed out that humans lay treasures where their heart is.[106] Those who live for this world lay treasures here on earth. However, those who are heavenly minded lay treasures in heaven. In other words, as good stewards, they use their treasures for God's glory. The apostle Paul made a similar exhortation in his Letter to the Colossians as Christ did in his Sermon on the Mount.[107]

Qualities of a Good Steward

A good steward demonstrates certain qualities. Jesus talked about these qualities in parables.

---

105. Matt 6:20.
106. Matt 6:19–21.
107. Col 3:1–2.

Expectant

A good steward is always expectant, looking for the master to ask for an accounting of his or her stewardship at any time. Jesus said that the world as we know it will come to an end when the gospel has been preached to the whole world as a witness to all the nations.[108] Disciples of Christ must be good stewards who expect their master to return at any moment.

Jesus told his disciples a parable about the expectant steward. He said a steward must always be dressed and ready for service and must keep his or her lamp burning like men waiting for their master to return from a wedding banquet so that they can receive him when he arrives. Jesus told them about the rewards that expectant stewards shall receive— the joy of dining with their master and being served by him. Jesus said it will be good for those servants whose master finds them ready, regardless of when he comes. He warned that disciples of Christ must be ready because he will return at an hour when they do not expect him.[109] Christians ought to be expectant stewards who long for the coming of the Lord Jesus Christ.

Heaven is the home of the disciple. Earth is a temporary assignment. Disciples must not become embroiled in the things of this world to the point that they live as if earth is their home. That is a recipe for being anything but a faithful and expectant steward who lives ever ready for Jesus's return and an eternity with him.

Faithful

Jesus also told his disciples a parable about the steward who is faithful and wise. A faithful and wise steward is one who carries out whatever assignment the master has given him or her while the master is absent. Jesus said the master will put them in charge of all his possessions when he returns. The Greek word used here for faithful is *pistos*, meaning faithful, to be trusted, or reliable, used here to describe servants of the Lord.[110] But

---

108. Matt 24:14.

109. Luke 12:35–40. See Johnson, *Gospel of Luke*, 205–6, commenting that all of Christian existence stands within an expectation—namely, Christ's return. Its fulfillment may be sure, but its timing is unknown. Therefore, the attitude of watchfulness is required, even if the return of the master appears delayed.

110. See Vine et al., *Vine's Complete Expository Dictionary*, 223 (New Testament Section). See also Strong's Reference Number 4103, defining *pistos* as faithful or reliable.

THE CHRISTIAN AS IMITATOR OF CHRIST

if the steward abandons his or her charge and begins to abuse his or her position, the master will surprise that steward by returning unexpectedly. The master will assign that steward a place with the unbelievers or hypocrites, an eternity separated from him where there will be weeping and gnashing of teeth.[111] In this context, the Greek word *apistos*, meaning unbelieving, is used in noun form in Luke's account of this parable to refer to the unfaithful steward as an unbeliever who will be assigned a place with the unbelievers.[112] Because a steward knows better and much is expected of a steward, Jesus said a steward who is found to be unfaithful when Christ returns will suffer greater punishment than someone who was ignorant of God's will. Jesus said much will be demanded of the one who is given much and much more will be asked of the one to whom more has been entrusted.[113]

The apostle Paul told the Corinthians how he and his fellow workers were servants of Christ and stewards of the mysteries of God. He said that it is required of a steward that one be found trustworthy.[114]

Before Jesus left the earth following his resurrection, he gave his disciples of all time the Great Commission. This commission consists of sharing the gospel about his redeeming grace with the whole world so that they might believe and have eternal life, baptizing them in the name of the Father and of the Son and of the Holy Spirit as a public declaration of their faith, and teaching them to obey everything Christ taught.[115] And as stewards of the gospel, just as Paul told the Corinthians, Christians are required to be faithful in carrying out the Great Commission.

Beyond this Great Commission that Jesus gave to disciples of all time, every disciple, follower, or imitator of Christ has a specific purpose, a specific assignment or calling that God has for them to carry out or fulfill on earth. It is up to every Christian to know what their assignment is and to be faithful in carrying out their assignment.

---

111. Matt 24:42–51; Luke 12:42–46.

112. See Vine et al., *Vine's Complete Expository Dictionary*, 223 (New Testament Section). *Apistos* is used in noun form in Luke to mean unbeliever. See also Strong's Reference Number 571, defining *apistos* as unbelieving.

113. Luke 12:47–48. See Johnson, *Gospel of Luke*, 204–6, noting that the household manager or steward was himself a slave just as those he oversaw. Despite his relative authority, he was equally subject to the authority of the master. The image of authority is one of service to others. If leaders do their work well, they will receive the reward of still greater authority. But if they abuse their privilege, they will be cut off completely.

114. 1 Cor 4:1–2. The NKJV says faithful instead of trustworthy.

115. Matt 28:18–20.

The apostle Paul is a fitting example of being faithful in carrying out one's assignment as a Christian. Earlier in his life as a Pharisee, Paul, who was then known as Saul, persecuted Christians for their faith in Christ, not realizing that Christ was the fulfillment of the Old Testament prophecies about the Messiah. While on his way to arrest Christians in Damascus, he encountered the living Christ through a flashing light from heaven that knocked him to the ground. Jesus spoke to him in an audible voice and told him to get up and go into the city where he would be told what he had been assigned to do.[116]

The Lord instructed a Christian in Damascus called Ananias to go and lay hands on and pray for Saul to regain his sight. The Lord calmed Ananias's fears about Saul and told him that he had chosen Saul to carry his name to the gentiles and their kings and to the people of Israel. The Lord said he was going to show Saul how much he must suffer for his name. Ananias obeyed the Lord and went and laid hands on Saul. Saul was filled with the Holy Spirit and regained his sight. He was baptized and began his ministry shortly thereafter and became known as the apostle Paul.[117]

The apostle Paul faithfully carried out his assignment. He took the gospel far and wide in three missionary journeys that were fraught with many challenges and much persecution. He said his life was worth nothing to him. All he wanted to do was to finish his course and his ministry to testify to the good news of God's grace that he received from the Lord Jesus.[118] In other words, Paul's only goal in life was to faithfully complete the assignment the Lord Jesus Christ gave him to preach the gospel. He was flogged, imprisoned, lashed, stoned, and shipwrecked. He dealt with dangers of all kinds and toiled faithfully, sometimes going without sleep or food.[119] He was later accused by the Pharisees and Sadducees of being a ringleader of the Nazarene sect, a troublemaker who was stirring up riots all over the world.[120] Aware that he would not get justice if he stood trial in Jerusalem, Paul appealed to Caesar.[121] He ended up in Rome as a prisoner. In his final Letter to his protégé Timothy, Paul told him that he

---

116. Acts 9:1–8; 22:10.

117. Acts 9:10–20.

118. Acts 20:24. The NIV speaks of finishing the race and completing the task the Lord Jesus gave him.

119. 2 Cor 11:23–27.

120. Acts 24:5.

121. Acts 25:8–12.

had fought the good fight, finished the race, and kept the faith.[122] He had been a faithful steward of the ministry that had been entrusted to him.

Wise

Jesus told a parable about ten virgins, five of whom were foolish and five wise. It was a parable about the kingdom of heaven. The foolish virgins took their lamps and went out to meet the bridegroom, but they did not carry any spare oil with them except what was in their lamps. The wise virgins, however, took along jars of oil. The bridegroom delayed coming until midnight, at which time his coming was announced and people were invited to come and meet him. The lamps of the foolish virgins were about to go out, so they asked the wise virgins for some of their oil. The wise virgins figured that if they shared their oil reserve with the other virgins, they might not have enough oil. They, therefore, refused to share their oil and asked the foolish virgins to go and buy some. While they were on their way to get more oil, the bridegroom arrived. The wise virgins went into the wedding banquet with him and the door was shut. When the foolish virgins returned, they pleaded with the bridegroom to open the banquet door, but he refused, saying he did not know them. Jesus then warned believers to keep watch because they do not know when the Lord will return.[123] A good Christian steward is one who is wise enough to live in anticipation of Christ's possible return at any moment.

Industrious

A good steward is one who is industrious. A good steward works hard to make the most of what has been entrusted to him or her, whether time, talent, or treasure.

---

122. 2 Tim 4:7.

123. Matt 25:1–13. See Culpepper, *Matthew*, 486–89, commenting that the bridegroom is the coming Son of Man. The wedding feast is the eschatological banquet, and the fates of the wise and foolish virgins warn of the coming judgment. The parabolic oil required for entrance into the kingdom is doing the Father's will or, by extension, keeping the law and teachings of Jesus. See also Harrington, *Gospel of Matthew*, 348–50, commenting that this parable contrasts characters, wise and foolish maidens, to show the need for constant watchfulness in the face of the coming Son of Man. The moral of the story is to watch because no one knows the day or the hour. The bridegroom is the Son of Man. The ten maidens represent members of the Christian community and offer positive and negative models about behavior in the face of the Son of Man's coming.

In the parables of the talents and the minas, two servants were industrious, but one was not. In the parable of the talents, the master called the servant lazy and worthless, and after taking the talent from him, ordered him to be thrown outside into the darkness where there will be weeping and gnashing of teeth.[124] In the parable of the minas, the mina was taken from the lazy servant, although he was not called worthless or thrown into the outer darkness.[125] Likewise, Christians who have been industrious with what has been entrusted to them will be given greater rewards and responsibilities in Christ's coming kingdom. However, those who have not been as faithful and industrious in stewarding what they were given will receive less in terms of rewards, position, and responsibility.

Productive/Fruitful

The parables of the talents and minas also reveal another quality of a good steward, that of fruitfulness and productivity. The first two servants in both parables were productive, whereas the third was not.

The Upshot of Good Christian Stewardship

It is abundantly clear that God takes good stewardship over what he entrusts to humanity very seriously. Jesus was the perfect steward. Being a good steward ought, therefore, to be a priority for everyone who professes to be a Christian. A Christian's time, talent, and treasure must be used in the service of God's kingdom and others, regardless of who they are, what they look like, or their life circumstances. This must be done with a full understanding of the fact that being a good steward has immense implications for both time and eternity. And the Holy Spirit, the Spirit of power and self-discipline, is able to give believers the strength and wisdom they need to be faithful stewards of God on earth.[126]

---

124. Matt 25:30 The NIV and the NKJV say servant while the NRSV says slave.
125. Luke 19:11–26.
126. 2 Tim 1:7.

7

Carrying Out the Great Commission

During his earthly ministry, Jesus was always about his Father's business with a sense of urgency.[1] He was constantly on the move on foot, preaching the good news in the towns and cities in Israel. When the people of Capernaum tried to keep him from leaving their town because of all the miracles he performed there, he told them that he must preach the good news of the kingdom of God to the other towns also, because that is why he was sent. So, he kept on preaching in the synagogues of Judea and throughout all of Galilee.[2] After Jesus's resurrection, he commanded his disciples of all time to follow his example by taking the gospel to all people, regardless of their nationality, ethnicity, skin color, or station in life, making disciples of them locally and globally.

This command Jesus gave his disciples is what has been called the Great Commission. In this chapter, we will look at the different elements of this Great Commission and its implications and practical applications for Christians of all time.

---

1. Mark 1:38–39; John 9:4.
2. Luke 9:43–44.

What Is the Great Commission?

After Jesus's resurrection, before his ascension, he told his disciples that all authority in heaven and on earth has been given to him by God the Father. God has highly exalted Jesus and given him a name that is above every name.[3] Based on this authority, Jesus charged his disciples to make disciples of all the nations. They were to baptize them in the name of the Father, Son, and Holy Spirit, and teach them to obey everything Jesus had commanded his disciples. This charge is known as the Great Commission.[4] Jesus promised to be with his disciples as they carried out the Great Commission, till the end of the age.[5]

The Gospel of Mark records that after Jesus gave his disciples the Great Commission, he ascended into heaven and sat down at the right hand of God, that the disciples went and preached everywhere, and that the Lord was with them, confirming his word by the signs that accompanied it.[6] Luke records in his Gospel account[7] and in the Acts of the Apostles that just before Jesus's ascension into heaven, he told his disciples not to leave Jerusalem until they had received the gift of the Holy Spirit that he had promised them. Jesus told them that they would receive power when the Holy Spirit came upon them, and that they would be his witnesses in Jerusalem, in all Judea and Samaria, and to the ends of the earth.[8] In other words, the disciples would need to be empowered by the Holy Spirit to carry out the Great Commission. They would not be able to do it in their own power.

---

3. Phil 2:9–11. After his ascension, God seated Jesus at his right hand in the heavenly realms, far above all rule and authority, power and dominion, and every title that can be given, whether in this present age or the age that is to come (Eph 1:18–21).

4. See Spurgeon, *Great Commission*, a compilation of some of Charles Spurgeon's most poignant sermons on the Great Commission.

5. Matt 28:18–20; Mark 16:15. See Harrington, *Gospel of Matthew*, 416, where he comments that as a summary of the entire Gospel, Matt 28:16–20 brings out the most important themes: the Father has given Jesus supreme and universal authority; the disciples are to share their discipleship not only with their fellow Jews but also with non-Jews; the Spirit of the risen Jesus will guide and protect the church until God's kingdom comes in its fullness. See also Culpepper, *Matthew*, 581–82, where he comments that Jesus enlarged the scope of the disciples' mission to all nations, not just Israel.

6. Mark 16:19–20.

7. Luke 24:49. See Johnson, *Gospel of Luke*, 403, where he comments that Luke associates the promise of the Holy Spirit with the promise to Abraham.

8. Acts 1:4–8. See John 14:16–18, where Jesus promised his disciples another helper or counselor, the Spirit of truth. See also John 14:26; 15:26; and 16:7, where Jesus tells his disciples about what the Holy Spirit would do in their lives.

The Greek word for disciple is *mathétés*, meaning a learner. But more than just a pupil, a disciple is also an adherent and, therefore, one who is an imitator of his or her teacher.[9] Jesus's Great Commission tells disciples to make disciples of others.[10]

This Great Commission was not just to the eleven disciples who accompanied Jesus to the mountain in Galilee from where he ascended to heaven. It was to all disciples of all time who constitute the body of Christ or the church.

After Jesus's resurrection, he breathed on his disciples and told them to receive the indwelling Holy Spirit.[11] But before they embarked on this Great Commission, Jesus instructed them to wait in Jerusalem until they had received the power or baptism of the Holy Spirit to embolden them to be his witnesses beginning in Jerusalem, in all Judea and Samaria, and to the ends of the earth.[12] Likewise, every Christian today needs the power of the Holy Spirit to embolden them to tell others about Jesus's saving grace. And it takes faithful believers to teach new believers or converts the word of God and how to live faithfully as disciples of Christ.

In the Great Commission, Jesus Christ charged his followers of all generations, who collectively constitute the body of Christ or the universal church, with the responsibility to do three things: make disciples of all nations; baptize them in the name of the Father, Son, and Holy Spirit; and teach them to obey all his commands. To do this will require sharing with everyone everywhere the gospel or good news of God's salvation through Jesus Christ, baptizing those who receive Jesus as their Savior, and teaching them to obey Jesus's commandments as recorded in his word.

The Great Commission: Making Disciples by Sharing the Good News

The first element of the Great Commission is the charge to make disciples of all nations. In order to make disciples of all nations, disciples of Christ

---

9. See Vine et al., *Vine's Complete Expository Dictionary*, 171 (New Testament Section). Also, Strong's Reference Number 3101, defining *mathétés* as learner, disciple, or pupil.

10. See Vine et al., *Vine's Complete Expository Dictionary*, 172 (New Testament Section). The Greek verb *matheteuo* is used in the active voice in Matt 28:19 to make disciples of all nations.

11. John 20:22.

12. Luke 24:49; Acts 1:8.

must share the gospel or good news with those who have not yet accepted Jesus Christ as Savior. During his earthly ministry, Jesus said that he had been anointed to preach good news to the poor and that he must preach the good news of the kingdom of God to the other towns outside his base in Capernaum because that is why he was sent.[13]

So, what exactly is the gospel or good news? The Greek word for gospel is *euaggelion*, meaning the good news. It is used in the New Testament to denote the good tidings of God's kingdom and salvation through faith in Jesus Christ based on his substitutionary death, burial, resurrection, and ascension.[14] To share the gospel is to bring or announce glad tidings, as conveyed by the Greek word *euaggelizó*, which is defined in English as to evangelize.[15]

Writing to the church in Corinth, the apostle Paul reminded them of the gospel that he had preached to them, which they had received and stood on. Paul reminded them that it is by this gospel that they were saved if they held firmly to it. The gospel is that Christ died for our sins as the Scriptures teach; that he was buried but rose on the third day as the Scriptures teach; and that there were many witnesses to his resurrection, including the disciples and as many as five hundred believers, many of whom were still living when Paul wrote to the Corinthians. Paul also made a point of reminding the Corinthians that the risen Christ appeared to him too.[16]

It was God who, out of his infinite love, reached out to humanity by sending his own Son to save humanity from the bondage of sin and eternal death so that they might live victoriously over sin and have eternal life.[17] Even though humanity was sinful, God showed his love for

---

13. Luke 4:18, 43. See Johnson, *Gospel of Luke*, 79–82, where he comments that Jesus is imaged as the prophetic spokesperson of God, that the salvation brought by Jesus would extend to all nations, and that many Jews later rejected the gospel because it was meant for all.

14. See Vine et al., *Vine's Complete Expository Dictionary*, 275 (New Testament Section). Also, Strong's Reference Number 2098, defining *euaggelion* as good news. It is used to denote the good news of the coming of the Messiah.

15. *Euaggelizó* means to proclaim glad tidings and *euangelistes* means a messenger of good or a preacher of the gospel. An evangelist is, therefore, a preacher of the gospel. See Vine et al., *Vine's Complete Expository Dictionary*, 208 and 276 (New Testament Section). Also, Strong's Reference Number 2097, defining *euaggelizó* to mean to announce good news. Also, Strong's Reference Number 2099, where *euaggelistés* is defined as an evangelist, a bringer of good news.

16. 1 Cor 15:1–8.

17. John 3:16.

humanity by sending Christ to die to redeem them from sin.[18] Christ was qualified to redeem humanity because he was sinless and, as the second person of the Triune God, was the brightness of God's glory and the express image of his person.[19]

Those who hear the gospel and receive it by believing in the redeeming work of Jesus Christ, repenting of their sins, and accepting the lordship of Jesus Christ become born again unto eternal life. This is what Peter preached to the Jews on the day of Pentecost in Jerusalem. He told them to repent and be baptized in the name of Jesus Christ for the forgiveness of their sins, and they would receive the gift of the Holy Spirit. This promise was not just for the Jews. It was for all people of all time, regardless of their nationality, ethnicity, skin color, or socioeconomic status.[20]

Part of the good news is that those who receive Jesus Christ as Savior, though once sinners, are now made righteous in him. Just as Abraham believed God and it was credited to him as righteousness, when one believes in the saving grace of God in Christ, it is credited as righteousness as an act of God's grace and love, and one is now justified as if one had never sinned.[21] There is, therefore, now no condemnation for those who are in Christ Jesus. Through Christ Jesus, the law of the Spirit of life has now set them free from the law of sin and death.[22] Thus, instead of being controlled by the power of sin, believers now have the indwelling Holy Spirit to help them live Christlike lives. Instead of being at odds with God, through faith in Christ believers are justified and at peace with God. God's grace is available to believers who now have access to him through faith in Christ.[23]

It is also part of the good news that, as a result of Christ's redeeming work, humanity can be restored to God and share in the riches of his glory. Paul prayed that the Ephesians would know the hope to which God

---

18. Rom 5:8.
19. Heb 4:15.
20. Acts 2:38–39.
21. Rom 4:5, 22–25. See Adeyemo, *Africa Bible Commentary*, 1358, commenting that when God credits our faith as righteousness, he is not rewarding our good deeds but displaying his grace. Trying hard to be good does not impress God. Only faith impresses God and that faith is seen in the confidence that God is faithful and will keep his promises. Salvation by faith may seem illogical to some, but that is the only way that God has provided for salvation.
22. Rom 8:1–2.
23. Rom 5:1–2.

had called them and the riches of his glorious inheritance in believers.[24] Christ lives in the believer through his Holy Spirit. This indwelling presence is the assurance of future glory and eternal life.[25]

All who have faith in Christ have become children of God. All who are baptized into Christ have clothed themselves with Christ. In this spiritual family of God, there is neither Jew nor Greek, slave nor free, male nor female. All believers are one in Christ Jesus without regard to nationality, ethnicity, skin color, or socioeconomic status. They have all become children of Abraham and inherited God's promise to bless all humanity through Abraham, through whom Christ descended.[26] They have become citizens of the kingdom of God or the kingdom of heaven and their names are enrolled or registered in heaven.[27] Like Abraham, they can look forward to the city not built with human hands, the city with foundations whose architect and builder is God.[28] They can look for a better country,[29] the heavenly Jerusalem,[30] the city that is to come where there are no more racial and class conflicts.[31] That is good news indeed.

Who Is Responsible for Sharing the Gospel or Good News?

Toward the end of his ministry, Jesus's disciples asked him about the signs that would signal his coming and the end of the age.[32] Jesus told them that the day of his coming is something that God has kept to himself. Even Christ, by deliberate choice, does not know when God will send

---

24. Eph 1:18.
25. Col 1:27.
26. Gal 3:26–29. See Adeyemo, *Africa Bible Commentary*, 1422, commenting that Christians baptized into Christ were taking on the virtues of Christ and differences between them had disappeared. They now all looked alike as members of Christ's family and categories like race, status, and gender are no longer important. See also Eric C. Redmond, "Letter to the Galatians," in McCaulley et al., *New Testament in Color*, 402, commenting that in Christ, all inherit the blessings of Abraham based on spiritual sonship. Paul recognizes egalitarian sonship with respect to inheritance and enfranchisement for all in Christ's kingdom.
27. Heb 12:23. The NRSV says enrolled, the NKJV says registered, and the NIV says names of the church of the firstborn are written in heaven.
28. Heb 11:10.
29. Heb 11:16.
30. Heb 12:22.
31. Heb 13:14.
32. Matt 24:3.

him back. Neither do the angels.[33] Jesus did tell his disciples about signs that would signal his coming and the end of the age. But he said that the end shall only come after the gospel of the kingdom has been preached in the whole world as a testimony to all nations.[34]

Jesus has now been gone for over two thousand years. It appears that he is being slow in carrying out his promise to return. But the apostle Peter helps us put all of this in proper perspective. He tells us that the Lord is not slow to fulfill his promise to return. On the contrary, he delays his coming because he wants everyone to be saved. He does not want anyone to perish. He wants all to come to repentance.[35] This should help everyone who professes to be a Christian, as well as the universal church, understand the paramount importance of the Great Commission. Its faithful execution will influence the timing of Christ's return.

God's word says everyone who calls on the name of the Lord will be saved. But before anyone can call on the name of the Lord, they must hear about him through the gospel and believe in him. And as Paul rhetorically asked the church in Rome, how can people hear about Jesus Christ without someone preaching to them, and how can someone preach unless that person has been sent?[36] In the Great Commission, Jesus sent all who believe in him to share the gospel with the whole world. Throughout the years, churches have sent and continue to send missionaries all over the world to preach the gospel to those who may not have heard it. The apostle Peter also told individual believers to be ready to give a gentle and respectful answer to everyone who asks about the reason for the hope that they have. In this way, many individual disciples also share the gospel as they tell others about their faith and the hope they have of eternal life through Christ.

Sharing the gospel by carrying out the Great Commission is the most important charge Jesus gave to his disciples. It is the only thing the Lord is waiting on his disciples of all time, individually and corporately, to do to prepare the way for his return. He is not waiting on Christians to

---

33. Matt 24:36.

34. Matt 24:14.

35. 2 Pet 3:9. See Mateus F. De Campos, "Second Letter of Peter," in McCaulley et al., *New Testament in Color*, 701–2, commenting on how Peter addresses the apparent lack of signs of divine intervention in judging evil by explaining God's perspective on time. What appears to be God's slowness—a passive lack of response—is in fact God's patience—an active and intentional response by which God mercifully withholds his judgment in order to give people the opportunity to repent.

36. Rom 10:13–15.

seize power or take over governments in the societies in which they live. He is not counting on them to influence the passage of laws or influence public policy. He is not waiting on them to influence cultural norms. He is not waiting on them to fight and win culture wars. He is only counting on them to carry out the Great Commission he gave them—to preach the gospel to every nation and to help transform people into Christlike people by discipling them to obey Jesus's commandments so that they will not perish but live in eternity with him when he returns.

The Example of Jesus Christ and the Apostles in Sharing the Good News

At the beginning of his ministry, Jesus went to the synagogue in Nazareth on the Sabbath and stood up to read. The scroll of the prophet Isaiah was handed to him. He read from a passage attributed to the Messiah, that the Spirit of the Lord was upon him; that he had been anointed to preach the gospel to the poor, heal the broken-hearted, proclaim liberty to the captives, recovery of sight to the blind, to set at liberty those who are oppressed, and to proclaim the acceptable year of the Lord. He then rolled back the scroll, handed it to the attendant, sat down, and told the congregation that the Scripture he just read had been fulfilled in their hearing that day.[37] Preaching the gospel was, therefore, a core part of Jesus's ministry.

Jesus began to preach about the kingdom of God after John the Baptist was imprisoned.[38] While in prison, John was kept informed about the things Jesus was doing. He sent messengers to Jesus to ask him if he was the expected Messiah, or whether they should be expecting someone else. Jesus told the messengers to go back and tell John what they had heard and seen. Blind eyes were seeing, the lame were walking, lepers were being healed, deaf ears were being opened, dead people were being raised, and the good news was being preached to the poor.[39] This included those who were poor in spirit and had humbled themselves to acknowledge their need for God, as well as those who were oppressed and disadvantaged and looked down on in society, especially by the wealthy and privileged. Jesus emphasized preaching the gospel as an essential part of his ministry.

37. Luke 4:16–21.
38. Matt 4:12–17.
39. Matt 11:4–5.

Jesus ministered in Capernaum on the Sabbath in the early days of his ministry. He taught the people, cast out demons, and healed many people. The people of Capernaum wanted to keep him there, but Jesus told them that he could not just stay there; he had to preach the good news of the kingdom of God to the other towns also, because that is why he was sent. So, he preached in the synagogues of Judea.[40]

At one point in his ministry, after a woman had anointed his feet with perfume, Luke records that Jesus traveled about from one town and village to another, proclaiming the good news of the kingdom of God.[41]

The apostles followed in Jesus's footsteps in preaching the gospel. At one point, Jesus gave his twelve disciples power and authority over all demons, as well as to cure diseases, and sent them out to preach the kingdom of God and heal the sick. The disciples left and went from village to village and through the towns preaching the gospel and healing people everywhere they went.[42]

Peter preached the gospel to Jews from every nation who had come to Jerusalem to celebrate the Feast of Pentecost. As a result of his gospel message, three thousand people repented of their sins, were baptized, and were added to the early church.[43]

When the early church in Jerusalem was being persecuted and the disciples were scattered, they preached the gospel wherever they went. Philip, a deacon[44] in the early church, took the gospel to Samaria during this period of persecution and many were saved.[45] Philip also shared the good news about Jesus with an Ethiopian eunuch who was the treasurer of the Ethiopian queen, Candace. He was traveling in his chariot along the road from Jerusalem to Gaza on his way back to Ethiopia. When they came across a body of water, the Ethiopian asked to be baptized and Philip baptized him.[46]

After God showed Peter in a vision not to call anyone unclean or impure, God sent Peter to preach the gospel to a gentile, a centurion in

---

40. Luke 4:31–44; Mark 1:38, where Jesus told his disciples that they must go to the nearby villages and preach there also. He traveled throughout Galilee, preaching in the synagogues.
41. Luke 8:1.
42. Mark 6:12–13; Luke 9:1–2, 6.
43. Acts 2:22–41.
44. Acts 6:1–6.
45. Acts 8:4–13.
46. Acts 8:26–39.

Caesarea called Cornelius. Cornelius and his family were devout, God-fearing people. Cornelius prayed to God regularly and gave generously to the needy. In answer to his prayers, God sent an angel to Cornelius to instruct him to send for Peter, who was in Joppa, a day's journey away. Peter hosted Cornelius's messengers overnight and set out for Caesarea with them the next day. When they arrived, Peter preached the gospel to them. Everyone in Cornelius's household received the Holy Spirit as Peter was preaching. They were all then baptized.[47]

Some of the disciples who were scattered as a result of the persecution of the early church went to places like Cyprus, Phoenicia, and Antioch in Syria, preaching the gospel to Jews. However, other disciples from Cyprus and Cyrene also went to Antioch and preached the gospel to gentiles too, telling them about the good news of the Lord Jesus Christ. Many people believed and turned to the Lord. The Jerusalem church sent Barnabas to Antioch when they heard of the harvest of souls there. When Barnabas arrived, many more people came to believe in the Lord. Barnabas went to Tarsus and brought Saul back with him to Antioch. Together, they taught and discipled many people for an entire year. It was the disciples at Antioch who were first called Christians.[48]

The apostle Paul told the church in Ephesus that it was a gift of God's grace by which he became a servant of the gospel. He said he was given the grace to preach the unsearchable riches of Christ to the gentiles. He also said that God's intent is for the church to be the revealer of the manifold wisdom of God.[49]

Paul told the church in Rome that he served God with his whole heart in preaching the gospel of his Son, Jesus. He told them that he prayed that a way would open for him to come to them because he was eager to preach the gospel to them.[50] Paul felt compelled to preach the gospel. He declared, "Woe to me if I do not proclaim the gospel!"[51] The resurrected Christ had commissioned him to preach the gospel, and he was faithful in carrying out his commission.[52] Paul saw his reward in preaching the gospel as being in his willingness to preach it free of charge so as not to

---

47. Acts 10.
48. Acts 11:19–26.
49. Eph 3:7–11.
50. Rom 1:9–10, 15.
51. 1 Cor 9:16. The NIV says, "Woe to me if I do not preach the gospel!"
52. Acts 9:15, 20.

abuse his authority in the gospel as an apostle of Christ.[53] Christians must also preach the gospel whether they are paid to do so or not.

Everyone who professes to be a Christian—a disciple, follower, or imitator of Christ—must have the same heart as Christ and the apostles did for the lost, and follow their example in sharing the good news with the lost.

The Example of the Early Church in Sharing the Good News

It was the church in Antioch that sponsored the apostle Paul's three missionary journeys that took the gospel to Europe. The church evidently had many anointed people in it. The Bible notes that some of them were prophets and teachers.[54] But the church did not just pick anyone to send. It was the Holy Spirit who gave direction for Saul and Barnabas to be set apart for the work to which the Lord had called them. And after Saul and Barnabas were set apart, the church fasted and prayed about their call, then laid hands on them to anoint them for their missionary journey.[55] This shows that churches must diligently and earnestly seek God's will and direction through fasting, prayer, and worship concerning missionary work, who to send, and where and when to send them. People who are sent must be called by God. If not, they will do more harm than good. Take, for example, the exportation of culture instead of the gospel and the condonation of harms like slavery and colonialism, oftentimes in the name of Christianizing those who were being harmed.

The first missionary journey took Paul and Barnabas to Cyprus. They preached in Salamis, where a young man called John Mark joined them as a helper; then in Paphos; Perga in Pamphylia, where John Mark left them to return to Jerusalem; then in Pisidian Antioch; Iconium; Lystra; and Derbe. They retraced their steps to strengthen the disciples in Lystra, Iconium, and Antioch, went through Pisidia and Pamphylia, and came back to Perga where they continued to preach the gospel. From there, they went to Attalia and sailed back to Antioch in Syria, where

---

53. 1 Cor 9:17–18. See Adeyemo, *Africa Bible Commentary*, 1388, commenting that Paul sees his preaching of the gospel as a duty and not as something he volunteered to do. However, he does have a choice as to whether to accept any monetary reward for his preaching and is proud that he refuses to do this and thus presents the gospel free of charge. This was clearly his regular practice.

54. Acts 13:1.

55. Acts 13:2–3.

CARRYING OUT THE GREAT COMMISSION

they gave a report to the church of what God had done through them among the gentiles.[56] Paul and Barnabas continued to teach and preach the gospel in Antioch upon their return.[57]

Paul invited Barnabas to join him on a second missionary journey to see how the people they had preached to during their first missionary journey were doing. Barnabas wanted John Mark to join them, but Paul disagreed because he had left them in Pamphylia to return to Jerusalem. So, Barnabas took John Mark and went with him to Cyprus, and Paul chose Silas and traveled with him through Syria and Cilicia, strengthening the churches.[58] Paul and Silas journeyed to Derbe and Lystra, where Paul took Timothy with them. They traveled from town to town strengthening churches in the faith and saw people being saved daily. They traveled throughout the region of Phrygia and Galatia, and on to Troas, where Luke the Gospel writer joined them. Before coming to Troas, while traveling through Phrygia and Galatia, it is important to note that the Holy Spirit prevented Paul and his companions from preaching the gospel in Asia. When they came to the border at Mysia, they wanted to cross into Bithynia, but the Holy Spirit would not let them, so they bypassed Mysia and went to Troas. At Troas, Paul had a vision in which a man from Macedonia was asking him to come and help them. This shows that missionaries must be sensitive to the Holy Spirit and constantly seek God's direction in their work. As a result of the Spirit's leading, from Troas they went to Samothrace, Neapolis, and Philippi in the district of Macedonia, where a wealthy woman by the name of Lydia and her household became believers in Jesus Christ and were baptized.[59]

After casting a demon out of a slave girl whose owners were profiting from her fortune telling, the owners, realizing that she could no longer tell fortunes and make money for them, stirred up trouble against Paul and Silas and dragged them before the authorities. They were flogged and thrown in prison. But that night, there was a violent earthquake as Paul and Silas sang and prayed in prison. The prison doors flew open, and their chains were loosened. But Paul and Silas did not escape. The jailer and his entire household ended up becoming believers. Paul and Silas left for Thessalonica, then Berea. To avoid troublemakers who followed Paul from Thessalonica to Berea, Paul went on to Athens while Silas and

---

56. Acts 13, 14.
57. Acts 15:35.
58. Acts 15:36–41.
59. Acts 16:1–15.

Timothy stayed in Berea. Paul then went to Corinth and on to Ephesus. He then sailed to Caesarea and continued on to his home church in Antioch, ending his second missionary journey.[60]

Paul set out on a third missionary journey after spending some time in Antioch, traveling throughout the region of Galatia and Phrygia, strengthening the disciples. He then went to Ephesus where he spent two years. After persecution arose in Ephesus and Paul's traveling companions, Gaius and Aristarchus, were seized, Paul left for Macedonia and arrived in Greece, where he stayed for three months. He was accompanied by several fellow workers, including Timothy and Gaius. Paul left back for Macedonia, sailing from Philippi to Troas, where his companions had gone on ahead of him. From Troas, Paul went on foot to Assos, where he boarded a ship to rejoin his companions who had boarded in Troas. From there, he went on to Miletus, where he sent for the Ephesians elders. When they arrived, Paul charged them to keep watch over themselves and their flock and warned them to guard against false prophets. From there he sailed to Tyre, then to Ptolemais, and on to Caesarea, where he stayed with Philip, the deacon and evangelist who shared the gospel with the Ethiopian eunuch, and then to Jerusalem, where he gave a detailed report of what God had done through his ministry among the gentiles.[61]

Jesus's disciples carried out the Great Commission and preached the gospel in Jerusalem, Judea, and Samaria, and Paul's three missionary journeys took the gospel "to the ends of the earth" just as Jesus had commanded.[62] It is now up to Christians everywhere, through the power of the Holy Spirit, to continue to share the gospel of Jesus Christ with others, and up to the church to sponsor missionaries to take the gospel all over the world, just as the church in Antioch in Syria did.

The Great Commission does not charge believers to go and preach about their culture or their political or ideological beliefs to others. The Great Commission does not charge believers to teach myths or historical perspectives that align with a certain ideology or agenda. It does not charge believers to go and take over governments or the world, or to

---

60. Acts 16:16–40; 17; 18:1–22.

61. Acts 18:23–28; 19; 20; 21:1–19.

62. Acts 1:8. See Adeyemo, *Africa Bible Commentary*, 1300, commenting that the disciples were to be witnesses to Jesus in the power of the Holy Spirit among all the nations. The way to establish the kingdom of God is making Jesus known among all the nations—literally to the ends of the earth. The task facing the disciples is so vast that they will only be able to perform it through the power of the Holy Spirit.

"Christianize" society. It does not commission Christians to go and fight crusades or "holy" wars. Jesus's only purpose in giving the Great Commission was to see people saved and discipled. The end result of all evangelizing or sharing of the good news is that people will repent of their sins, receive Jesus Christ as Savior and Lord, live lives that imitate him as his disciples, and live with him in eternity when he returns instead of facing eternal death in the lake of fire.

The Great Commission: Baptizing New Converts in the Name of the Father, Son, and Holy Spirit

The second element of the Great Commission is the charge to baptize those who receive the gospel and commit to becoming disciples of Jesus Christ. In the Great Commission, Jesus commanded his disciples to baptize those who believe in the name of the Father, and of the Son, and of the Holy Spirit.

The Greek word for the verb "baptize" is *baptizó*, meaning to dip.[63] Thus, new believers are to be immersed in water during baptism. Baptism is a public declaration of, and a witness to, the believer's newfound faith. It is also a public commitment to a new life in Christ. Immersion in water during baptism identifies the new believer with the death and burial of Jesus. It symbolizes the believer's death to sin. Being raised up out of the water after being baptized symbolizes being raised up, just as Christ rose from the dead to a new, righteous life in Christ.[64]

Not only did Jesus command disciples in the Great Commission to baptize new believers, but the apostles also commanded it. When Peter's preaching of the gospel at Pentecost brought conviction to the hearts of those who heard his message, they asked what they should do. Peter told them to repent and be baptized in the name of Jesus Christ for the forgiveness of their sins and the gift of the Holy Spirit.[65]

Later, when Peter preached the gospel to Cornelius and his household and they were filled with the Holy Spirit, Peter ordered that they be

---

63. See Vine et al., *Vine's Complete Expository Dictionary*, 50 (New Testament Section). Also, Strong's Reference Number 907, defining *baptizó* as to dip or sink.

64. Rom 6:3–7. See Adeyemo, *Africa Bible Commentary*, 1360, commenting that baptism symbolizes death to sin and represents a believer's union with Christ in his death and resurrection, which allows believers to share the blessing of a new and justified life. The old self has died. They cannot therefore go back to it.

65. Acts 2:37–39.

THE CHRISTIAN AS IMITATOR OF CHRIST

baptized in the name of Jesus Christ.[66] Although Peter did not say they should be baptized in the name of the Father, and of the Son, and of the Holy Spirit, saying only that they should be baptized in the name of Jesus Christ, this was enough since in Christ, all the fullness of the deity lives in bodily form. In other words, Jesus Christ embodies the Triune God—Father, Son, and Holy Spirit.[67]

Before Jesus began his public ministry, he himself led by example and submitted to baptism by John the Baptist. John tried to dissuade Jesus by pointing out that he was the one who needed to be baptized by Jesus, not the other way around. But Jesus said that it was proper to do this in order to fulfill all righteousness by publicly consecrating himself to God and his kingdom.[68] God used Jesus's baptism as the occasion to open up heaven and send the power of the Holy Spirit upon Jesus when he came up out of the water. He also used it as the occasion to audibly affirm Jesus as his Son with whom he is well pleased.[69]

Jesus was without sin and did not need to be baptized as an act of repentance from sin. But submitting to baptism identified him with the human race whom he came to redeem from sin and with the new move of God that was calling people to repent through John the Baptist. Identifying himself with the ministry of John the Baptist, whose ministry fulfilled Old Testament prophecies about preparing the way for the Messiah, also served as Jesus's identification of himself as the prophesied Messiah.[70]

The apostle James said that faith that is not accompanied by action is dead.[71] When one comes to faith in Christ, putting that faith into action by obeying his command to be baptized validates one's faith as genuine. Baptism itself does not and cannot save. One must be saved before being baptized. Baptism is a public affirmation of one's faith. But what if one comes to believe in Christ but dies without an opportunity to be baptized? That is what happened to the thief on the cross. He had no opportunity to be baptized. He believed in Jesus during his execution. But Jesus assured him that he would be with him in paradise that day.[72]

---

66. Acts 10:44–48.
67. Col 2:9.
68. Matt 3:13–15.
69. Matt 3:16–17; Mark 1:9–11; Luke 3:21–22; John 1:31–34.
70. Matt 3:3; Mark 1:2–3; and Luke 3:4, all quoting Isa 40:3. See also Mal 3:1.
71. Jas 2:17.
72. Luke 23:39–43.

Jesus gave the command to baptize those who receive the gospel and become born again. Being born again through repentance and faith in Jesus Christ is, therefore, a prerequisite to being baptized. Peter told the Jews at Pentecost to repent and then be baptized.[73] When Philip, a deacon in the early church, preached the good news of the kingdom of God to the Samaritans, they believed and were baptized.[74] Later when Philip shared the good news about Jesus with the Ethiopian eunuch who was on his way back to Ethiopia from Jerusalem, the Ethiopian believed and asked to be baptized when they came across a body of water.[75] It is unscriptural and pointless for one who has not received Christ as Savior to go through water baptism. This may happen when someone joins a local church even though he or she may not have been born again. In that event, baptism is just an empty ritual.

The Great Commission: Teaching Obedience to What Christ Commanded

The third and final element of the Great Commission is the charge to teach new converts to obey everything Jesus has commanded them.[76] This amounts to feeding them spiritual food—both the pure milk of God's word and solid food—depending on their maturity levels. The pure milk of the word includes the elementary teachings about Christ or principles of Christ—things like the need to repent from sin and acts that lead to spiritual death; faith in God; baptisms (water baptism and the baptism of the Holy Spirit); laying on of hands (for healing or the impartation of a spiritual gift); the resurrection of the dead (at the end of the age); and eternal judgment.[77] However, these teachings are only foundational. Believers must go on to mature in the faith by moving from learning

---

73. Acts 2:38.
74. Acts 8:12.
75. Acts 8:35–39.
76. Matt 28:20. See Harrington, *Gospel of Matthew*, 415–16, commenting that the disciples are commanded to carry on what was a major task of the earthly Jesus in the Gospel. The content of their teaching ("all that I have commanded you") and what was expected ("to observe") treats the teaching of Jesus as authoritative. The teacher par excellence commissions his disciples to carry on his teaching mission. See also Culpepper, *Matthew*, 584, where he comments that Jesus taught with authority, on the mountain and in the cities, the synagogues, and the temple. Now the Messiah hands this function on to his disciples. The transfer of authority is complete.
77. Heb 6:1–3.

these elementary or foundational teachings to more mature teaching or solid food, which teaches believers about God's righteousness, enables them to distinguish between good and evil,[78] and equips them to live self-controlled, obedient, and holy lives.[79]

If people who accept Jesus and are saved after hearing the gospel message are to be fed with the pure spiritual milk of the word, then there must be impure or adulterated milk, a version of the gospel or teaching that is infused with man-made concepts, traditions, philosophies, or ideologies. Such teaching may sound good because it has elements of the truth, but it is impure because it is not the whole truth as taught by Christ and the apostles. The only way to know if teaching is consistent with what Christ and the apostles taught is to measure it against the Bible. This is what the Christians in Berea did when Paul preached to them during his second missionary journey. They did not take whatever Paul preached to them as gospel. They searched the Scriptures themselves to fact-check what they heard.[80]

Jesus taught on numerous topics. In the Great Commission, Jesus did not give the impression that his teachings are just suggestions. He called them commandments. These commandments are what must be taught to new believers.

A few examples of Jesus's teachings or commandments are noteworthy here as a point of reference.

Christians Must Love God with All Their Heart and Their Neighbor as Themselves

The Pharisees came to Jesus once to test him with a question. They asked him which commandment in the law was the greatest. Jesus replied that it is to love the Lord God with all one's heart and with all one's soul and with all one's mind. He said it was the first and greatest commandment.[81]

---

78. Heb 5:13–14.

79. 1 Pet 1:13–16. See Sproul, *What Is the Great Commission?* This book explains that disciple-making requires much more than just sharing the gospel. See also West, *Great Commission, Soul Winning and Discipleship*, arguing that most churches have lost touch with fulfilling the Great Commission because while soul-winning is a vital part of the church's mission, it seems to have lost sight of biblical discipleship and holy living.

80. Acts 17:11.

81. Matt 22:34–38. Jesus was quoting Deut 6:5.

To love the Lord God with all one's heart is to love him unreservedly and wholeheartedly, not halfheartedly. To love him with all one's soul is to love him with all one's inner being, including one's emotions. To love him with all one's mind is to make him the primary focus of one's thoughts; to be more preoccupied with him in one's thoughts than with anyone or anything else. The one who loves God in this way desires to honor and please him through obedience. It is a love that is loyal to God and seeks God's honor and glory. It is a love that longs for God's presence.

When Jesus answered the Pharisees who asked him about the greatest commandment, he did not stop there. He added that there is a close second, which is to love one's neighbor as oneself.[82]

Jesus explained that these two commandments are the two commandments on which everything written in the law and the prophetic books hang. In other words, everything in the Old Testament law, including the Ten Commandments, and everything in the books of the prophets is designed to bring people to love God with total devotion and to love their neighbor, regardless of their nationality, ethnicity, skin color, or socioeconomic status, just as they love themselves. Imagine a world in which everyone who professes to be a Christian actually lived by this teaching. There would indeed be peace on earth and goodwill toward humanity.[83] And many of the evils of history like the holocaust, genocides, slavery, oppression, colonialism, and unprovoked wars would never have happened.

Christians Must Treat Others as They Would Want to Be Treated

In his extensive teaching in the Sermon on the Mount, Jesus included rules for living in the kingdom of God. These are rules for those who live under God's authority. They are rules for Christians. Among these rules

---

82. Matt 22:39–40. Jesus was quoting Lev 19:18. See Culpepper, *Matthew*, 430–32, commenting that Rabbis counted 613 commandments in the Torah. Jesus distilled them to their essence with these two commandments, which he placed on the same level. The heart is the innermost part of a person. When one loves God with one's whole heart, there can be no hypocrisy. The soul denotes one's entire being, life in totality. Mind denotes the power of thought. To love God with one's whole heart, soul, and mind, therefore, is to love God with one's whole being. One's strength is all of one's possessions. To love God with all one's strength is to not squander life on lesser pursuits or allow material goods to become false gods. To love one's neighbor as oneself is to place a necessary limitation on self-love.

83. Luke 2:14.

THE CHRISTIAN AS IMITATOR OF CHRIST

is what has been called the Golden Rule. Jesus taught that, in everything, one must do to others what one would have them do to one.[84] And just as he did when he laid out the two greatest commandments, he said that this rule sums up the law and the prophets. Together, the law and the prophets teach us to treat others in a manner that is right and just. They teach us to do no harm to others, just as we would ordinarily not do harm to ourselves. And Jesus said we are to do this in all circumstances—in everything. This would include all our dealings with others, whether in business, the workplace, the church, the home, and all relationships. Since no one wants to be discriminated against, oppressed, marginalized, or refused love and compassion, neither should anyone do any of that to another person.

Christians Must Treat All Other Christians as Family

Once, while Jesus was talking to a crowd, his mother and brothers came and stood outside the place where he was, desiring to speak to him. When he was informed that his mother and brothers were outside wanting to speak to him, Jesus asked a rhetorical question about who his mother and brothers were. He pointed to his disciples and said that they were his mother and brothers. He then stated that whoever does the will of his Father in heaven is his brother, sister, and mother.[85]

This means that anyone who professes to be a disciple, follower, or imitator of Christ must understand that they have become a member of the family of God. This spiritual family consists of all who have received Jesus Christ as Savior and have been born again, regardless of their nationality, ethnicity, skin color, or socioeconomic status. Christians may have blood relatives or relatives by marriage, but in God's eyes, their real family is this family of God. This family is also called the household of faith or the family of believers. The apostle Paul told the church in Galatia that they should do good to all, especially if they belong to the family of faith or the family of believers, no matter what they look like or their station in life.[86]

---

84. Matt 7:12; Luke 6:31.

85. Matt 12:46–50; Mark 3:31–35; Luke 8:19–21.

86. Gal 6:10. The NRSV uses family of faith. The NIV uses family of believers while the NKJV uses household of faith.

Unfortunately, there are professing Christians who, contrary to Jesus's teaching, would rather do good to someone who is not a member of the family of believers because they share the same nationality, skin color, ethnicity, or social class, but not to someone in the family of God who is of a different nationality, ethnicity, skin color, or social class.

Christians Must Give to the Poor and Needy Remembering That Jesus Takes It Personally

In the parable of the sheep and the goats, Jesus talked about his return to earth as King to judge the nations. At some point after his return, Jesus said he will separate the righteous (sheep) from the wicked (goats). He said the righteous will inherit the kingdom and the wicked will suffer eternal punishment. He said he (the King) will commend the righteous because they fed him when he was hungry, gave him drink when he was thirsty, took him in as a stranger, clothed him when he was naked, and visited him in prison. Jesus said the righteous will ask when they did all this for him and he will tell them that they did these things for him when they did it for the least of his brethren, believers who were suffering.

Jesus said that he will tell the wicked how they failed to feed him when he was hungry, give him drink when he was thirsty, take him in as a stranger, clothe him when he was naked, or visit him in prison. They too will ask when they failed to do all these things for him. He will respond that when they failed to do it for the least of his brethren, they failed to do it for him.[87]

Jesus's references in this parable to the hungry, the thirsty, the stranger, the naked, the sick, and the imprisoned are references to the poor, the needy, the vulnerable, and the outcast. This parable shows that Jesus regards showing love and compassion to the poor and needy, particularly to believers who are suffering, as tantamount to showing him love and compassion. And he promised an eternal reward for the righteous who do, and eternal punishment for the cursed who do not.[88]

---

87. Matt 25:31–46.

88. See Harrington, *Gospel of Matthew*, 358–60, where he notes that the usual interpretation of the parable of the sheep and the goats is as a judgment scene involving all humanity for treatment of all people in distress of some kind. But he argues that this judgment is of gentiles based on their treatment of Christians. See also Culpepper, *Matthew*, 499–500, agreeing that the sheep represent gentiles whose acts of mercy have fulfilled the weightier matters of the law and moved the King to show mercy on them.

The Great Commission: Not Teaching What Christ Did Not Command

Toward the end of his earthly ministry, Jesus told his disciples about things that would signal the end of the age and his second coming. He said that one of the signs will be the appearance of false prophets who will deceive many people.[89] In carrying out the Great Commission, disciples of Christ must not only teach all that Christ commanded and what the apostles taught, but they must also refuse to teach anything and refute teaching that is inconsistent with what Christ taught, keeping in mind that his divine power has given believers everything they need for life and godliness through the knowledge of him.[90]

Not Preaching Politics

Peter said that false teachers who start out well but become corrupted are like a dog that returns to its vomit. He described them as springs or wells without water who speak empty, boastful words that appeal to the sinful nature and drag back into error those who were escaping it. They promise people freedom even though they themselves live in bondage to corruption or depravity.[91] One author has charged some evangelicals as preaching libertarianism covered with a veneer of Christianity. He calls it Christian libertarianism and says it is not biblical Christianity, but ideological Christianity. It is individualistic libertarianism. Libertarianism calls for personal freedom and autonomy, or freedom from godly or even reasonable governmental restraint. It has shown opposition to government programs including the New Deal.[92]

And the "least of these" are those who believe in Jesus and act in his name. But see H. Daniel Zacharias, "Gospel of Matthew," in McCaulley et al., *New Testament in Color*, 82, commenting that the judgment scene is of people from all the nations standing before the Son of Man who separates the righteous from the unrighteous based on who has practiced solidarity with those on the margins, lifting them up, and ministering to their basic needs.

89. Matt 24:11.
90. 2 Pet 1:3.
91. 2 Pet 2:1, 17–22.
92. Hendricks, *Christians Against Christianity*, 136–42. See also Lawrence Lasisi, "Syncretism," in Adeyemo, *Africa Bible Commentary*, 900, discussing syncretism, which he describes as the mixing of different religious beliefs and systems. The church needs to relate to a world that is increasingly religiously and culturally pluralistic. Faith must be contextualized to allow meaningful local expression of it in specific cultures.

CARRYING OUT THE GREAT COMMISSION

Not Minimizing Jesus Christ to Suit a Christian Nationalism Agenda

Some in our day see Jesus Christ as not masculine enough, not macho enough or enough of a warrior-like personality to live up to their idea of a hero. One author has written insightfully about this militancy in conservative White evangelicalism.[93] She describes it as an ideology of militant masculinity that enshrines patriarchal authority and condones the callous display of power at home and abroad. It looks down on the humility and gentleness (and servanthood) that Jesus exemplified and taught, considering it the province of wusses.[94] It is characterized by Christian nationalism, believing that America is God's chosen nation, and a commitment to aggressive, militant White masculinity.[95] The author also writes about how American Christianity was transformed in the early twentieth century with southern evangelicals redefining Christian manhood to sanction aggression or violence to maintain order and protect, and notes that this doctrine came to unite White men in America.[96] Instead of holiness, humility, and love being the defining characteristics of the Christian man, the author writes that masculinity became the mark of the authentic Christian man.[97]

Many in Jesus's day wanted him to be a political leader who would free Israel from Roman rule. They wanted to rebrand Jesus as a political messiah with an earthly kingdom. But Jesus made it clear that his kingdom was not of this world.[98] When Salome, the mother of James and John, sought positions of power and influence for her sons in Jesus's kingdom, which she presumed to be of this world, the other disciples were indignant. But Jesus told them they were not to think and act like those who hold power in the gentile world, who are seen as strong and powerful for lording it over others—strongmen, if you will. But in the kingdom of God, whose values are the values that those who profess faith

---

However, none of this can compromise the cores or absolutes of the gospel message, and the supremacy of Jesus Christ as Lord and Savior cannot be sacrificed. So, the obvious question is whether the politico-religious philosophy of Christian libertarianism aligns with the absolutes of the gospel message.

93. Kobes Du Mez, *Jesus and John Wayne*.
94. Kobes Du Mez, *Jesus and John Wayne*, 3.
95. Kobes Du Mez, *Jesus and John Wayne*, 4.
96. Kobes Du Mez, *Jesus and John Wayne*, 17.
97. Kobes Du Mez, *Jesus and John Wayne*, 32.
98. Matt 18:36. One author has characterized Jesus as a first-century political revolutionary. Hendricks, *Politics of Jesus*, 5–10.

THE CHRISTIAN AS IMITATOR OF CHRIST

in Christ must exemplify, greatness is measured by serving and laboring for the kingdom, not by seeking political power, supremacy, or societal or world domination.[99]

Jesus is the Prince of Peace.[100] When his birth was announced by the angels to the shepherds in the field, they proclaimed a message of peace on earth among those whom he favors.[101] This is clearly antithetical to a theology of war and aggression that despises peacemaking. Peace, humility, and gentleness are part of the fruit of the Spirit.[102] The author states that although professing biblical principles such as biblical authority, the need to be born again, the centrality of Christ's atonement, and the need to carry out the Great Commission, these evangelicals mix in other beliefs, including the goal of reforming society, which Jesus did not include in the Great Commission.[103] The author describes many of them as theologically illiterate, holding views that are inconsistent with biblical truth. She writes that they have highly commercialized the faith, forged political alliances, and carved out an evangelical popular culture with adherents who may not even belong to a church;[104] that they've mixed religion and secular conservatism into a political alliance; that their heroes may not necessarily even be evangelical Christians;[105] and that they declared and are deeply engaged in the culture war.[106] Their heroes include the actor John Wayne because of his masculine image.[107]

The author writes about a syncretism that happened in southern evangelicalism where Christian theology was mixed with the lost cause after the Civil War, resulting in a southern brand of religion that saw Robert E. Lee as its patron saint. She writes that during the 1960s civil rights movement, conservative evangelicals saw it as unpatriotic to admit

---

99. Matt 20:20–26; Mark 10:35–45. In Mark's account, it was James and John themselves who asked Jesus for this honor.
100. Isa 9:6–7.
101. Luke 2:14. The NKJV adds goodwill toward men.
102. Gal 5:22.
103. Kobes Du Mez, *Jesus and John Wayne*, 5.
104. Kobes Du Mez, *Jesus and John Wayne*, 6–9.
105. Kobes Du Mez, *Jesus and John Wayne*, 10–11.
106. Kobes Du Mez, *Jesus and John Wayne*, 13.
107. Kobes Du Mez, *Jesus and John Wayne*, 31.

CARRYING OUT THE GREAT COMMISSION

racism in the nation's history. They saw a Republican president as an ally[108] and opposed integration.[109]

The author writes that evangelicals thrive on a politics of fear that feeds into the need for a masculine protector and ruthless power. She believes that, although not explicitly stated, evangelicals believe Jesus saves souls but has nothing more to offer; someone like John Wayne, whom they idolize, cannot save souls but will be a protector, a savior of one's hide or "ass," as she put it. In other words, they may trust in Christ for salvation, but not for supremacy and domination. The latter only comes by doing things their own way—through White militant patriarchy mixed with religion.[110] They believe violence, or the threat of violence, secures order, which is contrary to what Christ taught.[111] They believe that the end of Christian nationalism, a conflation of God and country, is justified by any means thought necessary to accomplish it.[112] This is contrary to Jesus's command to love one's neighbor, regardless of their nationality, ethnicity, or skin color, as oneself. It is also contrary to Jesus's command to do unto others as we would have them do unto us.

Some also mischaracterized Jesus as an aggressive and angry leader who picked fights with the religious leaders of his time and ordered his disciples around, thinking that portraying him this way would appeal to men.[113] Others, believing no real man would want to follow a meek Jesus, have sought to rebrand him as a "badass" who has called his disciples of all time to be "spiritual badasses" locally and globally.[114] And some point to the bloody wars of the Old Testament as justification for modern-day Christians to engage in culture and religious wars.[115]

Yes, Jesus did get angry at profiteers who had turned the temple in Jerusalem into a marketplace and were exploiting the poor.[116] But that did not make him an anger-filled leader. Jesus did not demonstrate

---

108. Kobes Du Mez, *Jesus and John Wayne*, 38.
109. Kobes Du Mez, *Jesus and John Wayne*, 38.
110. Kobes Du Mez, *Jesus and John Wayne*, 59.
111. Kobes Du Mez, *Jesus and John Wayne*, 111.
112. Kobes Du Mez, *Jesus and John Wayne*, 117.
113. Kobes Du Mez, *Jesus and John Wayne*, 194.
114. Kobes Du Mez, *Jesus and John Wayne*, 247, citing McDougall, *Jesus Was an Airborne Ranger*, 11, 101, 114, and 119.
115. Kobes Du Mez, *Jesus and John Wayne*, 247, citing Boykin and Weber, *Warrior Soul*, 18, 31–32.
116. Matt 21:12–13; Mark 11:15–17; Luke 19:45.

chronic anger. He did not sin even though he became angry. And it was not Jesus who picked fights with religious leaders. They were the ones who picked fights with him, always seeking to test and trap him. Jesus did not cower before them. He always engaged them. He outwitted them, which made them even angrier. They are the ones who were always seeking ways to kill him.[117] He confronted them with their hypocrisy because they pretended to be righteous when they were not. What is more, they were hindering others from experiencing the kingdom of God.[118] Jesus never bossed his disciples around. He did give his disciples authority and sent them out to preach, heal, and cast out demons.[119] He did send them on errands such as going to fetch him a colt to ride on into Jerusalem,[120] preparing an upper room for his last supper,[121] and going to buy food while traveling through Samaria.[122] But he was not doing this as some arrogant, worldly boss. In fact, Jesus told his disciples not to act like the gentiles who lorded it over others. Instead, they were to serve as he did.[123] And he even washed his disciples' feet.[124]

It is true that the Israelites fought many wars on their way to Canaan and after settling there. God gave them favor to win many battles against nations that practiced idolatry, including child sacrifices. David, their most famous warrior-king, fought and won many battles with God's help. After the Israelites settled in the promised land, God oftentimes used other nations to punish them for their idolatry and unfaithfulness to him. This was the case during the times of the Judges and after Israel chose to become a monarchy. The kingdom became divided into two after Solomon's reign—the northern kingdom of Israel (comprised of ten tribes) and the southern kingdom of Judah (comprised of two tribes). God used the Assyrians to destroy the northern kingdom in 722 BC[125] and the

---

117. Mark 11:18; Luke 19:47. Examples of other times when they plotted to kill Jesus include when he challenged their traditions about the Sabbath in Matt 12:14; Mark 3:6; and Luke 6:11. They plotted to kill him for raising Lazarus from the dead in John 11:49, 57. They wanted to kill him for helping a cripple on the Sabbath in John 5:18, and because he used a title of God (I AM) to refer to himself in John 8:58–59.

118. Matt 23:13.

119. Matt 10; Mark 6:7–13; Luke 10:1–20.

120. Mark 11:2; Luke 19:30.

121. Matt 26:17–19; Mark 14:12–13; Luke 22:7–13.

122. John 4:8.

123. Matt 20:25–28.

124. John 13:1–17.

125. 2 Kgs 17.

Babylonians to destroy the southern kingdom in 586 BC.[126] Both conquests led to exile for many Jews. But none of this means God loves war or is pleased with it. Jesus did not preach a gospel infused with advocacy for military, as opposed to spiritual, warfare.[127] Neither did his apostles.[128]

Moreover, isn't Christ the Prince of Peace?[129] Isn't he the one who said blessed are the peacemakers for they shall be called sons of God?[130] The peacemakers are those who have been reconciled to God through Christ,[131] and who strive to reconcile others to God, including their enemies. They seek to bring others along with them to heaven, not dispatch them to hell through war and bloodshed. And when he was about to leave the earth, didn't Jesus say that he was giving his peace to his disciples? Isn't his peace able to keep his followers from living in fear—fear that can provoke war?

Much of this repackaged or rebranded gospel goes against Jesus's teachings and is influenced by culture and ideology, not biblical truth. Jesus did not charge his disciples to study war and fight worldly battles for supremacy. He charged them to carry out the Great Commission and to be salt and light to an unsavory and dark world so that souls will be saved and lives transformed to pave the way for his return.[132]

The belief that Jesus Christ does not live up to the idea of a hero could not be farther from the truth. It is fueled by the same error that many in Jesus's day exemplified—namely, wanting Jesus's kingdom to be of this world because their focus is on this world. Jesus is the second person of the Triune God, the Holy Trinity. He is the full bodily representation of God. He gave up his throne in heaven and took on the form of a man to redeem sinful humanity. The apostle Paul pointed out that very rarely will anyone die for a righteous man, and that perhaps some might possibly dare to die for a good man. Yet, Christ died for sinners.[133] Jesus is a king who gave up his throne in heaven and came to earth to die a horrific, gruesome death on a cross,[134] a death that is considered

126. 2 Kgs 25; 2 Chr 36:15–21.
127. Matt 12:29; Mark 3:27.
128. Eph 6:12.
129. Isa 9:6.
130. Matt 5:9.
131. Rom 5:1.
132. Matt 24:14.
133. Rom 5:7–8.
134. Phil 2:6–8.

THE CHRISTIAN AS IMITATOR OF CHRIST

cursed,[135] being humanity's only hope of redemption. His death on the cross was not the end of the story. God raised him from the dead with his incomparably great power and seated him at his right hand in the heavenly realms far above all rule and authority, power and dominion, and every title that can be given, not only in this present age, but in the age to come. And God has placed all things under his feet.[136] Because Jesus did his Father's will, he has been given a name above every name. At his name, every knee will bow and every tongue, including those that call him a wuss, will confess that he is Lord, to the glory of God the Father.[137] He will rule the nations with an iron scepter when he returns in power and glory.[138] He will judge the living and the dead.[139] He does not need mere mortals that he created to help him remake his image into some sort of "macho man."

That is the good news about Jesus that anyone who professes to be a Christian should, with the help of the Holy Spirit, be sharing with everyone everywhere, regardless of their nationality, ethnicity, skin color, or socioeconomic status.

---

135. Gal 3:13, quoting Deut 21:22–23.

136. Eph 1:18–22. See Adeyemo, *Africa Bible Commentary*, 1428, commenting that Jesus is now seated at the right hand of the Father in a place of honor, power, and authority that far exceeds that of all other powers and titles, whether human, demonic, or angelic, both present and future. He has become the ruler of the universe. All spirit beings are subject to him and can be said to be under his feet. See also Esau D. McCaulley, "Letter to the Ephesians," in McCaulley et al., *New Testament in Color*, 418, commenting that Christ has not merely defeated death, but has ascended to God's right hand in power beyond all authorities, including the demonic grip of racism.

137. Phil 2:10–11. See M. Sydney Park, "Letter to the Philippians," in McCaulley et al., *New Testament in Color*, 464, where he comments that in his self-emptying, humility, and obedience to humiliating death, Christ reveals God's character. In response, God exalts him to the highest point by giving him the name that is above every name. It can only be God's own name, YHWH. God's honor and glory bestowed to Christ is all-extensive in its sovereignty as every being in all three dimensions of the world, whether living or dead, whether human or angelic, submits and confesses that Jesus Christ is Lord.

138. Ps 2:9, NIV; Rev 19:11–16.

139. 2 Tim 4:1.

The Great Commission: The Promise of Christ's Abiding Presence

Jesus promised his disciples, then and now, that as they carry out the Great Commission, he will be with them till the end of the age.[140] Jesus fulfilled this promise through his Holy Spirit, whom he sent as a helper to empower his disciples. Through the indwelling Holy Spirit, Christ's presence remains with his disciples. Jesus also abides with his disciples through his word. He is the Word.[141] He is with his disciples as they abide in him and his word abides in them.[142] Mark affirms that Jesus was indeed with his disciples as they preached everywhere, and that he confirmed his word through the signs that accompanied them.[143]

Jesus takes the Great Commission so seriously that he holds off his coming until the gospel has been preached to every nation to give people everywhere the opportunity to be saved. He wants no one to perish in hell. He wants everyone to have eternal life.[144] Christians must therefore grasp the immense importance of the Great Commission and, empowered by the Holy Spirit, diligently share this good news with everyone, regardless of nationality, ethnicity, skin color, or socioeconomic status, both locally and globally.

---

140. Matt 28:20. See Harrington, *Gospel of Matthew*, 415, commenting that the promise to be with the disciples until the end of the age envisions an abiding presence of the risen Lord among Christians. See also Culpepper, *Matthew*, 585, commenting that Jesus's last words are a promise, an assurance, that echoes the Lord's promise to Joshua. The risen one's presence communicates covenant faithfulness, deliverance in times of crisis, and empowerment for the church's mission. The Lord will be with his disciples, all who read or hear the gospel, until the end of the age—Immanuel.

141. John 1:1–2.

142. John 15:5–7.

143. Mark 16:20.

144. 2 Pet 3:9.

8

Committing to a Local Church

DURING HIS EARTHLY MINISTRY, Jesus was often found teaching in the temple, synagogues, people's homes, by the shore, and on mountainsides. He was also often found fellowshipping with all kinds of people, from his disciples to their families, friends like Lazarus and his sisters, tax collectors, and sinners. He was always engaging all kinds of people, from Pharisees, Sadducees, scribes, and teachers of the law to ordinary Jews on matters of faith. As imitators of Jesus Christ, Christians must also commit to a local assembly or church where they can fellowship and engage with others, grow from biblical teaching that equips them to serve, and benefit from discipleship that empowers them to treat the poor and people of all ethnicities like Jesus did.[1]

Jesus Christ is the head of the church.[2] The church is referred to as the body of Christ.[3] The Greek word for church is *ekklesia*,[4] meaning assembly. Although it originally referred to an assembly of citizens, a

---

1. See Jamieson, *Committing to One Another*, answering the question why join a church, expounding on the scriptural reason for becoming a church member, what it looks like to be a healthy member of the body, and how to serve in one's local congregation.

2. Col 1:18. See Adeyemo, *Africa Bible Commentary*, 1451 commenting that Paul presents Jesus as the head over humanity, creation, and his new creation, the church. The church is like a new society composed of those who have been reconciled to God by Jesus Christ.

3. 1 Cor 12:27; Eph 1:22–23.

4. See Vine et al., *Vine's Complete Expository Dictionary*, 42 and 122 (New Testament Section).

called-out assembly or a regularly convened political body,[5] and was also used to describe the congregation of Israel,[6] it is used primarily in the New Testament to denote a Christian congregation or assembly. References to the church may be references to a local church[7] or congregation,[8] or the universal church, that is, the church in general.[9]

There is only one way to become a member of the church or the body of Christ, and that is by being born again through faith in Jesus Christ. Jesus said that no one can see the kingdom of God unless he or she is born again, and no one can enter the kingdom of God unless he or she is born of water and the Spirit.[10] One who has not been born again can attend or join a local church, but that doesn't make that person a Christian or a member of the body of Christ.

After becoming a member of the body of Christ through regeneration or the new birth, can one be a faithful Christian and yet not commit to or belong to a local church where one worships with other believers, is discipled and taught God's word, serves, and helps support the work of the kingdom of God? There are some who profess to be Christians but insist that they do not have or need to belong to a local church; however, the Bible does not support this position. The writer of Hebrews exhorted the believers to whom he wrote not to give up meeting together.[11]

The Essence of Commitment

To make a commitment is to promise to do something, support someone or something, or behave in a particular way.[12] It can also be a firm deci-

---

5. As in Acts 19:39.
6. Acts 7:38.
7. Such as the church in Jerusalem in Acts 8:1.
8. Heb 2:12.
9. Matt 16:18; Eph 1:22.
10. John 3:3, 5. See Moloney, *Gospel of John*, 91–93, where he explains that Jesus was challenging Nicodemus to expand his notion of what the kingdom of God might be by saying one must be born again from above, meaning one must both be born of water in time (a ritual of rebirth solemnized by water baptism) and of the Spirit by experiencing the inbreaking of God.
11. Heb 10:25.
12. Oxford, "Commitment (n.)."

sion to do something,[13] an agreement or pledge to do something in the future,[14] or an obligation.[15]

The concept of commitment is at the heart of the Christian faith. Out of his immeasurable love for humanity, God committed his only Son to the redemption of a fallen world[16] and Jesus Christ committed himself to doing the Father's will[17] in laying down his life as a ransom for fallen humanity.[18] He committed himself, as did his disciples, to do the works of the one who sent him while it was still day because night comes when no one can work.[19] Jesus did his Father's will by going to the cross and finishing the work he came to do. After his resurrection, before he ascended to heaven, he made a commitment to be with his disciples of all time until the end of the age.[20]

Just as God demonstrated his love for us by committing his Son to our salvation, God wants the redeemed to also be committed to him. When a great number of people in Antioch believed the gospel and turned to the Lord, the leaders of the church in Jerusalem sent Barnabas there to minister to them. Barnabas encouraged the new believers to continue with the Lord. In other words, they were to make a wholehearted commitment to remain true to the Lord.[21] God also wants Christians to be committed to his word as their moral and spiritual compass.[22]

---

13. Cambridge, "Commitment (n.)."
14. Merriam-Webster, "Commitment (n.)."
15. Dictionary.com, "Commitment (n.)."
16. John 3:16; Rom 5:8.
17. Matt 26:39; Mark 14:36; Luke 22:42.

18. Matt 20:28; Mark 10:45. See Harrington, *Gospel of Matthew*, 287–89, where he comments that the word *ransom* describes the deliverance of a captive by means of a purchase. The giving of Jesus's life meant martyrdom. See also Boring, *Mark: A Commentary*, 302–3, interpreting Jesus's coming to lay down his life as a ransom for many as referring to the servant ministry of the Christ-event as a whole and to his death as salvific for everyone.

19. John 9:4. See Moloney, *Gospel of John*, 291–92, interpreting this to mean that Jesus was including his disciples in his work. The presence of the light of the world will not be limited to the historical life of Jesus, it will continue in the presence of Jesus in his associates, the disciples.

20. Matt 28:20. See Culpepper, *Matthew*, 585, commenting that Jesus's last words are a promise, an assurance, which echoes the Lord's promise to Joshua. The Lord will be with his disciples, all who read or hear the gospel, until the end of the age.

21. Acts 11:23.

22. David made and expressed this same commitment to God's word in Ps 119:11, 31, 33, 105.

Why Commit to a Local Church?

There are gifts that God gives to believers that are meant for the benefit of the church or the body of Christ. These gifts require a commitment on the part of the believer to be part of a local church where they can be used to build up the church. A believer cannot keep these gifts to himself or herself.

Paul gave the Corinthians direction on a number of issues, including spiritual gifts and their proper use in corporate worship. He explained that there are different kinds of manifestations of the Spirit that are given to individual believers by the Holy Spirit for the common good as the Holy Spirit determines or wills.[23] Believers are to also eagerly desire spiritual gifts that may be used for the benefit of the church in corporate worship.[24] These gifts include the message or word of wisdom, the message or word of knowledge, supernatural faith that transcends saving faith, gifts of healing, miraculous powers, prophecy, discerning or distinguishing between spirits, different kinds of tongues, and the interpretation of tongues.[25] The apostle Paul made it abundantly clear that these gifts must be exercised in love for the benefit of others in the body of Christ.[26] The apostle Peter also made this same point about gifts being used to serve others.[27] Those who demonstrate these spiritual gifts but whose lives are devoid of the qualities that characterize love—patience, kindness, humility, selflessness, temperance, forgiveness, truthfulness, trust, hope, and perseverance—qualities that are consistent with the fruit of the Spirit—are really not operating under the influence of the Holy Spirit and with God's approval. Paul characterized them as nothing, just mere noise makers attracting attention.[28] For this reason, believers are warned to test the spirits to see whether they are from God because there are many false prophets operating among believers with counterfeit gifts.[29] Paul emphasized the supremacy of love over spiritual gifts by pointing out that

---

23. 1 Cor 12:7, 11.

24. 1 Cor 12:31; 14:1.

25. 1 Cor 12:8–10. A believer may be given a combination of these gifts by the Holy Spirit, but believers are to also desire these gifts eagerly.

26. 1 Cor 12:7.

27. 1 Pet 4:10.

28. 1 Cor 13:1–7. Paul describes the one who speaks in angelic tongues without love as a resounding gong or a clanging cymbal. 1 Cor 13:1, NIV.

29. 1 John 4:1–3. The apostle John gives the litmus test of confessing both the divinity and humanity of Christ to distinguish between a spirit that is of the antichrist and one that is of God.

ultimately, when Christ returns at the end of the age and believers live in the presence of God in the new heaven and the new earth, believers will no longer need these spiritual gifts to strengthen them. However, they will still live together in love.[30]

Paul zeroed in on two particular gifts and their proper use in public worship—prophecy and speaking in tongues. Paul indicated that he would rather believers desire the gift of prophecy over the gift of speaking in an unknown tongue in public worship because the congregation will be strengthened, encouraged, or comforted by the prophetic utterance which they can understand. On the other hand, unless the message in an unknown tongue is interpreted and made intelligible to all, it does not benefit the congregation. Evidently the Corinthians were eager to have spiritual gifts, so Paul exhorted them to try to excel in gifts that build up or edify the church.[31]

In addition to the manifestations of the gifts of the Spirit, Paul also taught about grace gifts and ministry gifts, in which believers operate or function beyond the episodic manifestations of spiritual gifts in a church service or gathering of the body of Christ.

Regarding grace gifts, Paul told the church in Rome that every believer has been given a measure of faith by God and must use their different gifts, extended to them through God's grace, in exercise of that faith. The Greek word for gift in this context is *charisma*, meaning a gift of grace.[32] Believers with the gift of prophesying must use it in proportion to their faith. Those with a gift to serve, teach, or encourage must exercise those gifts. Those who have a gift to give toward the needs of others must do so generously. Those with a gift of leadership are to lead diligently and those with a gift of showing mercy to others must do so cheerfully.[33] These gifts represent abilities given to individual believers for the good of the congregation.

Regarding ministry gifts, Paul mentioned five ministry gifts in his Letter to the Ephesians[34] and seven ministry gifts in his first Letter to the

---

30. 1 Cor 13:8–10, 13.

31. 1 Cor 14:1–12.

32. See "*Charisma*" and "*Charis*" in Vine et al., *Vine's Complete Expository Dictionary*, 264 (New Testament Section). *Charis* in Greek means grace.

33. Rom 12:3–8. See Adeyemo, *Africa Bible Commentary*, 1369, commenting that believers must serve the community of believers with the ability God has given them, and that Paul is encouraging Christians to use their gifts to build up the church. The gifts must not be used selfishly, as they are given to build up the community.

34. Eph 4:11.

Corinthians.³⁵ Both Letters included gifts to serve as an apostle, prophet, or teacher. The Letter to the Ephesians added gifts to be an evangelist or pastor. The Letter to the Corinthians added gifts of healing, a special ability to help others, gifts of administration, and the gift to minister publicly in different kinds of tongues. And he made it clear that not all believers are given these ministry gifts to edify the body of Christ publicly. Although not all believers have the gift to bring a message in tongues to a congregation, every believer can receive the baptism of the Holy Spirit and the manifestation of speaking in another tongue as the disciples in Jerusalem, Paul, the Samaritans, the Ephesian disciples, and Cornelius's household did.³⁶ Spiritual gifts are given by Christ to spiritual leaders in the church to prepare believers for service so that the church body may be strengthened until believers are united in the faith and in the knowledge of Christ, maturing in the process, becoming more like Christ, and no longer gullible to false teaching. Through the use of these ministry gifts, believers will come to the point where they can speak the truth in love and grow in Christlikeness in every way.³⁷

All spiritual gifts are to be committed to and used for the building up and maturing of believers in the church. One cannot keep these gifts to oneself in isolation from the church. It is, therefore, inconsistent with God's intent for a believer not to belong to and commit to serving in a local church and using their God-given gifts to benefit other believers.

Biblical Metaphors that Illustrate the Importance of Committing to a Local Church

The Church Is a Spiritual House or Temple

In his Letter to believers scattered throughout Asia Minor, the apostle Peter referred to Jesus as a living stone and to the believers as living stones that are being built into a spiritual house. Jesus is the precious stone. Peter referred to Christ's rejection by Israel as a rejection by the builders. Although rejected, Peter said that Jesus Christ has become the chief cornerstone or capstone.³⁸

---

35. 1 Cor 12:28.
36. 1 Cor 12:29–30.
37. Eph 4:12–15.
38. 1 Pet 2:4–7. See Adeyemo, *Africa Bible Commentary*, 1519, commenting that Peter is referring to Christ as the chosen and precious cornerstone, a strong foundation

The apostle Paul used this same metaphor of the church as a building or temple when he wrote to the Ephesians. He described the believers as members of God's household, built on the foundation of the apostles and the prophets, with Christ Jesus himself as the chief cornerstone. Paul said that in Christ, the whole building is joined together and rises to become a holy temple in the Lord. And beyond being part of a spiritual building or temple, Paul said that each believer is also being built into a dwelling in which God lives by his Spirit.[39]

A stone building is made up of individual stones that have been fitted and framed together in such a way that they have become one whole structure. Stones are stacked under, above, and beside each other to support and hold each other together. This symbolizes Christians needing each other and standing together. It also symbolizes spiritual leaders providing covering and protection for the stones under them that submit to their authority. One cannot simply pull a stone out of a building. Nor can one do so without causing damage to the building. The church being a spiritual building, Paul said the apostles and prophets are the foundation and Jesus Christ is the capstone or chief cornerstone. And all believers are living stones who fit into this spiritual building or temple that rises in the Lord. A believer cannot, therefore, live independently of the church. That would be like an isolated stone that exists by itself and is not part of a building or structure. Such a believer does not fit God's design for the church.

The Church Is a Body

In his Letter to the Galatians, the apostle Paul told them of the grace gifts that Christ has given to people in the church to prepare believers to serve so that the church might be built up and become mature and Christlike. Believers will then grow in Christ, whom Paul described as the head of the body, the body being the church, and believers being the various parts of the body that are joined and held or knit together by every supporting ligament or joint. This body, connected to Christ as head, grows

---

stone on which it is safe to erect a building, hence the fact that the one who trusts in him will never be put to shame.

39. Eph 2:19–22; 1 Cor 6:19. See Adeyemo, *Africa Bible Commentary*, 1430, commenting that in ancient buildings, the cornerstone was highly valued because it tied the whole building together. This is precisely what Jesus Christ does for the church, which Paul describes as a new temple.

and builds itself up in love as every part of the body does its work, or as every believer in the church does his or her part.[40]

In his first Letter to the Corinthians, the apostle Paul again used the body as a metaphor to describe the church and its relationship to Jesus Christ. He said the body has many parts; yet it is still one body or unit. Likewise, all believers, regardless of identity, are members of the body of Christ. None of the parts of the body can function on their own or in isolation. No part is less important. The body is incomplete if a part is missing. Each part of the body needs the other parts. Even those parts of the body that may appear to be weaker are indispensable. That means a believer, regardless of their level of development, cannot isolate himself or herself from the body of Christ and refuse to commit to a local church.

In our own lives, we find out how important each body part is when we hurt a seemingly insignificant body part like a finger or a toe or lose the use of those body parts. Just as with the physical body, in the body of Christ, each member is equally important, although they may have different gifts and roles. This is to ensure that the body of Christ is not divided, but that members have equal concern for each other. The body's many parts have different functions, but each is equally important. In both the physical body and the body of Christ, when one part of the body hurts, the entire body hurts with it. If one part is honored, the whole body is honored.[41]

An Olympic track star's legs don't take all the glory for winning a race. Nor does the track star's neck take all the glory because a medal is hung around it. Certainly, it's not just the track star's legs that commiserate if he or she takes a tumble and does not finish the race. Likewise, in the church, if a church member suffers a loss, the church grieves with that person. And if a church member receives an honor, other church members celebrate with the honoree.

As members of the body of Christ, believers fellowship and worship together. In the times of the early church in Jerusalem, the believers there devoted themselves to the teachings of the apostles, to fellowship, the breaking of bread, and to prayer. They supported one another and got

---

40. Eph 4:7, 11–17.

41. 1 Cor 12:12–27. See Adeyemo, *Africa Bible Commentary*, 1392, commenting that regardless of their origins, all Christians are baptized by the Holy Spirit and filled with the same one Spirit. All are thus part of Christ's body. See also Gene L. Green, "First Letter to the Corinthians," in McCaulley et al., *New Testament in Color*, 345, commenting that Paul focuses on mutuality and the honor ascribed to even the lowliest member of the body. All members are necessary and should therefore receive honor.

together in their homes to fellowship and praise God together.[42] Likewise, in Troas, during Paul's second missionary journey, the church there came together on the first day of the week to break bread.[43]

One of the reasons for committing to a local church and gathering with other believers is for believers to encourage one another when they assemble together. The writer of Hebrews exhorted the believers to whom he wrote not to give up meeting together. Evidently, some were in the habit of doing so. He said encouraging one another was especially important since the day of the Lord, the day of Christ's return, is approaching.[44]

When someone accepts the Lord as Savior and becomes a believer, the Lord himself adds the person to the church[45] and the Holy Spirit baptizes or places that person into the body of Christ in spiritual fellowship and unity with other believers.[46] It is with this understanding that every believer must recognize the importance of committing to a local church and using their God-given gifts to serve others and build up the body of Christ for the work God has called the church to do.

The Church is a Household or Family

The apostle Paul told the Ephesians that, although gentiles were once without Christ and separated from God's people, as a result of Christ's having redeemed them with his own blood through his death on the cross, they were now members of the household of God.[47]

God has a family in heaven and on earth. Both are called by his name.[48] His family in heaven consists of believers who have finished their

---

42. Acts 2:42–47.
43. Acts 20:7.
44. Heb 10:25.
45. Acts 2:47.
46. 1 Cor 12:13.
47. Eph 2:11–13, 19. See Adeyemo, *Africa Bible Commentary*, 1430, commenting that Jesus Christ by his atoning death reconciled Jews and gentiles to one another and reconciled them both to God. He broke down the wall that divided Jews and gentiles. In Christ, they are both one, brothers and sisters with the other citizens and family members. See also Esau D. McCaulley, "Letter to the Ephesians," in McCaulley et al., *New Testament in Color*, 419, commenting that the gentiles were excluded from citizenship in Israel, foreigners to the covenants of promise, and separated from the Messiah. But through Christ, God has brought gentiles into a relationship with himself through the blood of his Son.
48. Eph 3:15.

race and gone to heaven. His family on earth consists of those who have received Jesus Christ as Lord and Savior and do his will. Jesus said whoever does the will of his Father in heaven is his brother, sister, and mother.[49] Believers who are living obedient lives are, therefore, members of the family of God. Through faith in Jesus Christ, they have all become God's children, having been baptized into Christ.[50] Paul told the Galatians that this family of God transcends racial, ethnic, gender, and social status, there being neither Jew nor Greek, slave nor free, male nor female.[51]

Paul described this family of God elsewhere as the household of faith. He urged believers to be good to all people especially members of the household of faith.[52] As a member of the family of God or the household of faith, a believer must commit to a local church where this family gathers, fellowships, prays, is discipled through the preaching of the word, teaching, and exhortation, and serves one another and the surrounding community to which it is called to be salt and light.

Practical Demonstrations of One's Commitment to the Local Church

Giving One's Time and Energy to the Local Church

One way of demonstrating one's commitment to the local church is to give one's time and energy to the church. This goes beyond attending church services and fellowship to committing time and energy to serve. As a follower of Christ, I committed significant time and energy to teaching adult Bible classes in the church for three decades. I taught Bible classes with the same degree of preparation and attention I gave to my classes as a university professor. I spent several hours each week using teacher's manuals and Bible study resources to study the lesson, prepare an outline, and put together insightful questions to provoke thought and facilitate interaction among class members. Every Sunday was like a workday, leaving early to teach my Bible class and attend church services,

---

49. Matt 12:50; Mark 3:35. See Boring, *Mark: A Commentary*, 110, explaining that becoming a disciple of Jesus brings one into a new family where believers are not only brothers and sisters to each other, but as Jesus's brother, belong with him as brothers and sisters to the family of God.

50. Gal 3:26–27.

51. Gal 3:28.

52. Gal 6:10.

and then spending a couple of hours after returning home to begin work on the following week's lesson.

At a local church that I attended while living in Virginia, dozens of people gave their lives to the Lord each Easter Sunday. Many came to church once a year, at Easter, and quite a number would respond to the gospel message and the invitation to give their lives to Christ. Following Jesus's Great Commission, these new converts were baptized in water and enrolled in a class specifically designed to teach new converts the basic truths about the word of God and living life as a faithful steward and disciple of Christ. I and a number of others taught these classes. The class included giving the new converts Bible quizzes to help them learn. I spent time grading them and returned them during the next class.

Other believers committed their time and energy in different ways. Some worked in the parking lot helping direct cars into parking spaces. Some served as ushers helping people find seats in an orderly manner. Others helped collect and count the offering. Some helped distribute communion elements. Some gave their time, energy, and talents to the music ministry. Some worked in security and others helped clean the church. Some served on deacon boards assisting the church leadership with the administration and the carrying out of the vision and mission of the church. In other churches that I have attended, many members have spent their time and energy doing these same things.

It is God who gives us our time on earth. Whatever time we spend on earth is by his grace. As Christians, committing some of that time to the work of his kingdom in a local church is an acknowledgment that we are only stewards of our time.

Giving One's Gifts and Talents to the Local Church

Another way of demonstrating the believer's commitment to the local church is by using his or her gifts and talents for the benefit of the local church. Believers have various God-given gifts that are meant for the benefit of the church or the body of Christ. Paul told the Corinthians that there are different kinds of manifestations of the Spirit that are given to individual believers by the Holy Spirit for the common good as the Holy

Spirit determines or wills[53] and spiritual gifts that may be used to benefit the church in corporate worship.[54]

As already seen earlier in this chapter, in addition to the manifestations of the gifts of the Spirit, there are also grace gifts and ministry gifts that believers are given for the benefit of the local church.

All spiritual gifts are, therefore, to be committed to the building up and maturing of believers in the church. They cannot be exercised without being a part of a local church.

Giving One's Treasure or Finances to Support the Work of the Local Church

Believers also demonstrate their commitment to the local church through their giving to support the mission and work of the local church. It takes resources to carry out the mission of the church, which includes the church's various ministries, both local and global. The church also needs resources for the remuneration of its full-time leadership and staff, the upkeep of its physical plant, and payment of utilities.

It is God who gives humans power to get wealth.[55] Therefore, all wealth is held in stewardship for God. As God's stewards, believers demonstrate their commitment to the local church when they give to support the work of the kingdom of God through that local church. This work includes local and global missionary work. It includes serving the communities in which local churches are embedded. And it also includes acts of benevolence to those in need, whether members of the local church, other affiliated churches, residents of the church's surrounding communities, or people who live in other communities or even countries.

The Christians in Macedonia are a good example of this. Although poor, they gave generously to help their fellow Christians in Judea. The Corinthians made a commitment to help likewise, and Paul urged them to follow through.[56] Paul sent fellow workers ahead of time to help them finish whatever arrangements they needed to make to finalize their gift.[57]

Commitment to a local church through giving is seen as an expression of the believer's relationship with God. Christians must first give

---

53. 1 Cor 12:7, 11.
54. 1 Cor 12:31; 14:1.
55. Deut 8:18.
56. 2 Cor 8:6–10, 24.
57. 2 Cor 9:5.

themselves to God as the Macedonians did, for it is that relationship of total surrender to God that grounds the Christian's giving. This relationship defines giving to the local church, which will show in the following ways. The giving will be done willingly from the heart, not reluctantly or under compulsion.[58] It will be in proportion to what one has or the measure of one's financial blessing.[59] It will be cheerful because God loves a cheerful giver.[60] It will be generous because one understands that the one who sows generously will also reap generously.[61] It will be sacrificial, thus making it even more meaningful to God.[62] It will be regular, set aside based on income as one earns,[63] and therefore also systematic.[64] Finally, it will be loving. It will flow out of love for God and the work of his kingdom on earth, and out of love for those who benefit from the believer's giving.

Although Christians do not live under the Old Testament law, like Jacob who promised to give a tenth of everything God gave him back to God,[65] believers may give a tithe of their income to God through the local church in recognition of God's provision and their stewardship. Believers may also bring offerings to the church as gifts to the Lord. These may be to express thanks for answered prayer or for a blessing, or it may support a specific need in the church or the work of missionaries.

---

58. 2 Cor 8:5. See Adeyemo, *Africa Bible Commentary*, 1406, commenting that the secret of the Macedonians' generosity was that they gave themselves first to the Lord. They and all their possessions became the Lord's property.

59. 2 Cor 8:12. See Adeyemo, *Africa Bible Commentary*, 230, commenting that the New Testament principle is to give in proportion to how God has blessed us.

60. "Cheerful" as used here comes from the Greek word *hilaros*, meaning cheerful. See Vine et al., *Vine's Complete Expository Dictionary*, 98 (New Testament Section). See also Strong's Reference Number 2431, defining *hilaros* as joyous or cheerful.

61. 2 Cor 9:6–7, 13.

62. Mark 12:41–44; Luke 21:1–4. See Johnson, *Gospel of Luke*, 316–19, commenting that the widow exemplifies the righteous poor who receive the good news, as shown by her response of disposing of her own possessions. The rich gave out of their excess, but the widow gave her very means of subsistence.

63. 1 Cor 16:1.

64. 1 Cor 16:2, NIV. The NKJV says to lay something aside on the first day of each week.

65. Gen 28:22.

Practical Ways in Which Committing to a Local Church Manifests Itself in Relationships with Other Believers

Because the church is a body of believers, committing to a local church involves a commitment to fellow believers. This commitment to other believers is not necessarily limited only to believers in one's local assembly or even denomination but extends to all true believers. And Christians should not feel they can only commit to a church whose members share the same nationality, ethnicity, skin color, or socioeconomic status. They must allow themselves to be led by God, through the Holy Spirit, to commit to a church where God has called them to be and where they can grow and serve the Lord and others. This commitment manifests itself in many ways. These include actions that believers engage in or do not engage in with respect to other believers in their local church and the church in general, as seen below.

Loving One Another

Loving one another is one way in which believers in the church demonstrate their commitment to each other. Jesus told his disciples that he was giving them a new commandment, which was to love one another as he had loved them. He said this was how everyone would know that they were his disciples.[66] It is significant that Jesus did not say that people would recognize Christians by their pronouncements of faith, their anointing, political influence, or even their miraculous or praiseworthy deeds. Instead, he said the key to being recognized as a Christian is the ability to love other believers genuinely, regardless of who they are, just as he had modeled for his disciples.

The apostle Peter told the believers to whom he wrote to love one another deeply from the heart with the sincere love they now had as a result of obeying the truth.[67] And the apostle John made it clear that whoever does not love does not know God because God is love. He also said that the one who claims to love God but hates another believer is a

---

66. John 13:34–35.

67. 1 Pet 1:22. See Adeyemo, *Africa Bible Commentary*, 1519, commenting that imitating Christ also means imitating his love for others. Christ cared for individuals who were bereaved, sick, hungry, and demon possessed. Christians, too, should love one another deeply from the heart. Our love for our fellow human beings should be steadfast, rooted in the transformation God's imperishable word has produced in us.

liar.[68] In other words, the evidence that we love God is the fact that we love other believers, including those who do not look like us because they are of a different nationality, ethnicity, or skin color, and those who come from different socioeconomic backgrounds. The Greek word for this love that Christ was talking about is *agapé*. It is a love which seeks the welfare of all[69] and does no ill to anyone.[70] It does not come from feelings and is not expressed only to people with whom one has some affinity.[71] It is the kind of love God has for humanity[72] and for his elect.[73] And it is only with the help of the indwelling Holy Spirit that Christians can demonstrate this love for others that distinguishes them as disciples of Christ.

Building Up One Another

In his Letter to the Romans, Paul exhorted them to make up their minds not to put any stumbling block or obstacle in the way of other believers that would cause their spiritual downfall. In other words, it is unacceptable to impose limitations on another's freedom in the Lord through fleshly criticism on matters where there is no right or wrong.[74] Rather, Paul urged the Romans to make every effort to do the kinds of things that help to edify or build each other up.[75] In his Letter to the Ephesians, Paul urged them to make peace and mutual upbuilding or edification of others the litmus test for what they say. He admonished them not to let evil talk come out of their mouths. Instead, whatever they said must meet the need to build up those to whom they spoke.[76]

---

68. 1 John 4:8, 20. See Miguel G. Echevarria, "Letters of John," in McCaulley et al., *New Testament in Color*, 718, where he comments that obeying the command to love one another reveals that we have been born of God, which is the same as experiencing new birth. Only the Holy Spirit enables us to love our neighbor. Failing to love others means we do not know God, otherwise we would share his love with others.

69. Rom 15:2.

70. Rom 13:10.

71. See Vine et al., *Vine's Complete Expository Dictionary*, 381–82 (New Testament Section). Also, Strong's Reference Number 26, defining *agapé* as love or goodwill.

72. John 3:16; Rom 5:8.

73. John 14:21.

74. Rom 14:1–6, 13.

75. Rom 14:19.

76. Eph 4:29 The NIV speaks of unwholesome talk.

Serving One Another

As we have already seen, believers in the body of Christ have been given various gifts by the Holy Spirit. But these gifts are not for the believer to hoard. They are to be used to serve others in the church—to edify others. They are for the common good.[77] The apostle Peter said that everyone must use whatever gift they have received to faithfully serve others as good stewards of the manifold grace of God.[78]

Encouraging One Another

The apostle Paul assured the believers in Thessalonica about the Lord's return, the resurrection of the dead in Christ, and the catching up of believers who are alive to meet with the Lord in the air and to be with him forever. The latter phenomenon is referred to as the rapture of the church. Not only did Paul tell the believers in Thessalonica these things to instill them with hope, but just as importantly, he exhorted them to encourage one another to keep the faith by reminding each other of this glorious future.[79]

Forgiving One Another

In his Letter to the Ephesians, the apostle Paul wrote to them about how to conduct themselves in the body of Christ. He urged them to be kind and tenderhearted toward each other, and to forgive each other just as God had forgiven them in Christ.[80]

In the model prayer that Jesus used to teach his disciples how to pray, he made several petitions to God. The fifth petition asked for forgiveness of sins but was conditioned on forgiving others for whatever wrongs they may have committed against the petitioner.[81] This means that in order to be forgiven for sin, the disciple must also forgive others. The requirement to forgive others means that being unforgiving is a sin that separates us from God. After completing the model prayer, Jesus

---

77. 1 Cor 12:7.
78. 1 Pet 4:10.
79. 1 Thess 4:13–18.
80. Eph 4:32. The NIV says to be kind and compassionate toward each other.
81. Matt 6:12; Luke 11:4.

returned to the issue of being unforgiving before moving on to address other issues by emphasizing that God will forgive us if we forgive others. On the other hand, God will not forgive us if we refuse to forgive others.[82] And Jesus never suggested that one should forgive only after the wrongdoer apologizes. Neither did he suggest that some wrongs are unforgivable.

When Jesus was still with his disciples, the apostle Peter asked him how many times he was supposed to forgive someone. Seven times? Peter evidently thought seven times would be plenty. After all, the number seven was also the number of completeness or perfection in Jewish numerology. Jesus's answer was that Peter would have to forgive, not seven times, but up to seventy times seven.[83] Jesus then proceeded to tell his disciples a parable in which he likened the kingdom of heaven to a king who settled his accounts receivable with his servants. One servant who owed 10,000 talents did not have the money to repay the debt. The king ordered that the servant be sold along with his family to repay the debt. However, the king had mercy when the servant begged for forgiveness, and he canceled the debt.

That same servant was owed one hundred denarii by a fellow servant who also begged for time to repay it. However, the servant who had been forgiven his debt refused to have mercy on his fellow servant and had him thrown into prison. When the king heard about what the unforgiving servant had done, he reversed his earlier decision and had the servant thrown into jail until his entire debt was repaid.[84]

A denarius or drachma was a daily wage in Jesus's time, meaning that one hundred denarii were a little over three months' wages. On the other hand, 10,000 talents amounted to a colossal sum, equal to 60 million denarii or drachmas. It would literally take multiple lifetimes for a servant earning a daily wage to pay it back. Jesus's use of this sum was a depiction of the debt of sin humankind could not possibly repay—a debt that was canceled only because Christ paid the debt with his own life. Jesus said at

---

82. Matt 6:14–15; Mark 11:25.

83. Matt 18:21–22.

84. Matt 18:21–34; Luke 17:3–4. See Harrington, *Gospel of Matthew*, 269–71, commenting that Jesus is making the point that there can be no limits to the willingness to forgive. Those who place limits on forgiving others will have limits placed on their forgiveness by God. To those who refuse to be merciful God will show strict justice. See also Culpepper, *Matthew*, 350–53, noting that counting how often one forgives is inimical to true forgiveness. We must forgive and keep on forgiving—and do so from the heart.

the end of the parable that this is how his heavenly Father will treat each of us unless we wholeheartedly forgive others from the heart.[85]

As unfair as it might seem, a disciple of Christ must forgive even the most egregious wrongs in order to remain in vital relationship with God. As desirable as an apology might be, the disciple cannot condition forgiveness on an apology and must be willing to forgive unconditionally. Of course, forgiveness does not mean a prior relationship can be maintained. Relationships are based on trust and where trust is completely destroyed, a relationship may no longer be possible. But there must still be forgiveness even if a relationship has to be permanently severed. This is especially true if the wrongdoer is an unbeliever. In the body of Christ, however, believers must always try to restore relationships that may have been strained or damaged by wrongdoing. In such cases, other believers in the church or church leaders may be able to assist in a process of reconciliation. If the wrongdoer still refuses to acknowledge wrongdoing, the believer must nonetheless forgive, except that now the wrongdoer is to be treated as an unbeliever and excluded from the church.[86]

God is not only able to forgive our sins, but he is also able to choose to forget our sin as a matter of his divine will.[87] Humans do not have that capacity. Even after one forgives, the memory of the wrong may remain and one might be tempted to take back the debt. It is, therefore, important to continually examine one's heart and affirm forgiveness whenever necessary.

Psychologists have said that forgiveness is really for the one who forgives and that refusing to forgive is harmful to one's own wellbeing.[88] In a real sense, beyond going against God's commands, refusing to forgive keeps one captive to the hurt and, ironically, gives the wrongdoer continued power over the one who refuses to forgive.

---

85. Matt 18:35.
86. Matt 18:15–17.
87. Isa 43:25; Mic 7:19; Heb 8:12.
88. See article by Herrera, "Let Go of Your Grudges," where he references the Stanford Forgiveness Project founded by Dr. Frederick Luskin and studies showing that forgiveness may help reduce anger, stress, and physical and mental health symptoms, including depression and damage to the cardiovascular system.

Admonishing and Exhorting One Another

In his Letter to the Colossians, the apostle Paul urged them to let the word of God, that is, the Scriptures, dwell in them richly as they taught and admonished one another with all wisdom and as they sang psalms, hymns, and spiritual songs with gratitude in their hearts to God. To admonish one another means to warn one another about something that is wrong based on the word of God. This could be because a believer is doing something that is inconsistent with the word of God or something that goes against their profession of faith in Christ.

The Old Testament gives us a stark example of a failure to admonish and the consequences of that failure in the family of Eli, the high priest of Israel. His sons, who ministered with him at the tent of meeting in Shiloh, slept with the women who served at the entrance of the tent of meeting. They also took portions of the meat the Israelites brought for sacrifice that were meant to be offered to the Lord. Although Eli confronted and rebuked his sons once because he had heard people talking about their misdeeds, he failed to admonish them to repent and cease and desist from their sinful acts. As a result, God sent a prophet to prophesy to Eli about the impending destruction of his house. This happened when the Philistines defeated the Israelites in battle and seized the ark of the covenant. Eli's two sons were killed in the battle and Eli fell backward and died of a broken neck when he heard the news.[89]

To admonish one another can also mean to exhort, urge, or encourage one another to do something, such as keeping the faith or staying the course. The author of Hebrews urged his audience not to give up meeting or assembling together. And as part of meeting or assembling together, they were to encourage one another, especially as the time for Christ's return nears, false teaching abounds, and persecution and trials mount.[90]

Refraining from Envying One Another

As can be seen in the above discussion, there are many things that believers do in their relationships with other believers as a result of their commitment to the local church. But there are also many things that believers must refrain from doing as a result of that commitment.

---

89. 1 Sam 2:12–17, 22–34; 4:1–18.
90. Heb 10:25.

One of the things believers must refrain from doing as a demonstration of their commitment to each other is envying one another. Envying someone involves wanting to be in their shoes or feeling aggrieved because of a blessing in their lives, a position they hold, or some favor they have. The one who envies is not happy for the one who is blessed. The apostle Paul urged the Galatians to live by the Spirit so that they would not gratify the desires of the sinful nature. He urged them to crucify the sinful nature with its passions and desires and keep in step with the Spirit. They were to avoid conceit and provoking and envying one another.[91]

Refraining from Hurting or Harming One Another

The apostle Paul reminded the Galatians that the entire Old Testament law is summarized in a single command—to love one's neighbor as oneself. And this love is made possible through the empowerment of the indwelling Holy Spirit in the life of the believer. He warned them that if they keep on biting or devouring each other, they should watch out or they will destroy each other.[92] The Living Bible, which is not a translation but a paraphrase based on the American Standard Version of the Bible, says not to be critical and catty lest believers ruin each other. This is essentially a warning that if love and unity are missing, the local church will self-destruct from members hurting and harming each other.

Refraining from Speaking Evil of One Another or Judging One Another

The apostle James, the head of the Jerusalem church, urged believers not to speak evil of each other or slander each other. Slandering or speaking evil of another person means saying things about them to others that are untrue and that reflect poorly on them. James also urged believers not to judge one another. Speaking evil of one another or judging one another violates God's law of love and constitutes judging that law. And when it comes to judging, James made it clear that there is only one lawgiver and

---

91. Gal 5:16–26. See Adeyemo, *Africa Bible Commentary*, 1423, commenting that the fighting in the Galatian church is an expression of their sinful nature. Such behavior indicates that those who practice it have no share in the kingdom of God. It is totally at odds with the behavior the Spirit desires.

92. Gal 5:15. See Adeyemo, *Africa Bible Commentary*, 1423, commenting that Paul compares the arguments disrupting the Galatian church to biting and devouring each other, and points out that this way of living is destructive for all who take part in it.

judge, and that is God, the one who has power to save and destroy. In light of that, no one is in a position to judge their neighbor.[93]

In his Letter to the Romans, the apostle Paul admonished them not to judge each other based on disputable matters that are governed by the level of one's faith. For example, believers are not to judge each other based on dietary choices. Paul also admonished them not to judge others based on how they viewed each day—whether they viewed each day equally or viewed some days, perhaps the Jewish feast days in Paul's day, as more special than the others. Instead of passing judgment on each other in these matters, Paul exhorted the Romans to make up their minds not to put any stumbling block or obstacle in the way of other believers.[94] Paul was saying that it is unacceptable to impose limitations on another's freedom in the Lord through fleshly criticism on matters where there is no right or wrong.

Benefits of Committing to a Local Church

As Christians imitate Christ's example and commit to engaging and fellowshipping with other believers in a local assembly, they will realize certain benefits.

In the early church, the believers' lives were characterized by continuing in the teaching of the apostles, fellowship, prayer, sharing meals, meeting each other's needs, gladness, praise, being regarded with favor, and having many others join their fellowship.[95]

Believers today can realize these same benefits when they commit to a local church. This commitment gives them the benefit of receiving biblical teaching or instruction under good pastoral leadership. Also, being a part of a local church alleviates isolation and loneliness as believers gather and fellowship together. This is especially true for believers who are single or widowed. And just as the early church members helped meet each other's needs, believers today can also benefit from the benevolence of others in the church in their times of need.

The early believers lived lives of unity and prayer. This led to effective outreach as God's power manifested itself in their ministry to their communities. The apostles did many signs and wonders and people were

---

93. Jas 4:11–12.
94. Rom 14:1–6, 13.
95. Acts 2:42–47.

filled with awe. People got saved every day and were added to the church. Committing to a local church where there is unity and devotion to prayer can unleash God's power to effectively reach lost souls.

Believers benefit tremendously from being part of a local church where they are able to receive love, comfort, admonition, exhortation, support, encouragement, instruction, and pastoral oversight.

In addition to these benefits, to commit to a local church is to be obedient to the exhortation to not forsake assembling together. When this commitment causes believers to walk together in love as God's family, receive biblical teaching, use their gifts to strengthen each other, and give of their time, energy, and resources to advance the work of the kingdom of God on earth, it all brings glory to the name of the Lord and equips them, with the help of the Holy Spirit, to live like Jesus did, including how he treated the poor and people of all ethnicities.

9

Treatment of the Poor

Jesus Christ loved, healed, delivered, preached to, and fed thousands of people, many of whom were poor. This chapter deals with how Christians, as followers and imitators of Jesus Christ, must treat the poor. It begins by examining what it means to be poor.

What Does It Mean to Be Poor?

A poor person is one who has very little money, not enough to meet basic needs,[1] someone lacking in material possessions,[2] or one with few possessions.[3] Being poor means one lacks the financial resources necessary to meet life's ordinary, everyday needs.

Poverty is the state or condition of being poor. At the end of the nineteenth century, it became more associated with having insufficient income to live appropriately than with pauperism, that is, receiving public or private assistance.[4] Of course, there are different levels of poverty. Some poor people may live at or just below the poverty line while others may be financially destitute, or "dirt poor," to use a colloquialism. In the

---

1. Oxford, "Poor (adj.)."
2. Merriam-Webster, "Poor (adj.)."
3. Cambridge, "Poor (adj.)."
4. Iceland, *Poverty in America*, 18.

United States, the official poverty rate in 2022 was 11.95 percent with 37.9 million people living in poverty.[5]

In the United States, the federal government, through the US Department of Health and Human Services, establishes poverty income guidelines each year for the contiguous states and the District of Columbia. These guidelines[6] determine financial eligibility for certain government programs such as the Supplemental Nutritional Assistance Program (SNAP) that offers eligible families food stamps, the National School Lunch Program, and Head Start. Under the guidelines for 2024, a one-person family would be entitled to certain benefits if their annual income were less than $15,060 a year. For a family of two or a family of four, they would be entitled to these benefits if their annual household income were less than $20,440 or $31,200, respectively. The 2024 poverty guidelines are based on the 2022 Census Bureau's poverty thresholds adjusted for price changes between 2022 and 2023 using the Consumer Price Index (CPI). The Census Bureau's poverty thresholds are used for statistical purposes, such as estimating the number of Americans in poverty each year. Families are considered to be in poverty if their total household income is lower than their family poverty threshold and individuals not living with family are considered to be in poverty if their individual income is lower than their individual poverty threshold.[7]

The Bible has numerous references to the poor, both in the Old and New Testaments. In the Old Testament, many of the references deal with treatment of the poor, as we shall see later in this chapter.

In the New Testament, many of these references occur during the time of Jesus's ministry. For example, when John the Baptist sent his disciples to ask Jesus if he was the Messiah, Jesus responded by telling them to go back and tell John what they were hearing and seeing—the blind were being given back their sight, the lame were walking, lepers were being cured, the deaf could hear, dead people were being raised, and the good news was being preached to the poor.[8] Many of the people Jesus referenced as having received a miracle would have been impoverished by their condition. Blindness, lameness, or leprosy would have prevented

---

5. United States Census Bureau, "National Poverty in America: January 2024."

6. Office of the Assistant Secretary for Planning and Evaluation. "Poverty Guidelines."

7. Poverty thresholds are issued each year for the prior year. See United States Census Bureau, "How the Census Bureau Measures Poverty."

8. Matt 11:5.

its sufferers from being able to work for a living. Therefore, their healing also gave them a chance to be freed from their poverty.

When Jesus was in Bethany in the home of Simon the leper, a woman came and poured a jar of expensive perfume on his head. The disciples were indignant that she had wasted the perfume. They felt it could have been sold and the proceeds given to the poor.[9] The Gospel of John has a different account of Mary, Lazarus's sister, anointing Jesus's feet with a very costly oil of spikenard as they prepared supper for him in their home. In John's account, it was Judas who made the comment about how wasteful the woman's gesture was, and how the perfume could have been sold and the proceeds given to the poor. John, however, notes that Judas did not say this because he cared about the poor; Judas was only concerned about himself because he was a thief. As treasurer of Jesus's ministry, the one who kept the money bag, he is reported to have been helping himself to the money. In both accounts, Jesus rebuked the objectors and told them to leave the woman alone. He remarked that they would always have the poor with them, but they would not always have him.[10]

While in the temple in Jerusalem, Jesus observed people putting their offerings in the treasury. He saw the rich put in large amounts and observed a widow putting in two copper coins or two mites, worth only a fraction of a penny. Jesus commented that the rich gave out of their wealth. However, out of her poverty, the widow gave all she had to live on. Her gift was, therefore, more than all the others.[11]

The Bible has many references, not just to the poor, but to the poor and needy. This raises the question as to whether the poor and needy are the same.

Before the Israelites entered Canaan, the Lord gave them instructions on many topics, including cancelation of fellow Israelites' debts every seventh year. God told the Israelites that they should cancel debts at the end of every seven years and there should be no poor people in the land if they followed his directive not to be hardhearted and tightfisted but openhanded, lending freely where necessary.[12] But because God knew that this directive would not be followed wholeheartedly, he said that there will always be poor people in the land. He therefore commanded

---

9. Matt 26:6–9; Mark 14:3–5. Mark notes that the disciples commented that it was worth a year's wages.

10. John 12:2–8.

11. Mark 12:41–44; Luke 21:1–3.

12. Deut 15:1–10.

them to be openhanded toward their poor and needy neighbors.[13] If a hired hand was poor and needy, regardless of his citizenship status, his wages were to be paid each day before sunset because he was counting on it. If he were not paid as required and he cried out to the Lord against the employer, the employer would be guilty of sin.[14]

Many psalms refer to the poor and needy. King Solomon penned a psalm about the reign of the Messiah, prophesying that the Messiah will deliver the needy when they call and the poor who have no helper; he will have pity on the poor and needy, save the lives of the needy, and redeem them from oppression and violence.[15] In a psalm by Asaph, in which he rebukes Israel's unjust judges, he exhorts judges to do justice to the afflicted and needy, to deliver the poor and needy, and to free them from the hand of the wicked.[16] In one proverb, King Lemuel, writing about what his mother taught him, recalls that she taught him to plead the cause of the poor and needy.[17] The prophet Ezekiel warned that God will hold accountable those who oppress the poor and needy[18] and the prophet Amos warned the wealthy women in the northern kingdom of Israel who oppressed the poor and crushed the needy that the time was coming when they would be led into captivity with fishhooks in their noses, as the Assyrians were known to do to their captives.[19]

These passages suggest that the terms *poor* and *needy* are used synonymously in the Bible. *Needy* in these contexts is not being used in the broader sense of someone who is clingy or who tends to need more emotional support or attention, though not necessarily poor.

---

13. Deut 15:11. See Adeyemo, *Africa Bible Commentary*, 230, 232, noting that God has a special concern for the poor and that all are called on to provide for the needy. The year for cancelling debts coincided with the seventh year in which the land was to be allowed to lie fallow so that the poor would have access to what grew naturally on it. See also Solomon Andria, "Generosity and Solidarity," in Adeyemo, *Africa Bible Commentary*, 231, noting that poverty does not come from God but resulted from the fall, and that sin lies behind the economic, social, political, environmental, and psychological factors that result in poverty.

14. Deut 24:14–15.

15. Ps 72:12–14.

16. Ps 82:3–4.

17. Prov 31:9. Some think King Lemuel is actually King Solomon or a fictional character created by King Solomon of an ideal king and queen mother. See Got Questions, "Who Was King Lemuel in Proverbs 31?"

18. Ezek 18:12.

19. Amos 4:1–2.

What Causes Poverty?

What Economists and Sociologists Say

Many Americans believe poverty results from individual failings while others believe circumstances are the primary factor.[20]

One author has pointed out that the persistence of poverty is not just an aggregation of individual failings, but that structural factors like features of the American economic system that produce income inequality and social inequities, as well as policy responses, are also responsible.[21]

Concentrated poverty has a variety of sources including lack of economic opportunities in many areas of the country and high levels of racial, ethnic, and class segregation.[22]

Individual characteristics, such as educational attainment, are a factor, but so also are structural factors like the way economic systems work and social inequality. Racial-ethnic gaps in poverty are due to educational attainment, prevalence of female-headed families, residential segregation, economic inequality, and discrimination. Past poverty, economic dislocation, wealth differentials, and family instability continue to be factors in poverty among minorities despite the decline of poverty in this group in the last fifty years. Single-parent families are more likely to be poor with the challenge of supporting a family on one income and paying for childcare while they work. They are also likely to be less educated. This makes them more vulnerable to poverty and material hardship.[23] A much higher proportion of jobs now require college graduates than before, and earnings of those with bachelor's degrees have risen. Meanwhile the less educated have lost ground as less skilled jobs have moved overseas where wages are lower.[24]

The Great Recession of 2007–2009 that followed the housing bubble resulted in higher poverty and greater food hardship.[25] The overall official poverty rate in the US rose from 12.3 percent in 2006, a year before the recession began, to 15 percent in 2011, two years after it ended. All

---

20. Iceland, *Poverty in America*, 79.
21. Iceland, *Poverty in America*, 3.
22. Iceland, *Poverty in America*, 7.
23. Iceland, *Poverty in America*, 8.
24. Iceland, *Poverty in America*, 86–87.
25. Iceland, *Poverty in America*, 9.

demographic groups experienced poverty increases except the elderly, who received fixed incomes from Social Security or pensions.[26]

Several government initiatives during the Great Recession kept 6.9 million people, including 2.5 million children, above the poverty line in 2010. These programs were implemented in 2009 and 2010 and included expansions of the Earned Income Tax Credit (EITC) and Child Tax Credit (CTC), the Making Work Pay Tax Credit, expansions in duration and level of unemployment insurance, and expansions of SNAP, more commonly known as food stamps. However, because all but the unemployment insurance program are noncash benefits, they were not captured in official poverty statistics.[27]

It has also been pointed out that there is substantial poverty and inequality in America today. It is believed that efforts to reduce poverty will be incremental at best because of deep divisions and ideological battles about how to address poverty and the proper role of government in society.[28]

Historically, during colonial times, poverty was attributed to individual misbehavior. But attitudes toward the elderly and children were more empathetic and communities accepted responsibility for caring for the elderly. In other words, it was felt that some poor were deserving of assistance and others were not.[29]

The Great Depression changed the attitude of blaming poverty on individual morality and misbehavior because the role of larger economic forces was plain for all to see.[30]

Social stratification is a cause of poverty. This is where social groups seek to maximize their rewards and limit others' access to resources and opportunities such as education or employment. Social stratification along racial, ethnic, or gender lines limits opportunities and increases poverty among some groups, although the degree of stratification across these groups diminished substantially in the US since the seventies.[31]

However, for Blacks, it has been estimated that a quarter of the Black-White wage gap is attributable to prejudice.[32] Also contributing to

26. Iceland, *Poverty in America*, 122.
27. Iceland, *Poverty in America*, 122–23.
28. Iceland, *Poverty in America*, 10, 163.
29. Iceland, *Poverty in America*, 12–13.
30. Iceland, *Poverty in America*, 17.
31. Iceland, *Poverty in America*, 89.
32. Iceland, *Poverty in America*, 92, citing Charles and Guryan, "Prejudices and

racial disparities in employment and education and reinforcing minority poverty is racial residential segregation, although this has improved in recent decades. Other factors such as the decline in the strength of unions, deindustrialization, and higher incarceration rates that impact employability, also contribute to poverty among Blacks. Thus, poverty is multidimensional, and this means that there is no single solution for it.[33]

It has been pointed out that when it comes to gender, women tend to have higher poverty rates than men because of lower employment and wage levels and a greater likelihood of being the heads of single-parent families. Labor market discrimination whereby women are paid less than men for the same work, and occupational sex-segregation whereby women are concentrated in certain jobs that pay less are factors in lower wage levels. There is also a gender wage gap whereby women who work full time year-round earn less than men who do. Women who worked full time year-round made 77 percent of what men made in 2011. The fact that a greater percentage of women tend to leave the labor force to have children and care for children and elderly relatives contributes to the gender wage gap. However, this gap is narrowing for women under thirty-five and will continue to do so with more women earning college degrees at all levels.[34]

In terms of marriage status, single-parent families with children headed by women are considerably more likely to be poor with 40.9 percent of such families being poor in 2011 compared to 8.8 percent of married-couple families with children. Having a single income, footing the cost of childcare and household expenses alone, and generally lower levels of education with resultant lower earnings, all contribute to higher poverty among female-headed families.[35]

Some have argued that culture plays a role in poverty. Americans' views on marriage and nonmarital childbearing have shifted and single parenthood is more socially accepted.[36] Arguments that high welfare benefits provide a disincentive to work and encourage dependency led to welfare reforms in the mid-1990s which ended cash benefits to poor female-headed families as long as they remained poor.[37]

Wages," 773–809.

33. Iceland, *Poverty in America*, 92–93.
34. Iceland, *Poverty in America*, 100–102.
35. Iceland, *Poverty in America*, 104.
36. Iceland, *Poverty in America*, 107–11.
37. Iceland, *Poverty in America*, 108, citing Murray, *Losing Ground*.

Earlier, the Job Opportunities and Basic Skills (JOBS) program under the Family Support Act of 1988 required single parents on welfare whose children were older than three to work in order to receive benefits or, if they could not get jobs, to enroll in education or job training to be paid for by the states and the federal government.[38] Then there was the Personal Responsibility and Work Opportunity Reconciliation Act (PRWORA) that was passed in 1996. It abolished the Aid to Families with Dependent Children (AFDC) program established under the Social Security Act of 1935 and replaced it with smaller grants to states under a program called Temporary Assistance to Needy Families (TANF). It required states to end welfare to recipients after two years regardless of whether they had found a job by that time and set a lifetime limit of five years on public assistance. The number of families receiving cash assistance dropped dramatically from five million in 1994 to 2.2 million in 2000. The employment rate among single mothers rose by 12 percent between 1994 and 1999 (from 60 percent to 72 percent) and their earnings also rose. However, a significant group of very disadvantaged women with few skills who could not find or maintain employment and who had physical and mental health issues were not helped by welfare reform and likely did worse.[39]

The poverty rate among female-headed families did decline in the 1990s coinciding with changing welfare policies that made it more difficult to receive benefits without working. The employment rate of never-married mothers who were most likely to have little education or job experience and long stays on the welfare rolls rose from 43 percent in 1992 to 65 percent in 1999. However, the percentage of single mothers who were employed fell from 76 percent in 2000 to 73 percent in 2007, and then to 68 percent in 2009 with the onset of the Great Recession.[40]

Post-pandemic, a deal between the Biden administration and Republican congressional leaders to raise the debt ceiling and avoid a default by the US on its bills included new work requirements for some able-bodied aid recipients in exchange for food aid under SNAP. The requirements do not apply to certain groups such as veterans, homeless people, and youth aging out of foster care. By 2025, able-bodied adults up to age fifty-four with no dependents will be required to work or attend at least eighty hours of job training programs a month to receive more

38. Iceland, *Poverty in America*, 137.
39. Iceland, *Poverty in America*, 138.
40. Iceland, *Poverty in America*, 106.

than three months of SNAP benefits within a three-year period. Despite these new work requirements, the Congressional Budget Office (CBO) estimates that eighty thousand people will be added to SNAP rolls in an average month.[41]

The subject of poverty and its causes is a very complex one indeed. In their attempts to provide a framework for examining this complex subject, other authors have described poverty as multidimensional, relational, and normative, the latter meaning that it is a matter of justice, not just economics.[42] They see thinking about poverty as having evolved from being viewed as self-inflicted to a social ill whose amelioration is a matter of justice. Later research has focused on factors such as the labor market, racism, and discrimination.[43] As a multidimensional phenomenon, these authors see poverty as a convergence of multiple factors such as disadvantage, social exclusion, segregation, crime, and incarceration. As a relational phenomenon, they see poverty as being a result of the convergence of factors such as exploitation of the poor, discrimination that disadvantages some groups, and public policies that exacerbate poverty. They see these policies as including concentrated policing and incarceration in poor communities of color.[44]

In a 2001 poll conducted by National Public Radio (NPR), the Kaiser Family Foundation, and the Harvard Kennedy School, respondents were roughly equally divided between two causes of poverty—people not doing enough to help themselves (48 percent) and circumstances beyond their control (45 percent). About half of affluent people polled felt the poor were not doing enough but poor people were more likely to blame circumstances for their financial state. Slightly more than half of those polled (52 percent) felt lack of motivation on the part of the poor was a major cause of poverty while a little over a third (35 percent) felt it was a minor cause of poverty.[45]

In a 2019 survey done by the Cato Institute on poverty, wealth, and work, Americans picked poor life choices (42 percent), drugs and alcohol (40 percent), and lack of job opportunities (29 percent) as the top three causes of poverty. Breakdown of families, and lack of work ethic were seen as the next two most responsible causes (29 percent each).

41. See Amiri, "Debt Deal Imposes New Work Requirements."
42. Desmond and Western, "Poverty in America," 305.
43. Desmond and Western, "Poverty in America," 306–7.
44. Desmond and Western, "Poverty in America," 308–12.
45. Lichter and Crowley, "Poverty in America."

When broken down along political lines, strong conservatives believe the top causes of poverty are poor life choices, lack of work ethic, breakdown of families, and drugs and alcohol, while liberals tend to believe that poverty is mainly caused by external forces that are beyond the control of individuals, such as discrimination, an unfair economic system, and lack of educational opportunities. Republicans emphasize personal choices and Democrats emphasize external forces. These different perspectives have implications for how these two political groups approach public policy solutions to poverty.[46]

What the Bible Says

Beyond what economists and sociologists have put forward as the causes of poverty, the Bible also has quite a bit to say about what causes poverty.

The writer of Proverbs counsels the lazy person to learn from the ant. The ant is diligent and industrious, storing up food in the summer for the winter months. The writer warns against laziness and procrastination, which he characterizes as sleep,[47] slumber, and folding of the hands. He warns that the one who lives this way will be overcome by poverty in the same way that a bandit or armed man suddenly comes on his unwitting victim.[48]

The writer notes that the lazy person does not sow seed in the spring, convincing themselves that it is still winter, and then begs because they have nothing come harvest time.[49] He warns that lazy hands make a person poor, but notes that diligent hands bring wealth.[50]

The writer also identifies stubbornness or a refusal to accept correction as another cause of poverty.[51] In other words, those who refuse wise counsel to correct error in their lives are likely to make poor decisions that negatively impact their finances.

Alcoholism and drug addiction are huge problems in modern-day society. Some have wrecked their finances because of problems with addiction. The writer of Proverbs warns of poverty because of alcoholism

---

46. Ekins, "What Americans Think."
47. Prov 20:13. Prov 23:21 says drowsiness clothes the drunken poor with rags.
48. Prov 6:6–11; 24:33–34.
49. Prov 20:4.
50. Prov 10:4, NIV.
51. Prov 13:18.

THE CHRISTIAN AS IMITATOR OF CHRIST

or drunkenness.[52] The writer also warns that love of pleasure can result in poverty.[53] This is probably a reference to the kind of riotous, wasteful lifestyle that ended up impoverishing the prodigal son in Jesus's parable about God's love.[54]

Sometimes people get sucked into easy-money or get-rich-quick schemes that look like sure bets. But these often turn out to be empty pursuits or fantasies.[55] People have collectively lost billions of dollars by investing in Ponzi schemes that promised great returns.[56]

The Bible does not always attribute poverty to one's own actions or inactions. The Old Testament law recognized that poverty may be the result of losing one's only means of support or because of one's calling. In this regard, the law of the tithe required that every three years, a tenth of that year's produce be stored in the towns and in the temple in Israel so that priests who got no allotment of land, widows and orphans who had no means of support, as well as immigrants who lived in those towns and had fallen on hard times, would have food to eat.[57] The law of the tithe was also an acknowledgment that poverty could result from losing a provider, as was the case with orphans and widows, or from not being able to own and farm land, as was the case with priests and immigrants.

The Bible acknowledges that poverty may be the result of societal injustice. During the time of the prophet Amos, Israel was economically prosperous but unjust and spiritually decadent. God sent Amos to prophesy to Israel to repent or perish. In one of his messages to the nation, Amos called the rich women of Samaria, Israel's capital, "cows of Bashan." They oppressed the poor and crushed the needy.[58] Amos re-

---

52. Prov 23:21.
53. Prov 21:17.
54. Luke 15:13–15.
55. Prov 28:19.
56. Investors lost about $65 billion in Bernie Madoff's Ponzi scheme.
57. Deut 14:28; Neh 13:10–13. See Adeyemo, *Africa Bible Commentary*, 230, commenting that the tithe should not be treated legalistically because the New Testament principle is to give in proportion to how God has blessed us. Those richly blessed may be able to give more than a tenth so a burden of guilt will not be laid on those who for a time and good reason are unable to give.
58. Amos 4:1–3. See Adeyemo, *Africa Bible Commentary*, 1036, noting that the luxury-loving women of Samaria had made themselves fat at the expense of the poor and were like the well-fed cows of fertile Bashan.

buked the rich for oppressing and trampling the poor, and for denying them justice in the courts by bribing judges.[59]

Poverty may sometimes be attributable to God's sovereign will.[60] Poverty may be part of one's divine calling, as it was with Jesus Christ. As the second person of the Triune God, Jesus was rich. Yet, to do the Father's will, he became poor by coming to earth and humbling himself unto death so that he might make rich those who believe in him.[61] Then there are priests and nuns who, believing they have been called by God, take vows of poverty as part of living lives devoted to the service of God and others.

Does Poverty Exist Only in Poor Nations?

Global data on poverty show that poverty does not only exist in poor countries. Although the US has virtually the highest gross national product (GNP) per capita in the world, one economist points out that it has higher levels of both absolute and relative poverty than other rich nations in Northern and Western Europe. It also has higher levels of relative poverty than just about all European countries, as well as lower levels of economic mobility than many of them. Differences in spending on programs that assist the lower-income population help explain these poverty differentials.[62]

It must be pointed out that poverty differs qualitatively in the US from the developing world where poverty is often measured in terms of having sufficient resources to stay alive. The US has more poverty than most countries with similar standards of living.[63] However, poverty in the developing world is about basic survival. In 2005, 1.4 billion people (25 percent of the world's population) lived in abject poverty on less than $1.25 a day, the threshold used by the World Bank to measure poverty. Of this number, 43 percent lived in South Asia and 29 percent in sub-Saharan Africa. However, this represented a decline from 1.9 billion people living on less than $1.25 a day in 1981.[64] Poverty in developing

---

59. Amos 5:11–12.
60. 1 Sam 2:7.
61. 2 Cor 8:9.
62. Iceland, *Poverty in America*, 7–8.
63. Iceland, *Poverty in America*, 61.
64. Iceland, *Poverty in America*, 62–64.

countries also differs qualitatively from poverty in the US and other developed countries in the sense that the poor in poor countries not only have difficulty meeting basic needs, but the countries in which they live have higher infant mortality rates and lower life expectancies.[65]

In terms of inequality, it is higher in the US than in Europe. Absolute poverty rates are higher in the US than in a majority of other developed countries, even though the median income in the US is substantially higher. Lower government transfers to low-income families in the US are the main reason. Government expenditures on social welfare programs as a percentage of GNP are considerably higher in European countries than in the US. Nevertheless, the majority of people born into any given quintile in the US move to a different one as adults.[66] And while the American safety net compares unfavorably to those of other rich nations, it does help keep millions of people out of poverty.[67]

It has been noted that the US government did the unimaginable during the pandemic by transforming itself into a European-style welfare state within weeks. Congress strengthened the social safety net by making Medicaid and food stamps more generous, creating new federal benefits like paid sick and caregiving leave and free school lunches, and making benefits like stimulus checks and child allowances nearly universal. It is estimated that the government spent about $5 trillion helping individuals and businesses since the pandemic began in March 2020. However, by the end of the first quarter of 2023, most of the programs had either ended or were set to expire soon, except for meals outside of school and food benefit increases, which have no expiration date. The expansion of the social safety net was designed to deal with the crisis caused by the pandemic. It did not reflect a fundamental, ideological shift in the way Americans view the role of government or the rights of citizens.[68]

In terms of economic mobility, Americans in the middle and top of the income distribution have just as much intergenerational mobility as those in other countries. But the lowest earners in America have the greatest difficulty moving up. The probability in the US is relatively high that a son whose father had earnings in the bottom quintile of the

---

65. Iceland, *Poverty in America*, 77–78.
66. Iceland, *Poverty in America*, 71–72.
67. Iceland, *Poverty in America*, 143.
68. Miller and Parlapiano, "U.S. Built." Housing vouchers expired in September 2023.

income distribution will also have earnings that will place him in the same quintile.[69]

Consequences of Poverty

There are many consequences of poverty. Studies show that children raised in poor families are less healthy, have lower cognitive development, social achievement, and emotional wellbeing. Poor people are more likely to die at younger ages. Low income and accompanying family instability and low levels of education are all contributing factors to the harmful effects of poverty. Poverty may also perpetuate itself as people who grow up in poor families are likely to also be poor themselves as adults.[70] In terms of psychological impacts, poor adolescents are likely to have lower self-esteem, act in antisocial ways, and likely to become delinquent.[71]

Poverty is costly to the national economy. For example, the costs associated with childhood poverty in the US total $500 billion a year—4 percent of Gross Domestic Product (GDP). These costs include lost earnings from low education, crime, and the health costs of being poor.[72]

Poverty's effects are multidimensional. Higher rates of poverty are associated with lower levels of education, employment, wages, and chronic health problems.[73]

Poverty has political consequences. It reduces public confidence in democratic institutions. The riots of the 1960s and the Los Angeles riots of 1992 were contributed to by a feeling of marginalization of Blacks in US cities. The unequal distribution of resources results in fragmentation in society.[74] Also, poor people are less likely to be fully engaged in democratic processes as they are more concerned about meeting basic day-to-day needs and may lack the means to get to polling stations or not be able to sacrifice hours off work to be engaged in the political process.

Food insecurity is another consequence of poverty. Food insecurity in America increased as a result of the Great Recession even though the

---

69. Iceland, *Poverty in America*, 74–76.
70. Iceland, *Poverty in America*, 3–4.
71. Iceland, *Poverty in America*, 3.
72. Iceland, *Poverty in America*, 4.
73. Iceland, *Poverty in America*, 89.
74. Iceland, *Poverty in America*, 4.

number of people receiving SNAP benefits increased by 70 percent between 2007 and 2011, with one in seven Americans receiving the benefit in 2011.⁷⁵

Other consequences of poverty include housing insecurity, unsafe neighborhoods, second-rate schools, and over-policed neighborhoods, all of which affect the quality of life and social mobility of the poor and contribute to higher incarceration rates.

These consequences make the issue of poverty and the Christian's attitude toward the poor important issues to ponder and act on.

Was Jesus Christ Poor?

As the second person of the Triune God, Jesus was rich. But, in order to do the Father's will, he became poor by coming to earth and humbling himself unto death so that he might make rich those who believe in him.⁷⁶ The Greek word used here to describe the poverty Jesus voluntarily assumed for humanity is *ptócheia*,⁷⁷ which signifies destitution or having nothing at all. It comes from the Greek verb *ptócheuó*, meaning to be poor as a beggar or to be destitute.⁷⁸

A scribe or teacher of the law came to Jesus once and openly committed to following Jesus wherever he went. Jesus responded by telling the scribe that foxes have holes or dens and birds of the air have nests but he, the Son on Man, had no place to lay his head.⁷⁹ Jesus was telling the scribe that following him or becoming his disciple comes at a cost. It requires being willing to surrender all. Jesus had surrendered all to do the Father's will. He left his throne in heaven and came to earth to redeem fallen humanity. In terms of an earthly occupation, with Jesus's father

---

75. Iceland, *Poverty in America*, 124, citing Isaacs, "Recession's Ongoing Impact."

76. 2 Cor 8:9.

77. See Vine et al., *Vine's Complete Expository Dictionary*, 478 (New Testament Section). See also Strong's Reference Number 4432, defining *ptócheia* as destitution or beggary.

78. See Vine et al., *Vine's Complete Expository Dictionary*, 476 (New Testament Section). See also Allen Dwight Callahan, "God's Only Begotten Thug," in Smith et al., *Bitter the Chastening Rod*, 39–52, noting that Jesus was penniless, landless, and homeless—a "thug" in the sense of one who has nothing. He inherited no earthly possessions, left no earthly possessions other than the clothes on his back, and was buried in a donated tomb.

79. Matt 8:19–20; Luke 9:57–58.

Joseph being a carpenter by trade,[80] Jesus must have learned the trade from Joseph because he too became a carpenter. He lived with his parents and siblings until he started his public ministry.[81]

After Jesus began his public ministry, he was always on the move. He went from town to town preaching the gospel, teaching about the kingdom of God, healing the sick, casting out demons, and doing good. He depended on the hospitality of others who took him in. He stayed in the homes of friends like Martha, the sister of Lazarus and Mary.[82] He sometimes stayed in the home of disciples like Peter.[83] The day Jesus came into Jericho and met Zacchaeus, he told Zacchaeus he would be spending the night at his house.[84] And before his crucifixion, he borrowed an upper room to celebrate the Passover with his disciples.[85] When he made his triumphal entry into Jerusalem, he rode on a borrowed donkey and a colt.[86] He did not own an animal of his own on which he travelled about as he preached from town to town. He walked wherever he went, except when he crossed the Sea of Galilee by boat. At one point he walked all the way from Judea to Galilee, going through Samaria where he stayed in the home of Samaritans for two days as their guest.[87] He even walked across the Sea of Galilee once, intending to go all the way to Bethsaida, right past his disciples who were in a boat on the water.[88]

As an infant, Jesus and his parents fled Israel and went and lived in Egypt as refugees. This was because when King Herod heard that magi from the east had come to Jerusalem looking for a newborn who was going to be king of the Jews, he became disturbed and came up with an evil plot to kill all the boys in Bethlehem and its vicinity who were two years of age and under. Before this happened, however, an angel of God warned Joseph in a dream to flee to Egypt with his family until further notice. It was not until Herod died that an angel appeared to Joseph in a dream and told him to take his family back to Israel.[89] Joseph might have

80. Matt 13:55–56.
81. Mark 6:3.
82. Luke 10:38–39; John 11:1.
83. Matt 8:14–16.
84. Luke 19:5.
85. Matt 26:17–19; Mark 14:12–16; Luke 22:7–13.
86. Matt 21:1–7; Mark 11:1–7; Luke 19:28–35; John 12:14.
87. John 4:3–4, 39–41.
88. Matt 14:22–27; Mark 6:45–50; John 6:16–20.
89. Matt 2:13–23. On Jesus's temporary refugee status, see Harrington, *Gospel of*

worked as a carpenter in Egypt to take care of his family. This could not have been easy considering the likelihood that he did not speak Egyptian.

Jesus's socioeconomic status did not change as an adult. As a full-time minister of the gospel, he did not own a home. Being always on the move, he was practically homeless.

How Did Jesus Treat the Poor?

At the start of his public ministry, Jesus went to the synagogue in Nazareth and was handed the scroll to read from the Scriptures. He opened the scroll to the book of Isaiah and read a prophetic passage about the ministry of the coming Messiah. He read that the Spirit of the Lord was upon the Messiah and that he had been anointed to preach good news to the poor, among other things. Jesus told his audience that he was the fulfillment of this Scripture.[90]

While John the Baptist was in prison, he sent his disciples to ask Jesus if he was the Messiah. Jesus responded by telling them to go back and tell John what they were hearing and seeing—the blind were being given back their sight, the lame were walking, lepers were being cured, the deaf could hear, dead people were being raised, and the good news was being preached to the poor.[91] Many of the people Jesus referenced would have been impoverished by their condition. Their healing, therefore, gave them a chance to be freed from their poverty.

When a woman came and poured a jar of expensive perfume on Jesus's head while he was in the home of Simon the Leper, the disciples were indignant that she had wasted the perfume. They felt it could have been sold and the proceeds given to the poor.[92] Jesus rebuked them and remarked that they would always have the poor with them and that they could help the poor whenever they wanted. But they would not always

---

Matthew, 44, commenting that Egypt, which came under Roman control in 30 BC was outside Herod's jurisdiction and that Egypt had been a place of refuge for Jews in biblical times. See also H. Daniel Zacharias, "Gospel of Matthew," in McCaulley et al., *New Testament in Color*, 49, commenting that the fact that Jesus and his parents were refugees for a time ought to shape current modern perspectives.

90. Luke 4:18–21, quoting Isa 61:1.

91. Matt 11:5.

92. Matt 26:6–9; Mark 14:3–5. Mark notes that the disciples commented that it was worth a year's wages.

have him.[93] Jesus was about to go to the cross. His disciples would not have him with them physically after that. Jesus was saying it was okay for the woman who poured perfume on him to honor him in this special way, as expensive as the perfume was. Unlike him, the poor were not going anywhere. They would always be there. People could help them at any time if they so desired.

Jesus's statement that there would always be poor people was a direct quote of a statement Moses made to the Israelites in the Old Testament before the Israelites entered the promised land of Canaan. Moses gave them many instructions from the Lord about how they were to live once they settled in Canaan. Among these were instructions on caring for the poor. Moses told them that there should not be poor people in the land if they followed God's directives to be kind to their neighbors. However, there would always be poor people in the land, presumably because this directive would not be followed wholeheartedly. Therefore, Moses commanded them to be openhanded toward the poor and needy in the land.[94]

Jesus expected his followers to give to the poor. He therefore taught them about the attitude they should have when they give to the poor, not if they give to the poor. Giving to the poor must come out of a sincere and genuine desire to be a blessing, not out of an ulterior motive or desire for public recognition or acknowledgment. Jesus said that when people give to the needy, they should not make a public spectacle out of it as the hypocrites did in the synagogues and streets in his day because they sought to be honored by others for their deeds. Jesus said the only reward they will get in such a case is the praise and recognition people give them. God will not praise or reward them because of their hypocrisy. Instead of making a public display of giving to the poor, Jesus instructed his disciples to give in such a way that even their left hand would not know what their right hand is doing. In other words, they are to give in secret or discreetly. Jesus said God, who sees their secret giving, will reward them openly.[95]

Jesus healed many people during his ministry. Lepers could not live in their communities because of the contagious nature of their condition. They obviously could not work or earn a living and would have been

---

93. Mark 14:3–7; John 12:2–8.
94. Deut 15:11.
95. Matt 6:1–4.

THE CHRISTIAN AS IMITATOR OF CHRIST

poor.[96] Healing them restored them to their place in society and gave them a chance to escape poverty. Many who were afflicted by sickness and disease would also likely have been poor. The woman who had been hemorrhaging for twelve years until she came to Jesus did not start out poor. However, she spent all her money on physicians and was still not well. Her condition had worsened when, in desperation, she came and touched Jesus's garment. Her healing meant she could now live a normal life.[97] The cripple who was brought on a bed by his friends to Jesus had to have been poor. He could not have been able to work for a living in his condition.[98] Neither could the blind, lame, and crippled people who lay by the pool of Bethesda waiting for a miracle. Among them was a man who had been crippled for thirty-eight years. Jesus healed him and gave him a chance to live a normal, productive life.[99] The same could be said about blind Bartimaeus whose sight Jesus restored. As a blind man, he was poor and sat by the road begging for alms. When Jesus healed him, he became a follower of Jesus.[100]

The man in Gadara who was possessed by a legion of demons lived a miserable, tormented life. He lived among the tombs. He would strip his clothes and cut himself. His condition had to have made him poor. When Jesus healed him by casting the demons out of him, he became an evangelist in the Decapolis, the ten cities in the region where he lived.[101]

At one point, as Jesus was entering a city called Nain, he saw a funeral procession heading out of the city to the cemetery. The mourners were carrying the coffin of a young man. His mother was a widow, and he was her only son. This means that she had no husband to provide for her. And now she had lost the only son who could. Jesus had compassion on her when he saw her weeping. He told her not to weep and came and touched the coffin. He spoke to the dead young man and raised him from the dead. Jesus presented him to his mother who would now have her means of support back.[102]

Jesus did all these miracles and acts of kindness out of a heart of love and compassion for people who were destitute and hurting. He

---

96. Matt 8:1–4; Mark 1:40–44; Luke 5:12–14; 17:11–19.
97. Matt 9:20–22; Mark 5:25–34; Luke 8:43–48.
98. Matt 9:2–8; Mark 2:1–12.
99. John 5:2–9.
100. Mark 10:46–52; Luke 18:35–43.
101. Mark 5:1–20; Luke 8:26–39.
102. Luke 7:11–15.

clearly cared about the poor and the needy. And, drawing on the indwelling Holy Spirit, who is called the Spirit of love,[103] all who profess to be Christians must do the same.

In the parable of the sheep and the goats, Jesus talked about his return to earth as king to judge the nations. At some point after his return, which will be after a period of great suffering known as the great tribulation, Jesus said he will separate the righteous (sheep) from the wicked (goats). He said the righteous will inherit the kingdom and the wicked will suffer eternal punishment. He said he (the king) will commend the righteous because they fed him when he was hungry, gave him drink when he was thirsty, took him in as a stranger, clothed him when he was naked, and visited him in prison. He said they did these things for him when they did it for the least of his brothers and sisters, believers who were suffering.

Jesus said that he will tell the wicked how they failed to feed him when he was hungry, give him drink when he was thirsty, take him in as a stranger, clothe him when he was naked, or visit him in prison. He said that when they failed to do it for the least of his brothers and sisters, they failed to do it for him.[104]

Jesus's references in this parable to the hungry, the thirsty, the stranger, the naked, the sick, and the imprisoned are references to the poor, the needy, the vulnerable, and the outcast. This parable shows that Jesus regards showing love and compassion to the poor and needy, particularly to believers who are suffering, as tantamount to showing him love and compassion. After all, Jesus did say that all who do his will are his family.[105] Jesus was full of love and compassion. As such, he regards demonstrating love and compassion as an essential element of true faith and of being his disciple or follower.

How Does God Feel About the Poor?

God has the same heart of love and compassion for the poor and needy that Jesus had. God is the one who strengthens the poor and the needy in their distress.[106] He is also their refuge from those who mistreat and

---

103. 2 Tim 1:7.
104. Matt 25:31–46.
105. Matt 12:50.
106. Ps 14:6.

THE CHRISTIAN AS IMITATOR OF CHRIST

oppress them. It is to him that they can cry out.[107] God is also the one who helps the poor and the needy[108] and the one who delivers and protects them from their oppressors.[109] He is the one who provides for the poor.[110]

When God gave the law to the Israelites before they entered Canaan, he instructed them not to charge interest on loans to fellow Israelites.[111] Moreover, they were to cancel the debts of poor people who had borrowed money every seven years.[112] This was to prevent them from being stuck in poverty. It was designed to give them a fresh start. God felt so strongly about not being tightfisted toward the poor that he exhorted the Israelites to be openhanded toward the poor. He warned them not to refuse to lend to a poor person because the year for canceling debts was approaching. He warned that if they did that and the poor person cried out to God against the person who refused to help them, the Lord would consider that person guilty of sin. On the other hand, if they were generous to the poor, God promised to bless them in all their work and in everything they did.[113]

If a poor borrower gave a cloak as a pledge or security for the loan, the lender was to return the cloak at sunset to the borrower so that the borrower could sleep in it and not be cold. Moreover, the lender was not to invade the borrower's privacy by entering the borrower's home to take the pledge. The lender was to wait outside for the borrower to bring it out.[114]

If property had been lost to a creditor, similar to what happens in modern foreclosure, the property was to be returned to the original owners in the Year of Jubilee, which was celebrated every fifty years. This was to guard against generational poverty. However, if before the Year of Jubilee came, the debtor who had sold property to the creditor acquired the means to redeem it or buy it back, he could do so by paying an amount that compensated for the difference in value between the date of foreclosure and the date of redemption.[115]

---

107. Isa 25:4.
108. Pss 40:17; 70:5.
109. Pss 12:5; 35:10.
110. Pss 68:10; 132:15.
111. Exod 22:25; Lev 25:35–36.
112. Deut 15:1–2.
113. Deut 15:7–10.
114. Deut 24:10–13.
115. Lev 23:22; 25:8–25.

TREATMENT OF THE POOR

God instituted the law of the tithe whereby every third year, the people were to bring a tenth of their produce and store it in their towns and the temple so that the Levites, who did not receive an allotment of land when the Israelites settled in the promised land, foreigners (immigrants), the fatherless, and widows would have enough food to eat.[116]

God also commanded the Israelites not to harvest all the produce of their land during harvest time. They were not to go back and harvest sheaves of corn that they had skipped or overlooked. They were not to beat all the olives from their olive trees by going over the trees a second time. And they were not to go over their vines again when they were harvesting grapes. They were also not to wholly reap the corners of their fields.[117] They were to leave the overlooked sheaves and leftover olives and grapes, known as gleanings, for the immigrants, fatherless, and widows to come and glean for food.[118] They were also to sow their land and gather its yield for six years but let the land lie fallow the seventh year so that the poor may eat what the land naturally produced.[119] In one of the most heartwarming love stories of the Old Testament, Ruth, a Moabitess who had immigrated to Israel with her mother-in-law, Naomi, met a kinsman of Naomi's called Boaz in whose fields she went and gleaned. They married and became the great grandparents of King David and ancestors of Jesus Christ.[120]

God's concern for the poor also extended to the working poor. He commanded the Israelites not to take advantage of hired hands who were poor and needy, whether they were immigrants or fellow Israelites. Those who hired them were to pay them their wages at sunset because they were poor and counting on their wages. God said he would count it as a sin against them if they did not do this and the poor cried out to him about it.[121]

If an Israelite sold himself to a creditor because he was unable to pay a debt, he was to work for the creditor until the Year of Jubilee and then he was to be released. Alternatively, he or a relative could pay for his redemption before the Year of Jubilee by paying the rate that a hired

---

116. Deut 14:28–29; Neh 13:12–13; Mal 3:10.
117. Lev 9:9–10; 23:22.
118. Deut 24:19.
119. Exod 23:10–11.
120. Ruth 2; 3; 4.
121. Deut 24:14–15.

hand would have been paid from the date of his redemption to the Year of Jubilee.[122]

If an Israelite was sold as a slave to another Israelite, he was to work for the slave master for six years and then be released in the seventh year. And when Hebrew slaves were released in the seventh year, they were not to be sent away empty handed as they might remain impoverished. The slave master was to liberally supply the newly freed slave from his flock, threshing floor, and winepress. This means they left with a supply of meat, grain, and wine until they could be gainfully employed. God said he was giving them this command to remind them that they too were slaves once in Egypt, and that it was he who redeemed them.[123] God, therefore, prevented the permanent impoverishment of the Hebrews by prohibiting lifelong enslavement.

The Bible says that righteousness and justice are the foundations of God's throne or his rule.[124] God is, therefore, a God of justice. He loves justice and hates injustice. In this world, the rich and powerful are not the ones who suffer injustice. It is the poor, the disenfranchised, and the outcasts. And God desires justice for them.

In one of David's psalms, blessing is pronounced on the one who considers the poor, and four specific promises are made about what God will do for them. First is a promise that the Lord will deliver them in time of trouble. Second is a promise that the Lord will preserve them and keep them alive. Third is a promise that the Lord will deliver them from the will of their enemies. And, finally, the promise is made that the Lord will strengthen them when they are sick.[125]

God promises to bless the one who is generous and shares his bread or food with the poor.[126] He promises that the one who gives to the poor will lack nothing. But he warns that the one who closes his eyes to the poor will receive many curses.[127]

God takes mistreatment of the poor personally. One proverb says that the one who oppresses the poor reproaches God, the poor's maker.

---

122. Lev 25:39–54.

123. Deut 15:12–15.

124. Ps 89:14.

125. Ps 41:1–3. In Matt 5:7, Jesus said blessed are the merciful for they shall obtain mercy.

126. Prov 22:9.

127. Prov 28:27. See Adeyemo, *Africa Bible Commentary*, *783*, noting the need to trust in God to supply our needs rather than being stingy.

However, the one who is kind to the needy honors God.[128] Another says that God will not answer the cries of those who shut their ears to the cry of the poor.[129] These passages show that mistreatment of the poor and insensitivity to their needs are offensive to God.

On the other hand, God shows how much he regards those who are generous toward the poor in how he responded to the kindness of Cornelius, a centurion in the Roman army based in Caesarea. He and his family were devout, God-fearing people. Not only did he give generously to those in need, but he was also a very prayerful man who prayed to God regularly. God was so moved by Cornelius's generosity and devotion that he sent an angel to tell Cornelius that his prayers and gifts to the poor had come up as a memorial offering before God, much like the aroma of sacrifice ascends to God. The angel directed Cornelius to send for the apostle Peter.[130]

Knowing that Jews did not entertain gentiles in their homes or enter the homes of gentiles, God spoke to Peter through a vision and told him not to call anything impure or common that God had cleansed or made clean. The Holy Spirit told Peter that three men had come to look for him and directed him to go with them because the Holy Spirit had sent them. Peter invited Cornelius's servants in when they arrived. They stayed with him overnight and he left with them the next day for Caesarea, a two-day journey.[131]

Peter preached the gospel to Cornelius and his household, relatives, and close friends. God poured his Holy Spirit on the gentiles, much to the astonishment of the Jewish believers who had accompanied Peter to Cornelius's house. They were all baptized with water in the name of the Lord Jesus Christ, and Peter and his companions stayed with them for a few more days.[132]

The gift of salvation and the Holy Spirit are the greatest gifts God can bestow on a person. Because of Cornelius's generosity to the poor and his devotion to God, he and those who were dear to him were blessed with these priceless gifts.

God's care and concern for the poor led him to institute laws for the protection of the poor before the Israelites settled in Canaan. God

---

128. Prov 14:31; 17:5.
129. Prov 21:13.
130. Acts 10:1–8.
131. Acts 10:9–24.
132. Acts 10:25–48.

THE CHRISTIAN AS IMITATOR OF CHRIST

warned the Israelites not to deprive immigrants or the fatherless of justice or take the cloak or garment of a widow as a pledge.[133] Immigrants, widows, and the fatherless were the most vulnerable people in society. They were the most likely to be poor. They were the least likely to have any influence or connections to those who did. They were, therefore, the most susceptible to being exploited and treated unjustly.

After the Israelites settled in Canaan and perverted justice, contrary to God's warning, he sent prophet after prophet to condemn injustice in the land and warn of the punishment that would ensue if they did not repent and change their unjust, ungodly ways.

The psalmist Asaph spoke out against injustice toward the poor in the courts. Judges were showing partiality to the wicked. The psalmist urged them to give justice to the weak and the orphan and maintain the rights of the lowly and destitute.[134]

God sent the prophet Isaiah to prophesy doom to Judah and Jerusalem for ungodliness and injustice. Isaiah warned that God would judge the leaders and elders of Judah for ruining the nation and plundering and crushing the poor.[135] He prophesied impending destruction and a complete reversal of fortunes for the rich who were obsessed with their wealth and comfort but indifferent to the poor. He prophesied impending doom.[136] This happened in 586 BC when the Babylonians conquered Judah, ransacked and destroyed the temple, and burned down Jerusalem.

Through the prophet Isaiah, God proclaimed woe against Judah's leaders for passing unjust laws and issuing oppressive decrees that denied the rights of the poor and denied justice to the oppressed. Isaiah accused them of making widows their prey and for robbing the fatherless. God's anger toward the nation would result in a day of disaster that would come from afar, a reference to the Babylonians, who would conquer Judah and take captives to Babylon. Many would be taken captive, and many others would die with no help in sight.[137]

---

133. Deut 24:17.

134. Ps 82:2–3. The NIV says to maintain the rights of the poor and oppressed. See Adeyemo, *Africa Bible Commentary*, 689–90, commenting that judges must be fair to all and not show partiality. Judges have a special responsibility to uphold the rights of the weak and poor and to make sure that widows and orphans are not oppressed.

135. Isa 3:14–15.

136. Isa 3:16–26.

137. Isa 10:1–4.

TREATMENT OF THE POOR

Before this happened, God refused to pay any attention to the empty, ritualistic fasts of the Jewish nation. Despite all their fasting, the Jews were wicked and oppressive. They did not care about the hungry, the homeless, or the naked. They lived lives of pleasure and exploited their workers.[138]

Things were no better in the northern kingdom of Israel in the prophet Amos's day. Creditors sold the poor for a pair of sandals.[139] The poor were trampled and the oppressed were denied justice in the courts.[140] God sent Amos, who was from the southern kingdom of Judah, to go and prophesy in the northern kingdom of Israel against these injustices, and to warn them of impending punishment.[141] He rebuked the upper-class women of Israel who lived lives of luxury at the expense of the poor and warned them of impending captivity. He prophesied that they would be led away with hooks in their noses.[142] The Assyrians conquered the northern kingdom of Israel in 722 BC. They took captives from Israel to Assyria and brought captives from other nations they had conquered to live in Israel.

God used other prophets to condemn the rich for exploiting the poor. The prophet Micah was a contemporary of the prophet Isaiah. Isaiah ministered in Jerusalem while Micah ministered in the countryside. He prophesied against Judah's corrupt leaders and unjust judges. He condemned injustice and oppression of poor peasants and villagers whose fields they seized and whose houses they took.[143] He prophesied the fall of the northern kingdom of Israel and its capital Samaria,[144] as well as the fall of the southern kingdom of Judah and its capital Jerusalem.[145]

After the people of Judah returned from exile in Babylon, the prophet Zechariah ministered to them and encouraged them to complete the rebuilding of the temple. He reminded them of how God had demanded

---

138. Isa 58:3–7.
139. Amos 2:6; 8:4–6.
140. Amos 2:7; 5:12.
141. Amos 2:6–16.
142. Amos 4:1–3. See Adeyemo, *Africa Bible Commentary*, 1036, commenting that the luxury-loving women of Samaria would eventually be treated like cattle, led away as captives with hooks in their noses or lips, which is how the Assyrians often treated those that they captured.
143. Mic 2:2.
144. Mic 1:6.
145. Mic 1:9–16; 3:9–12.

true justice, mercy, and compassion, and how he had commanded them not to oppress the widow and the fatherless. Unfortunately, God's commands had fallen on deaf ears and resulted in captivity. But now, by God's grace, they had been restored to the land.

Old Testament prophets are not the only ones who prophesied against injustice and the exploitation and oppression of the poor. Although James, the brother of Jesus and head of the church in Jerusalem, primarily wrote to the Jews living outside Israel about true saving faith that manifests itself in righteous living and good deeds, he also addressed social injustice and inequality like Amos did. He warned against discriminating against the poor in the church by showing favoritism to the rich and giving them preferential treatment. He reminded them that God has chosen those who are poor in the eyes of the world to be rich in faith because they do not trust in material possessions that they do not have. They trust in the Lord. James reminded his audience that it was the rich who were exploiting the poor, dragging them to court, and slandering the name of Jesus. He reminded them that favoritism is sin because it does not show genuine love for all.[146]

How the Early Church Treated the Poor

The early church in Jerusalem took care of the needs of believers. The community of believers was a mutually supportive one characterized by the sharing of possessions and resources. The believers in Jerusalem were not self-centered people. Instead, they were community-minded people. Some even sold their assets, houses, and lands, and made the proceeds available to their community of believers. As a result, there were no needy people among them. This means that those of them who were poor were provided for. Indeed, the church in Jerusalem even had a daily food distribution program that catered to the nutritional needs of the poor in the church, including widows. Seven deacons were selected to oversee this food distribution program after the Greek-speaking Jews alleged that the Hebrew- or Aramaic-speaking Jews were discriminating against their widows and neglecting them in the daily distribution.[147]

---

146. Jas 2:1–9.

147. Acts 2:44–46; 4:32–37; 6:1–6. See Johnson, *Acts of the Apostles*, 62, commenting that Luke communicated to his readers in vivid fashion that the gift of the Spirit brought about a community which realized the highest aspirations of human longing: unity, peace, joy, and the praise of God. See also Jordan J. Cruz Ryan, "Acts," in

TREATMENT OF THE POOR

Not only did the early church leaders show that they had a heart for the poor, but they also exhorted other ministers of the gospel to do the same. We see this in Paul's account to the Galatians of how God called him to preach the gospel to the gentiles and how he met with Peter after his conversion and, many years later, with the leaders of the church in Jerusalem. Paul said they had nothing to add to the gospel that he was preaching. However, he said that the only thing the leaders asked of him was that he continue to remember the poor. This resonated with Paul because, as he told the Galatians, this was the very thing that he was eager to do.[148]

Paul was actively involved in relief work for the poor. He appealed to the church in Corinth to follow through on the commitment they made a year earlier to contribute to the needs of the poor believers in Judea. He cited the example of the churches in Macedonia, pointing out that though they were extremely poor, their extreme poverty was outmatched by their rich generosity in contributing to an offering for the poor Judeans. Paul said that it was the Macedonians who urgently pleaded for the privilege of being part of this service to the believers in Judea. Paul was now asking the Corinthians to complete what they had eagerly begun, and to do it according to their means. Paul let them know that he would be sending Titus, with whom they were already acquainted, and several other men with him to collect this offering. Paul said he had been boasting to the Macedonians about the fact that the believers in the region of Achaia, where Corinth was located, were eager to give, and that this had stirred the Macedonians to action. He assured the Corinthians of God's blessing for their generosity.[149]

Paul told the Romans about this gift that the believers in Macedonia and Achaia made. Writing to them about his desire to visit them as part of a trip he wanted to make to Spain, the apostle Paul told the church in Rome that for now, he was headed to Jerusalem with a gift for the poor believers in Judea that had been given by the believers in Macedonia and Achaia. He said he wanted to get this gift to Jerusalem first and then head to Spain, hoping to visit the believers in Rome on the way.[150]

McCaulley et al., *New Testament in Color*, 337, where he notes an ideal community of followers of Jesus who eliminated poverty among themselves through sharing with those in need.

148. Gal 1:18–19; 2:1–10.
149. 2 Cor 8; 9.
150. Rom 15:23–28.

THE CHRISTIAN AS IMITATOR OF CHRIST

Despite the early church's concern for and support of the poor and needy in their midst, the apostle Paul made it clear that idleness was not to be tolerated. There were people in the church in Thessalonica who were idle. They were not working to take care of themselves. Evidently, some in the church believed that Jesus's return was imminent and, as a result, had abandoned their vocations and were no longer self-sufficient. They may have become dependent on the generosity of their church community and unable to contribute financially to the church. In his first Letter to the Thessalonians, Paul admonished them to work with their own hands so that they would win the respect of outsiders and not become dependent on anyone.[151]

Paul did not want others to emulate such idleness, so in his second Letter to the Thessalonians, he commanded the brethren to stay away from idle people. He reminded the Thessalonians how he and his fellow ministers worked day and night when they were in Thessalonica to take care of themselves so that they would not be a burden to the church in Thessalonica. They did not just help themselves to the church's charity. In that regard, Paul urged them to follow the example he and his fellow ministers set while with them. Paul reminded them that he had given them a rule while he was with them—that anyone unwilling to work should not eat. He commanded those who were idle in the church to settle down and earn the food they eat.[152] Paul also talked about work to the believers in Galatia. He exhorted those who stole before they became Christians to steal no more. Instead, they were to work for a living so that they could now be a blessing by sharing what they had with the needy.[153]

Paul did indeed lead by example as far as modeling hard work is concerned. He was a tentmaker who made and sold tents to support himself. In Corinth, during his second missionary journey, he made tents with Aquila and Priscilla, ministers of the gospel who had arrived from Rome.[154] On his way back to Jerusalem after his third missionary journey, he rendezvoused in Miletus with the Ephesian elders to encourage them

---

151. 1 Thess 4:11.

152. 2 Thess 3:6–12. See Adeyemo, *Africa Bible Commentary*, 1466 and 1468, noting that Paul's earlier advice to the Thessalonians (1 Thess 2:9 and 4:11) had not been taken seriously, leading him to make his point at greater length here, encouraging those who are already working to work hard because work allows us to meet our own needs and to contribute to the development of individuals and the community. Work is not a curse, but a task God has assigned us.

153. Eph 4:28.

154. Acts 18:1–3.

to keep watch over themselves and the flock they oversaw. Paul reminded them that he did not covet silver, gold, or clothing from anyone when he was in Ephesus despite his apostolic authority. Instead, he worked hard with his own hands. He said he had shown them how we must work hard so that we can help others. He reiterated what Jesus had taught—that it is more blessed to give than to receive.[155]

Contemporary Attitudes Toward the Poor

How do people feel about the poor in contemporary American society? What perceptions or beliefs do people have about the poor and what attitudes do they harbor toward them? Are these perceptions, beliefs, or attitudes necessarily consistent with reality? And are they consistent with biblical teaching?[156]

One perception or belief people have about the poor is that they are lazy. Another is that poor people do not work. However, contrary to that belief, over 60 percent of poor families have at least one worker in the family.[157] Lately, the United Way has drawn attention to people that it has described as ALICE—Asset Limited, Income Constrained, Employed. These are people who work hard. They earn above the federal poverty level but struggle to manage their most basic needs such as housing, food, transportation, childcare, healthcare, and access to basic technology. They oftentimes must decide between things like filling a prescription or repairing a vehicle, or between paying for childcare or paying the rent. They are essential workers who work in childcare, eldercare, and home health care, serve as cashiers, wait tables, or work as clerks. Households of color are disproportionately ALICE.[158]

---

155. Acts 20:17, 28, 33–35.

156. See Stephen Adei, "Wealth and Poverty," in Adeyemo, *Africa Bible Commentary*, 762, noting that nowhere do the Scriptures equate material poverty and piety, and Christians must work to remove the barriers that prevent people from escaping from poverty. See also Goza, *America's Unholy Ghosts*, 32 and 146, arguing that the White church in America has been influenced by the religious lie from Enlightenment philosophers that Christians don't need to relate to the poor and broken to relate to God who cares about the poor and broken as revealed in the Old and New Testaments.

157. Iceland, *Poverty in America*, 4.

158. United For ALICE is a United Way initiative to drive innovation, research, and action to improve life across the country for ALICE and for all.

Another popular belief is that poor people suck up a significant portion of the federal budget. However, the reality is that, apart from Medicaid, welfare programs are a modest share of federal spending.[159]

Another belief is that the majority of the poor people in America are Blacks. However, this is a myth, as only one quarter of the poor in America are Black, although that's an overrepresentation given their percentage of the population.[160]

A 2001 poll conducted by National Public Radio (NPR), the Kaiser Family Foundation, and the Harvard Kennedy School showed one persistent stereotype about the poor—namely, they are unmotivated, lack the aspiration to get ahead, or do not work hard to succeed. But the poll showed that more than half of poor people surveyed believed that most welfare recipients really want to work. At the time of the poll, however, for many low-income people, jobs were often unavailable, paid poorly, or did not provide health insurance. Many poor people, therefore, depended on public or familial assistance to make ends meet.[161]

A more recent 2019 Cato Institute national survey of 1,700 Americans on poverty, wealth, and work, showed that 70 percent of Americans have favorable feelings toward the poor, 8 percent have unfavorable feelings, and 21 percent are ambivalent about the poor. The majority of Republicans (65 percent), Democrats (78 percent), and Independents (64 percent) have favorable feelings toward the poor. However, 10 percent of Republicans, 6 percent of Democrats, and 11 percent of Independents have unfavorable feelings about the poor. Americans as a whole are more sympathetic toward the poor, although they do not dislike the rich, with 46 percent having favorable views of the rich compared to 70 percent having favorable views of the poor. More Democrats (78 percent) have favorable views of the poor than Republicans (65 percent).[162]

The Cato Institute survey showed how Americans in general view government welfare programs. As of the time of the survey, welfare recipients were 57 percent female, 43 percent male, 57 percent White, 22 percent Black, 11 percent Latino, and 2 percent Asian. The majority of Americans do not believe that welfare is designed to lift people out of poverty. Only 39 percent believe welfare lifts people out of poverty, while 60 percent believe that welfare is simply designed to provide for the basic

159. Iceland, *Poverty in America*, 5.
160. Iceland, *Poverty in America*, 4.
161. Lichter and Crowley, "Poverty in America."
162. Ekins, "What Americans Think."

needs of the poor. The majority of welfare recipients themselves believe that it is simply meant to provide for their basic needs. A little less than half of Americans (45 percent) believe that welfare makes poor people dependent and encourages them to stay poor, while a majority of Americans believe welfare gives poor people a chance to stand on their own two feet and start over afresh. Overwhelmingly (68 percent), welfare recipients believe it gives them a fresh start while only half of people who do not receive welfare believe it gives recipients a fresh start. Almost half of nonrecipients (49 percent) believe it creates dependency. Of those who had previously received benefits but were not at the time of the survey, a majority (56 percent) believe it gave them a fresh start but a significant minority (44 percent) worried that it created dependency.

Republicans generally (68 percent) feel welfare creates dependency while Democrats generally (71 percent) feel welfare helps people get back on their feet. Almost two-thirds of independents believe it gives recipients a fresh start. About two-thirds of African and Latino Americans do not believe welfare creates dependency, while White Americans are evenly divided along the lines of age, with those 65 and over (59 percent) believing that welfare creates dependency. A majority of Americans (54 percent) believe that welfare recipients would rather earn their own living, while 45 percent believe that they would rather stay on welfare. However, among those receiving welfare benefits, 65 percent believe that most poor people would rather earn their own living, while 34 percent felt recipients would rather stay on welfare. Nonrecipients were more evenly divided as to whether welfare recipients would rather earn their own living (50 percent) or stay on welfare (48 percent). Welfare recipients cited the cost of housing and lack of access to good jobs as hurdles to escaping poverty.[163]

A significant majority of Americans (77 percent) in the Cato Institute survey believed that the government has been ineffective in fighting poverty in the ten to fifteen years prior to the survey. A significant majority (72 percent) also believe the government just doesn't know how to fix poverty.[164] Almost three quarters of Americans (70 percent) would rather see the government attempt to address the root causes of poverty rather than spend more on welfare (29 percent). Most Americans (79 percent) also believe that more economic growth as opposed to more

---

163. Ekins, "What Americans Think."
164. Ekins, "What Americans Think."

welfare spending would be more effective in helping people escape poverty. However, 66 percent of Democrats would also like to see increased welfare spending, while 83 percent of Republicans would not. A minority of Americans (25 percent) think food assistance to the poor should be reduced, 41 percent think it should be increased, and 33 percent think it should stay the same. Two-thirds of Democrats would increase food assistance compared to 17 percent of Republicans. Among Republicans, 45 percent would cut food assistance and 38 percent would keep it about the same.[165]

Reflecting the stance against increased food assistance to the poor and the position that expanded government aid breeds dependency, an editorial in the *Wall Street Journal* took issue with increased post-pandemic government spending on food stamps in what it considers a food insecurity racket. It criticized increased government spending from $60 billion on food stamps in 2019 to $114 billion in 2021. It blamed this increase on the government's attempt to address food insecurity, which it described as a gauzy measure that overstates how many Americans do not consume enough calories, as opposed to addressing hunger. They suggested that the administration make food more affordable by reducing high inflation.[166] However, it must be noted that factors like the war in Ukraine, global supply-chain bottlenecks caused by the pandemic, and the zero-tolerance COVID policy in China that reduced production and exports, all contributed to high inflation. Whether these could have been controlled by any American administration is debatable.

It has been argued that these social and ideological conflicts and confusion about causes of poverty hinder efforts to reduce poverty and inequality.[167]

Historically, there's always been tension in America between offering aid in a humane manner to those who need it while not promoting so-called undesirable behaviors such as dependence on handouts or providing a disincentive to work.[168]

Colonists tended to assume responsibility for poor people that they regarded as part of their community, but not for others, and there was little social welfare for American Indians or Blacks during the colonial period. In the early 1800s as urbanization and industrialization began,

---

165. Ekins, "What Americans Think."
166. Editorial Board, "'Food Insecurity' Racket."
167. Iceland, *Poverty in America*, 3.
168. Iceland, *Poverty in America*, 5, 9.

able-bodied poor people were seen as lazy and morally degenerate.[169] However, the Great Depression changed the economic, social, and political landscape. With unemployment climbing from 3.2 percent in 1929 to 24.9 percent in 1933, it became evident that at least some of the new poverty resulted from socioeconomic factors that the needy could not control. Under several New Deal programs, grants were made available to the states, including $500 million in federal funds under the Federal Emergency Relief Act. Although Blacks tended to receive less aid than Whites due to discrimination, the programs ended up helping some Black families.[170]

The Social Security Act of 1935 provided social insurance in the form of pensions for the elderly, unemployment insurance for workers who became unemployed, public assistance in the form of aid to dependent children, and assistance to disabled children. The Act made the federal government assume responsibility for its citizens.[171]

The Food Stamp Act of 1964 provided funds for low-income families to buy food. Medicare provided health insurance for the elderly and Medicaid did the same for low-income families beginning in 1965. Benefits for the blind, disabled, and elderly were federalized in 1974 in the Supplemental Security Income program. Although a growing number of people were denouncing welfare by the late 1960s, social programs were expanded to help deserving needy citizens. These included the Earned Income Tax Credit (EITC) which provided tax rebates for low-income workers, and the Comprehensive Employment and Training Act (CETA), which subsidized public service jobs for the unemployed. However, many social programs such as childcare subsidies, food stamps, subsidized housing, unemployment insurance, aid to families with dependent children, and public and mental health services were slashed in the 1980s under the Reagan administration in the belief that there was widespread freeloading in the welfare system. In 1988, the Family Support Act introduced the Job Opportunities and Basic Skills program that required single parents on welfare with children over the age of three to work to receive assistance. They had to enroll in education or job-training programs paid for by the states and federal government if they could not get jobs.[172]

169. Iceland, *Poverty in America*, 131–32.
170. Iceland, *Poverty in America*, 135, citing Katz, *In the Shadow*, 224–54.
171. Iceland, *Poverty in America*, 135.
172. Iceland, *Poverty in America*, 136–37.

The Personal Responsibility and Work Opportunity Reconciliation Act (PRWORA) was passed in 1996. It ended Aid to Families with Dependent Children (AFDC) and replaced it with smaller grants to states that required assistance to welfare recipients to end after two years, whether they had found jobs or not, and set a lifetime limit on assistance at five years. The number of people receiving cash assistance, now known as Temporary Assistance to Needy Families (TANF, not AFDC) dropped from 5 million families in 1994 to 2.2 million in 2000. Although employment rates and incomes for single mothers generally rose after 1994 and continued to do so into the 2000s, some women with low skills and mental and physical problems fared worse after these reforms.[173]

The next most significant legislation benefiting poor and vulnerable populations was the Patient Protection and Affordable Care Act (ACA) of 2010 whose main purpose was to reduce the number of people without health insurance in the US. It also expanded Medicaid to more low-income families.[174] Although about twenty million people gained insurance coverage under the ACA, the Act, more popularly known as Obamacare, has been one of the most litigated federal programs in American history. Many opposed it as government overreach in instituting a social insurance program, while others defended it as addressing an unacceptable national problem. In the end, despite the numerous legal challenges, the ACA is still law.[175]

Social Security and Medicare make up the largest proportion of the American government's income-assistance spending. They keep the greatest number of people out of poverty, especially the elderly. The EITC benefits working families with low wages. Medicaid provides healthcare to low-income people.[176] The most controversial programs, such as cash welfare assistance, have for many years only consumed a small part of the budget.[177]

There are some who do not believe the government should provide any public support because people are completely responsible for their own welfare, while others think the government should provide a

---

173. Iceland, *Poverty in America*, 138.

174. Iceland, *Poverty in America*, 138–39.

175. The ACA was heavily litigated in state and federal courts but ultimately survived three Supreme Court challenges. For an article discussing the many legal challenges to the ACA, see Gluck et al., "Affordable Care Act's Litigation Decade," 1472.

176. Iceland, *Poverty in America*, 10, 130.

177. Iceland, *Poverty in America*, 155.

stronger safety net. There seems to be broad consensus, however, that there is a public responsibility to help those who lack the necessities of life; that people should support themselves as much as possible; and that policies promoting equity should not unduly hinder economic growth.[178]

There is evidence that welfare programs do have small, negative effects on behavior considered economically desirable as seen in the reduction in welfare rolls in the US and higher employment among single mothers after welfare reform in the US in the mid-1990s. Welfare benefits and disability insurance appear to moderately reduce employment.[179]

Growing divisions along the lines of race and ethnicity influence views on social safety nets. As in colonial times when communities supported their own but turned their backs on outsiders, some argue that racial polarization will hamper future efforts to alleviate poverty in America.[180]

It has been pointed out that American policies on poverty, which generally require poor people to work to be eligible for aid, differ from those of the developed world in that American policies emphasize stimulating economic growth and promoting individual liberty rather than ensuring income equality and collective well-being.[181]

In addition to government programs, there are many charitable organizations whose work centers on alleviating poverty locally, regionally, nationally, or globally, and people who give to support their work. Some operate homeless shelters. Some operate soup kitchens. Some operate food pantries. Some have food banks and feeding programs that help feed the poor. In addition to feeding the poor, others help with providing safe drinking water, shelter in times of natural disasters, or micro-credit to assist the poor to escape poverty. Some specialize in providing free health services in developing countries. Others assist refugees fleeing the ravages of war, political or religious persecution, or poverty. Some of these organizations are connected to churches or religious organizations and others are connected to the United Nations. Regardless of their affiliation and focus, all these charitable organizations depend on the generosity of people who have a heart to give to the poor, the vulnerable, and those who are hurting.

178. Iceland, *Poverty in America*, 145.
179. Iceland, *Poverty in America*, 146, citing Chen and Van der Klaauw, "Work Disincentive Effects," 757–84.
180. Iceland, *Poverty in America*, 151.
181. Iceland, *Poverty in America*, 130.

In the Cato Institute survey, nearly 71 percent of Americans said they had volunteered or donated money, food, or clothing to charity or a community group. Giving is not restricted to the wealthy. Half (50 percent) of Americans earning less than $20,000 gave to charity the year before the survey. Middle-class Americans give in larger numbers as their income increases, with 72 percent of those earning between $40,000–$59,000 giving to charity, and about 82 percent of those earning $60,000 or more a year giving to charity.[182]

How Should Modern-Day Christians Treat the Poor?

Anyone who professes to be a Christian—that is, a disciple, follower, or imitator of Jesus Christ—ought to treat the poor the same way Jesus did and have the same heart for the poor that God has.

Christians cannot forget that Jesus, the Son of God, took on human form and chose to come to earth as a poor, homeless man to give his life for others.

Jesus had compassion on people whose condition likely impoverished them. This included giving the blind their sight back, healing the lame, curing lepers, and opening deaf ears.[183] Sometimes his deep compassion led him to raise dead people on whom others who were helpless depended.[184] Modern-day Christians must demonstrate the same compassion for those who have been impoverished by physical disability and must be willing to help them in whatever way they can, whether by helping them directly, giving to charities that support them, or by volunteering with organizations that assist them.

Modern-day Christians must remember that Jesus takes kindness to the poor personally, as seen in the parable of the sheep and the goats.[185] Jesus's references to the hungry, thirsty, stranger, naked, sick, and the imprisoned in the parable are all references to the poor, the needy, the vulnerable, and the outcast. With the Holy Spirit's help, Christians must show kindness to these people in our modern-day world. Jesus regards showing love and compassion to the poor and needy, particularly to believers who are suffering, as tantamount to showing him love and compassion.

---

182. Ekins, "What Americans Think."
183. Matt 11:5.
184. Luke 7:11–15.
185. Matt 25:31–46.

TREATMENT OF THE POOR

Jesus was full of love and compassion. As such, one cannot profess to be his disciple, follower, or imitator and have a callous heart toward the poor. Like Jesus, a Christian must demonstrate love and compassion to all, especially those who belong to the family of faith.[186] Jesus said that all who do his will are his family.[187] Such compassion is an essential element of true faith and of being Jesus's disciple or follower.

Modern-day Christians must be willing to help other believers regardless of where they are. The believers in Macedonia and Achaia lived out this truth when they gave to help poor believers in a foreign country, Israel.[188] And just as the apostle Paul and the early church leaders in Jerusalem were eager to help the poor,[189] modern-day Christian leaders and Christians in general must likewise be willing and eager to assist the poor, especially those who are fellow believers, regardless of what they look like or where they live. Many churches have benevolence funds that are used to help church members who are facing some sort of hardship. These funds are collected from offerings made by others who have a heart to help needy fellow believers.

Because the poor cannot repay acts of kindness, Jesus said that such acts will be rewarded in the new heaven and new earth.[190] But before that happens, God also promises to bless the one who is generous and shares his food with the poor,[191] assuring that person that he or she will lack nothing.[192]

God's word says that he helps the poor and the needy[193] and provides for the poor.[194] How does he do this? By channeling resources through obedient servants who see themselves as faithful stewards. Modern-day Christians must heed God's exhortation about not being tightfisted toward the poor. He promises to bless the work and all the endeavors of those who are openhanded toward the poor.[195] The apostle Paul told the

---

186. Gal 6:10. The NIV says the family of believers.
187. Matt 12:50.
188. Rom 15:25.
189. Gal 2:10.
190. Luke 14:12–14.
191. Prov 22:9.
192. Prov 28:27.
193. Pss 40:17; 70:5.
194. Pss 68:10; 132:15.
195. Deut 15:7–10.

Philippians that God would meet all their needs because they had helped him in his time of need.[196]

God was so concerned about widows, orphans, and immigrants that he instituted the law of the tithe in ancient Israel whereby every third year, the people were to bring a tenth of their produce and store it in storehouses in their towns and the temple so these vulnerable people, as well as the Levites who did not receive an allotment of land when the Israelites settled in the promised land, would have enough food to eat.[197] Long before that, Jacob, Abraham's grandson, had made a commitment to give God a tenth of everything God gave him.[198] This would be Jacob's way of acknowledging that God was his source. Like Jacob, as an acknowledgment that God is their source, modern-day Christians must be open to giving a tenth or tithe of what God has given them to support the work of the kingdom of God and to help the poor, not because the Old Testament law legalistically compels them to do so.

Everything Jesus did for the poor was motivated by love and compassion. And that should be the motivation for acts of kindness by modern-day Christians to whom God has given his Holy Spirit, the Spirit of love. In the Cato Institute study, Americans were asked several questions to gauge their level of compassion.[199] The questions that were asked included whether they feel sympathy for those who are worse off, whether they sympathize with the homeless, and whether they suffer from other peoples' sorrows. The results were surprising, not when broken down along liberal and conservative lines, but when broken down along lines of those who profess to have faith and those who do not. The survey results showed that atheists and agnostics (62 percent) are more likely to score above average on empathy or compassion than those who identify with a religious tradition like Protestants (47 percent) and Catholics (36 percent). This raises the question as to whether some professing Christians understand that they are supposed to be imitators of Christ. Despite this difference in empathy levels, atheists, agnostics, Protestants, and Catholics were about equally likely to have volunteered or donated to a charitable cause in the past year.

---

196. Phil 4:15–19.
197. Deut 14:28–29; Mal 3:10.
198. Gen 28:20–22.
199. The study called this the Dispositional Compassion Index (DCI). Ekins, "What Americans Think."

Giving by a Christian must be in the same spirit of love and compassion out of which Christ gave all he had, not out of self-interest, such as reducing tax liability, or being admired. What if charitable donations were no longer tax deductible? Reducing tax liability from giving should be seen as an incidental benefit, but not the motivator for giving. Nor should giving be to attract praise or admiration. In the Sermon on the Mount, Jesus warned that a charitable deed that is done to attract praise or attention will receive no reward from God.[200] And the apostle Paul told the Corinthians that if he were to give away all his possessions but did not have love, he would gain nothing.[201] In other words, he would gain nothing in God's eyes or kingdom. Neither should giving be because the giver believes God expects it of them, as opposed to being motivated by love, compassion, a genuine willingness to be a blessing, and a desire to please God. In the most exhaustive instruction on giving in the New Testament, the apostle Paul told the Corinthians that giving must be done as one purposes in one's heart, not grudgingly or of necessity (feeling compelled), because God loves a cheerful giver.[202]

Beyond acts of kindness toward the poor, modern-day Christians must also be sensitive to how the poor are treated. They cannot participate in or condone mistreatment of the poor. God takes mistreatment of the poor personally and considers oppression of the poor as a personal reproach to him.[203] God refuses to hear the prayers of those who shut their ears to the cry of the poor.[204] In our highly polarized and politically charged society where government assistance to the poor is a perennial political football, modern-day Christians must remember how God takes mistreatment of the poor and insensitivity to their needs personally. In this regard, Christians must pay particular attention to the intersection of poverty and race because of the misconception that the majority of welfare recipients are Black, although the data show that the majority of welfare recipients are White.[205] Unfortunately, because of

---

200. Matt 6:1–4. See Harrington, *Gospel of Matthew*, 96, where he comments that Jesus's target is the aberrant style of those who make acts of personal piety, including almsgiving, into public displays, and that it is ostentatiousness in personal piety that is criticized here.

201. 1 Cor 13:3.

202. 2 Cor 9:7. The NIV says giving should not be done reluctantly or under compulsion.

203. Prov 14:31; 17:5.

204. Prov 21:13.

205. Welfare is used here to refer to the Supplemental Nutrition Assistance Program

this misconception, studies show that there are Whites who support cutting or restricting aid to the poor because they mistakenly assume Black people are benefiting and White people are being disadvantaged. Their opposition to welfare is, therefore, racially motivated.[206] This attitude is un-Christlike because it is contrary to the example Jesus Christ set. He showed compassion to all poor people and helped them regardless of their ethnicity.

As we saw earlier, many poor people do work. We also saw that many people are asset-limited, income-constrained employed (ALICE). They cannot make ends meet and have to make tough choices between necessities like rent and prescriptions. Modern-day Christians who own businesses or have managerial roles where they influence decisions about employment, pay, and benefits must remember that God's concern for the poor also extended to the working poor. He commanded the Israelites not to take advantage of hired hands who were poor and needy, whether they were immigrants or fellow Israelites. Those who hired them were to pay them their wages at sunset because they were poor and counted on their wages. God said he would count it as a sin against them if they did not do this and the poor cried out to him about it.[207] Modern-day Christians who hire and pay employees must treat and pay them fairly. They must remember that Jesus said that the worker deserves his wages, although that statement was made in the context of kingdom workers sharing the gospel.[208] In the same vein, Jesus also said that the worker is worthy of his food or worth his keep.[209]

Modern-day Christians must also remember that God is a God of righteousness and justice.[210] God loves justice and hates injustice. As such, modern-day Christians cannot participate in or condone injustice toward the poor. The rich and powerful are not the ones who suffer injustice in our world. It is the poor, the disenfranchised, and the outcast. The poor, and vulnerable people like immigrants, can get caught in the

---

or SNAP, popularly known as food stamps. See Hartline-Grafton and Vollinger, "New USDA Report."

206. See Chow, "Why More White Americans."

207. Deut 24:14–15; Lev 19:13, 33.

208. Luke 10:7.

209. Matt 10:10. See Adeyemo, *Africa Bible Commentary*, 1132, commenting that the twelve disciples Jesus sent to preach the gospel were not to worry about their material needs, for those who benefited from their ministries were expected to support them by supplying what they needed so that they could concentrate on their work.

210. Ps 89:14.

middle of political rhetoric and culture wars centering on immigration and welfare dependency. Modern-day Christians cannot forget that Jesus Christ and his family were, at one point, refugees from political injustice. They fled for their lives to Egypt at God's direction.

In ancient Israel, God sent prophet after prophet to condemn injustice. In the days of the early church, James, the leader of the church in Jerusalem, warned Christians against discriminating against the poor. He reminded them that God has chosen the poor to be rich in faith and to inherit the kingdom of God.[211] In our day, God continues to speak through his word about his love of justice and hatred of injustice.

Modern-day Christians must be willing to give to the poor. They must be willing to support the work of charitable organizations that assist the poor and needy throughout the world. Given God's love and concern for the poor, they must see this as part of supporting the work of the kingdom of God on earth.

In the final analysis, as imitators of Jesus Christ and with the help of the Holy Spirit, Christians must treat the poor just as Jesus, who was himself poor, did. They must have the same concern for the poor that God does. And as the apostle Paul taught and modeled, modern-day Christians must have a heart to help the poor without encouraging idleness, while also being cognizant of contemporary societal issues that complicate gainful employment. These include employment discrimination, mental health challenges, barriers to reentering society after incarceration, and low wages that disincentivize hard work. In this regard, professing Christians must commit to advocating and working for change. And it bears remembering that Jesus Christ promises a place in his kingdom for the righteous who show love and compassion to the poor and needy while warning of eternal punishment for those who withhold love and compassion from them.

---

211. Jas 2:1–9. See Adeyemo, *Africa Bible Commentary*, 1512, commenting that God is on the side of the poor, not because they are poor but because they are responsive to him and are near the kingdom. They inherit the kingdom for being rich in faith. See Also Daniel K. Eng, "Letter of James," in McCaulley et al., *New Testament in Color*, 643–44, noting that James is urging his marginalized hearers not to show favoritism to the rich, which reinforces the marginalization of the poor and perpetuates injustice.

10

Treatment of Others Based on Race

JESUS CHRIST LOVED, TREATED, and ministered to everyone he encountered without regard to their nationality, ethnicity, or the color of their skin, and Christians, as imitators of Christ, must do the same.

Over the decades, many studies have been done and countless papers and books written on race and racism. Many more will be written. But racism will continue to be the elephant in the room.

Is there still racism? Is racism always only an individual choice or act? Or is there such a thing as systemic or institutional racism, where laws, policies, and institutional cultures and practices help perpetuate racial disparities? How should a Christian—a born-again disciple, follower, or imitator of Jesus Christ—treat others on the basis of race?

What can Christians learn from the Bible's revelation about how God feels about race? And what can Christians learn from how Jesus, who came to show us the Father and who laid down his life as a ransom for the redemption of all humanity regardless of the color of their skin, treated others on the basis of their ethnicity?

In addressing how Christians must treat others based on race, we begin with the question of whether, during creation as recounted in the Bible, the Triune God created many races or just one race—the human race.

Is There More than One Race?

The Bible teaches that during creation, the Triune God—consisting of God the Father, God the Son, and God the Holy Spirit—created man, Adam, in the image of God. God formed him out of the dust of the earth and breathed life into him. God placed him in the garden of Eden to tend it and take care of it. Eden's geographical description in Genesis puts it in parts of Africa and the Middle East. It contained several rivers, including the Tigris and the Euphrates. These two rivers flow through Turkey, Iraq, Syria, Iran, Saudi Arabia, and Kuwait, emptying into the Persian Gulf. The geographic area described in Genesis as part of Eden included the whole land of Cush, which is where Ethiopia is believed to be today.[1]

Contrary to the biblical narrative about the garden of Eden, European Enlightenment ideas about White superiority led to claims that humans descended from a single creation in a European garden of Eden, a narrative repeated by Americans like Samuel Stanhope Smith, a Princeton theologian who later became president of Princeton in 1795. In 1787, he claimed in a speech to the American Philosophical Society that Adam and Eve were Europeans who lived in Europe, and that Europe was the cradle of humanity.[2] One European intellectual claimed that a catastrophic event in the garden of Eden sent survivors fleeing to Asia and Africa, even though the Bible makes clear that Adam and Eve were evicted from the garden of Eden and banished from it after they disobeyed God[3] and that God later scattered humans all over the earth following the Tower of Babel incident.[4]

Long before these European claims about the garden of Eden, Michelangelo had painted the famous *Creation of Adam* on the Sistine Chapel's ceiling, portraying Adam as a White man. And although Jesus Christ told the Samaritan woman he met at the well in Sychar that God is spirit and that those who worship him must worship him in spirit and in truth,[5] Michelangelo depicted God in his painting of the *Creation of Adam* as an elderly, white-bearded White man.

1. Gen 2:10–14.
2. See Kendi, *Stamped from the Beginning*, 50, 114. See also Goza, *America's Unholy Ghosts*, where he traces the imagining, institutionalization, and ingraining of racist ideas in America to the works of three Enlightenment philosophers—Thomas Hobbes, John Locke, and Adam Smith. He describes them as a philosophical, unholy "trinity."
3. Gen 1:26–28; 2:7–8, 18–25; 3:23–24.
4. Gen 11:1–9.
5. John 4:24.

God said it was not good for Adam to be alone, so he created Eve to be Adam's companion and helper. The Bible tells us that Adam and Eve wore no clothes. They were naked and unashamed of it.[6] The geographic description of Eden, including Ethiopia and the Middle East, puts them in a warm to moderate climate, which explains why they would be comfortable even though naked. It wasn't until after the fall that God clothed them minimally with the skin of an animal.[7]

No one knows exactly at what point in time Adam and Eve lived. After God created Adam, he gave Adam permission to eat of all of the trees in the garden but commanded him not to eat of the tree of the knowledge of good and evil. God warned him that he would die if he did.[8]

The Bible tells us that God made all people from one ancestor, from one man, Adam, or from one blood; and that God determined the set times for them and the exact places where they should live.[9] Adam and Eve were, therefore, the forbears or common ancestors of all humanity—the human race. In other words, God only created one race, not many races.

Although God commanded Adam not to eat of the tree of the knowledge of good and evil, Satan, the age-old serpent, was able to deceive Adam and Eve into doing just that, having convinced them that God was holding back on them and that they would become just like God if they did eat. In disobeying God, Adam and Eve sinned. This led to the curse—the fall of humankind, suffering, and death. It also led to the very first eviction, with Adam and Eve being banished from the garden of Eden.[10]

Because Adam and Eve were the forbears of the human race, their sin had consequences for all of the succeeding generations of humanity throughout the world. Their disobedience transmitted sin and death through the lifeblood of the human race.[11] As a result, all are born into sin and need a savior.[12] And God gave Jesus to humankind as that savior.[13]

---

6. Gen 2:18–25.

7. Gen 3:21.

8. Gen 2:7–17.

9. Acts 17:26. The NRSV says God made all people from one ancestor. The NIV says God made the nations from one man. The NKJV says God made every nation of men from one blood. See Lovchik, *Racism*, calling racism "reality built on a myth."

10. Gen 3:22–24.

11. Rom 5:12.

12. Rom 3:23.

13. John 3:16; Rom 6:23.

This sinfulness led to so much wickedness on the earth among the human race that the Bible says God regretted creating the human race. This wickedness led God to say that he would blot out from the earth the humans he had created[14] and led God to use a flood to destroy all humans except Noah, a righteous and blameless man, and his family. God did not create and has never referred to *races* or *men* when speaking of the human beings he created. He has always referred to *man, mankind,* or *humans,* depending on what translation one is reading.

Scientists have been studying human origins for quite a while now and there have been discoveries and hypotheses regarding modern human ancestry. Some of the interesting discoveries are the so-called Mitochondrial Eve in Africa, believed to be the ancestress of modern humans, and her male analog Y-Chromosomal Adam, believed to be the patrilineal ancestor of all living humans.[15]

The narrative that pervades the world that there are many races and that some are superior to others is contrary to the word and mind of God as revealed in the Bible. So, where did that narrative come from?

The Development of the Narrative and Social Construct of Race

It has been documented that the narrative that there is more than one race began with the Portuguese trade in African slaves and the creation of trans-Atlantic slave-trading policies in the mid-fifteenth century. The first slaves from West Africa were brought to Portugal by sailors commissioned by Prince Henry the Navigator and the first slave auction took place in 1444. Prince Henry's biographer, Gomes Eanes de Zurara, who was commissioned by Prince Henry's uncle King Alphonso V, described those of the slaves at the 1444 auction who were dark as black and ugly. Although he did not call the Black people that he described a *race*, he grouped them all together. The term *race* was used for the first time in 1481 by a French poet called Jacques de Breze and defined in a French dictionary for the first time in 1606 as meaning descent. That definition also introduced the idea of a good or bad race and, therefore, the

---

14. Gen 6:7. The NIV says God said he will wipe from the face of the earth mankind whom he had created. In the KJV and NKJV, God said he was sorry he made man, a reference to the entire human race.

15. Modern humans are called Homo sapiens. Scientists posit that they are preceded by pre-modern humans of various forms such as Neanderthals.

idea of a racial hierarchy. Gomes Eanes de Zurara described Africans as lost, beastly people, justifying their evangelization and enslavement.[16] These racist views of Africans were further reinforced by Leo Africanus, a well-educated Moroccan who had been captured and given to Pope Leo X, but freed before the pope's death. His 1526 book, *Cosmographia et geographia de Affrica*, published in 1550 under the title *Della descrittione dell'Africa* (*Description of Africa*) and translated into French and Latin in 1556, described Africans as lacking in reason, animalistic, and hypersexual. He and Zurara defined European thinking about Africa and Africans.[17]

Across the Atlantic, native populations in the Americas were grouped together as Indians or Blacks by Spanish and Portuguese colonizers in the fifteenth century. By 1735, humans had been divided into a racial hierarchy—White, Yellow, Red, and Black, with Whites at the top as the superior race, followed by Asians and American Indians, and with Africans at the bottom as the most inferior of the races.[18]

It should come as no surprise that the idea that there are many races and the narratives accompanying that idea were connected to slavery and the profiteering of slave trading. The narrative of race became justification for one of the world's most sinister sins. Never mind that this narrative contradicted the word of God as revealed in the Bible. The Portuguese used slavery as a guise for missionary work while profiting from it and convincing popes and Europeans that slavery was not about the money.[19] In other words, the Portuguese engaged in slavery in the name of God. Having received 185 slaves between 1434 and 1447, King Alphonso V is said to have derived more wealth from slave trading than taxes levied in his kingdom.[20]

---

16. Zurara's book, *The Chronicle of the Discovery and Conquest of Guinea*, was the first book on Africa, first published in 1453. See Kendi, *Stamped from the Beginning*, 22–25, 36. The dictionary that first defined race was the *Trésor de la langue française*, with an entry by Jean Nicot, a French diplomat. See Kendi, *How to Be an Antiracist*, 39–40.

17. Kendi, *Stamped from the Beginning*, 28–29.

18. The categorizations of races were done by Carl Linnaeus in his book *Systema Naturae*. Kendi, *How to Be an Antiracist*, 41.

19. Kendi, *How To Be an Antiracist*, 41–42; also, *Stamped from the Beginning*, 23.

20. Thomas, *Slave Trade*, 74; Zurara, *Chronicle of the Discovery*, xx-xl; Russell, *Prince Henry "the Navigator,"* 246; Kendi, *Stamped from the Beginning*, 24; *How to Be an Antiracist*, 42.

By the way, the word *slave* supposedly derives from the fact that Slavs from Eastern Europe were among those being sold as slaves by Moroccans and Turks to Europeans. *Slav* therefore became a root word for *slave*.[21]

Attempts to justify slavery took a tortured twist in the mid-seventeenth century with the idea that there were people like American Indians and Africans who belonged to a race that did not descend from Adam.[22] This idea of Blacks being of a different race than Adam and Eve was trumpeted loudly as pushback against abolitionism toward the end of the eighteenth century. One author based the theory of many creations on the biblical narrative of the Tower of Babel.[23] That story makes clear, however, that humanity had one language before people migrated all over the world and many other languages evolved.[24] Having had one language at one point supports the Bible story of the creation of one race, or monogenesis, not the creation of multiple races, or polygenesis. Not only did polygenesis contradict and twist biblical truth, but it also made God out to be an unjust and disingenuous God who deliberately disadvantaged some of his creation by making them inferior while subjecting them to the same expectations as those that he has supposedly endowed with superiority.

But that is essentially what John H. Van Evrie, a polygenist, claimed when he wrote in 1853 that God made the Negro an inferior being in every respect, while creating all White men equal.[25] Also in 1853, a reviewer of the novel *Uncle Tom's Cabin* refuted the notion that the souls of Negroes were being crushed by Whites, telling them that they were "nothing but niggers." The reviewer, a southern woman from Georgia, insisted that it was God, their maker, who had created Negroes to be "nothing but niggers."[26] This is despite the fact that the Bible says God does not show favoritism or partiality.[27]

---

21. Evans, *Open Wound*, 17–18; Kendi, *Stamped from the Beginning*, 23.

22. An idea known as polygenesis. Monogenesis is the idea that all humans are descended from one race.

23. Kames, *Sketches of the History of Man*, 4, 15. Henry Home, Lord Kames, was a Scottish judge and philosopher. See also, Long, *History of Jamaica*, 356, 364, 371, 475–78, pushing polygenesis. Also, Kendi, *Stamped from the Beginning*, 100–101.

24. Gen 11:1–9.

25. Van Evrie, *Negroes and Negro "Slavery,"* 221; Kendi, *Stamped from the Beginning*, 198.

26. De Bow, "Southern Slavery and Its Assailants"; Kendi, *Stamped from the Beginning*, 197.

27. Rom 2:11. The NIV says God does not show favoritism and the NKJV says that

THE CHRISTIAN AS IMITATOR OF CHRIST

This idea of a race not descended from Adam held sway throughout the so-called Age of Enlightenment and ruled American beliefs about race until 1859 when Charles Darwin, who had previously subscribed to the idea, debunked it in favor of natural selection, which became the new method to make racial distinctions and rankings supposedly based on biology. It was used by Darwinists to justify enslavement of Blacks while projecting the "White race" as evolving toward perfection. Nazis used eugenics, born out of biological racism, to commit genocide during the Second World War. This led to its rejection by academics, but not in popular thought.[28] Polygenesis was a widely held belief in America in 1850. Blacks were believed to be a different, inferior, animal-like species.[29]

One author has surmised that brilliant and powerful intellectuals like Gomes Eanes de Zurara produced the idea of race to justify racist policies like slave trading that promoted their economic, political, and cultural self-interest.[30]

Writing to his protégé Timothy, the apostle Paul warned that the love of money is the root of all kinds of evil, causing people to stray or err from true faith.[31] Slavery was probably the most evil manifestation of the love of money, and the narrative of race was constructed to justify this evil.

It is clear from the Bible that there are no races, just the human race. But there are many sub-groups or ethnicities within the human race. The human genome project found that all humans are genetically 99.9 percent identical, validating the biblical narrative that all humans descend from Adam and Eve. Nonetheless, segregationists categorize people into six races—White, Black, Latino, Asian, Native American, and Middle Eastern—and talk about maintaining White racial purity, as evidenced

---

there is no partiality with God.

28. See Kendi, *How to Be an Antiracist*, 51–52. The idea of a non-Adamic race was presented by Isaac La Peyrère in his book *Men Before Adam* in 1655. Darwin debunked the idea in *The Origin of Species* in 1859. Albion Small, the founder of American sociology, used natural selection to justify enslavement of Blacks.

29. Kendi, *Stamped from the Beginning*, 189. Books espousing polygenesis in the early 1850s included Nott and Gliddon, *Types of Mankind*; Van Evrie, *Negroes and Negro "Slavery"*; and Gobineau, *Inequality of Human Races*. Polygenesis was touted as a preeminently American science by the *New York Herald*. Kendi, *Stamped from the Beginning*, 198.

30. Kendi, *Stamped from the Beginning*, 42–43.

31. 1 Tim 6:10. The KJV says it is the root of all evil.

by the era of racial purity laws in America.[32] But talk of racial purity is a misnomer, there being only one race. People who profess to be Christians but nonetheless subscribe to the false narrative of race and even talk of racial purity couldn't be further from God's truth as revealed in the Bible. It is untenable to profess to be a follower of Christ while rejecting the biblical revelation of the creation of the human race and subscribing to a false worldly narrative that was concocted to justify the most egregious of sins—human chattel slavery.

With this tortured history behind the narrative of race in view, scholars have pointed out that race is not biological or scientific. It is a social construct or construction—a concept or idea originating in society whereby people are defined by things like ancestry, skin color, and hair texture. Nonetheless, this social construct has tangible economic, social, and political implications. It is a social categorization that is influenced by status or history and can change across cultures or be the subject of disagreements across and within racial groups. Categorizing people has psychological roots because people psychologically process cultural rules about race when they categorize people. Being "colored" for example, has different applications in America, where it refers to a person with Black ancestry, and South Africa where it refers to a person with mixed ancestry (Black and White). In these two countries, race is socially constructed differently in this respect and accords different advantages or privileges to this same group of people with mixed ancestry. Societies define race and give rewards and punishments based on that. The differences in how race is constructed across cultures shows that it is not scientific.[33]

Race has also been constructed differently across time. Take, for example, how François Bernier defined the superior or first race. He included Europeans and the people of North Africa, India, the Middle East, Southeast Asia, and the Americas, but excluded the people of northern Finland.[34] And consider the fact that although Europeans grouped Africans together into a race beginning in the fifteenth century, Africans

---

32. In *Loving v. Virginia*, 388 U.S. 1 (1967), racial purity laws in America criminalizing marriage between a White person and a non-White person were invalidated when the Supreme Court held the Virginia Racial Integrity Act of 1924 to be a violation of the equal protection and due process clauses of the fourteenth amendment to the constitution. The court found the statute to infringe on the fundamental right of marriage. American racial purity laws influenced Nazi Germany's anti-Jewish Blood Law. See Whitman, *Hitler's American Model*.

33. Hodson, "Race as a Social Construction."

34. Kendi, *Stamped from the Beginning*, 55–56.

themselves did not see themselves that way. They saw themselves as different ethnic groups. This was true even hundreds of years later in the seventeenth and eighteenth centuries during the slave trade, and probably didn't change until the twentieth century.[35]

Despite the fact that race is a social construct, many believe that race is a biological fact based on scientific distinctions, an idea that the media, government policy, and people who embrace a racial identity have reinforced. They believe categorizations based on physical attributes are objective, scientific, biological groupings, although they are really groupings that developed historically and have no biological significance beyond what society attributes to them. It has been pointed out that no races exist in nature; only physical differences that have been used to construct categories that are given meaning far beyond the physical differences themselves. These categories and meanings have changed over time, influenced by economic conditions and court rulings, and inconsistently designated in different societies.[36]

Based on this, the argument has been made that racism is "reality built on a myth";[37] race is a genetic mirage, albeit one with real consequences that cannot be ignored. It has been argued that the key to removing the mirage is to end the racism that shapes it.[38]

The True Origin of the Construct of Race

If race is a social construct that is not in accord with biblical truth, then it is based on a lie. That lie has led to another fundamental lie—the lie of the inherent superiority of Whites, presented as a distinct race, over those who belong to other so-called inferior races. Jesus called Satan a liar and the father of lies.[39] That being the case, disciples of Christ must discern that although human beings ostensibly came up with the social construct of race to promote their self-interests, Satan is the real source or origin of the lie about race—a lie that is contrary to God's truth as revealed in

---

35. Kendi, *How to Be an Antiracist*, 59–60.
36. Obach, "Demonstrating the Social Construction," 252–57.
37. See Lovchik, *Racism*.
38. Kendi, *How to Be an Antiracist*, 54–55.
39. John 8:44. See Moloney, *Gospel of John*, 280, where he explains that through lies and deceit, the devil robbed Adam of God's original promise of immortality, making him a liar and a murderer. Because of the devil's role of deceit and lies in human history, this makes him the father of lies.

the Bible. And as with all of Satan's lies, he offers great earthly rewards to those who buy into and act on his lies. These earthly rewards are the things of this world—wealth, power, privilege, and advantage—the same things he offered to Jesus during his temptation in the wilderness. For centuries, the color of one's skin in this construct of race has been used to define, and continues to be used to define, who has access to wealth, power, privilege, and advantage in a world system controlled by the god of this world—Satan. Those who have accepted and propagated this lie because it places them in the "superior" category have derived tremendous worldly gain from it. And those it minimizes by placing them in "inferior" categories have suffered because of it.

Racism—A Satanic Device

Racism is the belief that race is the primary determinant of human traits and capacities and that racial differences produce an inherent superiority of a particular race.[40] It is a form of prejudice in which a person believes in the superiority of their own race leading to mistreatment and discrimination. It is also used to refer to a system of oppression based on racial prejudice that is embedded into the fabric of society and its institutions, hence the reference to systemic, institutional, or structural racism.[41]

One author has defined racism as the marriage of racist policies (laws, rules, regulations, and procedures that have institutional, structural, or systemic qualities) and racist ideas that produces and normalizes racial inequities or disparities. Only those with racist power can make racist policy although all can discriminate, generally speaking. Racism is a collection of powerful racist policies fueled by racist ideas about the superiority or inferiority of a racial group, resulting in racial inequity. A racist is one who expressly (by action) or implicitly (by inaction) supports racist policies or expresses racist ideas.[42]

Racist ideas are used to justify racist policies that treat people differently or subject them to disadvantages because of their ethnicity. Some of these policies may appear to be neutral on their face but have disproportionate or disparate effects on racial minorities.

---

40. Merriam-Webster, "Racism (n.)."
41. Dictionary.com, "Racism (n.)."
42. Kendi, *How to Be an Antiracist*, 17–20, 22.

THE CHRISTIAN AS IMITATOR OF CHRIST

A racist believes that some are innately or inherently superior to others because of genetic or biological qualities they possess. Invariably, this belief boils down to differences in skin color. Racist beliefs and ideas are used to rationalize racially discriminatory policies that produce racial inequities.

From a spiritual perspective, however, a racist is one who opposes God's will for others of whom he or she disapproves because of their ethnicity or skin color. God endows everyone he creates with talents and abilities. He has a specific purpose for everyone he creates. He gives everyone gifts and abilities and an amount of time on earth to fulfill their God-given purpose. Those who embrace and practice racism and those who condone it put artificial barriers in the paths of those of whom they disapprove. They stand between God and the fulfillment of his purpose and plan for people of whom they disapprove based on "race." Peter acknowledged that he would have been opposing God if he hadn't accepted God's sovereignty to give the gift of the Holy Spirit and salvation to Cornelius, a gentile.[43] It is, therefore, the ultimate deception to think that one can oppose God in this way and still profess to love or serve God or be a disciple, follower, or imitator of Christ—a Christian.

If God only created one race, then the whole concept of many races and racism is a lie. If God is truth, and Satan is a liar and the father of lies, then racism must be one of Satan's cleverest lies.[44] In other words, racism is a satanic device designed to deceive and divide humankind. Paul didn't want the Corinthians to be ignorant of Satan's devices, and neither should modern-day Christians.[45] As a satanic device, racism is a sin trap. With it, Satan has deceived millions over centuries. Sin ultimately leads to death.[46] One might gain the world by buying into racism. But as a clever satanic device, it might be at the expense of one's soul.

One has to marvel at the ingenuity behind the crafting and spreading of racist ideas and racism beginning with Gomes Eanes de Zurara in the fifteenth century and continuing with numerous, powerful people across centuries, including European kings and queens, playwrights,[47]

---

43. Acts 11:17.

44. In a speech in the District of Columbia on April 16, 1888, the twenty-sixth anniversary of its emancipation, Frederick Douglass described the extreme financial exploitation of Blacks in the Jim Crow era as a satanic arrangement.

45. 2 Cor 1:10–11.

46. Rom 6:23.

47. Shakespeare's first Black character, Aaron, in his play *Titus Andronicus* was evil

popes, Puritan preachers, European and American politicians, scientists, authors, philosophers,[48] evangelicals, and founders of nations in the new world, and persisting to this very day with millions worldwide who have bought into it. The lure for buying into racism has been the rewards of riches, power, privilege, and advantage. As a lie backed by the power of Satan, the god of this evil world system, those who have bought into and profited from racism have found ways to malign and marginalize those who dare to oppose it. Take the case of Bartolome de Las Casas, for example. In 1510, he became the first ordained priest in the Americas (Hispaniola). First a supporter of the enslavement of natives and then the importation of Africans, he later became convinced before his death that slavery was evil and inconsistent with Christ's teachings. He disagreed with Gomes Eanes de Zurara, whose book he read, and regretted advocating for the importation of African slaves to Hispaniola. He tried and failed to close the door to African slavery and was labeled an extremist by the powerful forces behind slavery.[49]

The satanic forces behind slavery made it a venerable institution for centuries, enriching those who bought into it, and causing great devastation, sorrow, and suffering to the human beings who were enslaved and their descendants. Today, slavery has morphed into a more sophisticated twenty-first century phenomenon that includes human trafficking and new ways of oppressing people in slave-like conditions.[50]

Satan's intent in crafting and selling this lie is all about undermining God's will for humankind, destroying lives, and stealing souls. It is to accomplish the mission of his very existence, which Jesus alluded to when he described the mission of false shepherds and hirelings, who are of the devil and not of God, as being to steal, kill, and destroy.[51] He does

---

and oversexed, and Othello, a Black Moor, is called the "blacker devil" by his deceased wife's maid after Othello, who strangled his wife after being led to believe she had cheated on him, calls her an angel. See Barthelemy, *Black Face, Maligned Race*, 72–73, 91–93; Kendi, *Stamped from the Beginning*, 34–35.

48. Roman slavery was based on Aristotle's climate theory. Aristotle justified Greek slave holding on the belief that Greeks were superior due to their intermediate climate compared to those who lived in extreme hot or cold climates. The Puritans who came to America relied on Aristotle's theory to justify slavery. See Kendi, *Stamped from the Beginning*, 7.

49. Kendi, *Stamped from the Beginning*, 27.

50. Take, for example, mass incarceration and the wanton exploitation of prison labor.

51. John 10:10. See also Esau D. McCaulley, "Letter to the Ephesians," in McCaulley et al., *New Testament in Color*, 418, commenting that Christ's ascension to God's right

it extremely well, using deception and subterfuge, convincing many, as he did Adam and Eve, that they can align themselves with him, reap his rewards, and still please God and live free.

Does attributing racism to Satan as its mastermind absolve those who have bought into it and practiced or condoned it across the centuries from accountability? Absolutely not. God gave Adam and Eve his word. They were deceived by Satan to disobey God's word but that did not absolve them from accountability for exercising their free will to align themselves with Satan in disobedience to God's word. By the time Satan started weaving lies about race with the complicity of Europeans in the fifteenth century, the example of how Jesus Christ treated everyone he encountered regardless of their ethnicity or skin color and his teachings about loving one's neighbor as oneself and treating others as one would want to be treated had been known for over fourteen hundred years, leaving racists no excuse, especially if they claimed to be Christians. This is even more so when one considers that Jesus sent the Holy Spirit, the Spirit of truth, to guide believers into all truth.[52]

How Does God Feel About Racism?

God showed his disapproval of racism and prejudice very early in the Bible. Moses, who fled Egypt to Midian, married an Ethiopian woman by the name of Zipporah. Their sons Gershom and Eliezer were of mixed heritage, being part Jewish and part Ethiopian.[53] They may have had mixed heritage but, biblically speaking, they were not *mixed-blood*, *mixed-race*, or *biracial* children, as some might characterize them. Those terms are misnomers when viewed from a biblical perspective given that there is only one race and all humans are of one blood. It is to this diverse household that God went to find a servant-leader to lead his enslaved people out of Egypt into the land he had promised Abraham and his descendants hundreds of years earlier.[54]

---

hand in power beyond all authorities includes the demonic grip of racism that has stalked Blacks far too long.

52. John 16:13.
53. Exod 2:21; 18:3–4.
54. Exod 3:10. The Israelites had been slaves for 430 years. Exod 12:40. See Cain Hope Felder, "Race, Racism, and the Biblical Narratives," in Felder, *Stony the Road We Trod*, 135–37, where he discusses God's rebuke of the prejudice of Miriam and Aaron toward Moses's Egyptian wife and argues that negative attitudes toward Black people are entirely postbiblical.

After the Israelites crossed the Red Sea and moved through the wilderness toward the promised land, Aaron and Miriam, Moses's siblings, challenged his authority because he was married to an Ethiopian woman. Perhaps they felt that marrying an Ethiopian, a person of color, demonstrated a lapse in judgment on Moses's part. And if Moses had missed God on the issue of his choice of spouse, he was not the only one who could hear from the Lord. They could too. After all, God had appointed Aaron as Moses's spokesman to Pharaoh[55] and Miriam was described as a prophetess who led the Israelite women in song after crossing the Red Sea.[56]

Challenging Moses's authority by using his marriage to Zipporah as a pretext angered God, who struck Miriam with leprosy. Moses was God's appointed leader over his people—the person to whom he spoke directly. Challenging Moses meant having the audacity to challenge God's servant. Aaron's and Miriam's prejudice against Zipporah could not be used as an excuse. Moses ended up having to cry out to God to heal Miriam.[57]

God Accepts All Who Acknowledge, Love, and Serve Him

When the people of Israel were finally ready to enter Canaan after wandering in the wilderness for forty years because of their lack of faith in God to deliver on his promise after they came out of Egypt, Joshua, who now led the Israelites after Moses's death, sent a couple of spies to spy out the land. They went to the house of a prostitute named Rahab. The king of Jericho heard that spies had entered his country and were in Rahab's house, so he sent a message to Rahab to give up the men. But Rahab hid them and helped them escape.

Rahab had heard about how God had parted the Red Sea and given the Israelites, a ragtag group of former slaves, victory in battle over the kings of the Amorites. She was convinced that God had given Jericho to the Israelites. She figured that Jehovah, the God of the Israelites, was real and that he was the God in whom she was going to put her trust. She was willing to put her life in the hands of this God, so she made a deal

---

55. Exod 4:14–16. Aaron was later installed as high priest and his sons as priests. Exod 28:1.
56. Exod 15:20–21.
57. Num 12:1–15.

the Christian as imitator of Christ

with the spies to protect her and her family in return for her protection of the spies.[58]

The Israelites did conquer Jericho and save Rahab and her family. Rahab became a part of the nation of Israel.[59] Rahab appears later in the genealogy of Jesus. She married a man by the name of Salmon and had a son named Boaz.[60] Boaz later married a woman by the name of Ruth, a young widow who had returned with her widowed mother-in-law Naomi from the land of Moab.[61] Ruth and Boaz had a son by the name of Obed, who was the grandfather of King David.[62] Jesus is the root of David,[63] a descendant of Rahab and Ruth, two foreigners who put their faith in God and settled in Israel.

Jesus, the Son of God was, therefore, of mixed heritage, having Jewish, Canaanite, and Moabite ancestors in his lineage. This was a powerful debunking by God himself, the creator of the human race, of the lie and myth of racial purity. He knows his own work in creation—that he only created one race. Why would he then be concerned about racial purity? But God has always been concerned about spiritual purity. That was the sole reason why he forbade the Israelites from intermarrying with people from the nations he drove out of the land that he gave the Israelites. God specifically said that his concern was that they would turn the hearts of the Israelites from serving him to serving false gods, which would kindle his anger against them and result in their destruction.[64] Their unfaithfulness to God's requirements eventually led to their captivity and exile. When many among the remnant that returned from exile also failed to maintain spiritual purity and married foreign women from nations that did not serve God, Ezra, a scribe and spiritual leader of Israel, led them to repent.[65] Nehemiah, a contemporary of Ezra who served as governor, later led the Israelites to commit to maintaining spiritual purity by not

---

58. Josh 2.
59. Josh 6:25.
60. Matt 1:5; Luke 3:31.
61. Ruth 1:1–7.
62. Ruth 4:13–17.
63. Rev 5:5; 22:16.
64. Deut 7:1–4.
65. Ezra 9, 10. The foreign wives and their children were likely sent back to their people.

intermarrying with people from the neighboring nations who didn't serve God.[66] But this had nothing to do with racial purity.

God has the same concern today for believers' spiritual purity. The apostle Paul admonishes believers in Christ not to be unequally yoked or mismatched with unbelievers, which would include marrying an unbeliever.[67] Avoiding being unequally yoked does not justify segregation based on skin color, although many people, including some who profess to be Christians, have erroneously claimed that it does, and have acted on that false claim.

When Rahab and Ruth gave up their false gods for Jehovah, the God of Israel, and put their faith in him, the prohibition that they were off limits to the Israelites as spouses no longer applied. God had no reason to be concerned that they would lead an Israelite astray. He allowed them to be part of the lineage of Jesus to emphatically show that he accepts all who put their faith in him regardless of ethnicity or nationality. Jesus Christ came to reconcile humanity to God and to one another. He came to tear down the wall of hostility between Jew and gentile.[68] In Christ there is neither Jew nor Greek, slave nor free, male nor female.[69] He has made it possible for humanity to triumph over the deception of racism, racial superiority, so-called racial purity, and the division and hurts these falsehoods have brought upon humanity. Jesus Christ has made it possible for believers to belong to a spiritual, borderless nation, a royal priesthood, a holy nation of people who have been called out of the darkness of Satan's world of sin, deception, and lies to live in God's marvelous light.[70] One can't live in God's light, be a member of the family of God, yet harbor hatred and prejudice toward others, including other members of the family of God, discriminate against them, and make it difficult for them to fulfill their God-given purpose and potential because of the color of their skin.[71] But Satan deceives many to think they can.

66. Neh 9:38; 10:1–30.
67. 2 Cor 6:14. The NRSV and the HCSB use the word *mismatched*.
68. Eph 2:11–14.
69. Gal 3:28.
70. 1 Pet 2:9–10.

71. Matt 12:50; Mark 3:35. On believers belonging to a family that transcends ethnicity, nationality, class, and gender, see Boring, *Mark: A Commentary*, 110, explaining that becoming a disciple of Jesus brings one into a new family where believers are not only brothers and sisters to each other, but with Jesus as their brother belong with him as brothers and sisters to the family of God.

Who Does Satan Deceive with Racism?

Satan has succeeded in deceiving many who stand to benefit from racism because of the color of their skin. There are people who have bought into the lie of their superiority and the inferiority of others based on race or skin color who have reaped earthly rewards of wealth, power, privilege, and advantage.

But there is a flip side to racism. Satan not only tempts White people to buy into racism; he also tempts and deceives people of color who have been discriminated against and suffered great injustices throughout history to hate White people as the ones who have perpetrated and benefitted from these injustices. People of color have grieved through the centuries, and many continue to grieve today, about the impoverishment that accompanied slavery, Jim Crow, and systemic racism, while they've watched Whites transfer wealth and privilege from generation to generation. They grieve over the injustices that they see in many facets of society—education, employment, healthcare, the criminal justice system, and yes, even the church. Satan exploits this grief and deceives and tempts them to hate White people, whom they consider the enemy. He deceives many people of color to justify causing harm to White people in retaliation for the injustices they have suffered. Some have ambushed police officers in retaliation for what they perceive as police brutality against people of color. Some have committed crimes against White people and others show no empathy for crimes against White people, whether they are crimes that inflict physical harm or rob of perceived unjust wealth or even life.

Jesus taught against hating or retaliating against one's enemies. Instead, he taught his disciples to love their enemies, bless those who curse them, do good to those who hate them, and pray for those who persecute them.[72] Being able to do that is proof that one is a child of God—that one desires to be like one's Father in heaven.[73] Jesus also taught that we must forgive in order to be forgiven.[74] The apostle Paul told the Corinthians that the temptation to withhold forgiveness is a satanic device through which he takes advantage of the unforgiving.[75] The history of slavery in America shows that there are many examples of slaves who had deep

---

72. Matt 5:44.
73. Matt 5:45, 48.
74. Matt 6:12; 18:21–35; Luke 11:4.
75. 2 Cor 2:10–11.

faith and who seemed to have understood and been able to practice these principles, showing Christlike love and forgiveness to their masters and their families in spite of their dehumanizing and tragic circumstances. And God gave them joy and peace while they waited for freedom in their lifetime or their eternal reward if freedom eluded them. This often came across in the spirituals they sang. They understood that they could not be disciples, followers, or imitators of Christ and harbor hatred, resentment, bitterness,[76] and an unforgiving spirit in their hearts.[77] Unfortunately, this was often mistaken by their oppressors as evidence of their satisfaction with their condition and used to minimize the evils of slavery.

But there is another equally deceptive ploy Satan uses to deceive people on both sides of the racial divide. He convinces those who practice, condone, and benefit from racism that there is no heaven or hell, no day of judgment, or any accountability to a sovereign God after this life ends. Or, if they believe in God, he deceives them to be merely religious without becoming imitators of Christ who live in obedience to God's will. In this way, they can harm others by their racism and still believe they are godly people or even good Christians. On the flip side, Satan convinces those whose ancestors suffered oppression and who continue to be discriminated against and disadvantaged that there is no God. How could there be a God in the face of injustice and oppression? Or, if there is a God, then he is an unjust God to allow injustice and oppression. Many racial minorities have bought into this lie and refuse to believe in, or have anything to do with, God and his Son Jesus Christ. They do not seem to understand human freewill, the fall of humanity and its consequences, Satan's role in it, and God's provision for people to be able to live victorious, purposeful, godly lives in Jesus Christ in spite of it all.

Satan has deceived some ethnic minorities to believe that God is a White man's God, one who approves of oppression and injustice.[78] What they do not recognize is that people can create their own version of God, in essence, a god, an idol, whom they define to allow evil while calling it good. The version or brand of Christianity that Puritans and other European settlers concocted to justify slavery and oppression is not true Christianity. It is a perversion of it. It is inconsistent with the life

---

76. Heb 12:15.

77. Matt 6:15.

78. See Harris, *Is Christianity*, pointing out that Christianity is not a White man's religion.

and teachings of Jesus Christ and the heart and mind of God that Jesus revealed to humanity.

In all these cases—whether one believes that there is no God; that one can redefine him and live as one pleases and still think one is godly; that God is unjust and, therefore, not deserving of worship; or that he is a White man's God, Satan's aim is the same—to steal the souls of those he is able to deceive.

How Does Satan Pull Off His Lies About Race?

So, how does Satan manage to pull off these deceptions? How is he able to get people to buy into the idea that there are many races and that some are superior to others? And how does he get people to act on these lies? We get an idea of how Satan operates from the things he put Job through to try to destroy his faith and relationship with God. After Satan received permission from God to test Job, a band of people called the Sabeans raided Job's ranch, carried off his oxen and donkeys, and killed his servants who were ploughing and tending his herds.[79] The Chaldeans also formed three raiding parties, swept across the ranch, carried off Job's camels, and killed the servants who were tending them.[80] Where did the Sabeans and the Chaldeans get the idea to wreak this murderous havoc on Job's servants and rob him of his wealth? The account in Job clearly attributes it to the devil's influence. Perhaps he plants thoughts through the power of suggestion. That is why the apostle Paul told the Corinthians that the weapons with which we fight Satan are not worldly weapons. They are mighty through God to pull down strongholds that Satan tries to erect in our minds. Paul told the Corinthians to cast down imaginations, arguments, and pretensions that exalt themselves against the knowledge of God. These are thoughts that are contrary to what we know about God as revealed in his word. He told them to bring every thought captive to the obedience of Christ, knowing that it is through the power of suggestion and thoughts planted in the mind that Satan deceives people to do his bidding.[81]

---

79. Job 1:13–15.

80. Job 1:17. See Adeyemo, *Africa Bible Commentary*, 573, commenting that the disasters that befell Job must be understood to all come from a supernatural force if the conversation between God and Satan is taken seriously.

81. 2 Cor 10:4–5.

TREATMENT OF OTHERS BASED ON RACE

Slavery—The Most Sinister Form of Racism

Slavery is undoubtedly the most sinister form of racism, with colonialism not too far behind. The two often went hand in hand. In American slavery, human beings who believed they were superior subjected other human beings whom they believed were inferior to a lifetime of bondage as their property, profiting from their labor, skills, and God-given talents, while refusing to allow them to fulfill their God-given purpose and potential and God's will for their lives. And this was all based on their ethnicity or the color of their skin. Ironically, much of it was done in the name of God, with claims that slavery was for the benefit of the lost savages who were being enlightened and Christianized. In colonialism, European nations, finally forced by societal pressures to turn away from the evil and profits of slavery, used their military might to expropriate the land and wealth of nations of color, subjugating their people to forced rule in the process. Again, colonialism was framed as being for the benefit of the savages who needed to be enlightened. Colonialism was often accompanied by atrocities, including genocide, in order to carry out colonialist agendas.[82] Both slavery and colonialism were powered by the idea of White supremacy.

The first slaves from Africa were brought to Jamestown, Virginia, in 1619, four hundred years ago. Many were caught in raids, and some were sold as prisoners of war by African tribal leaders or by families who could not have fathomed the brutality and dehumanization of trans-Atlantic slavery. Many died while being transported across the Atlantic crammed and chained together in the berths of ships. Those that died were thrown into the ocean. Others were thrown into the ocean for being troublemakers because they resisted their captivity.

As with the rewards Satan offers to those who are willing to do his bidding, slavery in America brought great wealth to slave masters and businesses and institutions that were in the slavery supply chain—from shipbuilders, shipowners, the crew that operated slave ships, insurance companies that insured the ships and their human cargo, businesses that sold supplies to plantations, factories that processed raw materials from

---

82. Tens of thousands of native Hereros were killed in German concentration camps in former German South West Africa, now Namibia. See Stempel, "Lawsuit Against Germany." Also, Eligon, "Big Hole." A lawsuit by descendants of the Ovaherero and Nama people against Germany for reparations in federal court in New York was dismissed for lack of jurisdiction under the Foreign Sovereign Immunities Act. See Rukoro v. Federal Republic of Germany, 363 F.Supp.3d 436 (2019).

plantations, bankers that bankrolled plantation operations and cotton and tobacco factories, to colleges and universities that were financed by wealth from slavery.

How Does God Feel About Slavery?

Many have used the Bible to justify slavery. So, how does God really feel about slavery? The Israelites were slaves in Egypt for 430 years. God eventually freed them from slavery and brought them into the promised land. It was through the Israelites that he would reveal himself to humankind and bless humankind by sending his Son, the Messiah, Jesus Christ, to redeem a fallen world from sin. God told Moses, whom he called to lead his people out of Egyptian bondage, that he had seen the misery of his people in Egypt and heard their cries because of the slave drivers. He told Moses he was concerned about their suffering and had come to rescue them.[83]

Before the Israelites left Egypt, they asked their former slave masters for articles of silver, gold, and clothing. God gave the Israelites favor by predisposing the Egyptians to give them the things they asked for. The Bible says they plundered the Egyptians as a result.[84]

The Ten Commandments did not include one that said, "You shall not enslave." It did prohibit murder, but people killed and continue to kill anyway. It did prohibit stealing, adultery, false testimony, and wrongfully taking anything that belongs to another.[85] But people have disobeyed, done, and continue to do these things anyway. Would people not have enslaved others if God had prohibited it? Of course not. And God certainly knew that. Along those lines, Jesus said that Moses allowed men to divorce their wives by giving them a certificate of divorce because of the hardness of their hearts, although that is not what God intended from the beginning when he instituted marriage between a man and a woman

---

83. Exod 3:7–8. See Mitzi Smith, "Abolitionist Messiah: A Man Named Jesus Born of a Doulé," in Smith et al., *Bitter the Chastening Rod*, 52–70, arguing that based on the exodus event in the Bible, God is a God of liberation who stands firmly on the side of the enslaved in every era. See also Pohor, "Slavery," in Adeyemo, *Africa Bible Commentary*, 89, discussing the tragedy of slavery in its various forms, including modern human trafficking.

84. Exod 12:35–36.

85. Exod 20:13–17.

and forbade anyone to separate them or tear them asunder.[86] At least a certificate of divorce formalized the divorce and prevented the man from simply sending his wife away in summary fashion. In other words, Moses appeared to regulate divorce to protect the woman. In the same way, although the one who commanded people to love their neighbor as themselves would not have sanctioned slavery, he regulated it because of the hardness of peoples' hearts. He knew people would enslave anyway.

A Hebrew could be purchased as a slave in ancient Israel in Old Testament times. Slaves in Old Testament times were invariably debtors who were unable to repay their debts, whereas African slaves were captured in raids by western slave traders, sold as prisoners of war by other African tribes, or sold by family members in need of money. Although families that sold family members for money couldn't possibly have imagined what slavery in the Western Hemisphere was like, there being nothing comparable in their realm of experience, this hardly served to excuse selling family for profit.

As it turns out, God has something to say about this practice of capturing and selling others. Among the laws God gave to the Jews as they were about to enter Canaan was one that prescribed the ultimate punishment, the death penalty, for anyone who kidnapped and sold another person. God couldn't have been more emphatic about the abhorrence of this sin in his sight. Before the Civil War, free Blacks were sometimes kidnapped in northern states and sold into slavery in the South in an organized human trafficking scheme called the Reverse Underground Railroad. The passage of the Fugitive Slave Act in 1850 is said to have opened the door to mass kidnappings by northerners.[87] The movie *Twelve Years a Slave* was a moving depiction of the true-life story of Solomon Northup, a Black musician born free in New York State, who was tricked and kidnapped by two White men in 1841 and sold into slavery in Louisiana. Thousands of free slaves are believed to have been kidnapped and sold in this way.

Unlike slavery in America where a slave was a slave for life, God commanded the Israelites to hold Hebrew slaves for only six years and to free them in the seventh year without requiring them to buy their freedom. Under the Old Testament law, if a slave came to love a master who was kind, the slave could choose to stay after the sixth year along with

---

86. Matt 19:4–8; Mark 10:2–9.
87. Kendi, *Stamped from the Beginning*, 189–90.

THE CHRISTIAN AS IMITATOR OF CHRIST

the wife the master had given him and children from that union. But his stay after the sixth year was purely voluntary. Furthermore, a daughter who was sold as a slave could be redeemed or ransomed[88] by her father if she no longer pleased the master. The master had no right to sell her to foreigners.[89]

In American slavery, beginning with a 1662 Virginia law, a woman's condition determined the status of children she bore. Children born to a slave woman were automatically slaves for life even if the father was White, a change from English common law. One author noted how this made sexual exploitation of slave women by White men profitable.[90] Unlike in American slavery, where any slave woman, whether single, married, or engaged was fair game for a slave master's sexual appetites, under the Old Testament law it was considered a sin and a punishable offense for a man to sexually exploit a slave woman who was engaged to be married. The only reason the man was not to be put to death was because the woman was not free. But he was required to present a guilt offering of a ram for the priest to make atonement for his sin before the Lord.[91]

Unlike in American slavery where slaves could be beaten or lynched for any number of reasons, from talking back, to attempting to flee to freedom, God's commandments protected slaves from being unreasonably brutalized or killed without any consequences. A slave master was to be punished for beating his slave to death.[92] And if, as a result of beating his slave, a master blinded a slave in one eye or knocked out a tooth, he was to let the slave go free as compensation for maiming the slave.[93]

To prevent generational poverty and inequality, God instituted the Year of Jubilee. It occurred every fifty years from the time the Israelites entered the promised land. All slaves were to be freed in the Year of Jubilee and all ancestral lands that had been taken in payment of debt had to be returned to their original owners.[94] An Israelite who sold himself because

---

88. The Greek word for redeem as used here is *padah*, meaning to ransom. See Vine et al., *Vine's Complete Expository Dictionary*, 195 (Old Testament Section).

89. Exod 21:2–8.

90. Kendi, *Stamped from the Beginning*, 41.

91. Lev 19:20–22.

92. Exod 21:20.

93. Exod 21:26–27.

94. Lev 25:8–10. See Adeyemo, *Africa Bible Commentary*, 165, noting that the Jubilee Year was a sacred year when the slave population was liberated and allowed to return to their family property and clan.

of poverty was to be treated as a hired servant until the Year of Jubilee, when he and his family were to be released. God gave these regulations to govern Israelite slavery because the Israelites were his servants. He had redeemed them from slavery in Egypt. They, therefore, ultimately belonged to him, not to others.[95] And, through the Israelites, God has revealed himself to all humanity. He has made known that every human being belongs to him[96] and that he sent his Son to redeem every single one of them.[97] Those who accept that redemption belong to the household of God.

If an Israelite sold himself to a rich foreigner, he could redeem himself if he became able to do so, or one of his relatives could redeem him and treat him as a hired hand.[98] But even if he were not redeemed, he was to be let go in the Year of Jubilee.[99]

God did allow the Israelites to own slaves from among the nations that surrounded them. Foreign slaves could be passed on as an inheritance.[100] But they also benefited from the Year of Jubilee since liberty was to be proclaimed to all the inhabitants throughout the land in that year.[101]

The law gave further directions for how slaves were to be treated in the year of their release. When a Hebrew slave who had served his master for six years was released in the seventh year, he was not to be let go without enough supplies to sustain him and help him get a fresh start. The law required the master to not send him away empty handed. The master was to liberally supply him with animals from his flock, grain from his threshing floor, and wine from his wine press.[102] In other words, he wasn't supposed to be freed with absolutely no provision such that he would feel compelled to return to slavery. When God set the Israelites free after 430 years of slavery in Egypt, he made sure they did not leave empty handed. He directed the Israelites to ask their slave masters for articles of silver, gold, and clothing. God gave the Israelites favor by predisposing the Egyptians to give them the things they asked for. The Bible says that they plundered the Egyptians as a result.[103] This was unlike slavery in

95. Lev 25:42, 55.
96. Ps 24:1.
97. John 3:16.
98. Lev 25:47–53.
99. Lev 25:54.
100. Lev 25:44–46.
101. Lev 25:10.
102. Deut 15:12–14.
103. Exod 12:35–36.

America, where slaves were freed without any form of compensation. On the contrary, it was slave masters who received compensation for freeing their slaves.

In the District of Columbia, for example, by virtue of the District of Columbia Emancipation Act signed by President Abraham Lincoln in 1862, slave owners in the nation's capital were paid handsomely ($300) for every slave that they freed. A total of about three thousand slaves were believed to have been involved. The District of Columbia Emancipation Act also provided for the voluntary repatriation of the slaves who had been newly freed to Liberia or Haiti. The British had already set the precedent for paying slave owners, but not freed slaves, when slavery was abolished in the Caribbean colonies in the 1830s. England paid the equivalent of slightly more than $26 million to forty-six thousand slave owners when it abolished slavery in the Caribbean colonies in the 1830s (£20 million paid in 1833). Former slaves had to give four to six years of free labor to their former masters as part of the deal. No compensation was paid to the freed slaves.[104]

The thought of living in the same nation with freed slaves who had endured oppression and brutalization obviously made Whites in America uneasy and afraid. Sending freed slaves out of the country was one way they sought to address this fear. In 1800, legislators in Virginia had begun exploring with Thomas Jefferson the idea of sending free Blacks back to Africa or to an American colony in the Caribbean. Jefferson believed the races could not coexist as free and equal. He unsuccessfully explored sending them to Sierra Leone, England's colony for freed slaves dating back to 1792. The American Colonization Society was formed in 1816 to push for the deportation of free Blacks. In 1819, President James Monroe, former governor of Virginia, signed into law the Slave Trade Act, allocating $100,000 to send freed Blacks back to Africa. Land was obtained in West Africa near Sierra Leone for a settlement that was called Liberia. Its capital, Monrovia, was named for President Monroe. Only 154 Blacks left for Liberia in the decade after the settlement was established, in spite of the fact that all the legislatures in northern states supported sending freed Blacks back to Africa.[105] This history explains the outrage that was expressed regarding calls to send congresswomen of color who are citizens of the United States back to Africa for their

---

104. See Hunter, "When Slaveowners Got Reparations." See also Parry, "Scholars Behind the Quest."

105. Kendi, *Stamped from the Beginning*, 109, 144–48, 152–54.

political stances,[106] and chants to "Send her back" at a political rally, referring to one of the congresswomen.[107]

In 1852, Harriet Beecher Stowe, the author of *Uncle Tom's Cabin*, advocated that Blacks be sent back to Africa after being taught to become morally and intellectually mature.[108] In 1862, Congress allocated $600,000 to send Blacks to Haiti and Liberia. Abraham Lincoln, who believed Whites and Blacks could never be equal in America, favored sending Blacks to Liberia.[109] In 1870, during the Reconstruction period that began after slavery ended, President Ulysses S. Grant sought to annex the Dominican Republic as a place of possible emigration for Blacks, but the Senate did not ratify the annexation treaty.[110]

The failure to follow the biblical example of not letting a freed slave go empty handed resulted in the impoverishment of slaves and their continued dependence on former slave masters under slave-like conditions. It also meant a perpetuation of the effects of slavery. This was reinforced by Jim Crow laws in the South.

The apostle Paul addressed the issue of slavery in both subtle and not-so-subtle ways in his Letter to Philemon, a man Paul had led to Christ.[111] Philemon lived in Colossae. He was saved through Paul's ministry and the church in Colossae met in his house. Philemon's slave Onesimus ran away and came into contact with Paul during his initial imprisonment in Rome. Onesimus spent time with Paul and became useful to him. They became close enough for Paul to call him his son and his very heart in his Letter to Philemon.[112]

To protect the institution of slavery, Roman law made it a capital offense for a slave to run away. Paul knew this and was reluctant to send Onesimus back. He nonetheless did so with a strong petition for Philemon to receive Onesimus back, not as a slave, but as a brother in Christ

---

106. President Donald Trump called for progressive congresswomen to go back and fix the crime-infested places they originally came from. This was presumed to refer to Ilhan Omar of Minnesota, Rashida Tlaib of Michigan, Ayanna Pressley of Massachusetts, and Alexandra Ocasio-Cortez of New York. He did not mention them by name.

107. The chants at a rally in Greenville, North Carolina, were for congresswoman Ilhan Omar, an American citizen who came to America as a Somali refugee, to be sent back.

108. Kendi, *Stamped from the Beginning*, 194–95.

109. Kendi, *Stamped from the Beginning*, 218–19.

110. Kendi, *Stamped from the Beginning*, 251.

111. Phlm 1:19.

112. Phlm 1:10, 12.

THE CHRISTIAN AS IMITATOR OF CHRIST

and a friend and companion of Paul. Paul's short Letter lends a window into how he tackled the dilemma of slavery. He diplomatically set forth principles that would soften the harshness of slavery and eventually lead to its abolition. This Letter was written about AD 62, meaning that these principles were articulated in the very first century, fifteen centuries before American slavery.

Paul was a highly educated Jew and Roman citizen from an aristocratic background. Yet, as a disciple and apostle of Christ, he formed this tender bond with a slave at the bottom rung of the social ladder. In doing so, Paul was imitating Christ. And he urged the Corinthians to follow his example even as he followed Christ's example of putting the good of others above his own good in order that they might be saved.[113]

Paul started his Letter by reminding Philemon of how he had received forgiveness of sins from God and grace from Jesus Christ. Philemon was, therefore, obligated to extend the same grace to his runaway slave.[114] How could Philemon refuse to forgive Onesimus given this wisdom and truth with which Paul had appealed to him? Paul was essentially pointing to Christ as the model for Philemon to imitate and giving Philemon instructions on how a Christian master should relate to a Christian slave. After all, neither he nor the early church had the power to abolish slavery. These instructions, much like God's regulation of divorce, didn't imply approval. If God did not show favoritism based on nationality or ethnicity as Peter later discovered,[115] then slavery was untenable and could not be justified in the eyes of God.

Being Philemon's spiritual father, Paul could have stood on his apostolic authority to command Philemon to do the right thing, forgive Onesimus, set him free, and be reconciled to him as a brother in Christ, not as a slave. But Paul made clear he wasn't going to play that hand. Instead, this was something that Philemon ought to do out of love for Paul and Onesimus, who was now Paul's spiritual son too.[116]

If Paul had his way, he would keep Onesimus with him so that Onesimus could be useful to him as a prisoner in Rome. But Paul didn't want to impose his will on Philemon and was, therefore, reluctantly sending Onesimus back, not as a slave, but as a fellow brother in Christ. Paul

---

113. 1 Cor 11:1.
114. Phlm 1:3.
115. Acts 10:34.
116. Phlm 1:9–10.

wanted to impress upon Philemon that this was extremely important to him because Onesimus was his very heart and very dear to him.[117]

Paul told Philemon that any favor he did for Paul shouldn't be compelled. Rather it should be voluntary and spontaneous. Paul told Philemon he should welcome Onesimus just as he would welcome Paul himself, a partner in Christ's work. If Philemon were to welcome Onesimus just as he did Paul, what would that mean? It certainly would mean receiving Onesimus as a brother in Christ and letting him go free if that was Onesimus's desire. Paul does not state this bluntly but hints at it.[118]

Beyond running away and depriving Philemon of his property or chattel, as slaves were regarded, there is no evidence that Onesimus stole from Philemon. Not knowing if Onesimus had taken anything from Philemon other than himself, Paul promises to pay back Philemon if Onesimus owed him anything or had done something wrong.[119] In making that promise, Paul also reminded Philemon that he owed him his very life as the one who led him to salvation in Christ and the hope of eternal life. Taking Onesimus back as a brother in Christ and not as a slave would refresh Paul's heart.[120] Paul put subtle pressure on Philemon by saying he was confident Philemon would do more than he was asking. And what would doing more than forgiving Onesimus and being reconciled to him as a brother in Christ and not as a slave entail? Giving Onesimus his freedom, of course. Paul put even more pressure on Philemon by asking him to prepare a guest room for him to come and visit. If Paul were able to visit in the near future, he would obviously see for himself whether Philemon had done any of the things he had urged him to do.[121]

---

117. Phlm 1:12–16. Ironically, Onesimus means useful. Incidentally, Cotton Mather, a leading religious figure in colonial New England, was gifted a slave whom he named Onesimus. See Kendi, *Stamped from the Beginning*, 68–69.

118. Phlm 1:14, 17.

119. This was consistent with the Old Testament law of restitution and the New Testament principle of doing the right thing. See Lev 25:10; Deut 15:12; and Luke 19:8.

120. Phlm 1:18–20.

121. Phlm 1:22. See Lloyd A. Lewis, "African American Appraisal of the Philemon-Paul-Onesimus Triangle," in Felder, *Stony the Road We Trod*, 232–46, where he states his thesis that this triangular relationship fraught with the social barriers between master and slave is mitigated by Paul's careful use of language that reinforces the image of the church as a particular type of family. Onesimus is now a beloved brother just as Philemon is Paul's brother beloved of God and thus on par with Paul and his former master. It was now up to Philemon to determine how equal status under the gospel should govern Onesimus's status in his household. This makes Philemon good news, not justification of slavery.

THE CHRISTIAN AS IMITATOR OF CHRIST

So, when Paul tells slaves who had become Christians to obey their masters, it must be put in proper perspective. It was not an endorsement of slavery as slave masters took it to mean. Paul was instead asking them to be Christlike examples to their masters in spite of their tragic circumstances, remembering that the Lord himself suffered great injustice at the hands of wicked people, including many who had a form of godliness, and that the Lord would be their reward. He followed that by reminding slave masters to treat their slaves in a Christlike manner knowing that God, who is master to both slave master and slave alike, does not show favoritism.[122]

How God feels about slavery is seen in his Revelation to the apostle John that the evil world system run by Satan will be destroyed at the end of the age and that there will be no more cargoes of the bodies and souls of men.[123] The apostle Paul included slave traders among those he called lawbreakers and rebels, ungodly and sinful, unholy and irreligious.[124] Although slavery may have been legal at certain points in history because those who had power and benefited from it made it legal, it always violated the two greatest commandments—loving God with all of one's heart, soul, strength, and mind, and loving one's neighbor as oneself.

Slavery also violated the Golden Rule of treating others as one would want to be treated. Certainly no slave trader, enslaver, or beneficiary of the system of slavery would want to be a slave and treated as slaves were. And as early as 1688, the Mennonites rejected slavery based on the Golden Rule.[125]

Although God required a freed slave to be liberally supplied, slaves in America were sent away empty handed. That brings up the centuries-old issue of reparations. Many White Americans argue that slavery is a thing of the past, that the nation should move on, and that reparations are out of the question. But the issue of reparations has not gone away, and will not go away, because reparations originate from God himself. He told Abraham that his descendants would be enslaved in the future, that he would punish the nation that enslaved them, and that he would bring them out with great possessions.[126] He affirmed reparations to Mo-

---

122. Eph 6:5–9.

123. Rev 18:11–13.

124. 1 Tim 1:8–11. The NKJV uses the word *kidnappers* instead of *slave traders*. The KJV uses the word *men stealers*.

125. Kendi, *Stamped from the Beginning*, 52.

126. Gen 15:13–14.

ses when he called Moses to lead the Israelites out of Egypt and assured him that the Israelites would not leave empty handed. Rather, they would leave with articles of gold, silver, and clothing he would predispose the Egyptians to give to them.[127] God orchestrated reparations for the Israelites after 430 years of slavery in Egypt by predisposing the Egyptians to give the Israelites silver, gold, and clothing.[128] When God commanded the Israelites, upon settling in the promised land, to liberally supply freed slaves with provision, he said they were to do this remembering that they too were once slaves in Egypt before he redeemed them.[129] Reparations, therefore, represent an immutable divine principle.

Ironically, as already seen, although the American government never paid reparations to slaves or their descendants after emancipation, slave owners in the District of Columbia received reparations for freeing their slaves.[130] The National Coalition of Blacks for Reparations in America and the National Association for the Advancement of Colored People (NAACP) revived advocacy for reparations in the 1980s and 1990s, and scholars and activists have attempted to make a case for reparations in America and in the Caribbean.[131]

There's movement on the issue of reparations on a number of fronts. In 2018, the Catholic Sisters of the Religious of the Sacred Heart, who owned slaves in Louisiana and Missouri, created a reparations fund to finance scholarships for Blacks at their school in Louisiana. In 2019, Virginia Theological Seminary created a $1.7 million reparations fund. Princeton Theological Seminary committed to establishing a $27 million fund for scholarships and other initiatives to atone for its ties to slavery. Reparations funds have also been created by several episcopal dioceses that had ties to slavery. In 2019, the Chicago suburb of Evanston committed to paying reparations of $10 million over ten years to Black residents for discrimination and lack of access to housing. It has distributed $25,000 each to 140 mostly elderly residents who were at least eighteen and lived there between 1919 and 1969, when the city finally passed a fair

---

127. Exod 3:21–22.
128. Exod 12:35–36.
129. Deut 15:12–15.
130. See Hunter, "When Slaveowners Got Reparations."
131. See Bittker, *Case for Black Reparations*. See also Coates, "Case for Reparations"; Parry, "Scholars Behind the Quest"; and Goza, *Rebirth of a Nation*, arguing that reparations are necessary to heal America's racial wounds and live up to its democratic ideals.

housing ordinance. The money can go toward reducing mortgage debt, a down payment, or home repairs.[132]

In 2021, the Jesuits, a Catholic order that founded Georgetown University, pledged $100 million to atone for over one hundred years of slave labor and sales to finance its clergy, churches, and schools, including Georgetown.[133] In 2020, the state legislature in California commissioned a task force to study and develop reparations proposals for Blacks. The task force issued its report to the legislature in June 2023, surveying the ongoing and compounding harms experienced by Blacks as a result of slavery and its lingering effects on American society today, including political disenfranchisement, housing segregation, separate and unequal education, stolen labor and hindered opportunity, control over creative, cultural, and intellectual life, an unjust legal system, mental and physical harm, and the wealth gap. The task force has proposed a comprehensive reparations plan to address each of these aspects of this legacy. The plan will require spending billions of dollars and is expected to face an uphill battle for many of the proposals to be adopted. The plan includes encouraging the federal government to use the national racial wealth gap to determine federal-level reparations.[134] At the federal level, a bill has been introduced in the US House of Representatives every year since 1989 to establish a task force to study the issue of reparations. However, it has never made it to the floor for a vote.[135]

Is There Evidence of Systemic Racism and How Should a Christian Respond If There Is?

Research shows that most White Americans do not believe that racism is a systemic problem in America, and that acts of racial discrimination or injustice are engaged in by a few bad apples. They believe race is no longer a factor in life's opportunities and that there is a larger trend toward systemic racial equality.[136] But is this true? Is there evidence of systemic racism? Below I explore this issue in some key areas.

132. See Barrett, "Chicago Suburb Pays Reparations."
133. See Swarns, "Catholic Order Pledges $100 Million." The Jesuits sold 272 slaves in 1838 to save Georgetown from financial ruin.
134. California Task Force, *California Reparations Report*.
135. Barrett, "Chicago Suburb Pays Reparations."
136. See, for example, Quillian et al., "Hiring Discrimination," where they reference

Race and Education

Racism in education began when most of the southern states made it a crime to teach a slave to read and write.[137] Ironically, the prohibition itself was an indictment of the contradictions inherent in racism. Underlying it was the knowledge that, contrary to the myth that people of color were unintelligent and less than fully human, they were indeed intelligent human beings who could become literate if given the opportunity. It was feared that slaves would be able to read abolitionist and other literature and aspire to freedom. Only religious instruction was made available to slaves and free Blacks in many cases, although in some northern states, Blacks had access to formal schooling, oftentimes offered by religious organizations like the Quakers. After the 1831 slave revolt led by Nat Turner, an educated preacher, was put down, legislators in Virginia and other states passed harsher slave codes that restricted the education of Blacks.[138] Maryland prohibited its freed Blacks from attending public schools after abolishing slavery in 1864.[139]

School segregation is another manifestation of racism in public education. Public schools are located in school districts within counties. They are in urban, suburban, and rural areas all across America. These areas do not exist in a vacuum. They are embedded in neighborhoods, and because many neighborhoods in America are segregated, many schools reflect the segregated neighborhoods in which they are located. Funding for schools comes from a variety of sources. A significant portion of the funding comes from district property taxes and state budget appropriations. Some funding also comes from federal tax dollars. Many school districts also have foundations that raise money. This means that schools in affluent districts are better resourced than schools in poorer districts that are unable to provide the same quality of education as schools in more affluent districts. Efforts to address this inequality through the judicial system and forced busing have largely been unsuccessful. In 1896, the US Supreme Court in *Plessy v. Ferguson*[140] upheld the constitution-

---

polling data reinforcing these beliefs.

137. Arkansas, Kentucky, and Tennessee were the only slave states that did not outlaw educating slaves. See Christopher B. Span and Brenda N. Sanya, "Education and the Africa Diaspora," in Rury and Tamura, *Oxford Handbook*, 399–412.

138. Kendi, *Stamped from the Beginning*, 174.

139. Kendi, *Stamped from the Beginning*, 228.

140. 163 U.S. 537 (1896).

ality of racial segregation laws with respect to public facilities as long as segregated facilities were equal in quality—the so-called separate but equal doctrine. This was the law for fifty-eight years until it was overturned by *Brown v. Board of Education of Topeka*,[141] which held that state laws establishing racially segregated schools are unconstitutional even if the segregated schools are otherwise equal in quality.

White families opposed to integration moved out of school districts subject to desegregation orders. Some districts shut down schools and promoted White private schools with subsidized tuition through tuition grants or vouchers.[142] Many communities sought to beat desegregation orders by splitting from larger school districts. Many predominantly White municipalities have seceded or are attempting to secede from county school districts to form their own school districts in states like Alabama, California, Georgia, Louisiana, Tennessee, and Wisconsin. Thirty states have processes that allow new school districts to be created.[143]

School discipline is another area where racism manifests itself in education. A recent study by the nonpartisan Government Accountability Office (GAO) found that schoolchildren of color are subjected to more frequent and harsher discipline for similar infractions than White students. This was true even for Black students in affluent schools. The GAO found that in the 2013–2014 school year, Black students, who represented 15.5 percent of all public-school students, accounted for 39 percent of school suspensions. The disproportionate discipline affected both Black girls and boys, unlike any other group. The GAO analysis found that a higher percentage of Black boys was suspended more often than White boys in the most affluent schools, calling into question the claim that poverty, not race, underlies disproportionate school discipline.[144]

The Common Application that is used by one million high school students to apply to nine hundred colleges and universities recently indicated that beginning with the 2021–2022 admission cycle, it would remove a question about having faced school discipline after its own data showed that Black applicants answered yes more than twice as often as White applicants. Black women were three times as likely as White

141. 347 U.S. 483 (1954).

142. Stewart, "'Government School' Critics."

143. Campo-Flores, "New Districts Reignite." In 2017, seventy-one communities had sought to secede from their school districts in the previous two decades and forty-seven of them had succeeded. Ten of these were in Alabama.

144. Green, "Government Watchdog Finds Racial Bias."

women to answer yes. Those who answered yes submitted applications at a lower rate. The question, therefore, had a disparate impact on low-income applicants and applicants of color.[145]

Misperceptions about Black children being less innocent, more adultlike, and more responsible for their actions than White children lead to different treatment of Black children for normal childhood behavior, and to overpolicing and underprotection of Black children.[146] Children of color are also subjected to lower expectations and not encouraged or challenged to excel.

A study on racial attitudes and college attainment found that low expectations of minority students by White teachers may actually have a negative impact on the potential of some minority students to succeed in college. It found that the teachers in the study, which involved six thousand students, expected 58 percent of the White students but only 37 percent of the Black students to earn a four-year college degree. White teachers had the lowest expectations of Black male students. The study showed that high school teacher expectations influence the likelihood that similarly prepared students will graduate from college, highlighting the importance of teacher expectations and racial basis. It found that White teacher expectations place Black students at a disadvantage, and that this shows the need for bias training and stressing high expectations for White teachers.[147]

Researchers looking to understand the effect of teacher race on student persistence and performance believe that teachers sometimes treat students differently based on their own backgrounds and stereotypes. Research has shown that preschool teachers judge Black children more harshly for the same behavior; that White teachers are less likely to assign Black students to gifted programs even when they have comparable test scores with their White peers; and that White teachers have lower expectations of Black children's potential than Black teachers.[148] Researchers have proposed increasing teacher diversity, training teachers about biases and stereotypes, and getting teachers to affirm and set high expectations for all students as some of the effective solutions that can be

---

145. Korn, "College Common App."

146. Bernstein, "Let Black Kids Just Be Kids." Also, *Racial Innocence*.

147. Gershenson and Papageorge, "Power of Teacher Expectations," 64–70. See also Jaschik, "Expectations, Race and College Success."

148. Miller, "Does Teacher Diversity Matter."

THE CHRISTIAN AS IMITATOR OF CHRIST

deployed to address these problems. However, there is strong opposition in conservative circles to diversity and bias training.[149]

Higher education has also seen its fair share of racism. People of color were not allowed to attend colleges and universities during colonial times and early American history although many campuses were built with slave labor and were financially supported by slave traders.[150] Ivy League professors contributed to this state by coming up with intellectual arguments and pseudo-scientific research in defense of slavery. Presidents of colonial colleges like Increase Mather of Harvard, Samuel Stanhope Smith of Princeton, and John Augustine Smith of the College of William and Mary were overt White supremacists.[151] Historically Black Colleges and Universities (HBCUs) were founded to give people of color the opportunity to obtain a higher education. Many were private. But many were also established by states in segregated higher education systems. Nineteen historically Black universities were created by Congress in 1890 as land grants. Many universities in the South were segregated as recently as the 1960s. George Wallace, a governor of Alabama, famously pledged segregation now, tomorrow, and forever in his inaugural speech in 1963, and stood with others at the door of Foster Auditorium at the University of Alabama to block entry by two students of color.

Higher education is supposed to be a leveler of the playing field by giving students a pathway to the middle class and it has done that to a great extent. It has been documented, however, that wealth, often a proxy for race, plays a big role in the kinds of colleges and universities students attend, with more prestigious institutions offering greater opportunities.

Historically Black Colleges and Universities enroll only 10 percent of Black college and university students, yet they graduate 19 percent of Blacks with science, technology, engineering, and math (STEM) degrees, 50 percent of Black lawyers and doctors, and 80 percent of Black judges.[152] In spite of the great work HBCUs have done in educating people of color,

---

149. See Chronicle Staff, "DEI Legislation Tracker," documenting that thirteen states have passed laws prohibiting DEI (Diversity, Equity, and Inclusion) training in public colleges. See also Ellis and Thomas, "Trump's War on DEI," reporting on President Trump's freezing of DEI initiatives in the federal government by executive order.

150. See Wilder, *Ebony & Ivy*.

151. Kendi, *Stamped from the Beginning*, 57, 113–15, 133. Roderick Dew, a professor at William and Mary who later became president, was against sending free Blacks away since they were a source of cheap labor. Kendi, *Stamped from the Beginning*, 174.

152. Greenfield, "HBCUs Lead," discussing findings of a study by the United Negro College Fund (UNCF).

especially given the fact that two-thirds of their students are low-income students eligible for federal Pell grants, they tend to be less resourced and less able to compete with better resourced majority institutions in what they are able to offer. A federal analysis has documented how historically Black land-grant universities in sixteen states were underfunded to the tune of $13 billion from 1987 to 2020 in comparison to funding for White land grants in those states.[153]

Even the GI Bill that opened up higher education and the middle class to lots of former servicemen primarily benefited the White population. Many ethnic European Americans attained a college education in the 1940s and 1950s after the war, joined the professional ranks, and moved into suburban homes. Blacks did not benefit as much, being barred from attending many public colleges because of Jim Crow laws and restrictions in veterans' services. Blacks also were underrepresented in apprenticeship and job-training programs paid for by the GI Bill.[154] Research looking at state appropriations between 2006 (before the Great Recession) and 2015 in states where both the legislative and executive branches of government were controlled by Republicans, and the racial diversity of public university undergraduates in those states was substantial, showed that Republican-controlled states are less inclined to support higher education when the beneficiaries of state funding are more racially diverse compared to the overall state, and more inclined to support higher education when the beneficiaries are not as racially diverse. The funding differential during this study period was about $220 less per student in these states. The researchers found that cuts to higher education were less in these states when White students were overrepresented in public college enrollments compared with the state's overall population, and greater when White students were underrepresented compared with the state. Differences in appropriation levels were not found in Democrat-controlled states where White students were overrepresented. The authors conclude that these outcomes largely point to resentment among White Republican lawmakers against students of color.[155]

---

153. Knott, "States Underfunded." Only Delaware and Ohio equitably funded their Black land grants.

154. Carlson, "When College Was a Public Good."

155. See Kelderman, "'White Resentment,'" discussing a paper by Taylor et al., "Partisanship, White Racial Resentment." See also Taylor and Cantwell, *Unequal Higher Education*.

It has been observed that some states have been disinvesting in higher education as more immigrants, lower-income people, and people of color are accessing or desiring to access higher education. With this shift has also come a shift in the dialogue about the value of higher education from being a public good to an individual good. Some point to the fact that great advances in education like the establishment of land-grant universities and the GI Bill were made during times of strong White majorities, and that diversity in America has become an impediment to the welfare state which encompasses education. They see evidence of policy makers erecting barriers to higher education based on race and class. In Arizona, for example, per-student funding for higher education has dropped consistently over the last several decades as the percentage of non-White students has increased.[156] One author has pointed out how cuts to federal Pell Grants and other aid coupled with a shift to bank-based federal loans during President Reagan's administration reduced minority access to elite private institutions and started a trend toward ballooning student debt.[157] One study of 450 public colleges, for example, found more state support per student for predominantly White institutions than predominantly minority institutions, where students relied more on loans.[158]

Many students and their families have incurred significant debt loads to access the benefits of higher education. Total outstanding student loan debt owed by 42.2 million Americans currently stands at a whopping $1.6 trillion, higher than auto loan debt and credit card debt. Only mortgage debt, at $10.44 trillion, is higher. Young people saddled with debt are putting off marriage, buying a home, or having children.[159] A study of the cohort of students who began college in the 1995–1996 academic year showed that 57 percent of White students borrowed while 75 percent of Black students did. The median undergraduate loan amount for Black students was 3.5 times higher than for White students. Not only did Black students take out more loans, but they also had more difficulty paying them off than White borrowers. After twenty years since enrolling, 50 percent of the White borrowers had paid off their debt compared to 25 percent of Black borrowers,

---

156. Carlson, "When College Was a Public Good."

157. Fergus, *Land of the Fee*.

158. Hillman, "State Support." The study examined the relationship between state higher education appropriations and net tuition per full-time equivalent student from fiscal year 1980 to 2018.

159. See Lalijee, "Debt Is a Good Reason."

and Black borrowers owed $17,500 more. Black students borrowed $3,000 more on average. This makes Black student loan borrowers more likely to face long-term financial insecurity while exacerbating inequality. The White default rate in the cohort was 20 percent in the twenty years after enrolling while the Black default rate was 50 percent. The authors propose canceling as much student debt as possible given the fact that student loans, rather than opening doors, are blocking upward mobility for economically vulnerable students of color.[160]

But attempts by the Biden administration to forgive $430 billion of student loan debt to forty million student loan borrowers have run into legal obstacles. The Supreme Court struck down the administration's student loan forgiveness program in the Higher Education Relief Opportunities for Students Act (HEROES Act) of 2023 in the case of *Biden v. Nebraska*[161] and other attempts at loan repayment reductions and forgiveness under the Saving on a Valuable Education (SAVE) Plan have been blocked by the US Court of Appeals for the Eighth Circuit in the case of *Missouri v. Biden*.[162]

To complicate things further for graduates who took on debt to get a college education because they were led to believe that a college education was their ticket to the middle class, the governor of Pennsylvania, following Maryland's lead, has declared that 92 percent of jobs in state government, sixty-five thousand in all, now do not require a college degree.[163] Alaska, Colorado, Florida, Georgia, New Jersey, South Carolina, Utah, and Virginia have a similar policy.[164]

A recent report by the Education Trust found that despite the popularly held belief that affirmative action gives Black and Latino students an edge in higher education admissions, they are actually underrepresented in selective colleges and public two- and four-year colleges and universities. The report concludes that because higher education has historically used race to exclude some students, only race-conscious policies, not proxies like income, will be effective in achieving racial justice.[165]

160. Fisher, "White Borrowers," discussing a report by Sullivan et al., *Stalling Dreams*, from the Institute on Assets and Social Policy at Brandeis University.

161. 600 U.S. 477 (2023).

162. No. 24–2351, (Aug. 9, 2024).

163. See Thier, "Pennsylvania Is Axing."

164. See Arrojas, "These States Don't Require."

165. Report by Jones and Nichols, *Hard Truths*. The strategies suggested by the report include holistic admissions policies that include race as a factor and more federal

Ironically, the United States Supreme Court has disagreed with this conclusion in two cases filed against Harvard University and the University of North Carolina at Chapel Hill challenging their use of race as a factor in admissions.[166] The court set aside its own precedents going back to *California Board of Regents v. Bakke*,[167] in which the court allowed affirmative action programs that take race into account in a holistic review to play a role in college admissions since a diverse classroom environment is a compelling state interest under the Fourteenth Amendment.

In the aftermath of the Supreme Court's outlawing of affirmative action in college admissions, emboldened conservative organizations have filed a flurry of new lawsuits and revived previous cases that they had lost. Cases were filed against West Point and the University of Texas at Austin challenging their admissions policies, against Yale challenging its admissions and financial aid policies, against the University of Western Kentucky over minority scholarships, and against the University of Nebraska at Lincoln over a residency program for Black filmmakers. Other cases have been filed in Wisconsin over minority grants and there were plans to file additional challenges to scholarships and summer programs. Some have expressed the cynical view that these cases are not really about the constitution but represent a project to preserve White supremacy and attack pluralist democracy.[168]

Racism in education is inconsistent with equal opportunity, democratic ideals, and Christian principles. Policies and practices that disadvantage people of color do not reflect the character and teachings of Jesus Christ and do not imitate how Christ treated people. Legislators, policy makers, professors, teachers, and administrators in K-12 and higher education who devise or implement policies and practices that disadvantage people of color cannot reasonably believe that they are following or imitating Jesus Christ, or pleasing God. Neither can they believe they are imitating Christ when they underfund minority-serving institutions, close doors of opportunity to minorities to certain institutions, show bias in school discipline, induce underachievement in children of color through low expectations, and cause many people to not realize their God-given potential simply because of the color of their skin.

---

funding for HBCUs and minority-serving institutions.

166. Students for Fair Admissions v. Harvard University and Students for Fair Admissions v. University of North Carolina at Chapel Hill, 600 U.S. 181 (2023).

167. 438 U.S. 265 (1978).

168. See Knox, "New Legal Blitz."

Race and Employment

One could argue that racism in employment dates back to slavery when people of color were subjected to forced labor, many for long hours in produce and cotton fields under the harshest of conditions in the hot sun, without pay.

After the abolition of slavery through the Thirteenth Amendment to the US Constitution, Congress passed the Civil Rights Act of 1866. It was vetoed twice by President Andrew Johnson. His second veto was overridden, and it came into effect without presidential signature. It was ratified by Congress in 1870, two years after the Fourteenth Amendment came into effect.[169] The 1866 Civil Rights Act affirmed the citizenship of all persons born in the United States and gave citizens of every race and color the same right to make and enforce contracts as is enjoyed by White citizens.[170] The employment relationship is a contractual relationship. On the surface, the 1866 Civil Rights Act should have aided in preventing employment discrimination. However, with no federal penalties for violating the Act, it was practically useless in combatting employment discrimination. Victims of employment discrimination had no real legal recourse under the Act. The Act received new life after the passage of the Civil Rights Act of 1964, when the US Supreme Court reinterpreted it to prohibit racial discrimination by states and private parties.[171]

During Jim Crow in the South, racial discrimination in employment was overt, with laws called Black Codes that restricted Blacks to working as farm hands and domestics. Agricultural, domestic, and service workers, who have historically been predominantly people of color, were not afforded the same protections under the Fair Labor Standards Act. This law set a forty-hour workweek, provided for overtime, a federal minimum wage, and prohibited child labor. The National Labor Relations Act (the Wagner Act), which expanded collective bargaining rights of unions, excluded agricultural and domestic workers from its protections. Both laws were part of the New Deal, which lifted many out of poverty and helped them transition into the middle class after the Great Depression.

---

169. It was reenacted as Section 18 of the Enforcement Act of 1870.

170. Section one of the 1866 Civil Rights Act, 42 USC S1981.

171. In *Runyon v. McCrary*, 427 U.S. 160 (1976), the court held that the Act prohibits racial discrimination generally in making and enforcing private contracts. The court held that the statute prohibits a private school from discriminating on the basis of race.

Blacks were also exploited in industries such as coal mining, which powered iron and steel plants essential to US industrialization. They were discriminated against in hiring and paid less. Black men were imprisoned for minor offenses and then leased out as convicts by government agencies to work in coal mines, farms, quarries, railroad and road construction, and lumber operations.[172] Northern states did not have legal segregation. But they had de facto segregation, including job segregation.

Discrimination was also blatant in government jobs. President Woodrow Wilson fired fifteen out of seventeen Black federal supervisors and gave their jobs to Whites. The postmaster general and the treasury secretary under President Wilson ordered their departments to be segregated and Black federal workers across the country were fired or segregated in the workplace. Only public opposition from the NAACP prevented President Wilson from segregating the entire federal government.[173] Before this, the federal government had been integrated as a result of Reconstruction. Blacks who couldn't be logistically segregated because of the nature of their work had cages built around them to separate them from their White coworkers.[174]

In 1964, the most significant legislation in the fight against racial discrimination in employment, Title VII of the Civil Rights Act of 1964, was passed.[175] It prohibits discrimination in the terms and conditions of employment based on race, color, and national origin. Terms and conditions of employment include hiring, firing, pay, promotions, job assignments, access to training, layoff, and fringe benefits. Title VII also prohibited racial harassment that is severe or pervasive so as to create a hostile or offensive work environment. Racial discrimination is also prohibited when it results in an adverse employment decision such as firing or demotion. The Equal Employment Opportunity Commission (EEOC) was charged with enforcement of the Act. The 1964 Civil Rights Act was signed into law by President Lyndon B. Johnson. Incidentally, it must be noted that it wasn't just the federal government that passed civil rights legislation. Many states also passed fair employment practices laws and created fair employment practices agencies to enforce them.[176]

---

172. Feagin, *How Blacks Built America*, 34.

173. Wormser, "Segregation in the U.S. Government (1913)."

174. See Matthews, "Woodrow Wilson Was Extremely Racist."

175. 42 USC § 2000e.

176. National Conference of State Legislatures, "State Employment-Related Discrimination Statutes."

It is noteworthy that many Whites in the South left the Democratic Party for the Republican Party after the passage of the 1964 Civil Rights Act. Researchers have found that racially conservative attitudes led White southerners to leave the Democratic Party beginning in the 1950s after party leaders like Harry Truman began to advocate for civil rights during the last half of the twentieth century. White southerners went from being 80 percent Democrat before 1950 to 30 percent Democrat by the early 2000s.[177] White southerners, including professing Christians, were outraged by a law that would give people created in God's image the right to fulfill their God-given potential. The question is, did they believe that they were imitating Christ by opposing equality?

One can glean the extent of the problem of racial discrimination in employment when one considers the fact that Black workers constitute 13 percent of the working population in the US, but their racial discrimination claims constituted 26 percent of all the claims filed with the EEOC and state and local agencies, according to 2019 data.[178]

According to the EEOC's website, between 1997 and 2022 anywhere between 20,908 and 35,937 racial discrimination charges were filed with the EEOC every year. A significant percentage (ranging between 63.3 percent and 76.8 percent) were found to have no reasonable cause. The rest of the cases were resolved in any number of ways, including settlements that have ranged from an annual total of between $32.2 million and $112.7 million over the twenty-five-year period.[179]

Experts and former EEOC employees say the agency is underresourced with a smaller budget than it had in 1980 (adjusted for inflation) and 42 percent less staff, even though the labor force increased about 50 percent to 150 million people. The share of cases in which workers obtained relief for employment discrimination fell from about 19 percent in 2007 to about 13 percent in 2017.[180]

Conceding that racial discrimination is often subtle and difficult to measure and acknowledging the validity of field experiments or audit studies to assess discrimination, a recent metastudy analyzed data from

---

177. See Ordway, "'Racially Conservative' Attitudes," discussing a study by two Ivy League professors on the subject.

178. Jameel and Yerardi, "Workplace Discrimination Is Illegal."

179. US Equal Employment Opportunity Commission. "Title VII Race-Based Charge Receipts." This does not include charges filed with state or local fair employment practices agencies.

180. Jameel and Yerardi, "Workplace Discrimination Is Illegal."

twenty-four field experiments, which included data from over fifty-four thousand job applications covering more than twenty-five thousand positions. Field experiments consist of resume audits where fictitious resumes of Blacks and Whites with equivalent qualifications and ethnically identifiable names are sent, or in-person audits where trained pairs of testers, White and non-White, apply for jobs. Discrimination is measured by examining the rates of callback and invitations to in-person interviews. The study found that since 1990, White applicants received, on average, 36 percent more callbacks than Black applicants with equivalent qualifications, and that levels of discrimination against Black job applicants have not changed. This evidence of racial discrimination in hiring is in spite of the seemingly increased interest in diversity, equity, and inclusion. The authors of the analysis concluded that bias, whether conscious or not, continues to affect hiring decisions with little evidence of abating on its own.[181]

Another extensive analysis of literature concluded that the literature points toward consistent evidence of discrimination in access to employment but less consistent evidence of discrimination in wages. The authors felt the findings may in part be causally related because Blacks who break through the barriers to labor market entry are a more select sample, thus reducing measured racial wage disparities. The authors conclude that although great progress has been made since the early 1960s, the problem of racial discrimination remains as an important factor in shaping contemporary patterns of social and economic inequality.[182]

The resulting inequality from racism in employment has been long standing. A major study based on US census data found that the Black-White income gap is driven entirely by large differences in wages and employment rates between Black and White men. Black households experienced 25 percent to 45 percent lower median incomes than their White counterparts regardless of educational attainment and household structure in the preceding forty years.[183] In 2017, the median income for Black and Latino households was $40,258. For White households, it was $68,145.[184]

Many proposals have been made to address racial disparities in employment, including addressing exclusions from the protections of

181. Quillian et al., "Hiring Discrimination."
182. Pager and Shepherd, "Sociology of Discrimination," 181–209.
183. Chetty et al., "Race and Economic Opportunity," 711–83.
184. United States Census Bureau, "Real Median Household Income."

the Fair Labor Standards Act and the Wagner Act, eliminating employer exemptions from anti-discrimination laws, and abolishing the tipped minimum wage that disproportionately impacts workers of color in service jobs.[185]

Discriminating in employment against other human beings because of the color of their skin does not reflect the heart or character of God or Jesus Christ. Those who engage in it cannot possibly believe that they are imitating Jesus Christ who removed all barriers and distinctions among people. The apostle Paul noted that all who believe in Christ are children of God and that there is neither Jew nor Greek, slave nor free, male nor female, because all of Christ's disciples are one in Jesus Christ.[186] Racism is an un-Christian thing. Practicing or condoning it is un-Christian. It sets the one who engages in it against God because that person opposes God's will for the person discriminated against. It undermines the person's God-given potential and purpose. And where there is wage discrimination, it goes against the biblical principle that the worker deserves his or her wages.[187]

As a person of color, I have had my fair share of questionable experiences in the labor market. A major career goal of mine in the mid-1980s was to teach in a law school. I had the necessary credentials, including two master's degrees and a doctorate degree, all in law. I was licensed to practice law in New York, a state with one of the toughest bar exams, and had started to publish in law reviews/journals. I got several interviews with law schools at a recruiting venue in Illinois sponsored by the Association of American Law Schools. Participating law schools would come there to recruit law faculty. I only secured one campus interview over several years of participating in this event. One of the more memorable interviews was with a law school in Ohio. Interviews were done in thirty-minute slots. Recruiters had rooms at the hotel and cycled candidates in and out every thirty minutes. I arrived for my interview ahead of time. The previous candidate's interview ran over and ate into my slot by ten

---

185. Solomon et al., "Systematic Inequality and Economic Opportunity." The authors also advocate repealing Right-to-Work laws that allow states to ban unions from requiring workers who benefit from union collective bargaining activity to help pay for bargaining costs.

186. Gal 3:26–28. See Adeyemo, *Africa Bible Commentary*, 1422, noting that baptism in the early church signified identification with Christ, whereby believers took on Christ's characteristics and virtues. As a result, their differences disappeared, for now they all looked alike as members of Christ's family, as if they were "wearing" Christ.

187. Luke 10:7; 1 Tim 5:18.

minutes. He was a White male. He exited with lots of banter still going on with the recruiters who were two White males. They apologized and promised to give me "the same consideration." They asked me to have a seat. They asked only one question for my entire interview: "Do you have any questions for us?" My interview, which started ten minutes late, was over in ten minutes with ten minutes to spare in my allotted thirty minutes. I later read an article in the *National Law Journal*, which I recall having the title "Faculty at American Law Schools Still a Predominantly White Male Preserve." I did not apply to teach at an American law school again after reading that article. I was teaching law to business students at the time. I decided to be content with being a business law professor in business school. But let's be clear: under normal circumstances, no one with multiple degrees and professional licenses should have to give up on their professional goals because of a lack of equal opportunity.

Before I moved to Pennsylvania, I interviewed in Florida for a chief academic officer position at a school in southern Florida. I was to be picked up at eight o'clock in the morning to visit the flagship campus before returning to interview on the campus where the position was housed. I was in the hotel lobby shortly before eight waiting to be picked up, but nobody came to pick me up as arranged. There was no response when I called the office multiple times. Finally, at nine o'clock, a secretary picked up the phone. She came and picked me up and took me to the local campus. They scrambled for someone to pick me up and drive me to the flagship campus. By the time we got there, I had missed my first interview. Ironically, that interview was supposed to have been with the only Black administrator I met at the institution. We only had time for a brief meet-and-greet. It became clear to me that I was not a serious candidate. This was a sham interview. I did not receive an offer. No surprise there.

My wife also had a very memorable job interview experience in Pennsylvania. She had transitioned back to the workplace part time and was working as a bookkeeper for a small business, a home builder. She was ready to go back to work full time and responded to an ad for a payroll/bookkeeping position at a small accounting firm in a neighboring town from where we lived. They invited her for an interview. When she arrived, she was informed that the firm's receptionist was going to be trained for the bookkeeper position. She was asked if she was interested in being considered for the receptionist's position, knowing full well that she had an accounting degree with experience as an auditor and staff accountant. She declined.

A few weeks later, she received the oddest email on a Saturday from a CPA at the firm. She thanked my wife for taking time out of her day to interview for the receptionist position for which she never applied. The email said my wife's skill level was higher than what they needed for that position. The email said they would be sending a formal letter within the next week indicating that the receptionist position had been filled. My wife promptly wrote back the same day to tell her that she was unsure if the email had been sent to her in error since she never applied for the receptionist position. She reminded the sender that she applied for the payroll/bookkeeping position; that she was informed when she arrived for the interview that the receptionist would be trained for the position; that she had been invited to interview for the receptionist's job but had declined; and that she, therefore, did not need to be sent a formal letter about a position for which she had neither applied nor interviewed. Imagine how intrigued I am every time I bump into folks from the firm at a public event where we recite the pledge of allegiance together, collectively expressing our commitment to liberty and justice for all!

Apart from experiences in the job market, I've also had many questionable experiences in the workplace, only a few of which I will share. Many of these experiences occurred when I became the chief academic officer (CAO) at a small, rural campus of a major public research land-grant university in southcentral Pennsylvania with an all-White faculty. I was the eighth person to hold the post in the last fourteen years, the first—and still only—person of color in the position, and also the only Black person to be a tenured faculty member in the 121-year history of the campus.

On one occasion, after receiving a written peer review of teaching from a faculty member, I made several corrections and asked my staff assistant to ask him to make the corrections before including the letter in a tenure dossier. My staff assistant informed me that the faculty member said to tell me that he didn't give a "rat's—." I asked my staff assistant to tell him that I would be happy to send his review on if he didn't mind people thinking that he didn't have a good command of the English language. He came in and made all the changes. "You could edit the Bible, couldn't you," he bellowed, after making the changes. He couldn't bring himself to be gracious enough to thank me for correcting and editing his review letter and making it better. I assured him that the Bible is one book I would never attempt to edit.

As the CAO who oversaw faculty, I couldn't help but think about the fact that people do not normally harass, disrespect, or antagonize their supervisor. The first Black student, Ralph Brock, enrolled at the campus in 1903 and completed a forestry degree in 1906. He was hired to manage a seedling nursery and teach. He left shortly thereafter because of White students who antagonized him. He didn't feel the administration had adequately supported him. It is lamentable indeed that one hundred years later, a Black CAO had the same experiences with antagonistic White direct reports and contemplated leaving. It was clear to me that some of the faculty didn't think I belonged there. After I became chancellor of the campus, anonymous bogus hotline complaints became common but were always discredited after being investigated. I stayed at the campus, not because the behaviors stopped, but because of resilience and allies who encouraged and supported me. And I never went to work without a time of morning devotion consisting of prayer and Bible study. But the antagonism did take a toll. Among other things, I developed problems with my blood pressure and had trouble sleeping.

In spite of the antagonism, the university's top officials recognized my talents and contributions to the university and offered me a promotion to serve as interim chancellor at another campus in southwestern Pennsylvania. I eventually became the chancellor there. It was a great experience. I was generally very well received and appreciated there. I had the greatest staff. I left after a little less than four years to become chancellor of my original campus. I had left my family back there and wanted to be reunited with them. Moreover, the university's leadership was contemplating putting a technical college affiliated with the university in charge of the campus I ran, and that would not have been a good fit for me.

My evaluations as a chancellor were mostly reasonably positive. Of course, there were always the handful of negative comments. Some gave me low ratings across the board, even for "appreciation of diversity!" One evaluator said people probably couldn't relate to me because of the way I dressed and spoke. I decided that I would not dress less professionally or pretend to be less articulate to be relatable.

For the entire time I was at this campus in southcentral Pennsylvania, first as CAO and then as chancellor, I felt mostly tolerated, not appreciated. Many of the things I experienced would count as microaggressions.[188]

---

188. Defined as brief everyday exchanges that send denigrating messages to certain individuals because of their group membership. Sue, *Microaggressions in Everyday Life*,

This was very much unlike the campus where I served as chancellor in southwestern Pennsylvania, where I felt appreciated and valued. However, despite often shoddy treatment, there were people who showed me acts of kindness that were a great help—maintenance workers who met me at my parking spot on snow days and escorted me up the ramp into my office building to make sure I did not slip and fall; the occasional thank-you card from a colleague; colleagues who would ask about my family; and the occasional verbal acknowledgment that I was doing a good job. In a five-year review, one evaluator said I was the most effective administrator the campus has had in twenty-five years. In all of this, my greatest satisfaction has been the real, lasting, and impactful contributions I made to the university, especially to the education of students.

No one who claims to be a disciple, follower, or imitator of Jesus Christ can discriminate against another person because of the color of their skin and believe they are somehow doing God's will or following Christ's example. Denying someone the opportunity and right to work for a living, to be recognized or appropriately remunerated for their work, and to work free from hostility and harassment is unjust, ungodly, and un-Christlike. And God hates injustice. But he loves justice.[189]

Race and the Criminal Justice System

The criminal justice system is a multi-faceted network of state and federal laws and institutions and the people who enforce them. It comprises statutes that criminalize behavior; police officers who make arrests; prosecutors who make decisions about whether to prosecute, offer a plea deal, or try a case; judges who preside over trials, make findings of guilt or innocence in bench trials, and impose punishment following sentencing guidelines; juries who make findings of guilt or innocence in jury trials; jails and state and federal prison systems that house inmates; parole boards that hear and decide on parole requests; and parole officers who oversee those who are granted parole. Sadly, studies have found racial bias across the entire spectrum of the criminal justice system.

Sociologists trace policing in America to armed slave patrols that looked to apprehend runaway slaves. These government-funded armed

---

24. One author has bluntly called racial microaggressions racist abuse. See Kendi, *How to Be an Antiracist*, 47.

189. Isa 61:8.

THE CHRISTIAN AS IMITATOR OF CHRIST

policing organizations that sought to prevent slaves from escaping to freedom comprised ordinary White citizens. They evolved into police departments and in the South, they became the enforcers of Jim Crow laws. Some believe that this history of policing based on White fears of slave uprisings or flights to freedom continues to influence policing of Black people today in racial profiling and deadly encounters between White police officers and Black people.[190] It has been pointed out that Black people have been branded as criminals from the time they began to resist slavery in America. Since slavery was legal, their resistance was illegal. Slaves who revolted were never seen as freedom fighters. They were always cast as violent criminals.[191]

With the advent of the ubiquitous cellphone camera, video footage of shootings involving White police officers and unarmed Black men have proliferated, leading to protests and demands for justice and police reform. These video images have included the beating of Rodney King and the deaths of Philando Castile, Eric Garner, and George Floyd in police custody. According to a 2020 study, seventy people, more than 50 percent of them Black, died in police custody after complaining that they could not breathe. With Blacks constituting 12 percent of the American population, they are disproportionately overrepresented in this group.[192] Video footage of George Floyd's death, in particular, seems to have had an effect that other footage had not had before. The unbelievable casualness with which the officer slowly and painfully squeezed the life out of George Floyd—his knee on George Floyd's neck, his hands in his pocket, a supercilious look on his face as onlookers pleaded with him to take his knee off George Floyd's neck, with George Floyd pleading for his life, saying he could not breathe, while other police officers pinned down his back and legs and another kept onlookers at bay—shocked many Americans. Protesters poured into the streets, not just in America, but overseas also, during a pandemic when people were being urged to practice social distancing.

Various proposals for reform of policing have been put forward, ranging from better training to background and psychological testing, to holding officers accountable for bad behavior. In the Commonwealth of Pennsylvania, a couple of bills effecting reasonable reforms in policing

---

190. Feagin, *How Blacks Built America*.

191. Greene, *Negro in Colonial New England*, 15–17. Also Kendi, *Stamped from the Beginning*, 69.

192. See Baker et al., "Three Words."

such as thorough background checks, disclosure of employment information by law enforcement agencies, an electronic database of separation records of law enforcement officers, justification for hiring an officer whose separation records include red flags such as excessive force or filing a false report, mental health evaluations as a condition of continued employment, training on use of deadly force and de-escalation and reconciliation techniques, community and cultural awareness, and implicit bias, were signed into law by Governor Wolf after unanimous legislative approval in the summer after George Floyd's death.[193]

Another issue of grave concern in the American criminal justice system is the disparate punishment of Black people for the same crimes committed by White people. A recent study of nineteen hundred exonerations between 1989 and 2016 by the National Registry of Exonerations[194] found that Black people who are convicted of murder or sexual assault are significantly more likely than their White counterparts to be later found innocent. About 47 percent of the exonerations involved Black defendants. Forty percent of those convicted of murder are Black. Keep in mind that Blacks only constituted 12 percent of the US population in 2016 according to Census Bureau estimates. Half (50 percent) of those wrongfully convicted of murder are Black compared to the 36 percent White wrongful-conviction rate for murder. Thirty-one percent of Black people wrongfully convicted of murder were convicted of killing White people. The study's authors attribute the disparities to a variety of reasons, including the high incidence of crime in Black communities, misconduct (hiding evidence, witness tampering, and perjury), and racial bias. The study found misconduct in 76 percent of cases in which Black people were wrongfully convicted compared to 63 percent of the cases in which White people were wrongfully convicted. Wrongful convictions for sexual assault showed a similar pattern with 59 percent of exonerations going to Blacks and 34 percent to Whites. The study also found that innocent Blacks spent more time in prison waiting for their names to be cleared than innocent Whites.[195] These findings show that

---

193. These reforms are contained in HB1841 and HB1910, 2023–2024 Regular Session.

194. The National Registry of Exonerations is a University of Michigan Law School project that provides data on false convictions with a view to preventing them in the future.

195. Gross et al., *Race and Wrongful Convictions*. See also Chokshi, "Black People More Likely."

raw data on rates at which Blacks are charged with homicides must be put in proper context.[196]

According to the Sentencing Project, a nonprofit organization that advocates for the reduction of the prison population, Blacks are incarcerated at five times the rate of Whites in state prisons across the country. In the 1980s and 1990s, laws were passed around the country that increased penalties for drug possession around schools and public housing projects. These laws had a disproportionately negative impact on minority communities.[197] In Florida, for example, a 2016 study by the Sarasota Herald-Tribune found that Blacks receive longer sentences, sometimes twice as long, than Whites for the same crime under identical circumstances. The study found that judges disregard sentencing guidelines, sentencing Blacks to longer prison terms in 60 percent of felony cases. White judges gave Black defendants 20 percent more prison time in third-degree felony cases, which are the least serious felonies.[198] In New Jersey, a 2005 New Jersey Sentencing Commission study found that 96 percent of the inmates convicted under these harsher penalties were Blacks and Latinos due to the disproportionately high number of drug-free zones in urban, minority neighborhoods. In light of such racial disparities, Iowa, Connecticut, and Oregon became the first three states to require lawmakers to consider racial impact statements before passing criminal justice legislation.[199] New Jersey became the fourth state to do so.[200]

In 2005, in *United States v. Booker*,[201] the US Supreme Court invalidated a 1984 statute that required federal district court judges to impose sentences within the ranges of the sentencing guidelines set by the US Sentencing Commission, which were designed to reduce disparities in federal sentences. In a study by the US Sentencing Commission of federal judge sentences between 2005 and 2007, it found that sentences of Black men were on average 15.2 percent longer than the sentences of

---

196. Justice Department data showed that Blacks were charged with homicides at eight times the rate of Whites between 1980 and 2008.

197. Reinhard and King, "Racial Impact Bill."

198. Salman et al., "Florida's Broken Sentencing System."

199. Reinhard and King, "Racial Impact Bill." A study of the Iowa racial impact statement law by researchers at the Simpson College Urban Studies Institute did not show that it negatively or positively impacted passage of sixteen criminal justice bills between 2009 and 2013, although the researchers predicted that it could reduce disparities in incarceration rates over the next ten years.

200. Ramey, "New Jersey Requires."

201. 543 U.S. 220 (2005).

White men who had committed similar crimes. Between 2007 and 2011, the Commission's report found that sentences of Black men were 19.5 percent longer than those for White men who committed similar crimes. When sentences of probation were excluded from the analysis, sentences of Black men were 14.4 percent longer than those of similarly situated White men. The Commission did not imply that the disparities were the result of racial discrimination.[202] Nonetheless, the disparities are nothing short of striking.

The mass incarceration of people of color as a result of these racial injustices is the subject of much attention and debate. Sociologists have pointed out that the prison population, which is disproportionately Black and Latino, serves as a supply of low-wage workers, a prison-industrial complex that generates significant profits for private prisons and companies that use prison labor. According to one reporter, in 2016 it was estimated that Blacks, who were being imprisoned at six times the rate of Whites, made up 40 percent of the prison population, although they were only 12 percent of the nation's population. Many Fortune 500 companies and UNICOR, a federally created government corporation that operated 110 factories in seventy-nine prisons manufacturing products for the military, use this prison labor with prisoners being paid between one and ten dollars a day, much less than similar nonprison laborers.[203] Some sociologists have described this system as neoslavery and its workers as twenty-first century slaves.[204]

Another area of the criminal justice system where there are stark racial disparities is in the death penalty. Use of the death penalty has declined in the US. Nonetheless, a comprehensive analysis of executions and death sentences in 2019 showed glaring racial disparities depending on the race of the victim. Nearly half of murder victims nationwide are Black. However, in 2019, 80 percent (twenty-seven out of thirty-four) of death sentences involved White victims. Out of the twenty-two executions in 2019, sixteen (73 percent) involved White-only victims. The racial disparities become even more evident when one also looks at the race of the defendant. Of the thirty-four death sentences in 2019, seventeen, or 50 percent, were White defendants. Only one of those cases involved a Black victim. Twelve (35 percent) of the thirty-four defendants

---

202. Palazzolo, "Racial Gap in Men's Sentencing."
203. Feagin, *How Blacks Built America*, 40–42.
204. Feagin, *How Blacks Built America*, 42.

sentenced to death were Black and five (15 percent) were Latino, meaning that 50 percent of the death sentences were handed to people of color. Out of the twelve cases where Blacks were sentenced to death, only three involved Black victims. None of the death sentences of non-Blacks were for a Black-only victim.[205]

Since 1977, when executions resumed in the US, 308 Black defendants have been executed in cases involving at least one White victim, compared to thirty-four White defendants executed in cases involving at least one Black victim. Out of the 308 cases involving Black defendants, 294 involved White-only victims, and out of the thirty-four cases involving White defendants, twenty-one involved Black-only victims. Between 1980 and 2019, the proportion of Whites on death row had decreased from 54.4 percent to 42.2 percent, while the proportion of Blacks increased from 39.8 percent to 41.6 percent. The proportion of Latinos on death row increased from 4.4 percent to 13.4 percent during the same period. It has been noted that studies have consistently found racial disparities across the entire spectrum of the capital punishment process, be it policing, charging practices, jury selection, jury verdicts, and executions.[206]

The crack epidemic of the 1980s and the war on drugs led to serious racial disparities in the arrest and punishment of drug offenses. The Anti-Drug Abuse Act of 1986 imposed the same five-year mandatory minimum sentence for possession of five grams of crack as five hundred grams of powder cocaine, a hundred-to-one quantity disparity. Crack was used more by Blacks and cocaine by Whites. This quantity disparity translated into vast racial disparities in sentences for comparable offenses.

A recent year-long study of thirty years of data involving hundreds of thousands of arrest records and federal drug convictions showed some troubling facts. From 1991 to 2016, more Whites used crack than Blacks, but Blacks were sent to federal prison nearly seven times more often than Whites for crack offenses. The ratio of Black crack users imprisoned compared to White crack users from 1991 to 1995 was thirteen to one. Among drug offenders with little or no prior criminal history, Blacks were sent to federal prison for forty months longer on average than non-Hispanic Whites for crack and cocaine possession and distribution from 1991 to 2016. From 1984 to 2014, Blacks were arrested at twice the rate of

---

205. Death Penalty Information Center, "DPIC Analysis."

206. Death Penalty Information Center, "DPIC Analysis." Also, "Death Penalty in Black and White."

Whites for crack, cocaine, heroin, and opioid offenses. The study found that these disparities continue till this day. In 2016, for example, more Blacks (85,640) were arrested for cocaine than Whites (66,120) were for heroin and other opioids, even though opioids are more deadly. There were four times more arrests for cocaine than for opioid drugs in 2016. Nineteen of the ninety-four federal districts didn't send a single White defendant to federal prison on crack charges from 1991 through 1995. The study found that in Iowa, for example, where Blacks constitute just four percent of the population, they were eleven times more likely to be arrested for cocaine or narcotics offenses than Whites.[207]

With the opioid epidemic affecting White communities more, attitudes toward drug addiction softened. Opioid overdoses are believed to have accounted for four hundred thousand deaths between the late 1990s and 2020, far more than cocaine and crack overdoses. Yet the criminal justice system showed more compassion to opioid abusers, who are predominantly White, than to crack abusers, who are predominantly Black. The attitude toward opioid drug offenses has been more along the lines of rehabilitation instead of punishment. In 2016, Congress passed the Comprehensive Addiction and Recovery Act (CARA) to address the opioid epidemic through prevention, education, treatment, and recovery programs. It seeks to divert people arrested for low-level drug violations from the criminal justice system into treatment and other services and expand the use of naloxone by first responders to reverse opioid overdoses. Monies must be appropriated through the appropriations process each year to fund these initiatives.

In 2010, the quantity disparity between crack and powder cocaine was reduced by Congress from one-hundred-to-one down to eighteen-to-one in the Fair Sentencing Act of 2010, but not eliminated completely. In 2011, the US Sentencing Commission voted to apply the Act's sentencing guidelines to individuals sentenced before the law was enacted, giving an opportunity for federal judges to review their crack cocaine sentences for possible reduction. It was believed that over twelve thousand people, about 85 percent of them Black, stood to benefit.[208] However, the 2010 Act did not help those already convicted since it was not retroactive. To address this, in 2019, the FIRST STEP Act was passed.

207. Mullen et al., "Unfair System Arrested Millions."

208. See American Civil Liberties Union, "Fair Sentencing Act." The Brennan Center for justice has noted that the federal prison population increased 700 percent since 1980, disproportionately impacting minorities.

The Act shortens mandatory minimum sentences for nonviolent drug offenses and eases the "Three Strikes" law by reducing the mandatory life sentence for three or more convictions to twenty-five years. It also gives judges more discretion to deviate from mandatory minimum sentences when sentencing nonviolent drug offenders.[209] It made the Fair Sentencing Act retroactive, leading to the release of some seventeen hundred federal drug offenders, although it left the eighteen-to-one ratio in place. The ratio, a political compromise, is not based on science.[210] A follow-up study of the FIRST STEP Act about a year after its passage found that its sentencing reforms were off to a good start. It found that three thousand people serving outdated sentences for crack cocaine crimes were resentenced to shorter prison terms. It also estimated that two thousand people every year will receive 20-percent shorter prison sentences than they otherwise would have.[211]

Michelle Alexander, a professor and civil rights advocate, has described the American criminal justice system as the New Jim Crow. She argues that America has redesigned racial caste using the criminal justice system as a contemporary system of racial control that targeted Black men through the war on drugs. She points out how mass incarceration has relegated millions to permanent second-class status.[212]

All injustice is ungodly. Injustice that results in loss of freedom is troubling. But the worst form of injustice is the unjust imposition of the death penalty. A wrongful execution is the most egregious form of injustice. Between 2005 and 2021, governors in Georgia, South Carolina, and Virginia pardoned ten Black people, including one woman who was the only woman executed in Georgia in the twentieth century, for being wrongfully executed in those states between 1915 and 1951.[213] It bears mentioning here that when God gave the Israelites laws governing justice, he specifically forbade false charges and the execution of an innocent or honest person, resolving not to acquit those who are guilty of violating these laws.[214] Only God knows how many wrongful executions took place and how many people wrongfully sentenced to life in prison died before the advent of DNA technology. Thanks to DNA technology

209. See Grawert and Lau, "How the FIRST STEP Act."
210. Mullen et al., "Unfair System Arrested Millions."
211. Grawert, "What Is the First Step Act."
212. Alexander, *New Jim Crow*.
213. Death Penalty Information Center, "Posthumous Declarations of Innocence."
214. Exod 23:7, NIV.

and the work of organizations like the Innocence Project, there are people who were unjustly convicted and imprisoned who have been freed. Between 1973 and 2023, a total of 196 people (106 of them Black) who had been sentenced to death were exonerated.[215]

In the Old Testament, there were a number of sins and transgressions for which the death penalty could be imposed. One of them was adultery. Both the man and woman were to be put to death.[216] The story is well known of the teachers of the law and the Pharisees who brought a woman who was caught in adultery to Jesus as he taught in the temple. They referenced the Old Testament law that required that she be stoned to death and asked Jesus what he had to say about it. The Bible says this was a trap. They were looking for a way to accuse him. Perhaps they thought he would speak against the law of Moses and give them cause to impugn his legitimacy as a teacher. Jesus answered them by challenging the one among them who was without sin to be the first to throw a stone. They all dispersed. Jesus told the woman that he did not condemn her but told her to leave her life of sin.[217]

The teachers of the law and the Pharisees were demanding the imposition of the death penalty on the woman. The law demanded that both the man and woman caught in adultery be stoned. Yet they only dragged the woman before Jesus. They were about to commit an act of injustice by discriminating against the woman in the imposition of the death penalty. Jesus did not excuse her sin. He forgave her sin but refused to be complicit in an act of injustice. All the evidence of racial bias in the imposition of the death penalty in America should give every disciple of Christ or Christian pause. Jesus took exception to the injustice that was about to be visited on the woman who was brought before him. Her accusers wanted to execute her while letting the man with whom she

---

215. Death Penalty Information Center, "Innocence by the Numbers."

216. Lev 20:10.

217. John 8:1–11. See Moloney, *Gospel of John*, 260–62, commenting that the scribes and Pharisees knew what Moses would do in this situation. But they were anxious to place Jesus in a situation where he may be in conflict with Moses and the law. Jesus challenged those who challenged him and since none of them could claim to be without sin, they all exited in order of seniority. Jesus established a relationship with the accused woman by addressing her personally. And based on that relationship, Jesus could challenge her to sin no more. Jesus not only spared her physical life but gave her the possibility of a new life in relationship with God. In doing so, Jesus opposed the traditional defenders of the Mosaic tradition. He stood traditional values on their head if adherence to such values meant a woman was made a chattel and a necessary evil in a debate over a point of the law.

THE CHRISTIAN AS IMITATOR OF CHRIST

was caught in adultery go free. Because we live in a fallen world where there is injustice, no one can guarantee that every death sentence is just. The death sentence is draconian in nature. Unless overturned, it results in execution, an irrevocable act. It also has a spiritual dimension. Where the person executed has not been redeemed through faith in Jesus Christ, their execution dispatches them to hell and separates them from God for eternity. But God does not want anyone to perish. He patiently holds off final judgment because he wants everyone to come to repentance.[218]

Jesus Christ himself was unjustly subjected to capital punishment. He was accused of blasphemy by claiming to be the Son of God. The law required anyone who blasphemed the name of the Lord to be stoned to death.[219] However, the Pharisees knew that stoning Jesus was not a viable option considering his immense popularity. They therefore sought to hide behind Rome's power to execute criminals by bringing Jesus before Pilate, the governor, with their trumped-up charges.[220] Jesus had predicted his death on a cross.[221] That is why he came. The Pharisees and teachers of the law did not know that. As far as they were concerned, they were railroading Jesus. When Pilate saw that Jesus was innocent and wanted to release him, the Jews accused him of treason, saying Jesus claimed to be a king and, therefore, opposed Caesar, the Roman emperor. They told Pilate that if he let Jesus, one who opposed Caesar, go free, then Pilate himself was no friend of Caesar. Of course, Pilate would not want the emperor to hear that he had sided with one who opposed him. He handed Jesus over to be crucified.[222]

What happened to Jesus also happened to the apostle Paul. Jewish leaders who were upset with his ministry and the impact he was having accused him of being a troublemaker stirring up riots among Jews all

---

218. 2 Pet 3:9. See Mateus F. de Campos, "Second Letter of Peter," in McCaulley et al., *New Testament in Color*, 701–2, commenting on how Peter addresses the apparent lack of signs of divine intervention in judging evil by explaining God's perspective on time. What appears to be God's "slowness"—a passive lack of response—is in fact God's "patience"—an active and intentional response by which God mercifully withholds his judgment in order to give people the opportunity to repent.

219. Lev 24:16.

220. John 18:31.

221. John 12:32.

222. John 19:12–16.

over the world.²²³ Paul was tried by two governors before appealing to Caesar.²²⁴ Paul was eventually executed in Rome.²²⁵

The Savior of the world and the apostle who wrote nearly half of the books in the New Testament were both unjustly subjected to the death penalty by powerful leaders who opposed their message. Of course, God permitted it in order to fulfill his sovereign will. But knowing how the death penalty can be used as an instrument of injustice both in Jesus's day and ours, and with all the data and evidence we have, disciples of Christ—Christians—must be willing to follow Jesus's example of extending grace to the sinner who deserves death, as we saw him do with the woman caught in adultery. Puritan leaders like Cotton Mather supported the death penalty early in American history²²⁶ and many in America still do today despite the fact that it represents Old Testament justice. The Old Testament law was a foreshadow of what was to come—namely, the grace of God revealed in Jesus Christ. No one could be justified under the Old Testament law. It did not empower anyone to live a godly life. It condemned by pointing out one's sin. But under the new covenant established by Christ through his death and resurrection, one can be saved by faith through grace and live a godly life through the power of the indwelling Holy Spirit. Disciples of Christ should not prefer Old Testament justice over the example of Christ. But even in the Old Testament, God specifically forbade the killing of an innocent person and resolved not to acquit those who are guilty of violating that law.²²⁷

The racial injustices in the criminal justice system in America are just as displeasing to God. God loves justice but hates wrongdoing.²²⁸ And he requires that every human being do justice, love kindness, and walk humbly with him.²²⁹ One cannot claim him as one's God and not

---

223. Acts 24:5.

224. Acts 25:10. Paul was tried by governors Felix and Festus. Acts 24; 25.

225. In 2 Tim 4:6, Paul talked about his impending execution.

226. Kendi, *Stamped from the Beginning*, 61.

227. Exod 23:7.

228. Isa 61:8a.

229. Mic 6:8. See Adeyemo, *Africa Bible Commentary*, 1056, commenting that Micah pointed out that there was no need for more sacrifices. What the people needed to do was repent of their unbelief and injustice and obey the covenant laws. God had already told them what he desires. What he requires of them is good. What he forbids is evil. God alone is good and he wants his followers to act in accordance with his own character and to exercise justice, mercy, and humility. There is no point in carefully following the law's requirements for sacrifice while ignoring its demand for righteous

do that. Neither can one claim to be following or imitating Christ while devising unjust laws or perpetrating or condoning acts of injustice, including discriminatory punishment based on skin color or ethnicity.

Race and Healthcare

Regarding race and healthcare, researchers have provided abundant evidence of racial and ethnic disparities in the American healthcare system.

Healthcare in America is primarily employer-based. It was estimated that nearly 160 million Americans received health benefits through their employer before the pandemic. Employers receive tax breaks for providing health insurance, meaning that employer-sponsored insurance is government subsidized. Many American workers do not have employer-sponsored health insurance, including retired people and low-wage workers who sometimes work multiple jobs. Racial minorities are disproportionately represented among uninsured low-wage workers. The majority (60 percent) of Americans polled recently believe healthcare is a human right and that the government should ensure access for as many people as possible.[230]

In spite of the large numbers of uninsured, in 2022 it was reported that America spends about $4.5 trillion a year on healthcare,[231] more than any other nation, even though more people in America die of preventable causes than in any of the other industrialized nations.[232]

Since the passage of the Social Security Act in 1965, senior citizens who turn sixty-five are eligible for Medicare, a government-funded health insurance program that includes coverage for hospitalization, doctor's visits, and prescription drugs. Currently, 66.9 million people are enrolled in Medicare.[233]

Another way people obtain health insurance is through Medicaid, a health insurance program for the poor funded by states with subsidies from the federal government. The Medicaid program was authorized by the Social Security Act, the law that instituted Medicare. An estimated $532 billion was spent on Medicaid in 2015, with 63 percent of it coming

---

living.

    230. Interlandi, "Employer-Based Health Care."
    231. See Office of the Actuary, "National Health Expenditures 2022 Highlights."
    232. Radley, "Americans."
    233. Centers for Medicare and Medicaid Services, "Medicare Monthly Enrollment."

from the federal government. In 2017, it covered one in five Americans and four out of ten children, a total of seventy-four million people. This included two-thirds of the people in nursing homes and ten million adults and children with physical or mental disabilities.[234] Expenditures grew to $600 billion in 2017 and to almost $640 billion in 2019.[235] In 2019, according to the Centers for Medicare and Medicaid Services (CMS), Medicaid covered seventy-five million people, 40 percent of whom were children. Another 15 percent were disabled people. Enrollment was projected to reach eighty million in 2024 with an estimated expenditure of almost $840 billion.[236]

In 2010, with 46.5 million people uninsured, the Affordable Care Act (ACA) was passed, creating a mix of federal and state-sponsored health-insurance marketplace exchanges where people who did not have health insurance through their employer, Medicare, or Medicaid, were able to purchase government-subsidized health insurance. By 2013, the number of uninsured was down to forty-four million. By 2016, it was down to 26.7 million. It is estimated that more than twenty million previously uninsured people obtained health insurance through the ACA by 2016. Coverage gains were greatest among racial minorities, low-income people, and adults.[237]

The ACA became a great bone of contention between those who believe that private markets should address the problem of the uninsured, not government, and those who maintain that government should provide a solution because the private markets have not been able to provide one for decades. Those who favor a private solution argue that government should not be in the health insurance business, but those who favor a government solution point out that the government is already in the health insurance business, providing health insurance to millions through Medicare and Medicaid. The matter was the subject of prolonged litigation. In *National Federation of Independent Business v. Sebelius*,[238] the Supreme Court upheld the individual mandate in the ACA for most Americans to have health insurance by 2014, finding that

---

234. See Zernike et al., "In Health Bill's Defeat."
235. Vankar, "Medicaid—Statistics and Facts."
236. Vankar, "Medicaid—Statistics and Facts."
237. Garfield et al., *Uninsured and the ACA*.
238. 567 U.S. 519 (2012).

THE CHRISTIAN AS IMITATOR OF CHRIST

the penalty for violating the mandate functioned constitutionally as a tax and, therefore, a valid exercise of Congress's taxing power.

After Congress subsequently reduced the penalty to zero in the Tax Cuts and Jobs Act of 2017, a number of states, led by Texas, successfully argued in federal district court that the individual mandate was now unconstitutional since it could no longer be justified as a tax. After being upheld on appeal by the US Court of Appeals for the Fifth Circuit, the Supreme Court agreed to resolve the issue in March 2020. The Supreme Court held that neither the states nor the individuals challenging the law had the legal right to sue.[239] It had been feared that twenty million people would lose their health insurance if the ACA had been repealed.[240] Although many racial minorities gained insurance coverage under the ACA, 43 percent of those who gained health insurance under the ACA between 2010 and 2015 were White.[241]

Beginning in 2014, states were offered the opportunity to expand Medicaid coverage to more low-wage workers under sixty-five who earn below 133 percent of the Federal Poverty Level, a disproportionate percentage of whom are racial minorities. In 2019, Blacks and Latinos made up 51.9 percent of the poverty population even though they were 31.9 percent of the total population. Whites were 59.9 percent of the total population and 41.6 percent of the poverty population. Asians were 6.1 percent of the total population and 4.3 percent of the poverty population. Blacks were 13.2 percent of the total population but 23.8 percent of the poverty population. Latinos were 18.7 percent of the total population but 28.1 percent of the poverty population.[242] The federal government picked up 100 percent of the cost of the expansion for three years, and then phased down to 90 percent in 2020. Not all states took advantage of this opportunity. It seemed like the dividing line was the political affiliation of the state's governor, with Democratic governors signing on while Republican governors mostly did not. As of 2017, an estimated eleven million low-income adults were added to the program as a result of the

---

239. California v. Texas, 593 U.S. 659 (2021).

240. The ACA was dubbed "Obamacare" by those who oppose it. Many did not know that it was the same as the ACA. Some expressed support for the ACA but said they were against Obamacare. Its repeal would have disproportionately impacted racial minorities who gained healthcare through the ACA.

241. Garrett and Gangopadhyaya, *Who Gained Health Insurance Coverage*.

242. See Creamer, "Inequalities Persist Despite Decline."

TREATMENT OF OTHERS BASED ON RACE

expansion of Medicaid under the ACA.[243] Medicaid rolls expanded further during the COVID-19 crisis to cover people who lost their jobs due to the pandemic. In states that expanded Medicaid, the program covered 35.8 percent of unemployed adults between ages nineteen and sixty-four, compared to 16.4 percent of unemployed adults in the same age range in nonexpansion states.[244]

The COVID-19 pandemic exacerbated racial disparities in healthcare outcomes. Higher percentages of people of color died as a result of COVID-19. Many of them were on the front lines as essential workers whose employers stayed open and many were low-income earners who could not afford to not go to work.

Despite these grim realities, and with about 220,000 Americans dead from COVID-19 by the end of 2020, efforts to dismantle the ACA continued in full force with no published plan for a viable substitute until the Supreme Court ended repeal efforts in 2021.

This raises the question as to how disciples, followers, or imitators of Christ—Christians—should view access to healthcare and the ideological tussles over health insurance coverage. Jesus's life and ministry provide a lens with which to view this. Jesus Christ healed countless people during his three-year ministry. He didn't turn away any sick person who came to him for healing because of the person's ethnicity, nationality, or skin color. He charged no one for healing them. Ability to pay was not a barrier. The only requirement was faith[245]—that of the person in need of healing,[246] or that of someone else interceding on their behalf.[247] It would not be inaccurate to say that Jesus was a literal one-man universal healthcare system for the sick.

Jesus cared about people and their wellbeing more than how, where, or when they got healed. He healed on the Sabbath although it violated the tradition of the Pharisees. The Pharisees, who were the religious leaders of their day, were so much more concerned with their tradition than

---

243. Zernike et al., "In Health Bill's Defeat." See also Kaiser Family Foundation, "Status of State Medicaid," showing that ten states, including seven southern states, had not adopted Medicaid expansion.

244. Gangopadhyaya and Garrett, *Unemployment, Health Insurance*. This study is cited in Mann, "COVID-19 Crisis."

245. Jesus did not do many miracles in his hometown because of their unbelief or lack of faith. Matt 13:58; Mark 6:5.

246. Matt 9:22; Mark 5:34; Luke 8:48; 17:19.

247. Matt 8:8; 15:22–28; Mark 2:5–12; 7:24–30; Luke 5:20–26.

human need that they plotted to kill Jesus for healing a man with a withered hand on the Sabbath, as bewildering as that sounds.[248] Disciples and imitators of Christ in our day should, like Jesus, care more about people and their wellbeing than how that wellbeing is achieved. They should care more about whether someone can see a doctor or get care when sick than whether they are able to do so through the private health insurance market or a government-sponsored health insurance program. And, like Jesus who healed Jews and Samaritans alike and responded positively to a Roman centurion and a Canaanite mother who asked for healing for a servant and daughter, respectively, professing Christians should also care about all people having access to good healthcare so that they can live healthy lives and fulfill their God-given purpose and potential.

Race and the Church

The church is the body of Christ—those who have been redeemed by the blood of Jesus through faith in him. The only way to become a member of the church is to be born again through faith in Christ. One can belong to a church or become a member of a local church body without being a member of the church. In other words, one can be a member of a church and yet not be born again. Not all church members are disciples, followers, or imitators of Christ—Christians. As a result, the organized church, which should be the light of the world and the salt of the earth pointing lost sinners and the ungodly to Christ and discipling them to live Christ-like lives of love toward all humanity, has itself been complicit in the sin of racism.[249]

Prejudice is an ungodly thing, but unfortunately, it has been around since the early church. In the very early days of the church in Jerusalem, there was a program of food distribution to help out widows in the church. The first mention of prejudice in the early church was in connection with this program. Widows of the Greek-speaking Jews were being overlooked in the distribution of food. Preference was being given to the widows of the Hebrew-speaking Jews. The Greek-speaking Jews lodged

---

248. Matt 10:12–14; Mark 3:1–6; Luke 6:6–11.

249. See Goza, *America's Unholy Ghosts*, 32, 125, 146–47, arguing that the White church in America has been influenced by the religious lie from Enlightenment philosophers that Christians can be indifferent to injustice and yet intimate with God, though the Bible calls such indifference hardheartedness. This reshaped Christianity in America into Christian Stoicism.

a complaint with the twelve disciples. They, in turn, addressed all the other disciples and suggested that a group of seven men be selected to oversee the food distribution program so that the disciples could devote their time to prayer and the ministry of God's word.[250] These seven are believed to have been the very first deacons in the church.

In his early years, the apostle Peter harbored prejudice toward gentiles, but God would soon change that. God was moved by the prayers, devotion, and kindness of a Roman centurion called Cornelius who gave generously to the poor. Knowing that being kind and having a good heart are not enough for one to be saved and that Cornelius needed salvation in Jesus Christ, God had an angel instruct Cornelius in a dream to send for Peter to come and preach the gospel to his household. Knowing Peter's prejudice as a Jew and what his reaction would be to the invitation of a gentile to come into his home, God showed Peter in a vision that it was wrong to harbor prejudice toward anyone. Peter hosted Cornelius's servants and traveled with them the next day to Caesarea.

Peter was obedient to God's call to minister to Cornelius. He preached the gospel to Cornelius and his household and God gave Cornelius and his household the gift of the Holy Spirit. The Jewish believers who accompanied Peter were astonished that gentiles had received the Holy Spirit. Cornelius and his household were baptized in water as new believers. Peter stayed with them a few days before leaving. He learned that God does not show favoritism or partiality.[251]

Peter was criticized by the Jewish believers when he returned to Jerusalem for going into the home of gentiles and eating with them. Peter explained how God had shown him in a vision not to call anything impure that God has made clean, how the Holy Spirit instructed him to go to Cornelius's house to minister to him, and how Cornelius and his household had received the Holy Spirit. Peter asked how he could oppose God for giving gentiles the same gift he had given them. That took care of the objections and the Jews praised God for saving gentiles.[252] But Peter continued to struggle with prejudice.

In the church in Antioch, Peter had been eating with the gentile believers until some Jewish believers sent by James came from Jerusalem to Antioch. Being afraid of what the Jews from Jerusalem would say, Peter and the other Jews began to segregate themselves from the gentile

250. Acts 6:1–6.
251. Acts 10.
252. Acts 11:1–18.

THE CHRISTIAN AS IMITATOR OF CHRIST

believers. Paul opposed Peter to his face and rebuked him for his hypocrisy in discriminating against the gentile believers to please his fellow Jews. Paul told Peter that his behavior was not in line with the truth of the gospel.[253] Unfortunately, there are many today who condone racism in order to maintain rank and show solidarity with those in their racial subgroup who practice it. Practicing or condoning racism does not line up with the truth of the gospel that God so loved the world that he sent his son Jesus Christ to lay down his life for all of humanity regardless of the color of their skin. It also does not line up with the truth that God does not show favoritism or discriminate but accepts people from every nation who fear him and do the right thing.[254] Nor does it imitate Christ's example of accepting everyone he encountered regardless of their ethnicity, nationality, or skin color.

About having gone to Cornelius's house, Peter's question to his fellow Jewish believers about how he could oppose God contains an important truth. To be a racist is to oppose God's will for others of whom the racist disapproves because of the color of their skin or their ethnicity. It is to oppose God's sovereignty. People who think they can do that and still consider themselves imitators of Christ, which is what Christians are, are deceived.

The church has been complicit in racism for centuries. This complicity began with slavery and goes back to the fifteenth century when the Catholic Church gave Spain the right to colonize the New World and gave Portugal a monopoly over trade in West Africa. Pope Nicholas V gave Portugal the right to territories and trade along the West African coast, including the right to enslave Africans in perpetuity. Queen Isabela of Spain offered contracts for the shipment of slaves from West Africa to the Spanish colonies in the Americas. In search of economic wealth and power, other European nations competed for these contracts and joined in this trade in African slaves to the New World. When all was said and

---

253. Gal 2:11–14.

254. Acts 10:34–35. See Jordan J. Cruz Ryan, "Acts," in McCaulley et al., *New Testament in Color*, 250, commenting on God's acceptance of all people by arguing that, like Peter's message to Cornelius, the message we are challenged to proclaim includes the good news of the life of Jesus, the resurrection, and forgiveness of sins, as well as the message of ethnic egalitarianism in the eyes of God who shows no partiality. See also Johnson, *Gospel of Luke*, 194, commenting that Peter is coming to see that it is not membership in a particular nation or the observance of its specific customs that makes one acceptable to God, but rather the way of responding to God that comes from "the fear of the Lord," or in more precise terms, "faith."

TREATMENT OF OTHERS BASED ON RACE

done, 12.5 million Africans had been trafficked across the Atlantic by the time the slave trade ended.[255]

According to Gomes Eanes de Zurara, the biographer of Prince Henry the Navigator of Portugal, between 1434 and 1447, 927 slaves were brought to Portugal. Gomes Eanes de Zurara claimed that the great majority of them had found salvation, and that this was Prince Henry's greatest achievement. Of course, Prince Henry gained great wealth from slave ownership and slave trading. But this casting of slave trading in terms of saving the souls of slaves earned the blessing of Roman Catholic popes.[256]

The Bible was twisted in defense of slavery from the mid-sixteenth century until chattel slavery was abolished in the nineteenth century when an Englishman by the name of George Best came up with the narrative that Blacks were the descendants of Ham, Noah's youngest son. Noah cursed Canaan, Ham's son, to be a slave to Ham's two older brothers because Ham saw a drunken and naked Noah and told his brothers about it. It was the brothers, Shem and Japheth, who covered Noah while looking away from his naked body.[257] Incidentally, if the Canaanites were Ham's descendants through his son Canaan, then they were not African. The curse Noah pronounced on Canaan did not justify African slavery. And God showed that the curse was not absolute. God loved and accepted Rahab, a Canaanite who forsook Canaanite gods to serve Jehovah. God not only saved her life when the Israelites conquered Jericho, but he also honored her by placing her in the lineage of Jesus.[258]

The church in America has had a complicated history with race ever since Africans from Angola were brought to America as slaves in 1619. The Puritans who came to America from England believed they were superior. They learned it from Aristotle's climate theory, the foundation for Roman slavery, which argued the superiority of Greeks who lived in an intermediate climate and the inferiority of those who lived in extreme cold or hot climates,[259] and from other racist European ideas dating back

255. Elliot and Hughes, "No. 1/Slavery, Power and the Human Cost."

256. Kendi, *How to Be an Antiracist*, 42.

257. Gen 9:20–27. See Cain Hope Felder, "Race, Racism, and the Biblical Narratives," in Felder, *Stony the Road We Trod*, 128–32, where he argues that the original version of Gen 9:18–27 only referred to Ham and his error, and that a later version of the story, motivated by political developments in ancient Palestine, attempted to justify the subjugation of Canaanites by Shem's descendants (Israel) and was later used to sanction enslavement of Blacks.

258. Josh 6:25; Matt 1:5, recounting the genealogy of Jesus Christ.

259. See Garnsey, *Ideas of Slavery*, 114.

to Gomes Eanes de Zurara in the 1400s. They twisted the teachings of the apostle Paul to justify slavery and wrote it into colonial constitutions and laws in Virginia and New England in the 1620s and 1630s.[260] Paul did tell the Corinthians that what mattered is keeping God's commands and serving God where one is. He told them not to be troubled if they were a slave when God called them, although he said they should gain their freedom if they could and make the most of it.[261]

To justify slavery, Puritan colonists and ministers like John Cotton and Richard Mather adopted the false idea that the slave/master relationship was a loving family relationship, and that slaves and masters were equal in their souls but not their bodies. This idea was used to rationalize sharing the gospel with Africans without challenging slavery. Their grandson Cotton Mather led the movement to Christianize slaves in New England. The Puritans believed in bringing social order to the world through Christianity.[262] But let's be clear that Jesus's Great Commission was not about social order but about saving souls from the power of sin and the devil and transforming lives to become Christlike. Cotton Mather described the Puritan colonists in his sermons as a chosen people—"the English Israel." Those who opposed them were led by the devil, who was described as Black. He compared those who resisted slavery and desired equality to the devil resisting God. He taught that Africans were better off as slaves in America than as free barbarians in Africa. Not surprisingly, few Africans wanted to be Christians in the 1690s. The Religious Society of Negroes for which Cotton Mather wrote the rules, reminding them that they were miserable children of Noah, did not last.[263] It is ironic that Richard Mather saw himself as God-sent to the American colonies although he didn't preach the unadulterated truth of the Bible that Jesus came so that all, no matter who they are or their life circumstances, might have life and have it more abundantly. Instead, he preached a perverted gospel that condoned what false prophets do best—stealing, killing, and destroying, while doing it all in the name of God.

Church leaders like Jonathan Edwards and George Whitefield,[264] credited as the founders of the evangelical movement in America, owned

---

260. Kendi, *How to Be an Antiracist*, 17, 18, 22.

261. 1 Cor 7:17–21.

262. Kendi, *How to Be an Antiracist*, 33.

263. Kendi, *Stamped from the Beginning*, 59–63.

264. George Whitefield was co-founder of the University of Pennsylvania with Benjamin Franklin.

slaves and defended slavery. Roger Williams, the founder of the American Baptist church, supported slavery. Religious leaders defended slavery by claiming that they were doing their Christian duty in enslaving and converting Africans, whom they saw as inferior. One commentator has observed that evangelicals to this day are just as entangled with culture as Whitefield was in his day. He observes that now, as in Whitefield's day, evangelicals have a tendency to join hope to fear, philanthropy to religious bigotry, evangelism to geopolitics, and Protestantism to empire. He concludes that like Whitefield, evangelicals confuse earthly and heavenly politics.[265] Other authors have written about evangelical racism, evangelicals' un-Christian positions on White patriarchy and Christian nationalism, their partisan politics, and economic self-interests.[266]

The gospel was not shared with slaves until the 1720s, beginning in 1724 with Dr. Thomas Bray, commissary of Maryland, and a founder of the Anglican Church in America. Slave masters were opposed to the evangelization of slaves fearing that it would result in slaves becoming free upon baptism. To assuage them, colonial laws made clear that baptism did not demand that slaves be freed.[267] For example, a 1667 Virginia law denied freedom to baptized slaves.[268] Evangelists also harped on Bible verses exhorting slaves to obey their masters out of reverence for God and to serve them as if they were serving Christ himself even though Paul was not justifying slavery in urging slaves to be Christlike despite their tragic circumstances. He was asking them to imitate Christ no matter what, even in the face of injustice, so as to always glorify God in Christ.[269]

Cotton Mather, who led the movement to Christianize slaves in New England, claimed that Christianity allowed slavery, citing the

---

265. See Kennedy, "Did George Whitefield Serve," reviewing the book by Choi, *George Whitefield*.

266. See Butler, *White Evangelical Racism*, and Hendricks, *Christians Against Christianity*.

267. Kendi, *Stamped from the Beginning*, 49.

268. Kendi, *Stamped from the Beginning*, 73.

269. Eph 6:5–9 and Col 3:22–25 were the verses that were being used to justify slavery. See Adeyemo, *Africa Bible Commentary*, 1437, commenting that Christ gives worth and dignity to every human being since all are in Christ. The logical result of adopting such a Christlike attitude is the abolition of slavery. See also Emerson Powery, "Reading with the Enslaved: Placing Human Bondage at the Center of the Early Christian Story," in Smith et al., *Bitter the Chastening Rod*, 71–90, noting how enslavers in North America sadly repeated Jesus's words as recorded in passages like Luke 12:35–48 to justify slavery.

THE CHRISTIAN AS IMITATOR OF CHRIST

apostle Paul. He received a slave as a gift in 1706.[270] Evangelists did not preach on passages about freedom from slavery, such as those about God freeing the Israelites from slavery in Egypt. Instead, they preached a gospel that condoned slavery. Thomas Bray failed to convert many Blacks. They were not open to Christianity as it was being presented to them.[271] No surprise there.

Nonetheless, beginning in the 1730s to the end of the eighteenth century, a period known as the period of the Great Awakening or Revival, many slaves received the gospel. Tens of thousands of slaves are said to have received the gospel by 1800.[272] Jonathan Edwards, who had been influenced by Cotton Mather, was a leader in the movement that led to the Great Awakening beginning in 1733. His gospel was one of equality in soul but not body. It was a gospel of Negro subservience. Cotton Mather died in 1728, before the Great Awakening, but by the time he died, Adam, Christianity, Jesus, and God were erroneously and unbiblically associated with White Europeans.[273]

The preaching of a watered-down gospel to slaves was not unique to the American colonies. People connected to the church in England conceived of, and authored, the Slave Bible. While purporting to introduce slaves to the Christian faith, the Slave Bible selectively excluded most of the Bible, removing the portions that could inspire hope for freedom while emphasizing portions that were used to justify slavery, an institution that had enormous economic value to the British Empire.

Bibles have between sixty-six to seventy-eight books, depending on whether they are Protestant, Catholic, or Eastern Orthodox Bibles. The Slave Bible had fourteen.[274] There couldn't have been a more brazen example of the lack of a fear of God and a more gross misrepresentation of who God is—his nature, character, and desire for every human being created in his image to have an abundant life. And all this was done for

---

270. Kendi, *Stamped from the Beginning*, 68–69. He named the slave Onesimus, the name of the runaway slave in the book of Philemon.

271. Kendi, *Stamped from the Beginning*, 65.

272. See Sweeney, "Evangelical History in Black and White."

273. Kendi, *Stamped from the Beginning*, 74–75.

274. The Slave Bible is on exhibit in the Museum of the Bible in Washington, DC. The exhibition is titled *The Slave Bible: Let the Story Be Told*. The Black spiritual journey from the times of slavery when Black people were only offered a distorted view of God through the Slave Bible to today when Black theologians and Bible scholars produce a plethora of scholarship to augment Black voices on matters of faith, is remarkable. See, for example, Ware, *African American Theology*; and Brown, *Blackening of the Bible*.

worldly gain. Ironically, the fact that the authors of the Slave Bible lied about God to justify slavery is proof that they knew slavery was wrong and ungodly. It was a sad example of the organized church partnering with Satan, the father of lies and expert twister of the truth, to devise this scheme to misrepresent God in order to justify oppression and profit. And the thing about partnering with Satan is that he doesn't just go away because one begins to grapple with conscience. Once he gains a foothold, he seeks to turn it into a permanent stronghold. It shouldn't surprise anyone that humanity and the church continue to grapple with the legacy of slavery and racism to this day.

Evangelical condonation of slavery continued into the 1800s and what has been called the Second Great Awakening. Many slaves received the gospel during this period, a period that was characterized by segregated revivals, including those of Dwight Moody, who drew criticism from Frederick Douglass for placing caste above Christianity.[275] Frederick Douglass wrote that he recognized the widest possible difference between the Christianity of this land (America) and the Christianity of Christ. He also lamented the fact that the church and the slave prison stood next to each other; that the church-going bell and the auctioneer's bell chimed in with each other; and that the pulpit and the auctioneer's block stood in the same neighborhood.[276]

The South was dominated by Baptists and Methodists after the Second Great Awakening or Revival of 1800, with the Presbyterians also exerting influence of their own. The ministers of these denominations defended slavery. The establishment of a regional structure for churches whereby southern churches operated independently of their northern counterparts inspired the secession of the South and the onset of the Civil War. The Southern Baptists, for example, split from northern Baptists in 1845 over slavery to form their own denomination. Southern churches provided "moral" support for the Confederacy. Many of their ministers were Confederate chaplains. One such chaplain and leader of the southern Presbyterian Church, Henry Lewis Dabney, who also served as chief of staff to General Stonewall Jackson, advocated for slavery as biblically righteous.[277]

With the support of these religious leaders, the Confederacy believed it was fighting a holy war. Dabney ironically believed that the

---

275. Sweeney, "Evangelical History in Black and White."
276. PBS, "People and Ideas."
277. Wilson, "Robert Lewis Dabney," 79–89.

THE CHRISTIAN AS IMITATOR OF CHRIST

South's defeat was the devil's triumph,[278] although the South's defeat was consistent with God's professed hatred of robbery and iniquity and his love of justice.[279] Slavery was a grave sin and injustice that robbed Blacks of their humanity, freedom, and dignity, as well as the fruits of their labor and, hence, their wealth. Dabney felt Black equality would destroy the southern way of life and saw the church as the last place where there should be equality, when it should have been the very first. This led him to champion separate Black Presbyterian congregations after the Civil War ended.[280] He wanted to see a separate southern religion untainted by what he saw as a corrupt North and the abolitionists he loathed.

This separate southern religion became the foundation for a distinctive southern culture—an evangelical South.[281] But it is a religion or brand of Christianity that is contrary to the life and teachings of Jesus Christ. It is contrary to the kingdom of God Jesus preached, where all who have put their faith in Christ are children of God, there being neither Jew nor Greek, slave nor free, male nor female.[282] It is contrary to Jesus's teaching about the family of God—the diverse, multiethnic, and multinational family comprised of all who obey God's will.[283] It mixes racism, racial purity, and racial segregation with elements of God's word into a brand of "White Christianity" that is reminiscent of the syncretism of ancient Israel. Many in ancient Israel mixed the worship of God with idolatry and their own traditions. They despised the prophets God sent to warn them. They believed they were righteous and acceptable in the sight of God. They preferred false prophets who affirmed their false sense of righteousness and rejected and persecuted true prophets of God who told them that their religion was displeasing to God and that they needed to repent. Nonetheless, many modern-day White evangelicals continue to adhere to the same beliefs that people like Dabney espoused. It confounded the likes of Frederick Douglass in his day and continues to befuddle authentic Christians—disciples, followers, and imitators of Christ—to this day.

Another byproduct of the mixing of racial bigotry with Christian beliefs is seen in the activities of organizations such as the Ku Klux Klan

---

278. Wilson, "Robert Lewis Dabney," 82.
279. Isa 61:8.
280. Wilson, "Robert Lewis Dabney," 85.
281. Wilson, "Robert Lewis Dabney," 89.
282. Gal 3:26–28.
283. Matt 12:46–50; Luke 8:19–21.

TREATMENT OF OTHERS BASED ON RACE

(KKK). Some of its leaders were also leading members of churches. These organizations spoke of preserving "White Christianity" and the KKK used symbols such as a cross, the ultimate symbol of Christ's sacrificial love, in their rituals and lynchings.[284]

One has to wonder how people can live lives that are a far cry from the life and teachings of Jesus and the apostles and still believe that they are disciples, followers, or imitators of Jesus Christ—Christians on their way to heaven. Is it because they believe that once they pray the so-called sinner's prayer and invite Jesus into their lives, they have punched an irrevocable ticket to heaven regardless of whether they live contrary to Jesus's teachings, and in spite of his warning that not all who call him Lord will enter the kingdom of heaven, unless they do God's will?[285] If one believes that, then one can believe that one can live an unholy life, call good evil and evil good, condone injustice, shed blood, enslave and oppress others, worship and trust in power, wealth, and the things of this world, and lie and cheat one's way into heaven as long as one has prayed the sinner's prayer. But the Bible makes it clear that those who live like that cannot inherit the kingdom of God.[286] The Pharisees, the religious elite of Israel in Jesus's day, had all the external trappings of godliness—prayer, tithing, adherence to strict rules and traditions, and worship in the synagogue. But they were unjust, unmerciful, and unfaithful to God's truths. Jesus called them hypocrites, blind, and vipers on their way to hell.[287] They plotted to kill Jesus for healing a man with a crippled hand on the Sabbath[288] and for performing the most amazing miracle—bringing back to life a man who had been dead for four days.[289] And they did it all believing that they were righteous.

Perhaps another reason why people can live contrary to the teachings and example of Christ and still see themselves as Christians is because of

---

284. See Cone, *Cross and the Lynching Tree*, in which the author criticizes the White church for actively participating in the lynching of Black people throughout the nineteenth and twentieth century.

285. Matt 7:21–23. See Harrington, *Gospel of Matthew*, 109–10, where he comments that only those who do the Father's will can expect to enter the kingdom of heaven, whereas those who do not—whatever other achievements they have—will not enter. He argues that the division is between Jews who accept Jesus's interpretation of the Torah and those who do not.

286. 1 Cor 6:9–10; Eph 5:19–21; Rev 21:8; 22:14–15.

287. Matt 23:13–33.

288. Matt 12:13.

289. John 11:43–44, 53.

THE CHRISTIAN AS IMITATOR OF CHRIST

the history of racialization of Christianity beginning in colonial America. In 1680, after the governor of Virginia managed to quell a rebellion by Nathaniel Bacon, a planter who aimed to divert the anger of White laborers away from planters by enlisting them and enslaved Blacks to fight against neighboring American Indians, Virginia lawmakers pardoned the White rebels and prescribed thirty lashes for slaves who lifted a hand against any "Christian."[290] In other words, Virginia law now defined a Christian as a White person, whether they were born-again disciples, followers, or imitators of Christ or not. In 1705, Virginia lawmakers made it a requirement for one to be a "Christian White servant" in order to hold public office.[291] In so doing, not only did they deny Blacks the ability to hold public office, but they also appropriated *Christian* and made it synonymous with *White*. Then in 1712, after frustrated slaves longing for their freedom set fire to a building in New York, the Whites who came to put out the fire were described as "Christians." Nine "Christians" were reported to have died.[292] Many still use *Christian* in this sense today, seeing it as being synonymous with Whiteness, although being a Christian is not synonymous with White identity, nor does it have anything to do with the color of one's skin or one's ethnicity.

In spite of their tragic circumstances, many slaves came to know and worship the true God and his Son Jesus Christ whom he gave as a sacrifice for their sins. Satan was unable to use slavery to separate them from God in order to steal their souls even when worshiping God was fraught with danger. Before the end of the Civil War, most slaves worshiped after hours in secret gatherings in spite of prohibitions against such gatherings. As a result, the slave church was called the "invisible institution" by historians. There were grave consequences when they were caught in worship or prayer, sometimes leading to worse punishment than for committing a crime. Slaves were forbidden from calling on the name of God while being whipped. But slaves felt encouraged by Scriptures about God's justice. They identified with Christ's suffering and longed for freedom in time and eternity. However, other slaves were able to worship publicly in the back pews and galleries of White churches before the end of the Civil War, or in Black congregations of segregated denominations.[293]

---

290. Kendi, *Stamped from the Beginning*, 54.
291. Kendi, *Stamped from the Beginning*, 68.
292. Kendi, *Stamped from the Beginning*, 69.
293. See Sweeney, "Story of the Segregated."

While some evangelicals supported slavery and segregation, others fought against slavery and actively worked for its abolition. The Quakers were at the forefront of the abolitionist movement. They had fought through their own struggles with slavery but came to the conviction that it was wrong. They became the only large denomination to ban slave holding and free their slaves, although they still struggled with the idea of Blacks being equal.[294] Abolitionists preached against slavery as a sin and called for its abolition through repentance and love, messages that were unpopular with Americans who felt favored by God as settlers and pushed west. The importance of slavery to the economy and the fear of freeing millions of slaves, unless they were sent back to Africa—which the abolitionists opposed—were hurdles to abolition.[295] Wealth from slavery was not something that those who benefited from it were willing to give up as was the case with Pharaoh when the Israelites left Egypt.[296] The apostle Paul did warn his protégé Timothy that the love of money is the root of all sorts of evil and that it causes people who covet it to err from true faith.[297] Slavery was one of those evils. And fear was a byproduct of that evil. Ironically, it was those who had power who lived in fear, which speaks to the fact that there is no peace in ungodliness. On the other hand, as the apostle John taught, there is no fear in love because fear is the absence of love. And the evidence of the love of God in one's life is love for one's fellow human beings.[298] Slavery did not demonstrate love for fellow enslaved human beings.

The abolitionists preached repentance from the sin of slavery. One of its leaders, Theodore Weld, published two books against slavery.[299] William Lloyd Garrison, a Baptist, became a vocal abolitionist and publisher of a paper called *The Liberator*. He called for immediate abolition in the late 1820s and early 1830s, though not immediate, but rather,

---

294. See Jordan, *Slavery and the Meetinghouse*. See also Mitzi Smith, "Abolitionist Messiah: A Man Named Jesus Born of a Doulé," in Smith et al., *Bitter the Chastening Rod*, 52–70, arguing that Jesus's inaugural sermon in the temple taken from his reading of the book of Isaiah cast him as an abolitionist.

295. Stafford, "Abolitionists."

296. Exod 14:5.

297. 1 Tim 6:10.

298. 1 John 4:18–21.

299. Weld, *Bible Against Slavery*, contrasted biblical slavery where slaves had rights with American slavery where slaves, as property, had no rights. Weld et al., *American Slavery as It Is*, documented the testimonies of witnesses and active and former slave owners about the brutalities of slavery to generate outrage and condemnation.

THE CHRISTIAN AS IMITATOR OF CHRIST

gradual equality after civilizing Blacks.[300] Some churches came around to supporting the abolitionist cause, but most did not, and southern church denominations split from their northern counterparts. Charles Finney, an abolitionist and president of Oberlin College, predicted civil war and bloodshed two decades before it happened. Some abolitionists, disillusioned by the refusal of the nation to repent of the sin of slavery, lost their faith, a sad testament to the stronghold that Satan and the spirit of slavery had over the nation.

The civil war and bloodshed Charles Finney foresaw happened when Abraham Lincoln was elected and the South seceded.[301] This happened after Senator Jefferson Davis presented the South's platform of unlimited states' and enslavers' rights to the Senate in 1860. After almost two years of civil war beginning in April 1861, President Lincoln's Emancipation Proclamation came in January 1863, to William Lloyd Garrison's praise. Lincoln saw it as necessary to save the Union, not Blacks. But Black Christians saw it as an answer to prayer.[302]

Abolitionists saw the war as God's judgment for the nation's failure to repent of the sin of slavery.[303] Ironically, the Confederates believed that their cause was righteous. Many today still believe it was and deny the role of slavery in the war. Many argue that heritage and states' rights were the reasons for the Civil War.[304] In a fundraising letter for the Confederate Soldiers and Sailors Monument in Baltimore in 1901, the United Daughters of the Confederacy described the Confederate soldier as the purest, noblest, highest type of Christian warrior the world has ever produced.[305] If I could pick a Christian warrior that I could ascribe those superlatives to, it would be the apostle Paul. He taught us that our battle is not against flesh and blood but against evil forces;[306] that we should put on the whole armor of God;[307] that a soldier does not get entangled in

---

300. Kendi, *Stamped from the Beginning*, 162–68. Garrison did not support giving Blacks the right to vote until they had been educated. He retired after Lincoln's assassination, seeing his work as an abolitionist as over. Kendi, *Stamped from the Beginning*, 229, 233–34.

301. Stafford, "Abolitionists."

302. Kendi, *Stamped from the Beginning*, 218–21.

303. Stafford, "Abolitionists."

304. See Martinez, "For Civil-War Scholars."

305. See Levitz, "Daughters of Confederacy."

306. Eph 6:12.

307. Eph 6:13–17.

TREATMENT OF OTHERS BASED ON RACE

civilian affairs;[308] and that we should pray without ceasing.[309] Paul fought the good fight, finished his race, kept the faith,[310] preached to countless souls, established churches in Asia Minor and Europe, and wrote almost half of the New Testament.[311] He did so much damage to the kingdom of darkness that Satan harassed him at every turn.[312] He was a legitimate example of the noblest type of Christian warrior.

In spite of southerners putting Confederate soldiers and generals on spiritual pedestals, God obviously did not answer their prayers for victory in the Civil War, just as he did not honor King Zedekiah's hope for God's help against the Babylonians because of unrighteousness, oppression, and injustice in Judah.[313] During Zedekiah's reign, the people of Judah were violating the law by refusing to free Hebrew slaves in the seventh year.[314] But when defeat at the hands of the Babylonians was imminent, Zedekiah made a covenant with the people to obey this law by freeing their Hebrew slaves.[315] However, when the Babylonian army was temporarily diverted from its attack against Judah by war with Egypt, the people of Judah re-enslaved the slaves they had just freed.[316] As a result, God condemned them to die by sword, famine, and plague.[317] Many southerners believed that they were God's chosen people and that they would prevail in the war while enslaving, exploiting, and brutalizing Blacks. This thinking was nurtured by churches and clergymen in the South.[318] But slavery, which the South would in all likelihood have continued if they had won the war (a prospect which put slavery at the heart of the war, especially given Jefferson Davis's platform of unlimited

---

308. 2 Tim 2:4.
309. 1 Thess 5:17.
310. 2 Tim 4:7–8.
311. Acts 13–14; 15:36–40; 16–21.
312. 2 Cor 11:25.
313. Jer 21:1–5, 12–14. God told Jeremiah to tell Zedekiah that he (God himself) would fight against Zedekiah.
314. Exod 21:2–11; Deut 15:12–18.
315. Jer 34:8–10.
316. Jer 34:11.
317. Jer 34:12–20.
318. See Croskery, *Religious Rebels*, 18, 20–28, where the author cites many works on the influence of religion in the South's waging of the war.

THE CHRISTIAN AS IMITATOR OF CHRIST

enslavers' rights), was an egregious sin and, as the psalmist recognized, God does not hear those who cherish sin in their hearts.[319]

Southerners eventually accepted defeat by recognizing that either God did not favor the South, or he was punishing them for their sinful behavior.[320] On the other hand, radical northern Christians affected the course of the Civil War and Reconstruction, becoming a source of Union tenacity and helping frame the war as a war to end slavery.[321] The Union victory did indeed end slavery. But it didn't end racism, slavery's root, leading William Lloyd Garrison to say in 1876, as Reconstruction was coming to an end, that America must give up the spirit of racism based on skin color (complexional caste as he put it) or give up Christianity.[322] He was right. The truth is that the two are inconsistent. One cannot profess to be imitating Christ and serving a God who does not look on outward appearance or skin color, while practicing or condoning racism and racial discrimination. To think that one can is to misunderstand who Jesus is, who God is, and what it means to be a Christian—a disciple, follower, or imitator of Christ.

The church continued to support racial segregation after the Civil War, spurring the formation of Black churches. Blacks founded independent congregations like the AME (African Methodist Episcopal) Church, the AME Zion Church, or COGIC (Church of God in Christ).[323] The first AME Church was formed in 1787 in Philadelphia after White congregants removed Black congregants who were kneeling in prayer in a Whites-only section of St. George's Methodist Episcopal Church.[324]

In the modern era, Billy Graham reportedly did not desegregate his southern meetings until the Supreme Court declared the separate-but-equal doctrine as unconstitutional in *Brown v. Board of Education*. Reverend Graham was said to have angered many by inviting Dr. Martin Luther King Jr. to pray at a New York City crusade in 1957.[325] It was in that same year that John Buchanan, a prominent pastor in Alabama, claimed that segregation was ordained by God. It is estimated that less

---

319. Ps 66:18. See Adeyemo, *Africa Bible Commentary*, 672, commenting that sin always separates a person from God and is a hindrance to prayer.
320. See Beringer, *Elements of Confederate Defeat*, 166.
321. Howard, *Religion and the Radical*.
322. Kendi, *Stamped from the Beginning*, 256.
323. See Sweeney, "Story of the Segregated."
324. Equal Justice Initiative, "Racial Segregation in the Church."
325. See Sweeney, "Evangelical History in Black and White."

than twenty-four churches among the one hundred thousand or so White churches in the South in 1959, a mere couple of years after John Buchanan's statement, had any Black members.[326]

The church in America remained segregated through the Jim Crow era into the 1960s. One church historian notes that segregation and racial discrimination had the support of a distressing number of White evangelicals and mainstream Americans, not just the KKK, and that few White evangelicals helped in the fight for civil rights or were willing to discuss the implications of biblical faith for race relations and justice.[327] Other authors have written about divisive White evangelical politics fueled by racism, White patriarchy, nationalism, and economic self-interests.[328] Recall that Dr. King wrote his famous *Letter from Birmingham Jail* in response to a message in a Birmingham paper by eight White clergymen in Alabama who took exception to the nonviolent civil rights protests Dr. King led in Birmingham in defiance of a court order. They criticized Dr. King and his methods in their letter.

In 1963, Dr. King said that it was appalling that eleven o'clock on Sundays is the most segregated hour in Christian America. Dr. King's statement appears to continue to hold true. As recently as 2016, it was estimated that about 86 percent of churches in America lacked any meaningful racial diversity.[329]

Some denominations are still grappling with, and making efforts to atone for, their complicity in slavery and White supremacy. In 1995, the Southern Baptist Convention apologized for its support of slavery and segregation and condemned White supremacists in 2017. The Southern Baptist Theological Seminary issued a report in 2018 detailing its founders' slave holding, the support of its faculty for slavery, their concerns over the election of Abraham Lincoln, their support for scientific racism and the narrative that the war was not about slavery but about upholding the South's honor, and their opposition to Reconstruction.[330] Georgetown University, a Jesuit institution, recently acknowledged that its priests had sold 272 slaves in 1838 to save the institution, then Georgetown College, from closure. It has established a $400,000-a-year scholarship fund for

326. Equal Justice Initiative, "Racial Segregation in the Church."
327. See Sweeney, "Story of the Segregated."
328. See Butler, *White Evangelical Racism*. See also Kobes Du Mez, *Jesus and John Wayne*; and Hendricks, *Christians Against Christianity*.
329. See Equal Justice Initiative, "Racial Segregation in the Church."
330. See Hassan, "Oldest Institution."

descendants of these slaves.[331] The Jesuit conference of priests has since pledged to raise $100 million to benefit the descendants of these slaves and promote racial reconciliation efforts in the United States.[332] Princeton Theological Seminary announced a $27 million spend on scholarships to atone for its ties to slavery and Virginia Theological Seminary has established a $1.7 million reparations fund for using enslaved laborers.[333] These gestures and steps are an acknowledgment of past wrongs and a desire to make things right. They are important steps in the right direction.

Racism and slavery led to the Civil War after slave holding Confederate states seceded from the Union. Racism also led to pushback against Reconstruction, a resurrection of the spirit of bigotry, and Jim Crow; to monuments to those who almost destroyed the Union; to pushback against civil rights and equality; and to a point in history where we have come full circle with talk of a race war as those who fight for equality and those committed to inequality—who see life as a zero-sum game of winners and losers—clash. Some are actually chomping at the bit to start this race war. It was the motivation for the killing of nine members of the Emanuel AME church in Charleston, South Carolina, in 2015. In 2020, three police officers in Wilmington, North Carolina, were fired for racist language that included one of them saying he couldn't wait to start slaughtering Blacks in a civil war.[334] Many are arming themselves to the teeth fearing a civil war. Background checks in June 2020 for civilians seeking a license to carry a gun were at their highest in the twenty years that the FBI had been conducting checks. They were up 136 percent compared to a year before. A total of 7.8 million background checks were conducted in the three-month period from March to June 2020.[335] Ironically, it seems people, including some professing Christians, would rather arm themselves than choose Jesus's exhortation to love their neighbor as themselves and live in peace with one another.

This all shows the truth in Jesus's warning that one cannot serve two masters—that one cannot serve both God and money.[336] Many religious

---

331. See Swarns, "272 Slaves Were Sold."
332. See Swarns, "Catholic Order Pledges $100 Million."
333. See Swarns, "Georgetown's $400,000-a-Year Plan."
334. Slotkin, "North Carolina Police Chief."
335. See Wernau and Elinson, "Record Numbers of Americans."
336. Matt 6:24. The NRSV says one cannot serve God and wealth, the NIV says money, and the NKJV says mammon. See Harrington, *Gospel of Matthew*, 104, explaining the saying about not serving two masters as moving the theme of total commitment

leaders throughout the centuries, including popes, priests, and Protestant leaders of all denominations, have attempted to prove Jesus wrong by advocating for, supporting, and justifying slavery, colonialism, oppression, and the profits these evils brought, while doing it all in the name of God. They thought they had pulled it off, especially since they had great influence on the writing of history during their day. But as we look back in time and examine the historical record against God's will as he has revealed it in his word and against principles of common decency, it is as clear as day that they did not pull it off. It was only a question of time for their love of money and their hypocrisy to become openly exposed. Take, for example, the renaming of two halls at Georgetown University that had been named for two Catholic priests and former presidents of the university who were involved in the sale of 272 slaves in 1838 to help pay off the university's debt.[337] Mulledy Hall was renamed Freedom Hall and McSherry Hall was renamed Remembrance Hall. Truth and decency finally caught up with them, albeit posthumously.

Because racism has spiritual dimensions, Satan is not just going to throw up his hands and walk away because of efforts to remedy discrimination through social activism, the fight for civil rights, education, or criminal justice reform. As important as those things are, the remnant—the true disciples, followers, and imitators of Christ—will have to wage spiritual warfare to tear down the spiritual strongholds of racism. They must be willing to intercede and pray without ceasing for change in peoples' hearts and minds through the movement of the Holy Spirit. Empowered by the Holy Spirit, they must be willing to carry out the Great Commission that Jesus Christ entrusted to disciples of all time. Led by the Holy Spirit, they must model Jesus Christ and endeavor to live and treat others as he did. They must pray for a spirit of repentance and revival in the body of Christ that will spill over into the nation and bring repentance, reconciliation, solidarity, and healing to a racially fractured land. It was God himself who said that if, in the face of his wrath, his people who are called by his name will humble themselves and pray,

---

forward by imagining an attempt at divided commitment and judging it impossible. See also Adeyemo, *Africa Bible Commentary*, 1123, explaining that Mammon was the Carthaginian god of wealth and that a focus on material things can wrest our devotion from God to the god of wealth. Money should be our servant in the service of God, not a god to which we owe allegiance as slaves.

337. See Jaschik, "Georgetown Changes Building Names."

seek his face, and turn from their wicked ways, he will hear from heaven, forgive their sin, and heal their land.[338]

One author has suggested that the answer to racism is for people to make a commitment to being antiracists (not nonracists) who advocate for antiracist policies that create equal opportunity and reduce racial inequity, and who oppose and act to change racist policies that promote self-interest and create racial inequities, whether those racist policies are assimilationist or segregationist in nature. He argues that this necessitates seeing race as a power, as opposed to a social construct, and that it requires changing racist policies before attempting to change minds or morals through educational or moral suasion. Although he acknowledges that success is not guaranteed, he acknowledges that losing hope is not an option. The only option, as he sees it, is to fight for a chance to live in communion and to be forever free.[339]

The question is whether America has the will and moral courage to undertake this hard work. But even as some commit to this work, there are others who push back for ideological reasons, as seen in legislation prohibiting diversity, equity, and inclusion (DEI) training, offices, and staff.[340]

Because we live in a sinful, fallen world and racism is a sin, I wonder if people can become successful antiracists, even when willing, without becoming like Christ and being empowered by him through his Holy Spirit to live and relate to people as he did. He is the only one to ever inhabit this earth who was without sin and, therefore, not complicit in the sin of racism. From establishing the headquarters of his ministry in Galilee of the gentiles,[341] to being willing to go into Samaria to minister and stay and eat with Samaritans,[342] to laying down his life for all of humanity regardless of what they look like,[343] to establishing a new family of God where there is no Jew, gentile, male, female, slave, or free,[344] he is the only one who is able to work in us to will and to do God's good

---

338. 2 Chr 7:14.

339. Kendi, *How to Be an Antiracist*, 31–33, 208–9, 230–32, 238.

340. See Chronicle Staff, "DEI Legislation Tracker," documenting that thirteen states have passed laws prohibiting DEI training in public colleges. Five of the thirteen also prohibit DEI offices and staff along with four other states. See also Ellis and Thomas, "Trump's War on DEI," reporting on President Trump's freezing of DEI initiatives in the federal government by executive order.

341. Matt 4:15.

342. John 4:3–42.

343. Matt 20:28; Mark 10:45.

344. Gal 3:28.

pleasure.[345] And it is God's will that we love him with all our heart, soul, and mind, love our neighbor as ourselves,[346] and do unto others as we would have them do unto us.[347] No one can claim to be doing any of this by devising racist policies, concocting racist ideas, and discriminating against or oppressing others for worldly gain or out of ungodly self-interest. It is untenable to profess to be a Christian—an imitator of Christ—and also be a racist or condone racism. It is likewise untenable that people who professed to be Christians supported or profited from un-Christlike institutions like slavery.

The sin of racism, slavery, and discrimination, like any sin, calls for repentance. But somehow, it is one sin for which America, as a nation, seems unwilling to repent. Perhaps it is because of the fear that acknowledging this sin will mean having to reckon with it and make things right through some form of reparations, which many see as out of the question.

Some demand an apology for slavery. But nothing short of repentance, forgiveness, reconciliation, and solidarity will bring healing. Healing for a nation comes when the people of God humble themselves and pray and turn from their wicked ways.[348] Until the remnant in America leads the way in repentance, prayer, and a turning away from the sin of racism, healing will not come. There will always be hatred, conflict, fear, and suspicion, as some even talk of precipitating or preparing for a race war.[349]

Jesus loved all humanity. When he launched his public ministry, he left Nazareth and retuned to Galilee, where he established his headquarters in Capernaum. King Solomon gave twenty towns in this region to Hiram, king of Tyre, in exchange for timber from Lebanon to build the temple and palace in Jerusalem.[350] The upper part of Galilee bordered Phoenicia.[351] That region was called "Galilee of the gentiles." Isaiah had prophesied that the people of that region would see a great light.[352] The Gospel writer Matthew notes that Jesus centered his minis-

---

345. Phil 2:13.
346. Matt 22:34–40; Mark 12:28–31, NIV. Mark adds "and with all our strength."
347. Matt 7:12.
348. 2 Chr 7:14.
349. Efrink, "We Are Just Gonna."
350. 1 Kgs 9:11.
351. See Smith, *Smith's Bible Dictionary*, 203.
352. Isa 9:1–2.

THE CHRISTIAN AS IMITATOR OF CHRIST

try here to fulfill the prophecy in Isaiah.[353] It was, therefore, in a region of great diversity that Jesus carried out most of his ministry. He did not segregate himself from gentiles. Neither should Christians segregate themselves from others who look different. So-called racial segregation is un-Christlike and ungodly.

During his earthly ministry, Jesus was willing to go to the house of a Roman centurion to heal his servant, although Jews would normally not enter a gentile's home.[354] He was also willing to heal the demon-possessed daughter of a Canaanite woman while he was in the region of Tyre and Sidon.[355] Jesus did not withhold his favor from anyone because of the person's ethnicity or nationality. He went out of his way to Gadara to heal a non-Jew who was demon possessed so that he could fulfill his purpose as an evangelist.[356] He went through Samaria on his way from Judea to Galilee once just to minister to a Samaritan woman who, along with her townspeople, got saved.[357]

Unfortunately, contrary to Jesus's example, there is segregation in the church in America today as a carryover from the days of slavery. There are professing White Christians who do not want to belong to the same local church as ethnic minorities. Yet they believe they are on their way to heaven to worship God for eternity with these same believers that they want nothing to do with on earth. And there are those who have managed to "racialize" Jesus Christ. Although a Jew descended from Abraham—whom God called from Ur of the Chaldeans, now in modern-day Iraq—and although of mixed heritage having Jewish, Canaanite, and Moabite ancestors, many fixate on his skin color instead of the Savior that he is. They claim him as a White man and speak of "White Christianity," seeking to exclude others from a reimagined Christianity at odds with the Bible. And there are people of color who, reacting to all this, reject Christianity as a "White man's religion" or seek to construct their own Christ. In this way, Satan manages to use the device of race he has so cleverly engineered to deceive people on both sides of the racial divide.

Racism is a sin and Satan is its chief architect. It is also clearly evil, given the harm and destruction it has caused over the centuries and continues to cause to this day. It is one of the most fiendishly deceptive

---

353. Matt 4:15–16.
354. Matt 8:5–10; Luke 7:1–10.
355. Matt 15:21–28; Mark 7:24–30.
356. Mark 5:1–20; Luke 8:26–38.
357. John 4:3–42.

devices Satan has ever engineered. Because of its satanic origins, racism has spiritual dimensions. The strongholds of racism that Satan has erected in society will not come down without using the spiritual weapons of prayer, spreading the gospel, discipling people, and transforming lives to imitate Jesus Christ. The answer is not just more education and sensitivity training. These are useful to a point, but they do not have the power to transform a human being or tear down spiritual strongholds. Neither will antiracism legislation alone solve racism, as important as it is. Even the Ten Commandments that Moses received from God were unable to change people. And civil rights legislation has not changed the hearts and minds of racists. Only Jesus, living in the obedient disciple, follower, or imitator of Christ through his Holy Spirit, can bring transformative change. This means that the church, the body of Christ, God's remnant on earth, is key to ending racism. The answer to systemic racism and racist attitudes lies primarily in the transformation of souls through the power of the gospel. Indeed, one predominantly White church in Cincinnati, Ohio, has provided a model for other churches in its commitment to combat racial injustice through a faith-based program called Undivided. This program has been studied by a political scientist and author who has noted that the lessons learned by the church members that she tracked have the power to teach us all what an undivided society might look like and how we can help achieve it. The members came to believe, despite the challenges they experienced, in the transformative possibility for racial solidarity in a moment of deep divisiveness in America.[358] And because there is only one human race, racial solidarity is key, more so than racial reconciliation.

Commenting on chapters 3:21—4:25 of Paul's Letter to the Romans, a multiethnic pastor and theologian in a predominantly White multiethnic church has astutely noted that God's work of justifying a multiethnic people of Jews and gentiles should provide the motivation for diverse Christians to live in multiethnic Christian community when social location provides spaces to do so. He comments further that Paul's remarks should also provide the motivation for this diverse, justified people to work toward the flourishing of ethnically diverse image-bearers inside and outside the church by pushing against all forms of racial injustice and ethnic division in both churches and communities. God's work to justify a multiethnic group of Jews and gentiles by faith in Christ is a

---

358. See Han, *Undivided*.

significant biblical, theological, and spiritual truth that should guide us in our efforts against any form of racism or hostility against multiethnic Christian Communities.[359]

Other tools like antiracism legislation, education, and bias training, as important as they are, can only be supplemental in helping to dismantle racist policies, structures, and systems that Satan has craftily embedded in the fabric of society even as there is now great political and ideological pushback against using these tools to fight racism.

Meanwhile, the devil continues to deceive people with the lie of many races and racism. He has used it to offer wealth, power, privilege, and advantage to those who are willing to buy into the lie and act on it. In so doing, Satan has inflicted untold suffering on millions throughout the ages. His ultimate goal is to use racism to steal souls. How many souls have been, and will continue to be, lost to the lie about race? Only God knows. When Georgetown was about to sell slaves to save the institution from financial ruin, the priest who was the head of the Jesuit organization in Rome expressed fear that selling slaves to save Georgetown might be putting the Jesuits involved at risk of losing their very souls. He was persuaded to reconsider by other Jesuits including Georgetown's president at the time.[360] But one can't help but wonder whether the Holy Spirit, the eternal Spirit of truth, hadn't laid an eternal truth on the Jesuit's heart that souls were indeed at risk for this egregious evil. This is a truth that all, especially those who practice or condone racism today, must soberly ponder.

The Lunacy of Racism

Race is an unbiblical social construct used to identify people based on physical characteristics, ancestry, or culture. It is influenced by skin color, which is based on differing levels of a skin pigment called melanin. The fact that scientists trace all modern humans to common ancestors who lived in Africa 200,000 to 250,000 years ago exposes the lunacy of racism. Most humans can reportedly trace their ancestry to hunter-gatherers in East Africa.[361] The Human Genome Project estimated that human beings have between twenty thousand and twenty-five thousand genes. Human

---

359. See Jarvis J. Williams, "Letter to the Romans," in McCaulley et al., *New Testament in Color*, 295–96.

360. This fear was expressed by the Rev. Jan Roothnan. See Swarns, "272 Slaves Were Sold."

361. Zimmer, "Ancient DNA from West Africa."

beings share most genes in common—a whopping 99.9 percent, with less than 1 percent (0.1 percent) of total genes being slightly different between people. Geneticists have found more genetic diversity among populations in Africa than between Africa and the rest of the world. There is more genetic similarity between ethnic populations in West Africa and Western Europe than there is between ethnic populations in West and East Africa.[362] This has led one author to describe race as a genetic mirage.[363]

Researchers researching the range of skin pigmentation in Africa found four key areas of the genome where variation closely correlated with skin color differences. The strongest associations centered on a variant of one gene known to play a role in light skin color in European and southern Asian populations, and found to be common in populations in Ethiopia and Tanzania known to have ancestry from Southeast Asia and the Middle East.[364] Genetic variants of three other genes were found at the highest frequencies in the African population in Southern Africa as well as in Europeans.[365] The researchers also found a genetic region associated with skin pigmentation that included genes that protect against melanoma risk. The gene repairs DNA after exposure to ultraviolet light. The variants near these genes are found in populations living near areas with the highest ultraviolet light intensity, explaining why Africans don't get melanoma very often.[366] Ironically, the fact that darker skin is less susceptible to melanoma in itself makes nonsense of the idea of the inferiority of darker skin. The senior author of the study noted that there is lack of support for biological notions of race; that there is no such thing as an African (or Black) race because of the extreme variations in skin color on the African continent; and that in most cases the genetic variants associated with light skin arose in Africa.[367]

362. Roberts, *Fatal Invention*, 51–53.

363. Kendi, *How to Be an Antiracist*, 53.

364. This gene is the SLC24A5 gene. See University of Pennsylvania, "Genes Responsible for Diversity."

365. University of Pennsylvania, "Genes Responsible for Diversity." The genetic variants were variants of the MFSD12, OCA2, and HERC2 genes.

366. University of Pennsylvania, "Genes Responsible for Diversity." That gene is DDB1.

367. University of Pennsylvania, "Genes Responsible for Diversity," statement of Sarah Tishkoff, senior author.

THE CHRISTIAN AS IMITATOR OF CHRIST

Where Should Christians Go from Here?

Racism is a sin. It is ungodly. It is wrong. It is evil. And people innately know that. That is the reason why people deny being racist even when they know they are. One author has suggested that the denial is because of what the author calls the good/bad binary, whereby to be called a racist suggests being a bad, immoral person, and people push back against that and end up being unwilling to confront and deal with their own racism.[368] Other than overt White supremacists and avowed segregationists who make no bones about their racism, one will be hard pressed to get anyone else who practices or condones racism to admit to it. Some have noted that racial bias is largely unconscious, eliciting defensive reactions when pointed out, which in turn protects racial bias while causing racists to believe they are open minded. There is also the ideology of colorblindness whereby many Whites, including judges, policymakers, and legislators claim not to notice race or color, thus perpetuating racism by not addressing it.[369] When examined with a spiritual lens, this phenomenon of denying reality demonstrates and validates the truth that one cannot and will not repent of sin that one refuses to acknowledge. And that is one of the reasons why racism has persisted for centuries.

Racism is not a self-executing phenomenon. People with governmental power establish structures and systems through laws, rules, and regulations, and human actors devise policies and practices in both the public and private sectors, that discriminate against people of color. And, ironically, many insist that although the government has used race to disadvantage people of color for centuries, remedies to address these wrongs cannot be based on race because that would be discriminatory against the beneficiaries of centuries-long, government-sponsored racism.[370]

In light of Christ's love for all humanity and his example in ministering to people regardless of their ethnicity or life circumstances, professing Christians, as people who purport to imitate Christ, must soberly ponder whether they can practice or condone racism; believe that there are many races with some superior to others when that contradicts the biblical narrative that there is only one race created in the image of God;

368. DiAngelo, *White Fragility*, 71–73.

369. DiAngelo, *White Fragility*, 40–43. Also, Dovidio et al., *On the Nature of Prejudice*.

370. The Supreme Court outlawed the use of affirmative action in higher education admissions policies in *Students for Fair Admissions v. Harvard University* and *Students for Fair Admissions v. University of North Carolina at Chapel Hill*, 600 U.S. 181 (2023).

or believe that they will live together with disciples of Christ from every nation, tongue, and tribe in the new heaven and the new earth, even though they segregated themselves from them, wanted nothing to do with them, or may even have harmed them, on earth.

All disciples, followers, and imitators of Christ—Christians—who desire to do God's will on earth and live and treat others as Christ did can take comfort in the Bible's promise that there will come a day when heaven and earth will pass way and there will be a new heaven and a new earth—a day when Jesus Christ, the righteous Son of God, the King of kings and Lord of lords, will come and reign on earth with all those who put their trust in him and did his will. There will be no racism or segregation in Christ's kingdom. The apostle John saw an innumerable number of tribulation saints from every nation, tribe, people, and language wearing robes of white and waving palm branches, praising God before his throne. They were not worshiping God in segregated sections of heaven. They were all together before God's throne.[371] Racism will cause no more tears, pain, sorrow, and death in Christ's kingdom. God himself will wipe away the tears of all his saints.[372] It bears mentioning that it is that day for which many Negro spirituals expressed a deep yearning.

In the meantime, Christians—that is disciples, followers, and imitators of Christ—those who have accepted him as their Lord and Savior and desire to do his will, must, with the Holy Spirit's help, love him with all their heart, soul, strength, and mind, and their neighbor as themselves, regardless of their nationality, ethnicity, or skin color,[373] and do unto others, regardless of what they look like, as they would have others do unto

---

371. Rev 7:9, 14.

372. Rev 7:17; 21:1–4. See Blount, *Revelation*, 379–80, explaining the staggering results of God's direct relationship with the peoples participating in this covenant relationship. God will remove the cause of tears, including pain and even death itself. Also see Yong, *Revelation*, 243, noting that the covenantal language of the Old Testament is enlarged to include all the peoples of the earth, and that the promise of no more tears fulfills prophecy in Isa 25:8 and 65:17–19, and a promise made to the diverse tribulation multitude in Rev 7:17b.

373. Matt 22:37–40; Mark 12:30–31; Luke 10:27. Jesus said in Matthew's account that these are the two greatest commandments, and that the law and the prophets hang on them. See Goza, *America's Unholy Ghosts*, 129, arguing that what is needed is diverse intimacies to address injustices in a society divided by demographic differences and meaningful solidarity; and at 151, arguing that we need to rethink and rewrite the rules of the game and our relationships as Dr. Martin Luther King Jr., leading the prophetic Black church, partnered with President Lyndon B. Johnson to do through historic civil rights legislation.

them.[374] They must do what is just, love mercy, and walk humbly with God.[375] They must reject racism, White Christianity, racial purity, and racial segregation as un-Christlike. And therein lies a huge part of the antidote to racism as we work toward a more just and equitable society and wait for the appearing of the Lord Jesus Christ to make things right.

---

374. Matt 7:12; Luke 6:31. See Harrington, *Gospel of Matthew*, 105–6, commenting that the theological root of the Golden Rule is Lev 19:18, commanding love of others as oneself. The Golden Rule served as Jesus's summary of the law and the prophets. See also Johnson, *Gospel of Luke*, 112, commenting that Luke has Jesus demand of his followers a standard for human relationships that involves a "going beyond" or "more" than the norm of reciprocity. The ultimate norm here is "do as God would do." As God is kind toward all creatures, even those who are not themselves kind, even wicked, so are his disciples to be.

375. Mic 6:8.

Conclusion

A CHRISTIAN IS A disciple or imitator of Jesus Christ, a citizen of heaven who traverses this world on the narrow road that leads to eternal life. Jesus said few find this road, yet 2.4 billion people worldwide claim to have found it and wear the Christian label. Given that two disciples who found this road, Paul and Silas, were said to have turned the whole world upside down, could there really be 2.4 billion disciples on earth with the state the world is in?

Christian may be the most misunderstood and misused term in history. It was used in the Bible only to describe disciples of Christ, not just believers or people who had been born again. Jesus told those who had already believed in him that they could become his disciples only by continuing in his word, and that by doing so, they would know the truth and the truth would set them free from the power of sin. This truth includes the fact that God created only one race, a truth that should set every professing Christian free from the sin of racism and related notions of White Christianity, racial segregation, and racial purity. Was Jesus Christ, who was of Jewish, Canaanite, and Moabite heritage, racially impure? That is how unbiblical and absurd the notion of racial purity is.

Jesus Christ loved all humanity. He was kind and compassionate to everyone he encountered, and ministered to them regardless of their nationality, ethnicity, skin color, or socioeconomic status. As members of a diverse, blended family made up of all who do Christ's will, Christians must, with the Holy Spirit's help, imitate Christ's example of loving all humanity and being kind and compassionate to everyone they encounter, regardless of what they look like or their station in life.

Jesus was totally devoted to God. He spent much time with God in prayer and fasting and used the Scriptures to repel Satan's temptations. As imitators of Christ, Christians must draw on the Holy Spirit's power to live lives devoted to God in prayer, fasting, meditating on, and studying the Scriptures, so that they can become more like Christ and triumph over Satan's deceptions and temptations.

Jesus trusted God to the point of death because he trusted God to raise him from the dead. He surrendered to God's will and laid down his life to save humanity. As imitators of Christ, Christians must trust God's faithfulness in the same way that Jesus did. Christians demonstrate their trust in the Lord by doing what he commands—loving their neighbor as themselves, treating others as they would want to be treated, and loving other believers, regardless of what they look like or their station in life, as Christ has loved them. Through knowledge of the Scriptures, Christians will be able to discern and resist the devices and schemes that Satan uses to undermine faith in the Lord.

Jesus was a model of stewardship. He used all his time, energy, and anointing in the service of the kingdom of God. As imitators of Christ, Christians should also be faithful stewards of God who use their time, talents, and treasure to serve others, regardless of their nationality, ethnicity, skin color, or socioeconomic status, for God's glory.

Jesus was concerned about the souls he came to save. He spent his life faithfully preaching the good news and teaching in the temple in Jerusalem, in all the towns and cities of Israel, and the synagogues of Galilee and Judea. And he did it all on foot. Even when he was tired from walking all the way from Judea to Samaria, he ministered to a Samaritan woman as he sat beside the well from which she came to draw water. Jesus commissioned his disciples of all time to take this same good news to the whole world and to make disciples in every nation. Because a disciple is an imitator of Christ who lives by his word, Jesus was not commissioning his disciples to just make converts. He was commissioning them to become disciple makers who would disciple "little Christs" by teaching them to keep his commandments. Jesus did not commission his disciples to go and engage in Christian nationalism by taking over government, society, or the world. Nor did he send them to go and teach anything contrary to what he taught, such as Christian libertarianism.

Like Jesus, who could always be found in the synagogues on the Sabbath, preaching the good news and fellowshipping and engaging with others, professing Christians must also commit to engaging, fellowshipping, serving in, and supporting a local church where God can use them for his glory.

CONCLUSION

Jesus loved, ministered to, and showed compassion to the poor, regardless of their nationality, ethnicity, or skin color. Although, as the second person of the Triune God, he was a rich king in heaven, he traded heavenly royalty for earthly poverty to save humanity. He said he had nowhere to lay his head, being practically homeless. He fed thousands and healed lepers, cripples, the blind, mute people, and demon-possessed people whose condition had impoverished them. Jesus gave them hope and a new lease on life. Christians, as imitators of Christ, must likewise show love and compassion to the poor, regardless of their nationality or ethnicity. Jesus did not withhold love and compassion from the poor so that their suffering would drive them to God. Neither should any professing Christian do so under notions that assisting the poor breeds dependency, or that letting them suffer will drive them to faith and salvation in Christ.

Disproportionately more Black people happen to be poor based on their percentage of the American population. As a result, there is a misconception that most people on welfare are Black when, in fact, most of the people receiving welfare benefits are White. As a result of this intersection of race and poverty, there are some who favor cutting or limiting welfare benefits because they erroneously believe Black people are benefitting at the expense of White people.

The Triune God created only one race—the human race. Accordingly, God is no respecter of persons and Jesus loved everyone he encountered regardless of their nationality, ethnicity, or skin color. Every Christian must know this truth and reject the lie and sin of racism. To be a racist is to oppose God's will for someone because of the color of their skin or their ethnicity. One cannot imitate Christ and oppose God. One cannot imitate Christ and be a racist. There will be no racism, racial segregation, or talk of racial purity in Christ's millennial kingdom or in the new heaven and the new earth. Neither should these things exist among professing Christians on earth who are looking forward to Christ's coming kingdom. That kingdom will be filled with people from every nation, people, tribe, and language. If, for Christians, life on earth is a dress rehearsal for life in heaven, then as imitators of Christ, professing Christians must draw on the Holy Spirit's power to keep Jesus's commandments by loving God with all their heart, mind, soul, and strength, and their neighbor as themselves. They must do unto others as they would have others do unto them. And they must love one another as Christ has loved them, so that a world that operates contrary to Christ's teaching will know that they are indeed Christ's disciples.

THE CHRISTIAN AS IMITATOR OF CHRIST

Following the apostle Paul's admonition, everyone who professes to be a Christian must examine themselves to see if they are really in the faith.[1] They must soberly reflect on whether they are on the narrow road that leads to eternal life or the broad road that leads to destruction, whether they are born-again disciples, followers, or imitators of Jesus Christ, or merely putting on an act. If, upon an honest self-examination, one realizes that one is not the Christian one claims to be, then the question one must seriously ponder is what one is willing to do about it. If one is not willing to become the Christian one claims to be, then one's claim of being a Christian—that is, a disciple or imitator of Jesus Christ—is mere hypocrisy. Hypocrisy is the false assumption of an appearance of religion, pretending to be what one is not, pretending to believe what one does not, or acting in ways that contradict what one professes to be or believe.[2] The Greek word *hupokritēs*, from which hypocrite is derived, means an actor or hypocrite.[3]

Jesus hated hypocrisy. It roiled him to his core. He condemned the Pharisees for their hypocrisy. He said that the Pharisees themselves were not going to heaven, but that because of their hypocrisy, they were hindering others who wanted to go to heaven from doing so.[4]

Are there people in this world, perhaps millions or even billions of people, who have rejected Jesus Christ and are, therefore, being hindered from going to heaven because of the hypocrisy of people who claim to be Christians but who live contrary to what Jesus Christ modeled? That is a question that every professing Christian must soberly reflect on, considering the Bible's warning that everyone will face death, God's judgment, and an eternal destiny based on how they chose to live on earth.[5]

---

1. 2 Cor 13:5.

2. Merriam-Webster, "Hypocrisy (n.)."

3. See Vine et al., *Vine's Complete Expository Dictionary*, 317 (New Testament Section). See also, Strong's Reference Number 5273, defining *hupokritēs* as stage-actor or hypocrite.

4. Matt 23:13–36. See Adeyemo, *Africa Bible Commentary*, 1160, commenting that one of the central ideas in Jesus's pronouncement of woes on the teachers of the law and Pharisees is the ethical inconsistency in the lives of the teachers of the law and the Pharisees whom he repeatedly described as *hypocrites*, a word that originally meant an actor and came to mean someone who was false.

5. Heb 9:27 says that people are destined to die and after that to face judgment; 2 Cor 5:10 says all Christians will appear before the judgment seat of Christ; and Rev 20:15 says everyone whose name is not found in the Book of Life will be thrown into the lake of fire.

Bibliography

Adedoyin, Oyin. "Who Got a Lot Richer and Who Didn't During the Pandemic?" *Wall Street Journal*, Dec. 4, 2023. https://www.wsj.com/personal-finance/savings/who-got-a-lot-richer-and-who-didnt-during-the-pandemic-8dd238ab.

Adeyemo, Tokunboh, ed. *Africa Bible Commentary: A One-Volume Commentary Written by 70 African Scholars*. Grand Rapids: Zondervan Academic, 2010.

Alexander, Michelle. *The New Jim Crow: Mass Incarceration in the Age of Colorblindness*. New York: New Press, 2010.

Altrogge, Mark. "5 Spiritual Disciplines That Will Change Your Life (The First Is Key)." Bible Study Tools, updated Sept. 3, 2021. https://www.biblestudytools.com/bible-study/topical-studies/5-spiritual-disciplines-that-will-change-your-life-the-first-is-key.html.

American Civil Liberties Union. "Fair Sentencing Act." ACLU. https://web.archive.org/web/20231201074711/https://www.aclu.org/issues/criminal-law-reform/fair-sentencing-act.

Amerson, Melvin. *Stewardship in African-American Churches: A New Paradigm*. Nashville: Discipleship Resources, 2006.

Amiri, Farnoush. "Debt Deal Imposes New Work Requirements for Food Aid and That Frustrates Many Democrats." AP, June 3, 2023. https://apnews.com/article/debt-ceiling-food-aid-requirements-congress-democrats-7970ba06c4292dec8806e3d134 6a9a53.

Ammon, Francesca Russello. "How the Government Segregated America." *Chronicle of Higher Education* 63 (2017). https://www.chronicle.com/article/how-the-government-segregated-america/.

Anderson, Carol. *One Person, No Vote: How Voter Suppression Is Destroying Our Democracy*. New York: Bloomsbury, 2018.

Araujo, Ana Lucia. *Reparations for Slavery and the Slave Trade: A Transnational and Comparative History*. London: Bloomsbury Academic, 2017.

Arrojas, Matthew. "These States Don't Require a Degree for a Government Job." Best Colleges, updated June 10, 2024. https://www.bestcolleges.com/news/these-states-dont-require-degree-for-a-government-job/.

Arthur, Kay, et al. *How to Study Your Bible: Discover the Life-Changing Approach to God's Word*. Eugene, OR: Harvest House, 2013.

Associated Press. "A Timeline of Disaster and Displacement for Iraqi Christians." AP, Mar. 5, 2021. https://apnews.com/article/middle-east-islamic-state-group-saddam-hussein-baghdad-iraq-296b5588995cf7be62b49619bf1a7bb6.

BIBLIOGRAPHY

Baker, Mike, et al. "Three Words. 70 Cases. The Tragic History of 'I Can't Breathe.'" *New York Times*, June 29, 2020. https://www.nytimes.com/interactive/2020/06/28/us/i-cant-breathe-police-arrest.html.

Barrett, Joe. "Chicago Suburb Pays Reparations to Black Residents in a 'Test Run for the Whole Country.'" *Wall Street Journal*, July 10, 2023. https://www.wsj.com/articles/a-small-city-pays-reparations-in-a-test-run-for-the-whole-country-c1cb07fc.

Barthelemy, Anthony Gerard. *Black Face, Maligned Race: The Representation of Blacks in English Drama from Shakespeare to Southerne*. Baton Rouge: Louisiana State University Press, 1987.

Beckles, Hilary McD. *Britain's Black Debt: Reparations for Caribbean Slavery and Native Genocide*. Kingston, Jamaica: University of the West Indies Press, 2013.

Beringer, Richard, et al. *The Elements of Confederate Defeat: Nationalism, War Aims, and Religion*. Athens: University of Georgia Press, 1988.

Bernstein, Robin. "Let Black Kids Just Be Kids." *New York Times*, July 26, 2017. https://www.nytimes.com/2017/07/26/opinion/black-kids-discrimination.html.

———. *Racial Innocence: Performing American Childhood from Slavery to Civil Rights*. America and the Long 19th Century. New York: New York University Press, 2011.

Bittker, Boris I. *The Case for Black Reparations*. Boston: Beacon, 2003.

Blackmon, Douglas A. *Slavery by Another Name: The Re-Enslavement of Black Americans from the Civil War to World War II*. New York: Anchor, 2009.

Blount, Brian K. *Revelation: A Commentary*. New Testament Library. Louisville: Westminster John Knox, 2009.

Boring, M. Eugene. *Mark: A Commentary*. New Testament Library. Louisville: Westminster John Knox, 2006.

Boykin, Jerry, and Stu Weber. *The Warrior Soul: 5 Powerful Principles to Make You a Stronger Man of God*. Lake Mary, FL: Charisma House, 2015.

Brand, Chad, et al., eds. *Holman Illustrated Bible Dictionary*. Rev. ed. Nashville: Holman Reference, 2015.

Bridges, Jerry. *Trusting God*. Colorado Springs: NavPress, 2017.

Bright, Bill. *The Transforming Power of Fasting and Prayer: Personal Accounts of Spiritual Renewal*. Orlando: New Life, 1997.

Brown, Michael Joseph. *Blackening of the Bible: The Aims of African American Biblical Scholarship*. African American Religious Thought and Life. Harrisburg, PA: Trinity International, 2004.

Brundage, W. Fitzhugh. *The Southern Past: A Clash of Race and Memory*. Cambridge: Belknap, 2005.

Burke, Dennis. *How to Meditate God's Word*. Tulsa, OK: Harrison House, 1982.

Butler, Anthea. *White Evangelical Racism: The Politics of Morality in America*. Chapel Hill: Ferris and Ferris, 2021.

California Task Force to Study and Develop Reparation Proposals for African Americans. *The California Reparations Report*. June 29, 2023. https://oag.ca.gov/system/files/media/full-ca-reparations.pdf.

Cambridge Dictionary. "Christian (n.)." https://dictionary.cambridge.org/us/dictionary/english/christian.

———. "Christianity (n.)." https://dictionary.cambridge.org/us/dictionary/english/christianity?q=Christianity.

———. "Commitment (n.)." https://dictionary.cambridge.org/us/dictionary/english/commitment.

———. "Devil (n.)." https://dictionary.cambridge.org/us/dictionary/english/devil.
———. "Disciple (n.)." https://dictionary.cambridge.org/us/dictionary/english/disciple.
———. "Fasting (n.)." https://dictionary.cambridge.org/us/dictionary/english/fast?q=fasting.
———. "Follower (n.)." https://dictionary.cambridge.org/us/dictionary/english/follower.
———. "Imitator (n.)." https://dictionary.cambridge.org/us/dictionary/english/imitator.
———. "Meditation (n.)." https://dictionary.cambridge.org/us/dictionary/english/meditation.
———. "Poor (adj.)." https://dictionary.cambridge.org/us/dictionary/english/poor.
———. "Slander (v.)." https://dictionary.cambridge.org/us/dictionary/english/slander.
———. "Trust (v.)." https://dictionary.cambridge.org/us/dictionary/english/trust.
Campo-Flores, Arian. "New Districts Reignite School Segregation Debate." *Wall Street Journal*, Aug. 3, 2017. https://www.wsj.com/articles/school-secession-fight-grips-alabama-suburb-1501765200.
Carlson, Scott. "When College Was a Public Good." *Chronicle of Higher Education*, Nov. 27, 2016. https://www.chronicle.com/article/when-college-was-a-public-good/.
Carus, Paul. *The History of the Devil: With 350 Illustrations*. New York: Dover, 2008.
Centers for Medicare and Medicaid Services. "Medicare Monthly Enrollment." Data. CMS.gov, Mar. 25, 2024. https://data.cms.gov/summary-statistics-on-beneficiary-enrollment/medicare-and-medicaid-reports/medicare-monthly-enrollment.
Central Intelligence Agency. "People and Society." The World Factbook. https://www.cia.gov/the-world-factbook/countries/world/#people-and-society.
Charles, Kerwin Kofi, and Jonathan Guryan. "Prejudice and Wages: An Empirical Assessment of Becker's *The Economics of Discrimination*." *Journal of Political Economy* 116 (2008) 773–809. https://doi.org/10.1086/593073.
Chen, Susan, and Wilbert van der Klaauw. "The Work Disincentive Effects of the Disability Insurance Program in the 1990s." *Journal of Econometrics* 142 (2008) 757–84. https://doi.org/10.1016/j.jeconom.2007.05.016.
Chetty, Raj, et al. "Race and Economic Opportunity in the United States: An Intergenerational Perspective." *Quarterly Journal of Economics* 135 (2020) 711–83. https://doi.org/10.1093/qje/qjz042.
Choi, Peter Y. *George Whitefield: Evangelist for God and Empire*. Library of Religious Biography. Grand Rapids: Eerdmans, 2018.
Chokshi, Niraj. "Black People More Likely to Be Wrongfully Convicted of Murder, Study Shows." *New York Times*, Mar. 7, 2017.
Chow, Kat. "Why More White Americans Are Opposing Government Welfare Programs." npr, June 8, 2018. https://www.npr.org/sections/codeswitch/2018/06/08/616684259/why-more-white-americans-are-opposing-government-welfare-programs.
Chronicle Staff. "DEI Legislation Tracker." *Chronicle of Higher Education*, May 24, 2024. https://www.chronicle.com/article/here-are-the-states-where-lawmakers-are-seeking-to-ban-colleges-dei-efforts.
Coates, Ta-Nehisi. "The Case for Reparations." *Atlantic*, June 2014. https://www.theatlantic.com/magazine/archive/2014/06/the-case-for-reparations/361631/.
Cone, James H. *The Cross and the Lynching Tree*. Maryknoll, NY: Orbis, 2011.
Creamer, John. "Inequalities Persist Despite Decline in Poverty for All Major Race and Hispanic Origin Groups." United States Census Bureau, Sept. 15, 2020. https://www.census.gov/library/stories/2020/09/poverty-rates-for-blacks-and-hispanics-reached-historic-lows-in-2019.html.

BIBLIOGRAPHY

Croskery, Robert H. *Religious Rebels: The Religious Views and Motivations of Confederate Generals*. PhD diss., University of Western Ontario, 2012. https://ir.lib.uwo.ca/etd/1171/.

Culpepper, R. Alan. *Matthew: A Commentary*. New Testament Library. Louisville: Westminster John Knox, 2021.

Davidson, Kate. "It Would Take 228 Years for Black Families to Amass Wealth of White Families, Analysis Says." *Wall Street Journal*, Aug. 9, 2016. https://www.wsj.com/articles/BL-REB-36374.

Death Penalty Information Center. "The Death Penalty in Black and White: Who Lives, Who Dies, Who Decides." June 4, 1998. https://deathpenaltyinfo.org/facts-and-research/dpic-reports/in-depth/the-death-penalty-in-black-and-white-who-lives-who-dies-who-decides.

———. "DPIC Analysis: Racial Disparities Persisted in U.S. Death Sentences and Executions in 2019." Updated Sept. 25, 2024. https://deathpenaltyinfo.org/news/dpic-analysis-racial-disparities-persisted-in-the-u-s-death-sentences-and-executions-in-2019.

———. "Innocence by the Numbers." https://deathpenaltyinfo.org/policy-issues/innocence/innocence-by-the-numbers.

———. "Posthumous Declarations of Innocence." https://deathpenaltyinfo.org/policy-issues/innocence/posthumous-declarations-of-innocence.

De Bow, James D. B. "Southern Slavery and Its Assailants: The Key to Uncle Tom's Cabin." *De Bow's Review* 15 (1853) 486–96. https://quod.lib.umich.edu/m/moajrnl/acg1336.1-15.005/512:5?rgn=full+text;view=image.

Defoe, Daniel. *The Political History of the Devil*. Dover Books on the Occult. New York: Dover, 2016.

Dendle, Peter. *Satan Unbound: The Devil in Old English Narrative Literature*. Toronto: University of Toronto Press, 2001.

Desmond, Matthew, and Bruce Western. "Poverty in America: New Directions and Debates." *Annual Review of Sociology* 44 (2018) 305–18. https://doi.org/10.1146/annurev-soc-060116-053411.

DiAngelo, Robin. *White Fragility: Why It's So Hard for White People to Talk About Racism*. Boston: Beacon, 2018.

Dictionary.com. "Commitment (n.)." https://www.dictionary.com/browse/commitment.

———. "Racism (n.)." https://www.dictionary.com/browse/racism.

Dovidio, John F., et al., eds. *On the Nature of Prejudice: Fifty Years After Allport*. Malden, MA: Blackwell, 2005.

Dunbar, Erica Armstrong. *Never Caught: The Washingtons' Relentless Pursuit of Their Runaway Slave, Ona Judge*. New York: 37Ink/Atria, 2017.

Editorial Board. "The 'Food Insecurity' Racket." *Wall Street Journal*, Sept. 28, 2022. https://www.wsj.com/articles/the-food-insecurity-racket-snap-food-stamps-president-biden-hunger-white-house-11664317294.

Efrink, Tim. "'We Are Just Gonna Go Out and Start Slaughtering Them': Three Cops Fired After Racist Talk of Killing Black Residents." *Washington Post*, June 25, 2020. https://www.washingtonpost.com/nation/2020/06/25/wilmington-racist-police-recording/.

Egerton, John. "Adams v. Richardson: Can Separate Be Equal?" *Change* 6 (1974–75) 29–36. https://www.jstor.org/stable/40176648.

BIBLIOGRAPHY

Ekins, Emily. "What Americans Think About Poverty, Wealth, and Work." Cato Institute, Sept. 24, 2019. https://www.cato.org/publications/survey-reports/what-americans-think-about-poverty-wealth-work.

Eligon, John. "The Big Hole in Germany's Nazi Reckoning? Its Colonial History." *New York Times*, Sept. 11, 2018. https://www.nytimes.com/2018/09/11/world/europe/germany-colonial-history-africa-nazi.html.

Elliot, Mary, and Jazmine Hughes. "No. 1/Slavery, Power and the Human Cost: 1455–1775." *New York Times Magazine*, Aug. 19, 2019. https://www.nytimes.com/interactive/2019/08/19/magazine/history-slavery-smithsonian.html.

Ellis, Lindsay, and Ken Thomas. "Trump's War on DEI Freezes Diversity Work Across Federal Government." *Wall Street Journal*, Jan. 22, 2025. https://www.wsj.com/politics/policy/trumps-war-on-dei-freezes-diversity-work-across-federal-government-9a596d29?st=qWsdwM&reflink=article_email_share.

Equal Justice Initiative. *Lynching in America: Confronting the Legacy of Racial Terror*. 3rd ed. Montgomery, AL: Equal Justice Initiative, 2017. https://eji.org/wp-content/uploads/2005/11/lynching-in-america-3d-ed-110121.pdf.

———. "Racial Segregation in the Church." Equal Justice Initiative, Jan. 1, 2016. https://eji.org/news/history-racial-injustice-racial-segregation-in-church.

Evans, Bernard F. *Stewardship: Living a Biblical Call*. Collegeville, MN: Liturgical, 2014.

Evans, Tony. *Praying Through the Names of God*. Eugene, OR: Harvest House, 2014.

Evans, William McKee. *Open Wound: The Long View of Race in America*. Urbana: University of Illinois Press, 2009.

Fain, Paul. "College Degrees Lead to 'Good Jobs.'" Inside Higher Ed, July 26, 2017. https://www.insidehighered.com/news/2017/07/26/increasing-share-good-paying-jobs-go-college-graduates?utm_source=Inside+Higher+Ed&utm_campaign=7c2537cc65-DNU20170726&utm_medium=email&utm_term=0_1fcbc04421-7c2537cc65-197567609&mc_cid=7c2537cc65&mc_eid=56ca715c48.

Feagin, Joe R. *How Blacks Built America: Labor, Culture, Freedom, and Democracy*. New York: Routledge, 2016.

Felder, Cain Hope, ed. *Stony the Road We Trod: African American Biblical Interpretation*. Minneapolis: Fortress, 1991.

Fergus, Devin. *Land of the Fee: Hidden Costs and the Decline of the American Middle Class*. Oxford: Oxford University Press, 2018.

Fisher, Lauren. "White Borrowers? Almost Paid Off. Black Borrowers? Still Indebted." *Chronicle of Higher Education* 66 (2019). https://www.chronicle.com/article/white-borrowers-almost-paid-off-black-borrowers-still-indebted/.

Fletcher, Kingsley A. *Prayer and Fasting*. New Kensington, PA: Whitaker House, 1992.

Gangopadhyaya, Anuj, and Bowen Garrett. *Unemployment, Health Insurance, and the COVID-19 Recession*. Washington, DC: Urban Institute, 2020. https://www.urban.org/sites/default/files/publication/101946/unemployment-health-insurance-and-the-covid-19-recession_1.pdf.

Garfield, Rachel, et al. *The Uninsured and the ACA: A Primer—Key Facts About Health Insurance and the Uninsured Amidst Changes to the Affordable Care Act*. San Francisco: Henry J. Kaiser Family Foundation, 2019. https://files.kff.org/attachment/The-Uninsured-and-the-ACA-A-Primer-Key-Facts-about-Health-Insurance-and-the-Uninsured-amidst-Changes-to-the-Affordable-Care-Act.

Garnsey, Peter. *Ideas of Slavery from Aristotle to Augustine*. W. B. Stanford Memorial Lectures. Cambridge: Cambridge University Press, 1996.

Garrett, Bowen, and Anuj Gangopadhyaya. *Who Gained Health Insurance Coverage Under the ACA, and Where Do They Live?* Washington, DC: Urban Institute, 2016. https://www.urban.org/sites/default/files/publication/86761/2001041-who-gained-health-insurance-coverage-under-the-aca-and-where-do-they-live.pdf.

Gershenson, Seth, and Nicholas Papageorge. "The Power of Teacher Expectations: How Racial Bias Hinders Student Attainment." *Education Next* 18 (2018) 64–70. https://www.educationnext.org/power-of-teacher-expectations-racial-bias-hinders-student-attainment/.

Gluck, Abbe R., et al. "The Affordable Care Act's Litigation Decade." *Georgetown Law Journal* 108 (2020) 1471–534. https://www.law.georgetown.edu/georgetown-law-journal/wp-content/uploads/sites/26/2020/06/Gluck-Reagan-Turret_The-Affordable-Care-Act%E2%80%99s-Litigation-Decade.pdf.

Gobineau, Arthur de. *The Inequality of Human Races*. Translated by Adrian Collins. London: Heinemann, 1915.

González, Justo L. *Teach Us to Pray: The Lord's Prayer in the Early Church and Today*. Grand Rapids: Eerdmans, 2020.

Got Questions. "What Is the Biblical Significance of the Number Seven/7?" https://www.gotquestions.org/number-7-seven.html.

———. "Who Was King Lemuel in Proverbs 31?" https://www.gotquestions.org/King-Lemuel.html.

Goza, Joel Edward. *America's Unholy Ghosts: The Racist Roots of Our Faith and Politics*. Eugene, OR: Cascade, 2019.

———. *Rebirth of a Nation: Reparations and Remaking America*. Grand Rapids: Eerdmans, 2024.

Grawert, Ames. "What Is the First Step Act—and What's Happening with It?" Brennan Center for Justice, June 23, 2020. https://www.brennancenter.org/our-work/research-reports/what-first-step-act-and-whats-happening-it?ref=liberalcurrents.com.

Grawert, Ames, and Tim Lau. "How the FIRST STEP Act Became Law—and What Happens Next." Brennan Center for Justice, Jan. 4, 2019. https://www.brennancenter.org/our-work/analysis-opinion/how-first-step-act-became-law-and-what-happens-next.

Green, Erica L. "Government Watchdog Finds Racial Bias in School Discipline." *New York Times*, Apr. 4, 2018. https://www.nytimes.com/2018/04/04/us/politics/racial-bias-school-discipline-policies.html.

Greene, Lorenzo J. *The Negro in Colonial New England: 1620–1776*. New York: Columbia University Press, 1942.

Greenfield, Nathan M. "HBCUs Lead at Propelling Graduates into Middle Class." University World News, Dec. 3, 2021. https://www.universityworldnews.com/post.php?story=20211203090156622.

Gross, Samuel R., et al. *Race and Wrongful Convictions in the United States*. Irvine, CA: National Registry of Exonerations, 2017. https://repository.law.umich.edu/cgi/viewcontent.cgi?article=1121&context=other.

Grounds, Virginia. *Rock Solid Trust: Trusting God When Life Is Hard*. Bloomington, IN: Westbow, 2018.

Han, Hahrie. *Undivided: The Quest for Racial Solidarity in an American Church*. New York: Knopf, 2024.

BIBLIOGRAPHY

Harrington, Daniel J. *The Gospel of Matthew.* Sacra Pagina 1. Collegeville, MN: Liturgical, 2007.

Harris, Antipas L. *Is Christianity the White Man's Religion? How the Bible Is Good News for People of Color.* Downers Grove, IL: Intervarsity, 2020.

Hartline-Grafton, Heather, and Ellen Vollinger. "New USDA Report Provides Picture of Who Participates in SNAP." Food Research & Action Center, 2021. https://frac.org/blog/new-usda-report-provides-picture-of-who-participates-in-snap.

Hassan, Adeel. "Oldest Institution of Southern Baptist Convention Reveals Past Ties to Slavery." *New York Times*, Dec. 12, 2018. https://www.nytimes.com/2018/12/12/us/southern-baptist-slavery.html.

Hendricks, Obery M., Jr. *Christians Against Christianity: How Right-Wing Evangelicals Are Destroying Our Nation and Our Faith.* Boston: Beacon, 2021.

———. *The Politics of Jesus: Rediscovering the True Revolutionary Nature of Jesus' Teachings and How They Have Been Corrupted.* New York: Crown, 2007.

Hentz, Caroline Lee. *The Planter's Northern Bride.* Philadelphia: Peterson, 1854.

Herrera, Tim. "Let Go of Your Grudges. They're Doing You No Good." *New York Times*, May 19, 2019. https://www.nytimes.com/2019/05/19/smarter-living/let-go-of-your-grudges-theyre-doing-you-no-good.html.

Hickey, Marilyn. *The Power of Prayer and Fasting: 21 Days That Can Change Your Life.* New York: Warner Faith, 2006.

Hillman, Nick. "State Support for Public Higher Education—Trends and Data." University of Wisconsin–Madison, Apr. 22, 2019. https://web.education.wisc.edu/nwhillman/index.php/2019/04/22/state-support-for-public-higher-education-trends-and-data/.

History.com Editors. "Voting Rights Act of 1965." History, updated Jan. 10, 2023. https://www.history.com/topics/black-history/voting-rights-act.

Hodson, Gordon. "Race as a Social Construction." *Psychology Today*, Dec. 5, 2016. https://www.psychologytoday.com/us/blog/without-prejudice/201612/race-social-construction.

Horowitch, Rose. "Florida's 'Stop WOKE' Law to Remain Blocked in Colleges, Appeals Court Rules." NBC News, Mar. 17, 2023. https://www.nbcnews.com/politics/politics-news/floridas-stop-woke-law-remain-blocked-colleges-appeals-court-rules-rcna75455.

Howard, Victor B. *Religion and the Radical Republican Movement, 1860–1870.* Lexington: The University Press of Kentucky, 1990.

Hunter, Tera W. "When Slaveowners Got Reparations." *New York Times*, Apr. 16, 2019. https://www.nytimes.com/2019/04/16/opinion/when-slaveowners-got-reparations.html.

Iceland, John. *Poverty in America: A Handbook.* 3rd ed. Berkeley: University of California Press, 2013.

Interlandi, Jeneen. "Employer-Based Health Care, Meet Massive Unemployment." *New York Times*, June 29, 2020. https://www.nytimes.com/2020/06/29/opinion/sunday/coronavirus-medicare-for-all.html.

Isaacs, Julia B. "The Recession's Ongoing Impact on America's Children: Indicators of Children's Economic Well-Being Through 2011." Brookings, Dec. 20, 2011. https://www.brookings.edu/articles/the-recessions-ongoing-impact-on-americas-children-indicators-of-childrens-economic-well-being-through-2011/.

BIBLIOGRAPHY

Jameel, Maryam, and Joe Yerardi. "Workplace Discrimination Is Illegal. But Our Data Shows It's Still a Huge Problem." Vox, Feb. 28, 2019. https://www.vox.com/policy-and-politics/2019/2/28/18241973/workplace-discrimination-cpi-investigation-eeoc.

Jamieson, Bobby. *Committing to One Another: Church Membership*. 9Marks Healthy Church Study Guides. Wheaton, IL: Crossway, 2012.

Jaschik, Scott. "Expectations, Race and College Success." Inside Higher Ed, Oct. 23, 2017. https://www.insidehighered.com/news/2017/10/24/study-finds-high-school-teachers-have-differing-expectations-black-and-white.

———. "Georgetown Changes Building Names Tied to Slavery." Inside Higher Ed, Nov. 16, 2015. https://www.insidehighered.com/quicktakes/2015/11/16/georgetown-changes-building-names-tied-slavery.

Johnson, Luke Timothy. *The Acts of the Apostles*. Sacra Pagina 5. Collegeville, MN: Liturgical, 2006.

———. *The Gospel of Luke*. Sacra Pagina 3. Collegeville, MN: Liturgical, 1991.

———. *Living Jesus: Learning the Heart of the Gospel*. San Francisco: HarperCollins, 2000.

———. *The Real Jesus: The Misguided Quest for the Historical Jesus and the Truth of the Traditional Gospels*. San Francisco: HarperCollins, 1997.

Jones, Tiffany, and Andrew Howard Nichols. *Hard Truths: Why Only Race-Conscious Policies Can Fix Racism in Higher Education*. Washington, DC: Education Trust, 2020. https://edtrust.org/wp-content/uploads/2014/09/Hard-Truths-Why-Only-Race-Conscious-Policies-Can-Fix-Racism-in-Higher-Education-January-2020.pdf.

Jordan, Ryan P. *Slavery and the Meetinghouse: The Quakers and the Abolitionist Dilemma, 1820–1865*. Bloomington: Indiana University Press, 2007.

Kaiser Family Foundation. "Status of State Medicaid Expansion Decisions." KFF, Nov. 12, 2024. https://www.kff.org/status-of-state-medicaid-expansion-decisions/.

Kames, Henry Home, Lord. *Sketches of the History of Man*. Vol. 1. Edinburgh: Creech, 1807.

Katz, Michael B. *In the Shadow of the Poorhouse: A Social History of Welfare in America*. 10th anniv. ed. New York: Basic, 1996.

Keener, Craig S. *The Historical Jesus of the Gospels*. Grand Rapids: Eerdmans, 2012.

Kelderman, Eric. "Can 'White Resentment' Help Explain Higher-Education Cuts?" *Chronicle of Higher Education* 66 (2020). https://www.chronicle.com/article/can-white-resentment-help-explain-higher-education-cuts/.

Kempis, Thomas à. *The Imitation of Christ*. Mineola, NY: Dover, 2003.

Kendi, Ibram X. *How to Be an Antiracist*. New York: One World, 2019.

———. *Stamped from the Beginning: The Definitive History of Racist Ideas in America*. New York: Nation, 2016.

Kennedy, Rick. "Did George Whitefield Serve Two Masters?" *Christianity Today*, Feb. 22, 2019. https://www.christianitytoday.com/ct/2019/february-web-only/george-whitefield-peter-choi-evangelist-god-empire.html.

Knott, Katherine. "States Underfunded Historically Black Land Grants by $13 Billion Over 3 Decades." Inside Higher Ed, Sept. 20, 2023. https://www.insidehighered.com/news/government/2023/09/20/states-underfunded-black-land-grants-13b-over-30-years.

BIBLIOGRAPHY

Knox, Liam. "A New Legal Blitz on Affirmative Action." Inside Higher Ed, Sept. 20, 2023. https://www.insidehighered.com/news/admissions/traditional-age/2023/09/20/affirmative-action-lawsuits-return-vengeance.

Kobes Du Mez, Kristin. *Jesus and John Wayne: How White Evangelicals Corrupted a Faith and Fractured a Nation*. New York: Liveright, 2020.

Kochhar, Rakesh, and Mohamad Moslimani. "Wealth Surged in the Pandemic, but Debt Endures for Poorer Black and Hispanic Families." Pew Research Center, Dec. 4, 2023. https://www.pewresearch.org/race-ethnicity/2023/12/04/wealth-surged-in-the-pandemic-but-debt-endures-for-poorer-black-and-hispanic-families/.

Korn, Melissa. "College Common App Drops Question About Discipline, Citing Racial Disparities." *Wall Street Journal*, Sept. 30, 2020. https://www.wsj.com/articles/college-common-app-drops-question-about-discipline-citing-racial-disparities-11601494201

Krugler, David F. *1919, the Year of Racial Violence: How African Americans Fought Back*. New York: Cambridge University Press, 2014.

LaHaye, Tim. *How to Study the Bible for Yourself*. Eugene, OR: Harvest House, 2006.

Lalijee, Jason. "Debt Is a Good Reason to Get Divorced or Avoid Marriage Altogether, Americans Said in a Survey." Business Insider Nederland, Mar. 16, 2022. https://www.businessinsider.nl/debt-is-a-good-reason-to-get-divorced-or-avoid-marriage-altogether-americans-said-in-a-survey/.

Levitz, Jennifer. "Daughters of Confederacy 'Reeling' from Memorial Removals." *Wall Street Journal*, Aug. 21, 2017. https://www.wsj.com/articles/daughters-of-confederacy-reeling-from-memorial-removals-1503307806.

Lichter, Daniel T., and Martha L. Crowley. "Poverty in America: Beyond Welfare Reform." *Population Bulletin* 57 (2002). https://www.prb.org/wp-content/uploads/2021/02/06052002_57.2PovertyInAmerica.pdf.

Loewen, James W. *Lies Across America: What Our Historic Sites Get Wrong*. 20th anniv. ed. New York: New Press, 2019.

Long, Edward. *The History of Jamaica: Or, General Survey [. . .]*. 3 vols. London: Lowndes, 1774.

Lovchik, John. *Racism: Reality Built on a Myth*. Eugene, OR: Resource, 2018.

MacArthur, John, ed. *The MacArthur Topical Bible: A Comprehensive Guide to Every Major Topic Found in the Bible*. Nashville: Thomas Nelson, 2010.

Mann, Cindy. "The COVID-19 Crisis Is Giving States That Haven't Expanded Medicaid New Reasons to Reconsider." Commonwealth Fund, Apr. 15, 2020. https://www.commonwealthfund.org/blog/2020/covid-19-crisis-giving-states-havent-expanded-medicaid-new-reconsideration.

Martinez, Julia. "For Civil-War Scholars, a Settled Question That Will Never Die: What Caused the War?" *Chronicle of Higher Education* 64 (2017). https://www.chronicle.com/article/for-civil-war-scholars-a-settled-question-that-will-never-die-what-caused-the-war/.

Matthews, Dylan. "Woodrow Wilson Was Extremely Racist—Even by the Standards of His Time." Vox, Nov. 20, 2015. https://www.vox.com/policy-and-politics/2015/11/20/9766896/woodrow-wilson-racist.

McCaulley, Esau, et al., eds. *The New Testament in Color: A Multiethnic Bible Commentary*. Downers Grove: IVP Academic, 2024.

McDougall, John. *Jesus Was an Airborne Ranger: Find Your Purpose Following the Warrior Christ*. Colorado Springs: Multnomah, 2015.

BIBLIOGRAPHY

McKinley, Mike. *Am I Really a Christian?* 9Marks. Wheaton, IL: Crossway, 2011.
Merriam-Webster Dictionary. "Christian (n.)." Updated Jan. 1, 2025. https://www.merriam-webster.com/dictionary/Christian.
———. "Christianity (n.)." Updated Dec. 22, 2024. https://www.merriam-webster.com/dictionary/Christianity.
———. "Commitment (n.)." Updated Dec. 30, 2024. https://www.merriam-webster.com/dictionary/commitment.
———. "Devil (n.)." Updated Dec. 31, 2024. https://www.merriam-webster.com/dictionary/devil.
———. "Disciple (n.)." Updated Dec. 31, 2024. https://www.merriam-webster.com/dictionary/disciple.
———. "Fasting (n.)." Updated Dec. 26, 2024. https://www.merriam-webster.com/dictionary/fasting.
———. "Follower (n.)." Updated Dec. 26, 2024. https://www.merriam-webster.com/dictionary/follower.
———. "Hypocrisy (n.)." Updated Dec. 29, 2024. https://www.merriam-webster.com/dictionary/hypocrisy.
———. "Imitator (n.)." Updated Jan. 3, 2025. https://www.merriam-webster.com/dictionary/imitator.
———. "Meditation (n.)." Updated Dec. 26, 2024. https://www.merriam-webster.com/dictionary/meditation.
———. "Poor (adj.)." Updated Jan. 3, 2025. https://www.merriam-webster.com/dictionary/poor.
———. "Prayer (n.)." Updated Dec. 26, 2024. https://www.merriam-webster.com/dictionary/prayer.
———. "Racism (n.)." https://www.merriam-webster.com/dictionary/racism.
———. "Slander (v.)." Updated Dec. 26, 2024. https://www.merriam-webster.com/dictionary/slander.
———. "Steward (n.)." Updated Dec. 30, 2024. https://www.merriam-webster.com/dictionary/steward.
———. "Trust (v.)." Updated Jan. 2, 2025. https://www.merriam-webster.com/dictionary/trust.
Meyer, Joyce. *Unshakeable Trust: Find the Joy of Trusting God at All Times, in All Things.* New York: FaithWords, 2018.
Miller, Claire Cain. "Does Teacher Diversity Matter in Student Learning?" *New York Times*, Sept. 10, 2018. https://www.nytimes.com/2018/09/10/upshot/teacher-diversity-effect-students-learning.html.
Miller, Claire Cain, and Alicia Parlapiano. "The U.S. Built a European-Style Welfare State. It's Largely Over." *New York Times*, Apr. 6, 2023. https://www.nytimes.com/interactive/2023/04/06/upshot/pandemic-safety-net-medicaid.html.
Milton, John. *Paradise Lost.* London: Routledge, 1905.
Moloney, Francis J. *The Gospel of John.* Sacra Pagina 4. Collegeville, MN: Liturgical, 2006.
Moody, Dwight L. *How to Study the Bible.* Upd. ed. Abbotsford, WI: Aneko, 2017.
Morath, Eric, and Soo Oh. "As Wages Rise, Black Workers See the Smallest Gains." *Wall Street Journal*, updated Apr. 16, 2019. https://www.wsj.com/articles/as-wages-rise-black-workers-see-the-smallest-gains-11555437942.

Mullen, Shannon, et al. "An Unfair System Arrested Millions of Blacks, Urged Compassion for Whites." *Asbury Park Press*, June 17, 2020. https://www.app.com/in-depth/news/local/public-safety/2019/12/02/crack-heroin-race-arrests-blacks-whites/2524961002/.

Murray, Charles. *Losing Ground: American Social Policy, 1950–1980*. New York: Basic, 1984.

National Conference of State Legislatures. "State Employment-Related Discrimination Statutes." NCSL, July 2015. https://web.archive.org/web/20150824043248/http://www.ncsl.org/documents/employ/Discrimination-Chart-2015.pdf.

Nave, Orville J. *Nave's Topical Bible*. Nashville: Thomas Nelson, 1978.

Navigators. "How to Study the Bible." https://www.navigators.org/resource/how-to-study-the-bible/.

NCC Staff. "Andrew Johnson: The Most-Criticized President Ever?" National Constitution Center, July 31, 2019. https://constitutioncenter.org/blog/marking-the-passing-of-maybe-the-most-criticized-president-ever.

Nott, Josiah C., and George R. Gliddon. *Types of Mankind: Or, Ethnological Researches [. . .]*. Philadelphia: Lippincot, Grambo & Co., 1854.

Obach, Brian K. "Demonstrating the Social Construction of Race." *Teaching Sociology* 27 (1999) 252–57. https://doi.org/10.2307/1319325.

Office of the Actuary. "National Health Expenditures 2022 Highlights." CMS.gov, Dec. 13, 2023. https://www.cms.gov/newsroom/fact-sheets/national-health-expenditures-2022-highlights.

Office of the Assistant Secretary for Planning and Evaluation. "Poverty Guidelines." ASPE. https://aspe.hhs.gov/topics/poverty-economic-mobility/poverty-guidelines.

Ordway, Denise-Marie. "'Racially Conservative' Attitudes Led White Southerners to Leave Democratic Party." Journalist's Resource, Oct. 25, 2018. https://journalistsresource.org/politics-and-government/racism-white-southerners-democrats-republicans/.

Oxford Learner's Dictionaries. "Christian (n.)." https://www.oxfordlearnersdictionaries.com/us/definition/english/christian_2.

———. "Christianity (n.)." https://www.oxfordlearnersdictionaries.com/us/definition/english/christianity?q=christianity+.

———. "Commitment (n.)." https://www.oxfordlearnersdictionaries.com/us/definition/english/commitment?q=commitment.

———. "Devil (n.)." https://www.oxfordlearnersdictionaries.com/us/definition/english/devil?q=devil.

———. "Disciple (n.)." https://www.oxfordlearnersdictionaries.com/us/definition/english/disciple?q=disciple.

———. "Fasting (n.)." https://www.oxfordlearnersdictionaries.com/definition/english/fasting?q=fasting.

———. "Follower (n.)." https://www.oxfordlearnersdictionaries.com/us/definition/english/follower?q=follower.

———. "Imitator (n.)." https://www.oxfordlearnersdictionaries.com/us/definition/english/imitator?q=imitator.

———. "Meditation (n.)." https://www.oxfordlearnersdictionaries.com/definition/english/meditation?q=meditation.

———. "Poor (adj.)." https://www.oxfordlearnersdictionaries.com/us/definition/english/poor?q=poor.
———. "Prayer (n.)." https://www.oxfordlearnersdictionaries.com/definition/english/prayer?q=prayer.
———. "Slander (v.)." https://www.oxfordlearnersdictionaries.com/us/definition/english/slander_1?q=slander.
———. "Steward (n.)." https://www.oxfordlearnersdictionaries.com/us/definition/english/steward?q=steward.
———. "Trust (v.)." https://www.oxfordlearnersdictionaries.com/us/definition/english/trust_2.
Packer, J. I. *Praying the Lord's Prayer*. Wheaton, IL: Crossway, 2007.
Pager, Devah, and Hana Shepherd. "The Sociology of Discrimination: Racial Discrimination in Employment, Housing, Credit, and Consumer Markets." *Annual Review of Sociology* 34 (2008) 181–209. https://doi.org/10.1146/annurev.soc.33.040406.131740.
Palazzolo, Joe. "Racial Gap in Men's Sentencing." *Wall Street Journal*, Feb. 14, 2013. https://www.wsj.com/articles/SB10001424127887324432004578304463789858002.
Palmer, Earl F. *Trusting God: Christian Faith in a World of Uncertainty*. Vancouver, BC: Regent College Publishing, 2006.
Parry, Marc. "The Scholars Behind the Quest for Reparations." *Chronicle of Higher Education*, Nov. 14, 2017. https://www.chronicle.com/article/the-scholars-behind-the-quest-for-reparations/.
PBS. "People and Ideas: Civil War and Reconstruction." https://www.pbs.org/wgbh/americanexperience/features/godinamerica-civil-war-reconstruction/.
Pew Research Center. "Religious Landscape Study." https://www.pewresearch.org/religion/religious-landscape-study.
Phillips, Ulrich Bonnell. *American Negro Slavery: A Survey of the Supply, Employment and Control of Negro Labor as Determined by the Plantation Régime*. New York: Appleton, 1929.
Picca, Leslie Houts, and Joe R. Feagin. *Two-Faced Racism: Whites in the Backstage and Frontstage*. New York: Routledge, 2007.
Quillian, Lincoln, et al. "Hiring Discrimination Against Black Americans Hasn't Declined in 25 Years." *Harvard Business Review*, Oct. 11, 2017. https://hbr.org/2017/10/hiring-discrimination-against-black-americans-hasnt-declined-in-25-years.
Radley, David C., et al. "Americans, No Matter the State They Live In, Die Younger than People in Many Other Countries." Commonwealth Fund, Aug. 11, 2022. https://www.commonwealthfund.org/blog/2022/americans-no-matter-state-they-live-die-younger-people-many-other-countries.
Rainer, Thom S. *I Am a Christian: Discovering What It Means to Follow Jesus Together with Fellow Believers*. Carol Stream, IL: Tyndale Momentum, 2022.
Ramey, Corinne. "New Jersey Requires Racial-Impact Statements for Crime-Law Changes." *Wall Street Journal*, Jan. 16, 2018. https://www.wsj.com/articles/new-jersey-requires-racial-impact-statements-for-crime-law-changes-1516133956.
Ramirez, John. *Unmasking the Devil: Strategies to Defeat Eternity's Greatest Enemy*. New York: Destiny Image, 2015.

BIBLIOGRAPHY

Reinhard, Beth, and Kate King. "Racial Impact Bill in New Jersey Underscores National Justice Debate." *Wall Street Journal*, July 5, 2017. https://www.wsj.com/articles/racial-impact-bill-in-new-jersey-underscores-national-justice-debate-1499290581.

Roberts, Dorothy. *Fatal Invention: How Science, Politics, and Big Business Re-Create Race in the Twenty-First Century*. New York: New Press, 2011.

Rugaber, Christopher. "African-American Unemployment Hit Record Low in December." AP, Jan. 5, 2018. https://apnews.com/article/f41df97cf20b4d95b786c78fafb128fc.

Rury, John L., and Eileen H. Tamura, eds. *The Oxford Handbook of the History of Education*. New York: Oxford University Press, 2019.

Russell, Peter. *Prince Henry "the Navigator": A Life*. New Haven: Yale University Press, 2000.

Salman, Josh, et al. "Florida's Broken Sentencing System: Designed for Fairness, It Fails to Account for Prejudice." *Sarasota Herald-Tribune*, Dec. 12, 2016. https://www.ocala.com/story/news/crime/2016/12/13/floridas-broken-sentencing-system/24266823007/.

Sanders, Cheryl J. *Saints in Exile: The Holiness-Pentecostal Experience in African American Religion and Culture*. Religion in America. New York: Oxford University Press, 1999.

Schwartz, Sarah. "Map: Where Critical Race Theory Is Under Attack." EducationWeek, updated Nov. 1, 2024. https://www.edweek.org/policy-politics/map-where-critical-race-theory-is-under-attack/2021/06.

Scripture Union. "Discovery." https://scriptureunion.org/discovery/.

———. "Encounter with God." https://scriptureunion.org/encounters/.

Simms, William Gilmore. *The Sword and the Distaff: Or, "Fair, Fat, and Forty." A Story of the South, at the Close of the Revolution*. Philadelphia: Lippincott, Grambo & Co., 1852.

Slotkin, Jason. "North Carolina Police Chief Fires Three Officers over Racist Comments Caught on Tape." npr, June 25, 2020. https://www.npr.org/sections/live-updates-protests-for-racial-justice/2020/06/25/883358818/wilmington-n-c-police-fires-three-officers-over-racist-comments-caught-on-tape.

Smith, Mitzi J., et al., eds. *Bitter the Chastening Rod: Africana Biblical Interpretation After Stony the Road We Trod in the Age of BLM, SayHerName, and MeToo*. Minneapolis: Fortress Academic, 2023.

Smith, William. *Smith's Bible Dictionary*. Rev. ed. Nashville: Thomas Nelson, 1986.

Solomon, Danyelle, et al. "Systematic Inequality and Economic Opportunity." CAP20, Aug. 7, 2019. https://www.americanprogress.org/article/systematic-inequality-economic-opportunity/.

Sproul, R. C. *What is the Great Commission?* Crucial Questions. Sanford, FL: Ligonier Ministries, 2019.

Spurgeon, Charles H. *The Great Commission: A Sermon Collection*. Brentwood, TN: B&H, 2024.

Stafford, Tim. "The Abolitionists." *Christian History* 33 (1992). https://christianhistoryinstitute.org/magazine/article/abolitionists.

Stamps, Donald C., and John Wesley Adams, eds. *NIV Life in the Spirit Study Bible*. Grand Rapids: Zondervan, 2003.

Stanford, Peter. *The Devil: A Biography*. New York: Holt, 1996.

Staples, Brent. "When Southern Newspapers Justified Lynching." *New York Times*, May 5, 2018. https://www.nytimes.com/2018/05/05/opinion/sunday/southern-newspapers-justified-lynching.html.
Stempel, Jonathan. "Lawsuit Against Germany over Namibian Genocide Is Dismissed in New York." Reuters, Mar. 7, 2019. https://www.reuters.com/article/idUSKCN1QN2SM/.
Stewart, Katherine. "What the 'Government School' Critics Really Mean." *New York Times*, July 31, 2017. https://www.nytimes.com/2017/07/31/opinion/donald-trump-school-choice-criticism.html.
Stone, Nathan. *Names of God*. Moody Classics. Chicago: Moody, 2010.
Strong, James. *The New Strong's Concordance of the Bible: Concise Edition*. Nashville: Thomas Nelson, 1985.
———. *The New Strong's Exhaustive Concordance of the Bible*. Nashville: Thomas Nelson, 2010.
———. *Strong's Exhaustive Concordance of the Bible*. Peabody, MA: Hendrickson Academic, 2009.
———. "26. agapé." https://biblehub.com/greek/26.htm.
———. "96b. adokimos." https://biblehub.com/greek/96b.htm.
———. "265. hamartéma." https://biblehub.com/greek/265.htm.
———. "266. harmatia." https://biblehub.com/greek/266.htm.
———. "571. apistos." https://biblehub.com/greek/571.htm.
———. "647. apostasion." https://biblehub.com/greek/647.htm.
———. "907. baptizó." https://biblehub.com/greek/907.htm.
———. "1182. dekatos." https://biblehub.com/greek/1182.htm.
———. "1411. dunamis." https://biblehub.com/greek/1411.htm.
———. "1813. exaleiphó." https://biblehub.com/greek/1813.htm.
———. "1971. epipotheó." https://biblehub.com/greek/1971.htm.
———. "2097. euaggelizó." https://biblehub.com/greek/2097.htm.
———. "2098. euaggelion." https://biblehub.com/greek/2098.htm.
———. "2099. euaggelistés." https://biblehub.com/greek/2099.htm.
———. "2431. hilaros." https://biblehub.com/greek/2431.htm.
———. "2962. kurios." http://biblehub.com/greek/2962.htm.
———. "3101. mathétés." https://biblehub.com/greek/3101.htm.
———. "3126. mamónas." https://biblehub.com/greek/3126.htm.
———. "3623. oikonomos." https://biblehub.com/greek/3623.htm.
———. "4006. pepoithésis." http://biblehub.com/greek/4006.htm.
———. "4102. pistis." http://biblehub.com/greek/4102.htm.
———. "4103. pistos." https://biblehub.com/greek/4103.htm.
———. "4152. pneumatikos." https://biblehub.com/greek/4152.htm.
———. "4432. ptócheia." https://biblehub.com/greek/4432.htm.
———. "4559. sarkikos." https://biblehub.com/greek/4559.htm.
———. "4560. sarkinos." https://biblehub.com/greek/4560.htm.
———. "5007. talanton." https://biblehub.com/greek/5007.htm.
———. "5273. hupokrités." https://biblehub.com/greek/5273.htm.
Sue, Derald Wing. *Microaggressions in Everyday Life: Race, Gender, and Sexual Orientation*. Hoboken, NJ: Wiley, 2010.

BIBLIOGRAPHY

Sullivan, Laura, et al. *Stalling Dreams: How Student Debt Is Disrupting Life Chances and Widening the Racial Wealth Gap.* Waltham, MA: IASP, 2019. https://heller.brandeis.edu/iere/pdfs/racial-wealth-equity/racial-wealth-gap/stallingdreams-how-student-debt-is-disrupting-lifechances.pdf.

Swarns, Rachel L. "Catholic Order Pledges $100 Million to Atone for Slave Labor and Sales." *New York Times*, Mar. 16, 2021. https://www.nytimes.com/2021/03/15/us/jesuits-georgetown-reparations-slavery.html.

———. "Is Georgetown's $400,000-a-Year Plan to Aid Slave Descendants Enough?" *New York Times*, Oct. 30, 2019. https://www.nytimes.com/2019/10/30/us/georgetown-slavery-reparations.html#:~:text=In%20an%20interview%2C%20Mr.,t%20sufficient%2C%E2%80%9D%20he%20said.

———. "272 Slaves Were Sold to Save Georgetown. What Does It Owe Their Descendants?" *New York Times*, Apr. 16, 2016.

Sweeney, Douglas A. "Evangelical History in Black and White." EFCA, May 22, 2018. https://blogs.efca.org/posts/evangelical-history-in-black-and-white.

———. "The Story of the Segregated American Church." EFCA, June 5, 2018. https://blogs.efca.org/posts/the-story-of-the-segregated-american-church.

Taylor, Barrett J., and Brendan Cantwell. *Unequal Higher Education: Wealth, Status, and Student Opportunity.* American Campus. New Brunswick, NJ: Rutgers University Press, 2019.

Taylor, Barrett J., et al. "Partisanship, White Racial Resentment, and State Support for Higher Education." *Journal of Higher Education* 91 (2020) 858–87. https://doi.org/10.1080/00221546.2019.1706016.

Thier, Jane. "Pennsylvania Is Axing Its College Degree Requirement for 65,000 State Jobs, Calling It an 'Arbitrary Requirement.'" *Fortune*, Jan. 20, 2023. https://fortune.com/2023/01/20/pennsylvania-governor-josh-shapiro-axes-college-degree-requirements/.

Thomas, Hugh. *The Slave Trade: The Story of the Atlantic Slave Trade, 1440–1870.* New York: Simon & Schuster, 1997.

Thomas Nelson Publishing Staff. *The NKJV Open Bible.* Nashville: Thomas Nelson, 1997.

Thompsell, Angela. "Why Was Africa Called the Dark Continent? Victorian Era Adventure, Missionaries, and Imperialsim." ThoughtCo., updated Sept. 19, 2024. https://www.thoughtco.com/why-africa-called-the-dark-continent-43310.

Towns, Elmer L. *Praying the Lord's Prayer for Spiritual Breakthrough.* Bloomington, MN: Bethany House, 1997.

UC Davis Health. "Facts and Figures." https://health.ucdavis.edu/what-you-can-do/facts.html.

United States Census Bureau. "How the Census Bureau Measures Poverty." Updated June 15, 2023. https://www.census.gov/topics/income-poverty/poverty/guidance/poverty-measures.html.

———. "National Poverty in America Awareness Month: January 2024." Updated Jan. 4, 2024. https://www.census.gov/newsroom/stories/poverty-awareness-month.html.

———. "Real Median Household Income by Race and Hispanic Origin: 1967 to 2017." https://www.census.gov/content/dam/Census/library/visualizations/2018/demo/p60-263/figure1.pdf.

BIBLIOGRAPHY

University of Pennsylvania. "Genes Responsible for Diversity of Human Skin Colors Identified." ScienceDaily, Oct. 12, 2017. https://www.sciencedaily.com/releases/2017/10/171012143324.htm.

US Equal Employment Opportunity Commission. "Table E4e. Title VII Race-Based Charge Receipts and Resolutions by Type of Resolution FY1997–FY2023." Under Enforcement and Litigation Statistics, Tables and Downloads. https://www.eeoc.gov/data/enforcement-and-litigation-statistics-0.

Van Evrie, John H. *Negroes and Negro "Slavery": The First an Inferior Race; The Latter Its Normal Condition.* 3rd ed. New York: Van Evrie, Horton & Co., 1863.

Vankar, Preeti. "Medicaid—Statistics and Facts." statista, updated June 5, 2024. https://www.statista.com/topics/1091/medicaid/.

Velarde, Robert. "Devotional Bible Study Is Not an Option." Focus on the Family, Apr. 12, 2024. https://www.focusonthefamily.com/faith/devotional-bible-study-is-not-an-option/.

Vine, W. E., et al. *Vine's Complete Expository Dictionary of Old and New Testament Words.* Nashville: Thomas Nelson, 1985.

Ware, Frederick L. *African American Theology: An Introduction.* Louisville: Westminster John Knox, 2016.

Warren, Rick. *Rick Warren's Bible Study Methods: Twelve Ways You Can Unlock God's Word.* Grand Rapids: Zondervan, 1981.

Weems, Renita J. *Listening for God: A Minister's Journey Through Silence and Doubt.* New York: Touchstone, 2000.

Weld, Theodore Dwight. *The Bible Against Slavery: An Inquiry Into the Patriarchal and Mosaic Systems on the Subject of Human Rights.* 3rd ed. rev. New York: American Anti-Slavery Society, 1838.

Weld, Theodore Dwight, et al. *American Slavery as It Is: Testimony of a Thousand Witnesses.* New York: American Anti-Slavery Society, 1839.

Weller, Christian. "African-Americans' Wealth a Fraction of Whites Due to Systematic Inequality." *Forbes*, Feb. 14, 2019. https://www.forbes.com/sites/christianweller/2019/02/14/african-americans-wealth-a-fraction-that-of-whites-due-to-systematic-inequality/?sh=27d81f4b4554.

Wernau, Julie, and Zusha Elinson. "Record Numbers of Americans Try to Buy Guns." *Wall Street Journal*, July 14, 2020. https://www.wsj.com/articles/record-numbers-of-americans-try-to-buy-guns-11594719000.

West, Steve. *Great Commission: Soul Winning and Discipleship.* Maitland, FL: Xulon, 2013.

White, C. E. *Trusting God When You're Struggling: Overcoming Obstacles to Faith.* Devon, UK: CWM, 2020.

Whitman, James Q. *Hitler's American Model: The United States and the Making of Nazi Race Law.* Princeton: Princeton University Press, 2017.

Wilder, Craig Steven. *Ebony & Ivy: Race, Slavery, and the Troubled History of America's Universities.* New York: Bloomsbury, 2013.

Wilkinson, Bruce H. *The Prayer of Jabez: Breaking Through to the Blessed Life.* Sisters, OR: Multnomah, 2000.

Wilmore, Gayraud S. *Pragmatic Spirituality: The Christian Faith Through an Africentric Lens.* New York: New York University Press, 2004.

Wilson, Charles Reagan. "Robert Lewis Dabney: Religion and the Southern Holocaust." *Virginia Magazine of History and Biography* 89 (1981) 79–89. https://www.jstor.org/stable/4248454.

Wintour, Patrick. "Boris Johnson Among Record Number to Renounce American Citizenship in 2016." *Guardian*, Feb. 9, 2017. https://www.theguardian.com/politics/2017/feb08/boris-johnson-re.
Wormser, Richard. "Segregation in the U.S. Government (1913)." Thirteen PBS. https://www.thirteen.org/wnet/jimcrow/stories_events_segregation.html.
Wright, N. T. *The Lord and His Prayer*. Grand Rapids: Eerdmans, 2014.
Yong, Amos. *Revelation*. Belief, A Theological Commentary on the Bible. Louisville: Westminster John Knox, 2021.
Zernike, Kate, et al. "In Health Bill's Defeat, Medicaid Comes of Age." *New York Times*, Mar. 27, 2017. https://www.nytimes.com/2017/03/27/health/medicaid-obamacare.html.
Zimmer, Carl. "Ancient DNA from West Africa Adds to Picture of Humans' Rise." *New York Times*, Jan. 22, 2020. https://www.nytimes.com/2020/01/22/science/ancient-dna-africa.html.
Zurara, Gomes Eanes de. *The Chronicle of the Discovery and Conquest of Guinea*. Translated by Charles Raymond Beazley and Edgar Prestage. 2 vols. London: Hakluyt Society, 1896, 1899.

Index

Aaron, 207–9, 327
abolitionism, 319, 340, 353, 381n269, 387–88
Abraham, 37, 119, 166, 170, 193, 205–6, 209, 214, 226, 326, 342, 396
Achaia, 214, 299, 309
Adam and Eve, 2, 31, 39–40, 71–72, 119, 139, 140, 141–43, 148, 153, 315–16, 319–20, 326
adultery, 369–71
affirmative action, 351–52, 400n370
Affordable Care Act (ACA), 306, 373–75
African Methodist Episcopal (AME) Church, 390
Africans, 317–22, 325, 335, 378–81, 399
  See also slavery
agapé, 264
Agur, son of Jakeh, 156
Aid to Families with Dependent Children (AFDC), 279, 306
alcoholism, 281–82
Alexander, Michelle, 368
American Colonization Society, 338
American Indians, 304–5, 318–19, 386
Amos, 209, 275, 282–83, 297–98
Anakites, 181
Ananias, 44, 219
Andrew, 13, 15, 59, 96
angel of the Lord, 46, 145–46
antichrist, 21–22, 167
Anti-Drug Abuse Act of 1986, 366
Antioch, 26–27, 35, 56, 57, 74, 91–92, 116, 231, 232–34, 252, 377–78

antiracism, 394, 397–98
apology, 104, 267, 395
Aquila, 92, 123, 300
Aristarchus, 234
Arizona, 350
Armageddon, 21–22, 167
armor of God, 69n343, 126, 156n120, 162–63, 388
Asaph, 275, 296
asset-limited, income-constrained employed (ALICE), 301, 312
Assyrians, 4, 246–47, 275, 297, 297n142
Azariah (Abednego), 171–73

Babylon/Babylonians, 44–45, 88, 114–17, 120, 145, 171–72, 176, 247, 296–97, 389
background checks, 179, 363, 392
Bacon, Nathaniel, 386
Baptists, 383
baptizing new converts, 218, 224, 235–37
Barnabas, 56, 74, 92, 116, 231, 232–33, 252
Bartimaeus, 12, 290
Berea, 121, 152, 233–34, 238
Bernier, François, 321
Best, George, 379
Bible
  and creation, 2, 315–17
  death penalty, 369
  definitions of Christian, 25–26
  discerning false teaching, 147
  earliest mention of a steward, 193
  and evangelicals, 28, 29

425

INDEX

Bible (*cont.*)
   and fasting, 112–13
   friendship with the world is enmity with God, 42
   Jesus praying in, 15, 96–97
   metaphors of committing to a local church, 255–59
   and misinformation, 154
   multiple races narrative, 2, 19
   and poverty, 273–75, 281–83
   and powerful people, 180
   race and racism, 318–21, 326
   and slavery, 379
   study of the, 118–33, 147
   and tithes, 206
   use of the term Christian, 1, 26–28, 89
   who is the Lord, 166–67
Bible dictionaries, 130
Bibles, 154, 382. *See also* study Bibles
Biden administration, 279–80, 351
Biden v. Nebraska, 351
Black churches, 384, 386, 390
Black Codes, 353
Black land-grant universities, 348–50
Black people
   belief people have about the poor, 302
   criminal justice system, 362–69
   and education, 345–52
   and employment, 353–61
   narrative and social construct of race, 317–22
   and poverty, 277–78
   racialization of Christianity, 386–89
   and reparations, 343–44
   segregated churches, 384, 390–91
   sending free Blacks back to Africa, 338–39
   social welfare for, 304–5
   wage disparities, 277–78, 356
   See also race and racism
Boaz, 6, 174, 293, 328
body, church as, 256–58
Bray, Thomas, 381–82
Breze, Jacques de, 317
broad road, 69–70, 72, 78, 79, 86, 89, 406
Brock, Ralph, 360

Brown v. Board of Education of Topeka, 346, 390
Buchanan, John, 390–91

Caesar, 141, 219, 370–71
Caesarea, 27, 231, 234, 295, 377
Caesarea Philippi, 70
Caleb, 181–82, 189–90
California Board of Regents v. Bakke, 352
California reparations task force, 344
Canaan (Ham's son), 379
Canaanite woman, 4, 12, 175, 376, 396
Capernaum, 3–4, 7, 18, 19, 175, 222, 225, 230, 395
Caribbean colonies, 338
Casas, Bartolome de Las, 325
Catholic Sisters of the Religious of the Sacred Heart, 343
Cato Institute survey, 280, 302–4, 308, 310
Centers for Medicare and Medicaid Services (CMS), 373
centurion, 4, 12, 36, 53, 91, 175, 188, 230–31, 295, 376, 377, 396
Chaldeans, 149–50, 166, 170, 193, 332, 396
cheerful giving, 203, 212, 254, 262, 262n60, 311
Christian libertarianism, 144, 147, 242, 243n92, 404
Christian nationalism, 243–48
Christians, 25–93
   as an imitator of Christ, 59–62
   biblical references to, 1, 26–28, 89
   as church members, 376
   citizen of heaven, 62–69
   Civil War, 390
   definitions of, 25–26
   devotion to God, 16–18
   as a disciple of Christ, 56–58
   essence of who a Christian is, 90–93
   and fear, 160
   as a follower of Christ, 58–59
   followers of the Way, 29–30
   and forgiveness, 39–40
   future diverse kingdom, 24
   and healthcare, 375
   identifying characteristics of, 29–90

426

INDEX

indwelled by the Holy Spirit, 45–56
and justification, 37–39
living contrary to the life and teachings of Jesus, 384–86
modern-day Christians treatment of the poor, 308–13
must give to the poor and needy remembering that Jesus takes it personally, 241
must love God with all their heart and their neighbor as themselves, 238–39
must treat all other Christians as family, 240–41
must treat others as they would want to be treated, 239–40
names followers of Christ used to describe themselves, 28
narrow road that leads to eternal life, 69–90, 403, 406
other names used to describe believers, 29
and persecution, 187
and powerful people, 181
racialization of Christianity, 386
and racism, 393–94, 400–402
and redemption, 36
and regeneration, 30–36
and sanctification, 41–45
talent (gifts and abilities), 204
time on earth, 202
Christian warrior, 388–89
church and race, 376–98
citizenship, 35, 62, 66–69, 79, 84, 353
citizens of heaven, 35, 62–69, 79–80, 85, 91, 403
Civil Rights Act of 1866, 353
Civil Rights Act of 1964, 353–55
civil rights movement, 244–45
Civil War, 244–45, 335, 383–84, 386, 388–90, 392
colonialism, 8, 93, 149, 155, 232, 239, 333, 393
Colossae, 44, 74, 92, 339
commandments, 8, 19, 47, 65, 74, 89, 117, 127, 201, 224, 229, 238–41, 263, 336, 342, 404–5.
See also Ten Commandments

commitment to fellow believers, 263–70
admonishing and exhorting one another, 268
building up one another, 264
encouraging one another, 265
forgiving one another, 265–67
loving one another, 263–64
refraining from envying one another, 268–69
refraining from hurting or harming one another, 269
refraining from speaking evil or judging one another, 269–70
serving one another, 265
comparing the kingdom of God to a net parable, 65
Comprehensive Addiction and Recovery Act (CARA), 367
Comprehensive Employment and Training Act (CETA), 305
concordance, 130
Confederacy, 109, 383–84
Confederate Soldiers and Sailors Monument, 388
Congress, 284, 339, 348, 353, 367, 374
Congressional Budget Office (CBO), 280
Connecticut, 364
Corinthian church, 42–43, 61
Corinthians
church is a body metaphor, 257
faithful stewards, 218
and followers, 59
giving to the local church, 261
imitating Christ, 340
and imitation, 60
instruction on giving, 211–15, 311
and justification, 38–39
living on the narrow road, 75–76, 79, 82
manifestations of the Spirit, 260–61
ministry gifts, 254–55
and persecution, 186
picking up one's cross, 72
relief work for the poor, 299
and sanctification, 43–44
and self-examination, 75–76
sharing the good news, 225

INDEX

Corinthians (*cont.*)
    spiritual gifts, 253–55
    studying the Scriptures, 122–24
    talents (gifts and abilities), 202–3
    temptation to withhold forgiveness, 330
    weapons with which we fight Satan, 332
Cornelius, 53, 230–31, 295, 324, 377–78
corporate worship, 202, 207–9, 253, 261
Cosmographia et geographia de Affrica (Leo Africanus), 318
Cotton, John, 380
COVID-19 pandemic, 156, 284, 304, 375
crack epidemic of the 1980s, 366–68
Creation of Adam (Michelangelo), 315
criminal justice system, 361–72
cross, 70–72
culture wars, 69, 157, 229, 244–45, 313
Cyprus, 91–92, 231

Dabney, Henry Lewis, 383–84
daily devotionals, 130–31
Damascus, 44, 121, 219
Daniel, 112, 114, 171–73
Darius the Mede, 172–73
Darwin, Charles, 320
David, 6, 42, 45, 46, 90, 96, 120, 123, 149, 160, 163, 166, 183, 190, 201, 246, 294
Davis, Jefferson, 388–90
Day of Atonement, 112–13, 116–17
death penalty, 335, 365–71
debts, 104, 194, 266–67, 274, 275n13, 279, 292, 293, 335, 336, 350–51
Della descrittione dell'Africa (Description of Africa) (Leo Africanus), 318
Demas, 66–67, 79
Democrats, 281, 302–4, 355
denarius or drachmas, 13, 104, 196, 266
dependency, 278, 303–4, 405
Deuteronomy, 126
developing world, poverty in, 283–84
devil. *See* Satan
devotionals, 130–31
disciples
    biblical references to Christian, 1, 26–28, 89

    Christians are disciples of Christ, 56–58
    Christ's abiding presence, 249
    discerning false teaching, 147
    disciple of Christ as a steward of God, 194–200
    and fasting, 111–12
    follower of the Way, 29
    and followers, 59
    given the name Christian in the Bible, 89–90
    Great Commission, 91, 222–49
    and harvest, 107
    Holy Spirit as aid to remembering God's word, 127
    how to grow in faith and trust in the Lord, 188–91
    indwelled by the Holy Spirit, 47–55
    ineffective witnesses, 69
    Jesus preparing for impending death, 148
    making disciples by sharing the good news, 132, 224–35
    narrow road that leads to eternal life, 69–90
    not teaching what Christ did not command, 242–48
    and obedience, 128
    and Pentecost, 35
    and persecution, 186
    poor, treatment of, 288–89
    and prayer, 97–101, 105
    relationship with God, 101
    and sanctification, 41–43
    signs that would signal Jesus's coming, 227–28
    and stewardship, 217–18
    and worry, 184
District of Columbia Emancipation Act, 338, 343
diversity, equity, and inclusion (DEI), 394
divorce, 334–35
DNA technology, 368–69
Dominican Republic, 339
Douglass, Frederick, 324n44, 383–84

early church, 55–56, 230–35, 257–58, 270–71, 298–301, 376–77

INDEX

Earned Income Tax Credit (EITC), 277, 305–6
earthly rewards, 153, 323, 330
economic mobility, 283–85
Eden, 2, 24, 39–40, 71–72, 137, 140, 141, 315–16
education, 276–81, 285, 345–52
Education Trust, 351
Edwards, Jonathan, 380–82
Egypt, 181, 193, 287–88, 326, 327, 334, 337, 343, 382, 387, 389
ekklesia, 66–67, 250–51
Eli, 268
Eliezer, 193, 326
Elijah, 90, 112
Emancipation Proclamation, 388
Emanuel AME church, Charleston, SC, 392
employer-sponsored insurance, 372
employment and race, 353–61
England, 338, 379, 382
Enlightenment, 315, 320
Ephesians
    church as a building or temple metaphor, 256
    committing to a local church, 264–65
    gentiles now members of the household of God, 84, 258
    humanity restored to God, 226–27
    keep the unity of the Spirit through the bond of peace, 20
    ministry gifts, 203, 254–55
    and prayer, 106
    and sanctification, 44
    spiritual battles, 126, 156
Ephesus, 20, 30, 33, 44, 52, 60, 69n343, 75, 89, 92, 123, 152, 157, 231, 234, 301
Equal Employment Opportunity Commission (EEOC), 354–55
Esau, 206
Esther, 112, 114–15
eternal rewards, 58, 168–69, 178, 194, 241, 331
Ethiopian eunuch, 36, 92, 131–32, 230, 234, 237
eugenics, 320
Europe, 92–93, 283–84

evangelicals, 28, 29, 242, 243–45, 325, 380–81, 383–84, 387, 391
Evanston, IL, 343–44
expectant steward parable, 217
Ezekiel, 120, 129, 137–38, 275
Ezra, 109, 115–16, 328

Fair Labor Standards Act, 353, 357
Fair Sentencing Act of 2010, 367–68
faithful steward parable, 217–20
fakes who will populate the church parable, 64–65
false prophets, 73, 90, 92n477, 122n189, 150, 234, 242, 380, 384
family of God, 21, 41, 55, 62, 79, 83–86, 91, 227, 240–41, 258–59, 329, 384
Family Support Act of 1988, 279, 305
fasting, 17, 94, 111–18, 135, 136–37, 161–64
favoritism, 298, 313n211, 319, 319n27, 340, 342, 377–78
Feast of Tabernacles, 22, 53, 81
Federal Emergency Relief Act, 305
fellowshipping, 250, 257–58, 270, 404
female-headed families, 276, 278–79
Festival of Weeks, 50–51
field experiments or audit studies, 355–56
Finney, Charles, 388
firearms, 179–80
FIRST STEP Act, 367–68
Florida, sentencing system in, 364
Floyd, George, 362–63
folly of trusting in wealth parable, 178
food distribution program, 298, 376–77
food insecurity, 285–86, 304
Food Stamp Act of 1964, 305
food stamps, 273, 277, 279–80, 284, 286, 304–5
forgiveness, 36, 39–40, 61, 103–4, 226, 265–67, 330–31, 340
Fourteenth Amendment, 352, 353
free Blacks, 335, 338–39, 342, 345
Fugitive Slave Act of 1850, 335

Gadara, 3, 7, 143, 290, 396
Gadarenes, 7–8, 159

429

INDEX

Gaius, 234
Galatians
    carrying one's cross, 70–71
    church is a body metaphor, 256–57
    do good to all, 240
    and envy, 269
    family of God, 259
    and giving, 213–14
    and idolatry, 156
    narrow road that leads to eternal life, 75, 83, 86
    poor, treatment of, 299–300
    studying the Scriptures, 121
Galilee, 3–4, 14, 19, 47, 222, 224, 394, 395–96, 404
Garrison, William Lloyd, 387–88, 390
gender wage gap, 278
genealogy of Jesus, 6, 174, 328–29, 379
generosity, 211–12, 215, 295, 299–300, 307
Genesis, 315
gentiles
    Jews and gentiles reconciled to one another, 21n111, 258n47
    members of the household of God, 258
    multiethnic people of Jews and, 397–98
    names used to describe believers, 27, 29
    paradigm of family, 84
    and Peter, 295, 377–78
    public/earthly ministry of Jesus, 395–96
Georgetown University, 344, 391–93, 398
Gershom, 326
GI Bill, 349–50
giving, principles about, 211–14
God
    accepting of all who acknowledge, love and serve, 327–29
    call to minister to Cornelius, 377–78
    Christians indwelled by the Holy Spirit, 45–56
    Civil War, 388–90
    commitment, essence of, 252
    and creation, 315–17
    death penalty, 370–71
    disciple of Christ as a steward of, 194–200
    evangelical South, 384
    existence of, 142–43
    family of, 227, 240–41, 258–59
    and fasting, 117–18
    and forgiveness, 265–67
    giving to the local church, 261–62
    how does God feel about the poor, 291–98
    injustice, hatred of, 312–13, 361, 371–72
    and justification, 37–39
    law of the tithe, 205–10, 214, 282, 293, 310
    meditating on the Scriptures, 133–35
    model prayer, 103
    multiethnic group of Jews and gentiles, 397–98
    narrow road that leads to eternal life, 70–90
    new Jerusalem, 23–24, 80, 198
    one cannot serve both God and money, 155, 179, 194, 392–93
    origins of Satan, 139
    poor, treatment of, 309–13
    and prayer, 95–96
    race and racism, 315–17, 324–27, 330–32
    and regeneration, 31–35
    sanctification of the believer, 41–45
    sharing the good news, 225–27
    and slander, 140
    in Slave Bibles, 382–83
    and slavery, 334–44, 386–87
    studying the Scriptures, 118–33
    talent (gifts and abilities), 202–4
    treasure (money/finances), 204–16
    turning the hearts of disciples from, 151
    and war, 246–47
    will to be done on earth, 102
Golden Rule, 8, 182, 240, 342, 402n374
Goliath, 190
good and evil, 125, 140
good news, 224–35
Gospel of John, 128, 274

INDEX

Government Accountability Office (GAO), 346
Governor Felix, 29–30
grace gifts, 203, 254, 256–57, 261
Graham, Billy, 390
Grant, Ulysses S., 339
Great Awakening or Revival, 382–83
Great Commission, 69, 222–49
    baptizing new converts, 235–37
    Christians must give to the poor and needy remembering that Jesus takes it personally, 241
    Christians must love God with all their heart and their neighbor as themselves, 238–39
    Christians must treat all other Christians as family, 240–41
    Christians must treat others as they would want to be treated, 239–40
    Christ's abiding presence, 249
    defined, 223–24
    essence of who a Christian is, 91–93
    faithful stewards, 218
    not teaching what Christ did not command, 242–48
    and powerful people, 180
    and racism, 393
    sharing the good news, 224–35
    teaching obedience to what Christ commanded, 237–41
Great Depression, 156, 277, 305, 353
Great Recession of 2007–2009, 156, 276–77, 279, 285–86

Haiti, 338–39
Haman, 114–15
Hananiah (Shadrach), 171–73
Hanukkah, 73–74
Haran, 206
Harvard Kennedy School, 280, 302
Harvard University, 352
healing, 9–14, 273–74, 288–90, 375–76
healthcare and race, 372–76
health insurance, 305, 306, 372–76
heathen or pagan prayers, 100
heaven, 217, 227, 258–59
Hebrews, 60, 76, 124, 152, 158, 187, 189, 197, 200, 251, 258, 268

Hebrew slaves, 294, 335, 337, 389
higher education, 348–52
Higher Education Relief Opportunities for Students Act (HEROES Act), 351
Historically Black Colleges and Universities (HBCUs), 348–49
Holy Spirit
    aid to remembering God's word, 127
    and baptism, 50–54, 107, 203n55, 224, 235–36, 255
    Christians indwelled by, 45–56
    Christ's abiding presence, 249
    and faith, 169
    and fear, 183
    gift(s) of, 226, 260–61, 265, 295, 377
    Great Commission, 223–24, 393
    humanity restored to God, 227
    love and compassion, 291
    love one's neighbor as oneself, 86, 269
    loving one another, 264
    manifestations of, 202, 253
    Paul's missionary journeys, 233
    and prayer, 95, 108
    and regeneration, 32–35
    sanctification of the believer, 41–42
    Scriptures given by inspiration of, 120
    sent to disciples, 122–23, 148
    and slander, 140
    spiritual fellowship, 258
    and stewardship, 221
Human Genome Project, 320, 398–99
human race, 2, 31, 39, 142–44, 236, 314, 316–17, 320–21, 328, 397, 405
hypocrisy, 87, 209, 246, 289, 406

"I AM" statements, 29
idolatry, 79, 113, 156, 246, 384
inductive method, 129
industrious stewards, 220–21
intermarrying, 328–29
Iowa, 364, 367
Isaac, 206, 214
Isabela (Queen of Spain), 378

INDEX

Isaiah, 3–4, 33–34, 47, 85, 87, 109, 117, 132, 137–38, 229, 288, 296–97, 395–96

Israelites
- and fasting, 112–17
- God's word, 125–27
- and Isaiah, 87
- law of the tithe, 293, 310
- and Moses, 289
- poor, treatment of, 274–75, 292–98, 312
- and prayer, 109
- and Rahab, 327–29
- reparations for, 343
- and slavery, 334–37, 343
- temple taxes, 214
- ten spies, 181–82
- treasure (money/finances), 207–11
- and war, 246–47
- words of unbelief, 190

Israel of God, 83

Jabez, prayer of, 109–10
Jackson, Stonewall, 383
Jacob, 206–7, 214, 262, 310
James
- faith without works, 132–33, 189, 236
- follower of Christ, 59
- friendship with the world is enmity with God, 67
- poor, treatment of, 298, 313
- and prayer, 105–8
- refraining from speaking evil or judging one another, 269–70
- submit to God and to resist the devil, 150, 162

Jefferson, Thomas, 338
Jehovah, the God of Israel, 5–6, 21, 90, 174, 327–29, 379
Jeremiah, 114, 120
Jericho, 5–6, 12, 80, 174, 287, 327–28, 379
Jerusalem, 74, 91, 116, 213–15, 223–24, 227, 230–31, 257–58, 274, 296, 298–301
Jesuits, 344, 391–92, 398

Jesus Christ, 1–24
- abiding presence, 249
- and Abraham, 170
- ancestry, 5–6
- anointing in the Holy Spirit, 47–55
- baptize those who receive the gospel, 235
- Canaanite woman, 175
- capstone or chief cornerstone, 255–56
- Christian as disciple of, 56–58
- Christian is an imitator of, 59–62
- church is a body metaphor, 257
- commitment, essence of, 252
- creator of humanity, 2–3
- disciple of Christ as a steward of God, 194–200
- expectant stewards, 217
- false prophets, 150
- and fasting, 111–18
- fear of death, 158
- followers of the Way, 29–30
- and forgiveness, 265–67
- genealogy of, 6, 174, 328–29
- Great Commission, 180, 222–49
- and greed, 204–5
- as head of the church, 250–51
- and healing, 9–14, 273–74, 288–90, 375–76
- how to grow in faith and trust, 188–91
- and hypocrisy, 87, 209, 246, 289, 406
- "I AM" statements, 29
- love one's neighbor as oneself, 86, 143, 164, 326
- loving one another, 263–64
- making disciples by sharing the good news, 224–35
- meditating on the Scriptures, 135
- model of compassion, 9–15
- modern-day Christians treatment of the poor, 308–13
- not teaching what Christ did not command, 242–48
- and obedience, 128
- one cannot serve both God and money, 154–55, 179, 194, 392–93

INDEX

parables, 14–15, 64–65, 72–73, 100–102, 104, 105, 131, 146, 150–51, 155, 178, 194, 195–98, 204–5, 217–21, 241, 266–67, 291, 308
as perfect steward, 192, 221
personification or embodiment of the word of God, 118–19
poor, treatment of, 177–78, 273–74, 288–91
and possessions, 216
poverty voluntarily assumed by, 286–88
power over the Devil, 18–20
and prayer, 15–17, 94, 96–110
prepare disciples for his impending death, 148
Prince of Peace, 85, 244, 247
public/earthly ministry, 3–9, 32, 222, 225, 242, 250, 287–91, 395–96
race and racism, 314, 330–32, 400–402
return of, 21–23, 220, 227–29, 241, 258, 268, 291, 300
Roman centurion, 175
ruler of a future diverse kingdom, 20–24
Satan as deceiver/liar, 142–44
Satan as enemy, 146
and Satan's fate, 160
second person of the Triune God, 2–3, 119, 128, 226, 247
Sermon on the Mount, 239–40
sharing the good news, 225–27, 229–32
and slander, 140–41
son of God who loves all humanity, 3–9
temptation of, 125–27, 136, 161–62
total devotee of God, 15–18
trusting in, 165–91
and weapons, 179
who is the Lord, 166–67
worldly rewards, 152–53
and worry, 184–85
Jewish feasts, 81–82
Jews, 143, 230, 247, 295–98, 335, 370–71, 376–78, 396, 397–98
Jezebel, 90

Jim Crow, 330, 339, 349, 353, 362, 368, 391, 392
Joab, 149
Job, 105, 140, 141, 144–45, 147, 149, 151, 153, 156, 161, 185–86, 332
Job Opportunities and Basic Skills (JOBS) program, 279, 305
JOBS (Job Opportunities and Basic Skills) program, 279, 305
Joel, 51
John
account of Jesus, 118–19
Armageddon, battle of, 167
fear is the absence of love, 387
first Epistle, 75–76
follower of Christ, 59
and the Holy Spirit, 46
imitator of Christ, 60–61
loving one another, 263–64
no fear in perfect love, 159
not every spirit is of God, 55
and prayer, 106–7
Revelation, 21, 24, 44–45, 77–78, 85–86, 88, 91, 102, 161, 163, 342, 401
and rewards, 153
warning not to love the world, 148
John Mark, 232–33
Johnson, Andrew, 353
Johnson, Lyndon B., 354, 401n373
John the Baptist, 17–18, 32, 50, 86, 97, 101, 112, 229, 236, 273, 288
Joseph, 11, 193, 287–88
Joseph of Arimathea, 30, 57
Joshua, 133–34, 145–46, 153, 161–62, 173, 181–82, 189–90, 327
Judah, 113–18, 171, 176, 246, 296, 389
Judas, 47, 139, 149, 179n74, 274
Jude, 77
Judea, 91, 211–12, 222, 223–24, 230, 261, 299
Judges, 246
judgment, 71, 195–200
justice, 209, 280, 294, 296–98, 391
justification, 37–39

Kaiser Family Foundation, 280, 302
Kedorlaomer, king of Elam, 205–6

433

INDEX

King, Martin Luther Jr., 149, 390–91, 401n373
King Agrippa, 27, 44
King Alphonso V, 317–18
kingdom of God
    being born again, 251
    citizens of heaven, 62–66
    cleansing of the Holy Spirit, 49
    as diverse, 20–24
    established on earth, 102
    family of God, 227
    giving to the local church, 261
    and greatness, 243–44
    and harvest, 107
    hindering others from experiencing, 246
    and money, 155
    parable of the sower, 72–73, 131
    persecution of disciples, 186
    poor, treatment of, 310, 313
    righteous will inherit, 15, 43, 57, 75, 241, 291, 313, 385
    Satan's use of fear, 159
    sharing the gospel, 229–30
    wheat and the weeds parable, 146
    and worry, 184
kingdom of heaven, 62–65, 79, 87, 166, 220, 227, 385
kingdom of heaven parable, 64, 266–67
kingdom of heaven to a king parable, 104, 266
King Jehoshaphat, 113–14
King Lemuel, 275, 275n17
kings of Sodom and Gomorrah, 205–6
King Solomon, 166, 178, 184, 201, 275, 395
King Zedekiah, 389
Ku Klux Klan (KKK), 384–85

Laban, 206
labor market, 278, 356, 357
land grants, 348–49
land-grant universities, 348–50
law and the prophets, 8, 240
law of Moses, 113, 116, 133, 369
Lazarus, 88, 158
Lee, Robert E., 244–45
Leo Africanus, 318

Leo X (Pope), 318
leprosy, 9–10, 288–90
Letter from Birmingham Jail (King), 391
Letter to Philemon, 339–41
Letter to the Church in Rome, 44, 68, 74–75, 82, 106, 167, 203, 228, 231, 254, 299
Letter to the Colossians, 44, 55, 106–7, 144, 216, 268
Letter to the Romans, 84, 264, 270, 397–98
Levi, 133
Levites, 207–10, 293, 310
The Liberator, 387
Liberia, 338–39
Lincoln, Abraham, 338–39, 388, 391
Living Bible, 269
living stones metaphor, 255–56
local church, committing to, 250–71
    benefits of, 270–71
    biblical metaphors, 255–59
    church is a body, 256–58
    church is a household or family, 258–59
    church is a spiritual house or temple, 255–56
    commitment, essence of, 251–52
    commitment to fellow believers, 263–70
    encouraging one another, 265
    forgiving one another, 265–67
    giving one's gifts and talents, 260–61
    giving one's time and energy, 259–60
    giving one's treasures or finances, 261–62
    loving one another, 263–64
    practical demonstrations, 259–62
    refraining from envying one another, 268–69
    refraining from hurting or harming one another, 269
    refraining from speaking evil or judging one another, 269–70
    serving one another, 265
    why commit, 253–55
    See also commitment to fellow believers
Lord's Prayer, 101

INDEX

love and compassion, 9–15, 84–85, 86, 168–69, 241, 291, 308–13
love one's neighbor as oneself, 86, 143, 164, 182, 239, 245, 269, 326, 335, 392, 395
Loving v. Virginia, 321n32
Luke, 79, 97, 101, 120, 195, 198, 218, 223, 230, 233

Macedonia, 211–15, 233–34, 261–62, 299, 309
Malachi, 210–11, 215
mandatory minimum sentences, 368
Mark, 98, 223, 249
Martha, 80, 158
Mary, Lazarus's sister, 80, 274
Maryland, 345
masculinity, 243
mass incarceration, 365, 368
master's illustration parable, 194
Mather, Cotton, 371, 380, 381–82
Mather, Increase, 348
Mather, Richard, 380
Matthew, 98, 100–101, 150, 195, 395–96
Medicaid, 372–75
Medicare, 305, 306, 372–73
meditation, 134
Melchizedek, 124, 205–6
Mennonites, 342
Methodists, 383
Micah, 297
Michelangelo, 315
microaggressions, 360
Miletus, 300–301
millennial kingdom, 21–24, 68, 85, 102, 405
minas or pounds parable, 198–99, 221
ministry gifts, 203, 254–55, 261
Miriam, 326n54, 327
Mishael (Meshach), 171–73
missionary work, 93, 261, 318
Missouri v. Biden, 351
model prayer, 100–105, 265–66
modern-day Christians, 186, 187, 245, 308–13, 324
money or finances, 154–56, 178–79, 204–16
Monroe, James, 338

Moody, Dwight, 383
Moses, 112, 114, 119–20, 125, 126, 127, 133, 201, 209, 289, 326–27, 334–35, 342–43, 397
Mount Sinai, 112
mourning, 113
multiethnic groups, 397–98
mustard seed, 63

Nain, 12–13, 290
Naomi, 6, 174, 293, 328
National Association for the Advancement of Colored People (NAACP), 343, 354
National Coalition of Blacks for Reparations in America, 343
National Federation of Independent Business v. Sebelius, 373–74
National Labor Relations Act (Wagner Act), 353, 357
National Public Radio (NPR), 280, 302
National Registry of Exonerations, 363
native populations in the Americas, 318
Nazis, 320
Nebuchadnezzar, 171–72
Nehemiah, 115–16, 176, 207, 328–29
neoslavery, 365
new covenant, 49, 79, 83, 371
New Deal, 242, 305, 353
New England, 380–82
New Jersey Sentencing Commission, 364
new Jerusalem, 23–24, 80, 198
New Jim Crow, 368
New Testament
  Bible study, 128
  death penalty, 371
  ekklesia, 251
  and fasting, 116
  gospel or good news, 225
  instruction on giving, 211–14, 311
  name for the devil in, 141
  and prayer, 109–10
  references to the poor, 273
  talent in, 195–96
Nicholas V (Pope), 378
Nicodemus, 30–31, 63
Noah, 317, 379–80
NPR (National Public Radio), 280, 302

435

INDEX

obedience, 73–75, 89–90, 106, 125, 128, 237–41
Old Testament
    admonishing and exhorting one another, 268
    death penalty, 369, 371
    and harvest, 293
    love one's neighbor as oneself, 269
    Moses's statement to the Israelites, 289
    and poverty, 282
    and prayer, 109–10
    references to the poor, 273
    and slavery, 335–36
    talent in, 195
    and tithes, 214
    and war, 245
Olivet discourse, 73
Onesimus, 92, 339–41, 382n270
opioid epidemic, 367
Oregon, 364

parables
    comparing the kingdom of God to a net, 65
    expectant steward, 217
    faithful steward, 217–20
    fakes who will populate the church, 64–65
    folly of trusting in wealth, 178
    kingdom of heaven, 64, 266–67
    kingdom of heaven to a king, 104, 266
    master's illustration, 194
    minas or pounds, 198–99, 221
    parable of the sower, 72–73, 131, 150–51
    parable of the talents, 195–98, 221
    rich farmer's farm, 155
    rich man, 194, 204–5
    sheep and goats parable, 14–15, 241, 291, 308
    tax collector, 100–102
    ten virgins parable, 220
    unfaithful steward parable, 194
    wheat and the weeds parable, 146
Passover, 81–82, 98–99
Patient Protection, 306

Paul
    Abraham as example of justification by faith, 37
    admonishing and exhorting one another, 268
    ambassador in chains, 35
    building up one another, 264
    children of God, 21
    Christ coming to live in a believer through the Holy Spirit, 55
    Christian warrior, 388–89
    church as a building or temple metaphor, 256
    church is a body metaphor, 256–57
    citizens of heaven, 66
    death penalty, 370–71
    and division, 157
    do good to all, 86, 240
    early church treatment of the poor, 299–301
    encouraging one another, 265
    engaged citizenship, 68–69
    faithful stewards, 218–20
    family of God, 259
    and fasting, 116
    and fear, 159, 183
    fight the good fight, 167
    follower of the Way, 28, 29–30
    gentiles now members of the household of God, 258
    and gifts, 56
    giving to the local church, 261
    guard one's faith, 190
    humanity has no excuse for not believing in God, 142–43
    humanity restored to God, 226–27
    and idolatry, 156
    imitator of Christ, 60–61
    instruction on giving, 211–15, 311
    judge based on disputable matters, 270
    judgment seat of Christ, 197
    living on the narrow road, 70–76, 79, 82–83
    love of money, 155, 178, 320, 387
    love one's neighbor as oneself, 269
    manifestations of the Spirit, 260–61

INDEX

missionary journeys, 33, 36, 89, 92, 160, 233–34, 238, 258
modern-day Christians treatment of the poor, 309–13
opposition to Peter, 378
paradigm of family, 84
and Pentecost, 51
and persecution, 27–28, 152, 186–87
picking up one's cross, 72
and possessions, 216
and prayer, 106–7, 163
racism is a satanic device, 324
rarely will anyone die for a righteous man, 247
and regeneration, 32–36
and salvation, 32, 34
sanctification of the believer, 41–44
and sanctifications, 44
and self-examination, 75–76, 406
sharing the good news, 225
sharing the gospel, 231–32
and slavery, 339–42, 380, 381–82
some will abandon their faith, 144
spiritual battles, 126
spiritual gifts, 253–55
spiritual purity, 329
stewards of time on earth, 201–2
studying the Scriptures, 121–23
talents (gifts and abilities), 202–3
temptation to withhold forgiveness, 330
thoughts to entertain, meditate on, or think about, 150
treasure (money/finances), 204
triumph over Satan, 162
unity of the Spirit through the bond of peace, 20
wages of sin is death, 40
wander from the faith, 80
weapons with which we fight Satan, 332
Pennsylvania, 362–63
Pentecost, 33, 35, 50–52, 226, 230, 235–37
Personal Responsibility and Work Opportunity Reconciliation Act (PRWORA), 279, 306

Peter
and baptism, 235–37
citizen of heaven, 62, 66–68
and Cornelius, 53, 230–31
false teachers, 242
and forgiveness, 103–4, 266
and gentiles, 295, 377–78
growing in faith and trust in the Lord, 189
Jesus's return, 228
living stones metaphor, 255
love one another, 263
obedient follower of Jesus, 54
opposing God, 324
and Pentecost, 33, 51
and persecution, 152, 186
and prayer, 107, 110
and prophecy, 120
redeeming work of Jesus Christ, 226
and regeneration, 36
rewards for being a disciple, 58
and salvation, 34
serving one another, 265
sharing the gospel, 91
spiritual gifts, 253
studying the Scriptures, 123
temple taxes, 214
Pharaoh, 193, 327, 387
Pharisees, 11–12, 30–31, 87–88, 100, 122, 194, 209, 219, 238–39, 369–70, 375–76, 385, 406, 406n4
Philemon, 339–41
Philip, a deacon, 92, 131–32, 230, 234, 237
Philippi, 158, 167
Philippians, 80, 215, 310
Philistines, 113, 190, 268
Phoenicia, 231, 395
picking up one's cross, 70, 72
Pilate, 370
Plessy v. Ferguson, 345–46
political kingdom, 65–66
politics, 26, 66–68, 242–48
polygenesis, 319–20
Pontius Pilate, 66, 88, 140–41

437

INDEX

poor, treatment of, 272–313
    Christians must give to the poor and needy remembering that Jesus takes it personally, 241
    consequences of poverty, 285–86
    contemporary attitudes toward the poor, 301–8
    early church, 298–301
    how does God feel about, 291–98
    and Jesus Christ, 286–91
    modern-day Christians, 308–13
    poverty only in poor nations, 283–85
    and race, 311–12
    what causes poverty, 276–83
    what economists and sociologists say, 276–81
    what it means to be poor, 272–75
    what the Bible says, 281–83
Portugal, 317–18, 378–79
Potiphar, 193
poverty. *See* poor, treatment of
poverty income guidelines, 273
prayer, 15–17, 95–111, 161–64
Presbyterians, 383
Prince Henry the Navigator, 317, 379
Princeton Theological Seminary, 392
Priscilla, 92, 123, 300
prison labor, 365
professing Christians, 88–89, 106, 121, 128, 141, 153, 154, 160, 241, 355, 376, 392, 404–5
prophets, 119–21, 137–38, 253–55, 296–98, 384
Proverbs, 281–82
ptócheia, 286
Puritans, 331, 379–80

Quakers, 345, 387

race and racism, 314–402
    biological notions of race, 321–22, 324, 399
    and Christians, 400–402
    and the church, 376–98
    and the criminal justice system, 361–72
    and education, 345–52
    and employment, 353–61
    and God, 324–27, 330–32
    and healthcare, 372–76
    lunacy of racism, 398–99
    multiple races narrative, 2–3, 19, 314, 316–17, 318–19, 324
    narrative and social construct of race, 317–22
    and poverty, 276–78, 307, 311–12
    and Satan, 144, 323–26, 330–32, 396–98
    systemic racism, 344–98
    true origin of the construct of race, 322–23
Rahab, 5–6, 173–74, 327–29, 379
Reconstruction, 339, 354, 390, 391, 392
redemption, 36, 37, 248, 252, 292, 293–94, 314, 337
reform of policing, 362–63
regeneration, 30–36, 54
"Religious Landscape Study," Pew Research Center, 88–89
Religious Society of Negroes, 380
reparations, 342–44, 392
repentance, 32–33, 49, 228, 236–37, 370, 387, 395
Republicans, 281, 302–4, 349, 355
Revelation, 21, 44–45, 77–78, 85–86, 88, 91, 102, 161, 163, 342
Revival of 1800, 383
rich farmer's farm parable, 155
rich man parable, 194, 204–5
Roman centurion, 175, 376, 377, 396
Roman currency, 104
Ruth, 174, 293, 328, 329

Sabbath, 375–76
Sabeans, 149–50, 332
Sadducees, 219
saints, 44–45
Salmon, 6, 174, 328
Salome, 243
salvation, gift of, 58, 76, 169, 195, 295
salvation and regeneration, 31–35
Samaria, 91, 223–24, 230, 246, 282, 297, 396
Samaritans, 3, 4–5, 52–53, 237, 255, 287, 376, 394

INDEX

Samuel, 46, 113
sanctification, 41–45, 49
Sanhedrin, 31, 54, 107
Sarasota Herald-Tribune (newspaper), 364
Satan, 136–64
   accuser of the brethren, 144–46
   as adversary of Christians, 136, 141, 177
   as ancient serpent, 141
   attributes as revealed in the Bible, 139–50
   breaking bonds between disciples, 153
   causing division, 20, 157
   as deceiver/liar, 142–44, 322–23
   designs, schemes, and devices, 150–60
   and doubt, 182
   as enemy, 146–47
   fate of, 160–61
   getting disciples to fight spiritual battles with worldy weapons, 156–57
   getting people to worship money, 154–56
   inciting fear and anxiety, 158–60
   Jesus Christ, power over, 18–20
   Jesus's return, 22–23
   and justification, 38–39
   not wanting people to be saved, 150–51
   offering worldly rewards in exchange for doing things his way, 152–53
   one with power of suggestion, 149–50
   origins of, 137–39
   and persecution, 186
   as prince or ruler of this world, 148–49, 160
   race and racism, 144, 323–26, 330–32, 396–98
   and regeneration, 34–35
   as slanderer, 139–41
   and the soul, 71–72
   spreading misinformation and twisting the truth, 154
   and suffering, 185
   temptation of Jesus, 125–27, 136, 161–63
   and thief, 147
   triumphing over, 161–64
   turning the hearts of disciples from God, 151
   using persecution to discourage and undermine faith, 151–52
Saul, 39, 46, 166, 219, 231, 232
Saul of Tarsus (Paul), 57
Saving on a Valuable Education (SAVE) Plan, 351
school discipline, 346–47
Second Great Awakening, 383
segregated churches, 390–91
segregation in northern states, 354
segregation in schools, 345–46
Sentencing Project, 364
separate-but-equal doctrine, 346, 390
Sermon on the Mount, 9, 16–17, 69, 79, 99, 101, 105–6, 154–55, 184, 215, 216, 239–40, 311
sexual immorality, 42, 55n232, 57, 75n370, 77–79, 82
sharing the good news, 224–35
sheep and goats parable, 14–15, 241, 291, 308
Shiloh, 268
Sierra Leone, 338
Silas, 89, 233–34
Simon, 15, 52, 96–97
Simon Peter, 9, 59
Simon the Leper, 274, 288
single mothers, 278–79, 306
sinner's prayer, 61, 73, 78–79, 385
skin pigmentation, 399
Slave Bible, 382–83
slavery
   chattel slavery, 321, 379
   how does God feel about, 334–44
   and misinformation, 154
   and missionary work, 155
   and money, 155
   most sinister form of racism, 333–34
   narrative and social construct of race, 317–22

INDEX

slavery (cont.)
    and prayer, 109
    race and the church, 378–98
    race and the criminal justice system, 361–62
    Satan deceives with racism, 330–31
    satanic forces behind, 325
Slave Trade Act, 338
Smith, John Augustine, 348
Smith, Samuel Stanhope, 315, 348
Social Security, 277, 306
Social Security Act, 305, 372–73
social stratification, 277
Sodom and Gomorrah, 205
Solomon, 246
soul, 71
South, 383–84, 389–90, 391
Southern Baptist Convention, 391
Southern Baptist Theological Seminary, 391
Spain, 299, 318, 378
speaking in tongues, 52, 254, 255
spiritual disciplines, 94–135
    and fasting, 111–18
    meditating on the Scriptures (God's word), 133–35
    and prayer, 95–111
    studying the Scriptures (God's Word), 118–33
spiritual gifts, 202–3, 253–55, 261
spiritual purity, 328–29
Stephen, a deacon, 38, 74, 91, 131, 186
stewardship, 192–221
    areas of Christian stewardship, 200–216
    commitment to a local church through giving, 261–62
    defined, 192–94
    disciple of Christ as a steward of God, 194–200
    expectant stewards, 217
    faithful stewards, 217–20
    industrious stewards, 220–21
    and possessions, 216
    productive/fruitful stewards, 221
    qualities of a good steward, 216–21
    talent (gifts and abilities), 202–4
    and time, 200–202
    treasure (money/finances), 204–16
    upshot of good Christian stewardship, 221
    wise stewards, 220
St. George's Methodist Episcopal Church, 390
Stowe, Harriet Beecher, 339
Strong, James, 130
Students for Fair Admissions v. *Harvard*, 352n166
Students for Fair Admissions v. *University of North Carolina Chapel Hill*, 352n166
student loan debt, 350–51
study aids, 129–30, 132
study Bibles, 128–29, 132
Supplemental Nutrition Assistance Program (SNAP). *See* food stamps
syncretism, 244–45
Syria, 231
systemic racism, 330, 344–98

Tabitha (Dorcas), 110
talents, 195–200, 260–61, 324
Tarsus, 231
tax collector, 16–17, 86, 100–102, 198; parable, 100–102
Tax Cuts and Jobs Act of 2017, 374
teacher race, 347–48
teachers of the law, 86–87, 209, 250, 369–70, 406n4
temple taxes, 214
Temporary Assistance to Needy Families (TANF), 279, 306
temptation, 105, 111, 125–26, 136, 153, 161–63
Ten Commandments, 102, 119–20, 166, 180, 239, 334–35, 397
ten spies, 190
ten virgins parable, 220
Texas, 374
Thessalonians, 41, 60, 106, 121, 151–52, 300
Thessalonica, 121, 167, 215, 265, 300
Thirteenth Amendment, 353
Thomas, 29–30
"Three Strikes" law, 368

INDEX

Thyatira, 77–78
Timothy
    engaged citizenship, 68–69
    faithful stewards, 219–20
    and fear, 158–59, 183
    fight the good fight, 167
    guard one's faith, 190
    love of money, 155, 178, 320, 387
    Paul's missionary journeys, 233–34
    and persecution, 187
    picking up one's cross, 72
    and prayer, 107
    and salvation, 34
    some will abandon their faith, 144
    studying the Scriptures, 54, 122
    treasure (money/finances), 204
    wander from the faith, 80
tithes, 205–10, 214, 262, 282, 293, 310
Title VII of the Civil Rights Act of 1964, 354
Titus, 211
Tower of Babel, 315, 319
Transcendental Meditation, 134
treatment of the poor. *See* poor, treatment of
Triune God, 2–3, 96, 119, 124, 169, 226, 247, 283, 286, 314, 315, 405
Troas, 233–34, 258
Truman, Harry, 355
trusting in the Lord, 165–91
    and Abraham, 170
    benefits of, 187–88
    Canaanite woman, 175
    Daniel and his three friends, 171–73
    and doubt, 181–82
    and fear, 182–83
    how does one come to, 169–70
    how to grow in faith and trust, 188–91
    and money, 178–79
    in our day, 175–77
    and persecution, 186–87
    and powerful people, 180–81
    and Rahab, 173–74
    Roman centurion, 175
    and Ruth, 174
    and suffering, 185–86
    things that hinder, 181–87
    things that substitute for, 177–81
    trust, defined, 165–66
    and weapons, 179–80
    what it means to, 168
    what trusting looks like, 170–75
    who is the Lord, 166–68
    why trust in the Lord, 168–69
    and worry, 184–85
Turner, Nat, 345
Twelve Years a Slave (film), 335
two fish and five loaves, 13–14, 81, 97

Uncle Tom's Cabin (Stowe), 319
Undivided program, 397
unemployment and unemployment insurance, 156, 305, 307, 375
unfaithful steward parable, 194
unforgiving, 103–4, 265–66, 330–31
UNICOR, 365
Union, 390–92
United Daughters of the Confederacy, 388
United States Supreme Court
    Affordable Care Act (ACA), 306n175, 375
    Biden v. Nebraska, 351
    Brown v. Board of Education, 346, 390
    Civil Rights Act of 1964, 353
    college admissions, 352, 400n370
    Loving v. Virginia, 321n32
    Missouri v. Biden, 351
    National Federation of Independent Business v. Sebelius, 373–74
    Plessy v. Ferguson, 345–46
    student loans, 351
    United States v. Booker, 364–65
United Way, 301
University of North Carolina at Chapel Hill, 352
US Sentencing Commission, 364–65, 367

Van Evrie, John H., 319
Vashti (Queen), 114–15
Virginia, 26, 333, 336, 338, 345, 351, 368, 380, 386
Virginia Theological Seminary, 343, 392

INDEX

Wagner Act. *See* National Labor Relations Act (Wagner Act)
Wallace, George, 348
Wall Street Journal (newspaper), 304
wealth and money, worship of, 154–56, 178–79. *See also* money or finances
weapons, 156–57, 179–80, 332
Weld, Theodore, 387
welfare, 278–79, 302–7, 311–12
wheat and the weeds parable, 146
White Americans, 303, 342, 344
White Christianity, 3, 24, 84, 93, 144, 147, 151, 384–85, 396, 402
Whitefield, George, 380–81, 380n264
White southerners, 355
White supremacy, 333, 352, 391
wilderness, 5, 17, 46–47, 53, 77, 79, 112, 125–27, 166, 173, 182, 323, 327
Williams, Roger, 381
Wilmington, NC, 392

Wilson, Woodrow, 354
Wisconsin, 346, 352
wise stewards, 220
woman who poured perfume, 274, 288–89
women, 278–79, 306, 336, 346–47
words of unbelief and defeat, 189–90
working poor, 293, 312
work requirements for food aid, 279–80
wrongful convictions and executions, 363, 368–69

Year of Jubilee, 292–94, 336–37

Zacchaeus, 80–81, 198, 287
Zechariah, 22, 46, 116–17, 145, 297–98
Zerubbabel, 116, 145
Zipporah, 326–27
Zurara, Gomes Eanes de, 317–18, 320, 324–25, 379–80

www.ingramcontent.com/pod-product-compliance
Lightning Source LLC
Chambersburg PA
CBHW071222290426
44108CB00013B/1263